Windows Forensics

Windows Forensics

Philip Polstra

Windows Forensics

Copyright (c) 2016 by Pentester Academy

All rights reserved. No part of this publication may be reproduced, stored in a retrieval system, distributed, or transmitted in any form or by any means, including photocopying, recording, or other electronic or mechanical methods, without the prior written permission of the publisher, except in the case of brief quotations embodied in critical reviews and certain other noncommercial uses permitted by copyright law.

Although every precaution has been taken to verify the accuracy of the information contained herein, the author and publisher assume no responsibility for any errors or omissions. No liability is assumed for damages that may result from the use of information contained within.

First published: July 2016
Published by Pentester Academy, a division of Binary Security Innovative Solutions Pvt. Ltd.
http://www.PentesterAcademy.com

First Edition

Dedicated to my maker, hacker, and all-around-awesome daughter, Kathryn.

Contents

Acknowledgements xiii
Author Biography xv
Foreword xvii
Scripts, Videos, Teaching Aids, Community Forums and more xix
Introduction xxi

CHAPTER 1   **First Steps 1**
                    What is forensics? 1
                    Types of Forensics 1
                    Why use Linux for Windows Forensics? 2
                    General Principles 2
                          Maintaining Integrity 3
                          Chain of Custody 3
                          Standard Practices 4
                          Documentation 4
                    Phases of Investigation 4
                          Evidence Preservation and Collection 5
                          Evidence Searching 5
                          Reconstruction of Events 7
                    High-level Process 7
                          Every Child is Perfect, Just Ask The Parents 7
                    Building a Toolkit 8
                          Hardware 9
                          Software 9
                          Running live Linux in a virtual machine 15
                    Summary 19

CHAPTER 2   **Determining If There Was an Incident 21**
                    Opening a case 21
                    Talking to users 22
                    Documentation 22
                          If you are using a virtual machine, older may be better 23
                    Mounting known-good binaries 24

viii Contents

Minimizing disturbance to the subject system 26
    Using a USB drive to store data 26
    Using Netcat 26
    Sending data from the subject system 27
    Sending files 28
Using scripting to automate the process 31
    Scripting the server 32
    Scripting the client 35
Introducing our first subject system 38
Collecting volatile data 38
    Windows version 38
    Date and time information 39
    Networking information 40
    Using PS Tools 42
    Built-in commands, system internals, and miscellaneous 48
    Putting it together with scripting 53
Sure signs of compromise 55
Summary 55

CHAPTER 3 Live Analysis 57

There was an incident: now what? 57
Analyzing results from the initial scan 58
Getting file metadata 62
Using a spreadsheet program to build a timeline 63
Examining user command history 66
Collecting file hashes 66
Dumping RAM 68
    RAM acquisition from a virtual machine 68
    RAM acquisition with FTK Imager 69
Summary 72

CHAPTER 4 Creating Images 73

Shutting down the system 73
    Normal shutdown 74
    Pulling the plug 74
Image formats 74
    Raw format 74
    Proprietary format with embedded metadata 75
    Proprietary format with metadata in a separate file 75

Raw format with hashes stored in a separate file.............................. 75
Using dd.. 76
Using dcfldd.. 76
  Dc3dd.. 77
Hardware write blocking... 77
Software write blocking.. 78
  Udev rules... 79
  Live Linux distributions... 83
Creating an image from a virtual machine... 84
Creating an image from a physical drive... 84
Summary... 85

CHAPTER 5 Mounting Images 87

Partition basics... 87
Master boot record partitions... 87
Extended partitions.. 89
GUID partitions.. 90
Mounting partitions from an image file on Linux.................................. 91
Using Python to automate the mounting process.................................. 98
  Scripting or Programming Language.. 99
  Python 2 or Python 3.. 100
  MBR-based primary partitions.. 100
  Ranges in Python 2 and Python 3... 107
  MBR-based extended partitions.. 111
  GPT partitions.. 116
Summary... 124

CHAPTER 6 FAT Filesystems 125

FAT Basics.. 125
  Using Active@ Disk Editor... 126
Volume Boot Records... 130
  Examining the VBR in Active@ Disk Editor................................... 135
  Interpreting the VBR with Python.. 136
File Allocation Tables... 146
  Examining the FAT in Active@ Disk Editor.................................... 146
  Interpreting the FAT with Python... 148
Directories.. 152
  Short filenames... 152
  Long filenames... 154

Examining directories in Active@ Disk Editor 157
Using Python to interpret directories 160
The Sleuth Kit and Autopsy 182
The Sleuth Kit 182
Installing Autopsy on Linux 188
Autopsy basics 192
Deleted files 199
What happens when files are deleted 199
Examining deleted files in Active@ Disk Editor 200
Deleted files and Python 202
Summary 220

CHAPTER 7 File Forensics 221

Hiding Information 221
Mismatched extensions 221
Slack space 221
Unallocated space 223
Page file 223
File Signatures 223
Examining files in Active@ Disk Editor 223
Analyzing mounted images 232
The file utility 232
Detecting mismatched file extensions 236
Analyzing filesystem image files 239
Using Python to analyze a filesystem image 239
Using Linux system tools to analyze an image 251
File carving 255
Summary 259

CHAPTER 8 NTFS Filesystems 261

NTFS basics 261
The NTFS Volume Boot Record 264
The Master File Table 267
MFT basics 267
Attributes $10 and $30 272
The data attribute 278
Files small and large 278
Directories 284
The $90 attribute 286

Contents

The $A0 attribute and index buffers	289
Large directories	295
Off-the-shelf tools for examining directories	302
Deleted files	305
Python and NTFS	309
The VBR	311
MFT headers	315
MFT attribute headers	319
Standard information attribute	331
Filename attribute	342
Data attribute	347
Index root	350
Index allocations	356
Bitmap attributes	361
Attribute lists	365
Extracting files and directories	397
Timelines	403
Extracting information from an image	404
Importing into a spreadsheet	408
Importing into a database	410
Printing timelines	414
Understanding timestamps	418
Printing timelines on a file-by-file basis	420
Summary	423

CHAPTER 9 The Windows Registry 425

Registry basics	425
Extracting hive files	427
Examining the registry	428
Registry viewing tools	429
The SAM hive	431
The System hive	433
The Software hive	439
The User hive	443
Using RegRipper	446
SAM hive	449
System hive	449
Software hive	451
User hive	451
Summary	453

CHAPTER 10	Windows Artifacts	455
	The recycle bin	455
	Event logs	459
	Prefetch files	464
	User directories	465
	Miscellaneous artifacts	471
	Web browser history	473
	Summary	475

CHAPTER 11	Memory Forensics	477
	Introducing Volatility	477
	Volatility basics	478
	Examining processes	480
	Process lists	480
	Drilling down into a single process	484
	Finding malware	490
	More Volatility commands	494
	Summary	503

CHAPTER 12	Malware	505
	Is it in a database?	505
	First steps when examining an unknown file	506
	Packers	513
	Setting up a sandbox	515
	Examining executables	521
	32-bit executables	521
	64-bit executables	524
	Summary	526

CHAPTER 13	The Road Ahead	527
	Finishing the investigation	527
	Bigger is not always better	528
	Preparing for the next investigation	528
	Summary	529

Acknowledgements

First and foremost I would like to thank my wife and children for allowing me to take the time to write another book. This book would never have happened without their support.

Many thanks to Vivek Ramachandran and the whole Pentester Academy team for allowing this book to be possible. This book and related video course would never have been possible without their support.

Many thanks to Dr. Susan Baker for agreeing to edit a second book.

Finally, I would like to my many supportive friends in the information security community who have provided encouragement to me throughout the years.

Author Biography

Dr. Philip Polstra (known to his friends as Dr. Phil) is an internationally recognized hardware hacker. His work has been presented at numerous conferences around the globe including repeat performances at DEFCON, BlackHat, 44CON, GrrCON, MakerFaire, ForenSecure, and other top conferences. Dr. Polstra is a well-known expert on USB forensics and has published several articles on this topic. He has developed a number of video courses including ones on Linux forensics, USB forensics, Windows forensics, and reverse engineering.

Dr. Polstra has developed degree programs in digital forensics and ethical hacking while serving as a professor and Hacker in Residence at a private university in the Midwestern United States. He currently teaches computer science and digital forensics at Bloomsburg University of Pennsylvania. Bloomsburg is one of only six universities to achieve the National Security Agency and Department of Homeland Security Center of Academic Excellence designation in digital forensics. In addition to teaching, he provides training and performs penetration tests on a consulting basis. When not working, he has been known to fly, build aircraft, and tinker with electronics. His latest happenings can be found on his blog: http://polstra.org. You can also follow him at @ppolstra on Twitter.

Foreword

Hello All! ☺

Phil and I met online around six years back through SecurityTube.net and we've been great friends ever since. Over the years, we discussed interesting projects we could collaborate on and information security education was on top of our list as expected. Based on our discussions, Phil created an excellent "USB Forensics", "Linux Forensics" and "Windows Forensics" online courses for Pentester Academy! These courses were fantastic and well received by our students.

I'd always wanted to convert our online courses into books and Phil's "Linux Forensics" video course seemed like the best place to start this adventure! We launched the book last year at DEFCON and it has been a roaring success so far! We are now delighted to launch "Windows Forensics" as the next book in our forensics series and I'd like to take this opportunity to wish Phil and my publishing team at Pentester Academy bon voyage on this next adventure!

Finally but most importantly, I'd like to thank the SecurityTube.net and Pentester Academy community and our students for their love and support over the years! We would not be here today without you guys! You've made all our dreams come true. We cannot thank you enough.

Vivek Ramachandran
Founder, SecurityTube.net and Pentester Academy

Scripts, Videos, Teaching Aids, Community Forums and more

BOOK WEBSITE

We've created two mirror websites for the "Windows Forensics" book:

- http://www.pentesteracademy.com/books
- http://www.windowsforensicsbook.com

SCRIPTS AND SUPPORTING FILES

All Python and shell scripts have been made available for download on the website. We've tried our best to ensure that the code works and is error free but if you find any bugs please report them and we will publicly acknowledge you on the website.

VIDEOS

We are Pentester Academy and we love videos! Though the book is completely self-sufficient we thought it would be fun to have videos for a select few labs by the book author himself! You can access these for FREE on the book website.

COMMUNITY FORUMS

We would love to connect with our book readers – get their feedback and know from them firsthand what they would like to see in the next edition? Also, wouldn't it be great to have a community forum where readers could interact with each other and even with the author! Our book community forums do just that! You can access the forums through the website mentioned above.

TEACHING AIDS

Are you a professor or a commercial trainer? Do you want to use this book in class? We've got your covered! Through our website, you can register as a trainer and get access to teaching aids such as presentations, exercise files and other teaching aids.

WINDOWS FORENSICS BOOK SWAG!

Visit the swag section on our website and get your "Windows Forensics" T-Shirts, mugs, keychains and other cool swags!

Introduction

INFORMATION IN THIS CHAPTER:

- What this book is about
- Intended audience
- How this book is organized

WHAT THIS BOOK IS ABOUT

This book is about performing forensic investigations on subject systems running some form of the Windows operating system from a Linux workstation. Unlike the situation for Linux forensics in which you are normally responding to a suspected breach, there are a number of scenarios that might require you to perform Windows forensics. Given the popularity of Windows on desktop systems, it is very common for users to lose data which needs to be recovered. Many criminal and civil cases involve the collection of evidence from computers running Windows. Windows systems are frequently breached and/or infected with malware. A forensic analysis of an affected system can provide insight into exactly what has transpired on such systems.

Along the way we will learn how to better use Linux and the many tools it provides. In addition to covering the essentials of forensics, we will explore how to use Python, shell scripting, and standard Linux system tools to more quickly and easily perform forensic investigations. Readers of my **Linux Forensics** book will notice that some of the forensic tools used are the same regardless of whether the subject system is running Windows or Linux.

INTENDED AUDIENCE

This book is primarily intended to be read by forensics practitioners and other information security professionals. It describes in detail how to use free and open source tools to investigate computers running Windows from a Linux workstation. Forensic investigators who work primarily with Windows subjects who would like to learn more powerful techniques that Linux provides should find this book useful. This book should also prove useful to new investigators who want to investigate Windows systems without spending tens of thousands of dollars for proprietary software and equipment. The information contained within this book should allow a person to handle the majority of scenarios under which Windows forensics is likely to be performed.

The only knowledge a reader of this book is assumed to have is that of a normal Windows user. You need not be a Windows system administrator, hacker, or power user to learn from this book. Knowledge of Windows system administration, Python, shell scripting, and Assembly would be helpful, but definitely not required. Sufficient information will be provided for those new to these topics.

While I will attempt to describe some of the basics of using Linux as needed along the way, this is not a book on how to use Linux. There is a plethora of resources both online and in print on how to use Linux. This book will focus on how to use Linux, the operating system by programmers for programmers, in order to investigate Windows subject systems.

HOW THIS BOOK IS ORGANIZED

This book begins with a brief introduction to forensics. From there we will discuss acquiring the right tools and setting up a Linux forensic workstation. Our journey begins with a look at live analysis which is often the first step when performing forensic analysis as part of responding to a suspected incident. We then discuss the creation and analysis of forensic filesystem and memory images. Advanced attacks on Windows systems and malware round out our discussion.

Chapter 1: First Steps

Chapter 1 is an introduction to the field of forensics. It covers the various types of forensics and motivation for performing forensics on Windows systems. It also discusses phases of investigations, high-level processes , and step-by-step instructions for building a Linux forensic workstation.

Chapter 2: Was there an incident?

Chapter 2 walks you through what happens from the point when a client who suspects something has happened calls until you can be reasonably sure whether there was or was not an incident. It covers opening a case, talking to users, creating appropriate documentation, minimizing disturbance to the subject system, using scripting to automate the process, and collecting volatile data. It also provides a nice introduction to shell scripting.

Chapter 3: Live Analysis

Chapter 3 describes what to do before shutting down the subject system. It covers capturing file metadata, building timelines, collecting user command histories, performing log file analysis, hashing, dumping memory, and automating with scripting. A number of new shell scripting techniques and Linux system tools are also presented in this chapter.

Chapter 4: Creating Images

Chapter 4 starts with a discussion of the options for shutting down a subject system. From there the discussion turns to tools and techniques used to create a forensic image of a filesystem. Topics covered include shutting down the system, image formats, using dd and dcfldd, hardware and software write blocking, and live Linux distributions. Methods of creating images for different circumstances are discussed in detail.

Chapter 5: Mounting Images

Chapter 5 begins with a discussion of the various types of partitioning systems: Master Boot Record (MBR) based partitions, extended partitions, and GUID partition tables. Linux commands and techniques used to mount all types of partitions are presented. The chapter ends with an introduction to Python and how it can be used to automate the process of mounting partitions.

Chapter 6: FAT Filesystems

Chapter 6 covers the File Allocation Table (FAT) filesystem in detail. While the FAT filesystem is quite old, it is still in widespread use on removable media today. An extensive set of Python and shell scripts are presented in this chapter. This chapter provides advanced techniques for detecting alterations of metadata by an attacker.

Chapter 7: File Forensics

Chapter 7 discusses how to analyze individual files. Topics covered include using file signatures to determine file types, finding files with mismatched extensions, finding files of a certain type, and using tools like Scalpel to carve files from raw disk sectors. As always, Python and shell scripting are used to automate these tasks.

Chapter 8: NTFS Filesystems

This chapter contains an in-depth look at the default filesystem used by Windows today, NTFS. This chapter covers detecting alterations to metadata, extracting files from filesystem images, recovering deleted files, creating timelines, and importing metadata into databases and spreadsheets for analysis. Naturally, Python and shell scripting are leveraged heavily in order to automate these processes.

Chapter 9: The Windows Registry

The Windows registry is a treasure trove of information for the forensic investigator. This chapter provides insight into how the registry is organized and shows the reader how to extract pertinent information. A number of free tools are discussed in addition to the usual Python and shell scripts.

Chapter 10: Windows Artifacts

In addition to the useful information found in the registry, many important bits of evidence can be found in a few files. This chapter discusses these artifacts which include recycle bin files, event logs, prefetch files, user profile files, and web browsing history. In addition to Python and shell scripts, a number of free tools are presented in this chapter.

Chapter 11: Memory Analysis

Chapter 11 introduces the new field of memory analysis. The Volatility memory analysis framework is discussed in detail. This chapter covers getting process information, process maps, process dumps, command histories, using Volatility check plug-ins, retrieving network information, and obtaining in-memory executables.

Chapter 12: Malware

Chapter 12 provides an introduction to Windows malware analysis. It covers standard tools for investigating unknown files. It discusses obfuscation techniques and safety issues related to malware investigation.

Chapter 13: The Road Ahead

In this final chapter, tasks required to finalize an investigation are discussed. This chapter provides several suggestions for further study. General tips for a successful career involving forensics are also given.

CONCLUSION

Countless hours have been spent developing this book and accompanying scripts. It has been a labor of love, however. I hope you enjoy reading and actually applying what is in this book as much as I have enjoyed writing it.

For updates to this book, and also my latest endeavors, consult my website

http://philpolstra.com.

You can also contact me via my Twitter account,

@ppolstra.

Downloads related to the book and forms of community support
are available at Pentester Academy

http://pentesteracademy.com and **http://windowsforensicsbook.com**.

CHAPTER 1

First Steps

INFORMATION IN THIS CHAPTER:

- What is forensics?
- Types of forensics
- Why use Linux for Windows forensics?
- General principles
- Phases of investigation
- High-level process
- Building a toolkit

WHAT IS FORENSICS?

A natural question to ask yourself if you are reading a book on Windows forensics is: What is forensics anyway? If you ask different forensic examiners, you are likely to receive slightly different answers to this question. According to a recent version of the Merriam-Webster dictionary: "Forensic (n) belonging to, used in, or suitable to courts of judicature or to public discussion and debate." Using this definition of the word forensic my definition of forensic science is as follows:

Forensic science or forensics is the scientific collection of evidence of sufficient quality that it is suitable for use in court.

The key point to keep in mind is that we should be collecting evidence of sufficient quality that we can use it in court, even if we never intend to go to court with our findings. It is always easier to relax our standards than to tighten them later. We should also act like scientists; doing everything in a methodical and technically sound manner.

TYPES OF FORENSICS

When most people hear the term forensics they think about things they might have seen on shows such as CSI. This is what I refer to as physical forensics. Some of the more commonly encountered areas of physical forensics include fingerprints, DNA, ballistics, and blood spatter. One of the fundamental principles of physical forensics is Locard's Transfer (or Exchange) Principle. Locard essentially said that if objects interact, they transfer (or exchange) material. For example, if you hit something with your car, there is often an exchange of paint. As another example, when you touch a surface, you might leave fingerprints and take dirt on your shoes when you leave the area.

This book covers what I would refer to as digital forensics. Some like the term computer forensics, but I prefer digital forensics as it is much broader. We live in a world that is increasingly reliant on electronic devices such as smart phones, tablets, laptops, and desktop computers. Given the amount of information many people store on their smart phones and other small devices, it is often useful to examine those devices if they are suspected of some sort of crime. The scope of this book is limited to computers (which could be embedded) running a version of Windows.

There are many specializations within the broader space of digital forensics. These include network forensics, data storage forensics, small device forensics, computer forensics, and many other areas. Within these specializations there are further subdivisions. It is not unusual for forensic examiners to be highly specialized. My hope is that by the time you finish this book you will be proficient enough with Windows forensics to perform investigations in the majority of scenarios in which Windows forensics is relevant (data recovery, collecting evidence of illegal activities, confirming system breaches, etc.).

WHY USE LINUX FOR WINDOWS FORENSICS?

Presumably if you are reading this, you see the value in learning Windows forensics. However, you might question my assertion that Linux is ideally suited for performing investigations on Windows systems. Here are just a few of the reasons that a Linux forensic workstation makes the most sense.

Linux is the operating system "by programmers for programmers". As a result, there is a plethora of utilities for examining and manipulating data available for Linux, most of which are installed by default. For the few useful packages that are not already installed, just a few mouse clicks or keystrokes are needed to acquire them.

Linux provides the highest number of forensic tools. In addition to standard tools that can be used for forensics, many of the free and/or open source forensic applications are available in a Linux version. Because it is programmer-friendly, some of these forensic utilities appear first on the Linux platform. Most of the Windows-only programs can be easily run on Linux with the WINE (Wine Is Not an Emulator) facility. If you are unfamiliar with WINE, it allows Windows executables to be run directly on Linux by translating WIN32 API calls to native Linux system calls.

Linux is the most compatible system. If a filesystem exists, you can probably mount it on a Linux system. Additionally, no special software (such as FTK Imager from Access Data) is required to mount filesystem images.

Linux systems offer the best performance. The 64-bit versions of Linux have been available since two years prior to the availability of 64-bit microprocessors. Linux has a long history of delivering the best performance for any given set of hardware. Linux ships with a collection of highly-specialized and optimized utilities which further enhance performance of typical forensic investigation tasks. If your budget is limited, Linux is definitely the way to go.

GENERAL PRINCIPLES

There are a number of general guiding principles that should be followed when practicing forensics. These include maintaining the integrity of evidence, maintaining the chain of custody, following standard practice, and fully documenting everything. These are discussed in more detail below.

Maintaining Integrity

It is of the utmost importance that evidence not be altered while it is being collected and examined. We are fortunate in digital forensics that we can normally make an unlimited number of identical copies of evidence. Those working with physical forensics are not so lucky. In fact, in many cases difficult choices must be made when quantities of physical evidence are limited as many tests consume evidence.

The primary method of insuring integrity of digital evidence is hashing. Hashing is widely used in computer science as a way of improving performance. A hash function, generally speaking, takes an input of variable size and outputs a number of known size. Hashing allows for faster searches because computers can compare two numbers in one clock cycle versus iterating over every character in a long string which could require hundreds or thousands of clock cycles.

Using hash functions in your programs can add a little complication because more than one input value can produce the same hash output. When this happens, we say that a collision has occurred. Collisions are a complication in our programs, but when we are using hashes for encryption or integrity checking, the possibility of many collisions is unacceptable. To minimize the number of collisions we must use cryptographic hash functions.

There are several cryptographic hash functions available. Some still use the Message Digest 5 (MD5) to verify the integrity of images. The MD5 algorithm is no longer considered to be secure and the Secure Hash Algorithm (SHA) family of functions is preferred. The original version is referred to as SHA1 (or just SHA). SHA2 is currently the most commonly used variant and you may encounter references to SHA2 (224 bits), SHA256 (256 bits), SHA384 (384 bits), and SHA512 (512 bits). There is a SHA3 algorithm, but its use is not yet widespread. I normally use SHA256 which is a good middle ground offering good performance with a low chance of collisions.

We will discuss the details of using hashing in future chapters. For now the high level process is as follows. First, calculate a hash of the original. Second, create an image which we will treat as a master copy. Third, calculate the hash of the copy and verify that it matches the hash of the original. Fourth, make working copies of your master copy, then never use the master copy and original again. While it may seem strange, the hash on working copies should be periodically recalculated as a double check that the investigator did not alter the image.

Chain of Custody

Physical evidence is often stored in evidence bags. Evidence bags either incorporate a chain of custody form or have such a form attached to them. Each time evidence is removed from the bag the form is updated with who touched the evidence and what was done. The collection of entries on this form make up the chain of custody. Essentially the chain of custody is a guarantee that the evidence has not been altered and has been properly maintained.

In the case of digital forensics the chain of custody is still important. While we can make unlimited digital copies, we must still maintain the integrity of the original. This is also why a master copy should be made that is never used for any other purpose other than creating working copies as it prevents the need to touch the original other than for the one-time event of creating the master copy.

Standard Practices

Following standard practices makes your investigation easier. By following a written procedure accurately there is less explaining to do if you should find yourself in court. You are also less likely to forget something or make a mistake. If you follow standard practices there is also less documentation that has to be done. It used to be said, "Nobody was ever fired for buying IBM." Similarly, no forensics investigator ever got into trouble using written procedures that conform to industry standard practice.

Documentation

When in doubt document. It never hurts to overdo the documentation. As mentioned previously, if you follow standard written procedures, you can reference them as opposed to repeating them in your notes. Speaking of notes, I recommend handwritten notes in a bound notebook with numbered pages. This might sound strange to readers who are used to using computers for everything, but it is much quicker to jot notes onto paper. It is also easier to carry a set of handwritten notes to court.

The bound notebook has other advantages as well. No power is required to view these notes. The use of a bound notebook with numbered pages also makes it more difficult to alter your notes. Not that you would alter them, but a lawyer might not be beyond accusing you of such a thing. If you have difficulty finding a notebook with numbered pages you can number them yourself before use.

If you can work with someone else, it is ideal. Pilots routinely use checklists to make sure they do not miss anything. Commercial pilots work in pairs as extra insurance against mistakes. Working with a partner allows you to have a second set of eyes, lets you work more quickly, and also makes it even harder for someone to accuse you of tampering with evidence. History is replete with examples of people who have avoided conviction by accusing someone of evidence tampering and instilling sufficient doubt in a jury.

Few people love to do documentation. This seems to be true to a greater extent among technical people. There are some tools that can ease the pain of documenting your findings that will be discussed in later chapters of this book. An investigation is never over until the documentation is finished.

PHASES OF INVESTIGATION

There are three phases to a forensic investigation: evidence preservation and collection, evidence searching, and event reconstruction. It is not unusual for there to be some cycling between the phases as an investigation proceeds. These phases are described in more detail below.

Evidence Preservation and Collection

Medical professionals have a saying "First do no harm." For digital forensics practitioners our motto should be "Don't alter the data." This sounds simple enough. In actuality it is a bit more complicated as data is volatile. There is a hierarchy of volatility that exists in data found in any system.

The most volatile data can be found in CPU registers. These registers are high speed scratch memory locations. Capturing their contents is next to impossible. Fortunately, there is little forensic value in these contents. CPU caches are the next level down in terms of volatility. Like registers they are hard to capture and also, thankfully, of little forensic value.

Slightly less volatile than storage in the CPU are buffers found in various devices such as network cards. Not all input/output devices have their own storage buffers. Some low-speed devices use main system memory (RAM) for buffering. As with data stored in the CPU, this data is difficult to capture. In theory, anything stored in these buffers should be replicated in system memory assuming it came from or was destined for the target computer.

System memory is also volatile. Once power has been lost, RAM is cleared. When compared to previously discussed items, system memory is relatively easy to capture. In most cases it is not possible to collect the contents of system memory without changing memory contents slightly. An exception to this would be hardware-based memory collection. Memory acquisition will be discussed in greater detail in a later chapter.

Due to limitations in technology, until recently much of digital forensics was focused on "dead analysis" of images from hard drives and other media. Even when dealing with non-volatile media volatility is still an issue. One of the oldest questions in computer security and forensics is whether or not to pull the plug on a system you suspect has been compromised.

Pulling the plug can lead to data loss as anything cached for writing to media will disappear. On modern journaling filesystems (such as NTFS) this is less of an issue as the journal can be used to correct any corruption. If the system is shut down in the normal manner some malware will attempt to cover its tracks or even worse destroy other data on the system.

Executing a normal shutdown has the advantage of flushing buffers and caches. As previously mentioned, the orderly shutdown is not without possible disadvantages. As with many things in forensics, the correct answer as to which method is better is, "It depends." There are methods of obtaining images of hard drives and other media which do not require a system shutdown which further complicates this decision. Details of these methods will be presented in future chapters.

Evidence Searching

Thanks to the explosion of storage capacity it becomes harder to locate evidence within the sea of data stored in a typical computer with each passing year. Data exists at three levels, data, information, and evidence, as shown in Figure 1.1.

As shown in Figure 1.1, the lowest level of data is just raw data. Raw data consists of bits, normally organized as bytes, in volatile or non-volatile storage. In this category we find things such as raw disk sectors. It can be a challenge to use data at this level and on most modern systems there is plenty of data out there to pick through.

Above raw data we have information. Information consists of raw data with some sort of

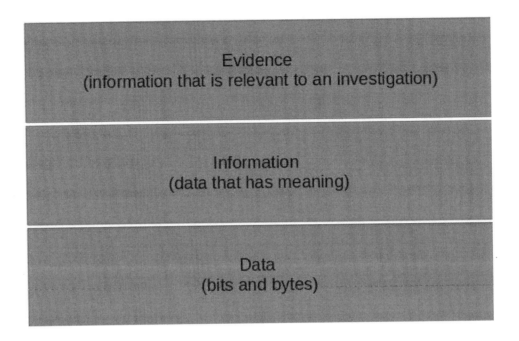

FIGURE 1.1.

The data hierarchy.

meaning attached to it. For example, an image has more meaning to a human than the bits that make up a JPEG file used to store the image. Even text files exist at this level in our hierarchy. Bringing many bytes of ASCII or Unicode values together gives them meaning beyond their collection of bytes.

At the highest level in our hierarchy is evidence. While there may be thousands or millions of files (collections of information) it is unlikely that the bulk of them have any relevance to an investigation. This leads us to ponder what it means for information to be relevant to an investigation.

As previously mentioned, forensics is a science. Given that we are trying to do science, we should be developing hypotheses and then searching for information that supports or refutes a hypothesis. It is important to remain objective during an investigation as the same piece of evidence might be interpreted differently based on people's preconceived notions.

It is extremely important that investigators do not become victims of confirmation bias. Put simply, confirmation bias is only looking at information that supports what you believe to be true while discounting anything that would refute what you believe. Given the amount of data that must be examined in a typical investigation, a hypothesis or two concerning what you think you will find is good (the owner of the computer did X, this computer was successfully exploited, etc.) to help guide you through the searching process. Do not fall into the trap of assuming your hypothesis or hypotheses are correct, however.

> ### CONFIRMATION BIAS IN ACTION
>
> #### Every Child is Perfect, Just Ask The Parents
> One of the best stories to describe confirmation bias goes as follows. Johnny loved magicians. One day his parents took him to see a famous magician, Phil the Great. At the end of the show the parents told Phil how much their son loved magic. Phil then offered to show them a trick. Johnny eagerly accepted.
>
> The magician proceeded to pull out a coin and move it back and forth between both hands then closed his fists and held out his hands. He asked Johnny to identify the hand containing the coin, which he did correctly. Now guessing correctly one time is not much of a feat, but this game was repeated many times and each time Johnny correctly guessed the hand containing the coin. While this was going on, the magician made comments like, "You must have excellent vision to see which hand contains the coin, You must be an expert on reading my facial expressions and that is how you know where the coin is."
>
> Eventually Johnny had correctly identified the hand with the coin fifty times in a row! His parents were amazed. They called the grandparents and told all of their friends about it on Facebook, Twitter, and other social media sites. When they finally thanked the magician and turned to leave, he shouted "goodbye" and waved with both hands. Each hand contained a coin.
>
> It was the parents' confirmation bias that led them to believe what they wanted to believe, that Johnny was a savant, and distracted them from the truth, the magician was indeed tricking them. Remain objective during an investigation. Do not let what you or your boss want to be true keep you from seeing contrary evidence.

Reconstruction of Events

In my mind trying to reconstruct what happened is the most fun part of an investigation. The explosion in size of storage media might make the searching phase longer than it was in the past, but that only helps to make the reconstruction phase that much more enjoyable. It is very unlikely that you will find all the evidence you need for your event reconstruction in one place. It is much more common to get little pieces of evidence from multiple places which you put together into a larger picture. For example, a suspicious process in a process list stored in a memory image might lead you to look at files in a filesystem image which might lead you back to an open file list in the memory image which in turn points toward files in the filesystem image. Putting all of these bits together might allow you to determine when and by whom a rootkit was downloaded and when and by which user it was subsequently installed.

HIGH-LEVEL PROCESS

While not every Windows forensics investigation is part of an incident response, it is one of the more common scenarios for those working outside of law enforcement. Additionally, with

CHAPTER 1 First Steps

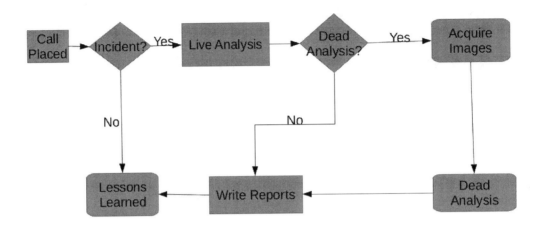

FIGURE 1.2.

High-level Process for Windows Incident Response

the exception of determining if there was an incident, much of this workflow will be relevant to other Windows investigations as well. The high level process for incident response is shown in Figure 1.2.

As can be seen in Figure 1.2, it all begins with a call. Someone believes that a breach (or something else) has occurred and they have called you to investigate. Your next step is to determine whether or not there was a breach. A small amount of live analysis might be required in order to make this determination. If no breach occurred, you get to document what happened and add this to your knowledge base.

If there was an incident, you would normally start with live analysis before deciding whether or not dead analysis is justified. If you deem it necessary to perform the dead analysis, you need to acquire some images and then actually perform the analysis. Whether or not you performed a dead analysis it isn't over until the reports are written. All of these steps will be discussed in detail in future chapters.

BUILDING A TOOLKIT

In order to do Windows forensics effectively you might want to acquire a few tools. Many of the forensic tools which run on Linux are free (most are also open source). In addition to the notebook discussed previously, some hardware and software should be in every forensic investigator's tool kit.

Hardware

You will likely want one or more external hard drives for making images (both RAM and hard disks). External hard drives are preferred as it is much easier to share with other investigators when they can just plug in a drive. USB 3.0 devices are the best as they are significantly faster than their USB 2.0 counterparts.

A write blocker is also helpful whenever an image is to be made of any media. Several hardware write blockers are available. Most of these are limited to one particular interface. If your budget affords only one hardware write blocker, I would recommend a SATA blocker as this is the most common interface in use at this time. Software write blockers are also a possibility. A simple software write blocker is presented later in this book.

Software

Software needs fall into a few categories: forensic tools, known-good binaries, and live Linux distributions. Ideally these tools are stored on USB 3.0 flash drives and perhaps a few DVDs if you anticipate encountering systems that cannot boot from a USB drive. Given how cheap USB flash drives are today, even investigators with modest budgets can be prepared for most situations.

There are a number of ways to install a set of forensic tools. The easiest method is to install a forensics oriented Linux distribution such as SIFT from SANS (http://digital-forensics.sans.org/community/downloads). Personally, I prefer to to run my favorite Linux and just install the tools rather than be stuck with someone else's themes and sluggish live system performance. The following script will install all of the tools found in SIFT on most Debian or Ubuntu based systems (unlike the SANS install script that works only on specific versions of Ubuntu).

```
#!/bin/bash
# Simple little script to load DFIR tools into Ubuntu and Debian
systems
# by Dr. Phil Polstra @ppolstra

# create repositories
echo "deb http://ppa.launchpad.net/sift/stable/ubuntu trusty main" \
   > /etc/apt/sources.list.d/sift-ubuntu-stable-utopic.list
echo "deb http://ppa.launchpad.net/tualatrix/ppa/ubuntu trusty main" \
   > /etc/apt/sources.list.d/tualatrix-ubuntu-ppa-utopic.list

#list of packages
pkglist="aeskeyfind
afflib-tools
afterglow
aircrack-ng
arp-scan
autopsy
```

```
binplist
bitpim
bitpim-lib
bless
blt
build-essential
bulk-extractor
cabextract
clamav
cryptsetup
dc3dd
dconf-tools
dumbpig
e2fslibs-dev
ent
epic5
etherape
exif
extundelete
f-spot
fdupes
flare
flasm
flex
foremost
g++
gcc
gdb
ghex
gthumb
graphviz
hexedit
htop
hydra
hydra-gtk
ipython
kdiff3
kpartx
libafflib0
libafflib-dev
libbde
libbde-tools
libesedb
libesedb-tools
libevt
```

```
libevt-tools
libevtx
libevtx-tools
libewf
libewf-dev
libewf-python
libewf-tools
libfuse-dev
libfvde
libfvde-tools
liblightgrep
libmsiecf
libnet1
libolecf
libparse-win32registry-perl
libregf
libregf-dev
libregf-python
libregf-tools
libssl-dev
libtext-csv-perl
libvshadow
libvshadow-dev
libvshadow-python
libvshadow-tools
libxml2-dev
maltegoce
md5deep
nbd-client
netcat
netpbm
nfdump
ngrep
ntopng
okular
openjdk-6-jdk
p7zip-full
phonon
pv
pyew
python
python-dev
python-pip
python-flowgrep
python-nids
```

```
python-ntdsxtract
python-pefile
python-plaso
python-qt4
python-tk
python-volatility
pytsk3
rsakeyfind
safecopy
sleuthkit
ssdeep
ssldump
stunnel4
tcl
tcpflow
tcpstat
tcptrace
tofrodos
torsocks
transmission
unrar
upx-ucl
vbindiff
virtuoso-minimal
winbind
wine
wireshark
xmount
zenity
regripper
cmospwd
ophcrack
ophcrack-cli
bkhive
samdump2
cryptcat
outguess
bcrypt
ccrypt
readpst
ettercap-graphical
driftnet
tcpreplay
tcpxtract
tcptrack
```

```
p0f
netwox
lft
netsed
socat
knocker
nikto
nbtscan
radare-gtk
python-yara
gzrt
testdisk
scalpel
qemu
qemu-utils
gddrescue
dcfldd
vmfs-tools
mantaray
python-fuse
samba
open-iscsi
curl
git
system-config-samba
libpff
libpff-dev
libpff-tools
libpff-python
xfsprogs
gawk
exfat-fuse
exfat-utils
xpdf
feh
pyew
radare
radare2
pev
tcpick
pdftk
sslsniff
dsniff
rar
xdot
```

```
ubuntu-tweak
vim"


#actually install
# first update
apt-get update

for pkg in ${pkglist}
do
        if (dpkg --list | awk '{print $2}' | \
            egrep "^${pkg}$" 2>/dev/null) ;
        then
                echo "yeah ${pkg} already installed"
        else
                # try to install
                echo -n "Trying to install ${pkg}..."
                if (apt-get -y install ${pkg} 2>/dev/null) ; then
                        echo "+++Succeeded+++"
                else
                        echo "----FAILED----"
                fi
        fi
done
```

Briefly, the above script works as described here. First, we run a particular shell (bash) using the special comment construct #!{command to run}. This is often called the "she-bang" operator or "pound-bang" or "hash-bang." Second, the lines with the echo statements add two repositories to our list of software sources. Technically, these repositories are intended to be used with Ubuntu 14.04, but they are likely to work with new versions of Ubuntu and/or Debian as well.

Third, a variable named pkglist is created which contains a list of the tools we wish to install. Fourth, we update our local application cache by issuing the command `apt-get update`. Finally, we iterate over our list of packages stored in pkglist and install them if they are not already installed. The test involves a string of commands, `dpkg --list | awk '{print $2}' | egrep "^${pkg}$" 2>/dev/null`. The command `dpkg --list` lists all installed packages and this list is then passed to `awk '{print $2}'` which cause the second word (the package name) to be printed, this is in turn passed to `egrep "^${pkg}$" 2>/dev/null` which checks to see if the package name exactly matches one that is installed (the ^ matches the start and the $ matches the end). Any errors are sent to the null device because we only care if there were any results.

In addition to the packages that are installed using the script above, you might want a few specialized utilities installed on your Linux forensic workstation. These will be discussed in detail as their use comes up in discussions in future chapters. Some of the larger packages that you might want to include are Active@ Disk Editor, FTK Imager, Autopsy, and Volatility.

Ideally, a set of known good system binaries should be installed to a flash drive in order to facilitate live response. This situation is a bit more complicated than the Linux equivalent. In order to have any chance of this working you will need to copy .cmd, .exe, .com, and .dll files from the the c:\windows directory and all of its subdirectories. This must be done for every version of Windows to be examined. Copying just the executables is not enough because any of the thousands of Windows Dynamic Link Libraries (DLL) may have been compromised.

Creating a set of known-good binaries is actually quite simple if you have the ability to mount a drive or filesystem image on your Linux workstation. If you attempt this be warned that you will need several gigabytes for each set of Windows binaries. Once the drive is mounted, the find facility can be used to copy all the required files using the following sequence of commands:

```
cd <Windows directory mount point>
find . -name "*.dll" -type f -exec cp {} <destination> \;
find . -name "*.exe" -type f -exec cp {} <destination> \;
find . -name "*.com" -type f -exec cp {} <destination> \;
find . -name "*.cmd" -type f -exec cp {} <destination> \;
```

On occasion a live Linux system installed on a bootable USB drive could be useful. Either a distribution such as SIFT can be installed by itself on a drive or the live system can be installed on the first partition of a larger USB drive and additional forensic tools on a second partition. If you are using a USB drive with multiple partitions, it is important to know that Windows systems will only see the first partition and then only if it is formated as FAT or NTFS.

THIS IS TAKING TOO LONG

Running live Linux in a virtual machine

If you decide to create a bootable SIFT (or similar) USB drive you will quickly find that it takes hours to install the packages from SIFT. This can tie up your computer preventing you from getting any real work done. However, there is a way to build the USB drive without tying up the machine. What you need to do is set up a virtual machine that can be run from a live Linux distribution on a USB drive. The following instructions assume you are running VirtualBox on a Linux host system.

VirtualBox ships with several tools. One of these is called vboxmanage. There are several commands vboxmanage supports. Typing `vboxmange -help` in a terminal will give you a long list of commands. This will not list the command that we need, however, as it is one of the internal commands.

In order to create a virtual disk that points to a physical device you must execute the following command as root: `vboxmanage internalcommands createrawvmdk -filename <location of vmdk file> -rawdisk <USB device>`. For example, if your thumb drive is normally mounted as /dev/sdb the following command could be used: `vboxmanage internalcommands createrawvmdk -filename /root/VirtualBox\ Vms/usb.vmdk -rawdisk /dev/sdb`. Note that you cannot just sudo this command as the regular user will have permission problems trying to run the virtual machine later. Creating this virtual drive and running VirtualBox is shown in Figure 1.3.

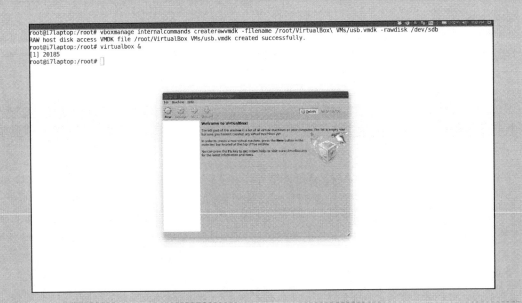

FIGURE 1.3.

Creating a virtual disk file that points to a physical USB drive.

Once the virtual disk file has been created, set up a new virtual machine in the normal manner. The creation of the live Linux virtual machine is shown in Figure 1.4 through Figure 1.6. Depending on the live Linux you have chosen, you may need to enable EFI support as shown in Figure 1.7. The virtual machine running for the first time is shown in Figure 1.8.

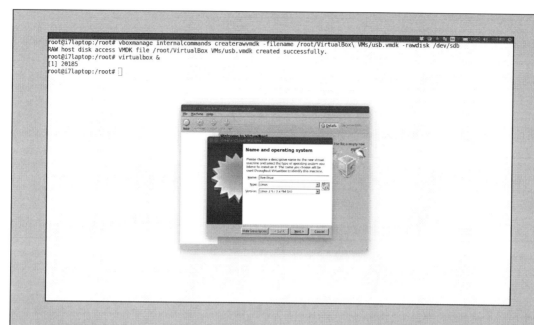

FIGURE 1.4.

Creating a virtual machine that runs a live Linux distribution from a USB drive.

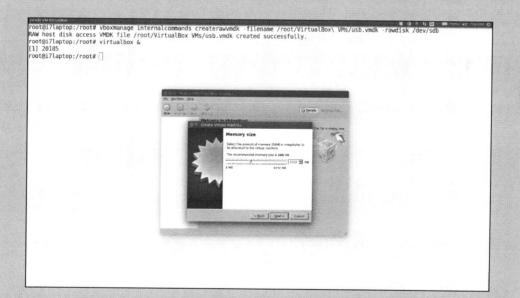

FIGURE 1.5.

Setting up memory for the live Linux virtual machine. Be certain to select the maximum amount of memory for better performance running a live distribution as everything is run from RAM.

18 **CHAPTER 1** First Steps

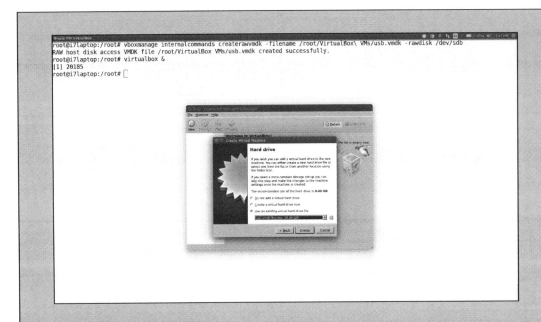

FIGURE 1.6.
Selecting the USB physical drive for the live Linux virtual machine.

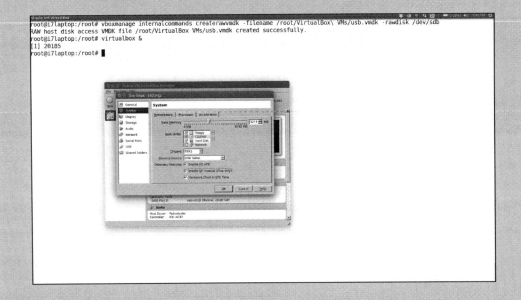

FIGURE 1.7.
Enabling EFI. Any operating system that uses the new UEFI boot system will likely need this box checked.

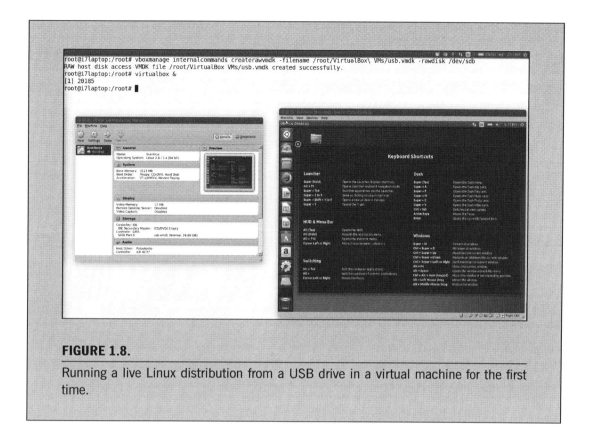

FIGURE 1.8.

Running a live Linux distribution from a USB drive in a virtual machine for the first time.

SUMMARY

In this chapter we have discussed all the preliminary items that should be taken care of before arriving on the scene after a suspected incident has occurred. We covered the hardware, software, and other tools that should be in your go bag. In the next chapter we will discuss the first job when you arrive, determining if there was an incident.

CHAPTER 2

Determining If There Was an Incident

INFORMATION IN THIS CHAPTER:

- Opening a case
- Talking to users
- Documentation
- Mounting known-good binaries
- Minimizing disturbance to the subject system
- Using scripting to automate the process
- Collecting volatile data
- Sure signs of compromise

OPENING A CASE

This chapter will address the highlighted box from our high-level process as shown in Figure 2.1. We will come to learn that there is often much involved in determining whether or not there was an incident. We will also see that some limited live response may be necessary in order to make this determination. As discussed previously, a suspected breach is only one of several

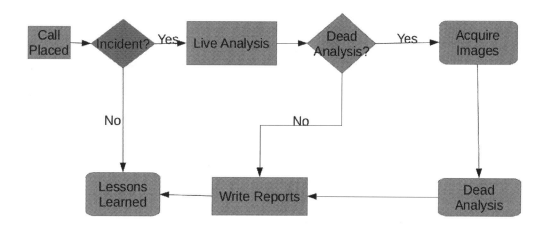

FIGURE 2.1.
The High-level Incident Response Process.

reasons for performing a forensic investigation. If you are not trying to determine if a breach occurred, you may safely skip ahead to Chapter 4 on creating system images.

Before you do anything else when you arrive on the scene, you should open a case file. This is not as complicated as it sounds. You could literally create a folder on your laptop with a case number. What should you use for a case number? Whatever you want. You might want a case number that is a year-number or you might prefer to use the date for a case number under the assumption that you will not be starting multiple cases on the same day. You could always append a number to the date if you had multiple cases in a given day.

You might also consider starting a new entry in your bound notebook (with the numbered pages). Some might prefer to wait until they are sure there was an incident before consuming space in their notebooks for a false alarm. My personal feeling on this is that notebooks are cheap and it is easier and cleaner if you start taking notes in one place from the very beginning.

TALKING TO USERS

Before you even think about touching the subject system you should interview the users. Why? Because they know more about the situation than you will. You might be able to determine that it was all a false alarm very quickly by talking to the users. For example, perhaps it was a system administrator who put a network card in promiscuous mode and not malware or an attacker. It would be far better for everyone if you found this out by talking to the administrator than after hours of investigating.

You should ask the users a series of questions. The first question you might ask is, "Why did you call me?" Was there an event that led to you being called in? Does the organization lack a qualified person to perform the investigation? Does the organization's policy on possible incidents require an outside investigator?

The second question you might ask is, "Why do you think there is a problem or incident?" Did something strange happen? Is the network and/or machine slower than normal? Is there traffic on unusual ports? Many Windows users will just shrug off strange behavior as a normal part of the Windows experience, but some more savvy users and administrators might notice behavior associated with malware.

Next you want to get as much information as you can about the subject (suspected victim) system. What is the system normally used for? Where did the system come from? Was it purchased locally or online, etc.? As many readers are likely aware, it has come to light that certain government entities are not above planting parasitic devices inside a computer that has been intercepted during shipment. Has the computer been repaired recently? If so, by whom? Was it an old, trusted friend or someone new? Malicious software and hardware are easily installed during such repairs.

DOCUMENTATION

As previously mentioned, you cannot over do the documentation. You should write down what the users told you during your interviews. In addition to the advantages already mentioned of using a notebook, writing notes in your notebook is a lot less distracting and intimidating for the users than banging away at your laptop keyboard or even worse filming the interviews.

You should also write down everything you know about the subject system. If it seems appropriate, you might consider taking a picture of the computer and screen. If you suspect that physical security has been breached, it is an especially good idea. You are now ready to actually touch the subject system.

VIRTUAL COMPLICATIONS

If you are using a virtual machine, older may be better

I have previously recommended the use of a USB 3.0 drive for performance reasons. If you are using a virtual machine to practice while you are going through this book, a USB 2.0 drive might be preferred. The reason for this is that some of the virtualization software seems to have issues dealing with USB 3.0 devices. At the time of this writing USB 2.0 devices seem to cause less troubles.

Regardless of the type of drive you have, the host operating systems will initially try to lay claim to any attached device. If you are using VirtualBox, you will need to check the appropriate device from the USB Devices submenu under Devices as shown in Figure 2.2.

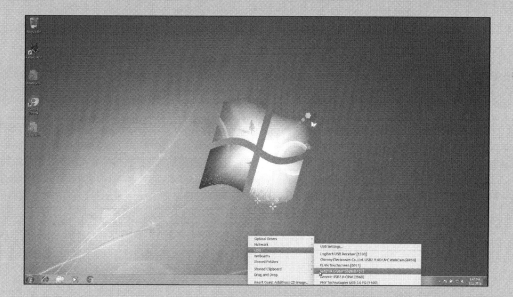

FIGURE 2.2.

Selecting a USB Drive. If your subject system is running inside a virtual machine, you will need to pass the device along to the virtual machine by selecting the device as shown here.

MOUNTING KNOWN-GOOD BINARIES

In most cases if you insert your USB drive with known-good binaries it will be automounted. If you ever receive the dreaded "scan and fix" message from Windows, be sure to press Cancel. This message really means that you used something other than Windows when you created the drive and if you allow Windows to "fix" it, you will likely end up with a truly broken drive. Once your drive is mounted, you should run a known-good command prompt (cmd.exe) located on your drive. However, you are not done after you run this command prompt. You must set your path to only point at the directories on your USB drive.

I should tell you a bit about how Windows handles Dynamic Link Libraries (DLL). The first thing to understand about Windows is that if a DLL needed by one of your applications is already loaded in memory, it will be used. Because of this, there is no way to guarantee that the known-good binaries on your USB drive will use the DLLs also on the USB drive.

The second thing you should understand about how DLLs are loaded is that there are multiple ways to change the search procedure. Creating the registry value HKEY_LOCAL_MACHINE\System\CurrentControlSet\Control\Session Manager\SafeDllSearchMode and setting it equal to one enables SafeDllSearchMode. When SafeDllSearchMode is enabled, the search order is as follows: directory from which the program was launched, the Windows system32 directory, the Windows system directory, the Windows directory, the current directory, and then directories listed in the %PATH% environment variable. Beginning with Windows XP Service Pack 2 (SP2), SafeDllSearchMode is enabled by default.

When SafeDllSearchMode is disabled, the DLL search order is as follows: directory from which the program was launched, the current directory, the Windows system32 directory, the Windows system directory, the Windows directory, and then directories listed in the %PATH% environment variable. To further complicate matters, the LoadLibraryEx function supports an alternate search order and the SetDllDirectory function also allows the standard directory list to be altered. The net of this complicated searching algorithm mess is that the best way to try and run your DLLs is to launch applications from the same directory in which the DLLs are stored. Even then there are no guarantees thanks to how in-memory DLLs are used first and to the possibility that LoadLibraryEx might have been used in the program you are trying to run.

Once everything is mounted, use the Windows Explorer to run your known-good cmd.exe as shown in Figure 2.3. Notice that you have the option to run this as an administrator. Be aware that if you select this option you may lose access to network drives for the currently logged in user. If you do not have an appropriate set of binaries for your subject system, you are left with the choice of performing live analysis with questionable binaries or skipping ahead right to creating images for dead analysis. At a minimum you might want to at least have an appropriate cmd.exe file that you use to launch the system utilities on the subject system.

Once the command prompt is run, the first order of business is to change to the correct directory (if you aren't already there) by typing `cd <path to known-good binaries>`. Next, you should set the %PATH% environment variable to point only at your known-good binaries using the command `set PATH=<path to known-good binaries>` as shown in Figure 2.4.

Minimizing disturbance to the subject system 25

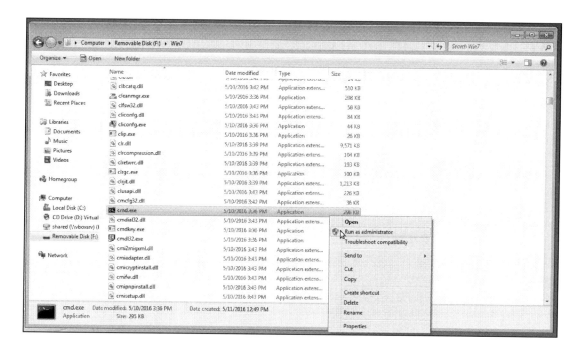

FIGURE 2.3.

Executing the known-good command prompt.

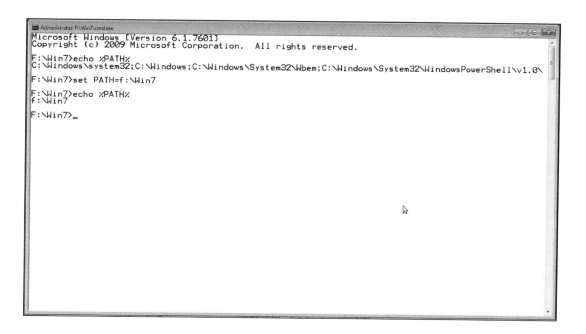

FIGURE 2.4.

Making the path point to known-good binaries.

MINIMIZING DISTURBANCE TO THE SUBJECT SYSTEM

Unfortunately, it is impossible to collect all the data from a running system without causing something to change. Your goal as a forensic investigator should be to minimize this disturbance to the subject system. There are two things you should never do if you can avoid it. First, don't install anything on the subject system. If you install new software, it will substantially change the system when configuration files, libraries, and executables are saved to the subject's media. The worst possible situation would be to compile something from source code as it will cause many temporary files to be created and will also consume memory (possibly pushing out other more interesting information) and affect a memory image should you choose to make one.

The second thing you should avoid is creating new files on the system. If you must use a tool that is not installed, have it on your response USB drive. Do not create memory or disk images and then store them on the subject system either!

You will definitely alter what is in RAM when you investigate a system. However, you should try to minimize your memory footprint. There are as couple of ways that you might accomplish these goals. Two popular solutions are to store data on USB media (which could be your response drive) or to use the netcat utility.

Using a USB drive to store data

Attaching a USB drive to the subject system is minimally invasive. A few larger USB 3.0 backup drives should be in your toolkit for just such occasions. It might be best to copy your system binaries to this drive first, should you end up going this route, to avoid having to mount more than one external drive.

Once the USB drive has been attached, you can use the techniques described earlier to operate with known-good system binaries and utilities. Log files and other data discussed in this chapter can be stored to the USB drive. Techniques described in later chapters can be used to store images on the USB drive. Even if you used the netcat utility (described next), having some USB backup drives on hand can make sharing images much easier. Naturally, whatever you do should be documented in your bound notebook.

Using Netcat

While using a USB drive meets our goals of not installing anything or creating new files on the subject system (with the exceptions noted above), it does not minimize our memory footprint. Copying to slow USB storage devices (especially USB 2.0 drives) is likely to result in a significant amount of caching which will increase our memory footprint. For this reason, the use of netcat is preferred when the subject system is connected to a network of reasonable speed and reliability.

Wired gigabit Ethernet is the most desirable media. If you are forced to use wireless networking, do your best to ensure your forensics workstation has a strong signal from the access point. If neither of these are an option, you may be able to connect your forensics laptop directly to the subject system via a crossover cable.

Realize that the subject system is probably set up to use Dynamic Host Configuration

Protocol (DHCP) so you will either need to use static IP addresses on both ends or install a DHCP server on your forensics laptop if you go the crossover cable route. If the subject system has only one network interface that must be disconnected, I recommend against using the crossover cable as it will disturb the system too much. To temporarily set up a static IP on your Linux workstation issue the command `sudo ifconfig {interface} down && sudo ifconfig {interface} {IP} netmask {netmask} up`, i.e. `sudo ifconfig eth0 down && sudo ifconfig eth0 192.168.1.1 netmask 255.255.255.0 up`.

On the Windows subject machine the IP address can be reset from an administrator command prompt. To bring up an administrator command prompt select All Programs from the Start Menu, then navigate to Accessories, and finally, right-click on the Command Prompt and select "Run as administrator". This process is shown in Figure 2.5. As shown in Figure 2.6, the command to set a static IP address on Windows from the command prompt is `netsh interface ip set address name="Local Area Connection" static <IP address> <subnet mask> <broadcast address>` assuming there is only one network adapter installed. If there is more than one network adapter, be sure to use the correct name in the command. Make sure you give each end a different IP on the same subnet!

Setting up a netcat listener

You will need to set up one or more listeners on the forensics workstation. The syntax for setting up a listener is pretty simple. Typing `netcat -l {port}` will cause a listener to be created on every network interface on the machine. Normally this information should be stored in a file by redirecting netcat's output using > or >>. Recall that the difference between > and >> is that > causes an existing file to be overwritten and >> appends data if the file already exists.

I recommend that you create a listener on the forensics workstation that receives the output of all the commands you wish to run on the subject system in a single log file. This keeps everything in one place. By default netcat will terminate the listener upon receiving the end-of-file (EOF) marker. The -k option for netcat will keep the listener alive until you press Control-C in the terminal where you started netcat. The command to start the log file listener is `netcat -k -l {port} >> {log file}`, i.e. `netcat -k -l 9999 >> example-log.txt`. This command is shown in Figure 2.7. Note that while I have used `netcat` here, this is a symbolic link to the same program pointed to by `nc` on most systems, so you can use whichever you prefer.

Sending data from the subject system

Windows systems do not ship with netcat like Linux systems do. To further complicate the situation there are multiple versions of netcat available for Windows. The full version of nmap (the network mapper) includes netcat. Because of nmap's dependencies, I recommend a standalone version of netcat. After a little Googling, you should find a website http://joncraton.org/blog/46/netcat-for-windows that contains a standalone netcat that should be installed to your incident response USB drive.

Now that you have a listener on the forensic workstation, it is easy to send data across the network using netcat. The general sequence for sending something for logging is `{command}`

28 CHAPTER 2 Determining If There Was an Incident

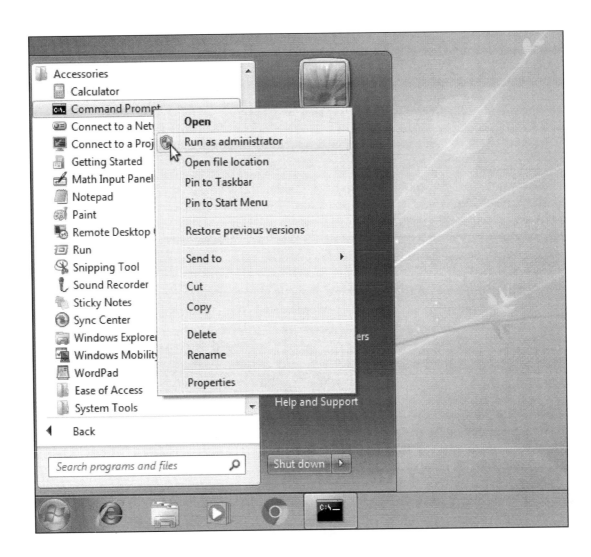

FIGURE 2.5.

Running a command prompt as the administrator.

`| nc {forensic workstation IP} {port}`. For commands that do not have output that makes it obvious what was run, you might want to send a header of sorts using the echo utility before sending the output of the command. This is demonstrated in Figure 2.8. The results of running the commands shown in Figure 2.8 are shown in Figure 2.9. Using scripting to automate this process is discussed later in this chapter.

Sending files

It is not unusual to extract suspicious files from a subject system for further study. Netcat is also handy for performing this task. In order to receive a file you should start a new listener on the

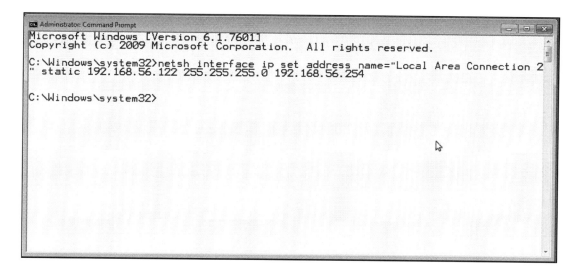

FIGURE 2.6.

Setting a static IP address from the Windows command prompt.

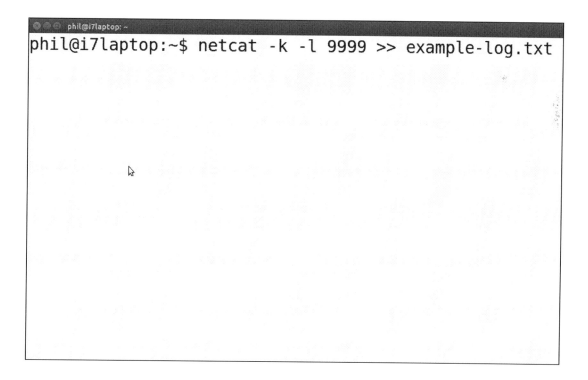

FIGURE 2.7.

Running a netcat listener on the forensics workstation.

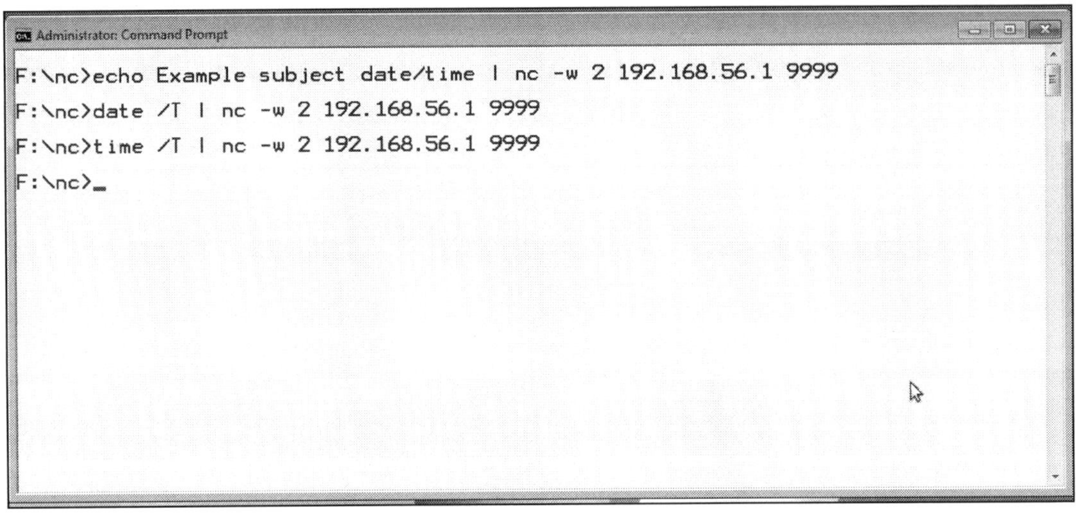
Administrator: Command Prompt
F:\nc>echo Example subject date/time | nc -w 2 192.168.56.1 9999
F:\nc>date /T | nc -w 2 192.168.56.1 9999
F:\nc>time /T | nc -w 2 192.168.56.1 9999
F:\nc>_

FIGURE 2.8.

Using netcat to send information to the forensics workstation.

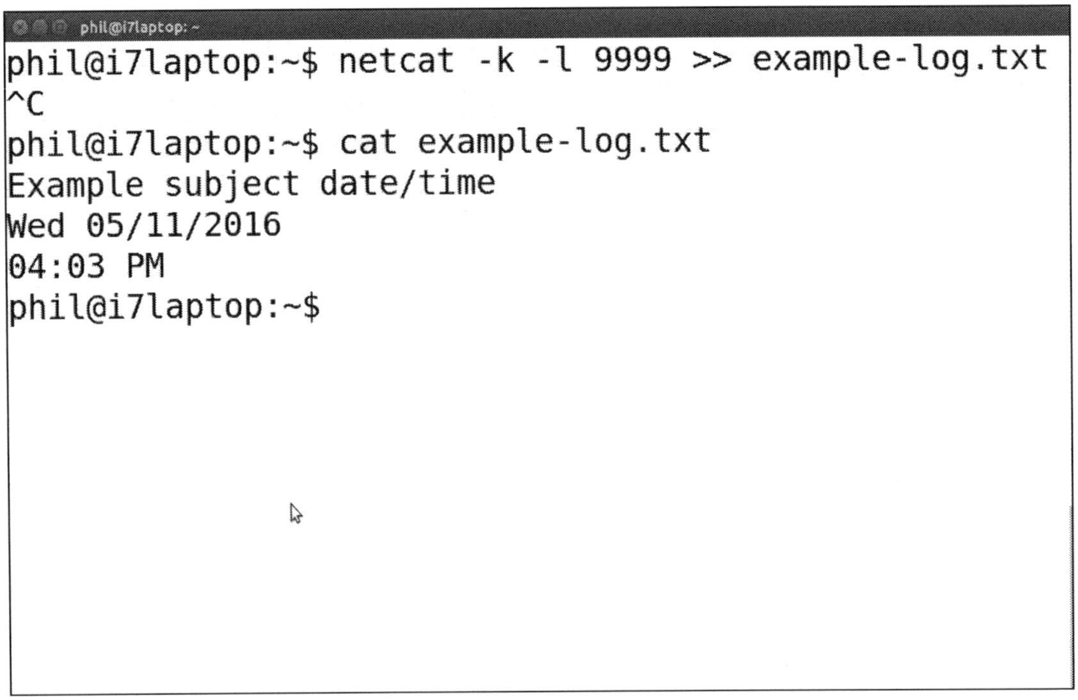
phil@i7laptop: ~
phil@i7laptop:~$ netcat -k -l 9999 >> example-log.txt
^C
phil@i7laptop:~$ cat example-log.txt
Example subject date/time
Wed 05/11/2016
04:03 PM
phil@i7laptop:~$

FIGURE 2.9.

Results received by listener from commands in Figure 2.8.

forensic workstation that does not use the -k option. In this case you want to end the listener after the file has been transmitted. The command is `nc -l {port} > {filename}`.

On the subject system the suspect file is redirected into the netcat talker. The syntax for sending the file is `nc {forensic workstation IP} {port} < {filename}`, i.e. `nc 192.168.1.119 4444 < notepad.exe`. The listener and talker for this file transfer are shown in Figure 2.10 and Figure 2.11, respectively.

USING SCRIPTING TO AUTOMATE THE PROCESS

It should be fairly obvious that our little netcat system described above is ripe for scripting. The first question one might ask is what sort of scripting language should be used. Many would immediately jump to using Python for this task. While I might like to use Python for many forensic and security tasks, it is not the best choice in this case.

There are a couple of reasons why shell scripting or Windows command scripts are a better choice, in my opinion. First, we want to minimize our memory footprint, and executing a Python interpreter runs counter to that goal. Second, a Python script that primarily just runs other programs is somewhat pointless. It is much simpler to execute these programs directly in a script. As an additional bonus for some readers, the scripts described here constitute a nice introduction to basic shell and command scripting.

```
phil@i7laptop:~$ nc -l 4444 > notepad.exe
phil@i7laptop:~$ ls -l notepad.exe
-rw-rw-r-- 1 phil phil 193536 May 11 16:20 notepad.exe
phil@i7laptop:~$
```

FIGURE 2.10.

Setting up a netcat listener to receive a file.

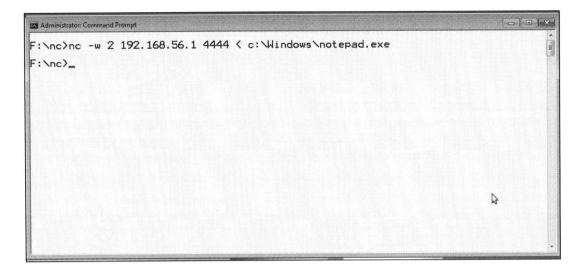

FIGURE 2.11.

Using netcat to send a file.

Scripting the server

The scripts shown below will create a new directory for case files and start two listeners. The first listener is used to log commands executed on the subject (client) machine and the second is used to receive files. A script to clean up and shut down the listeners is also presented. Here is the main script, start-case.sh:

```
#!/bin/bash
#
# start-case.sh
#
# Simple script to start a new case on a forensics
# workstation.  Will create a new folder if needed
# and start two listeners: one for log information
# and the other to receive files. Intended to be
# used as part of initial live response.
# by Dr. Phil Polstra (@ppolstra) as developed for
# PentesterAcademy.com.

usage () {
      echo "usage: $0 <case number>"
      echo "Simple script to create case folder and start listeners"
      exit 1
}
```

```
if [ $# -lt 1 ] ; then
      usage
else
      echo "Starting case $1"
fi

#if the directory doesn't exist create it
if [ ! -d $1 ] ; then
      mkdir $1
fi

# create the log listener
`nc -k -l 4444 >> $1/log.txt` &
echo "Started log listener for case $1 on $(date)" | nc localhost 4444

# start the file listener
`./start-file-listener.sh $1` &
```

This script starts with the special comment "#!" also known as the she-bang which causes the bash shell to be executed. It is important to run a particular shell as users are allowed to pick their own and might select something incompatible with your script. A # anywhere on a line begins a comment which terminates at the end of the line. The first several lines are comments that describe the script.

After the comments a function called usage is defined. To define a function in a shell script, simply type its name followed by a space, empty parentheses, another space, and then enclose whatever commands make up the function in curly brackets. Unlike compiled languages and some scripting languages, shell scripts require white space in the proper places or they will not function correctly. The $0 in the line `echo "usage: $0 <case number>"` is a variable that is set to the first command line parameter that was used to run the script, which is the name of the script file.

Note the use of double quotes in the echo commands. Anything enclosed in double quotes is expanded (interpreted) by the shell. If single quotes are used no expansion is performed. It is considered a good programming practice to define a usage function that is called when a user supplies command line arguments that do not make sense.

The line `if [ $# -lt 1 ] ;  then` begins an `if` block. The logical test is enclosed in square brackets. Note that there must be white space around the brackets and between parts of the logical test as shown. The variable $# is set to the number of command line arguments passed in to the script. In this script if that number is less than 1 the usage function is called, otherwise a message about starting a case is echoed to the screen. The variable $1 is the first command line parameter passed in (right after the name of the script) which is meant to be the case name. Observe that the `if` block is terminated with fi (if spelled backwards).

The conditional statement in the `if` block that starts with `if [ ! -d $1 ] ; then` checks to see if the case directory does not yet exist. The -d test checks to see that a directory with the name that follows exists. The ! negates (reverses) the test so that the code inside the if block is executed if the directory does not exist. The code simply uses mkdir to create the directory.

Next, the line `nc -k -l 4444 >> $1/log.txt` & starts a listener on port 4444 and sends everything received to a file in the case directory named log.txt. Note the command is enclosed in back ticks (backward single quotes). This tells the shell to please run the command. The & causes the command to be run in the background so that more things can be executed.

The next line simply echoes a banner which is piped to the listener in order to create a header for the log file. This line uses a bash shell trick. Any command(s) enclosed in parentheses preceded by a $ is(are) executed and the results can be used in another command. In this case $(date) is used to insert the current date and time. Finally, another script is also run in the background. This script starts the file listener process. This script is described next.

```
#!/bin/bash
#
# start-file-listener.sh
#
# Simple script to start a new file
# listener. Intended to be
# used as part of initial live response.
# by Dr. Phil Polstra (@ppolstra) as developed for
# PentesterAcademy.com.

# When a filename is sent to port 5555 a transfer on 5556
# is expected to follow.

usage () {
   echo "usage: $0 <case name>"
   echo "Simple script to start a file listener"
   exit 1
}

# did you specify a case name?
if [ $# -lt 1 ] ; then
   usage
fi

while true
do
   filename=$(nc -l 5555)
   nc -l 5556 > $1/$(basename $filename)
done
```

This script starts with the standard she-bang which causes the bash shell to be used. It also defines a usage function which is called if a case name is not passed in to the script. The real work in this script is in the while loop at the end. The line `while true` causes an infinite loop which is only exited when the user presses Control-C or the process is killed. Note that unlike the `if` block which is terminated with fi, the `do` block is terminated with `done` (not od).

The first line in the loop runs a netcat listener on port 5555 and sets the filename variable equal to whatever was received on this port. Recall that we have used this trick of running a command inside of $() to set a variable equal to the command results in the previous script. Once a filename has been received, a new listener is started on port 5556 (`nc -l 5556` on the next line) and the results directed to a file with the same name in a directory named after the case name, `> $1/$(basename $filename)` on the second half of the line. The first command line argument, which should be the case name, is stored in $1. The `basename` command is used to strip away any leading path for a file that is sent.

Once a file has been received, the infinite loop starts a new listener on port 5555 and the cycle repeats itself. The loop exits when the cleanup script, to be described next, is executed. The client side scripts that send log information and files will be discussed later in this chapter.

```
#!/bin/bash
#
# close-case.sh
#
# Simple script to start shut down listeners.
# Intended to be used as part of initial live response.
# by Dr. Phil Polstra (@ppolstra) as developed for
# PentesterAcademy.com.

echo "Shutting down listeners at $(date) at user request" | nc localhost 4444
killall start-case.sh
killall start-file-listener.sh
killall nc
```

This is our simplest script yet. First, we echo a quick message to our log listener on port 4444, then we use the killall utility to kill all instances of our two scripts and netcat. If you are wondering why we need to kill netcat since it is called by the scripts, recall that in some cases it is run in the background. Also, there could be a hung or in-process netcat listener or talker out there. For these reasons it is safest just to kill all the netcat processes.

Scripting the client

Now that we have a server (the forensic workstation) waiting for us to send information, we will turn our attention toward scripting the client (subject system). Because it would be bothersome to include the forensic workstation IP address and ports with every action, we will start by setting some environment variables to be used by other client scripts. A simple command script to do just that follows.

CHAPTER 2 Determining If There Was an Incident

```
@echo off
REM setup-client.cmd
REM Script to setup some variables for sending info via netcat
REM By Dr. Phil Polstra for PentesterAcademy.com
if not "%1"=="" SET RHOST=%1
if "%RHOST%"=="" SET RHOST=localhost
SET RPORT=4444
SET RFPORT=5555
SET RFTPORT=5556
```

This script begins by turning off command echoing on the first line. Notice that there is no she-bang as this is not a true shell script, just a collection of Windows commands. The lines beginning with REM are comments (remarks). Similarly to bash scripts that use $1, etc. to represent command line arguments, Windows uses %1, etc. for this purpose. The line if not "%1"=="" SET RHOST=%1 checks for the presence of a command line argument and sets the value of RHOST if something was passed in. The next line checks to see if RHOST is unset (nothing passed in) and sets it equal to localhost (127.0.0.1) as a default. The remaining lines simply set variables for the ports used by our scripts.

The following script will execute a command and send the results wrapped in a header and footer to the forensics workstation.

```
@echo off
REM Simple script to send a new log entry
REM to listener on forensics workstation. Intended to be
REM used as part of initial live response.
REM by Dr. Phil Polstra (@ppolstra) as developed for
REM PentesterAcademy.com.

REM defaults primarily for testing
if "%RHOST%"=="" SET RHOST=localhost
if "%RPORT%"=="" SET RPORT=4444

REM usage function
if "%1"=="" (
   echo usage: %0 command or script
   echo Simple script to send a log entry to listener
   exit
)

REM run the command
echo    ++++Sending log for %*   ++++ | nc -w 2 %RHOST% %RPORT%
%* | nc -w 2 %RHOST% %RPORT%
echo    ----end----   | nc -w 2 %RHOST% %RPORT%
```

After turning off command echoing and some comments, the script starts out with a couple of lines that will set RHOST and RPORT to default values if they have not already been set.

This is followed by a usage message which is displayed if no command to run was passed to the script. The only real work done in this script is in the last three lines. Readers of Linux Forensics will notice that the equivalent bash script accomplishes all of what these three lines do in one line. Unfortunately, due to the limits of Windows, this must be split up into three operations here versus a single atomic transaction that is possible with Linux.

There is also something new in this command script, the %* variable. %* is equal to the entire set of command line parameters passed to the script. We first use %* to create a header that reads "++++Sending log for {command with parameters} at {date} ++++". We then use %* on the next line to actually run the command and send the results to netcat. Finally, a "----end----" footer is added after the command output.

The last client script is used to send files to the forensic workstation for analysis. It will make a log entry, then send the filename to the appropriate port, then delay a few seconds to give the server time to create a listener to receive the file, and finally send the file. The script for doing this follows.

```
@echo off
REM Simple script to send a new file
REM to listener on forensics workstation. Intended to be
REM used as part of initial live response.
REM by Dr. Phil Polstra (@ppolstra) as developed for
REM PentesterAcademy.com.

REM defaults primarily for testing
if "%RHOST%"=="" SET RHOST=localhost
if "%RPORT%"=="" SET RPORT=4444
if "%RFPORT%"=="" SET RFPORT=5555
if "%RFTPORT%"=="" SET RFTPORT=5556

if "%1"=="" (
   echo usage: %0 filename
   echo Simple script to send a file to listener
   exit
)

REM log it
echo Attempting to send file %1 | nc -w 2 %RHOST% %RPORT%
REM send name
for /F %%i in ("%1") do @set BASENAME=%%~nxi
echo %BASENAME% | nc -w 2 %RHOST% %RFPORT%
nc -w 2 %RHOST% %RFTPORT% < %1
```

This script begins much like the previous script, but the last few lines require some explanation. Linux shell scripters have a utility known as basename available to them. Basename will strip away the path for any filename and return only the filename (including any extension). Windows lacks this utility, but there is some functionality in the FOR loop command that can be made to do the same thing. The line `for /F %%i in ("%1") do @set BASENAME=%%~nxi` will loop through the list of files passed in as the first parameter and execute the `set` command to store the base filename (represented by %%~nxi when executing the FOR command) in a variable called %BASENAME%. While it may seem strange to loop over a list of one item, this allows us to exploit functionality of the FOR command to perform an otherwise difficult task.

Once the base filename has been determined, it is sent to the filename listener. This filename is used to create the appropriate file. The last line uses the full pathname to send the file contents to the file data transfer port.

INTRODUCING OUR FIRST SUBJECT SYSTEM

Throughout this book we will work through a few example subject systems. If you wish to follow along, you may download the example images from the book support website. This website is also the place to get updates and other materials from this book. To keep things simple I will install this example system in a virtual machine using VirtualBox running on my Ubuntu 14.04 computer. Recall that I said earlier in this book that using a USB 2.0 response drive is less problematic when trying to mount the drive in a virtual machine.

Our first example is a Windows 7 64-bit system. I chose Windows 7 as our first sample because it is widely used among the new versions of Windows (Vista, 7, 8, and 10) at the time of this writing. Performing forensics on any of the newer versions of Windows starting with Vista is very similar. We will also discuss older versions of Windows, such as XP, in this book as people continue to run them even though Microsoft has terminated their support.

For readers of Linux Forensics, the samples used in this book are fundamentally very different. Whereas the majority of Linux forensic investigations are performed as part of incident response, the same cannot be said of Windows forensic investigations. Given this, we will use a larger set of example systems and will focus on the technical details of getting information from these systems. We will start from zero knowledge and show you how to extract relevant information.

COLLECTING VOLATILE DATA

There is plenty of volatile data that can be collected from the subject system. Collecting this data will help you make a preliminary determination as to whether or not there was an incident. Some of the more common pieces of data you should collect are discussed below.

Windows version

Depending on the situation you might not know the exact version of Windows that is being run. If the system is up and running, this is very easy to determine. Click on the Start button, then right click on Computer and select Properties as shown in Figure 2.12. You should see a window similar to Figure 2.13 which tells you the exact version of Windows installed and some other information.

Collecting volatile data

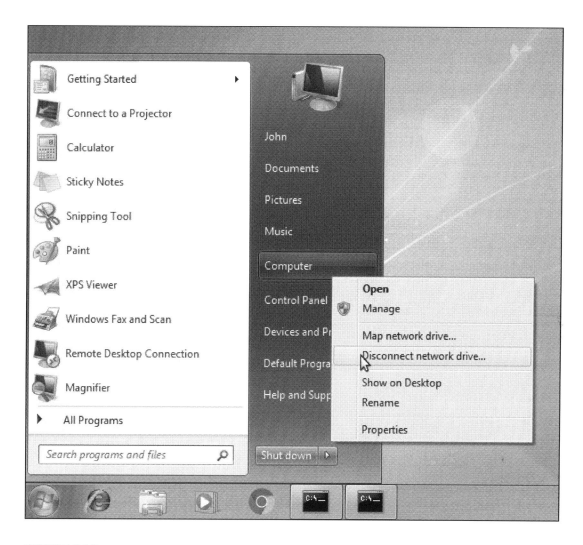

FIGURE 2.12.

Retrieving Windows version information.

Date and time information

One of the first things you want to collect is the date and time information. Why? The subject system might be in a different timezone from your usual location. Also, computer clocks are known to be bad at keeping good time. If the system has not been synchronized with a time server recently, the clock could be off and you will want to note this skew to adjust times in your reports. The `date /T` command outputs the date. The system time can be displayed using the `time /T` command.

We will use the scripts presented earlier in this chapter to make this initial scan of the machine simpler. First, run the cmd.exe from the known-good binaries on your response drive

CHAPTER 2 Determining If There Was an Incident

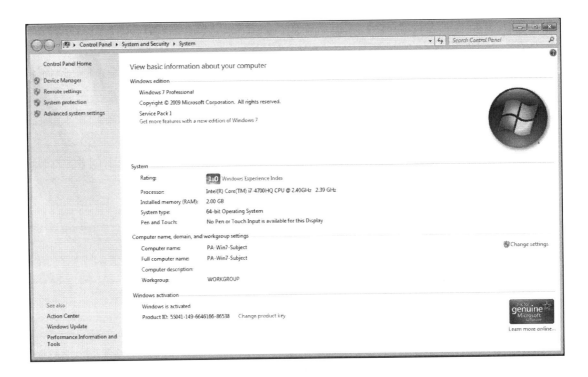

FIGURE 2.13.

Windows system information.

as described. Second, run the setup-client.cmd script passing it the forensic workstation's IP address. Third, create a case and start the listeners by running the start-case.sh script on the forensic workstation. You are now ready to send information to your forensic workstation. This process and sending the date and time is shown in Figure 2.14 and Figure 2.15.

Networking information

Windows provides a netstat utility that is similar, but not identical, to the Linux program of the same name. Running `netstat -h` at a comand prompt will provide a brief help screen with the most commonly used switches. The -a switch is used to list all connections and listening ports. The -n switch is used to display numerical forms of IP addresses. It is better to use the numerical addresses in case the subject's DNS server has been compromised. This command is likely to fail if run from a command prompt with administrator privileges. Partial results from `netstat -an` on the Windows 7 subject are shown in Figure 2.16. Many pieces of malware will create listeners on well-known ports. Depending on the sophistication of the malware, these listeners might be shown in the netstat results.

Another useful netstat switch is -r which will display routing information. A machine that has been compromised and/or infected with malware might alter the standard routing table. Results from running `netstat -r` on the Windows 7 subject are shown in Figure 2.17.

```
F:\>setup-client.cmd 192.168.56.1

F:\>send-log.cmd date /t
F:\>send-log.cmd time /t
F:\>
```

FIGURE 2.14.

Setting up the client and sending date and time.

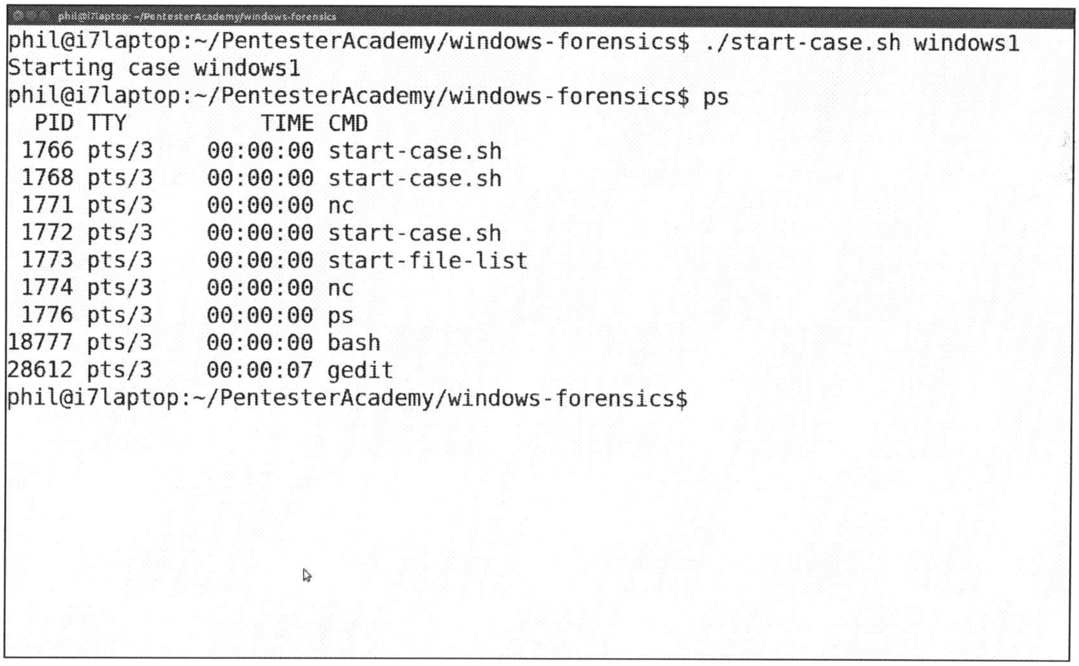

```
phil@i7laptop:~/PentesterAcademy/windows-forensics$ ./start-case.sh windows1
Starting case windows1
phil@i7laptop:~/PentesterAcademy/windows-forensics$ ps
  PID TTY          TIME CMD
 1766 pts/3    00:00:00 start-case.sh
 1768 pts/3    00:00:00 start-case.sh
 1771 pts/3    00:00:00 nc
 1772 pts/3    00:00:00 start-case.sh
 1773 pts/3    00:00:00 start-file-list
 1774 pts/3    00:00:00 nc
 1776 pts/3    00:00:00 ps
18777 pts/3    00:00:00 bash
28612 pts/3    00:00:07 gedit
phil@i7laptop:~/PentesterAcademy/windows-forensics$
```

FIGURE 2.15.

Creating a case and starting listeners.

CHAPTER 2 Determining If There Was an Incident

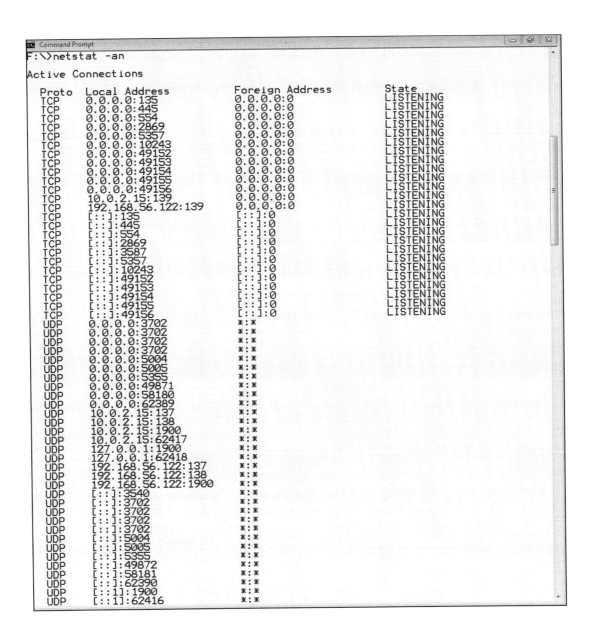

FIGURE 2.16.

Running netstat -an on a Windows 7 subject.

Using PS Tools

Given that the state of your subject system's binaries is unknown, it would be convenient to have another set of programs to extract information from the subject. Thankfully, Microsoft provides such utilities in its PS Tools package. Because Microsoft does update this package, I recommend that you Google this toolset in order to download the latest version.

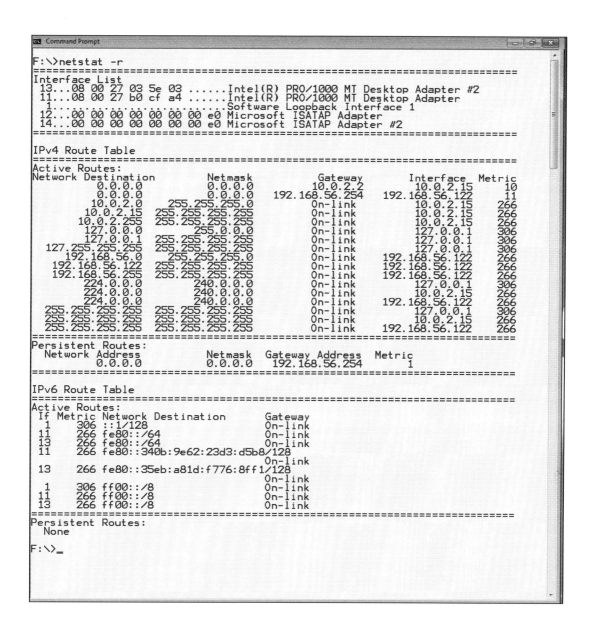

FIGURE 2.17.

Using netstat to display a routing table.

Most of the programs in the PS Tools package will require administrative privileges. In other words, they must be run from an administrative command prompt. The psLoggedon.exe program can be used to show currently logged on users, both local and remote. The results of running psloggedon.exe on the Windows 7 subject are shown in Figure 2.18. As seen in the figure, there are no remote logins to this subject machine.

Another program in the PS Tools suite, psfile, allows us to list or close any remotely opened

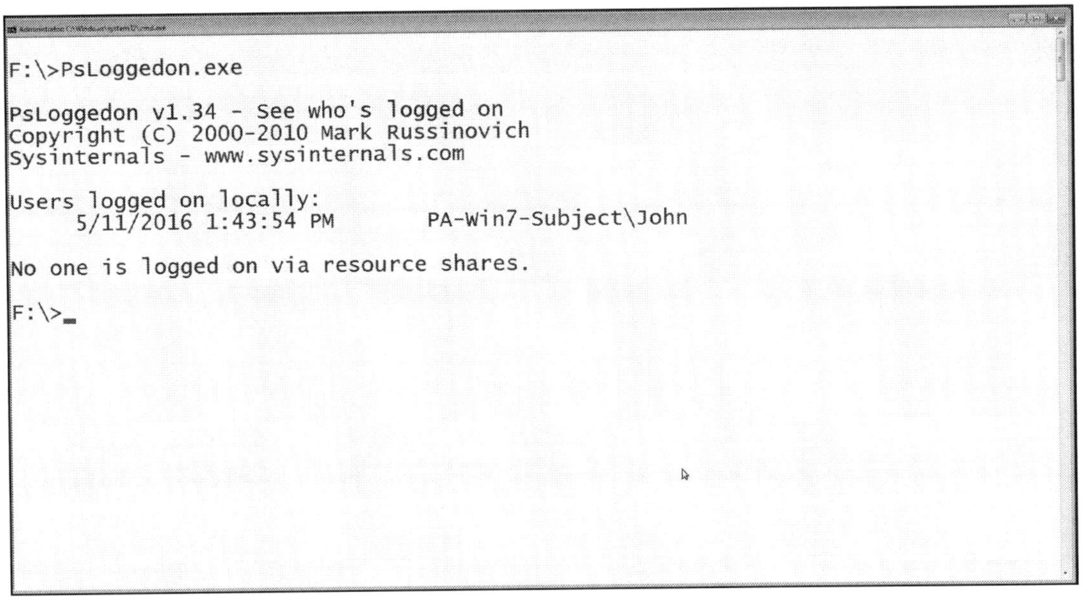

```
F:\>PsLoggedon.exe

PsLoggedon v1.34 - See who's logged on
Copyright (C) 2000-2010 Mark Russinovich
Sysinternals - www.sysinternals.com

Users logged on locally:
     5/11/2016 1:43:54 PM         PA-Win7-Subject\John

No one is logged on via resource shares.

F:\>
```

FIGURE 2.18.

Results from running psloggedon.exe on a Windows 7 subject.

files. The results of running `psfile /?` and then `psfile` are shown in Figure 2.19. From the figure you can see that nobody has currently opened any files on this machine remotely. There are two built-in commands that return the same information `openfiles` and `net files`. I recommend you run these as well. Any discrepancies between these tools is a likely indicator of compromise.

The pslist utility can be used to get a task list. Partial results of running `pslist /?` are shown in Figure 2.20. From this help screen we can see that the -d, -m, and -x flags will show thread detail, memory detail, and process information, respectively. Partial results of running `pslist -d -m -x` are shown in Figure 2.21. As with the psfile utility, you might wish to also run the built-in `tasklist` command with the /v (verbose) script to check for any inconsistencies that would point toward a compromise.

The psloglist utility can be used to retrieve system logs. We will discuss Windows systems logs and their various formats in greater details later in this book. Full information on the psloglist program can be found by running `psloglist /?`. One of the many switches supported by psloglist is -x which gives extended output. Partial results from running `psloglist -x` on the Windows 7 subject are shown in Figure 2.22.

There are a few miscellaneous programs that you might want to use if you suspect a system has been compromised. One such utility is `psping` which works just like the normal `ping` command. The PsGetsid tool will return the System ID (SID) for a particular user or the system. Results from running `psgetsid` and `psgetsid John` are shown in figure 2.23. The PsService program can be used to list the state of services on the subject computer. Partial results of running `psservice` are shown in Figure 2.24.

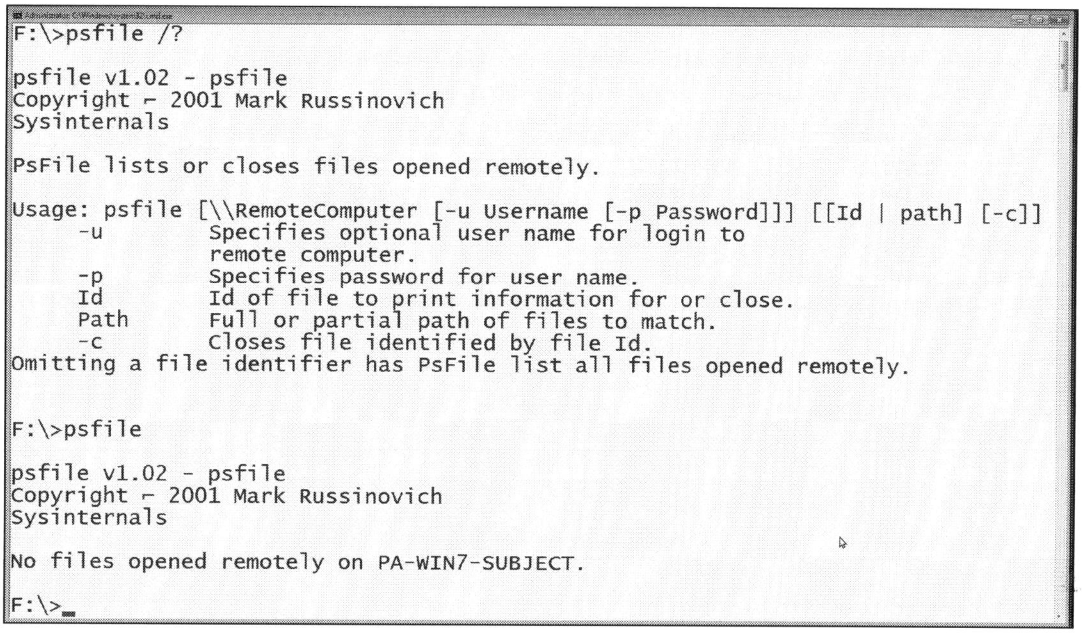

Collecting volatile data 45

```
F:\>psfile /?

psfile v1.02 - psfile
Copyright - 2001 Mark Russinovich
Sysinternals

PsFile lists or closes files opened remotely.

Usage: psfile [\\RemoteComputer [-u Username [-p Password]]] [[Id | path] [-c]]
      -u        Specifies optional user name for login to
                remote computer.
      -p        Specifies password for user name.
      Id        Id of file to print information for or close.
      Path      Full or partial path of files to match.
      -c        Closes file identified by file Id.
Omitting a file identifier has PsFile list all files opened remotely.

F:\>psfile

psfile v1.02 - psfile
Copyright - 2001 Mark Russinovich
Sysinternals

No files opened remotely on PA-WIN7-SUBJECT.

F:\>_
```

FIGURE 2.19.

Results from running psfile on a Windows 7 subject.

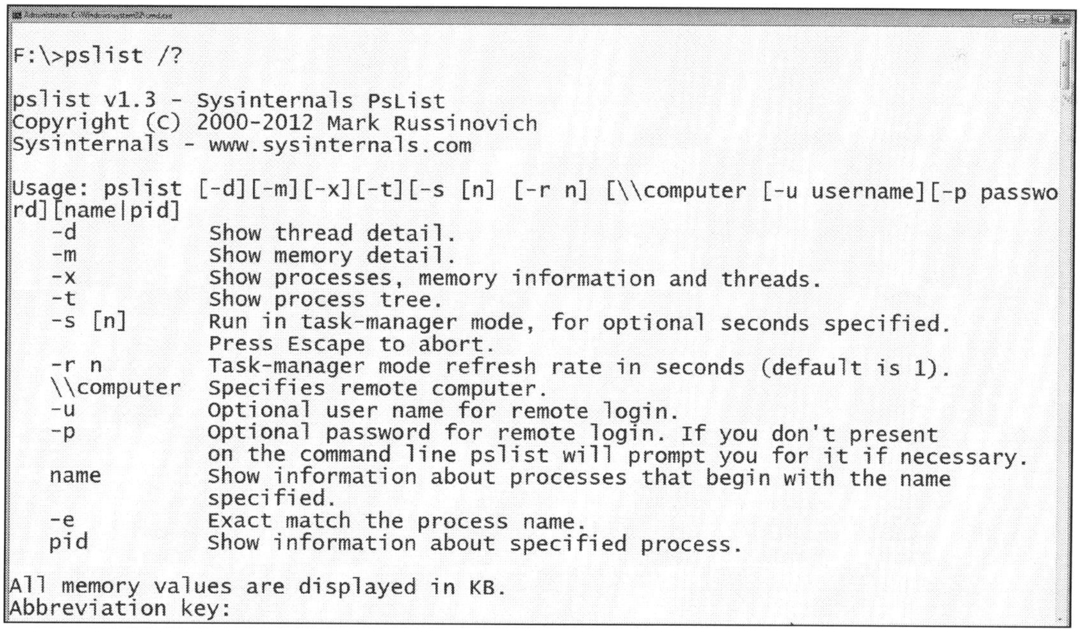

```
F:\>pslist /?

pslist v1.3 - Sysinternals PsList
Copyright (C) 2000-2012 Mark Russinovich
Sysinternals - www.sysinternals.com

Usage: pslist [-d][-m][-x][-t][-s [n] [-r n] [\\computer [-u username][-p passwo
rd][name|pid]
      -d        Show thread detail.
      -m        Show memory detail.
      -x        Show processes, memory information and threads.
      -t        Show process tree.
      -s [n]    Run in task-manager mode, for optional seconds specified.
                Press Escape to abort.
      -r n      Task-manager mode refresh rate in seconds (default is 1).
      \\computer Specifies remote computer.
      -u        Optional user name for remote login.
      -p        Optional password for remote login. If you don't present
                on the command line pslist will prompt you for it if necessary.
      name      Show information about processes that begin with the name
                specified.
      -e        Exact match the process name.
      pid       Show information about specified process.

All memory values are displayed in KB.
Abbreviation key:
```

FIGURE 2.20.

Pslist help screen.

```
Name                           Pid       VM      WS   Priv Priv Pk   Faults   NonP Page
svchost                        852   121984   32624  17696    22796    23522    42  222
 Tid Pri    Cswtch            State      User Time    Kernel Time    Elapsed Time
  856   9      302      Wait:UserReq    0:00:00.015    0:00:00.000   23:35:30.402
  860   8    92995      Wait:UserReq    0:00:00.000    0:00:00.062   23:35:30.402
  984   9       56      Wait:UserReq    0:00:00.000    0:00:00.015   23:35:28.787
  988   9      484   Wait:LpcReceive    0:00:00.000    0:00:00.000   23:35:28.787
  272  10      371      Wait:UserReq    0:00:00.000    0:00:00.000   23:35:27.257
  372   9      560      Wait:UserReq    0:00:00.015    0:00:00.000   23:35:25.143
  276  13      897      Wait:UserReq    0:00:00.015    0:00:00.015   23:35:25.006
 1072   8       71       Wait:Queue     0:00:00.000    0:00:00.000   23:35:23.260
 1076   9      639      Wait:UserReq    0:00:00.000    0:00:00.015   23:35:23.148
 1092   8      306      Wait:UserReq    0:00:00.015    0:00:00.000   23:35:22.856
 1104   2      294      Wait:UserReq    0:00:00.000    0:00:00.000   23:35:22.100
 1384  10       80      Wait:UserReq    0:00:00.000    0:00:00.000   23:35:15.373
 1432   9    10071      Wait:UserReq    0:00:00.000    0:00:00.015   23:35:13.857
 1548   9        3      Wait:UserReq    0:00:00.000    0:00:00.000   23:35:12.029
 1552   8       20      Wait:UserReq    0:00:00.000    0:00:00.000   23:35:12.029
 1644  10     1843      Wait:UserReq    0:00:00.000    0:00:00.000   23:35:11.748
 1804  10      900      Wait:UserReq    0:00:00.000    0:00:00.000   23:35:09.779
 1820  11     1770      Wait:UserReq    0:00:00.000    0:00:00.000   23:35:05.076
 1868   1      137      Wait:UserReq    0:00:00.000    0:00:00.000   23:35:01.342
 2824   8        9      Wait:UserReq    0:00:00.000    0:00:00.000   23:34:09.325
 2832   8        5      Wait:UserReq    0:00:00.000    0:00:00.000   23:34:09.325
 2836   8        1      Wait:UserReq    0:00:00.000    0:00:00.000   23:34:09.325
 2328  10      435      Wait:UserReq    0:00:00.000    0:00:00.031   23:33:11.778
 2208   9      285      Wait:UserReq    0:00:00.000    0:00:00.015   23:33:07.622
```

FIGURE 2.21

Partial results from running pslist -d -m -x on a Windows 7 subject.

```
System log on \\PA-WIN7-SUBJECT:
[5118] NetBT
    Type:      ERROR
    Computer:  PA-Win7-Subject
    Time:      5/12/2016 1:35:23 PM   ID:       4321
The name "WORKGROUP       :1d" could not be registered on the interface with IP a
ddress 10.0.2.15.
The computer with the IP address 10.0.2.2 did not allow the name to be claimed b
y
this computer.

    Data:
    0000: 00 00 00 00 04 00 32 00 00 00 00 00 E1 10 00 C0   ......2.........
    0010: 01 01 00 00 01 00 00 C0 11 01 00 00 00 00 00 00   ................
    0020: 00 00 00 00 00 00 00 00                           ........

[5117] Service Control Manager
    Type:      INFORMATION
    Computer:  PA-Win7-Subject
    Time:      5/12/2016 1:34:23 PM   ID:       7036
The Multimedia Class Scheduler service entered the stopped state.

    Data:
    0000: 4D 00 4D 00 43 00 53 00 53 00 2F 00 31 00 00 00   M.M.C.S.S./.1...
```

FIGURE 2.22.

Partial results from running psloglist -x on a Windows 7 subject.

Collecting volatile data

```
F:\>PsGetsid.exe

PsGetSid v1.44 - Translates SIDs to names and vice versa
Copyright (C) 1999-2008 Mark Russinovich
Sysinternals - www.sysinternals.com

SID for \\PA-WIN7-SUBJECT:
S-1-5-21-3073187811-2502202371-618229334


F:\>PsGetsid.exe John

PsGetSid v1.44 - Translates SIDs to names and vice versa
Copyright (C) 1999-2008 Mark Russinovich
Sysinternals - www.sysinternals.com

SID for PA-Win7-Subject\John:
S-1-5-21-3073187811-2502202371-618229334-1001


F:\>
```

FIGURE 2.23.

Using psgetsid to obtain the computer and user SID.

```
SERVICE_NAME: AeLookupSvc
DISPLAY_NAME: Application Experience
Processes application compatibility cache requests for applications as they are
launched
        TYPE               : 20 WIN32_SHARE_PROCESS
        STATE              : 1  STOPPED
                              (NOT_STOPPABLE,NOT_PAUSABLE,IGNORES_SHUTDOWN)
        WIN32_EXIT_CODE    : 0  (0x0)
        SERVICE_EXIT_CODE  : 0  (0x0)
        CHECKPOINT         : 0x0
        WAIT_HINT          : 0 ms

SERVICE_NAME: ALG
DISPLAY_NAME: Application Layer Gateway Service
Provides support for 3rd party protocol plug-ins for Internet Connection Sharing
        TYPE               : 10 WIN32_OWN_PROCESS
        STATE              : 1  STOPPED
                              (NOT_STOPPABLE,NOT_PAUSABLE,IGNORES_SHUTDOWN)
        WIN32_EXIT_CODE    : 1077 (0x435)
        SERVICE_EXIT_CODE  : 0  (0x0)
        CHECKPOINT         : 0x0
        WAIT_HINT          : 0 ms

SERVICE_NAME: AppIDSvc
```

FIGURE 2.24.

Partial results from running psservice on a Windows 7 subject.

Built-in commands, system internals, and miscellaneous

While we have managed to acquire quite a bit of information from our subject system using just a few tools, Microsoft does provide some built-in commands and also some downloads from their system internals family that can help us round out our picture of the subject system. Additionally, there are few third party utilities that may prove useful. Keep in mind that any built-in commands could have been compromised. The good news is that disagreement between tools is an almost certain indicator of compromise.

The built-in net command can provide much of the same functionality as some of the tools discussed earlier in this chapter. By executing `net sessions` from an administrator command prompt, remote logins can be listed. The results from running `net sessions` and psloggedon on a Windows 7 subject are shown in Figure 2.25.

The Logonsessions utility is part of the system internals family available from www.sysinternals.com. This program will list information about recent logins and optionally include running processes if the -p flag is used. Partial results of running `logonsessions -p` against a Windows 7 subject are shown in Figure 2.26.

Another useful tool from the system internals family is Listdlls. This program can be used to list DLLs from a single process or for the entire system. The -u switch causes only unsigned DLLs to be listed. This can be useful if you are trying to weed out some DLLs associated with malware from the plethora of DLLs normally loaded on a typical Windows system. You can also list DLL version information using the -v switch. Partial results from running `listdlls -v` against a Windows 7 subject are shown in Figure 2.27. Results from runing `listdlls -uv` are shown in Figure 2.28. Notice that the only unsigned DLL listed is associated with Listdlls.

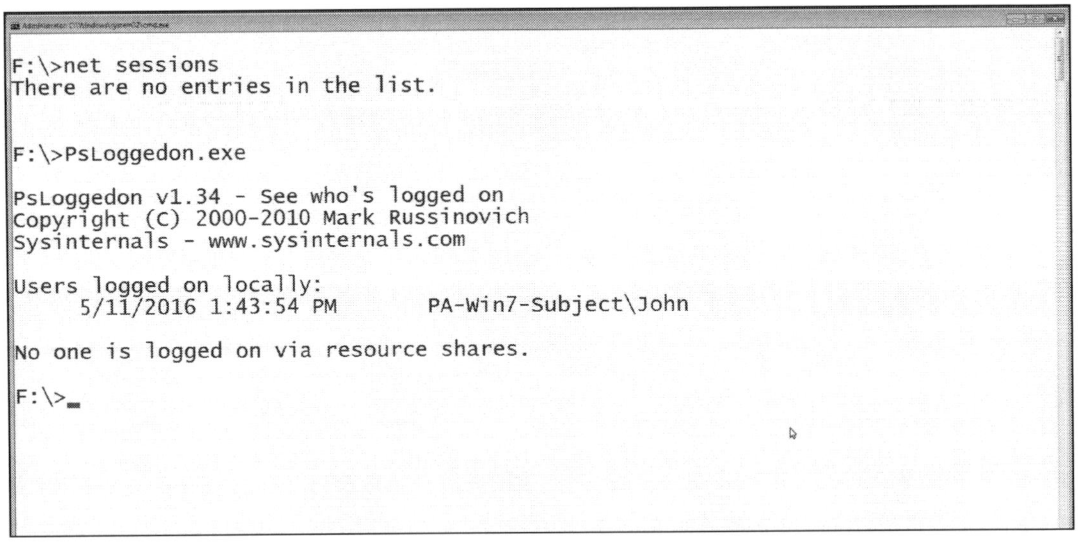

FIGURE 2.25.

Result from running both net sessions and psloggedon. Disagreement indicates a compromise.

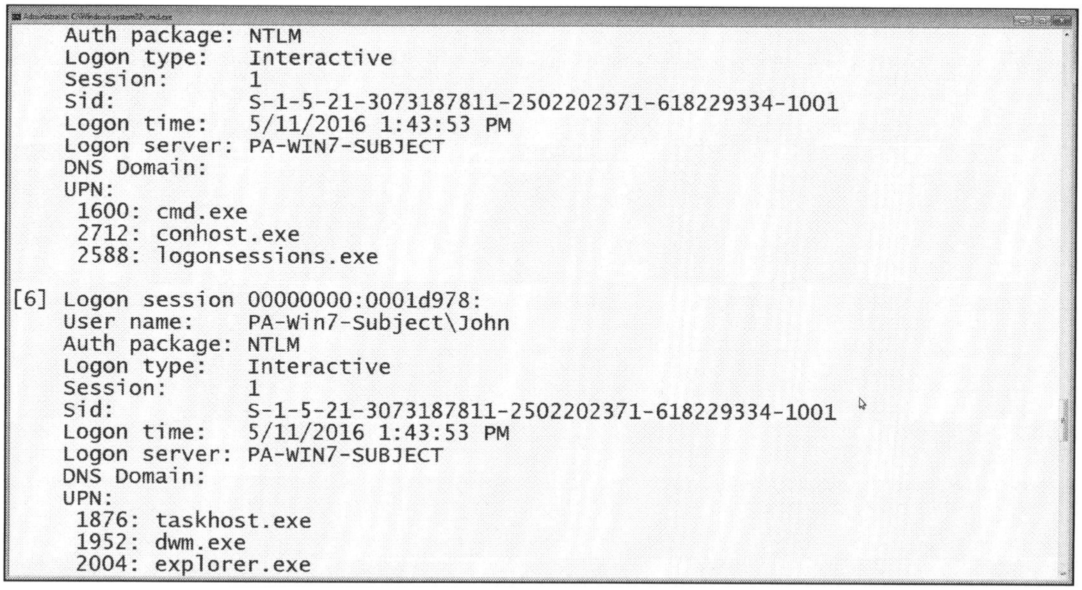

```
    Auth package: NTLM
    Logon type:   Interactive
    Session:      1
    Sid:          S-1-5-21-3073187811-2502202371-618229334-1001
    Logon time:   5/11/2016 1:43:53 PM
    Logon server: PA-WIN7-SUBJECT
    DNS Domain:
    UPN:
      1600: cmd.exe
      2712: conhost.exe
      2588: logonsessions.exe

[6] Logon session 00000000:0001d978:
    User name:    PA-Win7-Subject\John
    Auth package: NTLM
    Logon type:   Interactive
    Session:      1
    Sid:          S-1-5-21-3073187811-2502202371-618229334-1001
    Logon time:   5/11/2016 1:43:53 PM
    Logon server: PA-WIN7-SUBJECT
    DNS Domain:
    UPN:
      1876: taskhost.exe
      1952: dwm.exe
      2004: explorer.exe
```

FIGURE 2.26.

Partial results from running logonsessions -p on a Windows 7 subject.

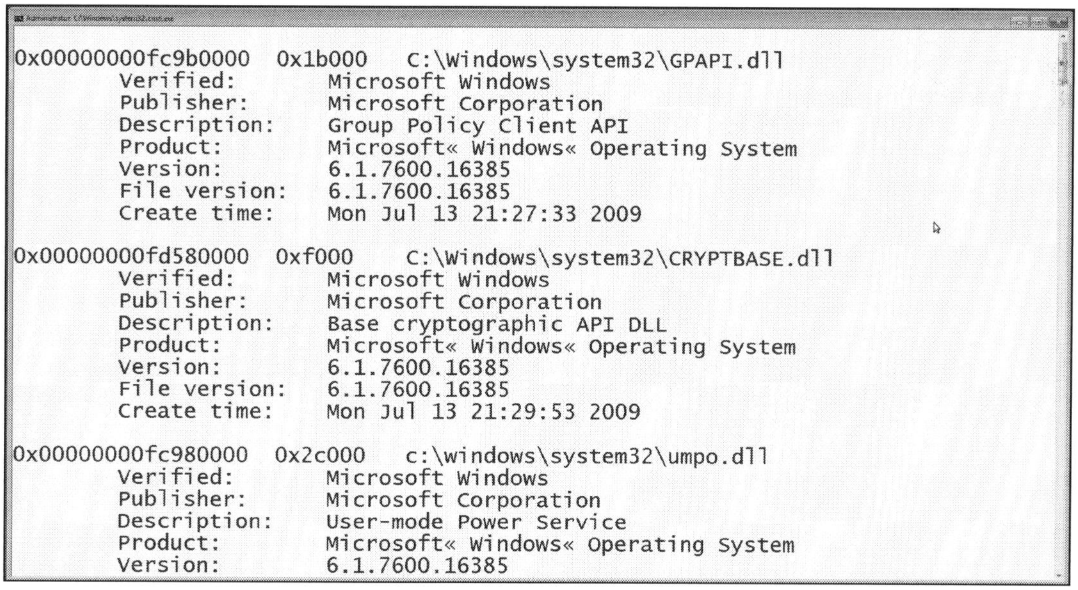

```
0x00000000fc9b0000    0x1b000    C:\Windows\system32\GPAPI.dll
        Verified:         Microsoft Windows
        Publisher:        Microsoft Corporation
        Description:      Group Policy Client API
        Product:          Microsoft« Windows« Operating System
        Version:          6.1.7600.16385
        File version:     6.1.7600.16385
        Create time:      Mon Jul 13 21:27:33 2009

0x00000000fd580000    0xf000     C:\Windows\system32\CRYPTBASE.dll
        Verified:         Microsoft Windows
        Publisher:        Microsoft Corporation
        Description:      Base cryptographic API DLL
        Product:          Microsoft« Windows« Operating System
        Version:          6.1.7600.16385
        File version:     6.1.7600.16385
        Create time:      Mon Jul 13 21:29:53 2009

0x00000000fc980000    0x2c000    c:\windows\system32\umpo.dll
        Verified:         Microsoft Windows
        Publisher:        Microsoft Corporation
        Description:      User-mode Power Service
        Product:          Microsoft« Windows« Operating System
        Version:          6.1.7600.16385
```

FIGURE 2.27.

Partial results from running listdlls -v against a Windows 7 subject.

50 CHAPTER 2 Determining If There Was an Incident

```
        Create time:    Mon Jul 13 21:34:20 2009
^C
F:\>listdlls -uv

ListDLLs v3.1 - List loaded DLLs
Copyright (C) 1997-2011 Mark Russinovich
Sysinternals - www.sysinternals.com
------------------------------------------------------------------------
Listdlls64.exe pid: 1368
Command line: listdlls  -uv

Base                    Size      Path
0x0000000040000000      0x4a000   F:\Listdlls64.exe
        Verified:       Unsigned
        Publisher:      Sysinternals
        Description:    Listdlls
        Product:        Sysinternals Listdlls
        Version:        3.10.0.0
        File version:   3.10.0.0
        Create time:    Thu Jun 23 16:53:25 2011

F:\>
```

FIGURE 2.28.

Listing only unsigned DLLs with listdlls -uv.

Windows makes extensive use of system handles. If you are unfamiliar with handles, they are a lot like pointers. Unlike pointers, handles can be used across programs and memory spaces. Essentially, they are references to a particular resource (window, file, object, etc.). The Handle utility also in the system internals family from www.sysinternals.com allows you to display handle information. Partial results from running `handle -a` against a Windows 7 subject are are shown in Figure 2.29.

TCPView is yet another tool from the system internals family. It comes with both a graphical and console tool. The console tool is called tcpvcon for TCP View console. Running tcpvcon with no arguments will list established network endpoints, whereas adding the -a switch will list all endpoints. Partial results from running `tcpvcon -a` on a Windows 7 system are shown in Figure 2.30.

The built-in ipconfig command can be used to determine several items for each network adapter on a system. Some of the information provided by this utility includes physical (MAC) and IP addresses, whether or not Dynamic Host Configuration Protocol (DHCP) is in use, default gateways, subnet masks, and DNS servers. Partial results from running `ipconfig /all` against a Windows 7 subject are shown in Figure 2.31.

Microsoft provides a tool, promqry, for determining if any of your network interfaces are in promiscuous mode. If you are not familiar with what this means, a network interface will normally drop any traffic it receives that is not meant for it. If an attacker wants to sniff traffic on a network, a well-connected network card in promiscuous mode can be a part of that attack. Partial results from running `promqry` on a Windows 7 subject are shown in Figure 2.32.

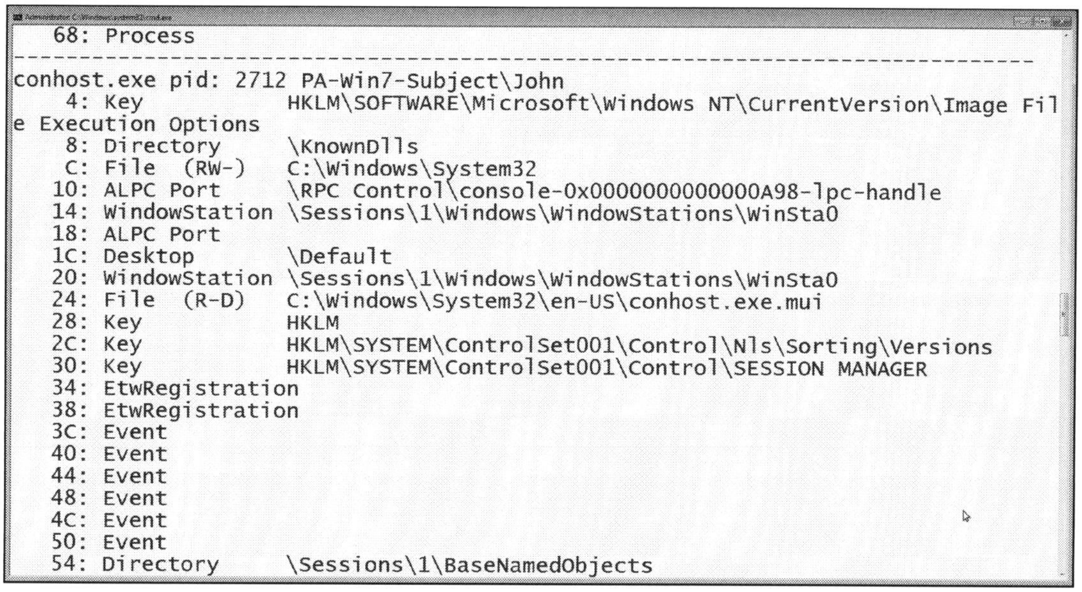

```
    68: Process
-----------------------------------------------------------------------
conhost.exe pid: 2712 PA-Win7-Subject\John
     4: Key             HKLM\SOFTWARE\Microsoft\Windows NT\CurrentVersion\Image Fil
e Execution Options
     8: Directory       \KnownDlls
     C: File   (RW-)    C:\Windows\System32
    10: ALPC Port       \RPC Control\console-0x0000000000000A98-lpc-handle
    14: WindowStation   \Sessions\1\Windows\WindowStations\WinSta0
    18: ALPC Port
    1C: Desktop         \Default
    20: WindowStation   \Sessions\1\Windows\WindowStations\WinSta0
    24: File   (R-D)    C:\Windows\System32\en-US\conhost.exe.mui
    28: Key             HKLM
    2C: Key             HKLM\SYSTEM\ControlSet001\Control\Nls\Sorting\Versions
    30: Key             HKLM\SYSTEM\ControlSet001\Control\SESSION MANAGER
    34: EtwRegistration
    38: EtwRegistration
    3C: Event
    40: Event
    44: Event
    48: Event
    4C: Event
    50: Event
    54: Directory       \Sessions\1\BaseNamedObjects
```

FIGURE 2.29.

Partial results from running handle -a against a Windows 7 subject.

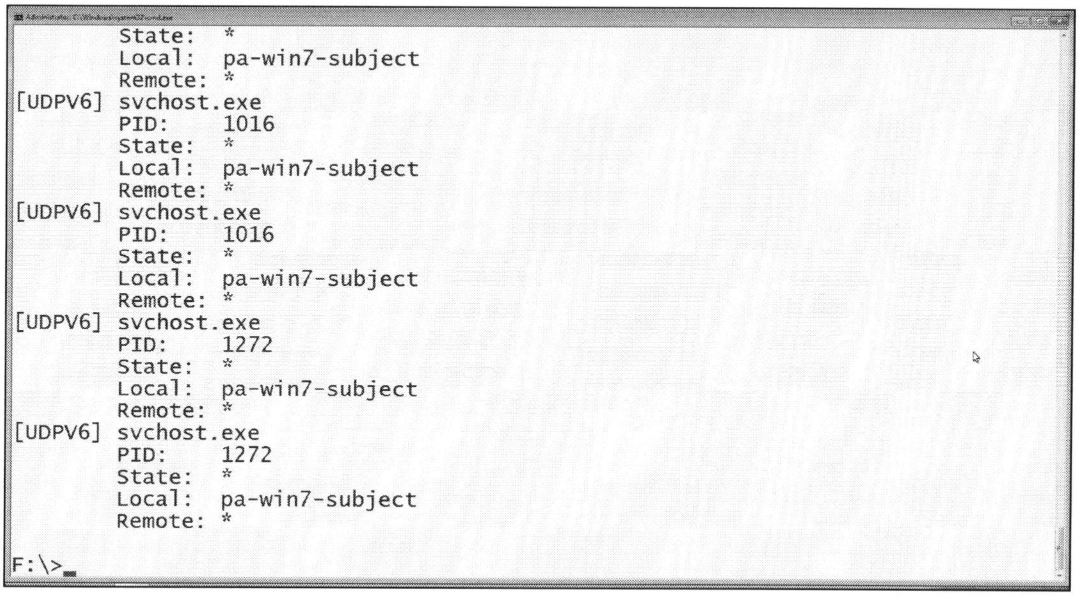

```
         State:   *
         Local:   pa-win7-subject
         Remote:  *
[UDPV6]  svchost.exe
         PID:     1016
         State:   *
         Local:   pa-win7-subject
         Remote:  *
[UDPV6]  svchost.exe
         PID:     1016
         State:   *
         Local:   pa-win7-subject
         Remote:  *
[UDPV6]  svchost.exe
         PID:     1272
         State:   *
         Local:   pa-win7-subject
         Remote:  *
[UDPV6]  svchost.exe
         PID:     1272
         State:   *
         Local:   pa-win7-subject
         Remote:  *
F:\>
```

FIGURE 2.30.

Partial results from running tcpvcon -a on a Windows 7 subject.

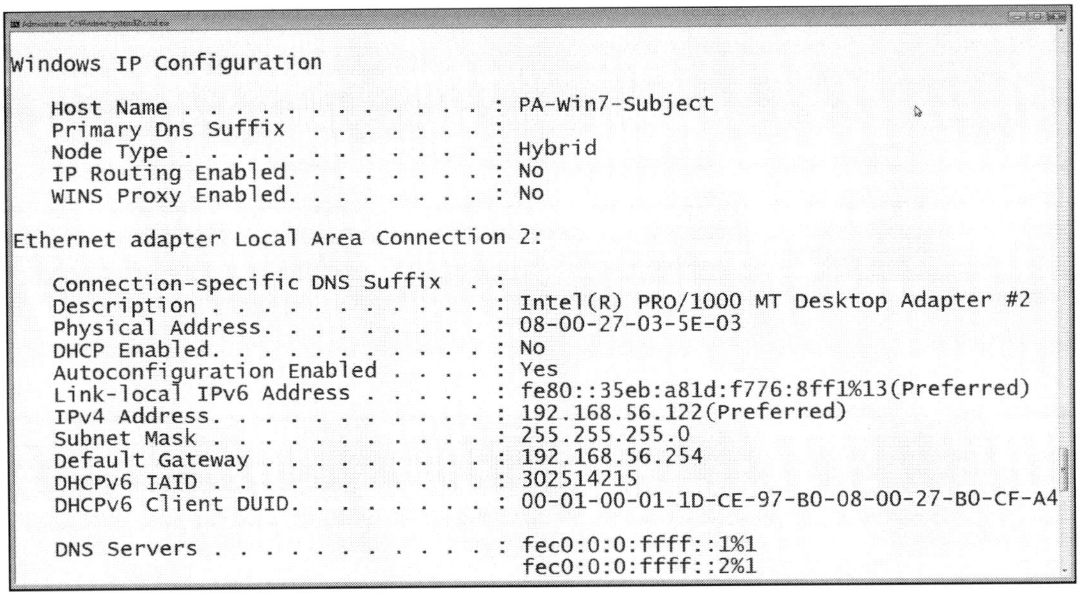

52 CHAPTER 2 Determining If There Was an Incident

```
Windows IP Configuration

    Host Name . . . . . . . . . . . . : PA-Win7-Subject
    Primary Dns Suffix  . . . . . . . :
    Node Type . . . . . . . . . . . . : Hybrid
    IP Routing Enabled. . . . . . . . : No
    WINS Proxy Enabled. . . . . . . . : No

Ethernet adapter Local Area Connection 2:

    Connection-specific DNS Suffix  . :
    Description . . . . . . . . . . . : Intel(R) PRO/1000 MT Desktop Adapter #2
    Physical Address. . . . . . . . . : 08-00-27-03-5E-03
    DHCP Enabled. . . . . . . . . . . : No
    Autoconfiguration Enabled . . . . : Yes
    Link-local IPv6 Address . . . . . : fe80::35eb:a81d:f776:8ff1%13(Preferred)
    IPv4 Address. . . . . . . . . . . : 192.168.56.122(Preferred)
    Subnet Mask . . . . . . . . . . . : 255.255.255.0
    Default Gateway . . . . . . . . . : 192.168.56.254
    DHCPv6 IAID . . . . . . . . . . . : 302514215
    DHCPv6 Client DUID. . . . . . . . : 00-01-00-01-1D-CE-97-B0-08-00-27-B0-CF-A4

    DNS Servers . . . . . . . . . . . : fec0:0:0:ffff::1%1
                                        fec0:0:0:ffff::2%1
```

FIGURE 2.31.

Partial results from running ipconfig /all against a Windows 7 subject.

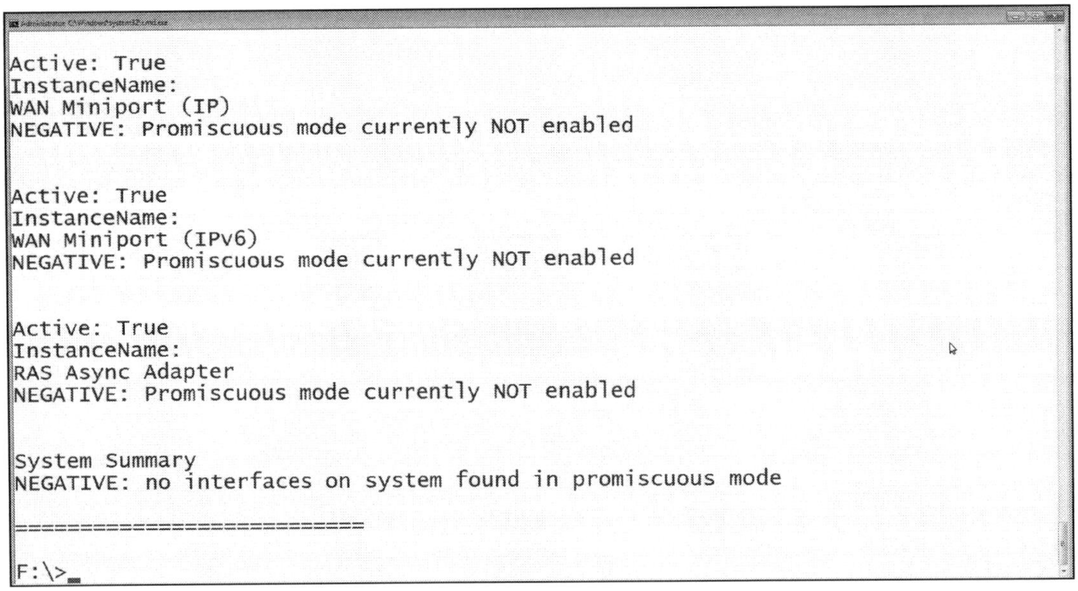

```
Active: True
InstanceName:
WAN Miniport (IP)
NEGATIVE: Promiscuous mode currently NOT enabled

Active: True
InstanceName:
WAN Miniport (IPv6)
NEGATIVE: Promiscuous mode currently NOT enabled

Active: True
InstanceName:
RAS Async Adapter
NEGATIVE: Promiscuous mode currently NOT enabled


System Summary
NEGATIVE: no interfaces on system found in promiscuous mode

============================

F:\>
```

FIGURE 2.32.

Partial results from running the Microsoft promqry tool on a Windows 7 system.

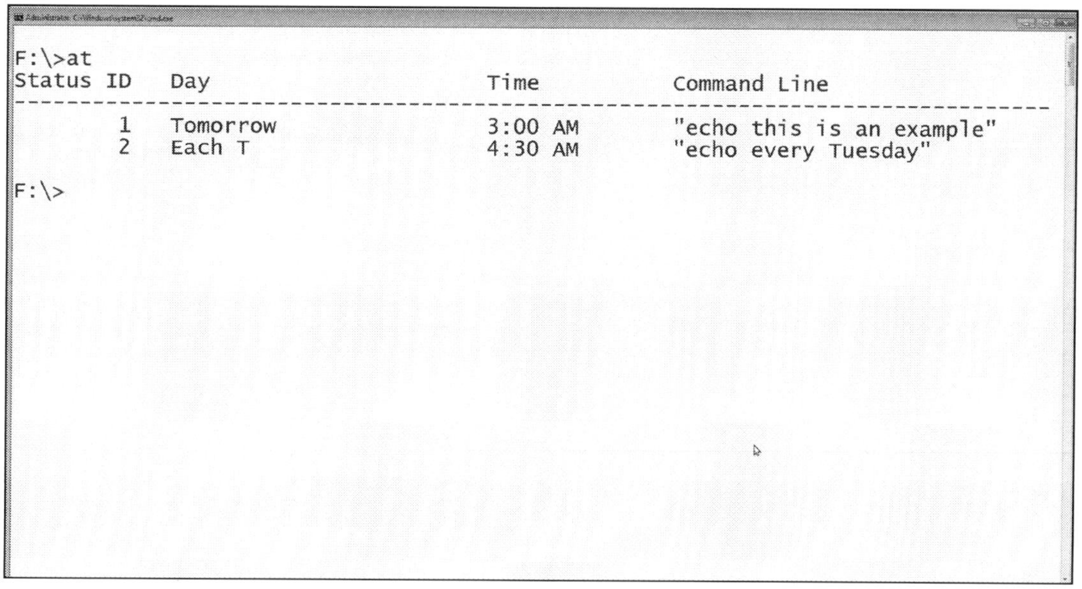

```
F:\>at
Status  ID   Day                   Time             Command Line
---------------------------------------------------------------------------
        1    Tomorrow              3:00 AM          "echo this is an example"
        2    Each T                4:30 AM          "echo every Tuesday"
F:\>
```

FIGURE 2.33.

Example output from the at command.

Jason Faulkner has written a tool called ClipOut. This program can be downloaded from jasonfaulkner.com. This utility will allow you to capture any text currently in the Windows clipboard. While not as useful as a user's command history, it is worth running this utility on the off chance you will find something.

Some malware will schedule things to run periodically. It is not unusual for system administrators to schedule periodic tasks on machines in their networks. The built-in at facility can be used by good and bad guys alike. Checking to see if something has been scheduled to run is as simple as running the at command. Consult the local system administrator to see what, if anything, should be scheduled to run. Example output from this command is shown in Figure 2.33.

Putting it together with scripting

There is no good reason to type all of the commands mentioned above by hand. Since you already are mounting a drive with your know-good binaries, it makes sense to have a script to do all the work for you on your response drive. A simple script for your initial scan follows. The script is straightforward and primarily consists of calling the send-log.cmd script presented earlier in this chapter. If you find that some of the PS Tools commands produce truncated output with this script, try increasing the wait time (-w option) for netcat in send-log.cmd. Another alternative is to use the netcat included with nmap if this seems to be problematic.

```
@echo off
REM initial-scan.cmd
REM
REM Initial scan script for Windows subjects
REM part of the solution create by Dr. Phil Polstra
REM as presented in Windows Forensics

REM send date and time
call send-log.cmd date /t
call send-log.cmd time /t

REM listening ports
call send-log.cmd netstat -an
REM routing
call send-log.cmd netstat -r

REM who is logged on
call send-log.cmd psloggedon.exe
call send-log.cmd net sessions
call send-log.cmd logonsessions -p

REM get file information
call send-log.cmd psfile
call send-log.cmd openfiles
call send-log.cmd net files

REM get task information
call send-log.cmd pslist -d -m -x
call send-log.cmd tasklist /v

REM get system logs
call send-log.cmd psloglist -x

REM get computer SID
call send-log.cmd psgetsid

REM get services
call send-log.cmd psservice

REM get DLL info
call send-log.cmd listdlls -v
call send-log.cmd listdlls -uv

REM get system handles
call send-log.cmd handle -a
```

```
REM get TCP information
call send-log.cmd tcpvcon
call send-log.cmd tcpvcon -a
call send-log.cmd ipconfig /all

REM check for promiscuous mode
call send-log.cmd promqry

REM check for text in the clipboard
call send-log.cmd clipout

REM check for scheduled tasks
call send-log.cmd at
```

SURE SIGNS OF COMPROMISE

There are a few clear signals that a system has been compromised. First, if the output of any of the commands presented in this chapter conflict, you have been breached. Second, if there are any processes listening on ports known to be associated with malware, the machine is infected. Third, if there are remote logins to the machine that should not exist, you have probably been the victim of an attack. If none of these are true, it does not mean that you have not been hacked and the situation may justify the effort to perform a fuller live analysis as described in the next chapter. If, however, any of these conditions are true, you should probably proceed directly to creating images (as discussed in Chapter 4) unless there is some compelling reason to perform further live analysis.

SUMMARY

We have covered quite a bit in this chapter. We discussed ways of minimizing disturbance to a subject system while determining if there was an incident. Several scripts to make this easy were presented. We ended this chapter with a set of scripts that can allow you to determine whether there was a compromise in mere minutes. In the next chapter we will discuss performing a full live analysis once you have determined that an incident occurred.

CHAPTER 3

Live Analysis

INFORMATION IN THIS CHAPTER:

- Analyzing the initial scan
- File metadata
- Timelines
- User command history
- Hashing
- Dumping RAM
- Automation with scripting

THERE WAS AN INCIDENT: NOW WHAT?

Based on interviews with the client and limited live response you are convinced there has been an incident, or at least the probability is high enough that further work is justified. Now what? It is time to delve deeper into the subject system before deciding if it must be shut down for dead analysis. The investigation has now moved into the next box as shown in Figure 3.1.

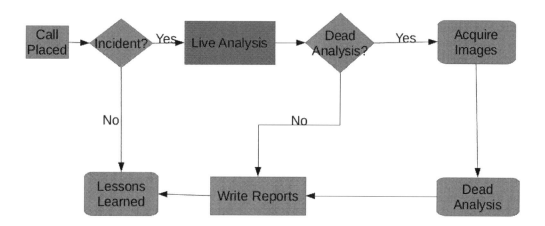

FIGURE 3.1.
The high-level incident response process.

Some systems can be shut down with minimal business disruption. In the case of our Windows 7 subject, this is a single user's desktop which is normally not terribly painful to take offline. Only one person is affected by taking the system down. His or her productivity has already been affected by malware that we have discovered. In a case like this you might decide to dump the RAM and proceed to dead analysis. If this is what you have chosen to do, you can safely skip ahead to the section of this chapter on dumping RAM.

ANALYZING RESULTS FROM THE INITIAL SCAN

If you have gotten this far in the process, you should begin by reexamining the network communications occurring on the subject. Before you can understand what a suspicious connection looks like, you need to understand a little about how ports and sockets work in TCP/IP.

Both TCP (connection-oriented) and UDP (connectionless) protocols rely on sockets. Sockets are essentially virtual data pipes that connect two processes which may or may not be on different machines. Each end of a socket has an address that consists of an IP address and socket number. Ports 0 – 1023 are referred to as well-known or privileged ports. The use of these ports is managed by the same people who assign IP addresses, Internet Assigned Numbers Authority (IANA). On most systems administrator privileges are required to start a listening process on these ports. Some of the best known ports in this range are 80 and 443 for HTTP (web) and HTTPS (secured web), respectively. Any services listening on these ports require a conversation with the local system administrator.

Ports 1024 – 49,151 are known as registered or user ports. Anyone can create a listening process on these ports. As a result, it is not unusual to see malware listening on these ports. It should be noted that legitimate applications can register these ports with IANA. If malware has sufficient privileges, it might install a listener on a privileged port.

Ports 49,152 – 65,535 are known as private or dynamic ports. These ports may be freely used by anyone without registration. It is extremely common for these ports to be used on the client side of Internet socket connections (web, etc.). All of the connections shown in Figure 3.2 are related to browsing a website. Note that all of the client side connections are using private ports, and the webserver side connections are using either port 443 or 80.

Malware can start a listener on any of these ports. Some malware use the same ports every time. One place that you can find a decent list of these ports is https://www.sans.org/security-resources/idfaq/which-backdoors-live-on-which-ports/8/4. A list of legitimate ports is built into your forensic workstation. The /etc/services file contains a listing of common ports and associated services. Because malware can use the same ports as legitimate services, a port number alone is not sufficient to determine if malware is present.

Just because you have not found any listeners does not mean you are malware free. Some malware might use a reverse connection. In other words, instead of setting up a listener, a connection is made to a remote system that is listening for infected machines. Not only does such a system get around the privilege issues related to well-known ports, it also makes it easier to get traffic through a firewall.

Walking through a process list is another good way to spot some malware. Two suspicious processes named bc are shown in Figure 3.3. On Unix and Linux systems bc is the basic calculator program. A little Googling reveals that on Windows bc is associated with the AES Shell

```
TCP    10.0.2.15:49774    204.186.48.25:443    ESTABLISHED
TCP    10.0.2.15:49775    204.186.48.24:443    ESTABLISHED
TCP    10.0.2.15:49776    172.217.4.77:443     ESTABLISHED
TCP    10.0.2.15:49777    204.186.48.24:443    ESTABLISHED
TCP    10.0.2.15:49778    204.186.215.32:443   ESTABLISHED
TCP    10.0.2.15:49779    204.186.48.24:443    ESTABLISHED
TCP    10.0.2.15:49781    204.186.215.45:443   ESTABLISHED
TCP    10.0.2.15:49783    31.13.69.245:80      TIME_WAIT
TCP    10.0.2.15:49784    31.13.69.245:80      TIME_WAIT
TCP    10.0.2.15:49785    31.13.69.245:80      TIME_WAIT
TCP    10.0.2.15:49786    31.13.69.245:80      TIME_WAIT
TCP    10.0.2.15:49787    31.13.69.245:80      TIME_WAIT
TCP    10.0.2.15:49788    148.137.10.10:80     TIME_WAIT
TCP    10.0.2.15:49789    148.137.10.10:80     TIME_WAIT
TCP    10.0.2.15:49790    148.137.10.10:80     TIME_WAIT
TCP    10.0.2.15:49791    148.137.10.10:80     TIME_WAIT
TCP    10.0.2.15:49792    148.137.10.10:80     TIME_WAIT
TCP    10.0.2.15:49794    31.13.69.203:80      ESTABLISHED
TCP    10.0.2.15:49795    31.13.69.203:80      ESTABLISHED
TCP    10.0.2.15:49796    31.13.69.203:80      ESTABLISHED
TCP    10.0.2.15:49797    31.13.69.203:443     ESTABLISHED
TCP    10.0.2.15:49798    31.13.69.203:443     ESTABLISHED
TCP    10.0.2.15:49799    31.13.69.203:443     ESTABLISHED
TCP    10.0.2.15:49800    31.13.69.228:443     ESTABLISHED
TCP    10.0.2.15:49801    31.13.69.203:443     ESTABLISHED
```

FIGURE 3.2.

Web traffic

```
2828  8        2        Wait:UserReq  0:00:00.000   0:00:00.000   16:48:09.901
2832  9     2031        Wait:UserReq  0:00:00.015   0:00:00.031   16:48:09.901
2964  8    41530        Wait:UserReq  0:00:00.546   0:00:00.046   16:48:05.463
1504  8    91882        Wait:Queue    0:00:13.375   0:00:07.390   16:47:10.026
3008  8        3        Wait:Queue    0:00:00.000   0:00:00.000   16:47:10.026
 336  8       13        Wait:Queue    0:00:00.000   0:00:00.000   16:46:49.979
1844  9     7622        Wait:Queue    0:00:00.203   0:00:00.140    2:28:48.662
1096  8        3        Wait:Queue    0:00:00.000   0:00:00.000    0:00:05.203

Name              Pid     VM      WS    Priv  Priv Pk   Faults   NonP Page
bc               2724   15036   2572    728    4192     3478      4    23
 Tid Pri  Cswtch          State      User Time  Kernel Time  Elapsed Time
2712  9     263      Wait:UserReq  0:00:00.046  0:00:00.015  16:44:54.745

Name              Pid     VM      WS    Priv  Priv Pk   Faults   NonP Page
bc               2808   81592  11552   6772    6804     3113     13   140
 Tid Pri  Cswtch          State      User Time  Kernel Time  Elapsed Time
2736 10 3975256      Wait:UserReq  0:00:00.093  0:00:00.031  16:44:54.651
2952 10       9      Wait:Executive 0:00:00.000 0:00:00.000  16:44:54.323
2972  9       2      Wait:Executive 0:00:00.000 0:00:00.000  16:44:54.307

Name              Pid     VM      WS    Priv  Priv Pk   Faults   NonP Page
cmd              2932   50760   3160   1892    1892      842      6    96
 Tid Pri  Cswtch          State      User Time  Kernel Time  Elapsed Time
2948  9      42      Wait:Executive 0:00:00.000 0:00:00.000  16:44:54.370

Name              Pid     VM      WS    Priv  Priv Pk   Faults   NonP Page
WUDFHost          552   43756   5676   1780    1844     1463      9    82
 Tid Pri  Cswtch          State      User Time  Kernel Time  Elapsed Time
2408  9      12      Wait:UserReq  0:00:00.000  0:00:00.000   3:01:11.734
```

FIGURE 3.3.

Suspicious processes in the process list. These are related to an AES Shell backdoor.

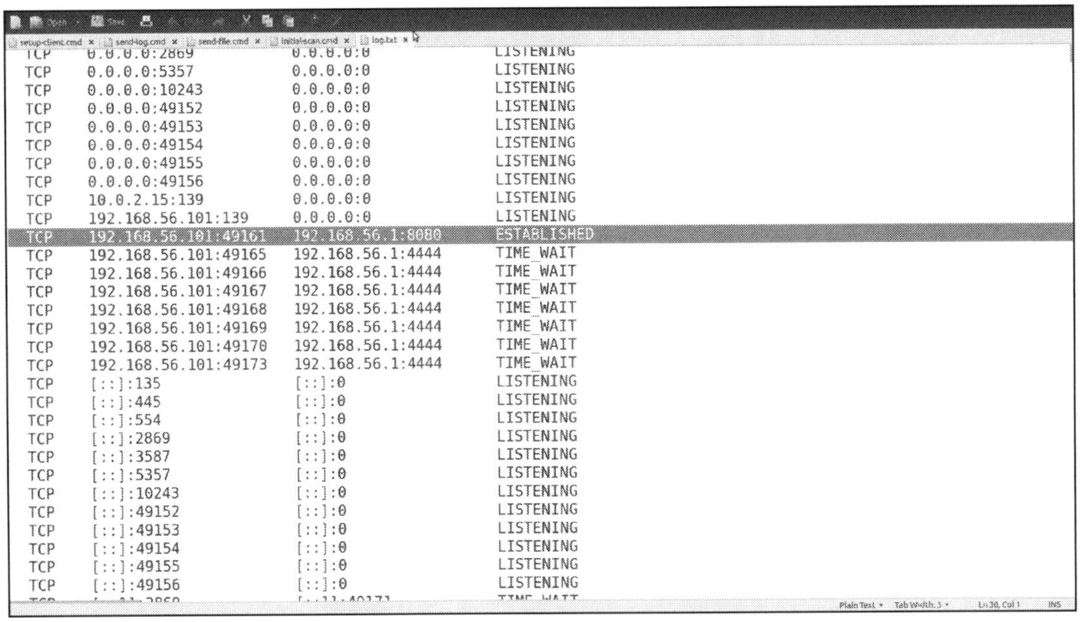

```
TCP    0.0.0.0:2869            0.0.0.0:0              LISTENING
TCP    0.0.0.0:5357            0.0.0.0:0              LISTENING
TCP    0.0.0.0:10243           0.0.0.0:0              LISTENING
TCP    0.0.0.0:49152           0.0.0.0:0              LISTENING
TCP    0.0.0.0:49153           0.0.0.0:0              LISTENING
TCP    0.0.0.0:49154           0.0.0.0:0              LISTENING
TCP    0.0.0.0:49155           0.0.0.0:0              LISTENING
TCP    0.0.0.0:49156           0.0.0.0:0              LISTENING
TCP    10.0.2.15:139           0.0.0.0:0              LISTENING
TCP    192.168.56.101:139      0.0.0.0:0              LISTENING
TCP    192.168.56.101:49161    192.168.56.1:8080      ESTABLISHED
TCP    192.168.56.101:49165    192.168.56.1:4444      TIME_WAIT
TCP    192.168.56.101:49166    192.168.56.1:4444      TIME_WAIT
TCP    192.168.56.101:49167    192.168.56.1:4444      TIME_WAIT
TCP    192.168.56.101:49168    192.168.56.1:4444      TIME_WAIT
TCP    192.168.56.101:49169    192.168.56.1:4444      TIME_WAIT
TCP    192.168.56.101:49170    192.168.56.1:4444      TIME_WAIT
TCP    192.168.56.101:49173    192.168.56.1:4444      TIME_WAIT
TCP    [::]:135                [::]:0                 LISTENING
TCP    [::]:445                [::]:0                 LISTENING
TCP    [::]:554                [::]:0                 LISTENING
TCP    [::]:2869               [::]:0                 LISTENING
TCP    [::]:3587               [::]:0                 LISTENING
TCP    [::]:5357               [::]:0                 LISTENING
TCP    [::]:10243              [::]:0                 LISTENING
TCP    [::]:49152              [::]:0                 LISTENING
TCP    [::]:49153              [::]:0                 LISTENING
TCP    [::]:49154              [::]:0                 LISTENING
TCP    [::]:49155              [::]:0                 LISTENING
TCP    [::]:49156              [::]:0                 LISTENING
```

FIGURE 3.4.

A remote connection related to the AES Shell backdoor.

backdoor. Some investigation reveals that there is a remote connection to port 8080 associated with this backdoor as shown in Figure 3.4.

You should look at the services running on the subject system. Talk to the local system administrator to verify that the set of services is as it should be. Another thing that can be done with this list is to ensure that the listening ports have a corresponding service. For example, the LanmanServer service is used for file and printer sharing. This service uses port 445. If there is a listener on this port and LanmanServer is not running then you likely have some malware trying to hide. This service is also widely attacked. One of the best known vulnerabilities in this service, MS08-067, went unpatched for years. The appropriate listening port and running service are shown in Figure 3.5 and Figure 3.6, respectively.

When looking at services, check that the firewall is running. If it is not running, that is a very bad sign. Even if it is running, you should check its settings at some point. A savvy attacker might adjust the firewall settings and add an exception for installed malware. Changes to the firewall as well as when it was started or stopped can be found in the system logs. Search on "firewall" in your text editor.

Another service that should be checked is RemoteRegistry. This service allows remote users to modify the registry on a Windows system. If this service is enabled, check with the local system administrator. In my opinion there is never a good reason to use this service. Another related service that should be checked is Remote Management.

Check the status of the Task Scheduler. On most systems this will be running. As usual, consult the local system administrator to determine the correct state of this service. It is com-

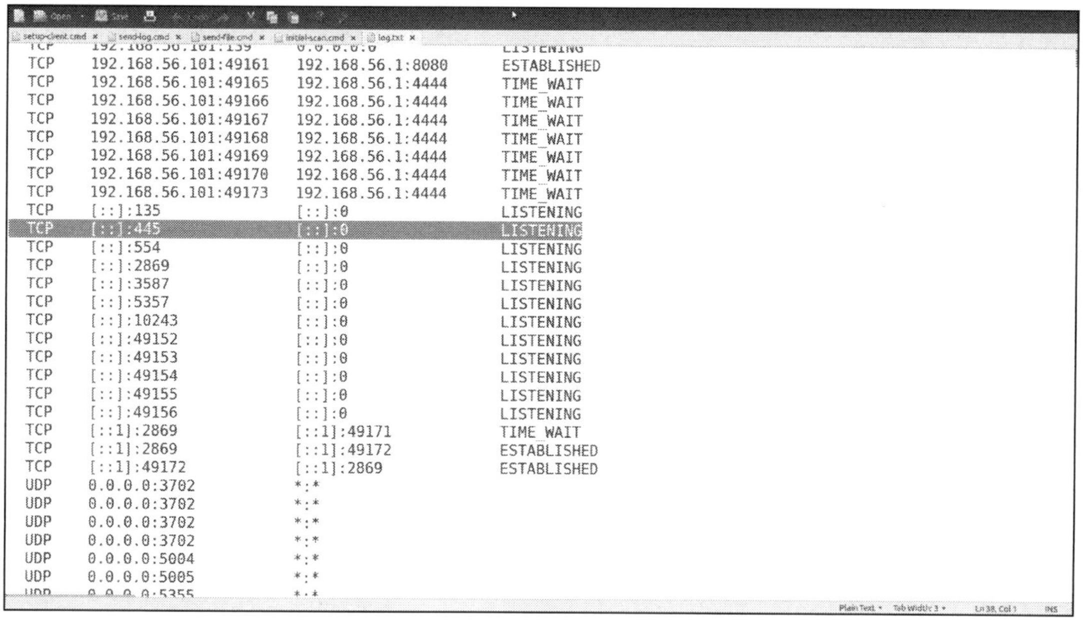
```
TCP    192.168.56.101:139     0.0.0.0:0              LISTENING
TCP    192.168.56.101:49161   192.168.56.1:8080      ESTABLISHED
TCP    192.168.56.101:49165   192.168.56.1:4444      TIME_WAIT
TCP    192.168.56.101:49166   192.168.56.1:4444      TIME_WAIT
TCP    192.168.56.101:49167   192.168.56.1:4444      TIME_WAIT
TCP    192.168.56.101:49168   192.168.56.1:4444      TIME_WAIT
TCP    192.168.56.101:49169   192.168.56.1:4444      TIME_WAIT
TCP    192.168.56.101:49170   192.168.56.1:4444      TIME_WAIT
TCP    192.168.56.101:49173   192.168.56.1:4444      TIME_WAIT
TCP    [::]:135               [::]:0                 LISTENING
TCP    [::]:445               [::]:0                 LISTENING
TCP    [::]:554               [::]:0                 LISTENING
TCP    [::]:2869              [::]:0                 LISTENING
TCP    [::]:3587              [::]:0                 LISTENING
TCP    [::]:5357              [::]:0                 LISTENING
TCP    [::]:10243             [::]:0                 LISTENING
TCP    [::]:49152             [::]:0                 LISTENING
TCP    [::]:49153             [::]:0                 LISTENING
TCP    [::]:49154             [::]:0                 LISTENING
TCP    [::]:49155             [::]:0                 LISTENING
TCP    [::]:49156             [::]:0                 LISTENING
TCP    [::1]:2869             [::1]:49171            TIME_WAIT
TCP    [::1]:2869             [::1]:49172            ESTABLISHED
TCP    [::1]:49172            [::1]:2869             ESTABLISHED
UDP    0.0.0.0:3702           *:*
UDP    0.0.0.0:3702           *:*
UDP    0.0.0.0:3702           *:*
UDP    0.0.0.0:3702           *:*
UDP    0.0.0.0:5004           *:*
UDP    0.0.0.0:5005           *:*
UDP    0.0.0.0:5355           *:*
```

FIGURE 3.5.

A listener on port 445 associate with Windows file and printer sharing.

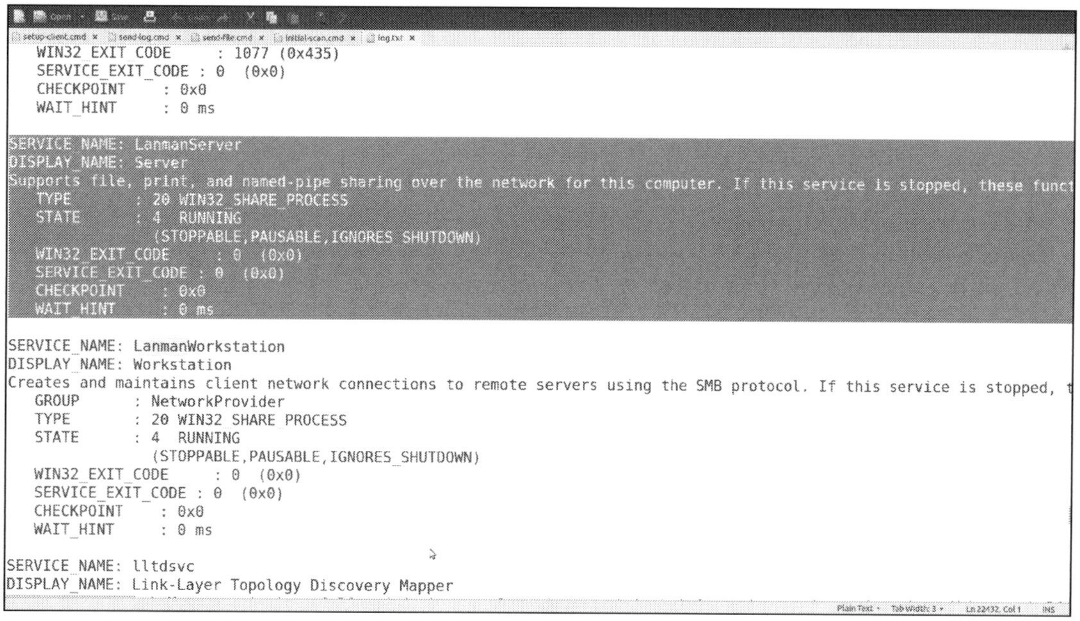
```
   WIN32_EXIT_CODE      : 1077 (0x435)
   SERVICE_EXIT_CODE : 0  (0x0)
   CHECKPOINT       : 0x0
   WAIT_HINT        : 0 ms

SERVICE_NAME: LanmanServer
DISPLAY_NAME: Server
Supports file, print, and named-pipe sharing over the network for this computer. If this service is stopped, these func
   TYPE          : 20 WIN32_SHARE_PROCESS
   STATE         : 4  RUNNING
                         (STOPPABLE,PAUSABLE,IGNORES_SHUTDOWN)
   WIN32_EXIT_CODE      : 0  (0x0)
   SERVICE_EXIT_CODE : 0  (0x0)
   CHECKPOINT       : 0x0
   WAIT_HINT        : 0 ms

SERVICE_NAME: LanmanWorkstation
DISPLAY_NAME: Workstation
Creates and maintains client network connections to remote servers using the SMB protocol. If this service is stopped, t
   GROUP         : NetworkProvider
   TYPE          : 20 WIN32_SHARE_PROCESS
   STATE         : 4  RUNNING
                         (STOPPABLE,PAUSABLE,IGNORES_SHUTDOWN)
   WIN32_EXIT_CODE      : 0  (0x0)
   SERVICE_EXIT_CODE : 0  (0x0)
   CHECKPOINT       : 0x0
   WAIT_HINT        : 0 ms

SERVICE_NAME: lltdsvc
DISPLAY_NAME: Link-Layer Topology Discovery Mapper
```

FIGURE 3.6.

The LanmanServer service in the service list.

mon for administrators to run important tasks like virus scans via this service which can lead attackers to disable it.

GETTING FILE METADATA

At this point in the investigation you should have a rough idea of approximately when an incident may have occurred. It is not unusual to start with some system directories and then go back to examine other areas based on what you find. It is the nature of investigations that you will find little bits of evidence that lead you to other little bits of evidence and so on.

A good place to start the live analysis is to collect file metadata which includes timestamps, permissions, and file sizes. Keep in mind that a sophisticated attacker might alter this information. In the dead analysis section of this book we will discuss ways of detecting this and how to recover some metadata that is not easily altered without specialized tools.

As always, we will leverage scripting to make this task easier and minimize the chances for mistakes. The following script builds on scripts from Chapter 2 in order to send file metadata to the forensic workstation. The data is sent in a structured manner that is easily handled by your Linux forensic workstation. Note that to keep this simple every file has a header describing it, but this is easily filtered out later.

```
@echo offer
REM simple script to collect file metadata for a specified directory
REM usage: get-fileinfo.cmd <directory, filename, or pattern>
REM Note: no recursion through subdirectories is performed
REM by Dr. Phil Polstra for PentesterAcademy.com

for %%i in (%1) do wmic datafile where name="%%i" get * /format:csv
```

The script takes a directory, filename, or pattern because you probably want to limit the scope of this command as it takes a while to run. All of the real work in this script is in the very last line. We have used the for loop and command line arguments (%1) in previous scripts. The use of `wmic` is new, however. Windows Management Instrumentation (WMI) is a set of standards used to communicate and share information between Windows programs and components. The `wmic` utility allows you to retrieve information from a component. In this case the component is a data file with a given name, and we retrieve all of its information (metadata). By combining this script with send-log.cmd, file metadata for important directories (such as \Windows and \Windows\System32) is easily sent to the forensic workstation.

A portion of what is received when send-log.cmd is used with this script to send file metadata for the \Windows directory is shown in Figure 3.7. There are extra blank lines in this thanks to the non-standard way that Windows appends a carriage return and newline to the end of each line (every other system uses just a newline). The headers for every line will be removed when we import the information into a spreadsheet in the next step.

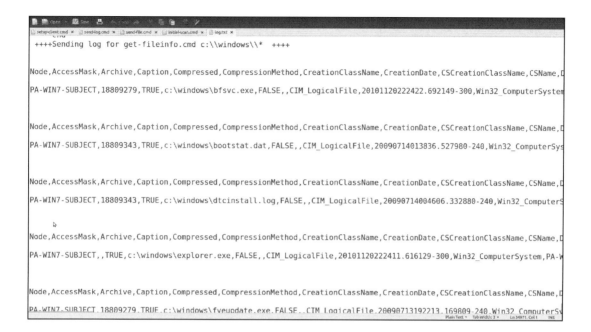

FIGURE 3.7.

Partial results from running get-fileinfo.com on the \Windows directory.

USING A SPREADSHEET PROGRAM TO BUILD A TIMELINE

Should you decide to perform a full dead analysis, a complete timeline can be built using techniques described later in this book. At this stage of the investigation having a file list that can be sorted by modification, creation, and access times based on output from the script in the previous section can be helpful. While not as nice as a proper timeline that intertwines these timestamps, it can be created in a matter of minutes.

The first step is to open the log.txt file for the case in your favorite text editor on the forensic workstation. Copy the appropriate lines and paste them to a new file. Save the file with a .csv extension and then open it in LibreOffice Calc (or your favorite spreadsheet program). You will be greeted with a screen such as that shown in Figure 3.8. Ensure that the comma check box is selected.

Once the file has been imported, it is easily sorted by selecting all of the pertinent rows and then choosing sort from the data menu. The entire spreadsheet can be selected by clicking on the square in the upper left corner above the 1 and to the left of the A. After this is done, sort the spreadsheet by column A. This should send all of the column headings to the very top or very bottom of the spreadsheet. If the headings end up at the bottom reverse the sort order.

Once this is done, select all but the bottommost row of headings and then delete it as shown in Figure 3.9. You should now have a proper CSV file that is easily sorted by name, timestamp, etc. Save this file. You might wish to save it in something other than CSV format if you want to change how it is displayed.

64 CHAPTER 3 Live Analysis

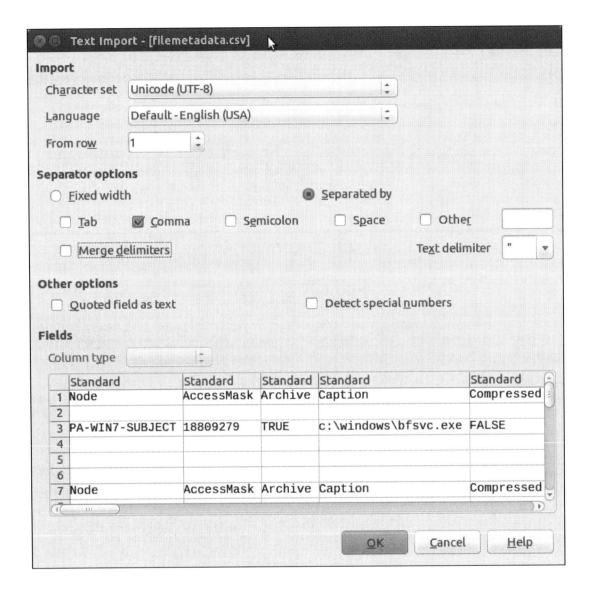

FIGURE 3.8.

Importing a CSV file with file metadata into LibreOffice Calc.

A similar technique can be used to sort by access, modification, or creation time. It might be desirable to copy and paste this spreadsheet onto multiple tabs (technically worksheets) and save the resulting workbook as a regular Calc file. The easiest way to copy information to a new sheet is to click in the blank square in the upper left corner (above the 1 and to the left of the A), press Control-C, go to the new sheet, click in the same upper left hand square, and then press Control-V.

The creation time tab of such a spreadsheet for our subject system is shown in Figure 3.10. The timestamps in this spreadsheet are of the form YYYYMMDDHHMMSS.mmmmmmSooo

Using a spreadsheet program to build a timeline

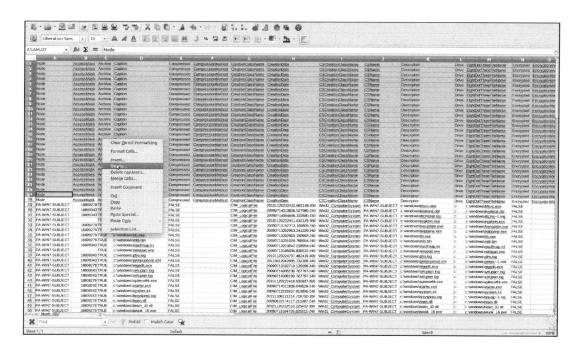

FIGURE 3.9.

Eliminating excess heading rows.

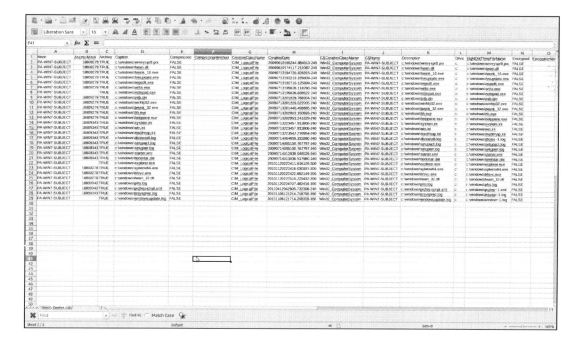

FIGURE 3.10.

File metadata for the \Windows directory sorted by creation timestamps.

where YYYY, MM, DD, HH, MM, SS, mmmmmm, S, and ooo are year, month, day, hours, minutes, seconds, fractional seconds, sign of offset from UTC time, and offset from UTC in minutes, respectively.

EXAMINING USER COMMAND HISTORY

Much like proper shells in Linux and Unix, Windows stores command prompt history. While use of the Windows command prompt is not nearly as common as utilizing a shell on Linux, there is always a chance that pertinent information may be found in this history. If you happen upon a live system with an open command prompt you may retrieve the command history using `doskey /history`. If you get any significant results you can use send-log.cmd to send this history to your forensic workstation.

COLLECTING FILE HASHES

There are a number of hash databases on the Internet that contain hashes for known-good and known-bad files. Is this the best way of finding malware? Absolutely not! That said, checking hashes is super quick compared to analyzing files with anti-virus software or attempting to reverse engineer them. A good hash database allows you to eliminate a large number of files from consideration. Occasionally you might find malware using hashes. Reducing the number of files you are forced to look at by eliminating known-good files from your analysis is much more useful, however.

Two popular free hash databases include https://www.owasp.org/index.php/OWASP_File_Hash_Repository by the Open Web Applications Security Project (OWASP), and http://www.nsrl.nist.gov/ from the National Institute of Standards and Technology. As of this writing they both support MD5 and SHA-1. Should they support more modern algorithms in the future, the script below is easily modified.

Unfortunately, unlike Linux, there is no standard way to compute hash values in every version of Windows. The newer versions of Windows have a built-in certutil program which can be used for this purpose. It has the unfortunate side effect of outputting three lines for every file. If you are dealing with an older version of Windows that lacks certutil, standalone applications such as md5sum (available at https://md5sum.codeplex.com/) and sha256sum (available from http://www.labtestproject.com/files/win/sha256sum/sha256sum.exe) are available. The simple script below can be used to compute MD5 hashes on multiple files. Naturally, this could be combined with send-log.cmd to send this list to the forensic workstation.

```
@echo off
REM Simple script to calculate MD5 sum as part of
REM initial live incident response.
REM Warning: This script might take a long time to run!
REM by Dr. Phil Polstra (@ppolstra) as developed for
REM PentesterAcademy.com.

For %%i in (%1) do certutil -hashfile %%i MD5
```

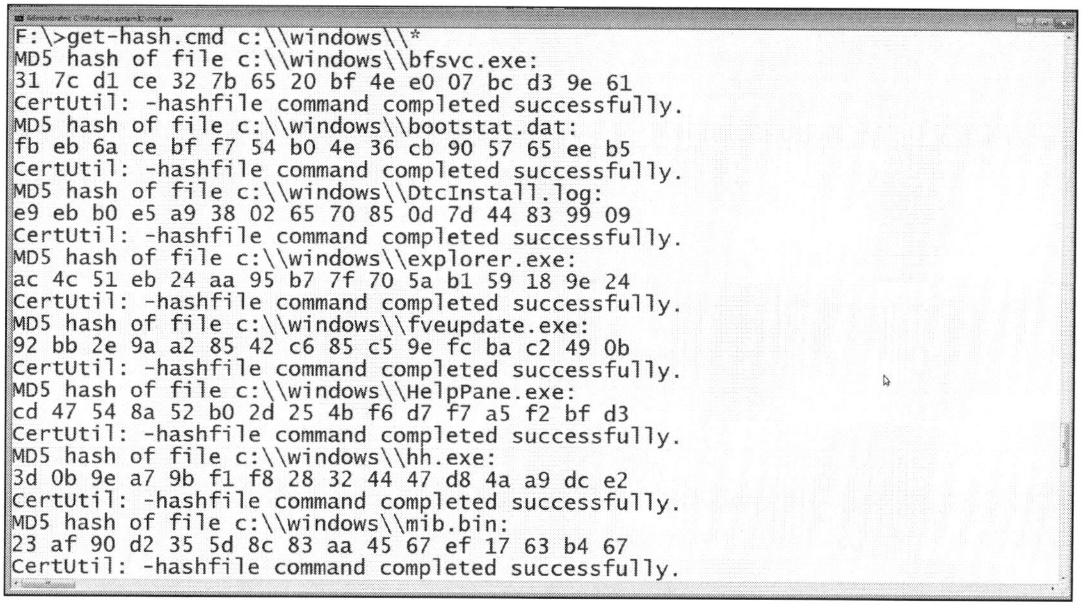

FIGURE 3.11.

Partial results from computing MD5 hashes on files in the \Windows directory.

Partial results from running this script on the \Windows directory are shown in Figure 3.11. These results can easily be transformed into a form that is easily parsed and put into a spreadsheet using something like the following one line Perl script on the forensic workstation:

```
perl -p -e
   's/^MD5 hash of (.*):$/\1;/;
   s/^CertUtil:.*$//;
   s/^\n//;
   s/;\n/;/' <file containing CertUtil output>
```

Here is a breakdown of this quick Perl script. The script should be entered on one line. It was broken up here to make it clearer. First we execute Perl and tell it to print every line in the file we pass it (-p) and then give it a short bit of Perl to run against every line in the file (-e). We then run one of the most basic Perl commands four times. The command is substitute and the syntax is s/<regular expression to match>/<what to substitute for matching text>/. If you are not familiar with regular expressions, they are powerful ways of defining patterns. A complete tutorial on regular expressions, also called regexs, is well beyond the scope of this book. There are a number of online resources, such as http://www.regular-expressions.info/, for those wanting to know more. The book *Mastering Regular Expressions* by Jeffrey E. F. Friedl (O'Reilly, 2006) is a great resource for those that prefer a book.

In regular expressions we have characters that match themselves (literals) and those with special meaning (metacharacters). Within the set of metacharacters we have things that match,

68 CHAPTER 3 Live Analysis

anchors, and quantity specifiers. Occasionally we want to treat metacharacters as literals and we do this by escaping them. Escaping a character is as simple as prepending the \ character before it.

Some of the more common matching metacharacters are character classes (lists of characters inside square brackets) which match any character in the list, and the period which matches any character except a newline. Because the period is a metacharacter, it must be escaped when you want to match a period.

Some of the most used quantity specifiers include *, +, and ? which indicate zero or more, one or more, and zero or one, respectively. Quantity specifiers apply to the thing (literal character, metacharacter, or grouping) just before them. For example, the regular expression A+ means one or more capital A's. As another example, [A-Z]?[a-z]+ would match any word that is written in all lower case letters with the possible exception of the first letter (breaking it down it is zero or one upper case letters followed by one or more lower case letters).

The carrot (^) and dollar sign ($) are used to anchor regular expressions to the start and end of a line, respectively. These anchors only make sense in the context of regular expression tools that process one line at a time. This is the default behavior in Perl.

Parts of a regular expression can be grouped together by enclosing them in parentheses. There are two reasons for using grouping. First, this allows a pattern to be repeated without typing in a regular expression more than once. Second, text that matches a grouping can be referred to later. This is often done when one value is to be substituted for another, as is the case in this script.

Lines in Perl are terminated with a semicolon (;). The first substitution matches a line that begins with (^) "MD5 hash of" followed by zero or more characters that are not newlines ((.*)) which are in turn followed by a colon at the very end of the line (:$), and all of this is replaced with whatever matched the first pattern in parentheses with a semicolon appended (\1;). The net effect of all of this is that only a line containing the filename and a semicolon remains.

The second substitution replaces any lines that begin with (^) CertUtil: followed by any non-newline characters to the end of the line (.*$) with an empty line. The third substitution removes any blank lines since it searches for lines that begin with a newline and replaces them with nothing. The final substitution replaces a semicolon followed by a newline with just a semicolon. This effectively puts the filename and hash on one line separated by a semicolon. Partial output from running this command on the \Windows directory is shown in Figure 3.12.

DUMPING RAM

What is the perfect way to capture a running system? Get a copy of what is in RAM. This allows you to exactly recreate the state of a machine. Okay, not exactly, but close enough for our investigative purposes. Some recently released tools such as Volatility make acquiring RAM images particularly useful. However getting these images today is not necessarily easy.

RAM acquisition from a virtual machine

If your subject happens to be running in a virtual machine, RAM acquisition becomes quite simple in most cases. If you are running the popular Oracle VirtualBox software, memory

```
phil@i7laptop:~/PentesterAcademy/windows-forensics/pawinsubject1$
phil@i7laptop:~/PentesterAcademy/windows-forensics/pawinsubject1$ perl -p -e 's/
^MD5 hash of file (.*):$/\1;/; s/^CertUtil:.*$//; s/^\n//; s/;\n/;/' hashes.txt
c:\\windows\\bfsvc.exe;31 7c d1 ce 32 7b 65 20 bf 4e e0 07 bc d3 9e 61
c:\\windows\\bootstat.dat;fb eb 6a ce bf f7 54 b0 4e 36 cb 90 57 65 ee b5
c:\\windows\\DtcInstall.log;e9 eb b0 e5 a9 38 02 65 70 85 0d 7d 44 83 99 09
c:\\windows\\explorer.exe;ac 4c 51 eb 24 aa 95 b7 7f 70 5a b1 59 18 9e 24
c:\\windows\\fveupdate.exe;92 bb 2e 9a a2 85 42 c6 85 c5 9e fc ba c2 49 0b
c:\\windows\\HelpPane.exe;cd 47 54 8a 52 b0 2d 25 4b f6 d7 f7 a5 f2 bf d3
c:\\windows\\hh.exe;3d 0b 9e a7 9b f1 f8 28 32 44 47 d8 4a a9 dc e2
c:\\windows\\mib.bin;23 af 90 d2 35 5d 8c 83 aa 45 67 ef 17 63 b4 67
c:\\windows\\msdfmap.ini;b9 fb 94 a8 da 62 71 1c 69 55 82 5d ef b2 5c 5a
c:\\windows\\notepad.exe;f2 c7 bb 8a cc 97 f9 2e 98 7a 2d 40 87 d0 21 b1
c:\\windows\\PFRO.log;24 c7 00 ad 56 c9 fa a7 b3 ac 2e 4e 2f b8 90 c6
c:\\windows\\Professional.xml;ff b8 b9 1b d1 9e 5b c1 0a 33 44 aa f3 48 80 f3
c:\\windows\\regedit.exe;2e 2c 93 78 46 a0 b8 78 9e 5e 91 73 92 84 d1 7a
c:\\windows\\setupact.log;c3 75 0b a4 08 ac e1 3c 57 25 a8 a9 9a 37 3d 63
c:\\windows\\splwow64.exe;d0 16 28 af 9f 7f b3 f4 15 b3 57 d4 46 fb e6 d9
c:\\windows\\Starter.xml;90 60 c3 c7 45 e7 b2 d8 e1 a8 1d d0 61 02 15 46
c:\\windows\\system.ini;28 6a 9e db 37 9d c3 42 3a 52 8b 08 64 a0 f1 11
c:\\windows\\TSSysprep.log;c6 cc 70 57 86 ac a3 31 7c 48 67 87 54 1b 11 1f
c:\\windows\\twain.dll;0b ea 3f 79 a3 6b 1f 67 b2 ce 0f 59 55 24 c7 7c
c:\\windows\\twain_32.dll;16 3a 95 97 5e 1d 88 19 e6 53 aa 3e 96 13 71 ca
c:\\windows\\twunk_16.exe;f3 6a 27 17 06 ed d2 3c 94 95 6a fb 56 98 11 84
```

FIGURE 3.12.

Partial results from applying the Perl one-liner to the CertUtil output from the \Windows directory.

can be acquired using tools that ship with the VirtualBox package. The following command is used to dump memory from a VirtualBox machine that is hosted on Linux: `vboxmanage debugvm <VM name> dumpvmcore --filename <image filename>`. An example of dumping the RAM from a Windows 7 subject is shown in Figure 3.13.

RAM acquisition with FTK Imager

There are a plethora of memory acquisition tools available, including some hardware devices. We will only cover one here. FTK Imager is an industry standard tool for creating disk images. Given that you will likely install this tool for other purposes, such as browsing filesystem images and extracting files, it makes sense to use it for memory acquisition.

Access Data makes a complete set of forensic tools. FTK Imager is a small part of this tool suite. Free versions of FTK Imager are available for download from http://accessdata.com/product-download. It is imperative that you download the FTK Imager Lite version. There are a couple of reasons for selecting this version. First, you do not have the hassle of registering it. Second, more importantly, FTK Imager Lite is a portable executable that is easily saved to your response drive, whereas the full versions must be installed. Recall that installing an application on the subject is the last thing you want to do, especially if you are planning on capturing a memory image.

CHAPTER 3 Live Analysis

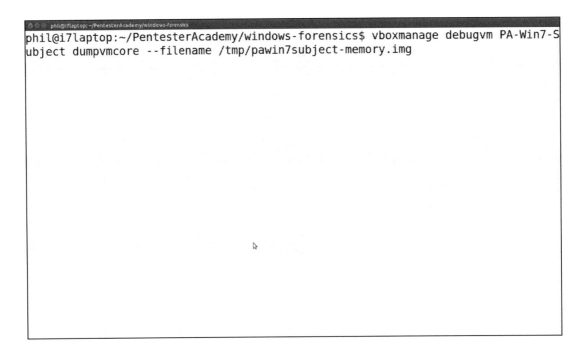

FIGURE 3.13.

Dumping memory from a virtual machine.

FIGURE 3.14.

Selecting Capture Memory in FTK Imager.

Capturing memory with FTK Imager is a very simple process. Run FTK Imager as an administrator as you will need elevated privileges to capture memory. Select Capture Memory from the File menu as shown in Figure 3.14.

Once you have selected Capture Memory, you will be greeted with a dialog box like the one shown in Figure 3.15. There are a couple of choices to be made. First, you need to decide where to put the image file. Previously in this book I have recommended that data be sent across a network. This is still an option. Depending on the networking situation on the subject, it may make more sense to store this file on your response drive. Either choice represents a compromise. Storing it to your response drive will result in more caching which can disturb your RAM image and sending a large quantity of data across the network can be painfully slow.

The second choice you must make is whether or not to capture the pagefile. Personally, I never bother to do this as it is easily obtained later from the filesystem image and the memory capture process is already slow enough. Speaking of speed, it typically takes about 15 minutes per gigabyte of RAM to perform this capture via FTK Imager to an attached USB drive.

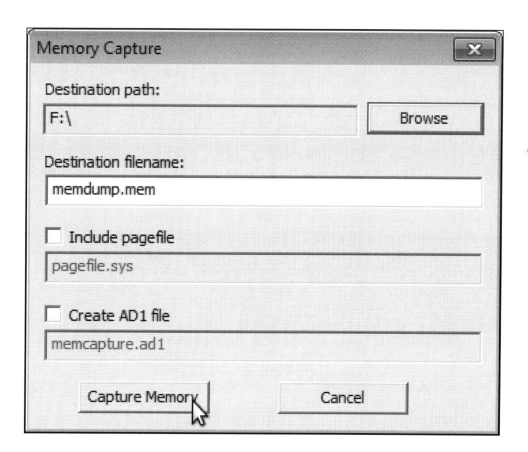

FIGURE 3.15.

Capturing a memory image to a USB drive via FTK Imager.

SUMMARY

In this chapter we have discussed multiple techniques that can be used to gather information from a system without taking it offline. This included collecting an image of system memory for later offline analysis. Analyzing this image will be be discussed later in this book (Chapter 11: Memory Analysis). In the next chapter we will turn our attention to traditional dead analysis which requires us to shut down the subject system.

CHAPTER 4

Creating Images

INFORMATION IN THIS CHAPTER:

- Shutting down the system
- Image formats
- Using dd
- Using dcfldd
- Hardware write blocking
- Software write blocking
- Udev rules
- Live Linux distributions
- Creating an image from a virtual machine
- Creating an image from a physical drive

SHUTTING DOWN THE SYSTEM

We are finally ready to start the traditional dead analysis process. We have now progressed to the next block in our high level process as shown in Figure 4.1 (assuming you are performing incident response). If some time has passed since you performed your initial scans and live

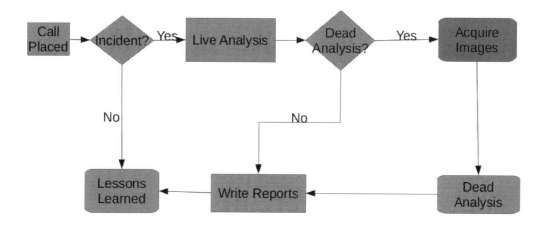

FIGURE 4.1.

High level forensic incident response process.

analysis captures described in the proceeding chapters, you may wish to consider rerunning some or all of the scripts.

As you prepare to shut down the system for imaging, you are faced with a decision to perform a normal shutdown or to pull the plug. Which is better? As with many things in forensics, there is not one right answer to this question for every situation. The investigator must weigh the pluses and minuses for each option.

Normal shutdown

A normal shutdown should, in theory, leave you with a clean filesystem. This, of course, assumes that a normal shutdown is possible with a system infected with malware. I have found that some rootkits prevent a normal shutdown. The biggest reason not to use a normal shutdown is that some malware might clean up after itself, destroy evidence, or even worse destroy other information on the system. With the modern journaling filesystems like NTFS, a clean filesystem is not as crucial as it was many years ago.

Pulling the plug

If we simply cut power to the subject system, the filesystem(s) may not be clean. As previously mentioned, this is not necessarily as serious as it was before journaling filesystems became commonplace.

The best thing this method has going for it is that malware does not have any chance to react. Given the information collected by running your scripts during the live analysis and memory image you have dumped, you are not likely to lose much, if any, information by pulling the plug. If you suspect a malware infection, this is your best option in most cases.

IMAGE FORMATS

As with the memory images, there are choices of formats for storing filesystem images. At a basic level you must decide between a raw format and a proprietary format. Within these choices there are still subchoices to be made.

Raw format

The raw format is nothing more than a set of bytes stored in the same logical order as they are found on the disk. Nearly every media you are likely to encounter utilizes 512 byte sectors. Whereas older devices formatted with FAT12 and FAT16 may use cylinders, heads, and sectors to address these sectors, the FAT32 and NTFS filesystems you are likely to encounter will almost certainly use Logical Block Addressing (LBA).

On media where LBA is used, sectors are numbered logically from 0 to {media size in bytes} / 512. The sectors are labeled LBA0, LBA1, etc. It is important to understand that this logical addressing is done transparently by the media device and therefore deterministic (does not depend on which operating system reads the filesystem, etc.). A raw image is nothing more than a large file with LBA0 in the first 512 bytes, followed by LBA1 in the next 512 bytes, and so on.

Because the raw format is essentially identical to what is stored on the media, there are numerous standard tools that can be used to manipulate them. For this and other reasons the raw format is very popular and supported by every forensic tool. Because raw images are the same size as the media they represent, they tend to be quite large.

Some investigators like to compress raw images. Indeed, some forensic tools can operate on compressed raw images. One thing to keep in mind should you choose to work with compressed images is that it limits your tool selection. It will also likely result in a performance penalty for many common forensic tasks such as searching.

Proprietary format with embedded metadata

EnCase is a widely used proprietary forensic tool. It is especially popular among examiners who focus on Windows systems. The EnCase file format consists of a header, the raw sectors with checksums every 32 kilobytes (64 standard sectors), and a footer. The header contains metadata such as the examiner, acquisition date, etc. and ends with a checksum. The footer has an MD5 checksum for the media image.

The EnCase file format supports compression. Compression is done at the block level which makes searching a little faster than it would be otherwise. The reason for this is that most searches are performed for certain types of files, and file headers at the beginning of blocks (sectors) are used to determine file type.

Proprietary format with metadata in a separate file

Halfway between the raw format and some sort of proprietary format is the use of multiple files to store an image. Typically one file is a raw image and the other stores metadata in a proprietary way. A number of imaging tools make this choice.

Raw format with hashes stored in a separate file

In my opinion, the best option is to acquire images in the raw format with hashes stored separately. This allows the image to be used with every forensic package available and adds standard Linux system tools to your toolbox. The hashes allow you to prove that you have maintained the integrity of the image during the investigation.

In a perfect world you would create an image of a disk and calculate a hash for the entire image and that would be the end of it. However, we do not live in a perfect world. As a result, I recommend that you hash chunks of the image in addition to calculating an overall hash.

There are a couple of reasons for this recommendation. First, it is a good idea to periodically recalculate the hashes as you work to verify you have not changed an image. If the image is large, computing the overall hash might be time consuming when compared to hashing a small chunk. Second, you may encounter media that is damaged. Certain areas may not read the same every time. It is much better to discard data from these damaged areas than to throw out an entire disk image if the hash does not match. Fortunately some of the tools to be discussed in this chapter do this hashing for you.

USING DD

All Linux systems ship with a bit-moving program known as dd. This utility predates Linux by several years. Its original use was for converting to and from ASCII (American Symbolic Code for Information Interchange) and EBCDIC (Extended Binary Coded Decimal Interchange Code). For those unfamiliar with EBCDIC, it was an encoding primarily used by IBM mainframes.

In addition to its conversion capabilities, dd is used for pushing data from one place to another. Data is copied in blocks, with a default block size of 512 bytes. The most basic use of dd is dd if=<input file> of=<output file> bs=<block size>. In Linux, where everything is a file, if the input file represents a device, the output file will be a raw image.

For example, dd if=/dev/sda of=sda.img bs=512 will create a raw image of the first drive on a system. I should point out that you can also image partitions separately by using a device file that corresponds to a single partition such as /dev/sda1, /dev/sdb2, etc. However, I recommend that you image the entire disk as a unit, unless there is some reason (such as lack of space to store the image) that prevents this.

There are a few reasons why I recommend imaging the entire drive if at all possible. First, it becomes much simpler to mount multiple partitions all at once using scripts presented later in this book. Second, any string searches can be performed against everything you have collected, including swap space. Finally, there could be data hidden in unallocated space (not part of any partition).

Does block size matter? In theory it does not matter as dd will faithfully copy any partial blocks so that the input and output files are the same size (assuming no conversions are performed). The default block size is 512 bytes. Optimum performance is achieved when the block size is an even multiple of the bytes read at a time from the input file.

As most devices have 512 byte blocks, any multiple of 512 will improve performance at the expense of using more memory. In the typical scenario (described later in this chapter) where an image is being created from media removed from the subject system, memory footprint is not a concern and a block size of 4 kilobytes or more is safely used. Block sizes may be directly entered in bytes or as multiples of 512 bytes, kilobytes (1024 bytes), or megabytes (1024 * 1024 bytes) using the symbols b, k, and M, respectively. For example, a 4 kilobyte block size can be written as 4096, 8b, or 4k.

There is one last thing I should mention before moving on to another tool. What happens when there is an error? The default behavior is for dd to fail. This can be changed by adding the option conv=noerror,sync to the dd command. When a read error occurs, any bad bytes will be replaced with zeros in order to synchronize the position of everything between the input and output files.

USING DCFLDD

The United States Department of Defense Computer Forensics Lab developed an enhanced version of dd known as dcfldd. This tool adds several forensic features to dd. One of the most important features is the ability to calculate hashes on the fly. The calculated hashes may be sent to a file, displayed in a terminal (default), or both.

In addition to calculating an overall hash, `dcfldd` can compute hashes for chunks of data (which it calls windows). As of this writing, `dcfldd` supports the following hash algorithms: MD5, SHA1, SHA256, SHA384, and SHA512. Multiple hash algorithms may be used simultaneously with hashes written to separate files.

The general format for using `dcfldd` to create an image with hashes in a separate file is `dcfldd if=<subject device> of=<image file> bs=<block size> hash=<algorithm> hashwindow=<chunk size> hashlog=<hash file> conv=noerror,sync`. For example, to create an image of the second hard drive on a system with SHA256 hashes calculated every 1GB, the correct command would be `dcfldd if=/dev/sdb of=sdb.img bs=8k hash=sha256 hashwindow=1G hashlog=sdb.hashes conv=noerror,sync`. If you wanted to calculate both SHA256 and MD5 hashes for some reason, the command would be `dcfldd if=/dev/sdb of=sdb.img bs=8k hash=sha256,md5 hashwindow=1G sha256log=sdb.sha256hashes md5log=sdb.md5hashes conv=noerror,sync`.

Dc3dd

Dcfldd is not the only enhanced version of dd available. Another fork of the dd program known as dc3dd is also available. There are some that prefer this to dcfldd. Dc3dd is available at https://sourceforge.net/projects/dc3dd/. Its commands are very similar to dcfldd. Consult the documentation if you opt to use this tool. Fans of this tool will point out that it is more up to date than dcfldd. It is not as lightweight as dcfldd which might be an issue if you are capturing an image directly on the subject system.

HARDWARE WRITE BLOCKING

You should have some means of assuring that you are not altering the subject's hard drives and/or other media when creating images. The traditional way to do this is to use a hardware write blocker. In many cases hardware write blockers are protocol (SATA, IDE, SCSI, etc.) specific.

Hardware write blockers tend to be a little pricey. A cheaper model might cost upwards of US$350. Because they are expensive, you might not be able to afford a set of blockers for all possible protocols. If you can only afford one blocker, I recommend you buy a SATA unit as that is by far what the majority of systems will be using. A relatively inexpensive blocker is shown in Figure 4.2. If you find yourself doing a lot of Linux response in data centers, a SCSI unit might be a good choice for a second blocker.

There are a few cheaper open-source options available, but they tend to have limitations. One such option is a microcontroller-based USB write blocker which I developed and described in a course on USB forensics at PentesterAcademy.com (http://www.pentesteracademy.com/course?id=16). However, I do not recommend the use of this device for large media, as it is limited to USB 2.0 full speed (12 Mbps). I may port this code to a new microcontroller that is capable of higher speeds (at least 480 Mbps) at some point, but for the moment I recommend the Udev rules method described later in this chapter.

FIGURE 4.2.

A Tableau SATA write blocker.

SOFTWARE WRITE BLOCKING

Just as hardware routers are really just pretty boxes running software routers (usually on Linux), hardware write blockers are almost always small computer devices running write blocking software. There are several commercial options for Windows systems. Naturally, most of the Linux choices are free and open source.

There is a kernel patch available to mount block devices automatically. You can also set something up in your favorite scripting language. Next I will describe a simple way to block anything connected via USB using udev rules.

Udev rules

Udev rules are the new way to control how devices are handled on Linux systems. Using the udev rules presented below, a "magic USB hub" can be created that automatically mounts any block device connected downstream from the hub as read-only.

Linux systems ship with a set of standard udev rules. Administrators may customize their systems by adding their own rules to the /etc/udev/rules.d directory. Like many system scripts (i.e. startup scripts), the order in which these rules are added is determined by the filename. Standard practice is to start the filename with a number which determines when it is loaded.

When the rules in the rules file below are run, all of the information required to mount a filesystem is not yet available. For this reason the rules generate scripts which call other scripts in two stages. The file should be named /etc/udev/rules.d/10-protectedmount.rules. Note that the vendor and product identifiers will be set with an install script to match your hub. This install script is presented later in this chapter.

```
ACTION=="add", SUBSYSTEM=="block", KERNEL=="sd?[1-9]",
ATTRS{idVendor}=="1a40", ATTRS{idProduct}=="0101", ENV{PHIL_
MOUNT}="1", ENV{PHIL_DEV}="%k", RUN+="/etc/udev/scripts/protmount.sh %k %n"
ACTION=="remove", SUBSYSTEM=="block", KERNEL=="sd?[1-9]",
ATTRS{idVendor}=="1a40", ATTRS{idProduct}=="0101", ENV{PHIL_
UNMOUNT}="1", RUN+="/etc/udev/scripts/protmount3.sh %k %n"

ENV{PHIL_MOUNT}=="1", ENV{UDISKS_PRESENTATION_HIDE}="1", ENV{UDISKS_
AUTOMOUNT_HINT}="never", RUN+="/etc/udev/scripts/protmount2-%n.sh"
ENV{PHIL_MOUNT}!="1", ENV{UDISKS_PRESENTATION_HIDE}="0", ENV{UDISKS_
AUTOMOUNT_HINT}="always"

ENV{PHIL_UNMOUNT}=="1", RUN+="/etc/udev/scripts/protmount4-%n.sh"
```

The general format for these rules is a series of statements separated by commas. The first statements, those with double equals ("==") are matching statements. If all of these are matched, the remaining statements are run. These statements primarily set environment variables and add scripts to a list of those to be run. Any such scripts should run quickly in order to avoid bogging down the system.

The first rule can be broken into matching statements and statements to be executed. The matching statements are `ACTION=="add"`, `SUBSYSTEM=="block"`, `KERNEL=="sd?[1-9]"`, `ATTRS{idVendor}=="1a40"`, `ATTRS{idProduct}=="0101"`. This matches when a new device is added, it is a block device, it is named /dev/sdXn (where X is a letter and n is a partition number), and its or a parents' USB vendor and product ID match those specified. If you only want to match the current device's attribute and not that of the parent, use ATTR{attributeName} instead of ATTRS{attributeName}. By using ATTRS we are assured the rule will be matched by every device attached downstream from the hub.

The part of the first rule containing commands to run is `ENV{PHIL_MOUNT}="1"`, `ENV{PHIL_DEV}="%k"`, `RUN+="/etc/udev/scripts/protmount.sh %k %n"`. These statements set an environment variable PHIL_MOUNT equal to 1, set another environment variable PHIL_DEV to the kernel name for the device (sda3, sdb1, etc.), and append /etc/udev/scripts/protmount.sh to the list of scripts to be run with the kernel name for the device and partition number passed in as parameters.

The second rule is very similar to the first, but it matches when the device is removed. It sets an environment variable PHIL_UNMOUNT to 1 and adds /etc/udev/scripts/protmount3.sh to the list of scripts to be run (the kernel device name and partition number are again passed in as parameters). The protmount3.sh and protmount4.sh scripts are used to clean up after the device is removed.

The next rule ENV{PHIL_MOUNT}=="1", ENV{UDISKS_PRESENTATION_HIDE}="1", ENV{UDISKS_AUTOMOUNT_HINT}="never", RUN+="/etc/udev/scripts/protmount2.sh" is run later just before the operating system attempts to mount the filesystem. If the PHIL_MOUNT variable has been set, we tell the operating system to hide the normal dialog that is displayed, never automount the filesystem (because it would not be mounted read-only), and add the protmount2.sh script to the list of things to be executed. If PHIL_MOUNT has not been set to 1, we set up the operating system to handle the device the standard way. The last rule causes protmount4.sh to run if the PHIL_UNMOUNT variable has been set.

We will now turn our attention to the scripts. Two of the scripts protmount.sh and protmount3.sh are used to create the other two, protmount2.sh and protmount4.sh, respectively. As previously mentioned, the reason for this is that all of the information needed to properly mount and unmount the filesystem is not available at the same time. The protmount.sh script follows.

```
#!/bin/bash

echo "#!/bin/bash" > "/etc/udev/scripts/protmount2-$2.sh"
echo "mkdir /media/$1" >> "/etc/udev/scripts/protmount2-$2.sh"
echo "chmod 777 /media/$1" >> "/etc/udev/scripts/protmount2-$2.sh"
echo "/bin/mount /dev/$1 -o ro,noatime /media/$1" >> "/etc/udev/scripts/protmount2-$2.sh"
chmod +x "/etc/udev/scripts/protmount2-$2.sh"
```

This script echoes a series of commands to the new script. The first line includes the familiar she-bang. The second line creates a directory, /media/{kernel device name} (i.e. /media/sdb2). The third line opens up the permissions on the directory. The fourth line mounts the filesystem as read-only with no access time updating in the newly created directory. The final line in the script makes the protmount2.sh script executable.

The protmount3.sh script is similar except that it creates a cleanup script. The cleanup script is protmount4.sh. The protmount3.sh script follows.

```
#!/bin/bash

echo "#!/bin/bash" > "/etc/udev/scripts/protmount4-$2.sh"
echo "/bin/umount /dev/$1" >> "/etc/udev/scripts/protmount4-$2.sh"
echo "rmdir /media/$1" >> "/etc/udev/scripts/protmount4-$2.sh"
chmod +x "/etc/udev/scripts/protmount4-$2.sh"
```

Software write blocking

An installation script has been created for installing this system. This script takes a vendor and product ID as required parameters. It also takes an optional second product ID. You might be curious as to why this is in the script. If you are using a USB 3.0 hub (recommended), it actually presents itself as two devices; one is a USB 2.0 hub and the other is a USB 3.0 hub. These two devices will have a common vendor ID but unique product IDs.

```bash
#!/bin/bash
#
# Install script for 4deck addon to "The Deck"
# This script will install udev rules which will turn a USB hub
# into a magic hub.  Every block device connected to the magic hub
# will be automatically mounted under the /media directory as read only.
# While this was designed to work with "The Deck" it will most likely
# work with most modern Linux distros.  This software is provided as is
# without warranty of any kind, express or implied.  Use at your own
# risk.  The author is not responsible for anything that happens as
# a result of using this software.
#
# Initial version created August 2012 by Dr. Phil Polstra, Sr.
# Version 1.1 created March 2015
#      new versions adds support for a second PID which is required
#      when using USB 3.0 hubs as they actually present as two hubs

unset VID
unset PID
unset PID2

function usage {
  echo "usage: sudo $(basename $0) --vid 05e3 --pid 0608 [--pid2 0610]"
  cat <<EOF

Bugs email: "DrPhil at polstra.org"

Required Parameters:
--vid <Vendor ID of USB hub>
--pid <Product ID of USB hub>

Optional Parameters:
--pid2 <Second Product ID of USB 3.0 hub>
EOF
exit
}

function createRule {
  cat > /etc/udev/rules.d/10-protectedmount.rules <<-__EOF__
```

CHAPTER 4 Creating Images

```
    ACTION=="add", SUBSYSTEM=="block", KERNEL=="sd?[1-9]",
ATTRS{idVendor}=="${VID}", ATTRS{idProduct}=="${PID}", ENV{PHIL_
MOUNT}="1", ENV{PHIL_DEV}="%k", RUN+="/etc/udev/scripts/protmount.sh %k %n"
    ACTION=="remove", SUBSYSTEM=="block", KERNEL=="sd?[1-9]",
ATTRS{idVendor}=="${VID}", ATTRS{idProduct}=="${PID}", ENV{PHIL_
UNMOUNT}="1", RUN+="/etc/udev/scripts/protmount3.sh %k %n"

    ENV{PHIL_MOUNT}=="1", ENV{UDISKS_PRESENTATION_HIDE}="1",
ENV{UDISKS_AUTOMOUNT_HINT}="never", RUN+="/etc/udev/scripts/
protmount2-%n.sh"
    ENV{PHIL_MOUNT}!="1", ENV{UDISKS_PRESENTATION_HIDE}="0",
ENV{UDISKS_AUTOMOUNT_HINT}="always"

    ENV{PHIL_UNMOUNT}=="1", RUN+="/etc/udev/scripts/protmount4-%n.sh"

__EOF__

if [ ! "$PID2" = "" ] ; then
   cat >> /etc/udev/rules.d/10-protectedmount.rules <<-__EOF__
    ACTION=="add", SUBSYSTEM=="block", KERNEL=="sd?[1-9]",
ATTRS{idVendor}=="${VID}", ATTRS{idProduct}=="${PID2}", ENV{PHIL_
MOUNT}="1", ENV{PHIL_DEV}="%k", RUN+="/etc/udev/scripts/protmount.sh %k %n"
    ACTION=="remove", SUBSYSTEM=="block", KERNEL=="sd?[1-9]",
ATTRS{idVendor}=="${VID}", ATTRS{idProduct}=="${PID2}", ENV{PHIL_
UNMOUNT}="1", RUN+="/etc/udev/scripts/protmount3.sh %k %n"

    ENV{PHIL_MOUNT}=="1", ENV{UDISKS_PRESENTATION_HIDE}="1",
ENV{UDISKS_AUTOMOUNT_HINT}="never", RUN+="/etc/udev/scripts/
protmount2-%n.sh"
    ENV{PHIL_MOUNT}!="1", ENV{UDISKS_PRESENTATION_HIDE}="0",
ENV{UDISKS_AUTOMOUNT_HINT}="always"

    ENV{PHIL_UNMOUNT}=="1", RUN+="/etc/udev/scripts/protmount4-%n.sh"

__EOF__
fi

}

function copyScripts {
   if [ ! -d "/etc/udev/scripts" ] ; then
     mkdir /etc/udev/scripts
   fi
   cp ./protmount*.sh /etc/udev/scripts/.
}
```

```
# parse commandline options
while [ ! -z "$1" ]; do
  case $1 in
    -h|--help)
      usage
      ;;
    --vid)
      VID="$2"
      ;;
    --pid)
      PID="$2"
      ;;
    --pid2)
      PID2="$2"
      ;;
  esac
  shift # consume command line arguments 1 at a time
done

# now actually do something
createRule
copyScripts
```

The script is straightforward. It begins with the usual she-bang, then a couple of environment variables are unset. We see a typical usage function, then a few functions are defined for creating and copying files. Finally, these functions are run at the end of the script.

Live Linux distributions

The preferred method of creating an image of a hard drive is to remove it from the subject system. However, this is not always practical. For example, some laptops (including the one I am currently using to write this book) must be disassembled to remove the hard drive as they lack access panels for this purpose. Booting a live Linux distribution in forensic mode can be the easiest option for these types of situations.

There are a couple of options available. Most any live Linux will work, but it never hurts to use a forensics-oriented distribution like SIFT. You can either install it to its own USB drive or use the same USB drive that you use for your known-good binaries. As I said earlier in this book, if you do this, you will need to format the drive with multiple partitions, and the first must be FAT in order for it to boot.

There are some that like to use a live Linux distribution on the forensic workstation. I recommend against doing this. My primary objection to doing this is that the performance is always relatively poor when running a live Linux distribution as everything is run in RAM. If you are just running the live Linux distribution for the write blocking, I recommend you just use my udev rules based blocking described earlier in this chapter.

```
phil@i7laptop:~/VirtualBox VMs/pfe1$ fdisk ./pentester-academy-subject1-flat.vmdk

Command (m for help): p

Disk ./pentester-academy-subject1-flat.vmdk: 19.3 GB, 19327352832 bytes
255 heads, 63 sectors/track, 2349 cylinders, total 37748736 sectors
Units = sectors of 1 * 512 = 512 bytes
Sector size (logical/physical): 512 bytes / 512 bytes
I/O size (minimum/optimal): 512 bytes / 512 bytes
Disk identifier: 0x0004565b

                              Device Boot      Start         End      Blocks   Id  System
./pentester-academy-subject1-flat.vmdk1   *      2048    33554431    16776192   83  Linux
./pentester-academy-subject1-flat.vmdk2       33556478    37746687     2095105    5  Extended
./pentester-academy-subject1-flat.vmdk5       33556480    37746687     2095104   82  Linux swap / Solaris

Command (m for help):
```

FIGURE 4.3.

Results of running fdisk against a virtual machine image.

CREATING AN IMAGE FROM A VIRTUAL MACHINE

While you are not as likely to need to create an image from a virtual machine professionally, you might wish to do so if you are practicing and/or following along with some of the examples from this book. If all you need is a raw image, you can use the tools that come with VirtualBox in order to create a raw image.

One downside of using the VirtualBox tools is that you will not get the hashes dcfldd provides. Another downside is that you will not get to practice using the tools you need for imaging a physical drive. The command to create the image from a Linux host is `vboxmanage clonehd <virtual disk image file> <output raw image file> --format RAW`.

If you are hosting your virtual machine on Linux, you can still use the standard tools such as dcfldd. The reason that this works is that Linux is smart enough to treat this virtual image file like a real device. This can be verified by running the command `fdisk <virtual disk image file>`. The results of running this command against a virtual machine hard drive are shown in Figure 4.3.

CREATING AN IMAGE FROM A PHYSICAL DRIVE

Creating an image from physical media is a pretty simple process if the media has been removed. You can use a commercial write blocker if you have one. Personally, I prefer to use

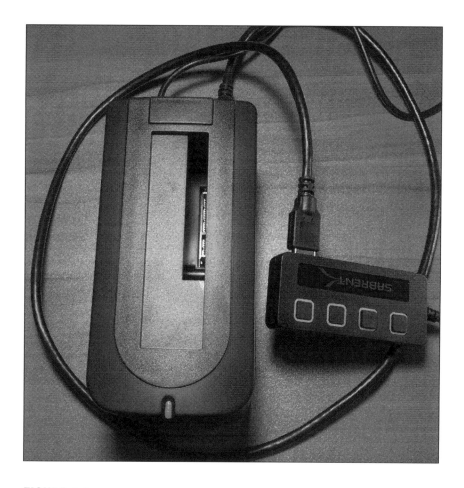

FIGURE 4.4.

An affordable disk imaging system.

the udev rules based system described earlier in this chapter. Regardless of what you use for write blocking, I strongly recommend you use USB 3.0 devices.

My personal setup consists of a Sabrent USB 3.0 hub model HB-UM43 which provides write blocking via my udev rules system and a Sabrent USB 3.0 SATA drive dock model DS-UBLK. This combination can be purchased from multiple vendors for under US$40. My setup is shown in Figure 4.4.

SUMMARY

In this chapter we discussed how to create disk images. This included imaging tools such as dcfldd, software and hardware write-blockers, techniques, and inexpensive hardware options. In the next chapter we will delve into the topic of actually mounting these images so we can begin our dead (filesystem) analysis.

CHAPTER 5

Mounting Images

INFORMATION IN THIS CHAPTER:

- Master Boot Record based Partitions
- Extended Partitions
- GUID Partition Table Partitions
- Mounting Partitions
- Using Python to Automate the Mounting Process

PARTITION BASICS

It was common for early personal computers to have a single filesystem on their hard drives. Of course it was also common for their capacities to be measured in single digit megabytes. Once drives started becoming larger, people began organizing them into partitions.

Initially up to four partitions were available. When this was no longer enough, an ineloquent solution, known as extended partitions, was developed in order to allow more than four partitions to be created on a drive. People put up with this kludge for decades before a better solution was developed. All of these partitioning systems will be discussed in detail in this chapter starting with the oldest.

Hard drives are described by the number of read/write heads, cylinders, and sectors. Each platter has circles of data which are called tracks. When you stack multiple circles on top of each other, they start to look like a cylinder and that is exactly what we call tracks that are on top of each other physically. Even when there is only one platter, there is a track on each side of the platter. The tracks are divided into chunks called sectors. Hard disk geometry is shown in Figure 5.1.

You will see entries for cylinders, heads, and sectors in some of the data structures discussed in this chapter. Most modern media use Logical Block Addressing (LBA), but these remnants of an earlier time are still found. Whether or not these values are used is another story.

MASTER BOOT RECORD PARTITIONS

The first method of having multiple partitions was to create something called a Master Boot Record (MBR) on the first sector of the hard disk. This was developed way back in the 1980s. A maximum of four partitions are permitted in the Master Boot Record. At most one of these four partitions can be marked as bootable. The overall format for an MBR is shown in Table 5.1.

Each of the partition entries in the MBR contains the information shown in Table 5.2.

Let's discuss these fields in the partition entries one at a time. The first entry is an active flag where 0x80 means active and anything else (usually 0x00) is interpreted as inactive. In the

88 CHAPTER 5 Mounting Images

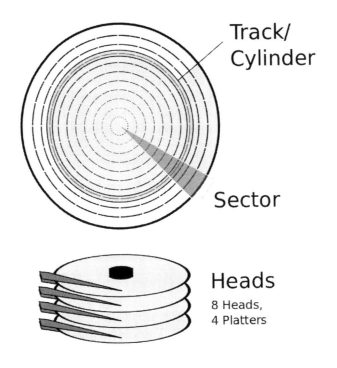

FIGURE 5.1.

Hard disk geometry.

Master *Boot* Record, active means it is bootable. For obvious reasons there can be at most one bootable partition. That does not mean that you cannot boot multiple operating systems, just that you must boot to some sort of selection menu program to do so.

The next entry is the starting head for the partition. This is followed by the starting sector and cylinder. Because the number of cylinders might exceed 255 and it is unlikely that so

Table 5.1. Master Boot Record Format

Offset	Length	Item
0 (0x00)	446 (0x1BE)	Boot code
446 (0x1BE)	16 (0x10)	First partition
462 (0x1CE)	16 (0x10)	Second partition
478 (0x1DE)	16 (0x10)	Third partition
494 (0x1EE)	16 (0x10)	Fourth partition
510 (0x1FE)	2 (0x2)	Signature 0x55 0xAA

Table 5.2. Partition Entry Format

Offset	Length	Item
0 (0x00)	1 (0x01)	Active flag (0x80 = bootable)
1 (0x01)	1 (0x01)	Start head
2 (0x02)	1 (0x01)	Start sector (bits 0-5); upper bits of cylinder (6-7)
3 (0x03)	1 (0x01)	Start cylinder lowest 8 bits
4 (0x04)	1 (0x01)	Partition type code (0x83 = Linux)
5 (0x05)	1 (0x01)	End head
6 (0x06)	1 (0x01)	End sector (bits 0-5); upper bits of cylinder (6-7)
7 (0x07)	1 (0x01)	End cylinder lowest 8 bits
8 (0x08)	4 (0x04)	Sectors preceding partition (little endian)
12 (0x0C)	4 (0x04)	Sectors in partition

many sectors would be in a single track, the upper two bits from the byte storing the sector are the upper two bits for the cylinder. This system allows up to 64 sectors per track and 1024 cylinders. Note that with only three bytes of storage, partitions must begin within the first eight gigabytes of the disk assuming standard 512 byte sectors.

The entry following the starting address is a partition type code. For Windows systems this type code is used to determine the filesystem type. Linux systems normally use 0x83 as the partition type and any supported filesystem may be installed on the partition. Partition type 0x82 is used for Linux swap partitions. Some of the more common types for Windows systems are 0x07, 0x0b, and 0x0c for NTFS, FAT32, and FAT32 with LBA, respectively. A complete list of type codes can be obtained by running the `fdisk` utility and entering the l (list type codes) command.

The cylinder/head/sector address of the end of the partition follows the partition type. The same format is used as that for the starting address of the partition. The number of sectors preceding the partition and total sectors occupy the last two positions in the partition entry. Note that these are both 32-bit values which allows devices up to two terabytes (2048 gigabytes) to be supported. Most modern devices use Logical Block Addressing (LBA), and the cylinder/head/sector addresses are essentially ignored.

EXTENDED PARTITIONS

When four partitions were no longer enough, a new system was invented. This system consists of creating one or more extended partitions in the four available slots in the MBR. The most common extended partition types are 0x05 and 0x85, with the former used by Windows

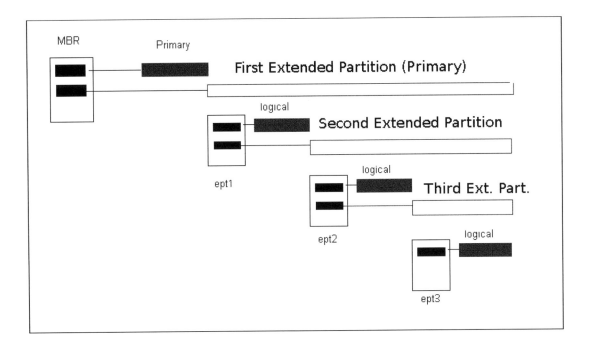

FIGURE 5.2.

Nested Extended Partitions.

and Linux and the later used only by Linux. Each extended partition becomes a logical drive with an MBR of its own. Normally only the first two slots in the extended partition MBR are used.

The addresses in partition entries in the extended partition's MBR are relative to the start of the extended partition (it is its own logical drive after all). Logical partitions in the extended partition can also be extended partitions. In other words, extended partitions can be nested which allows more than eight partitions to be created. In the case of nested extended partitions, the last partition is indicated by an empty entry in the second slot in that extended partition's MBR. Nested extended partitions are shown in Figure 5.2.

GUID PARTITIONS

The method of creating partitions is not the only thing showing its age. The Basic Input Output System (BIOS) boot process is also quite outdated. Under the BIOS boot process an ultramodern 64-bit computer is not started in 64-bit mode. It is not even started in 32-bit mode. The CPU is forced to regress all the way back to 16-bit compatibility mode. In fact, if you examine the boot code in the MBR, you will discover that it is 16-bit machine code.

The BIOS boot process has been replaced with the Unified Extensible Firmware Interface (UEFI) boot process. UEFI (pronounced ooh-fee) booting allows a computer to start in 64-bit mode directly. All 64-bit computers shipped today use UEFI and not BIOS for booting, although they support legacy booting from MBR-based drives. This legacy support is primarily intended to allow booting from removable media such as DVDs and USB drives.

A new method of specifying partitions was also created to go along with UEFI. This new method assigns a Globally Unique Identifier (GUID) to each partition. The GUIDs are stored in a GUID Partition Table (GPT). The GPT has space for 128 partitions. In addition to the primary GPT, there is a secondary GPT stored at the end of the disk (highest numbered logical blocks) to mitigate the chances of bad sectors in the GPT rendering a disk unreadable.

A drive using GUID partitioning begins with a protective MBR. This MBR has a single entry covering the entire disk with a partition type of 0xEE. Legacy systems that do not know how to process a GPT also do not know what to do with a partition of type 0xEE so they will ignore the entire drive. This is preferable to having the drive accidentally formated if it appears empty or unformatted.

As has been mentioned previously, modern systems use Logical Block Addressing (LBA). The protective MBR is stored in LBA0. The primary GPT begins with a header in LBA1 followed by GPT entries in LBA2 through LBA34. Each GPT entry requires 128 bytes. As a result, there are four entries per standard 512 byte block. While GPT entries are 128 bytes today, the specification allows for larger entries (with size specified in the GPT header) to be used in the future. Blocks are probably 512 bytes long, but this should not be assumed. The secondary GPT header is stored in the last LBA and the secondary GPT entries are stored in the preceding 32 sectors. The layout of a GPT-based drive is shown in Figure 5.3.

The GPT header format is shown in Table 5.3. When attempting to mount images of drives using GUID partitioning, this header should be checked in order to future proof any scripts should the default values shown in the table change.

The format for each partition entry is shown in Table 5.4. The format for the attributes field in these entries is shown in Table 5.5. Unlike MBR-based partitions with one byte to indicate partition type, GPT-based partitions have a 16-byte GUID for specifying the partition type. This type GUID is followed by a partition GUID (essentially a serial number) which is also 16 bytes long. You might see Linux documentation refer to this partition GUID as a Universally Unique Identifier (UUID).

The start and end LBA follow the UUID. Next comes the attributes and then the partition name which can be up to 36 Unicode characters long. Attribute fields are 64 bits long. As can be seen in Table 5.5, the lowest three bits are used to indicate a system partition, firmware partition, and support for legacy boot. System partitions are not to be changed and firmware partitions are to be completely ignored by operating systems. The meaning of the upper 16 bits of the attribute field depends on the partition type.

MOUNTING PARTITIONS FROM AN IMAGE FILE ON LINUX

Linux is the best choice for a forensic platform for several reasons regardless of operating system used by the subject system. One of the many reasons that this is true is the ease with which an image file can be mounted. Once filesystems in an image have been mounted, all of the standard system tools can be used as part of the investigation.

Linux tools, such as `fdisk`, can also be used directly on an image file. This fact might not

92 CHAPTER 5 Mounting Images

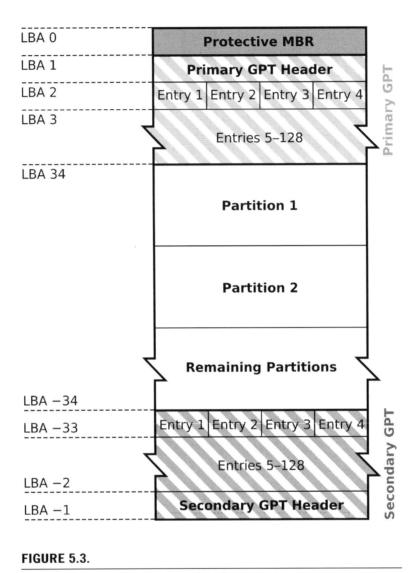

FIGURE 5.3.

Layout of a drive with GUID partitioning.

be immediately obvious, but we will show it to be true. The key to being able to use our normal tools is Linux's support for loop devices. In a nutshell, a loop device allows a file to be treated as a block device by Linux.

The command for running `fdisk` on an image is simply `fdisk <image file>`. After `fdisk` has been run, the partition table is easily printed by typing `p <enter>`. The key piece of information you need for each partition to be mounted is the starting sector (LBA). The results of running `fdisk` and printing the partition table for a Windows virtual machine image are shown in Figure 5.4. Note that in most cases we do not need to know the partition type as the Linux `mount` command is smart enough to figure this out on its own.

Table 5.3. GUID Partition Table Header Format.

Offset	Length	Contents
0 (0x00)	8 bytes	Signature ("EFI PART" or 0x5452415020494645)
8 (0x08)	4 bytes	Revision in Binary Coded Decimal format (version 1.0 = 0x00 0x00 0x01 0x00)
12 (0x0C)	4 bytes	Header size in bytes (92 bytes at present)
16 (0x10)	4 bytes	Header CRC32 checksum
20 (0x14)	4 bytes	Reserved; must be zero
24 (0x18)	8 bytes	Current LBA (where this header is located)
32 (0x20)	8 bytes	Backup LBA (where the other header is located)
40 (0x28)	8 bytes	First usable LBA for partitions
48 (0x30)	8 bytes	Last usable LBA for partitions
56 (0x38)	16 bytes	Disk GUID
72 (0x48)	8 bytes	Starting LBA of array of partition entries
80 (0x50)	4 bytes	Number of partition entries in array
84 (0x54)	4 bytes	Size of a single partition entry (usually 128)
88 (0x58)	4 bytes	CRC32 checksum of the partition array
92 (0x5C)	--	Reserved; must be zeros for the rest of the block

Table 5.4. GUID Partition Table Entry Format.

Offset	Length	Item
0 (0x00)	16 (0x10)	Partition type GUID
16 (0x10)	16 (0x10)	Unique partition GUID
32 (0x20)	8 (0x08)	First LBA
40 (0x28)	8 (0x08)	Last LBA
48 (0x30)	8 (0x08)	Attributes
56 (0x38)	72 (0x48)	Partition name (UTF-16 encoding)

Table 5.5. GUID Partition Table Entry Attributes Format.

Bit	Content	Description
0	System partition	Must preserve partition as is
1	EFI Firmware	Operating system should ignore this partition
2	Legacy BIOS boot	Equivalent to 0x80 in MBR
3-47	Reserved	Should be zeros
48-63	Type specific	Varies by partition type (60=RO, 62=Hidden, 63=No automount for Windows)

The single primary partition in the image from Figure 5.4 begins at sector 63. In order to mount this image we need to first create a mount point directory by typing `sudo mkdir <mount point>`, i.e., `sudo mkdir /media/win-c`. Next we need to mount the filesystem using the `mount` command. The general syntax for the command is `mount [options] <source device> <mount point directory>`.

The options required to mount an image in a forensically sound way are ro (read-only) and noatime (no access time updating). The second option might seem unnecessary, but it insures

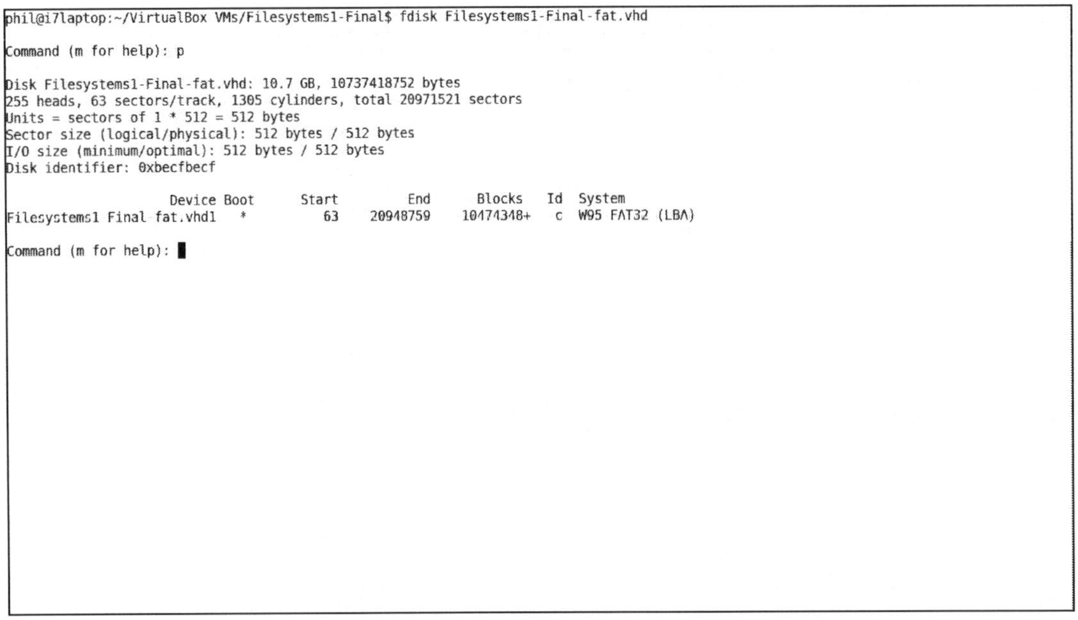

```
phil@i7laptop:~/VirtualBox VMs/Filesystems1-Final$ fdisk Filesystems1-Final-fat.vhd

Command (m for help): p

Disk Filesystems1-Final-fat.vhd: 10.7 GB, 10737418752 bytes
255 heads, 63 sectors/track, 1305 cylinders, total 20971521 sectors
Units = sectors of 1 * 512 = 512 bytes
Sector size (logical/physical): 512 bytes / 512 bytes
I/O size (minimum/optimal): 512 bytes / 512 bytes
Disk identifier: 0xbecfbecf

                 Device Boot      Start         End      Blocks   Id  System
Filesystems1 Final fat.vhd1   *          63    20948759    10474348+   c  W95 FAT32 (LBA)

Command (m for help):
```

FIGURE 5.4.

Running fdisk on an image file. Note that root privileges are not required to run fdisk on an image. The starting sector will be needed later for mounting.

that certain internal timestamps are not updated accidentally. Mounting an image file requires the loop and offset options.

Putting all of these together, the full mount command is `sudo mount -o ro,noatime, loop,offset=<offset to start of partition in bytes> <image file> <mount point directory>`. The offset can be calculated using a calculator or a little bash shell trick. Just like commands can be executed by enclosing them in $(), you can do math on the command line by enclosing mathematical operations in $(()).

Using our bash shell trick, the proper command is `sudo mount -o ro,noatime, loop,offset=$(( <starting sector> * 512 )) <image file> <mount point directory>`. The series of commands to mount the image from Figure 5.4 are shown in Figure 5.5.

What if your image contains extended partitions? The procedure is exactly the same. An image with an extended partition is shown in Figure 5.6. Note that `fdisk` translates the relative sector addresses inside the extended partition to absolute addresses in the overall image. Also note that the swap partition inside the extended primary partition starts two sectors into the partition. The first sector is used by the extended partition's mini-MBR and the second is just padding to make the swap partition start on an even-numbered sector.

The mini-MBR from the extended partition in the image from Figure 5.6 is shown in Figure 5.7. The partition type, 0x82, is highlighted in the figure. Recall that this is the type code for a Linux swap partition. Notice that the second MBR entry is blank indicating that there are no extended partitions nested inside this one. The `dd` command was used to generate this figure.

A quick way to view a single sector from an image is to issue the command `dd skip=<sector number> bs=<sector size> count=1 if=<image file>`

```
phil@i7laptop:~/VirtualBox VMs/Filesystems1-Final$ sudo mkdir /media/win-c
[sudo] password for phil:
phil@i7laptop:~/VirtualBox VMs/Filesystems1-Final$ sudo mount -o ro,noatime,loop,offset=$(( 63 * 512 )) Filesystems1-Final-fat.vhd /media/win-c
phil@i7laptop:~/VirtualBox VMs/Filesystems1-Final$ ls /media/win-c
AUTOEXEC.BAT       CONFIG.SYS              ftk-imager   NTDETECT.COM   Program Files            WINDOWS
boot.ini           Dev-Cpp                 IO.SYS       ntldr          Recycled
castle-wolfenstein Documents and Settings  MSDOS.SYS    PAGEFILE.SYS   System Volume Information
phil@i7laptop:~/VirtualBox VMs/Filesystems1-Final$
```

FIGURE 5.5.

Mounting a single primary partition from an image file.

96 CHAPTER 5 Mounting Images

```
phil@i7laptop:~/VirtualBox VMs/pfe1$ dd skip=33556478 bs=512 count=1 if=pentester-academy-subject1-flat.vmdk | xxd
1+0 records in
1+0 records out
512 bytes (512 B) copied, 6.1522e-05 s, 8.3 MB/s
0000000: 0000 0000 0000 0000 0000 0000 0000 0000  ................
0000010: 0000 0000 0000 0000 0000 0000 0000 0000  ................
0000020: 0000 0000 0000 0000 0000 0000 0000 0000  ................
0000030: 0000 0000 0000 0000 0000 0000 0000 0000  ................
0000040: 0000 0000 0000 0000 0000 0000 0000 0000  ................
0000050: 0000 0000 0000 0000 0000 0000 0000 0000  ................
0000060: 0000 0000 0000 0000 0000 0000 0000 0000  ................
0000070: 0000 0000 0000 0000 0000 0000 0000 0000  ................
0000080: 0000 0000 0000 0000 0000 0000 0000 0000  ................
0000090: 0000 0000 0000 0000 0000 0000 0000 0000  ................
00000a0: 0000 0000 0000 0000 0000 0000 0000 0000  ................
00000b0: 0000 0000 0000 0000 0000 0000 0000 0000  ................
00000c0: 0000 0000 0000 0000 0000 0000 0000 0000  ................
00000d0: 0000 0000 0000 0000 0000 0000 0000 0000  ................
00000e0: 0000 0000 0000 0000 0000 0000 0000 0000  ................
00000f0: 0000 0000 0000 0000 0000 0000 0000 0000  ................
0000100: 0000 0000 0000 0000 0000 0000 0000 0000  ................
0000110: 0000 0000 0000 0000 0000 0000 0000 0000  ................
0000120: 0000 0000 0000 0000 0000 0000 0000 0000  ................
0000130: 0000 0000 0000 0000 0000 0000 0000 0000  ................
0000140: 0000 0000 0000 0000 0000 0000 0000 0000  ................
0000150: 0000 0000 0000 0000 0000 0000 0000 0000  ................
0000160: 0000 0000 0000 0000 0000 0000 0000 0000  ................
0000170: 0000 0000 0000 0000 0000 0000 0000 0000  ................
0000180: 0000 0000 0000 0000 0000 0000 0000 0000  ................
0000190: 0000 0000 0000 0000 0000 0000 0000 0000  ................
00001a0: 0000 0000 0000 0000 0000 0000 0000 0000  ................
00001b0: 0000 0000 0000 0000 0000 0000 0000 00fe  ................
00001c0: ffff 82fe ffff 0200 0000 00f0 3f00 0000  ............?...
00001d0: 0000 0000 0000 0000 0000 0000 0000 0000  ................
00001e0: 0000 0000 0000 0000 0000 0000 0000 0000  ................
00001f0: 0000 0000 0000 0000 0000 0000 0000 55aa  ..............U.
phil@i7laptop:~/VirtualBox VMs/pfe1$
```

FIGURE 5.7.

A mini-MBR from an extended partition. The highlighted byte is for the partition, 0x82, which indicates this is a swap partition. Note that the second entry is blank indicating there are no nested extended partitions under this one.

| xxd. The command used to generate Figure 5.7 was dd skip=33556478 bs=512 count=1 if=pentester-academy-subject1-flat.vmdk | xxd. It is important to realize that dd uses blocks (with a default block size of 512) whereas mount uses bytes. This is why we do not have to do any math to use dd.

The commands required and also the results of mounting the primary partition from Figure 5.6 are shown in Figure 5.8. Notice that my Ubuntu system automatically popped up the file browser window shown. This is an example of behavior that can be customized using udev rules as described earlier in this book.

What if your subject sytem is using GUID Partition Tables (GPT)? The results of running fdisk against such a system are shown in Figure 5.9. The only partition displayed covers the entire disk and has type 0xEE. This is the protective MBR discussed earlier in this chapter. Note that fdisk displays a warning that includes the correct utility to run for GPT drives.

The results of running parted on the GPT drive from Figure 5.9 are shown in Figure 5.10. In the figure we see a system partition which is marked as bootable, several NTFS partitions, an ext4 and Linux swap partitions. This is a computer that came preloaded with Windows 8.1 with secure boot (which really means make it difficult to boot anything other than Windows) which has had Linux installed after the fact.

You may have noticed that the results displayed in Figure 5.10 specify the start and stop of partitions in kilobytes, megabytes, and gigabytes. In order to mount a partition we need to

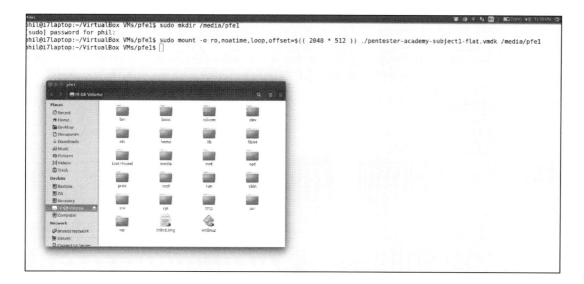

FIGURE 5.8.

Mounting a Linux partition in an image from the command line.

```
phil@i7laptop:~$ sudo fdisk /dev/sda

WARNING: GPT (GUID Partition Table) detected on '/dev/sda'! The util fdisk doesn't support GPT. Use GNU Parted.

The device presents a logical sector size that is smaller than
the physical sector size. Aligning to a physical sector (or optimal
I/O) size boundary is recommended, or performance may be impacted.

Command (m for help): p

Disk /dev/sda: 1000.2 GB, 1000204886016 bytes
255 heads, 63 sectors/track, 121601 cylinders, total 1953525168 sectors
Units = sectors of 1 * 512 = 512 bytes
Sector size (logical/physical): 512 bytes / 4096 bytes
I/O size (minimum/optimal): 4096 bytes / 4096 bytes
Disk identifier: 0x13a203d8

   Device Boot      Start         End      Blocks   Id  System
/dev/sda1               1  1953525167   976762583+  ee  GPT
Partition 1 does not start on physical sector boundary.

Command (m for help):
```

FIGURE 5.9.

Running fdisk on a drive that uses GUID Partition Tables.

```
phil@i7laptop:~$ sudo parted /dev/sda
GNU Parted 2.3
Using /dev/sda
Welcome to GNU Parted! Type 'help' to view a list of commands.
(parted) print
Model: ATA ST1000LM024 HN-M (scsi)
Disk /dev/sda: 1000GB
Sector size (logical/physical): 512B/4096B
Partition Table: gpt

Number  Start   End     Size    File system     Name                         Flags
 1      1049kB  106MB   105MB   fat32           EFI system partition         boot
 2      106MB   1050MB  944MB   ntfs            Basic data partition         hidden, diag
 3      1050MB  1184MB  134MB                   Microsoft reserved partition msftres
 4      1184MB  401GB   400GB   ntfs            Basic data partition         msftdata
 5      401GB   963GB   561GB   ext4
 7      963GB   979GB   16.0GB  linux-swap(v1)
 6      979GB   1000GB  21.5GB  ntfs            Basic data partition         hidden, diag

(parted)
```

FIGURE 5.10.

Result of running parted on the GPT drive from Figure 5.9.

know the exact start of each partition. The unit command in `parted` allows us to specify how these values are displayed. Two popular choices are s and B which stand for sectors and bytes, respectively. The results of executing the `parted` print command using both sectors and bytes are shown in Figure 5.11.

Once the starting offset is known, mounting a partition from a GPT image is exactly the same as the preceding two cases (primary or extended partitions on MBR-based drives). The `parted` utility can be used on MBR-based drives as well, but the default output is not as easy to use. Next we will discuss using Python to make this mounting process simple regardless of what sort of partitions we are attempting to mount.

USING PYTHON TO AUTOMATE THE MOUNTING PROCESS

Automation is a good thing. It saves time and also prevents mistakes caused by fat-fingering values. Up to this point in the book we have used shell scripting and Windows command scripting for automation. In order to mount our partitions we will utilize the Python scripting language. As this is not a book on Python, I will primarily only be describing how my scripts work. For readers that want a more in-depth coverage of Python, I highly recommend the Python course at PentesterAcademy.com (http://www.pentesteracademy.com/course?id=1).

You might ask why we are switching to Python. This is a valid question. There are a couple of reasons to use Python for this task. First, we are no longer just running programs and pushing

```
(parted) unit s p
Model: ATA ST1000LM024 HN-M (scsi)
Disk /dev/sda: 1953525168s
Sector size (logical/physical): 512B/4096B
Partition Table: gpt

Number  Start        End          Size         File system  Name                         Flags
 1      2048s        206847s      204800s      fat32        EFI system partition         boot
 2      206848s      2050047s     1843200s     ntfs         Basic data partition         hidden, diag
 3      2050048s     2312191s     262144s                   Microsoft reserved partition msftres
 4      2312192s     783713399s   781406208s   ntfs         Basic data partition         msftdata
 5      783718400s   1880309759s  1096591360s  ext4
 7      1880309760s  1911560191s  31250432s    linux-swap(v1)
 6      1911560192s  1953523711s  41963520s    ntfs         Basic data partition         hidden, diag

(parted) unit B p
Model: ATA ST1000LM024 HN-M (scsi)
Disk /dev/sda: 1000204886016B
Sector size (logical/physical): 512B/4096B
Partition Table: gpt

Number  Start          End            Size          File system  Name                         Flags
 1      1048576B       105906175B     104857600B    fat32        EFI system partition         boot
 2      105906176B     1049624575B    943718400B    ntfs         Basic data partition         hidden, diag
 3      1049624576B    1183842303B    134217728B                 Microsoft reserved partition msftres
 4      1183842304B    401263820799B  400079978496B ntfs         Basic data partition         msftdata
 5      401263820800B  962718597119B  561454776320B ext4
 7      962718597120B  978718818303B  16000221184B  linux-swap(v1)
 6      978718818304B  1000204140543B 21485322240B  ntfs         Basic data partition         hidden, diag

(parted)
```

FIGURE 5.11.

Changing the default units in parted to shown partition boundaries in sectors and bytes.

bytes around. Rather, we are reading in files, interpreting them, performing calculations, and then running programs. Second, we are looking to build a library of code to use in our investigations. Having Python code that interprets MBR and GPT data is likely to be useful further down the road.

WHAT IS IT GOOD FOR?

Scripting or Programming Language

You will see me refer to Python as a scripting language in this book. Some might say that it is a programming language. Which is correct? They are both correct. In my mind a scripting language is an interpreted language that allows you to quickly do work. Python certainly meets this criterium.

To me a programming language is something that is used to create large programs and software systems. There are some that certainly have done this with Python. However, I would argue that Python is not the best choice when performance is an issue and the same program will be run many times without any code modifications. I'm sure that anyone who has ever run a recent version of Metasploit would agree that running large programs written in interpreted languages can be painful.

> ## WHAT VERSION?
>
> ### Python 2 or Python 3
> Python is widely used by professionals in the information security and forensics industry. There are a number of reasons for this. First, Python is a very simple language that can be used to teach children about programming. In fact, my daughter learned to program in Python when she was only nine years old. Second, Python is a very full and rich language that allows data to be processed easily. Third, because it is so popular, there are a large number of Python modules available for almost anything an information security or forensic practitioner is likely to want.
>
> Another reason that hackers seem to like Python is that it allows the creation of short scripts. There are two versions of Python available today, Python 2.x and Python 3.x. Python 3 is intended to be a cleaned-up and more consistent version of Python. Because of this, Python 3 is intentionally incompatible with Python 2. Because the install base of Python 2 is large (it is normally pre-installed on Linux systems) and it allows the user to be a little less careful, it seems to be preferred by many hackers.
>
> Readers of **Linux Forensics** will note that book was written using Python 2. I have made the decision to move to Python 3 in this book for a few reasons. First, Python 2 does not get all of the new features and updates. Only some of the new features are backported to Python 2. Second, Python 3 has a number of performance enhancements that are not available or not implemented by default in Python 2. Third, Python 3 is consistent, whereas Python 2 is not. Some of the implications of this are that the same code does the same thing regardless of context and that all functions (most notably print) are treated the same. Fourth, Unicode support is slightly better in Python 3. Fifth, support for Python 2 will eventually end completely. For these reasons I have decided that it is worth a little extra effort to make the move to Python 3.

MBR-based primary partitions

We will start with the simplest case, primary partitions from MBR-based drives. I have broken up the mounting code into three separate scripts for simplicity. Feel free to combine them if that is what you prefer. It is open source after all. The following script will mount primary partitions from an MBR-based image file.

```
#!/usr/bin/python3
# This is a simple Python script that will
# attempt to mount partitions from an image file.
# Images are mounted read-only.
#
# Developed for PentesterAcademy by Dr. Phil Polstra
```

```
import sys
import os.path
import subprocess
import struct

class Mbr():
    ''' Master Boot Record class
    Accepts a sector (512 bytes) and creates an MBR object.
    The MBR object can be queried for its attributes.
    The data is stored in a tuple using struct.unpack.'''
    def __init__(self, sector):
        '''This constructor expects a 512-byte MBR sector.
        It will populate the ._mbrTuple.'''
        fmt=('<446s' + # Boot code
            # partition 1
            'B' + # Active flag 0x80 is active (bootable)
            'B' + # Start head
            'B' + # Start sector only bits 0-5 bits 6-7 for cylinder
            'B' + # Start cylinder (upper 2 bits in previous byte)
            'B' + # partition type code
            'B' + # End head
            'B' + # End sector
            'B' + # End cylinder
            'I' + # Sectors preceeding partition
            'I' + # Sectors in partition
            # partition 2
            'B' + # Active flag 0x80 is active (bootable)
            'B' + # Start head
            'B' + # Start sector only bits 0-5 bits 6-7 for cylinder
            'B' + # Start cylinder (upper 2 bits in previous byte)
            'B' + # partition type code
            'B' + # End head
            'B' + # End sector
            'B' + # End cylinder
            'I' + # Sectors preceeding partition
            'I' + # Sectors in partition
            # partition 3
            'B' + # Active flag 0x80 is active (bootable)
            'B' + # Start head
            'B' + # Start sector only bits 0-5 bits 6-7 for cylinder
            'B' + # Start cylinder (upper 2 bits in previous byte)
            'B' + # partition type code
            'B' + # End head
            'B' + # End sector
```

CHAPTER 5 Mounting Images

```
            'B' + # End cylinder
            'I' + # Sectors preceeding partition
            'I' + # Sectors in partition
            # partition 4
            'B' + # Active flag 0x80 is active (bootable)
            'B' + # Start head
            'B' + # Start sector only bits 0-5 bits 6-7 for cylinder
            'B' + # Start cylinder (upper 2 bits in previous byte)
            'B' + # partition type code
            'B' + # End head
            'B' + # End sector
            'B' + # End cylinder
            'I' + # Sectors preceeding partition
            'I' + # Sectors in partition
            '2s') # Signature should be 0x55 0xAA
        self._mbrTuple=struct.unpack(fmt, sector)

    def isActive(self, partno):
        return self._mbrTuple[1+10*(partno-1)]==0x80

    def startHead(self, partno):
        return self._mbrTuple[2+10*(partno-1)]

    def startSector(self, partno):
        # return lower 6 bits of sector
        return self._mbrTuple[3+10*(partno-1)] % 64

    def startCylinder(self, partno):
        # add in the upper 2 bits if needed
        return (self._mbrTuple[4+10*(partno-1)] +
            256 * self._mbrTuple[3+10*(partno-1)]//64)

    def partitionType(self, partno):
        return self._mbrTuple[5+10*(partno-1)]

    def isEmpty(self, partno):
        return self.partitionType(partno)==0

    def endHead(self, partno):
        return self._mbrTuple[6+10*(partno-1)]

    def endSector(self, partno):
        # return lower 6 bits of sector
        return self._mbrTuple[7+10*(partno-1)] % 64
```

```python
    def endCylinder(self, partno):
        # add in the upper 2 bits if needed
        return (self._mbrTuple[8+10*(partno-1)] +
            256 * self._mbrTuple[7+10*(partno-1)]//64)

    def reservedSectors(self, partno):
        '''Sectors preceeding this partition'''
        return self._mbrTuple[9+10*(partno-1)]

    def totalSectors(self, partno):
        return self._mbrTuple[10+10*(partno-1)]

    def validSignature(self):
        return self._mbrTuple[41]==b'\x55\xAA'

    def prettyPrint(self):
        print('MBR signature valid:', self.validSignature())
        for i in range(1, 5):
            print('Partition', i, 'information:')
            if self.isEmpty(i):
                print('\tEntry is empty.')
            else:
                print('\tBootable:', self.isActive(i))
                print('\tStart head:', self.startHead(i))
                print('\tStart sector:', self.startSector(i))
                print('\tStart cylinder:', self.startCylinder(i))
                print('\tPartition type:', self.partitionType(i))
                print('\tEnd head:', self.endHead(i))
                print('\tEnd sector:', self.endSector(i))
                print('\tEnd cylinder:', self.endCylinder(i))
                print('\tReserved sectors:', self.reservedSectors(i))
                print('\tTotal sectors:', self.totalSectors(i))


def usage():
    print("usage " + sys.argv[0] + " <image file>\nAttempts to mount partitions from an image file")
    exit(1)

def main():
    if len(sys.argv) < 2:
        usage()

    notsupParts = [0x05, 0x0f, 0x85, 0x91, 0x9b, 0xc5, 0xe4, 0xee]
    swapParts = [0x42, 0x82, 0xb8, 0xc3, 0xfc]
```

```python
   # read first sector
   if not os.path.isfile(sys.argv[1]):
      print("File " + sys.argv[1] + " cannot be opened for reading")
      exit(1)

   with open(sys.argv[1], 'rb') as f:
      sector = f.read(512)

   mbr=Mbr(sector) # create MBR object

   if mbr.validSignature():
      print("Looks like a MBR or VBR")
      mbr.prettyPrint()

      for i in range(1,5):
         if not mbr.isEmpty(i):
            if mbr.partitionType(i) in notsupParts:
               print("Sorry GPT and extended partitions are "
                  "not supported by this script!")
            else:
               if mbr.partitionType(i) in swapParts:
                  print("Skipping swap partition")
               else:
                  mountpath = '/media/part%s' % str(i)
                  if not os.path.isdir(mountpath):
                     subprocess.call(['mkdir', mountpath])
                  mountopts = ('loop,ro,noatime,offset=%s'
                     % str(mbr.reservedSectors(i) * 512))
                  subprocess.call(['mount', '-o', mountopts,
                     sys.argv[1], mountpath])
   else:
      print("Doesn't appear to contain valid MBR")

if __name__ == "__main__":
   main()
```

Let's break down the preceding script. It begins with the usual she-bang; however, this time we are running the Python 3 interpreter instead of the bash shell. Just as with shell scripts, all of the lines beginning with "#" are comments. We then import Python libraries sys, os.path, subprocess, and struct which are needed to get command line arguments, check for the existence of files, launch other processes or commands, and interpret values in the MBR, respectively.

Next we define a class Mbr which is used to decode the four partition entries in the MBR. The class definition includes a Python multi-line comment known as a docstring. Three double quotes on a line start or stop the docstring. Like many object-oriented languages, Python uses classes to implement objects. However, Python is different from other languages in that it uses indentation to group lines of code together and does not use a line termination character such as the semicolon used by numerous languages.

The line `class Mbr():` tells the Python interpreter that a class definition for the Mbr class follows on indented lines. The empty parentheses indicate that there is no base class. In other words, the Mbr is not a more specific (or specialized) version of some other object. Base classes can be useful as they allow you to more easily and eloquently share common code, but they are not used extensively by people who use Python to write quick and dirty scripts to get things done.

The line `def __init__(self, sector):` inside the Mbr class definition begins a function definition. Python allows classes to define functions (sometimes called methods) and values (also called variables, parameters, or data members) that are associated with the class. Every class implicitly defines a value called self that is used to refer to an object of the class type. With a few exceptions (not described in this book) every class function must have self as the first (possibly only) argument it accepts. This argument is implicitly passed by Python. We will talk more about this later as I explain this script.

Every class should define an __init__ function (that is a double underscore preceding and following init). This special function is called a constructor. It is used when an object of a certain type is created. The __init__ function in the Mbr class is used as follows:

```
mbr = Mbr(sector)
```

This creates a new object called mbr of the Mbr type. If we want to print its contents we can call its prettyPrint function like so:

```
mbr.prettyPrint()
```

Back to the constructor definition. We first build a somewhat lengthy format string called fmt. The fmt variable is an example of a local variable. Local variables are created inside functions (the constructor in this case) and go away when the containing function exits. As previously mentioned, Python uses indentation to group code and there is no line termination character. One way to split long bits of code across multiple lines is to use unclosed parentheses as we have done here. An appropriate format string for each entry in the MBR is concatenated together to create a format string describing the entire MBR. The hash (#) sign is used to start a comment that continues to the end of the line. All of these comments make the code easier to understand and reduce the chances of fat-fingering the format string.

The format string in the constructor is used by the unpack function found in the struct module to interpret and then store the MBR on the line that reads

```
self._mbrTuple=struct.unpack(fmt, sector)
```

The Python struct module documentation can be found at https://docs.python.org/3.5/library/struct.html. As a general rule, python.org should be the first place to look for answers to questions about Python or any standard modules. The purpose of the struct module is to perform conversions to and from Python values and C structures.

Full details on how to create a format string can be found at the webpage referenced in the preceding paragraph. Some of the most commonly used items are B, H, I, Q, and s which represent unsigned 1-byte, 2-byte, 4-byte, 8-byte integers, and strings, respectively. Signed integers use lowercase letters that correspond with the unsigned counterparts of the same size. The less-than sign (<) at the beginning of the format string indicates that little endian values are used with no alignment. When storing multi-byte values the greater valued (most significant) bytes or smaller valued (least significant) bytes can be listed first which is known as big endian and little endian format, respectively. By default struct will align values on standard memory boundaries (usually 4 or 8 bytes) which is not what we want when reading or writing from binary files.

Given the proper format string struct.unpack can take the 512-byte MBR sector and convert it to a set of values. These values must be stored somewhere. In this case that somewhere is in a data member called _mbrTuple. Note that this is referred to as `self._mbrTuple` in the code. The self. prefix is required to avoid creating a local variable that would go away once the constructor exits. Preceding a data member name with a single underscore is a common practice in Python and is a polite request for others not to attempt to access this data member directly.

What kind of thing is _mbrTuple? As the name suggests it is a tuple. Python supports lists which are similar to arrays in other languages. An array is a collection of items that are accessed by an integer index. The first item in an array is item 0. If an array is named myArray, the first, second, and third items would be referenced as myArray[0], myArray[1], and myArray[2], respectively. The biggest difference between an array and a list is that arrays must contain items of the same type, but a Python list can contain items of any type (including other lists and complex objects). A Python tuple is an immutable (unchangeable) list. A list is easily created by enclosing values in square brackets ([]) such as `myList = [1, 2, 3.14, 'Bob']`. A tuple is created in the same way, but with parentheses, i.e., `myTuple = (1, 2, 3.14, 'Bob')`.

Following the Mbr constructor we see a series of accessors that simply return an item from the _mbrTuple data member. With the exception of the signature and boot code, all of these values pertain to one of the four partitions. Partition 1 entries begin with the active flag in item 1 and there are ten entries per partition which leads to the following formula for calculating the tuple index for an active flag:

$$index = 1 + 10 * (partionNumber - 1)$$

A similar formula is used for the other nine entries for each partition. Note that these formulas could be simplified if desired. I have left them in this format to make it more clear where they come from.

There are a couple of operators in these accessors that may be unfamiliar to some readers. The modulus (%) operator is used in startSector and endSector. The modulus operator gives the remainder when integer division is performed. Integer division is what you first learned in grammar school before you learned about decimals and fractions. For example 7 % 4 is 3 because 4 goes into 7 once with a remainder of 3. In startSector and endSector the net of taking the sector number modulus 64 (2 to the 6th power) is to strip off the upper two bits which are the upper two bits of the cylinder number. The integer division (//) operator is used in startCylinder and endCylinder in order to divide the sector number by 64 to retrieve the upper two bits of the cylinder number. Speaking of integer division, this is one place where Python 2 is not consistent. Some of the time in Python 2 when you use the standard division (/) operator

> **OBJECT OR LIST?**
>
> ### Ranges in Python 2 and Python 3
>
> Ranges are a place where things have been optimized in Python 3 by default. In Python 2 using `range(5000000)` in your code will result in a list containing the numbers 0 through 4999999. If all you are using the range for is to create a looping variable this is an incredible waste of computing resources. You need to create a list that stores five million items, each of which will only be used one time. Things like this can bring your computer to a crawl.
>
> In order to prevent this problem in Python 2 an xrange class was created. If a loop was to be iterated a large number of times, the for statement might be altered slightly to read something like `for i in xrange(5000000)`. This class would store starting value, ending value, step, and current location. Each time the next item for the "list" is fetched the proper value would be returned making this transparent to any code relying on this range.
>
> In Python 3 an object is created every time you use range. This is easily verified by running a Python 2 shell and printing a range and then doing the same in a Python 3 shell. In Python 2 `print(range(4))` will print [0, 1, 2, 3] and in Python 3 it will print range(0,4).

you get integer division and sometimes you get floating point division. It depends on what you are dividing. In Python 3 / performs floating point division all of the time and // yields integer division every time.

The prettyPrint function in Mbr is a little easier to understand than the constructor and accessors. First the function checks to see if the MBR signature is valid. Then it loops through the four partition records. The Python `for` statement is used for this loop. A range is used to set the value of i for each iteration of this loop. In Python ranges are half open intervals. In other words, `range(1,5)` represents the integers 1 through 5 exclusive (1 through, but not including 5) or 1, 2, 3, and 4. If the starting value is omitted, zero is used. For example, `range(4)` would yield 0, 1, 2, 3.

For each partition this function first checks to see if the partition entry is empty. If so, it just prints "Entry is empty." If it is not empty whether it is bootable, its type, starting sector, and total sectors are displayed. The print function used here shows another difference between Python 2 and Python 3. In Python 2 `print` is a statement and parentheses are not required to surround any parameters passed to it. In Python 2 `print "Hello"` is valid. In Python 3 print is just a function so parentheses must be used. Fortunately, surrounding arguments with parentheses works equally well in both versions of Python. For example, `print("Hello")` works for both versions.

The script creates a usage function similar to what we have done with our shell scripts in the past. Note that this function is not indented and, therefore, not part of the Mbr class. The function does make use of the sys library that was imported in order to retrieve the name of this script using `sys.argv[0]` which is equivalent to $0 in our shell scripts.

We then define a main function. As with our shell scripts, we first check that an appropriate number of command line arguments are passed in, and if not, display a usage message and exit. Note that the test here is for less than 2 command line arguments. There will always be one command line argument, the name of the script being run. In other words, if len(sys.argv) < 2: will only be true if you passed in no arguments.

We then created a list for partitions which are not supported by this script and also swap partitions which are not normally mounted. Note that we have not restricted this script to only mounting Windows partitions. There is little reason to do so and there is also the chance that a subject system contains both Windows and Linux partitions. More information on examining any Linux partitions can be found in Linux Forensics.

Once we have verified that you passed in at least one argument, we check to see if the file really exists and is readable, and if not, display an error and exit, in the following lines of code:

```
if not os.path.isfile(sys.argv[1]):
   print("File " + sys.argv[1] + " cannot be opened for reading")
   exit(1)
```

The next two lines might seem a bit strange if you are not a Python programmer (yet). This construct is the preferred way of opening and reading files in Python as it is succinct and insures that your files will be closed cleanly. Even some readers who use Python might not be familiar with this method as it has been available for less than a decade and I have seen some recently published Python books in forensics and information security still teaching people the old, non-preferred way of handling files. The two lines in question follow.

```
with open(sys.argv[1], 'rb') as f:
   sector = f.read(512)
```

To fully understand why this is a beautiful thing, you need to first understand how Python handles errors. Like many other languages Python uses exceptions for error handling. At a high level exceptions work as follows. Any risky code that might generate an error (which is called throwing an exception) is enclosed in a try block. This try block is followed by one or more exception catching blocks that will process different errors (exception types). There is also an optional block that is called every time the program exits the try block whether or not there was an error called a finally block. The two lines above are equivalent to the following:

```
try:
  f = open(sys.argv[1], 'rb')
  sector = f.read(512)
except Exception as e:
  print 'An exception occurred:', e
finally:
  f.close()
```

The file passed into the script is opened as a read-only binary file because the 'rb' argument passed to open specifies the file mode. When the file is opened, a new file object named f is created. The read function of f is then called and the first 512 bytes (containing the MBR) are read. Regardless of any errors the file is closed cleanly before execution of the script proceeds.

Because the file is opened in binary mode, read returns a bunch of bytes as opposed to a string. This is another place where Python 2 and Python 3 differ. In Python 3 a "normal" string in other languages such as C and C++ that consists of a bunch of bytes containing ASCII (American Symbolic Code for Information Interchange) values, one byte per character, is stored as a bytes object. A Python 3 string (str) is stored in Unicode and the number of bytes per character can vary depending on the encoding (codec) in use. Because the word bytes is overused in computer science you may often hear people refer to Python 3 bytes as binary strings or byte strings. Creating a binary string is as simple as prefixing any quotes around text with a lowercase b, i.e., myBinaryString=b'Hello World!'.

Once the MBR has been read, we do a sanity check. If the file is not corrupted or the wrong kind of file, the last two bytes should be 0x55 0xAA. This is the standard signature for an MBR. If the MBR appears valid, we print out the information using the Mbr prettyPrint method. We then use a for loop to iterate over the four partitions. If they are not swap partitions or in the unsupported list, we will attempt to mount them.

The first thing we do when attempting to mount a partition is determine a mount path which will be /media/partN, where N is the partition number. The line mountpath = '/media/part%s' % str(i) will create a string with this path which is stored in the mountpath variable. When applied to strings, the % operator causes items in a list or tuple to be substituted into a string. If there is only one item to be substituted, it can follow the % (there is no need to create a list or tuple with one item). For example, "Hello there %s, I see you are %d years old today." % ('Bob', 42) would create a string with the value "Hello there Bob, I see you are 42 years old today."

The line if not os.path.isdir(mountpath): checks for the existence of this mountpath directory. If it does not exist, it is created on the next line. The next line uses subprocess.call() to call an external program or command. This function expects a list containing the program to be run and any arguments.

On the next line the string substitution construct is used once again to create a string with options for the mount command complete with the appropriate offset. Note that str(mbr.reservedSectors(i) * 512) is used to first compute this offset and then convert it from a numeric value to a string as required by the % operator. Finally, we use subprocess.call() to run the mount command.

Only one thing remains in the script that requires explanation, and that is the last two lines. The test if __name__ == "__main__": is a common trick used in Python scripting. If the script is executed, the variable __name__ is set to "__main__". If, however, the script is merely imported, this variable is not set. This allows the creation of Python scripts that can both be run and imported into other scripts thereby allowing code to be reused.

If you are new to Python, you might want to take a break at this point after walking through our first script. You might want to reread this section if you are still a bit uncertain about how this script works. Rest assured that things will be a bit easier as we press on and develop new scripts.

The results of running our script against an image file from a Windows system are shown in Figure 5.12. Figure 5.13 depicts what happens when running the script against an image from an Ubuntu 14.04 system.

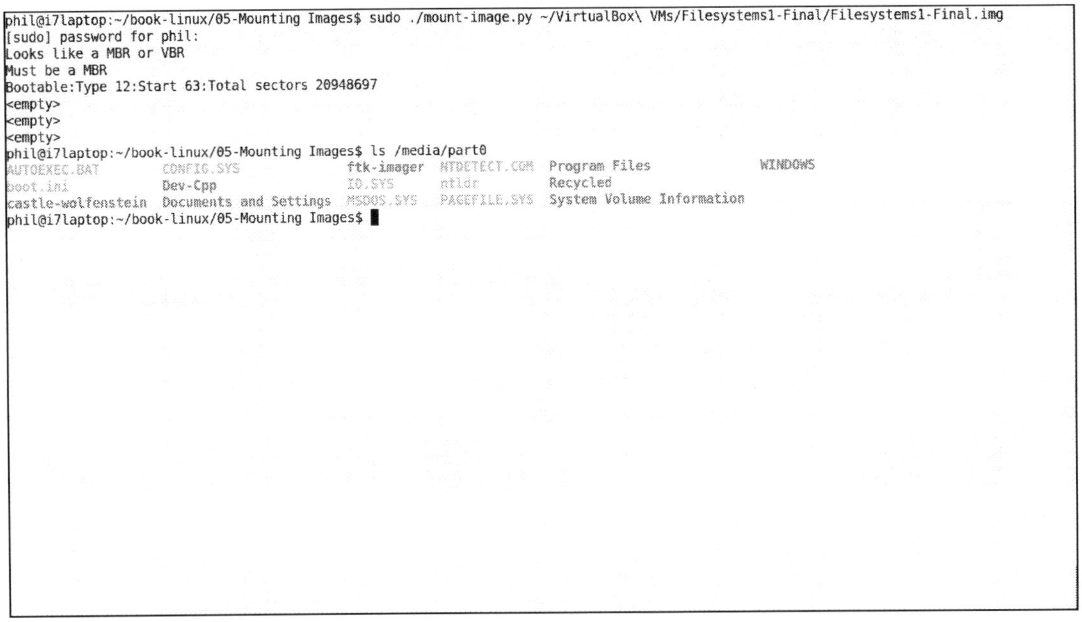

CHAPTER 5 Mounting Images

FIGURE 5.12.

Running the Python mounting script against an image file from a Windows system.

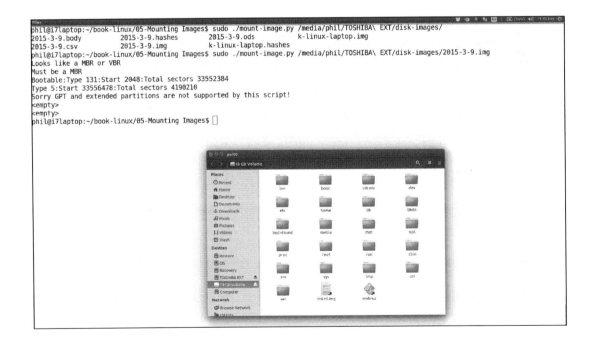

FIGURE 5.13.

Running the Python mounting script against an image file from an Ubuntu 14.04 system.

MBR-based extended partitions

The following script will attempt to mount anything in extended partitions that were skipped over in the previous script:

```
#!/usr/bin/python3
# This is a simple Python script that will
# attempt to mount partitions inside an extended
# partition from an image file.
# Images are mounted read-only.
#
# Developed for PentesterAcademy by Dr. Phil Polstra

import sys
import os.path
import subprocess
import struct

class Mbr():
   ''' Master Boot Record class
   Accepts a sector (512 bytes) and creates an MBR object.
   The MBR object can be queried for its attributes.
   The data is stored in a tuple using struct.unpack.'''
   def __init__(self, sector):
      '''This constructor expects a 512-byte MBR sector.
      It will populate the ._mbrTuple.'''
      fmt=('<446s' + # Boot code
         # partition 1
         'B' + # Active flag 0x80 is active (bootable)
         'B' + # Start head
         'B' + # Start sector only bits 0-5 bits 6-7 for cylinder
         'B' + # Start cylinder (upper 2 bits in previous byte)
         'B' + # partition type code
         'B' + # End head
         'B' + # End sector
         'B' + # End cylinder
         'I' + # Sectors preceeding partition
         'I' + # Sectors in partition
         # partition 2
         'B' + # Active flag 0x80 is active (bootable)
         'B' + # Start head
         'B' + # Start sector only bits 0-5 bits 6-7 for cylinder
         'B' + # Start cylinder (upper 2 bits in previous byte)
         'B' + # partition type code
         'B' + # End head
         'B' + # End sector
```

CHAPTER 5 Mounting Images

```
            'B' + # End cylinder
            'I' + # Sectors preceeding partition
            'I' + # Sectors in partition
            # partition 3
            'B' + # Active flag 0x80 is active (bootable)
            'B' + # Start head
            'B' + # Start sector only bits 0-5 bits 6-7 for cylinder
            'B' + # Start cylinder (upper 2 bits in previous byte)
            'B' + # partition type code
            'B' + # End head
            'B' + # End sector
            'B' + # End cylinder
            'I' + # Sectors preceeding partition
            'I' + # Sectors in partition
            # partition 4
            'B' + # Active flag 0x80 is active (bootable)
            'B' + # Start head
            'B' + # Start sector only bits 0-5 bits 6-7 for cylinder
            'B' + # Start cylinder (upper 2 bits in previous byte)
            'B' + # partition type code
            'B' + # End head
            'B' + # End sector
            'B' + # End cylinder
            'I' + # Sectors preceeding partition
            'I' + # Sectors in partition
            '2s') # Signature should be 0x55 0xAA
        self._mbrTuple=struct.unpack(fmt, sector)

    def isActive(self, partno):
        return self._mbrTuple[1+10*(partno-1)]==0x80

    def startHead(self, partno):
        return self._mbrTuple[2+10*(partno-1)]

    def startSector(self, partno):
        # return lower 6 bits of sector
        return self._mbrTuple[3+10*(partno-1)] % 64

    def startCylinder(self, partno):
        # add in the upper 2 bits if needed
        return (self._mbrTuple[4+10*(partno-1)] +
            256 * self._mbrTuple[3+10*(partno-1)]//64)

    def partitionType(self, partno):
        return self._mbrTuple[5+10*(partno-1)]
```

```python
   def isEmpty(self, partno):
      return self.partitionType(partno)==0

   def endHead(self, partno):
      return self._mbrTuple[6+10*(partno-1)]

   def endSector(self, partno):
      # return lower 6 bits of sector
      return self._mbrTuple[7+10*(partno-1)] % 64

   def endCylinder(self, partno):
      # add in the upper 2 bits if needed
      return (self._mbrTuple[8+10*(partno-1)] +
         256 * self._mbrTuple[7+10*(partno-1)]//64)

   def reservedSectors(self, partno):
      '''Sectors preceeding this partition'''
      return self._mbrTuple[9+10*(partno-1)]

   def totalSectors(self, partno):
      return self._mbrTuple[10+10*(partno-1)]

   def validSignature(self):
      return self._mbrTuple[41]==b'\x55\xAA'

   def prettyPrint(self):
      print('MBR signature valid:', self.validSignature())
      for i in range(1, 5):
         print('Partition', i, 'information:')
         if self.isEmpty(i):
            print('\tEntry is empty.')
         else:
            print('\tBootable:', self.isActive(i))
            print('\tStart head:', self.startHead(i))
            print('\tStart sector:', self.startSector(i))
            print('\tStart cylinder:', self.startCylinder(i))
            print('\tPartition type:', self.partitionType(i))
            print('\tEnd head:', self.endHead(i))
            print('\tEnd sector:', self.endSector(i))
            print('\tEnd cylinder:', self.endCylinder(i))
            print('\tReserved sectors:', self.reservedSectors(i))
            print('\tTotal sectors:', self.totalSectors(i))
```

```python
def usage():
   print("usage " + sys.argv[0] + \
       " <image file>\nAttempts to mount extended partitions from " + \
       "an image file")
   exit(1)

def main():
   if len(sys.argv) < 2:
      usage()

   extParts = [0x05, 0x0f, 0x85, 0x91, 0x9b, 0xc5, 0xe4]
   swapParts = [0x42, 0x82, 0xb8, 0xc3, 0xfc]

   # read first sector
   if not os.path.isfile(sys.argv[1]):
      print("File " + sys.argv[1] + " cannot be openned for reading")
      exit(1)

   with open(sys.argv[1], 'rb') as f:
      sector = f.read(512)

   mbr=Mbr(sector) # create MBR object

   for i in range(1,5):
      if not mbr.isEmpty(i):
         if mbr.partitionType(i) in extParts:
            print("Found an extended partion at sector %s" % \
                  str(mbr.reservedSectors(i)))
            bottomOfRabbitHole = False
            extendPartStart = mbr.reservedSectors(i)
            extPartNo = 5
            while not bottomOfRabbitHole:
               # get the linked list MBR entry
               f=open(sys.argv[1], 'rb')
               f.seek(extendPartStart * 512)
               llSector = f.read(512)
               f.close()
               if len(llSector)==512:
                  extMbr=Mbr(llSector)
                  # try and mount the first partition
                  if extMbr.partitionType(1) in swapParts:
                     print("Skipping swap partition")
                  else:
                     mountpath = '/media/part%s' % str(extPartNo)
                     if not os.path.isdir(mountpath):
```

```
                    subprocess.call(['mkdir', mountpath])
                    mountopts = 'loop,ro,noatime,offset=%s' \
                        % str((extMbr.reservedSectors(1) + \
                            extendPartStart) * 512)
                    print("Attempting to mount extend part type" + \
                        "%s at sector %s" \
                        % (hex(extMbr.partitionType(1)), \
                        str(extendPartStart + extMbr.reservedSectors(1))))
                    subprocess.call(['mount', '-o', mountopts, \
                        sys.argv[1], mountpath])
                if extMbr.isEmpty(2):
                    bottomOfRabbitHole = True
                    print("Found the bottom of the rabbit hole")
                else:
                    extendPartStart += extMbr.reservedSectors(2)
                    extPartNo += 1

if __name__ == "__main__":
    main()
```

This script starts out vary similar to the previous script until we get into the main function. The first difference is the definition of two lists: extParts and swapParts that list extended partition and swap partition types, respectively. We then read the MBR as before and verify that it looks like an MBR should. Things really start to diverge from the previous script at the following lines:

```
            if mbr.partitionType(i) in extParts:
                print("Found an extended partition at sector %s" \
                    % str(mbr.reservedSectors(i)))
                bottomOfRabbitHole = False
                extendPartStart = mbr.reservedSectors(i)
                extPartNo = 5
```

In these lines we check to see if we have found an extended partition. If so, we print a message and set a few variables. The first variable named bottomOfRabbitHole is set to False. This variable is used to indicate when we have found the lowest level in a set of nested extended partitions. The start sector of the primary extended partition is stored in extendPartStart. This is necessary because addresses inside an extended partition are relative to the extended partition, but we need absolute addresses to mount the partition(s). Finally, we set a variable extPartNo equal to 5 which is traditionally used as the partition number for the first logical partition within an extended partition.

The line `while not bottomOfRabbitHole:` begins a while loop. A while loop is executed as long as the condition listed in the while loop is true. Within the while loop we use our `with open` construct as before to read the mini-MBR at the start of the extended partition with one small addition to the previous script. The line `f.seek(extendPartStart * 512)` is new. Because the mini-MBR is not located at the start of the file (LBA0) we must seek ahead to the appropriate place. The offset we need is just the sector number multiplied by the size of a sector (512).

Next we read the entries in the mini-MBR and create a new Mbr object called extMbr. Recall that only the first two entries of this mini-MBR are used. If the first entry (extMbr.partitionType(1)) is a swap partition, we skip it. Otherwise, we attempt to mount it. The mounting code is the same as that found in the previous script.

We then check the second entry in the mini-MBR (extMbr.isEmpty(2)). If it is empty (partition type is zero), there are no nested extended partitions and we are done. If this is not the case, we add the starting sector of the nested extended partition to extendPartStart and increment extPartNo so things are setup properly for our next iteration of the while loop.

GPT partitions

Now that we have covered systems using the legacy MBR-based method of partition, let's move on to GUID-based partitions. Hopefully within the next few years this will become the only system you have to handle during your investigations. As I said previously, this new system is much more straightforward and elegant. Our script for automatically mounting these partitions follows.

```
#!/usr/bin/python3
#
# mount-image-gpt.py
#
# This is a simple Python script that will
# attempt to mount partitions from an image file.
# This script is for GUID partions only.
# Images are mounted read-only.
#
# Developed for PentesterAcademy by Dr. Phil Polstra

import sys
import os.path
import subprocess
import struct

supportedParts = ["EBD0A0A2-B9E5-4433-87C0-68B6B72699C7",
"37AFFC90-EF7D-4E96-91C3-2D7AE055B174",
"0FC63DAF-8483-4772-8E79-3D69D8477DE4",
"8DA63339-0007-60C0-C436-083AC8230908",
"933AC7E1-2EB4-4F13-B844-0E14E2AEF915",
"44479540-F297-41B2-9AF7-D131D5F0458A",
"4F68BCE3-E8CD-4DB1-96E7-FBCAF984B709",
"B921B045-1DF0-41C3-AF44-4C6F280D3FAE",
"3B8F8425-20E0-4F3B-907F-1A25A76F98E8",
```

```
"E6D6D379-F507-44C2-A23C-238F2A3DF928",
"516E7CB4-6ECF-11D6-8FF8-00022D09712B",
"83BD6B9D-7F41-11DC-BE0B-001560B84F0F",
"516E7CB5-6ECF-11D6-8FF8-00022D09712B",
"85D5E45A-237C-11E1-B4B3-E89A8F7FC3A7",
"516E7CB4-6ECF-11D6-8FF8-00022D09712B",
"824CC7A0-36A8-11E3-890A-952519AD3F61",
"55465300-0000-11AA-AA11-00306543ECAC",
"516E7CB4-6ECF-11D6-8FF8-00022D09712B",
"49F48D5A-B10E-11DC-B99B-0019D1879648",
"49F48D82-B10E-11DC-B99B-0019D1879648",
"2DB519C4-B10F-11DC-B99B-0019D1879648",
"2DB519EC-B10F-11DC-B99B-0019D1879648",
"49F48DAA-B10E-11DC-B99B-0019D1879648",
"426F6F74-0000-11AA-AA11-00306543ECAC",
"48465300-0000-11AA-AA11-00306543ECAC",
"52414944-0000-11AA-AA11-00306543ECAC",
"52414944-5F4F-11AA-AA11-00306543ECAC",
"4C616265-6C00-11AA-AA11-00306543ECAC",
"6A82CB45-1DD2-11B2-99A6-080020736631",
"6A85CF4D-1DD2-11B2-99A6-080020736631",
"6A898CC3-1DD2-11B2-99A6-080020736631",
"6A8B642B-1DD2-11B2-99A6-080020736631",
"6A8EF2E9-1DD2-11B2-99A6-080020736631",
"6A90BA39-1DD2-11B2-99A6-080020736631",
"6A9283A5-1DD2-11B2-99A6-080020736631",
"75894C1E-3AEB-11D3-B7C1-7B03A0000000",
"E2A1E728-32E3-11D6-A682-7B03A0000000",
"BC13C2FF-59E6-4262-A352-B275FD6F7172",
"42465331-3BA3-10F1-802A-4861696B7521",
"AA31E02A-400F-11DB-9590-000C2911D1B8",
"9198EFFC-31C0-11DB-8F78-000C2911D1B8",
"9D275380-40AD-11DB-BF97-000C2911D1B8",
"A19D880F-05FC-4D3B-A006-743F0F84911E"]

def printGuid(packedString):
    if len(packedString) == 16:
        outstr = format(struct.unpack('<L', packedString[0:4])[0], 'X').zfill(8) \
            + "-" + \
            format(struct.unpack('<H', packedString[4:6])[0], 'X').zfill(4) \
            + "-" + \
            format(struct.unpack('<H', packedString[6:8])[0], 'X').zfill(4) \
            + "-" + \
            format(struct.unpack('>H', packedString[8:10])[0], 'X').zfill(4) \
            + "-" + \
```

```python
            format(struct.unpack('>Q', b"\x00\x00" + packedString[10:16])[0],\
        'X').zfill(12)
    else:
        outstr = "<invalid>"
    return outstr

class GptRecord():
    def __init__(self, recs, partno):
        self.partno = partno
        offset = partno * 128
        self.empty = False
        # build partition type GUID string
        self.partType = printGuid(recs[offset:offset+16])
        if self.partType == "00000000-0000-0000-0000-000000000000":
            self.empty = True
        self.partGUID = printGuid(recs[offset+16:offset+32])
        self.firstLBA = struct.unpack('<Q', recs[offset+32:offset+40])[0]
        self.lastLBA = struct.unpack('<Q', recs[offset+40:offset+48])[0]
        self.attr = struct.unpack('<Q', recs[offset+48:offset+56])[0]
        nameIndex = recs[offset+56:offset+128].find(b'\x00\x00')
        if nameIndex != -1:
            self.partName = recs[offset+56:offset+56+nameIndex].decode("utf-8",\
        "replace")
        else:
            self.partName = recs[offset+56:offset+128].decode("utf-8",\
        "replace")

    def printPart(self):
        if not self.empty:
            outstr = str(self.partno) + ":" + str(self.partType) + ":" \
                + str(self.partGUID) + \
                ":" + str(self.firstLBA) + ":" + str(self.lastLBA) + ":" + \
                str(self.attr) + ":" + self.partName
            print(outstr)


class Mbr():
    '''Master Boot Record class
    Accepts a sector (512 bytes) and creates an MBR object.
    The MBR object can be queried for its attributes.
    The data is stored in a tuple using struct.unpack.'''
    def __init__(self, sector):
        '''This constructor expects a 512-byte MBR sector.
        It will populate the ._mbrTuple.'''
        fmt=('<446s' + # Boot code
```

```
# partition 1
'B' + # Active flag 0x80 is active (bootable)
'B' + # Start head
'B' + # Start sector only bits 0-5 bits 6-7 for cylinder
'B' + # Start cylinder (upper 2 bits in previous byte)
'B' + # partition type code
'B' + # End head
'B' + # End sector
'B' + # End cylinder
'I' + # Sectors preceeding partition
'I' + # Sectors in partition
# partition 2
'B' + # Active flag 0x80 is active (bootable)
'B' + # Start head
'B' + # Start sector only bits 0-5 bits 6-7 for cylinder
'B' + # Start cylinder (upper 2 bits in previous byte)
'B' + # partition type code
'B' + # End head
'B' + # End sector
'B' + # End cylinder
'I' + # Sectors preceeding partition
'I' + # Sectors in partition
# partition 3
'B' + # Active flag 0x80 is active (bootable)
'B' + # Start head
'B' + # Start sector only bits 0-5 bits 6-7 for cylinder
'B' + # Start cylinder (upper 2 bits in previous byte)
'B' + # partition type code
'B' + # End head
'B' + # End sector
'B' + # End cylinder
'I' + # Sectors preceeding partition
'I' + # Sectors in partition
# partition 4
'B' + # Active flag 0x80 is active (bootable)
'B' + # Start head
'B' + # Start sector only bits 0-5 bits 6-7 for cylinder
'B' + # Start cylinder (upper 2 bits in previous byte)
'B' + # partition type code
'B' + # End head
'B' + # End sector
'B' + # End cylinder
'I' + # Sectors preceeding partition
'I' + # Sectors in partition
'2s') # Signature should be 0x55 0xAA
```

```python
            self._mbrTuple=struct.unpack(fmt, sector)

        def isActive(self, partno):
            return self._mbrTuple[1+10*(partno-1)]==0x80

        def startHead(self, partno):
            return self._mbrTuple[2+10*(partno-1)]

        def startSector(self, partno):
            # return lower 6 bits of sector
            return self._mbrTuple[3+10*(partno-1)] % 64

        def startCylinder(self, partno):
            # add in the upper 2 bits if needed
            return (self._mbrTuple[4+10*(partno-1)] +
                256 * self._mbrTuple[3+10*(partno-1)]//64)

        def partitionType(self, partno):
            return self._mbrTuple[5+10*(partno-1)]

        def isEmpty(self, partno):
            return self.partitionType(partno)==0

        def endHead(self, partno):
            return self._mbrTuple[6+10*(partno-1)]

        def endSector(self, partno):
            # return lower 6 bits of sector
            return self._mbrTuple[7+10*(partno-1)] % 64

        def endCylinder(self, partno):
            # add in the upper 2 bits if needed
            return (self._mbrTuple[8+10*(partno-1)] +
                256 * self._mbrTuple[7+10*(partno-1)]//64)

        def reservedSectors(self, partno):
            '''Sectors preceeding this partition'''
            return self._mbrTuple[9+10*(partno-1)]

        def totalSectors(self, partno):
            return self._mbrTuple[10+10*(partno-1)]

        def validSignature(self):
            return self._mbrTuple[41]==b'\x55\xAA'
```

```python
    def prettyPrint(self):
        print('MBR signature valid:', self.validSignature())
        for i in range(1, 5):
            print('Partition', i, 'information:')
            if self.isEmpty(i):
                print('\tEntry is empty.')
            else:
                print('\tBootable:', self.isActive(i))
                print('\tStart head:', self.startHead(i))
                print('\tStart sector:', self.startSector(i))
                print('\tStart cylinder:', self.startCylinder(i))
                print('\tPartition type:', self.partitionType(i))
                print('\tEnd head:', self.endHead(i))
                print('\tEnd sector:', self.endSector(i))
                print('\tEnd cylinder:', self.endCylinder(i))
                print('\tReserved sectors:', self.reservedSectors(i))
                print('\tTotal sectors:', self.totalSectors(i))

def usage():
    print("usage " + sys.argv[0] + " <image file>\nAttempts to mount
partitions from an image file")
    exit(1)

def main():
    if len(sys.argv) < 2:
        usage()

    # read first sector
    if not os.path.isfile(sys.argv[1]):
        print("File " + sys.argv[1] + " cannot be openned for reading")
        exit(1)
    with open(sys.argv[1], 'rb') as f:
        sector = f.read(512)
    mbr=Mbr(sector)
    if mbr.validSignature():
        if mbr.partitionType(1) != 0xee:
            print("Failed protective MBR sanity check")
            exit(1)
        # check the header as another sanity check
        with open(sys.argv[1], 'rb') as f:
            f.seek(512)
            sector = f.read(512)
        if sector[0:8] != b"EFI PART":
            print("You appear to be missing a GUI header")
            exit(1)
```

```
        print("Valid protective MBR and GUI partion table header found")
        with open(sys.argv[1], 'rb') as f:
            f.seek(1024)
            partRecs = f.read(512 * 32)
        parts = [ ]
        for i in range(0, 128):
            p = GptRecord(partRecs, i)
            if not p.empty:
                p.printPart()
                parts.append(p)
        for p in parts:
            if p.partType in supportedParts:
                print("Partition %s seems to be supported attempting to mount"\
                    % str(p.partno))
                mountpath = '/media/part%s' % str(p.partno)
                if not os.path.isdir(mountpath):
                    subprocess.call(['mkdir', mountpath])
                mountopts = 'loop,ro,noatime,offset=%s' % str(p.firstLBA * 512)
                subprocess.call(['mount', '-o', mountopts, sys.argv[1], mountpath])


if __name__ == "__main__":
    main()
```

Let's walk through this code. It begins with the normal she-bang. Then we import the same four libraries as in the previous scripts. Next we define a very long list of supported partition types. As you can see from this list, Linux supports most any partition type.

We define a simple helper function to print the GUIDs from the packed strings used to store the GPT entries on these lines:

```
def printGuid(packedString):
    if len(packedString) == 16:
        outstr = format(struct.unpack('<L', \
            packedString[0:4])[0], 'X').zfill(8) + "-" + \
            format(struct.unpack('<H', \
            packedString[4:6])[0], 'X').zfill(4) + "-" + \
            format(struct.unpack('<H', \
            packedString[6:8])[0], 'X').zfill(4) + "-" + \
            format(struct.unpack('>H', \
            packedString[8:10])[0], 'X').zfill(4) + "-" + \
            format(struct.unpack('>Q', \
            "\x00\x00" + packedString[10:16])[0], 'X').zfill(12)
    else:
        outstr = "<invalid>"
    return outstr
```

This helper function uses the same `struct.unpack` method found in the previous scripts. One difference is that the first three parts of the GUID are stored in little endian format and the last two are big endian. That is why the first three calls to `struct.unpack` have '<' in their format strings and the last two have '>'. Also, the last call to unpack might look a bit strange. All that I've done here is add two bytes of leading zeros to the value because there is no unpack format specifier for a 6-byte value, but there is one for an 8-byte value.

We have introduced a new function, `format`, in this helper function. As the name implies, `format` is used to print values in a specified way. Our chosen format, 'X', specifies hexadecimal with upper case letters. Once we have a string containing our value we run `zfill()` on the string to add leading zeros in order for our GUIDs to print correctly. As a simple example, the expression `format(struct.unpack('<L', b'\x04\x00\x00\x00')[0], 'X').zfill(8)` evaluates to the string "00000004".

Next we define a GptRecord class. It expects a list of partition table entries (all 128 of them) and an index into the table as inputs. Only the following lines require any explanation in this class:

```
nameIndex = recs[offset+56:offset+128].find(b'\x00\x00')
if nameIndex != -1:
   self.partName = \
     recs[offset+56:offset+56+nameIndex].encode('utf-8', 'replace')
else:
   self.partName = \
     recs[offset+56:offset+128].encode('utf-8', 'replace')
```

Why are these lines here? I have found that sometimes Unicode strings such as those used to store the partition name in the GPT are null-terminated (with 0x00 0x00), and there may be random junk after the terminating null character. The first line in this code fragment uses `find` to see if there is a null character in the name. If the string is found then nameIndex is set to its position. If the string is not found, the `find` function returns -1. Looking at the `if` block you will see that if a null was found, we only use characters before it to store the partition name. Otherwise, we store all of the name.

The Mbr class still has not gone away. This class is used to read the protective MBR as a sanity check. You will see that the main function starts out the same as before by reading the first sector and using Mbr to parse it. The second sanity check causes the script to exit if the first partition is not type 0xEE, which indicates a GPT drive.

The third sanity check reads the GPT header in the second sector and checks for the string "EFI PART" which should be stored in the first eight bytes of this sector. If this final check passes, the image is reopened and the next 32 sectors containing the 128 GPT entries are read.

We then have a `for` loop in this code:

```
for i in range(0, 128):
   p = GptRecord(partRecs, i)
   if not p.empty:
      p.printPart()
      parts.append(p)
```

```
phil@i7laptop:~/PentesterAcademy/linux-forensics$ ./mount-image-gpt.py gpt.img
Valid protective MBR and GUI partion table header found
0:DE94BBA4-06D1-4D40-A16A-BFD50179D6AC:D18DD83C-B67A-4EDB-91D1-492C806CAD20:2048:1333247:1:Basic data partition
1:C12A7328-F81F-11D2-BA4B-00A0C93EC93B:F51DD64C-717D-4588-9497-12AD87D33D96:1333248:1865727:0:EFI system partition
2:E3C9E316-0B5C-4DB8-817D-F92DF00215AE:B5134F0A-6679-464A-BA64-404A24F466ED:1865728:2127871:0:Microsoft reserved partition
3:EBD0A0A2-B9E5-4433-87C0-68B6B72699C7:C0849437-058C-426E-87BD-EFA7112DEECC:2127872:832661075:0:Basic data partition
4:EBD0A0A2-B9E5-4433-87C0-68B6B72699C7:443717F0-C75E-4424-8694-95138DDFB720:1418598400:1465137151:1:Basic data partition
5:0FC63DAF-8483-4772-8E79-3D69D8477DE4:7A8DFD95-C09E-4897-A8E5-027868453443:832661504:1379536503:0:
6:0657FD6D-A4AB-43C4-84E5-0933C84B4F4F:2AEECCF2-EF1B-4C19-8EAC-3F444AC90754:1379536896:1418598399:0:
Partition 3 seems to be supported attempting to mount
mkdir: cannot create directory '/media/part3': Permission denied
mount: only root can do that
Partition 4 seems to be supported attempting to mount
mkdir: cannot create directory '/media/part4': Permission denied
mount: only root can do that
Partition 5 seems to be supported attempting to mount
mkdir: cannot create directory '/media/part5': Permission denied
mount: only root can do that
phil@i7laptop:~/PentesterAcademy/linux-forensics$
```

FIGURE 5.14.

Mounting GUID-based partitions from an image file. Note: the script was intentionally run without root privileges to prevent mounting of an image that was corrupted.

Non-empty partitions are printed and added to the parts list. You may be wondering why I do not stop once an empty record has been encountered. It is valid, though somewhat unusual, to have empty entries in the middle of the GPT.

Once the entire GPT has been parsed, we iterate over the parts list and attempt to mount any supported partitions. The methods used are the same as those from the previous mounting scripts. The results of running this script against an image using GUID partitions is shown in Figure 5.14. Note that this script was intentionally run without root privileges so that the mounts would fail as the image used was corrupted.

SUMMARY

We have covered a lot of ground in this chapter. We discussed the basics of mounting different types of partitions found in image files. Some readers may have learned a little Python along the way as we discussed how Python could be used to automate this process. In the next chapter we will discuss the inner workings of the File Allocation Table (FAT) filesystem in detail.

CHAPTER 6

FAT Filesystems

INFORMATION IN THIS CHAPTER:

- FAT basics
- Using Active@ Disk Editor
- Volume Boot Records
- File allocation tables
- Directories
- The Sleuth Kit
- Autopsy
- Automation with Python
- Deleted files

In this chapter we will begin the discussion of traditional filesystem analysis. Even though dead analysis encompasses more than just filesystem analysis, some use the terms interchangeably. Forensic investigators have been performing dead analysis for decades. As a result, this is a very mature and well understood field. In order to get the most from dead analysis a solid understanding of the underlying filesystem(s) is required. This chapter discusses the File Allocation Table (FAT) filesystem which has been in DOS since the beginning and still persists in Windows to this day. FAT has become a de facto standard which is used inside and outside of Windows.

FAT BASICS

The File Allocation Table (FAT) filesystem has been with us for quite a while. The original FAT filesystem was used on the 5.25 inch floppy diskettes. The FAT filesystem gets its name from one of its key components, the file allocation table. There are three variants for FAT which are named by the size of entries (in bits) in this file allocation table: FAT12, FAT16, and FAT32.

The FAT12 filesystem was first used on 5.25 inch floppy disks which had a rather limited capacity of 160 kilobytes. Because space was limited on these floppies, a 12-bit (1.5 bytes or a byte plus a nybble) was all that could be spared for each FAT entry. As storage expanded and hard drives became commonplace the maximum capacity of a FAT12 filesystem was much less than what could be stored on a hard drive and the FAT16 filesystem was developed with 16-bit (2 byte) entries. Eventually FAT16 was also incapable of keeping up with improvements in storage and the FAT32 filesystem was developed. Whereas the FAT12 and FAT16 filesystems differ only in the size of FAT entries, FAT32 added some additional performance enhancing features.

CHAPTER 6 FAT Filesystems

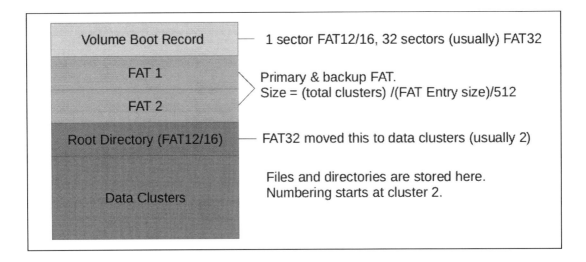

FIGURE 6.1.

FAT filesystem layout.

The overall layout of a FAT filesystem is shown in Figure 6.1. The filesystem begins with a Volume Boot Record (VBR) which describes the filesystem to the operating system. This is followed by a primary and backup file allocation table. For FAT12 and FAT16 filesystems the root directory comes next. Following these structures we find sectors used to store data. These sectors are organized into clusters consisting of a power of two sectors (1, 2, 4, 8, etc.). The first available data cluster is cluster number 2 (there is no cluster 0 or 1).

Using Active@ Disk Editor

LSoft Technologies makes a nice freeware disk editor called Active@ Disk Editor (ADE). This tool is available in both a Windows and a Linux version. In earlier versions of ADE the Linux version was really just the Windows version which used WINE (Wine Is Not an Emulator) to run under Linux. If you are unfamiliar with WINE it is a tool that translates Windows API calls into native Linux system calls. In the most recent version of ADE the Linux version is a proper Linux executable. ADE may be downloaded from http://disk-editor.org.

I recommend installing both the Windows and Linux versions of ADE. The main reason for this recommendation is that I have seen different bugs come and go with each new release. Since the code base has split, I have observed several instances where something works perfectly in one edition and not at all in the other. You might also consider using the Way Back Machine at http://archive.org to download ADE version 5 if certain features do not seem to work in either edition of ADE version 6.

When you first run ADE you will likely be asked to select a disk image as shown in Figure 6.2. Upon clicking the ellipsis (...) button to browse for an image file you will be greeted with a dialog like the one from Figure 6.3. Be sure to select "All Files" from the drop down box in the lower right corner to display all of your image files.

FAT Basics

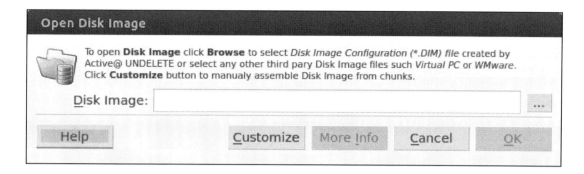

FIGURE 6.2.
Opening a disk image in Active@ Disk Editor.

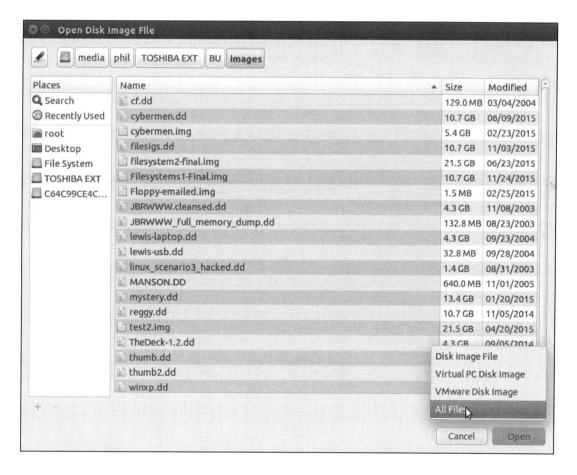

FIGURE 6.3.
Showing all image files in a directory.

Once a disk image has been loaded into ADE, you should see a window similar to Figure 6.4. Notice that underneath a "Disk Image" item any partitions in the image will be listed. In order to get a logical view of the volume either right click on the appropriate volume and select "Open in Disk Editor" from the menu (as shown in Figure 6.4) or select it and press the "Open in Disk Editor" button. This should open a new tab with the logical view of the volume. If you skip this step, you will not be able to navigate to a specific cluster and some of the ADE features will not be available.

After opening a volume in the disk editor, a new tab that ends in "- Volume" will be created. Normally a template view is displayed as shown in Figure 6.5. If no template is displayed, select View->Windows->Template from the ADE menu as shown in the figure. In some cases ADE will automatically select the correct template and in others you must ensure that the correct template is selected in the drop down menu. If the information in the template appears to be incorrect, you may have accidentally reset the template position. To fix this, simply right click on the start of the appropriate sector and select "Set Template Position" from the pop up menu as shown in Figure 6.6. ADE has several nice features not found in expensive commercial packages such as item highlighting and tool tips (descriptions that appear when you hover the mouse over an item).

The Navigate button is one of the most commonly used items in ADE. As can be seen in Figure 6.7, Navigate will take you to various components of the volume (or disk). It will also allow you to go to a particular offset or sector, although separate buttons and hot keys are also

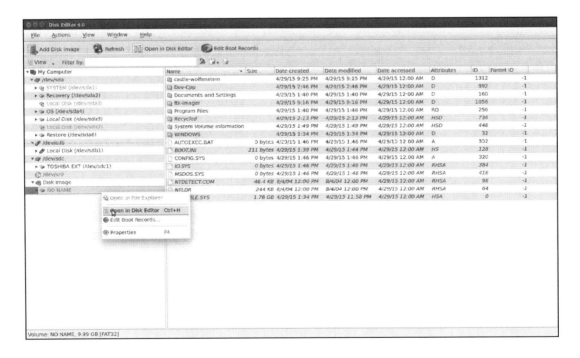

FIGURE 6.4.

Opening a volume in Active@ Disk Editor. Note this logical view is required in order to use cluster numbers.

FAT Basics

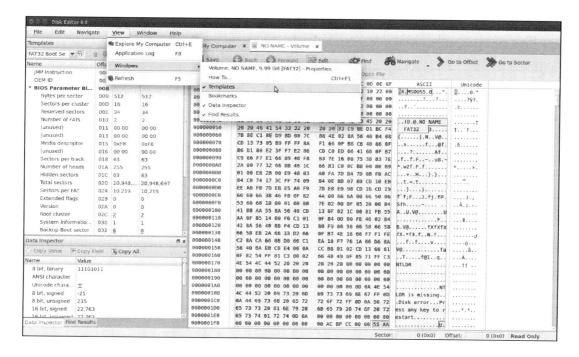

FIGURE 6.5.

Showing the template view in Active@ Disk Editor.

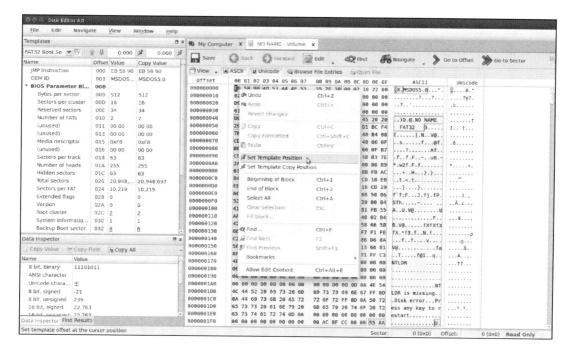

FIGURE 6.6.

Setting the template position in Active@ Disk Editor.

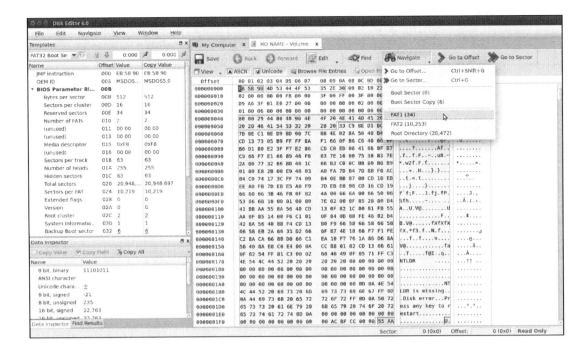

FIGURE 6.7.

The Active@ Disk Editor Navigate button.

available for these purposes. Note that sector numbers and offsets are relative to the volume or disk depending on whether you are on the volume or raw data tabs, respectively.

VOLUME BOOT RECORDS

The Volume Boot Record (VBR) is used to describe a filesystem to the operating system. The fields in the first 28 bytes of the VBR are the same for all versions of FAT, but the later fields will differ. The reason for this has to do with some of the fields being too small for later versions of FAT (FAT16 and FAT32). FAT12 and FAT16 use one sector for the VBR. FAT32 uses multiple sectors because it adds a backup boot sector, more space for bootstrap code, and extra information. The exact number of sectors used by FAT32 varies, but 32 is a common number. The first 28 bytes of the VBR that are common to all FAT variants are summarized in Table 6.1.

The first three bytes of the VBR contain a jump to bootstrap code. Storing parameters at the beginning of a program and then jumping over them is a common technique used by Assembly programmers. The first byte should be 0xEB which is the operation code for a short jump in 16-bit Intel architectures. A short jump allows a program to jump forward up to 127 bytes or jump backward up to 128 bytes. The third byte is unneeded for a short jump and normally has the value of 0x90 which is the no-operation (NOP) code. The NOP instruction is widely use for padding.

The second item in the VBR is the OEM name. For FAT filesystems the OEM name can

Table 6.1. First 28 bytes of a FAT Volume Boot Record.

Offset	Length	Item
0 (0x00)	3 (0x3)	Jump to bootstrap
3 (0x03)	8 (0x08)	OEM name (who made this filesystem?)
11 (0x0B)	2 (0x02)	Bytes/sector (probably 512)
13 (0x0D)	1 (0x01)	Sectors/cluster (usually power of 2)
14 (0x0E)	2 (0x02)	Reserved sectors before filesystem (1 or 32)
16 (0x10)	1 (0x01)	Copies of FAT (probably 2)
17 (0x11)	2 (0x02)	Root directory entries (0 for FAT32)
19 (0x13)	2 (0x02)	Filesystem sector if under 32 MB (65,536 sectors)
21 (0x15)	1 (0x01)	Media descriptor (F0 = floppy, F8 = everything else)
22 (0x16)	2 (0x02)	Sectors/FAT (will show 0 for FAT32)
24 (0x18)	2 (0x02)	Sectors/track
26 (0x1A)	2 (0x02)	Number of heads

indicate what version of Windows was used to create the volume. Common OEM names include MSWIN4.0, MSWIN4.1, and MSDOS5.0, for Windows 95, Windows 98, and Windows XP, respectively.

The third item in the VBR is the number of bytes per sector. This is almost certainly 512 (0x200). While newer solid state media could easily support a larger sector size, nearly every device still uses 512 byte sectors at the time of this writing. Part of the reason for this is that Windows did not support any other value prior to Windows 7. The fourth item in the VBR is the number of sectors per cluster. This value is normally a power of 2 with 1, 2, 4, 8, and 16 being common choices depending on media size.

The fifth item in the VBR is the number of reserved sectors. This is the number of sectors before the first FAT begins. Typically this will be 1 for FAT12 and FAT16 and 32 for FAT32. It is certainly possible to have more than these minimums (which merely reflect the size of the VBR itself). On USB flash drives it is not unusual for the first 2048 sectors to be reserved regardless of whether the drive has an MBR or just a single partition with a VBR only.

The sixth item in the VBR is the number of File Allocation Tables (FATs). Because the FAT is critical for FAT filesystems there are normally two copies. It is certainly possible to have only one or more than two. However, I have never seen such a filesystem (with the exception of something called exFAT).

The seventh item in the VBR is the number of root directory entries. In FAT12 and FAT16 the root directory is stored in a special place before the data clusters. The number of

32-byte directory entries must be known in order to calculate the number of sectors occupied by the root directory. Because FAT32 stores the root directory in the data clusters, this value will be zero for FAT32 filesystems. Having the root directory in a known location can speed up processing but limits the number of files and directories in the root directory. This is the reason that the root directory was moved out to the data clusters with all the other directories in FAT32.

The eighth item in the VBR is a 2-byte value for the total number of sectors in the filesystem. If there are more than 65,535 sectors (32MB using standard sectors), this value will be zero and a 4-byte field that occurs later will be populated. Following this comes the media descriptor. This will most like be 0xF8 which indicates a hard drive or something that emulates a hard drive. A floppy disk will have a media descriptor of 0xF0.

A 2-byte value for sectors per FAT follows the media descriptor. For FAT32 filesystems this value will be zero as the field is too small. A 4-byte field that occurs later will be populated with the appropriate value for FAT32. The last two fields in the first 28 bytes of the VBR are sectors per track and number of heads. These entries are likely ignored for most modern media.

The remaining items for FAT12 and FAT16 are shown in Table 6.2.

Offset 28 (0x1C) houses the number of hidden sectors. These are sectors that precede the partition. This could be the MBR, reserved sectors, other partitions, or some combination of these. Next we see the total number of sectors as a 4-byte value. This field is only populated if there are more than 65,535 sectors in which case the earlier field for total sectors should be zero.

At offset 36 (0x20) a logical drive number is found. In this system the first drive is 0x80, the second is 0x81, etc. This value may be used in assigning drive letters. The next field is 24 bytes long and may contain an extended boot signature if the first byte is 0x29. Extended boot signatures are summarized in Table 6.3. These pieces of extra information are not needed in order to correctly interpret the filesystem.

The extended boot signature contains a 4-byte partition serial number. Recall that the MBR contains a serial number for the entire disk. FAT partitions may have a volume label. If one

Table 6.2. Remaining VBR items specific to FAT12 and FAT16.

Offset	Length	Item
28 (0x1C)	4 (0x4)	Hidden sectors (preceding this partition)
32 (0x20)	4 (0x04)	Filesystem sectors if over 32MB (64k sectors)
36 (0x24)	1 (0x01)	Logical drive number (0x80, 0x81...)
38 (0x26)	24 (0x18)	Extended boot signature if 1st byte 0x29
62 (0x48)	448 (0x1C0)	Bootstrap code (16-bit assembly)
510 (0x1FE)	2 (0x02)	Signature (0x55 0xAA)

Table 6.3. Extended boot signatures.

Offset	Length	Item
38 (0x26)	1 (0x1)	0x29 indicates an extended signature follows
39 (0x27)	4 (0x04)	Partition serial number
43 (0x2B)	11 (0x0B)	Volume label or "NO NAME"
54 (0x36)	8 (0x08)	Human readable filesystem type

has been set, it may be found in the extended boot signature and/or the first entry of the root directory. Rather than leave the field blank, the string "NO NAME" is stored if no label has been assigned. The extended boot signature ends with a human readable filesystem type such as FAT12, FAT16, or FAT32. This value is strictly informational and should not be relied upon.

The last two items in a FAT12 or FAT16 VBR are 448 bytes of bootstrap code and the signature 0x55 0xAA in the last two bytes of the sector. The bootstrap code is 16-bit Intel Assembly code. The reason that 16-bit code is used instead of 32-bit or 64-bit code is to maintain backward compatibility with the original IBM PC running MSDOS.

The remaining entries for FAT32 are summarized in Table 6.4.

The FAT32 specific part of the first sector in the VBR begins with three 4-byte fields for hidden sectors, total sectors (if more than 65,535), and sectors per FAT, respectively. The next item, mirror flag, is new. If bit 7 in this field is set, then only one FAT is in use and the lowest four bits (bits 0-3) designated the active FAT. I have never seen this feature be utilized. A filesystem version follows the mirror flag.

Because the FAT12 and FAT16 VBRs are one sector long and needed to boot the system from a partition, they are often referred to as boot sectors. Even though the FAT32 VBR is more than one sector long, it too is sometimes called a boot sector. To further confuse the issue, others mean only the first sector of the VBR when referring to the FAT32 boot sector. As if that were not bad enough, some will use the FAT32 boot sector to indicate the first two sectors in the VBR.

Because the root directory has been moved to the data clusters, its location must be stored in the VBR. Given that the root directory is created when the partition is formated, the directory is almost always stored in the first available cluster (cluster 2). The next two fields describe the location of two new elements that were added in FAT32, the Filesystem Information (FSINFO) block sector and backup boot sector, respectively. Theses sectors are relative to the start of the VBR. The most common values are 1 and 6 for the FSINFO block and backup boot sector, respectively. The FSINFO block will be described later in this section.

As with FAT12 and FAT16, the FAT32 VBR contains a logical drive number, extended boot signature, bootstrap code, and the standard signature of 0x55 0xAA at the end of the first sector. The logical drive number and extended boot signature have the same format regardless of the version of FAT in use. There are only 420 bytes available for bootstrap code in the first sector of a FAT32 VBR. There is another sector available for additional bootstrap code, but I have never seen it be used.

Table 6.4. FAT32 specific entries in the first VBR sector.

Offset	Length	Item
28 (0x1C)	4 (0x04)	Hidden sectors (preceding this partition)
32 (0x20)	4 (0x04)	Filesystem sectors if over 32MB (64k sectors)
36 (0x24)	4 (0x04)	Sectors/FAT
40 (0x28)	2 (0x02)	Mirror Flag (b7=1 single FAT then b0-3 tell which)
42 (0x2A)	2 (0x02)	Filesystem version
44 (0x2C)	4 (0x04)	First cluster of root directory (probably 2)
48 (0x30)	2 (0x02)	FSINFO sector number in reserved area (probably 1)
50 (0x32)	2 (0x02)	Backup boot sector number in reserved area (usually 6)
64 (0x40)	1 (0x01)	Logical drive (0x80, 0x81, ...)
66 (0x42)	24 (0x18)	Extended boot signature (same as FAT12/FAT16)
90 (0x5A)	420 (0x1A4)	Bootstrap code
510 (0x1FE)	2 (0x02)	Signature (0x55 0xAA)

Table 6.5. The Filesystem Information block.

Offset	Length	Item
0 (0x00)	4 (0x4)	Signature RRaA
484 (0x1E4)	4 (0x04)	Start marker rrAa
488 (0x1E8)	4 (0x04)	Free clusters (0xFFFFFFFF = unknown)
492 (0x1EC)	4 (0x04)	Last allocated cluster (0xFFFFFFFF = unknown)
508 (0x1FC)	4 (0x04)	Signature (0x00 0x00 0x55 0xAA)

The Filesystem Information (FSINFO) block was introduced with FAT32. Normally the FSINFO block is found in the second sector of the VBR. The FSINFO block is summarized in Table 6.5.

As can be seen from Table 6.5, the FSINFO block is mostly empty. The main reason this was added was to speed up cluster allocations. By knowing how many free clusters are available the operating system can determine how likely contiguous clusters will be available to store a new file. If the last allocated cluster is known, it serves as a good starting point to look for free space for a new file as most filesystems are filled from low to high clusters. The information stored in the FSINFO block is not authoritative and is used solely for improving performance.

Examining the VBR in Active@ Disk Editor

The VBR for a FAT filesystem is shown in Figure 6.8. Interpreting the jump instruction (0xEB 0x58 0x90) we see that it calls for a short jump ahead 0x58 bytes. The 0x90 is a no-operation (NOP) instruction used for padding. If the jump were not there, execution would continue at position 0x02. Adding 0x02 to 0x58 yields 0x5A which should be the position of our boot code. According to ADE the bootstrap code does in fact begin at position 0x5A.

The next block (highlighted in green) contains the OEM name of "MSDOS5.0". As previously mentioned, this indicates the filesystem was created by Windows XP. The next block (highlighted in yellow) contains the essential BIOS parameters that are needed to read the

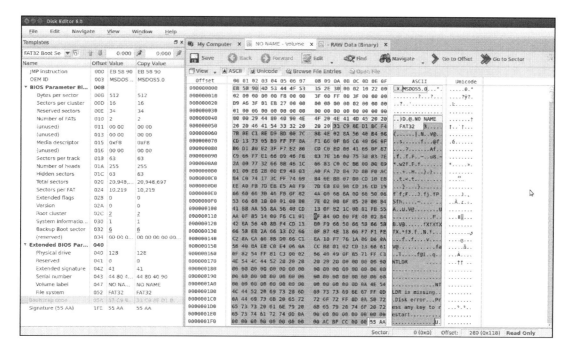

FIGURE 6.8.

Examining a FAT VBR in Active@ Disk Editor.

CHAPTER 6 FAT Filesystems

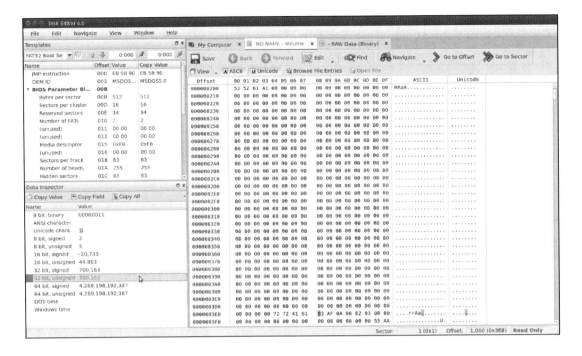

FIGURE 6.9.

Examining the FSINFO block in Active@ Disk Editor.

partition. From this block we can see that we have standard 512-byte sectors with 16 sectors per cluster, 34 reserved sectors (sectors before the first FAT), 63 hidden sectors (sectors before this partition), 20,948,697 total sectors, 10,219 sectors per FAT, the root directory is in cluster 2 as expected, the FSINFO block is in the following sector, and the backup boot sector is in the sixth VBR sector as anticipated.

The extended BIOS parameter block (highlighted in magenta) indicates that this is the first drive (128 or 0x80), an extended signature is present (field is 41 or 0x29), the serial number is 0x44 0x80 0x40 0x90, there is no volume label, and this is likely a FAT32 filesystem. Recall that the human readable filesystem in the extended BIOS parameter block is not authoritative. The sector ends with the correct signature (0x55 0xAA). Note that ADE also displays values found in the backup boot sector.

The FSINFO block is shown in Figure 6.9. Using the data interpreter we see that there are 700,163 free clusters on this disk. As shown in Figure 6.10 the last allocated cluster was 994. Recall that this information is not authoritative.

Interpreting the VBR with Python

The ability to interpret the VBR with Python can be extremely useful. At first it may not appear to be worth the effort. Where the real value is found in creating the VBR parsing code is having the ability to locate other items in a FAT filesystem such as the FATs, root directory, clusters, etc. Before any of these tasks can be performed the VBR must be properly read. The following code will read a FAT VBR.

```
#!/usr/bin/python3
# This is a simple Python script that will
# attempt to read VBR(s) from an image file.
# Developed for PentesterAcademy by Dr. Phil Polstra

import struct
import sys
import os.path
from mbr import Mbr

__all__=['Vbr']

class Vbr:
    def __init__(self, buffer):
        self.getVbr(buffer)

    def jumpCode(self):
        return self._vbrTuple[0]

    def oemName(self):
        return self._vbrTuple[1]

    def bytesPerSector(self):
        return self._vbrTuple[2]

    def sectorsPerCluster(self):
        return self._vbrTuple[3]

    def reservedSectors(self):
        return self._vbrTuple[4]

    def copiesOfFat(self):
        return self._vbrTuple[5]

    def rootDirectoryEntries(self):
        return self._vbrTuple[6]

    def totalSectors(self):
        if self._vbrTuple[7]==0:
            return self._vbrTuple[13]
        else:
            return self._vbrTuple[7]
```

```python
def mediaDescriptor(self):
    return self._vbrTuple[8]

def sectorsPerFat(self):
    if self._vbrTuple[9]==0:
        return self._vbrTuple[14]
    else:
        return self._vbrTuple[9]

def sectorsPerTrack(self):
    return self._vbrTuple[10]

def heads(self):
    return self._vbrTuple[11]

def hiddenSectors(self):
    return self._vbrTuple[12]

def mirrorFlags(self):
    return self._vbrTuple[15]

def filesystemVersion(self):
    if self._fat32:
        return self._vbrTuple[16]
    else:
        return None

def rootDirectoryCluster(self):
    if self._fat32:
        return self._vbrTuple[17]
    else:
        return None

def fsinfoSector(self):
    if self._fat32:
        return self._vbrTuple[18]
    else:
        return None

def backupBootSector(self):
    if self._fat32:
        return self._vbrTuple[19]
    else:
        return None
```

```python
def logicalDrive(self):
    if self._fat32:
        return self._vbrTuple[21]
    else:
        return self._vbrTuple[14]

def serialNumber(self):
    if self._fat32:
        return self._vbrTuple[24]
    else:
        return self._vbrTuple[17]

def volumeLabel(self):
    if self._fat32:
        return self._vbrTuple[25]
    else:
        return self._vbrTuple[18]

def filesystemType(self):
    if self._fat32:
        return self._vbrTuple[26]
    else:
        return self._vbrTuple[19]

def bootCode(self):
    if self._fat32:
        return self._vbrTuple[27]
    else:
        return self._vbrTuple[20]

def validSignature(self):
    if self._fat32:
        return self._vbrTuple[28]==b'\x55\xAA'
    else:
        return self._vbrTuple[21]==b'\x55\xAA'

def isFat32(self):
    return self._fat32

def mirrorFlags(self):
    if self._fat32:
        return self._vbrTuple[15]
    else:
        return None
```

CHAPTER 6 FAT Filesystems

```
def sectorFromCluster(self, cluster):
   '''Given a cluster number returns a sector number
   relative to the start of the volume.  The sector
   for cluster 2 is first calculated'''
   sector=(self.copiesOfFat()*self.sectorsPerFat()+
      self.reservedSectors()+
      self.rootDirectoryEntries()//16) #FAT12/16
   sector+=(cluster-2)*self.sectorsPerCluster()
   return sector

def offsetFromCluster(self, cluster):
   '''Gives offset within volume image for a given
   cluster number'''
   return (self.bytesPerSector()
            * self.sectorFromCluster(cluster))

def clusterFromSector(self, sector):
   cluster=(sector-self.copiesOfFat()
         * self.sectorsPerFat()-
      self.reservedSectors()-
      self.rootDirectoryEntries()//16)//(
      self.sectorsPerCluster())+2
   return cluster

def clusterFromOffset(self, offset):
   return self.clusterFromSector(offset//
            self.bytesPerSector())

def sectorFat1(self):
   return self.reservedSectors()

def sectorFat2(self):
   return self.reservedSectors()+self.sectorsPerFat()

def getVbr(self, buffer):
   # first 28 bytes are common to all formats
   fmtStart=('<3s' + # 0 jump to bootstrap
      '8s' +  # 1 OEM name
      'H' +   # 2 bytes/sector
      'B' +   # 3 sectors/cluster
      'H' +   # 4 reserved sectors
      'B' +   # 5 copies of FAT
      'H' +   # 6 root directory entries (0 for FAT32)
      'H' +   # 7 total number of sectors if <32MB
      'B' +   # 8 media descriptor (F8 or F0)
```

```
                    'H' +   # 9 sectors/FAT for FAT12/16 or 0 for FAT32
                    'H' +   # 10 sectors per track
                    'H' )   # 11 number of heads
            fmt32=(         # The end part for FAT32
                 'I' +   # 12 hidden sectors
                 'I' +   # 13 total number of sectors if >32MB
                 'I' +   # 14 sectors/FAT for FAT32
                 'H' +   # 15 mirror flags B7=1 single FAT in B0-3
                 'H' +   # 16 filesystem version
                 'I' +   # 17 root directory cluster (normally 2)
                 'H' +   # 18 FSINFO sector (usually 1)
                 'H' +   # 19 backup boot sector (usually 6)
                 '12s' +# 20 reserved
                 'B' +   # 21 logical drive (0x80, 0x81, etc)
                 's' +   # 22 reserved
                 'B' +   # 23 if 0x29 next 3 fields are present
                 '4s' +  # 24 serial number
                 '11s' +# 25 volume label
                 '8s' +  # 26 filesystem type as string
                 '420s'+# 27 boot code
                 '2s')   # 28 should be 0x55 0xaa
            fmt1216=(   # The end part for FAT12/16
                 'I' +  # 12 Number of hidden sectors
                 'I' +  # 13 Total number of sectors (>32MB)
                 'B' +  # 14 Logical drive number (0x80, 0x81,...)
                 'B' +  # 15 Unused
                 'B' +  # 16 Extended boot signature (0x29).
                 '4s' +# 17 Serial number of partition
                 '11s'+# 18 Volume Label or "No Name"
                 '8s' +# 19 File system type (FAT12, etc.)
                 '448s'+# 20 Bootstrap
                 '2s') # 21 Signature 0x55 0xAA
            # is this FAT32? If reserved sectors !=1 ->FAT32
            self._fat32=(struct.unpack('<H', buffer[14:16])!=1)
            if self._fat32:
                fmt = fmtStart + fmt32
            else:
                fmt = fmtStart + fmt1216

            self._vbrTuple=struct.unpack(fmt, buffer)


def usage():
    print("usage " + sys.argv[0] + " <image file>\n"+
        "Reads VBR(s) from an image file")
    exit(1)
```

```python
def main():
    if len(sys.argv) < 2:
      usage()

    notsupParts = [0x05,0x0f,0x85,0x91,0x9b,0xc5,0xe4,0xee]
    swapParts = [0x42, 0x82, 0xb8, 0xc3, 0xfc]

    # read first sector
    if not os.path.isfile(sys.argv[1]):
       print("File " + sys.argv[1] +
             " cannot be openned for reading")
       exit(1)

    with open(sys.argv[1], 'rb') as f:
       sector = f.read(512)

    mbr=Mbr(sector) # create MBR object

    if mbr.validSignature():
       print("Looks like a MBR or VBR")
       mbr.prettyPrint()

       for i in range(1,5):
          if not mbr.isEmpty(i):
             if mbr.partitionType(i) in notsupParts:
                print("Sorry GPT and extended partitions" +
                      " are not supported by this script!")
             else:
                if mbr.partitionType(i) in swapParts:
                   print("Skipping swap partition")
                else:
                   # let's try and read the VBR
                   with open(sys.argv[1], 'rb') as f:
                      f.seek(mbr.reservedSectors(i)*512)
                      sector=f.read(512)
                      vbr=Vbr(sector)
                      if vbr.validSignature():
                         print('Found Volume with type',
                               vbr.filesystemType())
                         print('Volume label:', vbr.volumeLabel())
                         print('Total sectors:', vbr.totalSectors())
                         s=vbr.sectorFromCluster(14)
                         print('Cluster 14:', s)
                         print('Sector:', vbr.clusterFromSector(s))
```

```
        else:
            print("Doesn't appear to contain valid MBR")

if __name__ == "__main__":
    main()
```

This file has many similarities with the previous mbr.py script. We begin by importing a few modules. The line `from mbr import Mbr` is new. This line imports the Mbr class from the previous script using a different form of import which allows you to import only part of a module and also frees you from having to prefix all function calls with the module name and period.

Lazy programmers that want to import everything from a module using this alternate syntax can use `from <module> import *`. By default this will import everything from a module. However, the module programmer can override this behavior by creating a list named __all__ that lists all of the items that should be exported. For example, in this script the line __all__=['Vbr'] causes only the Vbr class (and not the main and usage functions) to be exported.

The Vbr class constructor simply calls the getVbr helper method which builds a format string and uses struct.unpack to intrepret the VBR and store its fields in a tuple. Three strings are defined in this method fmtStart, fmt32, and fmt1216, which apply to the common 28 bytes at the start, remaining fields for FAT32, and remaining fields for FAT12 or FAT16, respectively. The code for getVbr follows.

```
    def getVbr(self, buffer):
        # first 28 bytes are common to all formats
        fmtStart=('<3s' +  # 0 jump to bootstrap
            '8s' +   # 1 OEM name
            'H' +    # 2 bytes/sector
            'B' +    # 3 sectors/cluster
            'H' +    # 4 reserved sectors
            'B' +    # 5 copies of FAT
            'H' +    # 6 root directory entries (0 for FAT32)
            'H' +    # 7 total number of sectors if <32MB
            'B' +    # 8 media descriptor (F8 or F0)
            'H' +    # 9 sectors/FAT for FAT12/16 or 0 for FAT32
            'H' +    # 10 sectors per track
            'H' )    # 11 number of heads
        fmt32=(          # The end part for FAT32
            'I' +    # 12 hidden sectors
            'I' +    # 13 total number of sectors if >32MB
            'I' +    # 14 sectors/FAT for FAT32
            'H' +    # 15 mirror flags B7=1 single FAT in B0-3
            'H' +    # 16 filesystem version
            'I' +    # 17 root directory cluster (normally 2)
            'H' +    # 18 FSINFO sector (usually 1)
```

```
            'H' +   # 19 backup boot sector (usually 6)
            '12s' +# 20 reserved
            'B' +   # 21 logical drive (0x80, 0x81, etc)
            's' +   # 22 reserved
            'B' +   # 23 if 0x29 next 3 fields are present
            '4s' +  # 24 serial number
            '11s' +# 25 volume label
            '8s' +  # 26 filesystem type as string
            '420s'+# 27 boot code
            '2s')   # 28 should be 0x55 0xaa
        fmt1216=(   # The end part for FAT12/16
            'I' +   # 12 Number of hidden sectors
            'I' +   # 13 Total number of sectors (>32MB)
            'B' +   # 14 Logical drive number (0x80, 0x81,...)
            'B' +   # 15 Unused
            'B' +   # 16 Extended boot signature (0x29).
            '4s' +# 17 Serial number of partition
            '11s'+# 18 Volume Label or "No Name"
            '8s' +# 19 File system type (FAT12, etc.)
            '448s'+# 20 Bootstrap
            '2s') # 21 Signature 0x55 0xAA
        # is this FAT32?  If reserved sectors !=1 ->FAT32
        self._fat32=(struct.unpack('<H', buffer[14:16])!=1)
        if self._fat32:
            fmt = fmtStart + fmt32
        else:
            fmt = fmtStart + fmt1216

        self._vbrTuple=struct.unpack(fmt, buffer)
```

The bulk of the Vbr class consists of accessors which primarily return items from the tuple stored in the class. Note that for items that occur after the common entries at the beginning of the VBR, the code will select the appropriate tuple item based on whether or not the filesystem is FAT32. For FAT12 and FAT16 filesystems the value None is returned for values that only pertain to FAT32.

Several useful functions are also defined for calculating a sector from a cluster, offset from a cluster, cluster from a sector, cluster from an offset, and starting sector for each FAT. These functions will be used in later scripts. In fact, all of the later scripts from FAT filesystems rely on these methods.

The main function starts the same as that from the mbr.py script. The only thing that has been added is an attempt to read in a VBR and perform a few simple tests. Note that the filesystem type has not been checked in this simple script so if it is run against an image containing anything other than FAT partitions, it will likely fail. The main function code follows.

```python
def main():
   if len(sys.argv) < 2:
      usage()

   notsupParts = [0x05,0x0f,0x85,0x91,0x9b,0xc5,0xe4,0xee]
   swapParts = [0x42, 0x82, 0xb8, 0xc3, 0xfc]

   # read first sector
   if not os.path.isfile(sys.argv[1]):
      print("File " + sys.argv[1] +
            " cannot be openned for reading")
      exit(1)

   with open(sys.argv[1], 'rb') as f:
      sector = f.read(512)

   mbr=Mbr(sector) # create MBR object

   if mbr.validSignature():
      print("Looks like a MBR or VBR")
      mbr.prettyPrint()

      for i in range(1,5):
         if not mbr.isEmpty(i):
            if mbr.partitionType(i) in notsupParts:
               print("Sorry GPT and extended partitions" +
                     " are not supported by this script!")
            else:
               if mbr.partitionType(i) in swapParts:
                  print("Skipping swap partition")
               else:
                  # let's try and read the VBR
                  with open(sys.argv[1], 'rb') as f:
                     f.seek(mbr.reservedSectors(i)*512)
                     sector=f.read(512)
                     vbr=Vbr(sector)
                     if vbr.validSignature():
                        print('Found Volume with type',
                              vbr.filesystemType())
                        print('Volume label:', vbr.volumeLabel())
                        print('Total sectors:', vbr.totalSectors())
                        s=vbr.sectorFromCluster(14)
                        print('Cluster 14:', s)
                        print('Sector:', vbr.clusterFromSector(s))
   else:
      print("Doesn't appear to contain valid MBR")
```

FILE ALLOCATION TABLES

The FAT filesystem gets its name from the file allocation table(s) it uses. Each cluster has an entry in the FAT. The entries for clusters 0 and 1 have a special meaning. Cluster 2 is the first data cluster on a FAT filesystem. FAT12, FAT16, and FAT32 have 12-bit (1.5-byte), 16-bit (2-byte), and 32-bit (4-byte) entries in the FAT, respectively.

A value of zero in a cluster's FAT entry indicates that the cluster is unallocated (available). A value of 2 through the highest cluster number on the filesystem indicates that a cluster is in use and whatever is stored there continues to the indicated cluster. An end-of-file (EOF) marker in a cluster's FAT entry indicates that the cluster is in use and whatever is stored in the cluster (file or directory) ends in the cluster. The EOF marker for FAT12, FAT16, and FAT32 is 0xFFF, 0xFFFF, and 0x0FFFFFFF, respectively. The list of clusters that comprise a file or directory is referred to as a cluster chain because of the way the FAT must be traversed in order to retrieve a file or directory.

A special value is used to indicate a bad cluster. The bad cluster value for FAT12, FAT16, and FAT32 is 0xFF7, 0xFFF7, and 0x0FFFFFF7, respectively. Because most modern media handle bad sectors in hardware, it is rare to find bad clusters in the FAT. If you find clusters marked as bad in the FAT, you should examine the clusters to ensure someone is not attempting to hide data. Technically the end of file is indicated by a value from the bad cluster value plus one through the values listed in the preceding paragraph, but I have yet to see a FAT filesystem that did not use the highest value in this range (the one ending in F).

Finding the location of a FAT entry for FAT16 and FAT32 filesystems is very simple. The offset from the start of the FAT is simply (cluster number) * (FAT entry size). For example, cluster 500 in a FAT32 filesystem has its FAT entry 500 * 4 or 2000 bytes from the start of the FAT.

Things are slightly more complicated with FAT12 thanks to each entry being one and a half bytes long. FAT entries for a FAT12 filesystem are most easily read in three byte chunks. The start of the chunk is at (cluster number) // 2 * 3 bytes from the start of the FAT. Here // is used to indicate integer division. The entries are coded as follows: 0xBC 0xFA 0xDE, which corresponds to 0xABC and 0xDEF for the left and right entries, respectively. Even clusters use the left entry and odd clusters use the right one. Notice that the nybbles in the middle byte cross over each other and go to the outside. You may never encounter a FAT12 filesystem, but if you do, you now know how to read them.

As previously stated, the first two entries in the FAT have special meanings. The very first byte in the FAT contains a media descriptor which should match the one found in the VBR. This should be 0xF0 for a 3.5 inch floppy disk and 0xF8 for virtually everything else. The cluster 1 entry normally has the value 0xFFF, 0x7FFF, or 0xFFFFFFFF for FAT12, FAT16, and FAT32, respectively.

Examining the FAT in Active@ Disk Editor

Examining the FAT in ADE is as simple as opening an image and using the Navigate button to go to a FAT as shown in Figure 6.11. If you did not already know that this was a FAT32 filesystem, the fact that all of the values are clearly aligned on 4-byte boundaries should make that apparent. The start of a 12-bit FAT is shown in Figure 6.12. Note how this FAT only

File Allocation Tables

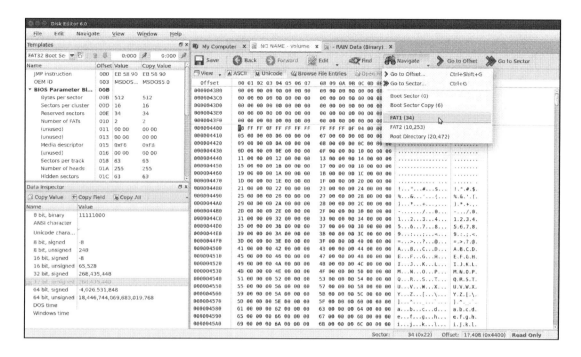

FIGURE 6.11.
Examining a FAT in Active@ Disk Editor.

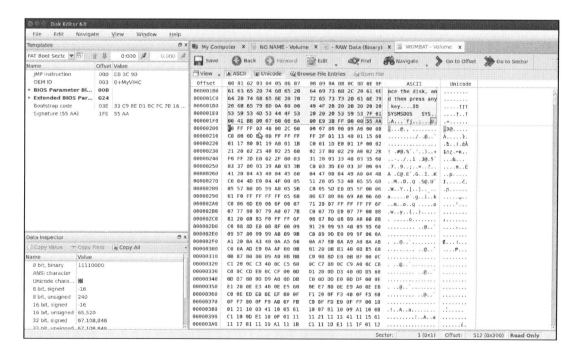

FIGURE 6.12.
A 12-bit FAT in Active@ Disk Editor.

148 CHAPTER 6 FAT Filesystems

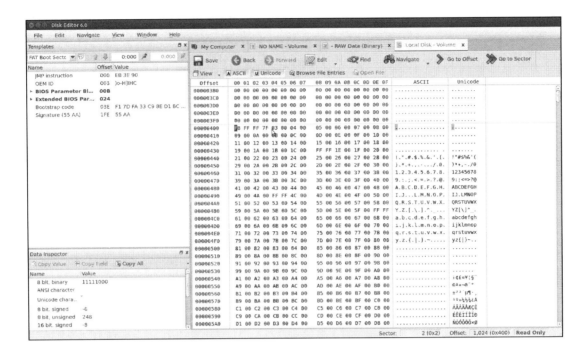

FIGURE 6.13.

A 16-bit FAT in Active@ Disk Editor.

makes sense when examined in three byte chunks. Using the algorithm presented above and the values in positions 03-05 (0x03 0x40 0x00) we see that file that the begins in cluster 2, continues in cluster 3 (left entry), and then in cluster 4 (right entry). A 16-bit FAT is shown in Figure 6.13.

Interpreting the FAT with Python

Interpreting FAT entries and chasing cluster chains is very tedious for all but the smallest of files. This is a good place to use a little Python. The following script creates a Fat class which will prove useful in future scripts.

```
#!/usr/bin/python3
# This is a simple Python script that will
# attempt to read FAT entries from an image file.
# Developed for PentesterAcademy by Dr. Phil Polstra

import struct
import sys
import os.path
from mbr import Mbr
from vbr import Vbr
```

```python
__all__=['Fat']

class Fat:
    def __init__(self, buffer):
        # determine FAT type
        if buffer[1:8]==b'\xFF\xFF\x0F\xFF\xFF\xFF\xFF':
            self._fatBits=32
        elif buffer[1:4]==b'\xFF\xFF\x7F':
            self._fatBits=16
        else:
            self._fatBits=12
        self._fat=buffer

    def fatBits(self):
        return self._fatBits

    def fatEntry(self, cluster):
        if cluster==None:
            return None
        if self._fatBits==32:
            return struct.unpack('<I',self._fat[cluster*4:cluster*4+4])[0]
        elif self._fatBits==16:
            return struct.unpack('<H',self._fat[cluster*2:cluster*2+2])[0]
        else:
            offset=(cluster//2)*3
            if cluster%2==0: # left entry
                return (struct.unpack('<B',self._fat[offset:offset+1])[0]+
                    256*struct.unpack('<B', self._fat[offset+1:offset+2])[0]%16)
            else: # right entry
                return (struct.unpack('<B', self._fat[offset+2:offset+3])[0]*16+
                    struct.unpack('<B', self._fat[offset+1:offset+2])[0]//16)

    def isAllocated(self, cluster):
        if cluster:
            return self.fatEntry(cluster)!=0
        else:
            return False

    def nextCluster(self, cluster):
        if cluster==None:
            return None
        retVal=self.fatEntry(cluster)
        # is this the end of the chain?
        if (retVal==0 or
            (self._fatBits==32 and retVal==0x0FFFFFFF) or
```

150 CHAPTER 6 FAT Filesystems

```python
                (self._fatBits==16 and retVal==0xFFFF) or
                (self._fatBits==12 and retVal==0xFFF)):
                return None
            else:
                return retVal

    def isEnd(self, cluster):
        return self.nextCluster(cluster)==None

    def clusterChain(self, cluster):
        '''Given a starting cluster, this function
        returns a list of clusters that make up a
        cluster chain.'''
        chain=[]
        nextC=cluster
        while self.isAllocated(nextC):
            chain.append(nextC)
            nextC=self.nextCluster(nextC)
        return chain

def usage():
    print("usage " + sys.argv[0] + " <image file>\n"+
        "Reads FAT Entries from an image file")
    exit(1)

def main():
    if len(sys.argv) < 2:
        usage()

    notsupParts = [0x05, 0x0f, 0x85, 0x91, 0x9b, 0xc5, 0xe4, 0xee]
    swapParts = [0x42, 0x82, 0xb8, 0xc3, 0xfc]

    # read first sector
    if not os.path.isfile(sys.argv[1]):
        print("File " + sys.argv[1] + " cannot be openned for reading")
        exit(1)

    with open(sys.argv[1], 'rb') as f:
        sector = f.read(512)

    mbr=Mbr(sector) # create MBR object

    if mbr.validSignature():
        print("Looks like a MBR or VBR")
        mbr.prettyPrint()
```

```
        for i in range(1,5):
            if not mbr.isEmpty(i):
                if mbr.partitionType(i) in notsupParts:
                    print("Sorry GPT and extended partitions "
                        "are not supported by this script!")
                else:
                    if mbr.partitionType(i) in swapParts:
                        print("Skipping swap partition")
                    else:
                        # let's try and read the VBR
                        with open(sys.argv[1], 'rb') as f:
                            f.seek(mbr.reservedSectors(i)*512)
                            sector=f.read(512)
                            vbr=Vbr(sector)
                            if vbr.validSignature():
                              print('Found Volume with type', vbr.filesystemType())
                                print('Volume label:', vbr.volumeLabel())
                                print('Total sectors:', vbr.totalSectors())
                                s=vbr.sectorFromCluster(14)
                                print('Cluster 14:', s)
                                print('Sector:', vbr.clusterFromSector(s))
                                # grab the FAT
                                f.seek(mbr.reservedSectors(i)*512+
                                    vbr.sectorFat1()*512)
                                fatRaw=f.read(512*vbr.sectorsPerFat())
                                fat=Fat(fatRaw)
                              print('Cluster 3 allocated:',fat.isAllocated(3))
                              print('Chain starting at 3:',fat.clusterChain(3))
        else:
            print("Doesn't appear to contain valid MBR")

if __name__ == "__main__":
    main()
```

The Fat constructor examines the first few bytes of the FAT in order to determine if it is FAT12, FAT16, or FAT32. The correct number of bits for the FAT is stored in the _fatBits class variable. Recall that an underscore before a function or variable name is a polite request to not access it directly from outside of the class.

The fatEntry method simply returns the FAT entry for a given cluster. First a sanity check is performed to ensure that a cluster number was given. Then our old friend struct.unpack is used to return a value for the FAT entry. The code for FAT32 and FAT16 is straightforward. The situation for FAT12 is a bit more complicated. First, the offset to a 3 byte chunk is calculated on the line `offset=(cluster//2)*3`. Second, a check is made to determine if the cluster number is even in which case the left entry pertains to the cluster on the line `if cluster%2==0:`. If this is the case, %16 (modulus 16) is applied to the middle byte to isolate the low nybble, then the resulting value is multiplied by 256 and added to the first byte. If the cluster number is odd (else clause), the third byte in the chunk is shifted one nybble to the left by multiplying its value by 16, then the high nybble of the center byte is isolated by applying //16 (integer division by 16) and that value is added to the last byte.

The remaining methods in Fat use fatEntry. The isAllocated method simply checks to see if a FAT entry is non-zero. The nextCluster method retrieves a FAT entry and returns it if the entry is not equal to an EOF marker. The isEnd method uses nextCluster to test for the existence of another cluster in the chain. Finally, the clusterChain method first creates an empty list and then uses a while loop to walk through a cluster chain until the end is reached while adding clusters to the list.

The main function is the same as that for the vbr.py script with a few lines added to check some of the Fat methods. The new lines are as follows:

```
# grab the FAT
f.seek(mbr.reservedSectors(i)*512+
vbr.sectorFat1()*512)
fatRaw=f.read(512*vbr.sectorsPerFat())
fat=Fat(fatRaw)
print('Cluster 3 allocated:',fat.isAllocated(3))
print('Chain starting at 3:',fat.clusterChain(3))
```

DIRECTORIES

With the possible exception of the root directory (FAT12 and FAT16 only), FAT directories are stored in the data clusters. Entries in FAT directories are 32 bytes long which means that a standard 512-byte sector can store 16 directory entries. Initially only short 8.3 filenames were supported which consisted of up to 8 characters for the filename and 3 characters for the file extension (type). Later Microsoft introduced a kludge that allows longer filenames to be supported.

Short filenames

The short filename directory entry is summarized in Table 6.6.

The first field is the filename. Note that there are eight characters for the base name and three for the extension. The period separating the base name and extension is implied, not stored. If there is an extension, the period is automatically inserted into the filename.

The second entry in a FAT directory record stores the file attributes. These are stored in a bit vector where a 1 in a bit indicates that attribute is present. Only bits 0 through 5 are used and the top two bits must always be zero. The meaning of the bits 0 through 5 in ascending order are read-only, hidden, system, volume label, directory, and archive. The hidden attribute causes a file to be omitted from directory listings unless defaults have been changed. This is often combined with the system attribute to prevent users from tampering with system files which can break their systems. The volume label, if one exists, is normally found in the first entry of

Table 6.6. FAT directory entry (short filename).

Offset	Length	Item
0 (0x00)	11 (0x0B)	File name
11 (0x0B)	1 (0x01)	Attributes
14 (0x0E)	4 (0x04)	Creation Time & Date
18 (0x12)	2 (0x02)	Last Access Date (no time)
20 (0x14)	2 (0x02)	Starting cluster high word (FAT32)
22 (0x16)	4 (0x04)	Modified Time & Date
26 (0x1A)	2 (0x02)	Starting cluster low word
28 (0x1C)	4 (0x04)	File size in bytes (0 for directories)

the root directory. If it exists, it should match the volume label in the VBR. The archive bit is set whenever a file is changed. The idea of this attribute is to speed up backups of a filesystem as the backup software could tell what has changed since the previous backup, assuming that the software clears this flag after backing up a file.

The creation time and date follows the attributes. Something to keep in mind with any FAT timestamps is that these fields are not required to be populated. The FAT filesystem is used by many small devices and operating systems other than DOS/Windows. The specification defines these fields but does not require them to be updated. The format for times and dates is summarized in Figure 6.14.

As can be seen from Figure 6.14, times are stored as 2-byte values with a 2 second resolution. The minute value spans the two bytes. The reason for only two seconds of resolution is that anything higher would require an additional bit which would increase the size on disk to three bytes. Remember that the FAT filesystem was developed decades ago when disk space was at a premium.

As shown in Figure 6.14, dates are stored as 2-byte values in FAT directories. The month value spans the two bytes. Years are stored as an offset from 1980. This essentially makes the DOS epoch January 1, 1980 (in contrast to the Unix/Linux epoch of January 1, 1970).

The last access date follows the creation time and date in a directory entry. Note that there is no time in this field. There are a few likely reasons why this is so. First, the write times for old media such as floppy disks is slow enough that constantly updating access times in directories would be pretty painful. Second, space was at a premium when this system was first developed.

We have previously discussed the workings of the file allocation table and how it can be used to trace a cluster chain. The directory entry stores the starting cluster for each file or

	Bits	Length (bits)	Item
Time	B11-B15	5	Hours
Time	B5-B10	6	Minutes
Time	B0-B4	5	Double seconds
Date	B9-B15	7	Years since 1980
Date	B5-B8	4	Month
Date	B0-B4	5	Day

FIGURE 6.14.

FAT times and dates.

directory. In other words, it tells you where the cluster chain starts. The high word (two bytes) follows the last access date in a directory entry. For FAT12 and FAT16 this value will be zero as it is unneeded.

The last three fields in a directory record are the modified time and date, starting cluster low word, and the file size in bytes. As a reminder, just because the modification timestamp field exists, that does not mean it is updated. For directories the file size is reported as zero.

With the exception of the root directory, every directory on a filesystem is a subdirectory. All of these subdirectories begin with two special entries: "." and "..". The first entry ("." or dot) is a reference to the current directory. The second entry (".." or dot dot) refers to the parent directory. While these two entries do consume space, they speed up directory traversal and reduce the workload on the CPU.

Long filenames

The ability to handle longer filenames was added in Windows 95. These long filename entries are also 32 bytes long. These entries contain no metadata (timestamps, attributes, size, etc.), only filename chunks. Whereas 8.3 filenames are stored in ASCII, long filenames are stored in Unicode. Long filename entries grow upward from (come before) the corresponding short filename entry. Long filename entries are summarized in Table 6.7.

The sequence number is used to ensure that the entries are being interpreted properly and also indicate the final long filename chunk. Only bits 0-4 are for the chunk sequence number. Bit 6 (0x40) is used to indicate the final chunk. For example, a file that had a long filename requiring two chunks of storage would have a sequence number of 0x01 for the first chunk (just

Table 6.7. Long filename directory entries.

Offset	Length	Item
0 (0x00)	1 (0x1)	Sequence number B0-B4; B6(0x40)=final part
1 (0x01)	10 (0x0A)	Part of filename in Unicode
11 (0x0B)	2 (0x02)	Always 0x0F 0x00
13 (0x0D)	1 (0x01)	Checksum for short filename
14 (0x0E)	12 (0x0C)	Part of filename in Unicode
26 (0x1A)	2 (0x02)	Always 0x00 0x00
28 (0x1C)	4 (0x04)	Part of filename in Unicode

before the short filename entry) and a sequence number of 0x42 for the last chunk (just before the first chunk).

The first 5 characters (10 bytes in Unicode) begin at offset 1 in the entry. Following this is two bytes which must be 0x0f and 0x00. In the short entry the first byte is used to store attributes, and if this byte were interpreted as an attribute, it would correspond to a read-only, hidden, system, volume label, which makes absolutely no sense. This serves as extra protection against the entry being misinterpreted.

Position 13 (0x0D) in a long filename entry contains a checksum for the short filename entry. This is a double check to ensure that long filename entries are consistent and applied to the correct file. In position 14 another 6 characters (12 bytes in Unicode) of the filename are stored. This is followed by the value 0x00 0x00 at position 26 (0x1A). The starting cluster low word is stored in this position in a short filename entry. In the case of FAT12 or FAT16 having a zero in this field is invalid. The long filename entry ends with two more characters of the filename. Each chunk can store up to 13 characters (5 + 6 + 2) of the filename.

What happens when a file is deleted from a FAT filesystem? The first byte in any directory entries associated with the file is changed to 0xE5. This is a marker used by DOS/Windows to indicate that a directory entry may be reused. The clusters are marked as available (but not cleared) in the FATs. Depending on the version of Windows, the starting cluster high word may be zeroed out for FAT32 filesystems. This can make recovering deleted files from FAT32 volumes somewhat challenging. The process for recovering deleted files is presented later in this chapter.

CHAPTER 6 FAT Filesystems

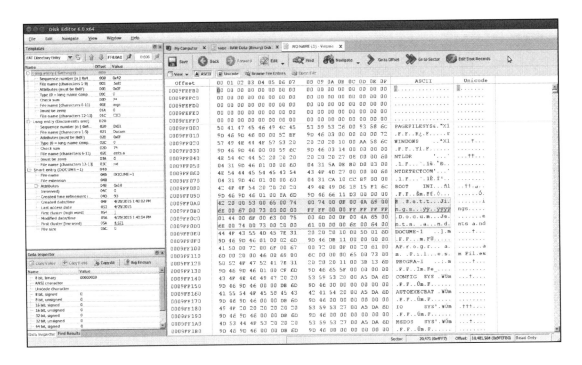

FIGURE 6.15.
Examining a directory with a long filename in Active@ Disk Editor.

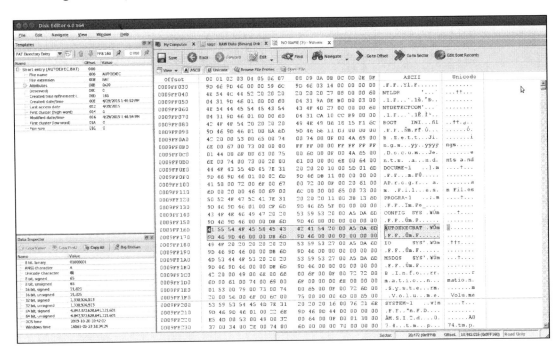

FIGURE 6.16.
Active@ Disk Editor skipping entries when navigating a directory with long filenames.

Examining directories in Active@ Disk Editor

Active@ Disk Editor includes a template for examining FAT directory entries. The template supports both long and short filename entries. A directory entry for a subdirectory with a long filename is shown in Figure 6.15. Notice that the short filename (the one with all the metadata) appears last and that the long filename entries with sequence numbers 0x01 and 0x42 grow upward from this entry as described previously in this chapter.

As can be seen in Figure 6.15, some of the Unicode filename chunks are not displayed correctly in the Unicode column in ADE. The reason for this is that the sequence number at the start of these entries causes Unicode strings to start on an odd offset. All hex editors, including ADE, will assume Unicode values begin at even offsets. Note that the last long filename entry contains a Unicode null (0x00 0x00) and the remaining unused space is filled with the value 0xFF 0xFF. This is common.

ADE provides up and down arrows in the template view in order to traverse directories and other items (that we will talk about later in this book). When examining directories containing long filenames ADE will often skip over entries or become confused. Figure 6.16 shows what happened after the down arrow was pressed when the directory from Figure 6.15 ("Documents and Settings") was selected. Note how ADE skipped over "Program Files" and "CONFIG. SYS".

Getting ADE back on track when it has become confused by long filename directory entries is rather simple. Right click on the start of the directory entry you wish to view and select Set

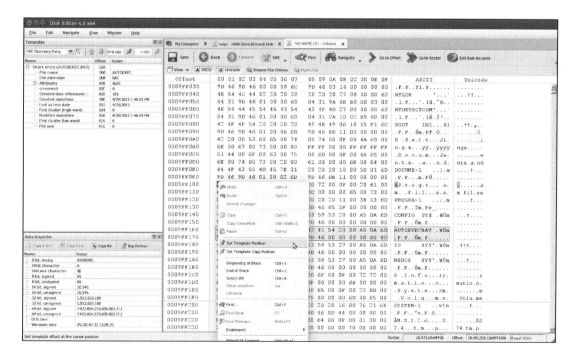

FIGURE 6.17.

Resetting the template position when viewing directories in Active@ Disk Editor.

158 CHAPTER 6 FAT Filesystems

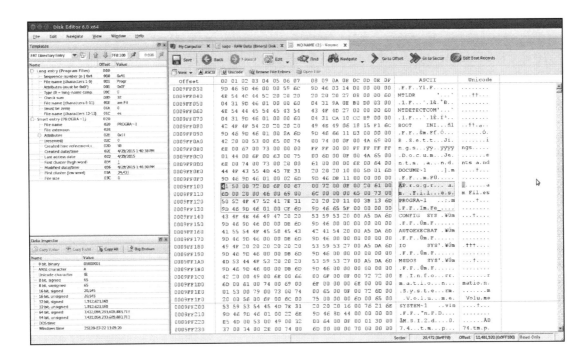

FIGURE 6.18.

Viewing a directory entry in Active@ Disk Editor after resetting the template position.

Template Position as shown in Figure 6.17. The directory should then be shown correctly as in Figure 6.18.

Viewing a file or directory from its directory entry in ADE is quite simple. You will notice that the first cluster high word and low word both appear as hyperlinks in the template view. Clicking on either hyperlink will bring you to the first cluster of a file or directory as appropriate. A subdirectory is shown in Figure 6.19. Note the first two entries that are a self reference ("." or dot) and pointer to the parent directory (".." or dot dot) as discussed previously in this chapter.

As mentioned earlier in this chapter, when a file is deleted, the first byte in each of its directory entries is changed to 0xE5. This can confuse ADE, especially when files and directories with long filenames are deleted. The problem seems to stem from the 0xE5 being incorrectly interpreted as a sequence number for a very long filename. This issue is demonstrated in Figure 6.20. Resetting the template position to point to a non-deleted file or a deleted short filename entry will fix this problem.

As we learned earlier in this chapter, the first entry in the root directory can be a volume label. If this entry exists it should match the volume label found in the VBR. It seems to be more common to find this directory entry in FAT12 and FAT16 filesystems. The volume label for a floppy disk is shown in Figure 6.21.

Directories

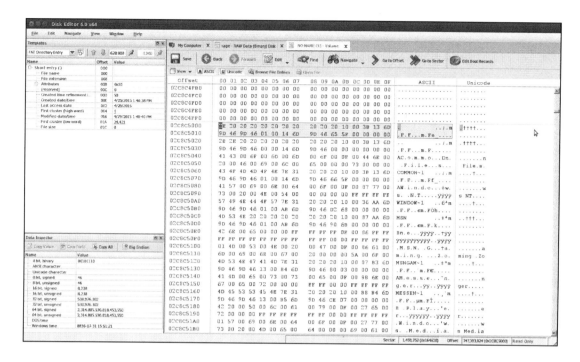

FIGURE 6.19.

Examining a subdirectory in Active@ Disk Editor.

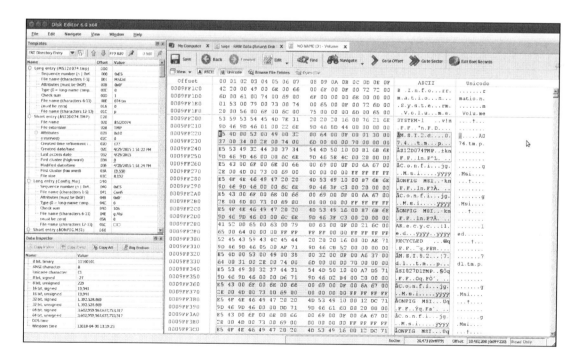

FIGURE 6.20.

Active@ Disk Editor confused by directory entries from deleted items with long filenames.

CHAPTER 6 FAT Filesystems

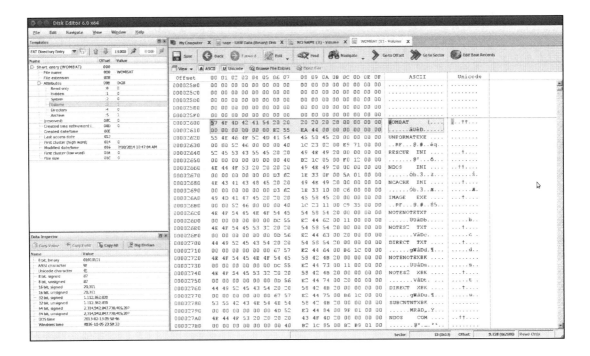

FIGURE 6.21.

Examining a directory entry for a volume label in Active@ Disk Editor.

Using Python to interpret directories

We will develop some Python code (in a module) that can be used to interpret FAT directory entries. This code will build on previous work for interpreting the MBR, VBR, and FAT. This new Python module begins with a she-bang line, some comments, imports and a list of exported classes and functions.

```
#!/usr/bin/python3

# This is a simple Python script that will
# attempt to read FAT directory entries from an image file.
# Developed for PentesterAcademy by Dr. Phil Polstra

import os.path
import sys
import struct
from mbr import Mbr
from vbr import Vbr
from fat import Fat

__all__=['Directory', 'FileEntry', 'DirEntry', 'timeTupleToString',
    'dateTupleToString']
```

Next we define a few helper functions. These functions will be used to interpret and easily print times and dates. As with previous scripts, struct.unpack is used to interpret the binary values from a filesystem image. The fatTime and fatDate functions use a combination of the modulus operator and integer division to isolate certain bits in these two byte values. The modulus operator (%) is used to strip off upper bits using the formula bits = value % 2^(least significant bit of portion to discard). For example, the day is found in the lowest 5 bits of the date field and 2 to the 5th power is 32 which is why the line of code reads `day=val%32`. Integer division removes lower bits in accordance with the formula bits=value // 2^(least significant bit to retain). For example, the hours are stored in bits 11 through 15 of the time field, and 2 to the 11th power is 2048 which leads to the line of code that reads `hours=val//2048`. Note that fatTime and FatDate both return tuples.

```
# helper functions for conversions
def fatTime(buffer):
    '''This function accepts a byte string
    that should be 2 bytes long and returns
    a tuple (hour, minutes, seconds)'''
    val=struct.unpack('<H', buffer)[0]
    seconds = 2*(val%32) # lowest 5 bits * 2
    hours=val//2048 # top 5 bits
    minutes=(val%2048)//32 # middle 6 bits
    return (hours, minutes, seconds)

def fatDate(buffer):
    '''This function accepts a byte string
    that should be 2 bytes long and returns
    a tuple (year, month, day)'''
    val=struct.unpack('<H', buffer)[0]
    day=val%32 # lowest 5 bits
    year=1980 + val//512 # top 7 bits +1980
    month=(val%512)//32 # middle 4 bits
    return (year, month, day)

def timeTupleToString(hms):
    '''Covert hour, minute, second tuple to
    a pretty string'''
    if len(hms)!=3:
        return "None"
    (hour, minute, second)=hms
    if hour:
        return "%02d:%02d:%02d" % (hour, minute, second)
    else:
        return "None"

def dateTupleToString(ymd):
    '''Convert year, month, day tuple to
```

```
    a pretty string'''
    if len(ymd)!=3:
        return "None"
    (year, month, day)=ymd
    if year:
        return "%04d-%02d-%02d" % (year, month, day)
    else:
        return "None"
```

A DirEntry class is created in order to represent a 32-byte directory entry. Multiple 32-byte entries are required for files and directories with long filenames. A FileEntry class will be used to represent all 32-byte entries associated with a single file or directory. The DirEntry constructor follows.

```
class DirEntry:
    def __init__(self, buffer):
        '''This class represents a raw directory
        entry. It is created by a buffer that
        should be 32 bytes long'''
        # is this a deleted entry?
        if buffer[0:1]==b'\xE5':
            self._deleted=True
        else:
            self._deleted=False
        # is this a long filename entry?
        if buffer[11:13]==b'\x0F\x00':
            self._longEntry=True
            self._sequenceNumber=struct.unpack('<B', buffer[0:1])[0]
            self._lastEntry=(self._sequenceNumber&0x40!=0)
            self._checksum=struct.unpack('<B', buffer[13:14])[0]
            fn=buffer[1:11]+buffer[14:26]+buffer[28:32]
            # is there an Unicode null in string?
            if fn.find(b'\x00\x00')>0:
                self._filename=fn[:fn.find(b'\x00\x00')+1].decode('utf-16')
            elif fn.find(b'\xFF\xFF')>0:
                self._filename=fn[:fn.find(b'\xFF\xFF')].decode('utf-16')
            else:
                self._filename=fn.decode("utf-16")
        else:
            # this is a short entry
            self._longEntry=False
            # this if is to prevent Unicode decoding errors
            if buffer[0:1]==b'\xE5':
                self._basename='_'+buffer[1:8].decode('utf-8')
```

```
        else:
            self._basename=buffer[0:8].decode('utf-8')
            self._extension=buffer[8:11].decode('utf-8')
        self._basename=self._basename.rstrip()
        self._extension=self._extension.rstrip()
        # any nulls in the name?
        if self._basename.find('\x00')>0:
            self._basename=self._basename[:self._basename.find('\x00')]
        if self._extension.find('\x00')>0:
            self._extension=self._extension[:self._extension.find('\x00')]
        self._attributes=struct.unpack('<B', buffer[11:12])[0]
        (self._createHour, self._createMinute, self._createSecond)=\
            fatTime(buffer[14:16])
        (self._createYear, self._createMonth, self._createDay)=\
            fatDate(buffer[16:18])
        (self._accessYear, self._accessMonth, self._accessDay)=\
            fatDate(buffer[18:20])
        self._startCluster=(65536*
            struct.unpack('<H', buffer[20:22])[0] +
            struct.unpack('<H', buffer[26:28])[0])
        (self._modifyHour, self._modifyMinute, self._modifySecond)=\
            fatTime(buffer[22:24])
        (self._modifyYear, self._modifyMonth, self._modifyDay)=\
            fatDate(buffer[24:26])
        self._filesize=struct.unpack('<I', buffer[28:32])[0]
```

The constructor first checks the value of the first byte (`buffer[0:1]`) to see if it contains 0xE5 which indicates a deleted entry. As a reminder, slice notation is being used. In order to include a substring, part of a list, etc. the syntax is `myThing[<starting index>:<ending index+1>]`.

All long filename entries should have the value 0x0F 0x00 in positions 11 and 12. This fact is used to determine if the current entry is used to store a long filename. The sequence number is retrieved and the bitwise AND operator is used to check if this is the last entry (`self._sequenceNumber&0x40!=0`).

All 26 bytes that might contain a long filename chunk in Unicode are concatenated together. The find command is used to check for the presence of a Unicode null (0x00 0x00). If one is found, the binary string is truncated after the null and then converted from a binary string to a normal string using decode. The encoding used here is UTF-16 in which all values are two bytes long. If no embedded Unicode nulls were found, a check is made for the value of 0xFF 0xFF. If this value is found, the binary string is truncated before the first 0xFF 0xFF before decode is used to obtain a normal string. This step might seem unnecessary, but I have seen values padded with 0xFF 0xFF that lack a terminating null. If neither of these conditions are true the entire binary string is converted to a normal string.

If the current entry is a short filename entry, all of the metadata is retrieved. First decode is used to convert the base filename and file extension to normal strings. The encoding used is UTF-8 which will correctly interpret ASCII strings. Note that decode is required here to convert the binary string to a normal string, even though Unicode is not used. After conversion, rstrip is used on both parts of the name to remove trailing spaces.

Sometimes if the short filenames do not require all available space they are null terminated and other times they are padded with trailing spaces. This is why a check is made for trailing nulls. After the filename is successfully stored, struct.unpack and our helper functions are used to retrieve the remaining items. Something that might appear strange to new Python programs are lines where a tuple is used to assign multiple values simultaneously. For example, the line (self._createHour, self._createMinute, self._createSecond) = fatTime(buffer[14:16]) calls the fatTime function and then simultaneously sets _createHour, _createMinute, and _createSecond.

Several accessors are defined in the DirEntry class. These are all straightforward. For values that do not apply to long filename entries the value of None is returned. The accessor definitions follow.

```
def longEntry(self):
    return self._longEntry

def deleted(self):
    return self._deleted

def attributes(self):
    if self.longEntry():
        return None
    else:
        return self._attributes

def filename(self):
    if self._longEntry:
        return self._filename
    else:
        if len(self._extension)==0 or \
            self._extension=='   ':
            return self._basename
        else:
            return self._basename+'.'+self._extension

def createTime(self):
    if self._longEntry:
        return (None, None, None)
    else:
        return (self._createHour, self._createMinute, \
            self._createSecond)
```

```python
def createDate(self):
   if self._longEntry:
      return (None, None, None)
   else:
      return (self._createYear, self._createMonth, self._createDay)

def modifyTime(self):
   if self._longEntry:
      return (None, None, None)
   else:
      return (self._modifyHour, self._modifyMinute, self._modifySecond)

def modifyDate(self):
   if self._longEntry:
      return (None, None, None)
   else:
      return (self._modifyYear, self._modifyMonth, self._modifyDay)

def accessDate(self):
   if self._longEntry:
      return (None, None, None)
   else:
      return (self._accessYear, self._accessMonth, self._accessDay)

def startCluster(self):
   if self._longEntry:
      return None
   else:
      return self._startCluster

def filesize(self):
   if self._longEntry:
      return None
   else:
      return self._filesize
```

The FileEntry class is used to represent the collection of 32-byte entries (DirEntry class) that pertain to a single file or directory. The design decision was made to represent every deleted long filename entry as a separate FileEntry object. This was done to avoid complications. It is certainly possible that a file with a long filename is deleted and then some, but not all, of the long filename entries are used for another file. Attempting to group together an incomplete set of entries would result in an error. Additionally, the long filename entries are not normally all that interesting for the forensic investigator as he or she is normally more interested in file contents than names and all of the pertinent metadata is contained in the short filename entry. The FileEntry constructor follows.

```python
class FileEntry:
    '''This class represents a file entry
    which may contain multiple raw directory
    entries.  A deleted file with a long
    name will result in multiple file
    entries.  This is done to avoid problems
    if part of the complete entry gets
    reused.'''
    def __init__(self, buffer, offset=0):
        '''Takes a buffer containing directory
        entries with an optional offset.  If
        the first entry encountered is a long
        entry it will scan forward until the
        short entry is found.'''
        self._dirEntries=[]
        # is this an empty slot?
        if buffer[offset:offset+1]==b'\x00':
            return
        # is the first entry deleted?
        de=DirEntry(buffer[offset:offset+32])
        if de.deleted():
            # deleted entries get their own spot
            self._dirEntries.append(de)
            return
        # is this a long entry?
        if de.longEntry():
            # scan forward till short entry
            oset=offset+32
            while de.longEntry():
                self._dirEntries.append(de)
                if buffer[oset:oset+1]==b'\x00':
                    break
                de=DirEntry(buffer[oset:oset+32])
                oset+=32
            # now add the short entry
            self._dirEntries.append(de)
        else:
            # just a short entry
            self._dirEntries.append(de)
```

The constructor starts by creating an empty list to store 32-byte director entries (DirEntry objects). Next, it checks to see if the first byte is zero which indicates we are at the unused space at the end of the directory entries. A DirEntry object is created if the entry is not empty.

The new DirEntry object is checked to see if it is deleted. If so, it is appended to the list and the constructor exits. Deleted entries will always be the only entry inside a FileEntry object (see discussion above).

If the DirEntry object represents a long filename entry, we add it to our list and keep scanning forward until a short filename entry is found. For entries with long filenames the _dirEntries variable will contain a list of long filename entries and one short filename entry in the same order as they are found on disk. If the DirEntry object represents a short filename entry, it is simply appended to the _dirEntries list as the only entry.

Several accessors are defined for the FileEntry class. These methods are straightforward and use only a few new techniques not yet encountered in this book. The accessors follow.

```
def entries(self):
    return len(self._dirEntries)

def empty(self):
    return len(self._dirEntries)==0

def deleted(self):
    # deleted files have a single entry
    if self.empty():
        return False
    else:
        return self._dirEntries[0].deleted()

def hasLongFilename(self):
    if self.empty():
        return False
    else:
        return self._dirEntries[0].longEntry()

def hasShortFilename(self):
    if self.empty():
        return False
    else:
        return not self._dirEntries[self.entries()-1].longEntry()

def longFilename(self):
    if not self.hasLongFilename():
        return None
    else:
        # is this a single deleted entry?
        if self.entries()==1:
            return self._dirEntries[0].filename()
        else:
            # all but the last entry contain the filename
            fn=""
            for i in range(self.entries()-2, -1,-1):
                fn+=self._dirEntries[i].filename()
            return fn
```

```python
def shortFilename(self):
    if self.empty() or \
       self._dirEntries[self.entries()-1].longEntry():
        return None
    else:
        return self._dirEntries[self.entries()-1].filename()

def attributes(self):
    if self.empty() or \
       self._dirEntries[self.entries()-1].longEntry():
        return None
    else:
        return self._dirEntries[self.entries()-1].attributes()

def readOnly(self):
    if self.attributes():
        return (self.attributes()&0x01)!=0
    else:
        return False

def hidden(self):
    if self.attributes():
        return (self.attributes()&0x02)!=0
    else:
        return False

def systemFile(self):
    if self.attributes():
        return (self.attributes()&0x04)!=0
    else:
        return False

def volumeLabel(self):
    if self.attributes():
        return (self.attributes()&0x08)!=0
    else:
        return False

def directory(self):
    if self.attributes():
        return (self.attributes()&0x10)!=0
    else:
        return False
```

```python
    def archive(self):
        if self.attributes():
            return (self.attributes()&0x20)!=0
        else:
            return False

    def createTime(self):
        if not self.hasShortFilename():
            return (None, None, None)
        else:
            return self._dirEntries[self.entries()-1].createTime()

    def createDate(self):
        if not self.hasShortFilename():
            return (None, None, None)
        else:
            return self._dirEntries[self.entries()-1].createDate()

    def accessDate(self):
        if not self.hasShortFilename():
            return (None, None, None)
        else:
            return self._dirEntries[self.entries()-1].accessDate()

    def modifyTime(self):
        if not self.hasShortFilename():
            return (None, None, None)
        else:
            return self._dirEntries[self.entries()-1].modifyTime()

    def modifyDate(self):
        if not self.hasShortFilename():
            return (None, None, None)
        else:
            return self._dirEntries[self.entries()-1].modifyDate()

    def startCluster(self):
        if not self.hasShortFilename():
            return None
        else:
            return self._dirEntries[self.entries()-1].startCluster()

    def filesize(self):
        if not self.hasShortFilename():
            return None
```

```
        else:
            return self._dirEntries[self.entries()-1].filesize()

    def __str__(self):
        '''Used by print().'''
        if self.hasLongFilename():
            return '<LFN> '+self.longFilename()
        else:
            return self.shortFilename()

    def prettyPrint(self):
        if self.empty():
            print('<Empty>')
            return
        print('Deleted:', self.deleted())
        if self.hasLongFilename():
            print('Long filename:', self.longFilename())
        if self.hasShortFilename():
            print('Short filename:', self.shortFilename())
        print('Start cluster:', self.startCluster())
        print('Filesize:', self.filesize())
        if self.attributes():
            print('Attributes: %02X' % self.attributes())
        print('Created:', dateTupleToString(self.createDate()),
            timeTupleToString(self.createTime()))
        print('Accessed:', dateTupleToString(self.accessDate()))
        print('Modified:', dateTupleToString(self.modifyDate()),
            timeTupleToString(self.modifyTime()))
```

One new technique used in the FileEntry accessors is the inclusion of a third parameter for the range function. The general syntax for range is range(start, stop, step). The default value of step is one. In the longFilename method the filename starts in the second to last entry (the last entry should be the short filename entry) and then grows backwards toward the first entry. Setting step to -1 in the for loop allows the filename to be constructed correctly.

In addition to prettyPrint, the FileEntry class defines a __str__ method. This method is implicitly called whenever a string representation of the object is needed. The most common example of where this is used would be when a FileEntry object is passed to print. Note that this returns a string that contains the filename, but not all the metadata printed out in prettyPrint.

We define a Directory class that is used to represent a collection of FileEntry objects found in the appropriate clusters for a directory. This class is very simple and straightforward thanks to all of the effort we put into DirEntry and FileEntry. The code for this class follows.

```
class Directory:
    '''This class represents a directory as a collection
    of fileEntry objects.  The directory is created by
    passing the constructor all of the appropriate clusters.'''
```

```python
    def __init__(self, buffer):
        self._dirEntries=[]
        # while we haven't hit the end add entries
        offset=0
        while offset < len(buffer):
            if buffer[offset:offset+1]==b'\x00':
                break
            de=FileEntry(buffer, offset)
            offset+=32*de.entries() # skip to next file
            self._dirEntries.append(de)

    def entries(self):
        return len(self._dirEntries)

    def entry(self, numb):
        if numb >= self.entries():
            return None
        return self._dirEntries[numb]

    def list(self):
        for de in self._dirEntries:
            de.prettyPrint()
```

The main function from our previous fat.py script can be used with a couple of additional lines to test the new code on the root directory. As mentioned previously, we will make better use of this code later. The additional lines are as follows.

```
        # now grab the Root Directory
        cchain=fat.clusterChain(2)
        rdBuffer=b''
        for clust in cchain:
            f.seek(mbr.reservedSectors(i)*512+
                512*vbr.sectorFromCluster(clust))
            rdBuffer+=f.read(512*vbr.sectorsPerCluster())
        rd=Directory(rdBuffer)
        rd.list()
```

The entire directory module that we have developed in this section follows.

```
#!/usr/bin/python3

# This is a simple Python script that will
# attempt to read FAT directory entries from an image file.
# Developed for PentesterAcademy by Dr. Phil Polstra
```

```python
import os.path
import sys
import struct
from mbr import Mbr
from vbr import Vbr
from fat import Fat

__all__=['Directory', 'FileEntry', 'DirEntry', 'timeTupleToString',
   'dateTupleToString']

# helper functions for conversions
def fatTime(buffer):
   '''This function accepts a byte string
   that should be 2 bytes long and returns
   a tuple (hour, minutes, seconds)'''
   val=struct.unpack('<H', buffer)[0]
   seconds = 2*(val%32) # lowest 5 bits * 2
   hours=val//2048 # top 5 bits
   minutes=(val%2048)//32 # middle 6 bits
   return (hours, minutes, seconds)

def fatDate(buffer):
   '''This function accepts a byte string
   that should be 2 bytes long and returns
   a tuple (year, month, day)'''
   val=struct.unpack('<H', buffer)[0]
   day=val%32 # lowest 5 bits
   year=1980 + val//512 # top 7 bits +1980
   month=(val%512)//32 # middle 4 bits
   return (year, month, day)

def timeTupleToString(hms):
   '''Covert hour, minute, second tuple to
   a pretty string'''
   if len(hms)!=3:
      return "None"
   (hour, minute, second)=hms
   if hour:
      return "%02d:%02d:%02d" % (hour, minute, second)
   else:
      return "None"

def dateTupleToString(ymd):
   '''Convert year, month, day tuple to
   a pretty string'''
```

```python
        if len(ymd)!=3:
            return "None"
        (year, month, day)=ymd
        if year:
            return "%04d-%02d-%02d" % (year, month, day)
        else:
            return "None"

class DirEntry:
    def __init__(self, buffer):
        '''This class represents a raw directory
        entry.  It is created by a buffer that
        should be 32 bytes long'''
        # is this a deleted entry?
        if buffer[0:1]==b'\xE5':
            self._deleted=True
        else:
            self._deleted=False
        # is this a long filename entry?
        if buffer[11:13]==b'\x0F\x00':
            self._longEntry=True
            self._sequenceNumber=struct.unpack('<B', buffer[0:1])[0]
            self._lastEntry=(self._sequenceNumber&0x40!=0)
            self._checksum=struct.unpack('<B', buffer[13:14])[0]
            fn=buffer[1:11]+buffer[14:26]+buffer[28:32]
            # is there an Unicode null in string?
            if fn.find(b'\x00\x00')>0:
                self._filename=fn[:fn.find(b'\x00\x00')+1].decode('utf-16')
            elif fn.find(b'\xFF\xFF')>0:
                self._filename=fn[:fn.find(b'\xFF\xFF')].decode('utf-16')
            else:
                self._filename=fn.decode("utf-16")
        else:
            # this is a short entry
            self._longEntry=False
            # this if is to prevent Unicode decoding errors
            if buffer[0:1]==b'\xE5':
                self._basename='_'+buffer[1:8].decode('utf-8')
            else:
                self._basename=buffer[0:8].decode('utf-8')
            self._extension=buffer[8:11].decode('utf-8')
            self._basename=self._basename.rstrip()
            self._extension=self._extension.rstrip()
            # any nulls in the name?
            if self._basename.find('\x00')>0:
                self._basename=self._basename[:self._basename.find('\x00')]
```

```python
            if self._extension.find('\x00')>0:
                self._extension=self._extension[:self._extension.find('\x00')]
            self._attributes=struct.unpack('<B', buffer[11:12])[0]
            (self._createHour, self._createMinute, self._createSecond)=\
                fatTime(buffer[14:16])
            (self._createYear, self._createMonth, self._createDay)=\
                fatDate(buffer[16:18])
            (self._accessYear, self._accessMonth, self._accessDay)=\
                fatDate(buffer[18:20])
            self._startCluster=(65536*
                struct.unpack('<H', buffer[20:22])[0] +
                struct.unpack('<H', buffer[26:28])[0])
            (self._modifyHour, self._modifyMinute, self._modifySecond)=\
                fatTime(buffer[22:24])
            (self._modifyYear, self._modifyMonth, self._modifyDay)=\
                fatDate(buffer[24:26])
            self._filesize=struct.unpack('<I', buffer[28:32])[0]

    def longEntry(self):
        return self._longEntry

    def deleted(self):
        return self._deleted

    def attributes(self):
        if self.longEntry():
            return None
        else:
            return self._attributes

    def filename(self):
        if self._longEntry:
            return self._filename
        else:
            if len(self._extension)==0 or \
                self._extension=='   ':
                return self._basename
            else:
                return self._basename+'.'+self._extension

    def createTime(self):
        if self._longEntry:
            return (None, None, None)
        else:
            return (self._createHour, self._createMinute, self._createSecond)
```

```python
    def createDate(self):
        if self._longEntry:
            return (None, None, None)
        else:
            return (self._createYear, self._createMonth, self._createDay)

    def modifyTime(self):
        if self._longEntry:
            return (None, None, None)
        else:
            return (self._modifyHour, self._modifyMinute, self._modifySecond)

    def modifyDate(self):
        if self._longEntry:
            return (None, None, None)
        else:
            return (self._modifyYear, self._modifyMonth, self._modifyDay)

    def accessDate(self):
        if self._longEntry:
            return (None, None, None)
        else:
            return (self._accessYear, self._accessMonth, self._accessDay)

    def startCluster(self):
        if self._longEntry:
            return None
        else:
            return self._startCluster

    def filesize(self):
        if self._longEntry:
            return None
        else:
            return self._filesize

class FileEntry:
    '''This class represents a file entry
    which may contain multiple raw directory
    entries. A deleted file with a long
    name will result in multiple file
    entries. This is done to avoid problems
    if part of the complete entry gets
    reused.'''
    def __init__(self, buffer, offset=0):
        '''Takes a buffer containing directory
```

```
            entries with an optional offset.  If
            the first entry encountered is a long
            entry it will scan forward until the
            short entry is found.'''
            self._dirEntries=[]
            # is this an empty slot?
            if buffer[offset:offset+1]==b'\x00':
                return
            # is the first entry deleted?
            de=DirEntry(buffer[offset:offset+32])
            if de.deleted():
                # deleted entries get their own spot
                self._dirEntries.append(de)
                return
            # is this a long entry?
            if de.longEntry():
                # scan forward till short entry
                oset=offset+32
                while de.longEntry():
                    self._dirEntries.append(de)
                    if buffer[oset:oset+1]==b'\x00':
                        break
                    de=DirEntry(buffer[oset:oset+32])
                    oset+=32
                # now add the short entry
                self._dirEntries.append(de)
            else:
                # just a short entry
                self._dirEntries.append(de)

    def entries(self):
        return len(self._dirEntries)

    def empty(self):
        return len(self._dirEntries)==0

    def deleted(self):
        # deleted files have a single entry
        if self.empty():
            return False
        else:
            return self._dirEntries[0].deleted()

    def hasLongFilename(self):
        if self.empty():
            return False
```

```python
        else:
            return self._dirEntries[0].longEntry()

    def hasShortFilename(self):
        if self.empty():
            return False
        else:
            return not self._dirEntries[self.entries()-1].longEntry()

    def longFilename(self):
        if not self.hasLongFilename():
            return None
        else:
            # is this a single deleted entry?
            if self.entries()==1:
                return self._dirEntries[0].filename()
            else:
                # all but the last entry contain the filename
                fn=""
                for i in range(self.entries()-2, -1,-1):
                    fn+=self._dirEntries[i].filename()
                return fn

    def shortFilename(self):
        if self.empty() or \
           self._dirEntries[self.entries()-1].longEntry():
            return None
        else:
            return self._dirEntries[self.entries()-1].filename()

    def attributes(self):
        if self.empty() or \
           self._dirEntries[self.entries()-1].longEntry():
            return None
        else:
            return self._dirEntries[self.entries()-1].attributes()

    def readOnly(self):
        if self.attributes():
            return (self.attributes()&0x01)!=0
        else:
            return False

    def hidden(self):
        if self.attributes():
            return (self.attributes()&0x02)!=0
```

```python
        else:
            return False

    def systemFile(self):
        if self.attributes():
            return (self.attributes()&0x04)!=0
        else:
            return False

    def volumeLabel(self):
        if self.attributes():
            return (self.attributes()&0x08)!=0
        else:
            return False

    def directory(self):
        if self.attributes():
            return (self.attributes()&0x10)!=0
        else:
            return False

    def archive(self):
        if self.attributes():
            return (self.attributes()&0x20)!=0
        else:
            return False

    def createTime(self):
        if not self.hasShortFilename():
            return (None, None, None)
        else:
            return self._dirEntries[self.entries()-1].createTime()

    def createDate(self):
        if not self.hasShortFilename():
            return (None, None, None)
        else:
            return self._dirEntries[self.entries()-1].createDate()

    def accessDate(self):
        if not self.hasShortFilename():
            return (None, None, None)
        else:
            return self._dirEntries[self.entries()-1].accessDate()
```

```python
def modifyTime(self):
    if not self.hasShortFilename():
        return (None, None, None)
    else:
        return self._dirEntries[self.entries()-1].modifyTime()

def modifyDate(self):
    if not self.hasShortFilename():
        return (None, None, None)
    else:
        return self._dirEntries[self.entries()-1].modifyDate()

def startCluster(self):
    if not self.hasShortFilename():
        return None
    else:
        return self._dirEntries[self.entries()-1].startCluster()

def filesize(self):
    if not self.hasShortFilename():
        return None
    else:
        return self._dirEntries[self.entries()-1].filesize()

def __str__(self):
    '''Used by print().'''
    if self.hasLongFilename():
        return '<LFN> '+self.longFilename()
    else:
        return self.shortFilename()

def prettyPrint(self):
    if self.empty():
        print('<Empty>')
        return
    print('Deleted:', self.deleted())
    if self.hasLongFilename():
        print('Long filename:', self.longFilename())
    if self.hasShortFilename():
        print('Short filename:', self.shortFilename())
    print('Start cluster:', self.startCluster())
    print('Filesize:', self.filesize())
    if self.attributes():
        print('Attributes: %02X' % self.attributes())
    print('Created:', dateTupleToString(self.createDate()),
        timeTupleToString(self.createTime()))
```

```python
        print('Accessed:', dateTupleToString(self.accessDate()))
        print('Modified:', dateTupleToString(self.modifyDate()),
            timeTupleToString(self.modifyTime()))

class Directory:
    '''This class represents a directory as a collection
    of fileEntry objects.  The directory is created by
    passing the constructor all of the appropriate clusters.'''
    def __init__(self, buffer):
        self._dirEntries=[]
        # while we haven't hit the end add entries
        offset=0
        while offset < len(buffer):
            if buffer[offset:offset+1]==b'\x00':
                break
            de=FileEntry(buffer, offset)
            offset+=32*de.entries() # skip to next file
            self._dirEntries.append(de)

    def entries(self):
        return len(self._dirEntries)

    def entry(self, numb):
        if numb >= self.entries():
            return None
        return self._dirEntries[numb]

    def list(self):
        for de in self._dirEntries:
            de.prettyPrint()

def usage():
    print("usage " + sys.argv[0] + " <image file>\n"+
        "Reads FAT Directory Entries from an image file")
    exit(1)

def main():
    if len(sys.argv) < 2:
      usage()

    notsupParts = [0x05, 0x0f, 0x85, 0x91, 0x9b, 0xc5, 0xe4, 0xee]
    swapParts = [0x42, 0x82, 0xb8, 0xc3, 0xfc]

    # read first sector
    if not os.path.isfile(sys.argv[1]):
        print("File " + sys.argv[1] + " cannot be openned for reading")
        exit(1)
```

```python
with open(sys.argv[1], 'rb') as f:
    sector = f.read(512)

mbr=Mbr(sector) # create MBR object

if mbr.validSignature():
    print("Looks like a MBR or VBR")
    mbr.prettyPrint()

    for i in range(1,5):
        if not mbr.isEmpty(i):
            if mbr.partitionType(i) in notsupParts:
                print("Sorry GPT and extended partitions are not \
                    supported by this script!")
            else:
                if mbr.partitionType(i) in swapParts:
                    print("Skipping swap partition")
                else:
                    # let's try and read the VBR
                    with open(sys.argv[1], 'rb') as f:
                        f.seek(mbr.reservedSectors(i)*512)
                        sector=f.read(512)
                        vbr=Vbr(sector)
                        if vbr.validSignature() and vbr.isFat32():
                            print('Found Volume with type', vbr. \
                                filesystemType())
                            print('Volume label:', vbr.volumeLabel())
                            print('Total sectors:', vbr.totalSectors())
                            s=vbr.sectorFromCluster(2)
                            print('Cluster 2:', s)
                            print('Sector:', vbr.clusterFromSector(s))
                            # grab the FAT
                            f.seek(mbr.reservedSectors(i)*512+
                                vbr.sectorFat1()*512)
                            fatRaw=f.read(512*vbr.sectorsPerFat())
                            fat=Fat(fatRaw)
                            print('Cluster 2 allocated:',fat.isAllocated(2))
                            print('Chain starting at 2:',fat.clusterChain(2))
                            # now grab the Root Directory
                            cchain=fat.clusterChain(2)
                            rdBuffer=b''
                            for clust in cchain:
                                f.seek(mbr.reservedSectors(i)*512+
                                    512*vbr.sectorFromCluster(clust))
                                rdBuffer+=f.read(512*vbr.sectorsPerCluster())
                            rd=Directory(rdBuffer)
                            rd.list()
```

```
        else:
            print("Doesn't appear to contain valid MBR")

if __name__ == "__main__":
    main()
```

THE SLEUTH KIT AND AUTOPSY

Many years ago Brian Carrier built a command line forensic toolkit called The Sleuth Kit (TSK). This tool was based on The Coroner's Toolkit (TCT) by Dan Farmer and Wietse Venema. While TCT is a Linux/Unix only tool, TSK also supports Windows. Brian Carrier also developed a graphical front end for TSK known as Autopsy.

The Sleuth Kit

The Sleuth Kit (TSK) is easily installed using the package manager for your favorite Linux system. If you are using a Linux based on Debian or Ubuntu, the command is `sudo apt-get install sleuthkit`. You can also download the source code from http://sleuthkit.org, but this is not really necessary in most cases. When you build from scratch, you will have the option to include Expert Witness Format (EWF) file support. This is the format used by EnCASE tools. You should have no need for this support when working with the open source tools described in this book.

The tools in TSK work at different levels: disk, partition, file name, file metadata, and block. Tools that work at the disk level begin with "mm". Three tools exist at this level: mmstat, mmls, and mmcat. The results of running `mmstat` against FAT and NTFS filesystems is shown in Figure 6.22. Note that when using the default switches only the image type of "dos" is displayed.

The `mmls` command is used to list partition information for a filesystem image. The results of running this command on an image are shown in Figure 6.23. Notice how TSK has a somewhat different way of labeling partitions. The MBR and unallocated space before the single partition are each given a partition number. The leftover unallocated space after the partition is likewise assigned a partition number.

The `mmcat` command is use to extract the contents of a specific partition and send it to standard out. When working with raw images on Linux this utility is completely unnecessary as the same thing can be accomplished with the built in `dd` tool. Using mmcat to display the start of a FAT partition (first few bytes of the VBR) is shown in Figure 6.24.

There is only one tool at the partition level in TSK, `fsstat`. This tool can be used to gather filesystem details. Partial results from running this command against a FAT32 partition are shown in Figure 6.25. Note that the -o <starting sector of partition> switch must be used to select and examine the correct partition. If you only want to know the filesystem type, the -t flag will print only the type.

There are three commands `fls`, `ffind`, and `fcat` at the file name level in TSK. All of these commands require an offset in sectors to the start of a partition as a parameter. The ls command in Linux is used to list files in directories similar to the dir command in Windows. Partial results

```
phil@i7laptop:~/sleuthkit$ mmstat /media/phil/TOSHIBA\ EXT/BU/images/Filesystems1-Final.img
dos
phil@i7laptop:~/sleuthkit$ mmstat /media/phil/TOSHIBA\ EXT/BU/images/mystery.dd
dos
phil@i7laptop:~/sleuthkit$
```

FIGURE 6.22.

Running mmstat on FAT and NTFS images.

```
phil@i7laptop:~/sleuthkit$ mmls /media/phil/TOSHIBA\ EXT/BU/images/Filesystems1-Final.img
DOS Partition Table
Offset Sector: 0
Units are in 512-byte sectors

     Slot       Start        End          Length       Description
000: Meta       0000000000   0000000000   0000000001   Primary Table (#0)
001: -------    0000000000   0000000062   0000000063   Unallocated
002: 000:000    0000000063   0020948759   0020948697   Win95 FAT32 (0x0c)
003: -------    0020948760   0020971519   0000022760   Unallocated
phil@i7laptop:~/sleuthkit$
```

FIGURE 6.23.

Runing mmls on a Windows XP image containing a FAT filesystem.

CHAPTER 6 FAT Filesystems

```
phil@i7laptop:~/sleuthkit$ mmcat /media/phil/TOSHIBA\ EXT/BU/images/Filesystems1
-Final.img 2 | xxd |head
0000000: eb58 904d 5344 4f53 352e 3000 0210 2200  .X.MSDOS5.0...".
0000010: 0200 0000 00f8 0000 3f00 ff00 3f00 0000  ........?...?...
0000020: d9a6 3f01 eb27 0000 0000 0000 0200 0000  ..?..'..........
0000030: 0100 0600 0000 0000 0000 0000 0000 0000  ................
0000040: 8000 2944 8040 904e 4f20 4e41 4d45 2020  ..)D.@.NO NAME
0000050: 2020 4641 5433 3220 2020 33c9 8ed1 bcf4       FAT32   3....
0000060: 7b8e c18e d9bd 007c 884e 028a 5640 b408  {......|.N..V@..
0000070: cd13 7305 b9ff ff8a f166 0fb6 c640 660f  ..s......f...@f.
0000080: b6d1 80e2 3ff7 e286 cdc0 ed06 4166 0fb7  ....?.......Af..
0000090: c966 f7e1 6689 46f8 837e 1600 7538 837e  .f..f.F..~..u8.~
phil@i7laptop:~/sleuthkit$
```

FIGURE 6.24.

Using mmcat to display the start of a partition. Note that dd can just as easily be used when dealing with raw images.

```
FILE SYSTEM INFORMATION
--------------------------------------------
File System Type: FAT32

OEM Name: MSDOS5.0
Volume ID: 0x90408044
Volume Label (Boot Sector): NO NAME
Volume Label (Root Directory):
File System Type Label: FAT32
Next Free Sector (FS Info): 36344
Free Sector Count (FS Info): 11202608

Sectors before file system: 63

File System Layout (in sectors)
Total Range: 0 - 20948696
* Reserved: 0 - 33
** Boot Sector: 0
** FS Info Sector: 1
** Backup Boot Sector: 6
* FAT 0: 34 - 10252
* FAT 1: 10253 - 20471
* Data Area: 20472 - 20948696
--More--
```

FIGURE 6.25.

Partial output from fsstat. The command to produce this output is: fsstat -o <first sector of partition> <image file>.

```
phil@i7laptop:~/sleuthkit$
phil@i7laptop:~/sleuthkit$ fls -o 63  /media/phil/TOSHIBA\ EXT/BU/images/Filesys
tems1-Final.img |more
r/r 3:     PAGEFILE.SYS
d/d 4:     WINDOWS
r/r 5:     ntldr
r/r 6:     NTDETECT.COM
r/r 7:     boot.ini
d/d 10:    Documents and Settings
d/d 12:    Program Files
r/r 13:    CONFIG.SYS
r/r 14:    AUTOEXEC.BAT
r/r 15:    IO.SYS
r/r 16:    MSDOS.SYS
d/d 19:    System Volume Information
d/d * 21:         MSI2d074.tmp
d/d * 23:         Config.Msi
d/d * 25:         Config.Msi
d/d 27:    Recycled
d/d * 29:         MSI827d1.tmp
d/d * 31:         Config.Msi
d/d * 33:         Config.Msi
d/d 35:    Dev-Cpp
d/d 37:    ftk-imager
```

FIGURE 6.26.

Partial result from running the fls command against a FAT32 filesystem.

from running fls against a FAT32 image are shown in Figure 6.26. The numbers in the listing are starting clusters. An asterisk before the number indicates a file is deleted.

The ffind command can be used to find any filenames associated with a particular cluster in a FAT filesystem. The command will search through directory entries looking for the given cluster. The results of running ffind are shown in Figure 6.27.

The fcat command can be used to extract a file from a filesystem image by its fully qualified pathname. The results of running this command to extract a short file are shown in Figure 6.28. Note that for this command the pathname is listed before the image filename.

TSK commands at the file metadata level start with "i". The "i" stands for inode which is a structure used to store metadata in Linux filesystems. For a FAT filesystem the inode becomes a cluster number. The istat command can be used to obtain statistics for a given cluster. The results from running this command against the cluster which contains a /boot.ini file are shown in Figure 6.29.

The icat command is much like fcat with the exception that a starting cluster number must be supplied instead of a fully qualified pathname. The results of running this command against the same boot.ini file from Figure 6.28 are shown in Figure 6.30. Note that the cluster number comes after the filesystem image file.

Block level commands in TSK begin with "blk". These commands expect a sector number. The most basic block command is blkstat. This command will retrieve statistics about a

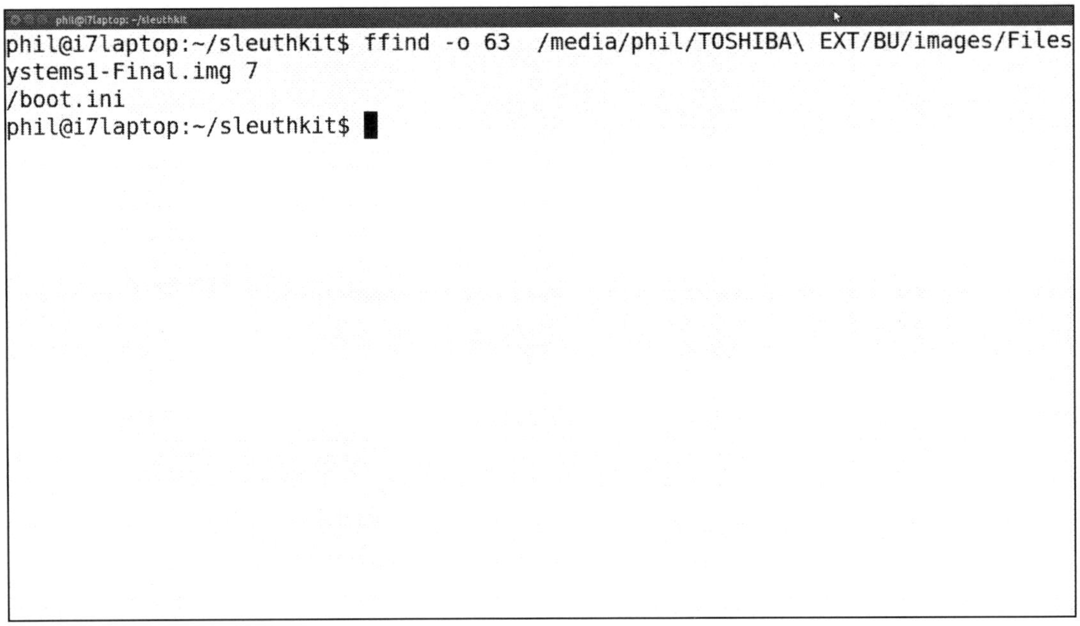

CHAPTER 6 FAT Filesystems

```
phil@i7laptop:~/sleuthkit$ ffind -o 63  /media/phil/TOSHIBA\ EXT/BU/images/Filesystems1-Final.img 7
/boot.ini
phil@i7laptop:~/sleuthkit$
```

FIGURE 6.27.

Running ffind against a FAT filesystem.

```
phil@i7laptop:~/sleuthkit$ fcat -o 63   /boot.ini /media/phil/TOSHIBA\ EXT/BU/images/Filesystems1-Final.img
[boot loader]
timeout=30
default=multi(0)disk(0)rdisk(0)partition(1)\WINDOWS
[operating systems]
multi(0)disk(0)rdisk(0)partition(1)\WINDOWS="Microsoft Windows XP Professional" /noexecute=optin /fastdetect
phil@i7laptop:~/sleuthkit$
```

FIGURE 6.28.

Using fcat to extract a file from an image.

```
phil@i7laptop:~/sleuthkit$ istat -o 63   /media/phil/TOSHIBA\ EXT/BU/images/Files
ystems1-Final.img 7
Directory Entry: 7
Allocated
File Attributes: File, Hidden, System
Size: 211
Name: boot.ini

Directory Entry Times:
Written:        2015-04-29 13:44:20 (EDT)
Accessed:       2015-04-29 00:00:00 (EDT)
Created:        2015-04-29 13:39:34 (EDT)

Sectors:
1140280 0 0 0 0 0 0
0 0 0 0 0 0 0
phil@i7laptop:~/sleuthkit$
```

FIGURE 6.29.

Running istat against a cluster in a FAT filesystem used to store a small file.

```
phil@i7laptop:~/sleuthkit$ icat -o 63   /media/phil/TOSHIBA\ EXT/BU/images/Filesy
stems1-Final.img 7
[boot loader]
timeout=30
default=multi(0)disk(0)rdisk(0)partition(1)\WINDOWS
[operating systems]
multi(0)disk(0)rdisk(0)partition(1)\WINDOWS="Microsoft Windows XP Professional"
/noexecute=optin /fastdetect
phil@i7laptop:~/sleuthkit$
```

FIGURE 6.30.

Using icat to extract a file by its starting cluster.

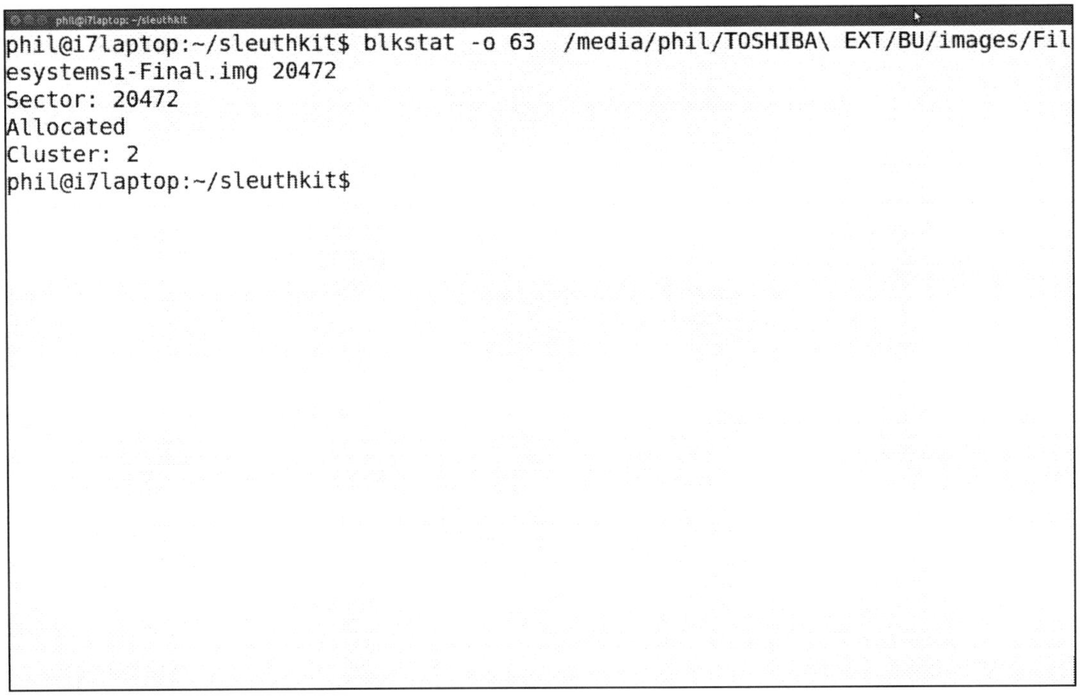

```
phil@i7laptop:~/sleuthkit$ blkstat -o 63  /media/phil/TOSHIBA\ EXT/BU/images/Fil
esystems1-Final.img 20472
Sector: 20472
Allocated
Cluster: 2
phil@i7laptop:~/sleuthkit$
```

FIGURE 6.31.

Running blkstat against the starting sector of cluster 2. The sector number was obtained by running other higher level TSK commands.

sector such as whether or not it is allocated and the cluster within which it is contained, if any. The results of running this command against the starting sector of cluster 2 (which contains the root directory) are shown in Figure 6.31.

The `blkcat` command can be used to extract a sector from a filesystem image. When dealing with raw images this command is unnecessary as the same functionality is provided by dd. Using this command to extract the start of the root directory is shown in Figure 6.32.

I have not presented an exhaustive list of TSK commands here. Rather, I have only listed the commands you are most likely to use when examining FAT filesystems. See http://wiki.sleuthkit.org for additional documentation if you are interested.

Installing Autopsy on Linux

There are a few options if you want to run Autopsy on a Linux workstation. The easiest is just to run the Windows version with WINE. Recall that WINE (WINE Is Not an Emulator) is a tool that allows Windows applications to be run on Linux by translating Win32 API calls to native Linux system calls. If you just want to get to work with the minimum of hassle this is a good option. You might be tempted to install Autopsy from system repositories. Be warned that you will likely get a very old version this way (2.x versus 4.x at the time of this writing).

```
phil@i7laptop:~/sleuthkit$ blkcat -o 63   /media/phil/TOSHIBA\ EXT/BU/images/File
systems1-Final.img 20472  |xxd |head
0000000: 5041 4745 4649 4c45 5359 5326 0093 586c  PAGEFILESYS&..Xl
0000010: 9d46 9d46 0000 52bf 9d46 0300 0000 0072  .F.F..R..F.....r
0000020: 5749 4e44 4f57 5320 2020 2010 00aa 586c  WINDOWS    ...Xl
0000030: 9d46 9d46 0000 596c 9d46 0314 0000 0000  .F.F..Yl.F......
0000040: 4e54 4c44 5220 2020 2020 2027 0800 0060  NTLDR      '...`
0000050: 0431 9d46 0100 0060 0431 9a0e b0d0 0300  .1.F...`.1......
0000060: 4e54 4445 5445 4354 434f 4d27 0000 0060  NTDETECTCOM'...`
0000070: 0431 9d46 0100 0060 0431 ca10 ccb9 0000  .1.F...`.1......
0000080: 424f 4f54 2020 2020 494e 4906 1815 f16c  BOOT    INI....l
0000090: 9d46 9d46 0100 8a6d 9d46 6611 d300 0000  .F.F...m.Ff.....
phil@i7laptop:~/sleuthkit$
```

FIGURE 6.32.

Using blkcat to extract a sector from an image.

The latest version of Autopsy can be built from source. I will outline this process in this section. Be aware that there could be small changes to this process by the time you are reading this book. The most up-to-date instructions can be found in the BUILDING.txt file inside the Autopsy source code on github.com. This file can be found at https://github.com/sleuthkit/autopsy/blob/develop/BUILDING.txt.

The first step to build Autopsy is to get Java set up correctly. As of this writing you will need Oracle's Java Development Kit (JDK) version 1.8.0_66 or higher. This version is likely not found in your system repositories so you must download it from Oracle's website.

Once you have properly installed the JDK you will need to download the code for The Sleuth Kit (TSK) and build it. This is rather easy to do using git. The command is `git clone https://github.com/sleuthkit/sleuthkit.git`. Running this command is shown in Figure 6.33. If you get an error saying git is not installed, install it using `sudo apt-get install git`.

If you look at the INSTALL.txt file in your downloaded TSK source directory it will tell you that you can simply run the configure script in order to generate a makefile. This configure script will be missing, however. In order to properly build this file you will need the automake, autoconf, and libtool packages which can be installed using the command `sudo apt-get install automake autoconf libtool`. Once the required packages are installed, the configure script can be created by running `./bootstrap`. These steps are shown in Figure 6.34.

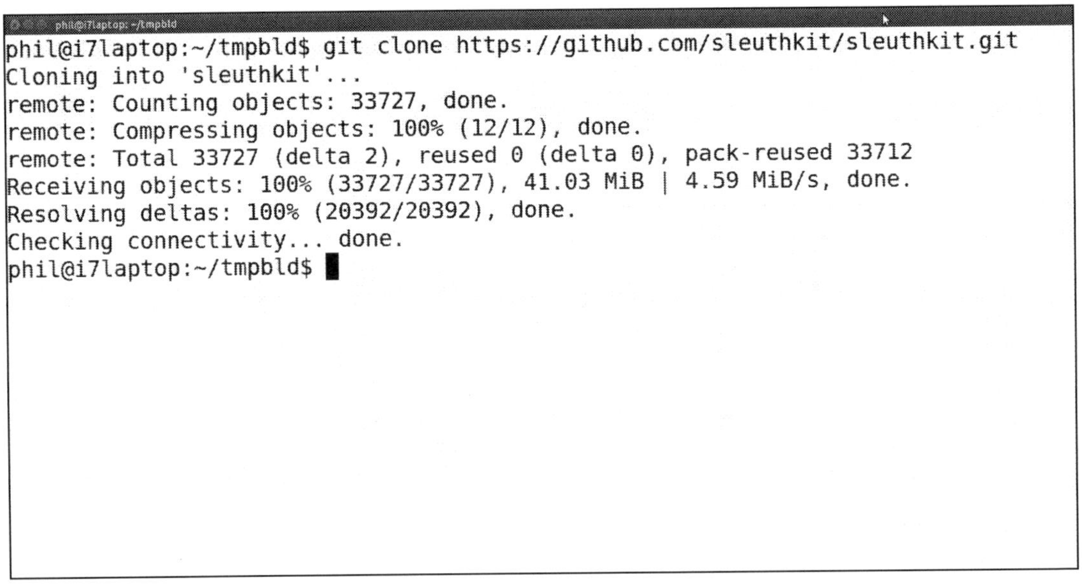

CHAPTER 6 FAT Filesystems

```
phil@i7laptop:~/tmpbld$ git clone https://github.com/sleuthkit/sleuthkit.git
Cloning into 'sleuthkit'...
remote: Counting objects: 33727, done.
remote: Compressing objects: 100% (12/12), done.
remote: Total 33727 (delta 2), reused 0 (delta 0), pack-reused 33712
Receiving objects: 100% (33727/33727), 41.03 MiB | 4.59 MiB/s, done.
Resolving deltas: 100% (20392/20392), done.
Checking connectivity... done.
phil@i7laptop:~/tmpbld$
```

FIGURE 6.33.

Downloading TSK source code with git.

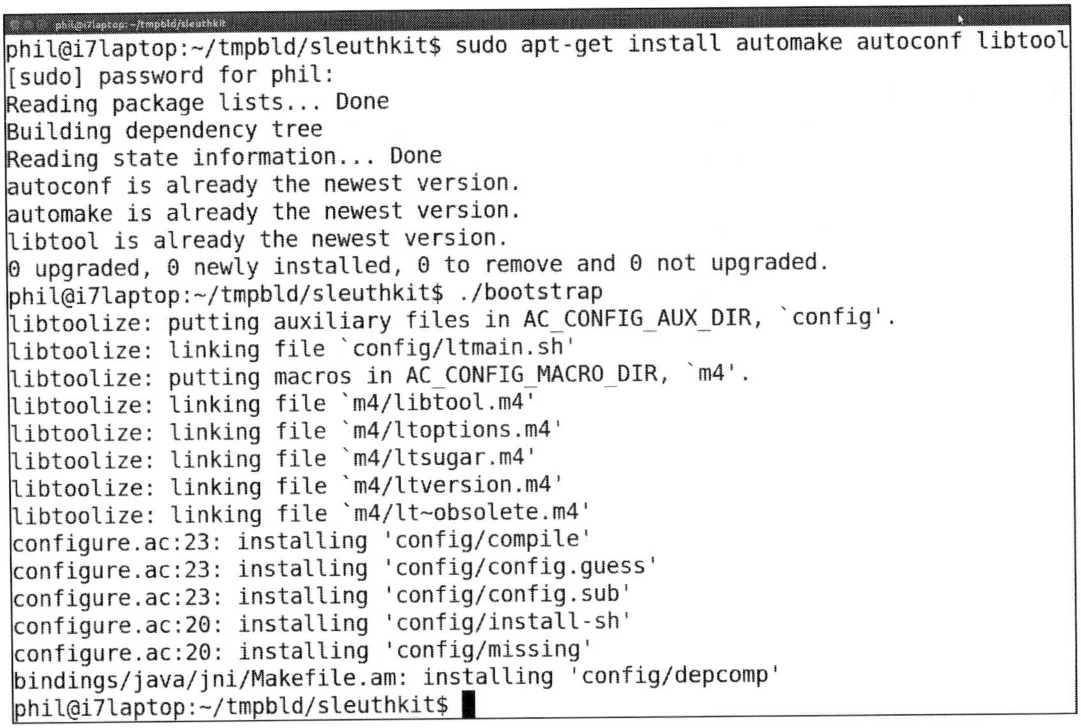

```
phil@i7laptop:~/tmpbld/sleuthkit$ sudo apt-get install automake autoconf libtool
[sudo] password for phil:
Reading package lists... Done
Building dependency tree
Reading state information... Done
autoconf is already the newest version.
automake is already the newest version.
libtool is already the newest version.
0 upgraded, 0 newly installed, 0 to remove and 0 not upgraded.
phil@i7laptop:~/tmpbld/sleuthkit$ ./bootstrap
libtoolize: putting auxiliary files in AC_CONFIG_AUX_DIR, `config'.
libtoolize: linking file `config/ltmain.sh'
libtoolize: putting macros in AC_CONFIG_MACRO_DIR, `m4'.
libtoolize: linking file `m4/libtool.m4'
libtoolize: linking file `m4/ltoptions.m4'
libtoolize: linking file `m4/ltsugar.m4'
libtoolize: linking file `m4/ltversion.m4'
libtoolize: linking file `m4/lt~obsolete.m4'
configure.ac:23: installing 'config/compile'
configure.ac:23: installing 'config/config.guess'
configure.ac:23: installing 'config/config.sub'
configure.ac:20: installing 'config/install-sh'
configure.ac:20: installing 'config/missing'
bindings/java/jni/Makefile.am: installing 'config/depcomp'
phil@i7laptop:~/tmpbld/sleuthkit$
```

FIGURE 6.34.

Generating the configure script by installing required tools and executing the bootstrap script.

Running the configure script should generate a Makefile. If you are missing any required libraries or tools, the script will tell you. If this happens, simply install the required item and rerun configure. Compiling TSK once you have a Makefile is as simple as typing `make` from within the main sleuthkit directory. While you should not need it yet, you may wish to set the JDK_HOME environment variable by typing `export JDK_HOME=<directory where you installed JDK>`. TSK can be optionally installed for all users by running `sudo make install`.

Autopsy needs a Java archive (JAR) file. To build this file simply change to the bindings/java subdirectory in the sleuthkit source tree and type `ant dist-PostgreSQL`. The TSK_HOME environment variable must be set to point to the newly built TSK by running `export TSK_HOME=<main sleuthkit directory>`.

With the underlying TSK utilities and libraries installed it is time to download the Autopsy source code by typing `git clone https://github.com/sleuthkit/autopsy.git` from your home directory (or wherever you would like to put the source code) as shown in Figure 6.35.

After the Autopsy source code has been downloaded, it can be built using ant. The ant utility is frequently used to build Java applications. The Autopsy documentation states that all is required is to change to the autopsy source directory and type `ant`. I have found this to not be the case. Rather, I get an error related to the file Tsk_DataModel_PostgreSQL.jar as shown in Figure 6.36.

```
phil@i7laptop:~/tmpbld$ git clone https://github.com/sleuthkit/autopsy.git
Cloning into 'autopsy'...
remote: Counting objects: 123885, done.
remote: Compressing objects: 100% (209/209), done.
remote: Total 123885 (delta 125), reused 0 (delta 0), pack-reused 123600
Receiving objects: 100% (123885/123885), 413.60 MiB | 4.49 MiB/s, done.
Resolving deltas: 100% (67213/67213), done.
Checking connectivity... done.
Checking out files: 100% (2572/2572), done.
phil@i7laptop:~/tmpbld$
```

FIGURE 6.35.

Downloading Autopsy source code with git.

```
-javac-init-nbjdk:

-javac-init-bootclasspath-prepend:

-javac-init-no-bootclasspath-prepend:

-javac-init:

init:

findTSK:
     [echo]   TSK_HOME: /home/phil/tmpbld/sleuthkit/

getTSKJars:

BUILD FAILED
/home/phil/tmpbld/autopsy/netbeans-plat/8.1/harness/suite.xml:187: The following
 error occurred while executing this line:
/home/phil/tmpbld/autopsy/Core/build.xml:31: The following error occurred while
executing this line:
/home/phil/tmpbld/autopsy/Core/build.xml:21: Warning: Could not find file /home/
phil/tmpbld/sleuthkit/bindings/java/dist/Tsk_DataModel_PostgreSQL.jar to copy.

Total time: 1 minute 20 seconds
phil@i7laptop:~/tmpbld/autopsy$
```

FIGURE 6.36.

Error related to missing Tsk_DataModel_PostgreSQL.jar file when building Autopsy.

This problem is easily fixed by changing to the bindings/java/dist subdirectory in the sleuthkit source tree (not autopsy!) and copying the Tsk_DataModel.jar file to the correct filename by typing `cp Tsk_DataModel.jar Tsk_DataModel_PostgreSQL.jar`. Now that Autopsy can find the appropriate JAR file, change back to the root Autopsy source code directory and rerun `ant`. The tools should now build successfully. To run Autopsy execute `ant run` from the root Autopsy directory. You should eventually (perhaps minutes later) be greeted with a screen such as the one shown in Figure 6.37. Again, you do not need to build Autopsy to run it under Linux, so you can revert to running the Windows version using WINE if you run into difficulties building it from scratch.

Autopsy basics

In order to use Autopsy you must first create a case. This is easily done from the welcome screen or the Case menu. When you select Create New Case you will be greeted with a screen such as the one shown in Figure 6.38.

After clicking Next you should see the additional information screen as shown in Figure 6.39.

Once a case has been created, Autopsy will prompt you to add a data source as shown in Figure 6.40. Note that Autopsy asks for a timezone in order to correctly display time-

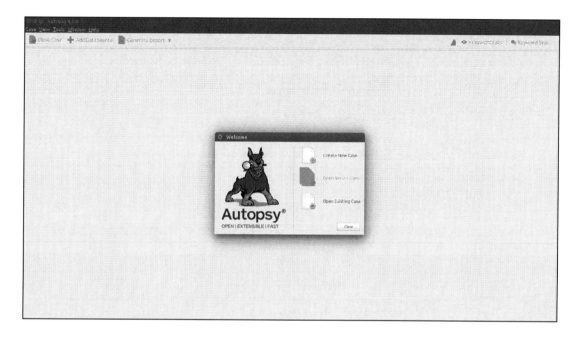

FIGURE 6.37.

The Autopsy start screen after successfully building TSK and Autopsy from source on Linux.

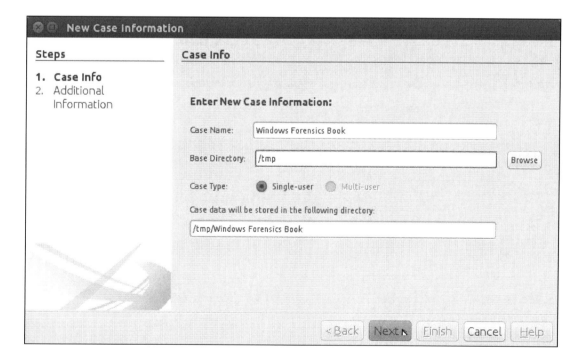

FIGURE 6.38.

Creating a case in Autopsy.

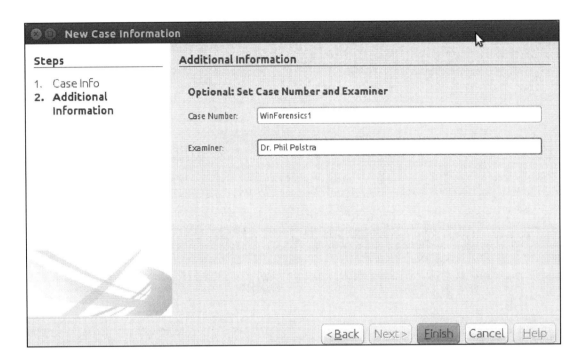

FIGURE 6.39.

Entering additional information when creating a case.

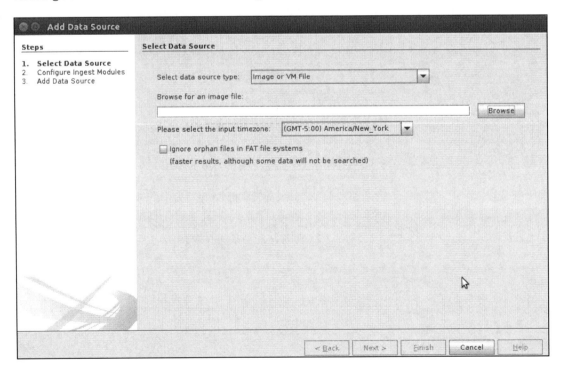

FIGURE 6.40.

Adding a data source in Autopsy.

stamps. This is especially useful if the subject system and forensic workstation are in different timezones.

Once a data source has been selected, you must tell Autopsy which ingest modules to run. Only select modules you think you will need. The initial ingestion can take hours to run. For example, the 20 gigabyte image used for some of the figures in this chapter took over six hours to ingest into Autopsy! The ingest configuration screen is shown in Figure 6.41.

In the hours that it takes to ingest a filesystem image into Autopsy the tool can still be used to a limited extent. A caveat of using Autopsy while it is still ingesting is that the screen might flicker and it might often take you back to the main case page. This can be rather frustrating if you are trying to examine a file several levels down in the directory tree.

Starting at the top of a case tree you should see a Data Sources branch. If you expand this, you should see any images that you have added to the case and also any partitions inside the images. Part of the root directory for a FAT32 image is shown in Figure 6.42. The files with red X's on their icons are deleted files. Note that this uses the same partition labeling scheme as the underlying TSK discussed earlier in this chapter.

The Views branch of a case tree has three subbranches: File Types, Deleted Files, and File Size. The File Types branch will show several commonly interesting file types including images, videos, audio, archives, documents, and executables. Personally, I do not find the

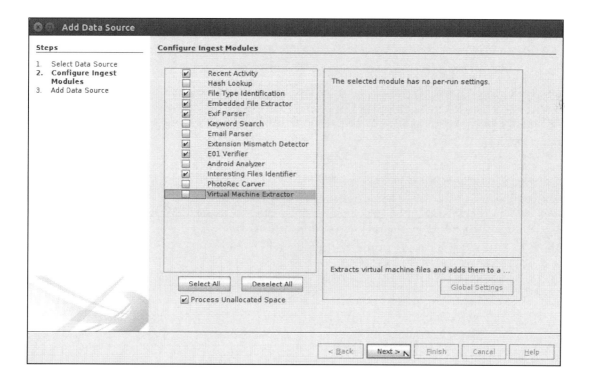

FIGURE 6.41.

Configuring ingest modules when adding a data source. Unselect unnecessary ingest modules in order to speed up processing times.

CHAPTER 6 FAT Filesystems

FIGURE 6.42.

Examining filesystem images in Autopsy.

Deleted Files view terribly useful as it often has thousands of files, most of which are likely not recoverable. The File Size view can help you locate larger files. Notice that there are less than fifty files larger than 50 megabytes out of thousands in this image. These views are shown in Figure 6.43.

The Results tree is where Autopsy displays all of the information found when running various ingest modules. Some of the standard ingest modules include EXIF metadata, extension mismatch detection, user accounts, web bookmarks, web cookies, web downloads, web history, web searches, keyword hits, hash set hits, and e-mail messages. We will discuss where the ingest modules get this information in detail later in this book. At that time a number of stand-alone tools that can be used outside of Autopsy will be presented. Some of the web searches performed are displayed in Figure 6.44.

Autopsy can be used to generate a timeline by selecting Timeline from the Tools menu. It can take some time to generate a timeline from a typical filesystem image. A much faster and more general method for creating timelines is described in this book. One of the Autopsy timeline views is shown in Figure 6.45.

Several reports which are primarily just the results from ingest modules in a convenient format are available. These reports are created by selecting Generate Report from the Tools menu. An example HTML report is shown in Figure 6.46.

Deleted files

FIGURE 6.43.

The standard views in the Autopsy case tree.

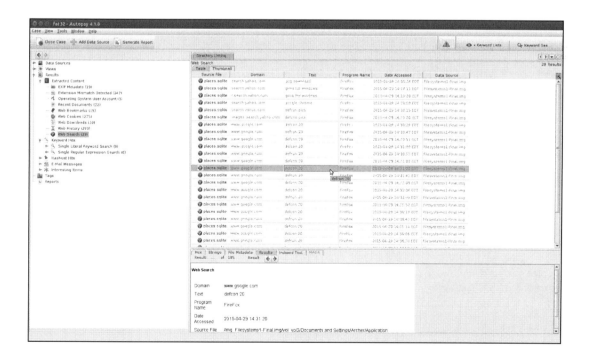

FIGURE 6.44.

Examining users' web searches in Autopsy.

198 CHAPTER 6 FAT Filesystems

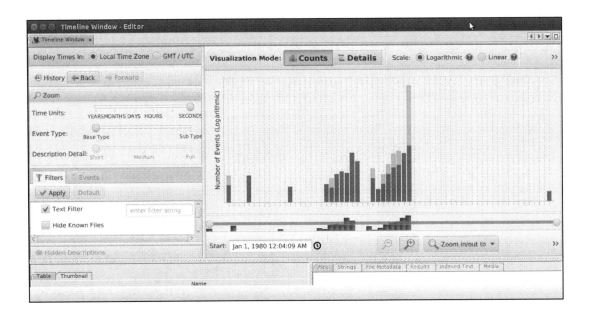

FIGURE 6.45.

Creating and viewing a timeline in Autopsy.

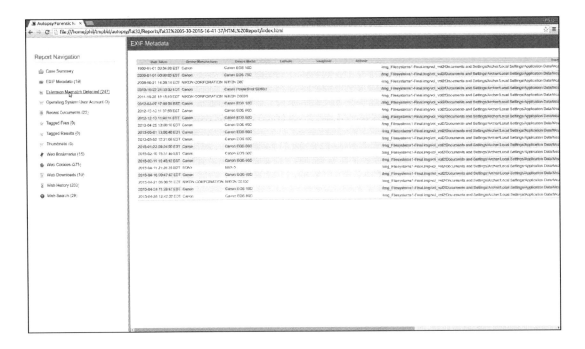

FIGURE 6.46.

An HTML report generated by Autopsy.

DELETED FILES

It is not unusual for a forensic investigator to attempt to recover deleted files. There are a number of tools that have been created over the years to facilitate deleted file recovery. As we shall soon see, it is not possible to recover a deleted file all of the time. While the FAT filesystem is quite simple, it is also one of the hardest filesystems to deal with when it comes to deleted file recovery.

What happens when files are deleted

When a file is deleted, the information is not normally erased from the media. If recovery is attempted immediately, the chances for success are good. The probability of successfully recovering a deleted file goes down with each successive file operation on the filesystem.

When a file or directory is deleted, the first byte in the directory entry or entries (if it has a long filename) is changed to 0xE5. This marks the entry as available for reuse. For FAT32 filesystems the high word of the starting cluster may be zeroed out depending on the version of Windows in use. No other changes are made to the directory entry or entries.

In the FATs any clusters that were used by the file or directory are marked as available. In other words, each of these FAT entries are set equal to zero. There are three basic recovery scenarios: a single cluster file, a contiguous multiple cluster file, and a fragmented multiple cluster file.

The easiest recovery scenario is the single cluster file. If the filesystem is FAT12 or FAT16, recovery is guaranteed provided the cluster has not been reused. If you are forced to deal with a FAT32 filesystem, recovery may still be possible. In this case some intelligent guessing of the starting cluster high word can be performed. It is typical for files to be stored in higher numbered clusters than their containing directory. A good initial guess for the cluster high word is that of the containing directory. Each possible high word can be tested until the file size and type match that of the deleted file.

The medium difficult recovery scenario involves a contiguous (not fragmented) multiple cluster file on a FAT12 or FAT16 filesystem. Recovery is likely in this scenario provided the clusters have not been reused. While this situation may not seem likely, multiple studies have found that the majority of files are contiguous. If the file was stored on a FAT32 filesystem and the starting cluster high word has been zeroed out, successful recovery is far from guaranteed. The problem is that there are usually multiple high words that would appear to match. There is no way to know for certain that the file was contiguous, so all of the possible high word values could be incorrect.

The most difficult recovery scenario involves a fragmented file. If you are extra unlucky, the file is stored on a FAT32 filesystem and the starting cluster high word has been zeroed out. It is typical for files to grow toward higher numbered clusters (even if they are fragmented). If you have a FAT12 or FAT16 filesystem the most likely candidate for the correct cluster chain would be the set of the first n available clusters beginning with the file's starting cluster where the file requires n clusters to be stored. The chances of this cluster chain being correct go down as the volume begins to fill (once the end of the disk is reached, Windows will start using lower numbered clusters) and if many fragmented files have recently been deleted (the file clusters might be intertwined). As with the other scenarios, multiple possibilities must be

CHAPTER 6 FAT Filesystems

evaluated if the file was stored on a FAT32 filesystem and the starting cluster high word has been zeroed out. Some of the possible techniques involve file analysis which is the subject of the next chapter.

After reading this section you might think that recovering deleted files is somewhat hopeless. However, there is good news. Today most systems use NTFS on internal drives and deleted file recovery is much simpler than with FAT. FAT filesystems are primarily used on removable media which are much less likely to be fragmented. Even in cases where no discernible filesystem is present a technique known as file carving (described in the next chapter) can be used.

Examining deleted files in Active@ Disk Editor

Examining files and directories deleted from FAT12 and FAT16 filesystems is fairly easy using ADE. The process is as follows. When navigating a directory look for any entries that begin with 0xE5. Ignore any long filename entries. Right click on the appropriate short filename entry and choose Set Template Position from the popup menu. You may also need to ensure that the template is set to FAT Directory Entry. With the template set correctly a hyperlink for the first cluster should be displayed in the template view as shown in Figure 6.47. The results of clicking on the hyperlink are shown in Figure 6.48. Note that this seems to match the directory entry for a text file of length 0x2D.

The directory entry for a deleted directory is shown in Figure 6.49. The corresponding

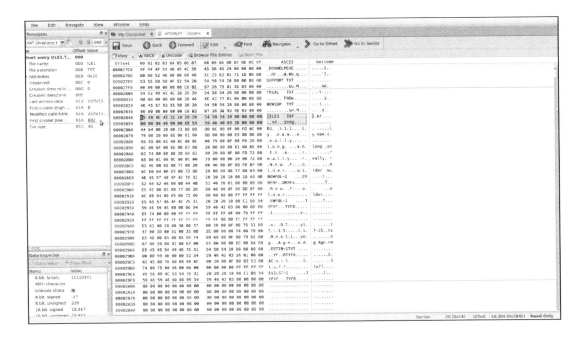

FIGURE 6.47.

Examining a deleted file's directory entry in Active@ Disk Editor.

Deleted files

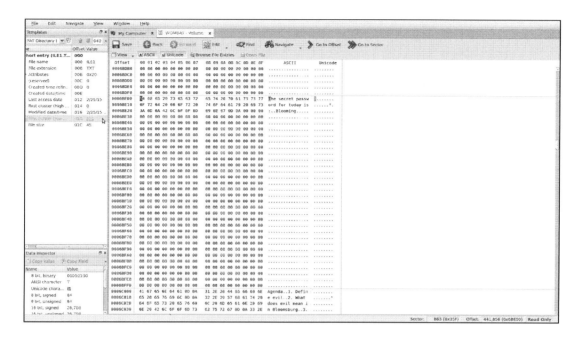

FIGURE 6.48.
A deleted text file's contents.

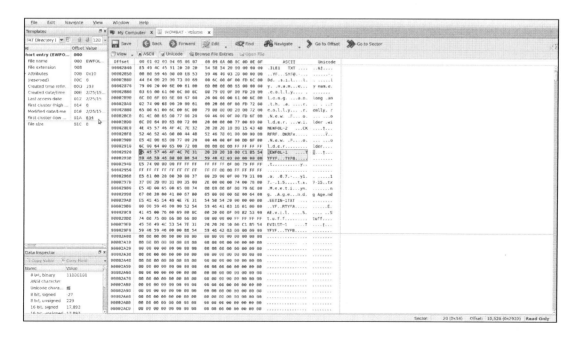

FIGURE 6.49.
Examining a deleted directory's directory entry in Active@ Disk Editor.

202 CHAPTER 6 FAT Filesystems

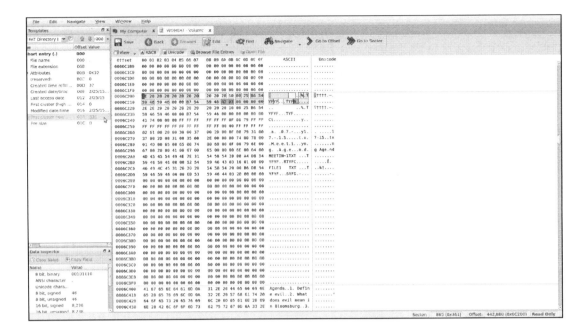

FIGURE 6.50.

A deleted directory's contents.

cluster appears in Figure 6.50. Notice how the subdirectory starts with the appropriate dot and dot dot entries. The dot entry correctly points to the current cluster.

The directory entry for a JPEG file deleted from a FAT16 filesystem on a compact flash card is shown in Figure 6.51. Note that the file started in cluster 3,634 and occupied multiple clusters. The results of clicking on the hyperlink are shown in Figure 6.52. As we will learn in the next chapter, this file has the correct signature for a JPEG file.

We can examine one of the FATs to verify that the appropriate clusters are marked as available. Since this is a FAT16 filesystem each FAT entry uses two bytes. Therefore, the offset from the start of the FAT for cluster 3634 is 3634 * 2 = 7268 or 0x1C64. The first FAT can be found at offset 0x0200 which gives the offset for the appropriate entry as 0x1E64. Navigating to this offset as shown in Figure 6.53 reveals a large block of available clusters.

The directory entry for a file deleted from a FAT32 filesystem is shown in Figure 6.54. Notice that the starting cluster high word appears to have been zeroed out. This is easily confirmed by clicking on the hyperlink. Recovery of this file is best achieved with the assistance of some Python scripting or other tool.

Deleted files and Python

As we have seen in the previous section, in some cases recovering deleted files from a FAT filesystem can be quite simple. However, there are many cases that are far from easy. Python

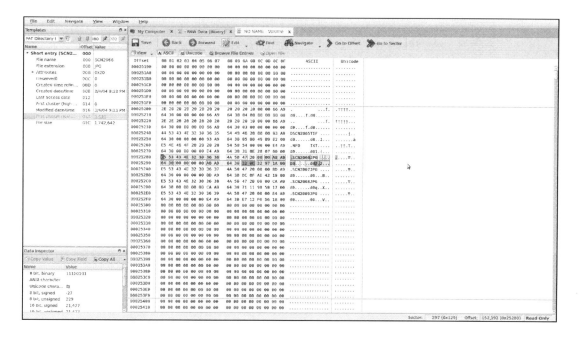

FIGURE 6.51.

Examining a JPEG file deleted from a FAT16 filesystem on a compact flash card.

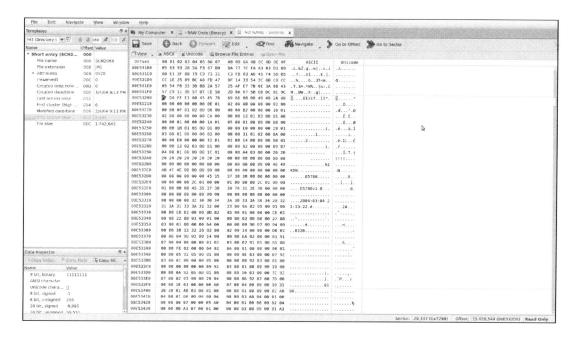

FIGURE 6.52.

The first sector of a deleted JPEG file.

204 CHAPTER 6 FAT Filesystems

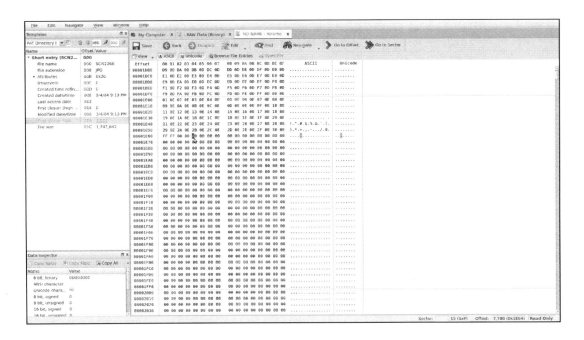

FIGURE 6.53.

Verifying that clusters are unallocated by checking the FAT.

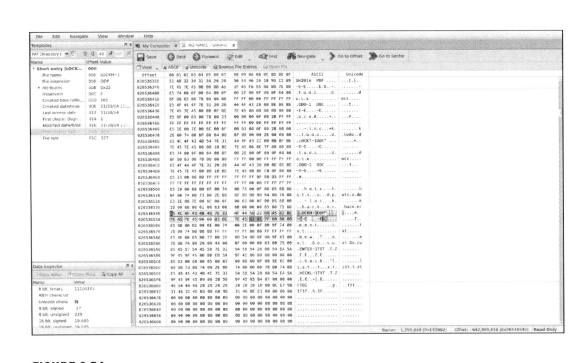

FIGURE 6.54.

A file deleted from a FAT32 filesystem that has a zeroed out starting cluster high word.

can help automate the recovery process and increase the chances of success. In this section we will create a Python script that leverages our previously developed code.

```
!/usr/bin/python3
'''This script will list and optionally attempt
to recover deleted files on a FAT filesystem
given the directory's starting cluster and an
image file.

Created by Dr. Phil Polstra
for PentesterAcademy.com'''

import os.path
import sys
import struct
from mbr import Mbr
from vbr import Vbr
from fat import Fat
from directory import *

__all__=['DeletedEntry', 'DeletedList']

class DeletedEntry(FileEntry):
    '''This class extends the FileEntry class
    to include support for deleted files.  It
    will give the probability of recovery and
    also attempts to recover a deleted file.'''
    def __init__(self, buffer, offset=0, fat32=True, clusterSize=4096):
        '''FAT32 might zero out the high word for the
        starting cluster, so we need to know if this is
        a 32-bit FAT filesystem when attempting recovery.'''
        super().__init__(buffer, offset)
        self._fat32=fat32
        self._clusterSize=clusterSize
```

The script begins with the usual she-bang line and a few imports followed by a list of items to be exported if this file is imported by another script. The DeletedEntry class does something new. It inherits from the FileEntry class created earlier. When a class inherits from another, it will contain all of the methods and data members from the parent class. The line `super().__init__ (buffer, offset)` causes the base class (FileEntry) constructor to be called. The super() function will return an object of the parent class type for any class. After calling this parent constructor, the two new data members, _fat32 and _clusterSize, are initialized. It is true that a Vbr object has these two new pieces of information, but including a Vbr object for every deleted entry would lead to poor performance.

Next we define a method for DeletedEntry called definitelyNotRecoverable. The following conditions make it impossible to recover a deleted file: the file is not deleted, the entry contains a long filename chunk (no metadata), if it is not a FAT32 filesystem and the starting cluster low word is zero, if it is not a FAT32 filesystem and the starting cluster is allocated (too late, the cluster was reused), and if it is a FAT32 filesystem and the starting cluster high word has not been zeroed and the starting cluster is allocated. The code for this method follows.

```
def definitelyNotRecoverable(self, fat):
    '''A file is definitely not recoverable if it
    is a long filename entry or the starting
    cluster is zero or the starting cluster is
    allocated.'''
    if not self.deleted():
       return True
    if self.hasLongFilename():
       return True
    if not self._fat32 and self.startCluster()==0:
       return True
    if (not self._fat32 and
       fat.isAllocated(self.startCluster()) ):
       return True
    if (self._fat32 and
       self.startCluster()//65536>0 and
       fat.isAllocated(self.startCluster()) ):
       return True
    return False
```

There are two conditions under which a file is definitely recoverable. Both involve a file or directory that fits within a single cluster. If the filesystem is FAT12 or FAT16 and the starting cluster is unallocated the file is recoverable. If the filesystem is FAT32 and the the starting cluster high word has not been zeroed out and the starting cluster is unallocated the file is recoverable. A definitelyRecoverable method and __str__ method for DeletedEntry follow.

```
def definitelyRecoverable(self, fat):
    '''A file is definitely recoverable if it
    is less than a cluster long and the cluster
    is unallocated.  We could also check the
    RAM slack but that would require access
    to the filesystem image.'''
    if not self.deleted():
       return False
    if (not self._fat32 and
       self.filesize() <= self._clusterSize and
       not fat.isAllocated(self.startCluster()) ):
       return True
```

```
        if (self._fat32 and
           self.startCluster()//65536>0 and
           self.filesize() <= self._clusterSize and
           not fat.isAllocated(self.startCluster()) ):
            return True
        return False

    def __str__(self):
        '''Method for print.  Will print
        will print <DEL> before filename.'''
        prefix=''
        if self.deleted():
            prefix='<DEL>'
        return prefix + super().__str__()
```

Armed with methods to determine if success is guaranteed or impossible we now add a recoverFile method to DeletedEntry. This method calls two helper methods: _recoverFileFat16 (which also does FAT12) and _recoverFileFat32. Recall that starting any class variable or method with a single underscore is a polite request that the item not be touched directly from outside the class. The code for recoverFile and _recoverFileFat16 follows.

```
    def recoverFile(self, imageFile, offset, fat, vbr, hiwordGuess=0):
        '''Attempt to recover the file given the image
        filename, offset to the start of the partition
        in bytes, and the FAT & VBR objects (because you probably
        had it and this will speed up the process).
        Returns the number of candidate files recovered.'''
        # first check that it isn't hopeless
        if self.definitelyNotRecoverable(fat):
            return 0
        if self._fat32:
            return self._recoverFileFat32(imageFile, offset, fat, vbr,\
                hiwordGuess)
        else:
            return self._recoverFileFat16(imageFile, offset, fat, vbr)

    def _recoverFileFat16(self, imageFile, offset, fat, vbr):
        '''Recover a file from a FAT16 or FAT12 filesytem.
        Accepts the image filename, offset in bytes to the
        start of the partition and FAT object.'''
        fname=self.shortFilename()
        # first check for the easy case
        if self.definitelyRecoverable(fat):
            # The file is less than a cluster long
            with open(imageFile, 'rb') as f:
```

CHAPTER 6 FAT Filesystems

```
            f.seek(offset + vbr.offsetFromCluster(self.startCluster()))
            fileContent=f.read(self._clusterSize)
    with open(fname, 'wb') as f:
        f.write(fileContent)
    return 1 # one candidate file recovered
# this check shouldn't be needed unless this is called directly
if not self.definitelyNotRecoverable():
    # get the candidate cluster chain
    cchain=self._getCandidateChain(imageFile, offset, fat, vbr, 0)
    if len(cchain)==0: # got nothing
        return 0
    with open(imageFile, 'rb') as f:
        with open(fname, 'wb') as g:
            for i in cchain:
                f.seek(offset+vbr.offsetFromCluster(i))
                fileContent=f.read(self._clusterSize)
                g.write(fileContent)
    return 1
return 0
```

The recoverFile method is straightforward. First it checks if the situation is hopeless in which case it returns zero (the method returns the number of candidate files recovered). Then it simply calls _recoverFileFat32 or _recoverFileFat16 as appropriate.

The _recoverFileFat16 method first checks for the easy case where the file is definitely recoverable. In this case the appropriate cluster is read and then written out to a file with the correct short filename except that the first character will be an underscore. If the file might be recoverable another helper method _getCandidateChain is called. The method will attempt to rebuild a cluster chain. It will begin at the starting cluster and then add any unallocated clusters to the list until the chain contains the appropriate number of clusters. If no suitable cluster chain can be found an empty one is returned. The code for this method follows.

```
def _getCandidateChain(self, imageFile, offset, fat, vbr, hiword):
    '''Given a start cluster hi word this method returns
    a list of cluster numbers for a file.  For FAT12/16
    the hi word should just be zero.  If the hi word is
    not zero then additional checks are performed to
    make sure a bunch of empty clusters at the end
    of the disk are not being matched.'''
    clusters=self.filesize()//self._clusterSize
    if self.filesize()%self._clusterSize !=0:
       clusters+=1 # add a partial cluster
    ramSlack=512-self.filesize()%512
    fileSlack=(self._clusterSize-self.filesize()%self._clusterSize)//512
    candidateChain=[]
    # if the starting cluster is allocated it is a no-go
```

```
    if fat.isAllocated(self.startCluster()%65536 +
       hiword*65536):
       return candidateChain
# short circuit for FAT12/16
foundClusters=0
if not self._fat32 or \
   self.startCluster()//65536>0:
   for i in range(self.startCluster(),
      vbr.totalSectors()//vbr.sectorsPerCluster()):
      if not fat.isAllocated(i):
         candidateChain.append(i)
         foundClusters+=1
      if foundClusters >=clusters:
         break
   return candidateChain
# if we made it this far it is FAT32
for i in range(self.startCluster() + 65536*hiword,
   vbr.totalSectors()//vbr.sectorsPerCluster()):
   if not fat.isAllocated(i):
      candidateChain.append(i)
      foundClusters+=1
   if foundClusters >=clusters:
      # now check that none of these clusters is all
      # zeroes - true that could be legit, but it is
      # very unlikely that such a file has any forensic
      # significance
      with open(imageFile, 'rb') as f:
         for j in candidateChain:
            f.seek(offset +
            vbr.offsetFromCluster(j))
            fileContent=f.read(self._clusterSize)
            if fileContent==b'\x00'*self._clusterSize:
               # the entire cluster was blank
               return []
         #one final check of RAM slack
         f.seek(offset +
            vbr.offsetFromCluster(candidateChain[clusters-1]+1)-
            512 * fileSlack - ramSlack)
         fileContent=f.read(ramSlack)
         if fileContent==b'\x00'*ramSlack:
            return candidateChain
         else:
            return []
```

This method begins by calculating the appropriate number of clusters required to store the file. It then calculates the RAM and file slack for the file. To understand this method you must first understand slack space. Slack space is leftover space in the last cluster of a file. This is broken down into two pieces: RAM slack and file slack.

RAM slack is the partial sector in the slack space. It is so named because a long time ago (over twenty years ago) when DOS or Windows needed to write a file to disk it would copy 512 byte chunks of RAM. If anything just happened to be in RAM right after the data to be written, it was also written to disk. This was done for performance reasons. It did not take long for people to figure out that this was a really bad idea from a security standpoint. For the last few decades this RAM slack always contains zeroes unless someone has explicitly tried to hide data in this space. The _getCandidateChain method relies on this RAM slack being zeroed out as a check to see if a cluster could be the last one in a chain.

File slack is the whole sectors in the slack space. These sectors are not zeroed out and may contain parts of old files. With the increased use of compressed file formats file slack has become less useful in forensic investigations.

Returning to _getCandidateChain, after calculating the RAM and file slack, the starting cluster is checked to see if it is allocated. If it is, an empty chain is returned. For FAT12, FAT16, or FAT32 without a zeroed out starting cluster high word, the chain consists of the set of clusters with the lowest cluster number that is greater than the starting cluster number.

The logic for a FAT32 filesystem when the starting cluster high word has been zeroed is a bit more involved. A best guess at the starting cluster high word is used in this case. The set of candidate clusters is created in a similar manner to the FAT12 or FAT16 case. These clusters are checked to see if any of them contain nothing but zeros. This is certainly possible, but such a file likely has little forensic significance anyway. If the clusters check out, the RAM slacked is checked in the last cluster to see that it contains only zeros.

The _recoverFileFat32 method first checks for a file that is definitely recoverable. If successful recovery is guaranteed, the file is created and the method returns 1. The _getCandidateChain method is used to build a candidate cluster chain with the passed in starting cluster high word guess. If this seems successful, a candidate file is created and the method returns 1. If this guess did not pan out, we increment the high word and try again. If this seemed successful, the file is created and 1 is returned. Finally, if none of these things worked out, we run through all of the possible starting cluster high words, create files for all valid candidates and return the number of candidates found. The _recoverFileFat32 method follows.

```
def _recoverFileFat32(self, imageFile, offset, fat, vbr, hiwordGuess):
    '''Recover a file from a FAT32 filesytem.
    Accepts the image filename, offset in bytes to the
    start of the partition and FAT object.'''
    fname=self.shortFilename()
    # first check for the easy case
    if self.definitelyRecoverable(fat):
        # The file is less than a cluster long
        with open(imageFile, 'rb') as f:
            f.seek(offset + vbr.offsetFromCluster(self.startCluster()))
            fileContent=f.read(self._clusterSize)
```

```python
            with open(fname, 'wb') as f:
                f.write(fileContent)
            return 1 # one candidate file recovered
    # this check shouldn't be needed unless this is called directly
    if not self.definitelyNotRecoverable(fat):
        # get the candidate cluster chain
        # start with the suggested hiword
        cchain=self._getCandidateChain(imageFile, offset, fat, vbr,\
            hiwordGuess)
        if len(cchain)>0: # got something
            with open(imageFile, 'rb') as f:
                with open(fname, 'wb') as g:
                    for i in cchain:
                        f.seek(offset+vbr.offsetFromCluster(i))
                        fileContent=f.read(self._clusterSize)
                        g.write(fileContent)
            return 1
        # if the best guess hiword is not it, try the next hiword
        cchain=self._getCandidateChain(imageFile, offset, fat, vbr,\
            hiwordGuess+1)
        if len(cchain)>0: # got something
            with open(imageFile, 'rb') as f:
                with open(fname, 'wb') as g:
                    for i in cchain:
                        f.seek(offset+vbr.offsetFromCluster(i))
                        fileContent=f.read(self._clusterSize)
                        g.write(fileContent)
            return 1
        # if we are here then we're getting desperate will
        # cycle through the hiwords
        candidates=0
        for i in range(0,
            vbr.totalSectors()//vbr.sectorsPerCluster()//65536):
          cchain=self._getCandidateChain(imageFile, offset, fat, vbr, i)
          if len(cchain)>0: # got something
              candidates+=1
              with open(imageFile, 'rb') as f:
                  with open(fname+str(candidates), 'wb') as g:
                      for j in cchain:
                          f.seek(offset+vbr.offsetFromCluster(j))
                          fileContent=f.read(self._clusterSize)
                          g.write(fileContent)
        return candidates

    return 0
```

We create a DeletedList class that inherits from Directory. This class is used to store only deleted entries from a passed in directory. Note that other than the constructor all of this class is implemented in the parent Directory class. The code for this class follows.

```python
class DeletedList(Directory):
    '''This class creates a list of deleted
    files from a raw directory buffer.'''

    def __init__(self, buffer, fat32=True, clusterSize=4096):
        self._dirEntries=[]
        # while we haven't hit the end add entries
        offset=0
        while offset < len(buffer):
            if buffer[offset:offset+1]==b'\x00':
                break
            de=FileEntry(buffer, offset)
            if buffer[offset:offset+1]==b'\xE5':
                de=DeletedEntry(buffer, offset, fat32, clusterSize)
                self._dirEntries.append(de)
            offset+=32*de.entries() # skip to next file
```

These new classes are used in order to list and attempt to recover files from a directory in a specific cluster. The main method builds upon the main method used in a previous script. After reading the MBR, VBR, and FAT, it will read in the directory in the passed in cluster. From there it will create a DeletedList object and then iterate over the entries in the list in order to attempt recovery. The complete script follows.

```python
#!/usr/bin/python3
'''This script will list and optionally attempt
to recover deleted files on a FAT filesystem
given the directory's starting cluster and an
image file.

Created by Dr. Phil Polstra
for PentesterAcademy.com'''

import os.path
import sys
import struct
from mbr import Mbr
from vbr import Vbr
from fat import Fat
from directory import *

__all__=['DeletedEntry', 'DeletedList']
```

```python
class DeletedEntry(FileEntry):
    '''This class extends the FileEntry class
    to include support for deleted files.  It
    will give the probability of recovery and
    also attempts to recover a deleted file.'''
    def __init__(self, buffer, offset=0, fat32=True, clusterSize=4096):
        '''FAT32 might zero out the high word for the
        starting cluster, so we need to know if this is
        a 32-bit FAT filesystem when attempting recovery.'''
        super().__init__(buffer, offset)
        self._fat32=fat32
        self._clusterSize=clusterSize

    def definitelyNotRecoverable(self, fat):
        '''A file is definitely not recoverable if it
        is a long filename entry or the starting
        cluster is zero or the starting cluster is
        allocated.'''
        if not self.deleted():
            return True
        if self.hasLongFilename():
            return True
        if not self._fat32 and self.startCluster()==0:
            return True
        if (not self._fat32 and
            fat.isAllocated(self.startCluster()) ):
            return True
        if (self._fat32 and
            self.startCluster()//65536>0 and
            fat.isAllocated(self.startCluster()) ):
            return True
        return False

    def definitelyRecoverable(self, fat):
        '''A file is definitely recoverable if it
        is less than a cluster long and the cluster
        is unallocated.  We could also check the
        RAM slack but that would require access
        to the filesystem image.'''
        if not self.deleted():
            return False
        if (not self._fat32 and
            self.filesize() <= self._clusterSize and
            not fat.isAllocated(self.startCluster()) ):
            return True
```

```python
            if (self._fat32 and
                self.startCluster()//65536>0 and
                self.filesize() <= self._clusterSize and
                not fat.isAllocated(self.startCluster()) ):
                return True
            return False

    def __str__(self):
        '''Method for print.  Will print
        will print <DEL> before filename.'''
        prefix=''
        if self.deleted():
            prefix='<DEL>'
        return prefix + super().__str__()

    def recoverFile(self, imageFile, offset, fat, vbr, hiwordGuess=0):
        '''Attempt to recover the file given the image
        filename, offset to the start of the partition
        in bytes, and the FAT & VBR objects (because you probably
        had it and this will speed up the process).
        Returns the number of candidate files recovered.'''
        # first check that it isn't hopeless
        if self.definitelyNotRecoverable(fat):
            return 0
        if self._fat32:
            return self._recoverFileFat32(imageFile, offset, fat, vbr, \
                hiwordGuess)
        else:
            return self._recoverFileFat16(imageFile, offset, fat, vbr)

    def _recoverFileFat16(self, imageFile, offset, fat, vbr):
        '''Recover a file from a FAT16 or FAT12 filesytem.
        Accepts the image filename, offset in bytes to the
        start of the partition and FAT object.'''
        fname=self.shortFilename()
        # first check for the easy case
        if self.definitelyRecoverable(fat):
            # The file is less than a cluster long
            with open(imageFile, 'rb') as f:
                f.seek(offset + vbr.offsetFromCluster(self.startCluster()))
                fileContent=f.read(self._clusterSize)
            with open(fname, 'wb') as f:
                f.write(fileContent)
            return 1 # one candidate file recovered
        # this check shouldn't be needed unless this is called directly
```

```python
        if not self.definitelyNotRecoverable():
            # get the candidate cluster chain
            cchain=self._getCandidateChain(imageFile, offset, fat, vbr, 0)
            if len(cchain)==0: # got nothing
                return 0
            with open(imageFile, 'rb') as f:
                with open(fname, 'wb') as g:
                    for i in cchain:
                        f.seek(offset+vbr.offsetFromCluster(i))
                        fileContent=f.read(self._clusterSize)
                        g.write(fileContent)
            return 1
        return 0

    def _recoverFileFat32(self, imageFile, offset, fat, vbr, hiwordGuess):
        '''Recover a file from a FAT32 filesytem.
        Accepts the image filename, offset in bytes to the
        start of the partition and FAT object.'''
        fname=self.shortFilename()
        # first check for the easy case
        if self.definitelyRecoverable(fat):
            # The file is less than a cluster long
            with open(imageFile, 'rb') as f:
                f.seek(offset + vbr.offsetFromCluster(self.startCluster()))
                fileContent=f.read(self._clusterSize)
            with open(fname, 'wb') as f:
                f.write(fileContent)
            return 1 # one candidate file recovered
        # this check shouldn't be needed unless this is called directly
        if not self.definitelyNotRecoverable(fat):
            # get the candidate cluster chain
            # start with the suggested hiword
            cchain=self._getCandidateChain(imageFile, offset,
                fat, vbr, hiwordGuess)
            if len(cchain)>0: # got something
                with open(imageFile, 'rb') as f:
                    with open(fname, 'wb') as g:
                        for i in cchain:
                            f.seek(offset+vbr.offsetFromCluster(i))
                            fileContent=f.read(self._clusterSize)
                            g.write(fileContent)
                return 1
            # if the best guess hiword is not it, try the next hiword
            cchain=self._getCandidateChain(imageFile, offset,
                fat, vbr, hiwordGuess+1)
```

```python
            if len(cchain)>0: # got something
                with open(imageFile, 'rb') as f:
                    with open(fname, 'wb') as g:
                        for i in cchain:
                            f.seek(offset+vbr.offsetFromCluster(i))
                            fileContent=f.read(self._clusterSize)
                            g.write(fileContent)
                return 1
            # if we are here then we're getting desperate will
            # cycle through the hiwords
            candidates=0
            for i in range(0,
                vbr.totalSectors()//vbr.sectorsPerCluster()//65536):
                cchain=self._getCandidateChain(imageFile, offset, fat, vbr, i)
                if len(cchain)>0: # got something
                    candidates+=1
                    with open(imageFile, 'rb') as f:
                        with open(fname+str(candidates), 'wb') as g:
                            for j in cchain:
                                f.seek(offset+vbr.offsetFromCluster(j))
                                fileContent=f.read(self._clusterSize)
                                g.write(fileContent)
            return candidates

        return 0

    def _getCandidateChain(self, imageFile, offset, fat, vbr, hiword):
        '''Given a start cluster hi word this method returns
        a list of cluster numbers for a file.  For FAT12/16
        the hi word should just be zero.  If the hi word is
        not zero then additional checks are performed to
        make sure a bunch of empty clusters at the end
        of the disk are not being matched.'''
        clusters=self.filesize()//self._clusterSize
        if self.filesize()%self._clusterSize !=0:
            clusters+=1 # add a partial cluster
        ramSlack=512-self.filesize()%512
        fileSlack=(self._clusterSize-self.filesize()%self._clusterSize)//512
        candidateChain=[]
        # if the starting cluster is allocated it is a no-go
        if fat.isAllocated(self.startCluster()%65536 +
            hiword*65536):
            return candidateChain
        # short circuit for FAT12/16
        foundClusters=0
```

```python
        if not self._fat32 or \
            self.startCluster()//65536>0:
            for i in range(self.startCluster(),
                vbr.totalSectors()//vbr.sectorsPerCluster()):
                if not fat.isAllocated(i):
                    candidateChain.append(i)
                    foundClusters+=1
                if foundClusters >=clusters:
                    break
            return candidateChain
        # if we made it this far it is FAT32
        for i in range(self.startCluster() + 65536*hiword,
            vbr.totalSectors()//vbr.sectorsPerCluster()):
            if not fat.isAllocated(i):
                candidateChain.append(i)
                foundClusters+=1
            if foundClusters >=clusters:
                # now check that none of these clusters is all
                # zeroes - true that could be legit, but it is
                # very unlikely that such a file has any forensic
                # significance
                with open(imageFile, 'rb') as f:
                    for j in candidateChain:
                        f.seek(offset +
                        vbr.offsetFromCluster(j))
                        fileContent=f.read(self._clusterSize)
                        if fileContent==b'\x00'*self._clusterSize:
                            # the entire cluster was blank
                            return []
                    #one final check of RAM slack
                    f.seek(offset +
                        vbr.offsetFromCluster(candidateChain[clusters-1]+1)-
                        512 * fileSlack - ramSlack)
                    fileContent=f.read(ramSlack)
                    if fileContent==b'\x00'*ramSlack:
                        return candidateChain
                    else:
                        return []

class DeletedList(Directory):
    '''This class creates a list of deleted
    files from a raw directory buffer.'''

    def __init__(self, buffer, fat32=True, clusterSize=4096):
        self._dirEntries=[]
```

```python
        # while we haven't hit the end add entries
        offset=0
        while offset < len(buffer):
            if buffer[offset:offset+1]==b'\x00':
                break
            de=FileEntry(buffer, offset)
            if buffer[offset:offset+1]==b'\xE5':
                de=DeletedEntry(buffer, offset, fat32, clusterSize)
            self._dirEntries.append(de)
            offset+=32*de.entries() # skip to next file

def usage():
    print("usage " + sys.argv[0] + " <image file> <cluster>\n"+
        "Reads FAT Directory Entries from an image file")
    exit(1)

def main():
    if len(sys.argv) < 3:
      usage()

    notsupParts = [0x05, 0x0f, 0x85, 0x91, 0x9b, 0xc5, 0xe4, 0xee]
    swapParts = [0x42, 0x82, 0xb8, 0xc3, 0xfc]

    # read first sector
    if not os.path.isfile(sys.argv[1]):
        print("File " + sys.argv[1] + " cannot be openned for reading")
        exit(1)

    with open(sys.argv[1], 'rb') as f:
        sector = f.read(512)

    mbr=Mbr(sector) # create MBR object

    if mbr.validSignature():
        print("Looks like a MBR or VBR")
        mbr.prettyPrint()

        for i in range(1,5):
            if not mbr.isEmpty(i):
                if mbr.partitionType(i) in notsupParts:
                    print("Sorry GPT and extended partitions are"
                    " not supported by this script!")
                else:
                    if mbr.partitionType(i) in swapParts:
                        print("Skipping swap partition")
```

```
            else:
                # let's try and read the VBR
                with open(sys.argv[1], 'rb') as f:
                    f.seek(mbr.reservedSectors(i)*512)
                    sector=f.read(512)
                    vbr=Vbr(sector)
                    if vbr.validSignature() and vbr.isFat32():
                     print('Found Volume with type', vbr.filesystemType())
                        print('Volume label:', vbr.volumeLabel())
                        print('Total sectors:', vbr.totalSectors())
                        s=vbr.sectorFromCluster(2)
                        print('Cluster 2:', s)
                        print('Sector:', vbr.clusterFromSector(s))
                        # grab the FAT
                        f.seek(mbr.reservedSectors(i)*512+
                            vbr.sectorFat1()*512)
                        fatRaw=f.read(512*vbr.sectorsPerFat())
                        fat=Fat(fatRaw)
                        # now grab the Directory
                    print('Fetching directory in cluster', sys.argv[2])
                        cchain=fat.clusterChain(int(sys.argv[2]))
                        rdBuffer=b''
                        for clust in cchain:
                            f.seek(mbr.reservedSectors(i)*512+
                                512*vbr.sectorFromCluster(clust))
                            rdBuffer+=f.read(512*vbr.sectorsPerCluster())
                        rd=DeletedList(rdBuffer, vbr.isFat32(),
                            512*vbr.sectorsPerCluster())
                        for j in range(rd.entries()):
                            delFile=rd.entry(j)
                            print(delFile)
                            if delFile.hasShortFilename():
                                print('\tDefinitelyNotRecoverable:',
                                    delFile.definitelyNotRecoverable(fat))
                                print('\tDefinitelyRecoverable:',
                                    delFile.definitelyRecoverable(fat))
                            delFile.recoverFile(sys.argv[1],
                                mbr.reservedSectors(i)*512,
                                fat, vbr,
                                int(sys.argv[2])//65536)
    else:
        print("Doesn't appear to contain valid MBR")

if __name__ == "__main__":
    main()
```

SUMMARY

In this chapter we have learned to extract information from a FAT filesystem. We discovered how to use tools such as Active@ Disk Editor and Autopsy to aid in gathering evidence. We also learned a bit of Python along the way and leveraged this to interpret FAT filesystem structures and also to recover deleted files. In the next chapter we will go from looking at low level filesystem structures to examining files themselves before diving back down into the weeds to look at NTFS filesystems.

CHAPTER 7

File Forensics

INFORMATION IN THIS CHAPTER:

- Hiding Information
- Slack space
- File signatures
- The file utility
- File carving
- File forensics with Active@ Disk Editor
- Automation via shell scripts and Python

HIDING INFORMATION

Now that we have covered the low level details of the FAT filesystem, we will discuss looking at filesystem images at the file level. In other words, we will look at collections of sectors which may be organized into files without any regard to filesystem metadata. The first topic in this chapter is information hiding.

There are a number of places information can hide on media. In some cases a user has intentionally attempted to hide information and in others the data is not easily obtained when interacting with a filesystem in the standard way. Ways of intentionally hiding information include changing file extensions, inserting data in slack space, and storing things in unallocated space. Data stored in unallocated space, slack space, and page (swap) files by Windows can be difficult to retrieve yet useful in certain types of investigations.

Mismatched extensions

Unlike other operating systems such as Linux and OS X, Windows stupidly uses a file's extension and nothing else in order to determine its file type. Windows stores a mapping of file extensions to programs that can interpret that file type in the registry (more about this later in the book). If a user changes a file extension, it can make the file appear corrupted to the casual observer. In order to prevent this situation Windows will warn you if you attempt to change a file extension. Techniques described later in this chapter can be used to find files with mismatched extensions.

Slack space

Slack space is leftover space in the last cluster of a file. It is rare for a file to be exactly a multiple of a cluster size. As shown in Figure 7.1, slack space is broken into two components. The

FIGURE 7.1.

Slack space. Partial sectors of slack are RAM slack and full sectors are file slack.

first component, RAM slack, consists of unused space in the last sector (not cluster!) used by the file. File slack is the whole sectors in the unused space in the last cluster. Files may have no slack, only RAM slack, only file slack, or both RAM and file slack.

RAM slack gets its name from the fact that DOS and Windows originally would write whatever followed data to be written to disk in RAM to the media in order to write 512 bytes at a time. It did not take long for people to figure out that writing potentially sensitive information to the disk in this manner was a really bad idea. For decades these leftover bytes in the last sector have been zeroed out. If you encounter anything other than zeros in RAM slack today it is cause for further investigation. The portion of the last sector which is being used by the file is simply the file size modulus 512. The RAM slack is then the total sector size minus the used portion which yields the following equation for RAM slack: RAM slack = 512 − (file size) % 512.

While RAM slack is now zeroed out by the operating system, the same can not be said for file slack. Any unused sectors in the last cluster of a file are left alone by Windows. If a cluster has only been used once, the extra sectors will likely be filled with zeros. If, however, a cluster was reused, the file slack can contain portions of old files. Just as a user can intentionally store data in RAM slack, this is also possible with file slack. There is no easy way to determine that information has been manually inserted into file slack as it is very common to find data there. Techniques for recovering information from file slack will be covered later in this chapter. The total slack is given by the following formula: (cluster size) − (file size) % (cluster size). As the file slack is the whole sectors of slack, the formula for file slack in sectors is simply ((cluster size) − (file size) % (cluster size))//512. Recall that // indicates integer division.

Unallocated space

Unallocated space comes in several forms. When a disk is partitioned, some sectors might lie outside of any partition. When a filesystem is created on a partition, a few sectors might be unused due to the fact that a filesystem may require a total sector count that is divisible by a certain number (usually a power of two). Finally, there can be sectors in a volume that are currently marked as unallocated or even defective. One of the many advantages to running Linux is that all of these types of unallocated space are easily searched using standard system tools that are likely installed by default on your Linux workstation.

Page file

Like many modern operating systems, Windows uses virtual memory. Systems that employ virtual memory usually also implement swapping. What this means is that when available RAM begins to run low, chunks of RAM are written to disk to allow the currently executing process sufficient RAM to execute. Programs have little control over this process. While some programmers might ensure that sensitive information (such as passwords) are not stored on disk unencrypted, if the information is stored in RAM in clear text it is always possible that it will end up stored in a swapping file. On Windows systems this file is often called a page file. The default page file location is c:\pagefile.sys. The same Linux system tools used to search unallocated space can be used to search this file.

FILE SIGNATURES

For many files the first few bytes (the file header) have well known values. Some files also have well known endings (footers). The header and/or footer combination is known as a file signature. By knowing these signatures it is easy to detect mismatched file extensions, find files in unallocated space, and locate file fragments in the page file. Gary Kessler maintains one of the most comprehensive file signature lists at http://www.garykessler.net/library/file_sigs.html. We will examine some of the more common file signatures in this section.

Examining files in Active@ Disk Editor

Viewing raw file contents in Active@ Disk Editor (ADE) is as simple as selecting a file on the My Computer tab, right clicking on it, and selecting Open in Disk Editor from the popup menu as shown in Figure 7.2. A file named book.docx is shown in Figure 7.3. This file has the signature of an Adobe Portable Document File (PDF). As can be confirmed at Gary Kessler's site, a PDF begins with %PDF-X.x.%, where X.x is the PDF version, and ends with %%EOF.

A file named buddy.doc is shown in Figure 7.4. This is an older format Microsoft Office document. These older office documents begin with 0xD0 0xCF 0x11 0xE0. The easy way to

CHAPTER 7 File Forensics

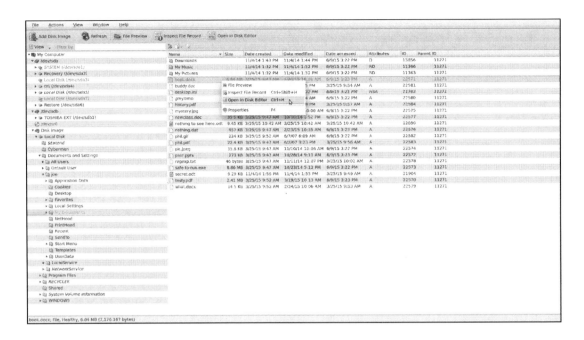

FIGURE 7.2.
Examining raw file data in Active@ Disk Editor.

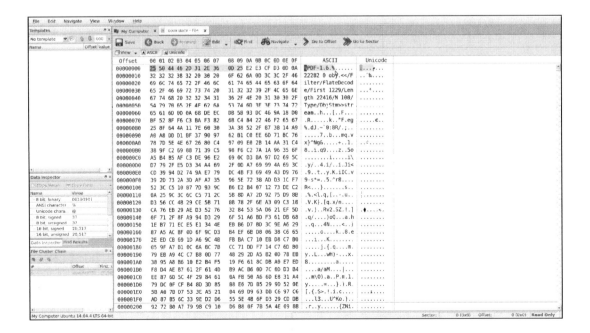

FIGURE 7.3.
An Adobe Portable Document File (PDF). Note that the file extension is mismatched.

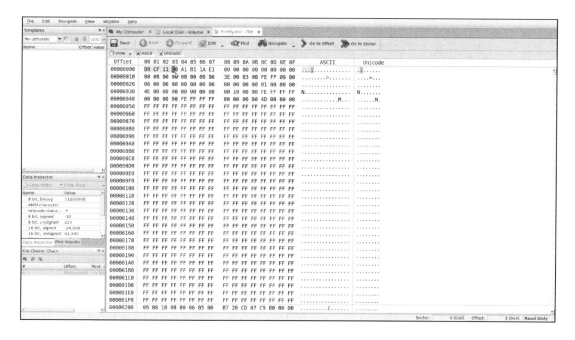

FIGURE 7.4.

An older format Microsoft Word document.

remember this signature is that it spells out "docfile-0". It is often difficult to distinguish a Word document, Excel spreadsheet, or PowerPoint presentation from each other as they all begin with the same header. I have found that the easiest way to make the determination is to scroll to the end of the file and then browse backward. The end of the file will often contain text that makes it clear which type of file you are looking at. Incidentally, one nice feature of OpenOffice or LibreOffice is that they will open any office documents even if the extension is wrong.

Technically the "docfile-0" signature does not indicate a Microsoft Office document. Rather, this indicates a Compound Binary File (CBF) format. The CBF format is used to store data for other programs, including some not made by Microsoft.

A bitmap file is shown in Figure 7.5. Note that because the file signature consists solely of the letters "BM" at the start of the file, searching for these files will lead to many false positives. Incidentally, bytes 2 through 5 are the file size as a 4-byte unsigned little endian integer. This could be used to eliminate some of the false positives.

A JPEG image file is shown in Figure 7.6. There are three different JPEG signatures. The one shown in the figure is common with JPEG generated by a photo editing program such as Photoshop or the GIMP (GNU Image Manipulation Program). This signature is 0xFF 0xD8 0xFF 0xE0 0xXX 0xXX JFIF, where 0xXX 0xXX is the size of a table in the JPEG. The other common JPEG signature is similar, 0xFF 0xD8 0xFF 0xE1 0xXX 0xXX Exif. This format is commonly seen in raw images downloaded from digital cameras. The third, much less popular, format has a signature of 0xFF 0xD8 0xFF 0xE8 0xXX 0xXX SPIFF.

An Open Document Text (ODT) file is shown in Figure 7.7. Many of the modern document

226 CHAPTER 7 File Forensics

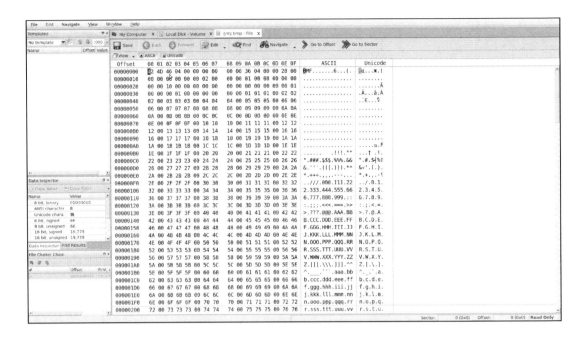

FIGURE 7.5.

A bitmap file. Note that positions 2 through 5 contain the file size.

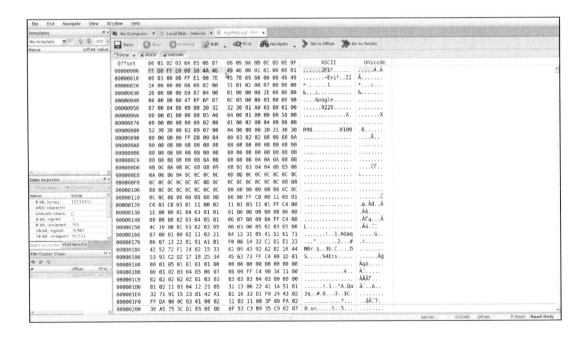

FIGURE 7.6.

A JPEG image file. Note that there are three separate JPEG formats.

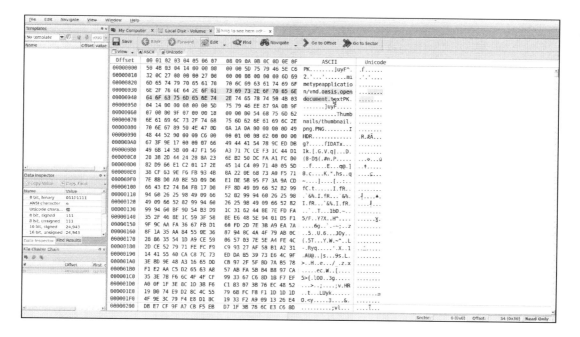

FIGURE 7.7.

An Open Document Text (ODT) file created with OpenOffice or LibreOffice. Note that the string "open.document.text" on the third line makes this file easy to identify.

formats have gone to an Extensible Markup Language (XML) format. This is in fact what the x stands for in .docx, .xlsx, and .pptx file extensions. Because XML files can be rather verbose, most of these new formats are also compressed. A compressed file begins with "PK". How can you discern one compressed file format from another? The key is to look through the file in order to find the "files" embedded in the archive. The open document files from LibreOffice or OpenOffice are the easiest to identify as there is normally a mimetypeapplication field right at the top of the file that tells you exactly what is in the archive.

The beginning of a new format PowerPoint (pptx) file is shown in Figure 7.8. You can see from the "PK" in the first two bytes that this file is compressed. In this case you can tell it is a PowerPoint file from the string "ppt/_rels/presentation.xml" starting at offset 0xFE. Normally it is easier to identify Microsoft Office documents by going to the end of the file and looking backwards. The end of the same file is shown in Figure 7.9. Note the repeated references to a top level ppt directory. The end of a new format Word document is shown in Figure 7.10. In this case the top level directory is word.

The start of a Graphic Interchange Format (GIF) image file is shown in Figure 7.11. The file signature for this format is GIF8xa, where x is either 7 or 9 (for 1987 and 1989 versions of the format). This is a popular image format as it supports animations. Another popular image format, the Portable Network Graphic (PNG), is shown in Figure 7.12. The file begins with "%PNG".

A Microsoft executable file is shown in Figure 7.13. The file signature "MZ" represents the initials of the developer that created this format. An easy way to remember this signature is to

228 CHAPTER 7 File Forensics

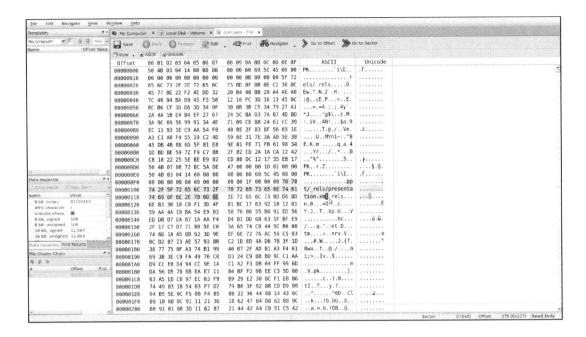

FIGURE 7.8.

The start of a new format PowerPoint file. The "PK" in the first two bytes indicates a compressed file.

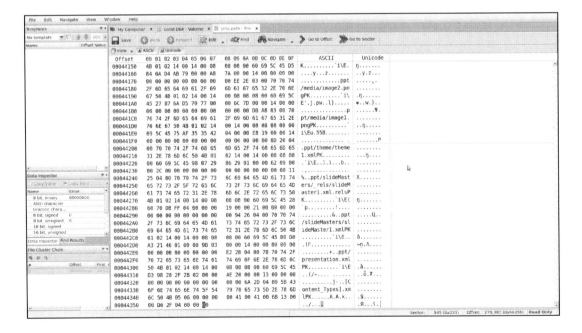

FIGURE 7.9.

The end of a new format PowerPoint file. The repeated references to a top level ppt directory indicate this is a PowerPoint file.

File Signatures 229

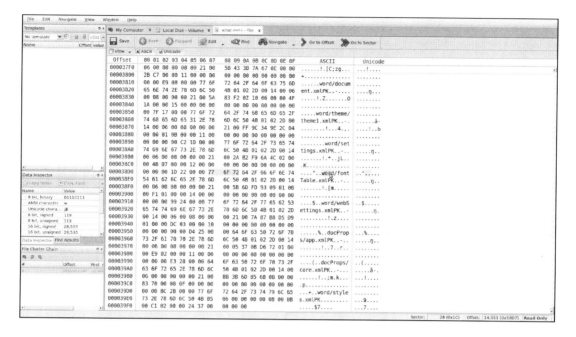

FIGURE 7.10.

The end of a new format Word file. The repeated references to a top level word directory indicate this is a Word file.

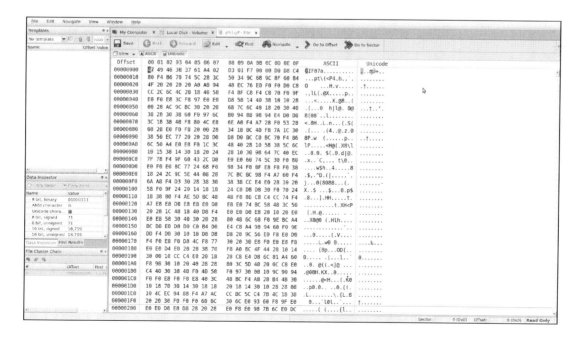

FIGURE 7.11.

The start of a GIF image file.

230 CHAPTER 7 File Forensics

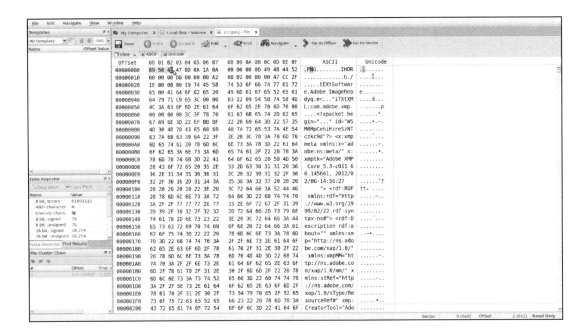

FIGURE 7.12.

The start of a PNG image file. Note that for unknown reasons the 0x89 in the first byte is not displayed correctly as "%".

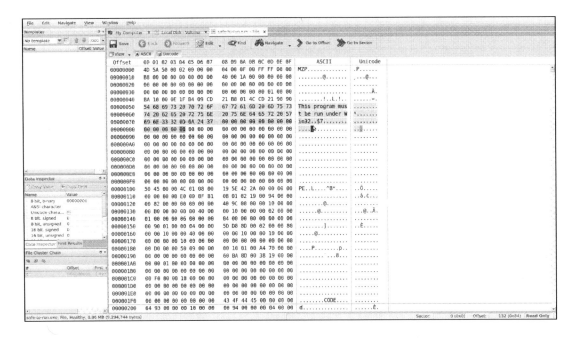

FIGURE 7.13.

A Microsoft executable. The string "This program must be run under Win32" indicates that this is a 32-bit Windows executable.

sound it out as "Microsoft ex-Zah-cute-able". While you might immediately think this means a .exe file, there are several other executables that use this format such as .com files, DLLs, drivers, Program Information Files (PIF), and screen savers. You can tell this particular file is a 32-bit Windows program from the message on the sixth line, "This program must be run under Win32". The "PE" at offset 0x100 also indicates that this is a Portable Executable.

ADE has a find utility which can easily be used to find files of a certain type if you know the file signature. To search through a volume make it the active tab in ADE and then click on the Find button. You should see a dialog like the one shown in Figure 7.14. In this case a per block search is being performed in order to locate PDF files which begin with the string "%PDF". You have the option of searching for the next match or finding all occurrences. When using Find All the results are presented on the Find Results tab as shown in Figure 7.15. Regardless of which find option you choose, be certain to start looking at the beginning of object.

The above technique can be used with any file signature in order to locate files of a certain type. This technique will include files stored in unallocated clusters which can either be deleted

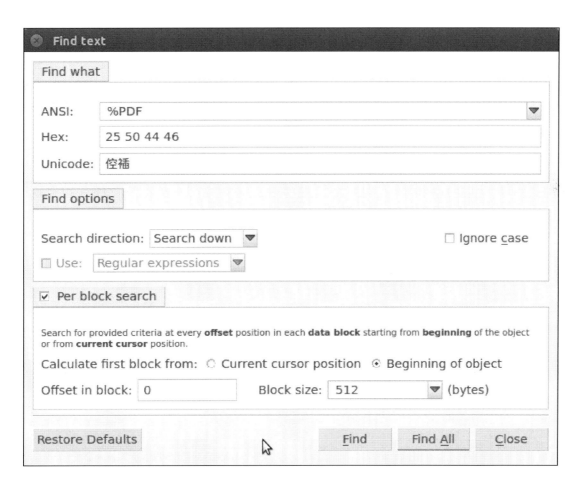

FIGURE 7.14.

Finding PDF files in Active@ Disk Editor.

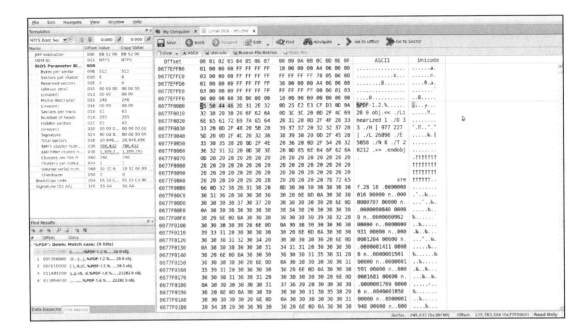

FIGURE 7.15.

Result from using a per block search to find PDF files in Active@ Disk Editor.

or intentionally hidden. To search an entire image, simply open the entire image in ADE and then use the Find button on the raw image tab. ADE also supports regular expression (including extended regular expression) searches if you know how to build regular expressions.

ANALYZING MOUNTED IMAGES

One of the many advantages of using Linux is that raw filesystem image files are easily mounted. Once an image has been mounted, all of the standard Linux system utilities can be used for analysis. Scripts were presented earlier in this book that allow partitions in raw disk images to be easily mounted.

The file utility

As has been stated previously, unlike Windows, Linux does not care about file extensions. Linux will correctly select the appropriate program to open a file. The primary reason that this is possible is the existence of an extensive file signature database in a library that ships with Linux. This library can be tapped using the file utility. A user's "My Documents" directory is shown in a Linux file explorer in Figure 7.16. Note how nothing.dat and phil.pdf are correctly interpreted as being a zip archive and image file, respectively, despite having the wrong file extension.

Analyzing mounted images 233

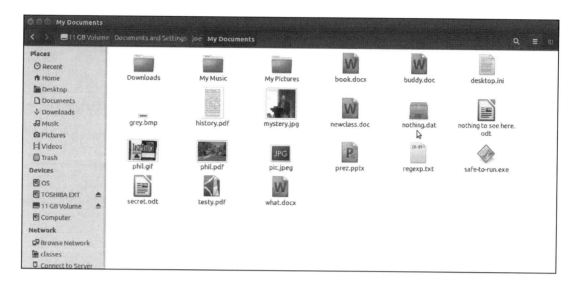

FIGURE 7.16.

Linux correctly interprets file types regardless of file extensions.

The syntax from running the file utility is simply `file <filename>`. Note that this utility does support wild cards in the filename. It also supports recursion should you wish to parse an entire directory tree. The output from running file on a set of files is shown in Figure 7.17.

Notice that the result from the file utility go beyond simple file type identification. The Word documents include authors and timestamps. The image files include size and specification version information. Even the text file results contain additional information.

One of the general philosophies of Unix/Linux is that an operating system should provide a set of programs that do one thing very well which can be combined together to perform almost any task. The general file finder utility in Linux is called find. The general syntax for find is `find <starting directory> [options] [commands]`. By default find will print out files that match the pattern given, if any. Running `find .` will print out all files at or below the current directory. Partial output from this command is shown in Figure 7.18.

As can be seen in Figure 7.18, many of the Windows files and directories have spaces in their filenames. This can make it problematic to pass the results to another program for further processing. One way to solve this problem is to use the -print0 option for the find command. This causes a null character to follow each result instead of the default newline.

The standard way to connect two utilities together in Linux is to pipe the results of one command to the next using the vertical pipe (|). The syntax is simply `<command 1> | <command 2>`. We can use this method to pipe our find results to a while loop which runs the file utility on each of the results. The command is `find . -print0 | while read -d $'\0' fname; do file "$fname"; done`.

The while loop uses the read command. The normal syntax for this command is `read <variable name>`. This will cause one line at a time to be read from standard input and assigned to a variable for each pass through the while loop. This continues until no more

CHAPTER 7 File Forensics

```
phil@i7laptop:/media/part1/Documents and Settings/joe/My Documents$ file *
book.docx:              PDF document, version 1.6
buddy.doc:              Composite Document File V2 Document, Little Endian, Os: Windows, Version 5.
1, Code page: 1252, Title: Excel Timeline Template, Author: Vertex42 LLC, Last Saved By: Jon, Name o
f Creating Application: Microsoft Excel, Last Printed: Wed May 19 06:56:18 2004, Create Time/Date: M
on Mar 29 05:50:20 2004, Last Saved Time/Date: Wed Mar  7 23:09:45 2007, Security: 0
desktop.ini:            ASCII text, with CRLF line terminators
Downloads:              directory
grey.bmp:               PC bitmap, Windows 3.x format, 8 x 2 x 8
history.pdf:            PDF document, version 1.2
My Music:               directory
My Pictures:            directory
mystery.jpg:            JPEG image data, JFIF standard 1.01
newclass.doc:           Composite Document File V2 Document, Little Endian, Os: Windows, Version 6.
1, Code page: 1252, Author: wkrum, Template: Normal.dotm, Last Saved By: Polstra, Philip, Revision N
umber: 13, Name of Creating Application: Microsoft Office Word, Total Editing Time: 01:36:00, Last P
rinted: Wed Feb  8 14:53:00 2006, Create Time/Date: Wed Oct 29 19:09:00 2014, Last Saved Time/Date:
Thu Oct 30 18:52:00 2014, Number of Pages: 4, Number of Words: 855, Number of Characters: 4874, Secu
rity: 0
nothing.dat:            Zip archive data, at least v2.0 to extract
nothing to see here.odt: OpenDocument Text
phil.gif:               GIF image data, version 87a, 676 x 467
phil.pdf:               JPEG image data, JFIF standard 1.02
pic.jpeg:               PNG image data, 219 x 162, 8-bit/color RGB, non-interlaced
prez.pptx:              Zip archive data, at least v2.0 to extract
regexp.txt:             ASCII text, with no line terminators
safe-to-run.exe:        PE32 executable (GUI) Intel 80386, for MS Windows
```

FIGURE 7.17.

Results from running the file command on a set of files.

```
phil@i7laptop:/media/part1/Documents and Settings/joe/My Documents$
phil@i7laptop:/media/part1/Documents and Settings/joe/My Documents$ find .
.
./book.docx
./buddy.doc
./desktop.ini
./Downloads
./Downloads/LibreOffice_4.3.3_Win_x86.msi
./grey.bmp
./history.pdf
./My Music
./My Music/Desktop.ini
./My Music/Sample Music.lnk
./My Pictures
./My Pictures/Desktop.ini
./My Pictures/Sample Pictures.lnk
./mystery.jpg
./newclass.doc
./nothing to see here.odt
./nothing.dat
./phil.gif
./phil.pdf
./pic.jpeg
./prez.pptx
./regexp.txt
./safe-to-run.exe
./secret.odt
```

FIGURE 7.18.

Partial output from running "find .".

input is received. In our case we want to use a null character as a delimiter and not the default newline. This is why we have added "-d $'\0'" as an option to our command. Putting this all together we see that `while read -d $'\0' fname;` will read results from the find command one at a time and store them in a loop variable named fname. In Linux shell scripting the semicolon ends a line without requiring the enter key to be pressed. This effectively allows multiple commands to be entered on one line.

The code to be executed in a while loop comes after the `do` keyword. A single command `file "$fname";` is executed each time through the loop. In Linux shell scripts variables are created or set by simply stating their name. When the variable is referenced, a dollar sign ($) is added before the name. The double quotes around $fname are needed to properly handle filenames with spaces. The while loop is closed with the `done` keyword. Partial results from this one line script are shown in Figure 7.19.

I could use the one line script above to parse an entire filesystem and print out the file type information. If I am looking for a particular file type, I can use yet another Linux utility to get results that match a pattern. The utility to use is the GNU Regular Expression Parser (GREP). As previously mentioned, a regular expression is a pattern. At this point we will not dive into writing complex regular expressions. Rather, we will exploit the fact that a literal string is itself a (rather boring) regular expression. By piping the results from our one line script to `grep JPEG`, we can obtain a list of all JPEG files on a system. Partial results from running the command `find . -print0 | while read -d $'\0' fname; do file "$fname"; done | grep JPEG` are shown in Figure 7.20. This same idea can be used with other file

```
phil@i7laptop:/media/part1/Documents and Settings/joe/My Documents$ find . -print0 | while read -d $
'\0' fname; do file "$fname"; done
.: directory
./book.docx: PDF document, version 1.6
./buddy.doc: Composite Document File V2 Document, Little Endian, Os: Windows, Version 5.1, Code page
: 1252, Title: Excel Timeline Template, Author: Vertex42 LLC, Last Saved By: Jon, Name of Creating A
pplication: Microsoft Excel, Last Printed: Wed May 19 06:56:18 2004, Create Time/Date: Mon Mar 29 05
:50:20 2004, Last Saved Time/Date: Wed Mar  7 23:09:45 2007, Security: 0
./desktop.ini: ASCII text, with CRLF line terminators
./Downloads: directory
./Downloads/LibreOffice_4.3.3_Win_x86.msi: Composite Document File V2 Document, Little Endian, Os: W
indows, Version 6.2, Code page: 0, Title: Installation database, Subject: LibreOffice 4.3, Author: T
he Document Foundation, Keywords: Install,MSI, Comments: LibreOffice, Name of Creating Application:
Windows Installer, Security: 0, Template: Intel;1033, Last Saved By: Intel;1077, Revision Number: {8
7C753BB-81E3-403B-BD87-6293F870B20B}4.3.3.2;{87C753BB-81E3-403B-BD87-6293F870B20B}4.3.3.2;{4B17E523-
5D91-4E69-BD96-7FD81CFA81BB}, Number of Pages: 200, Number of Characters: 32
./grey.bmp: PC bitmap, Windows 3.x format, 8 x 2 x 8
./history.pdf: PDF document, version 1.2
./My Music: directory
./My Music/Desktop.ini: ASCII text, with CRLF line terminators
./My Music/Sample Music.lnk: MS Windows shortcut, Item id list present, Points to a file or director
y, Has Relative path, Read-Only, Directory, ctime=Wed Nov  5 00:30:05 2014, mtime=Wed Nov  5 00:30:1
1 2014, atime=Wed Nov  5 00:30:11 2014, length=0, window=hide
./My Pictures: directory
./My Pictures/Desktop.ini: ASCII text, with CRLF line terminators
./My Pictures/Sample Pictures.lnk: MS Windows shortcut, Item id list present, Points to a file or di
rectory, Has Relative path, Read-Only, Directory, ctime=Wed Nov  5 00:30:05 2014, mtime=Wed Nov  5 0
```

FIGURE 7.19.

Partial results from running: find . -print0 | while read -d $'\0' fname; do file "$fname"; done.

```
phil@i7laptop:/media/part1/Documents and Settings$ find . -print0 | while read -d $'\0' fname; do file "$fname"; done | grep JPEG |more
./All Users/Documents/My Pictures/Sample Pictures/Blue hills.jpg: JPEG image data, JFIF standard 1.02
./All Users/Documents/My Pictures/Sample Pictures/Sunset.jpg: JPEG image data, JFIF standard 1.02
./All Users/Documents/My Pictures/Sample Pictures/Water lilies.jpg: JPEG image data, JFIF standard 1.02
./All Users/Documents/My Pictures/Sample Pictures/Winter.jpg: JPEG image data, JFIF standard 1.02
./joe/Local Settings/Application Data/Google/Chrome/User Data/Default/Cache/f_000029: JPEG image data, JFIF standard 1.01
./joe/Local Settings/Application Data/Google/Chrome/User Data/Default/Cache/f_00002a: JPEG image data, JFIF standard 1.01
./joe/Local Settings/Application Data/Google/Chrome/User Data/Default/Cache/f_00002e: JPEG image data, JFIF standard 1.01
./joe/Local Settings/Application Data/Google/Chrome/User Data/Default/Cache/f_000033: JPEG image data, JFIF standard 1.01
./joe/Local Settings/Application Data/Google/Chrome/User Data/Default/Cache/f_000037: JPEG image data, JFIF standard 1.01
./joe/Local Settings/Application Data/Google/Chrome/User Data/Default/Cache/f_00003a: JPEG image data, JFIF standard 1.01, comment: "CREATOR: gd-jpeg v1.0 (using IJG JPEG v80), quality = 75"
./joe/Local Settings/Application Data/Google/Chrome/User Data/Default/Cache/f_00003c: JPEG image data, JFIF standard 1.01, comment: "CREATOR: gd-jpeg v1.0 (using IJG JPEG v80), quality = 75"
./joe/Local Settings/Application Data/Google/Chrome/User Data/Default/Cache/f_00003d: JPEG image data, JFIF standard 1.01, comment: "CREATOR: gd-jpeg v1.0 (using IJG JPEG v80), quality = 75"
./joe/Local Settings/Application Data/Google/Chrome/User Data/Default/Cache/f_00003e: JPEG image data, JFIF standard 1.01, comment: "CREATOR: gd-jpeg v1.0 (using IJG JPEG v80), quality = 75"
./joe/Local Settings/Application Data/Google/Chrome/User Data/Default/Cache/f_00003f: JPEG image dat
```

FIGURE 7.20.

Using GREP to find files of a specific type.

types. In a typical investigation you would likely want to capture the results to a file by adding something like "> jpeg-list.txt" to the end of the command.

Detecting mismatched file extensions

In this section we will create a simple shell script for detecting files with mismatched extensions. You might wonder why we would choose to use a shell script and not a Python script for this purpose. The answer lies in the power of the file utility described in the previous section. It is straightforward to write a shell script that leverages the functionality of the file utility. The script follows.

```
#!/bin/bash
# Simple script to check for mismatched extensions
# Created by Dr. Phil Polstra
# for PentesterAcademy.com

find "$1" -print0 | while read -d $'\0' file
do
        resp=$(file "$file")
        filename=$(basename "$file")
        ext="${filename##*.}"
```

Analyzing mounted images

```
# check for mismatch
if [ "${ext^^}" == "PNG" ]; then
      if [[ ! $resp =~ "PNG image" ]]; then
            echo "*** $filename is mismatched"
            echo $resp
      fi
elif [ "${ext^^}" == "JPG" ]; then
      if [[ ! $resp =~ "JPEG image" ]]; then
            echo "*** $filename is mismatched"
            echo $resp
      fi
elif [ "${ext^^}" == "JPEG" ]; then
      if [[ ! $resp =~ "JPEG image" ]]; then
            echo "*** $filename is mismatched"
            echo $resp
      fi
elif [ "${ext^^}" == "GIF" ]; then
      if [[ ! $resp =~ "GIF image" ]]; then
            echo "*** $filename is mismatched"
            echo $resp
      fi
elif [ "${ext^^}" == "MP4" ]; then
      if [[ ! $resp =~ "MPEG v4" ]]; then
            echo "*** $filename is mismatched"
            echo $resp
      fi
elif [ "${ext^^}" == "MP3" ]; then
      if [[ ! $resp =~ "MPEG" ]]; then
            echo "*** $filename is mismatched"
            echo $resp
      fi
elif [ "${ext^^}" == "PDF" ]; then
      if [[ ! $resp =~ "PDF document" ]]; then
            echo "*** $filename is mismatched"
            echo $resp
      fi
elif [ "${ext^^}" == "DOC" ]; then
      if [[ ! $resp =~ "Composite Document File" ]]; then
         if [[ ! $resp =~ "Microsoft WinWord" ]]; then
               echo "*** $filename is mismatched"
               echo $resp
         fi
      fi
elif [ "${ext^^}" == "DOCX" ]; then
      if [[ ! $resp =~ "Microsoft Word 2007" ]]; then
```

```
                    echo "*** $filename is mismatched"
                    echo $resp
                fi
            elif [ "${ext^^}" == "XLS" ]; then
                if [[ ! $resp =~ "Composite Document File" ]]; then
                    if [[ ! $resp =~ "Microsoft Excel" ]]; then
                        echo "*** $filename is mismatched"
                        echo $resp
                    fi
                fi
            elif [ "${ext^^}" == "XLSX" ]; then
                if [[ ! $resp =~ "Microsoft Excel 2007" ]]; then
                    echo "*** $filename is mismatched"
                    echo $resp
                fi
            elif [ "${ext^^}" == "PPT" ]; then
                if [[ ! $resp =~ "Composite Document File" ]]; then
                    if [[ ! $resp =~ "Microsoft PowerPoint" ]]; then
                        echo "*** $filename is mismatched"
                        echo $resp
                    fi
                fi
            elif [ "${ext^^}" == "PPTX" ]; then
                if [[ ! $resp =~ "Microsoft PowerPoint 2007" ]]; then
                    echo "*** $filename is mismatched"
                    echo $resp
                fi
            elif [ "${ext^^}" == "EXE" ]; then
                if [[ ! $resp =~ "executable" ]]; then
                    echo "*** $filename is mismatched"
                    echo $resp
                fi
            fi
        fi
done
```

As usual, the script begins with a she-bang line that forces it to be run with bash even if that is not the shell currently in use. Next we use the same find command and while loop as in our one line script, but what is inside the loop has been greatly expanded. The first line inside the loop uses the $(command) construct to run the file utility on a file and store the results in the resp variable. The next line, filename=$(basename "$file"), also uses this construct and the basename command to strip the path from the fully qualified filename and stores just the filename in the filename variable.

The line ext="${filename##*.}" uses a new technique. In general, the variable filename can be referenced as $filename or ${filename}. The second form is considered safer. The reason for this is that if another variable had a name that was a substring of filename, the shell might insert the wrong value. This is in fact the case in this script as there is another variable named file. In other words, without the curly brackets "$filename" could be interpreted as "${file}name". Not only is using the curly brackets safer, it also enables certain variable manipulations. The construct ${filename##*.} returns just the file extension, if any, from the filename.

The remaining code in the while loop is just a series of tests for common file extensions. The construct "${ext^^}" is used to convert the file extension to uppercase before the comparison. In Linux shell scripts tests are enclosed in square brackets. The line if ["${ext^^}" == "PNG"]; then will perform a test to see if the file extension in uppercase is equal to "PNG". Notice the spaces around the brackets and ==. These spaces are not optional in shell scripting! Linux shell scripts support if statements with multiple elif clauses. The elif keyword is short for "else if". If blocks are terminated with fi, which is just if spelled backwards. Many other things in shell scripting use this reverse spelling for block termination.

If the file extension matches in the if clause, a second test is performed. Note that, unlike Python, the indentation in the above script is optional. Indenting nested blocks does make code more readable, however. The second test is an extended test that is specific to the bash shell. These extended tests must be enclosed in double square brackets. The test used (=~) might look familiar to PERL programmers. This is a containment test. The line if [[! $resp =~ "PNG image"]]; then is interpreted as if not $resp contains the string "PNG image". If a file has a PNG extension but the file utility does not say it is a PNG file, a message is printed out with the echo command.

All of the tests in this script follow the same pattern. There is a small variation for the older Microsoft Office files as there is more than one possible result returned by the file utility. In those cases a third test has been added. It is worth noting that these tests could have been combined into a single test. I chose not to do this in order to make the script easier to read and understand.

Should you wish to check additional file types not covered by this script, new types are easily added. Copy and paste one of the test blocks and change the extension test. Run the file utility against a file of the target type and update the response test to check for any unique string in the response. Running this script against all user directories on a mounted image is shown in Figure 7.21. The Linux time utility was used to measure the execution time for this script.

ANALYZING FILESYSTEM IMAGE FILES

Just because filesystem images are easily mounted on a Linux system does not mean that you must mount them. There are certain pieces of information that are just as easily obtained either way. As we will see, some things (such as searching unallocated space) are best performed directly on a filesystem image file.

Using Python to analyze a filesystem image

We have seen that the file utility is very powerful and allows easy identification of files in a mounted filesystem image. One limitation of this utility is that it cannot be used on files inside a filesystem image that has not been mounted. There is a Python module, magic, that exports the

CHAPTER 7 File Forensics

```
phil@i7laptop:~/book-windows/07-File Forensics$ time ./extension-mismatch.sh /media/part1/Documents\ and\ Settings/
*** book.docx is mismatched
/media/part1/Documents and Settings/joe/My Documents/book.docx: PDF document, version 1.6
*** phil.pdf is mismatched
/media/part1/Documents and Settings/joe/My Documents/phil.pdf: JPEG image data, JFIF standard 1.02
*** pic.jpeg is mismatched
/media/part1/Documents and Settings/joe/My Documents/pic.jpeg: PNG image data, 219 x 162, 8-bit/color RGB, non-interlaced
*** prez.pptx is mismatched
/media/part1/Documents and Settings/joe/My Documents/prez.pptx: Zip archive data, at least v2.0 to extract
*** testy.pdf is mismatched
/media/part1/Documents and Settings/joe/My Documents/testy.pdf: ISO Media, MPEG v4 system, version 1

real    0m8.509s
user    0m3.953s
sys     0m4.578s
phil@i7laptop:~/book-windows/07-File Forensics$
```

FIGURE 7.21.

Running the extension mismatch shell script. Note the detailed responses that were obtained in mere seconds.

functionality of the underlying libraries used by the file utility. The magic module can be used to create a Python script that searches for specific file types in a filesystem image.

The script starts with a she-bang line as usual followed by several imports. Because the magic module has not yet been ported to Python 3 at the time of this writing, the she-bang line explicitly runs Python 2. The imported modules are magic, optparse, re, and os for determining file types, parsing command line options, performing regular expression search, and checking for file existence, respectively.

```
#!/usr/bin/python2
'''Simple Python script to find
various types of files from an
image file.  Sectors are searched
directly and the offset and sector number
are returned.

As developed by Dr. Phil Polstra
for PentesterAcademy.com.'''

# import the file info library
# note this is Python 2.x only
```

```
# and that is why this script is
# in Python2
import magic
# process command line options
import optparse
# Regular Expressions
import re
# file existance
import os
```

Next we define a base class, FileFinder, that has two methods. The first method, matches, accepts a buffer containing the start of a file and returns True if it appears to be of the desired type. The second method, fileType, returns a string that describes the type of file. The actual functionality for these methods will be implemented in derived classes. The code for several of these classes follows.

```
'''Base class for file finder
merely defines some methods.'''
class FileFinder:
    def matches(self, buffer):
        return False
    def fileType(self):
        return 'Generic'

'''JPEG Finder'''
class JpegFinder(FileFinder):
    def matches(self, buffer):
        mag=magic.from_buffer(buffer)
        if re.search("JPEG image", str(mag)):
            return True
        else:
            return False
    def fileType(self):
        return 'JPEG'

'''PNG Finder'''
class PngFinder(FileFinder):
    def matches(self, buffer):
        mag=magic.from_buffer(buffer)
        if re.search("PNG image", str(mag)):
            return True
        else:
            return False
    def fileType(self):
        return 'PNG'
```

```python
'''GIF Finder'''
class GifFinder(FileFinder):
    def matches(self, buffer):
        mag=magic.from_buffer(buffer)
        if re.search("Gif image", str(mag)):
            return True
        else:
            return False
    def fileType(self):
        return 'GIF'

'''BMP Finder'''
class BmpFinder(FileFinder):
    def matches(self, buffer):
        mag=magic.from_buffer(buffer)
        if re.search("PC bitmap", str(mag)):
            return True
        else:
            return False
    def fileType(self):
        return 'Bitmap'

'''Image Finder works will all image types'''
class ImageFinder(FileFinder):
    def __init__(self):
        self.finders=[]
        self.finders.append(JpegFinder())
        self.finders.append(PngFinder())
        self.finders.append(GifFinder())
        self.finders.append(BmpFinder())

    def matches(self, buffer):
        for finder in self.finders:
            if finder.matches(buffer):
                return True
        return False
    def fileType(self):
        return 'Image'

'''PDF Finder'''
class PdfFinder(FileFinder):
    def matches(self, buffer):
        mag=magic.from_buffer(buffer)
        if re.search("PDF document", str(mag)):
            return True
```

```
            else:
                return False
        def fileType(self):
            return 'PDF'

'''EXE Finder'''
class ExeFinder(FileFinder):
        def matches(self, buffer):
            mag=magic.from_buffer(buffer)
            if re.search("executable", str(mag)):
                return True
            else:
                return False
        def fileType(self):
            return 'Executable'

'''Zip Finder'''
class ZipFinder(FileFinder):
        def matches(self, buffer):
            mag=magic.from_buffer(buffer)
            if re.search("archive", str(mag)):
                return True
            else:
                return False
        def fileType(self):
            return 'Zip'

'''Powerpoint Finder'''
class PptFinder(FileFinder):
        def matches(self, buffer):
            mag=magic.from_buffer(buffer)
            if re.search("Composite Document File", str(mag)):
                return True
            elif re.search("PowerPoint", str(mag)):
                return True
            else:
                return False
        def fileType(self):
            return 'Powerpoint'


'''Word Finder'''
class DocFinder(FileFinder):
        def matches(self, buffer):
            mag=magic.from_buffer(buffer)
```

244 CHAPTER 7 File Forensics

```
            if re.search("Composite Document File", str(mag)):
                return True
            elif re.search("Microsoft Word", str(mag)):
                return True
            elif re.search("Microsoft WinWord", str(mag)):
                return True
            else:
                return False
        def fileType(self):
            return 'Word'

'''Excel Finder'''
class XlsFinder(FileFinder):
        def matches(self, buffer):
            mag=magic.from_buffer(buffer)
            if re.search("Composite Document File", str(mag)):
                return True
            elif re.search("Microsoft Excel", str(mag)):
                return True
            else:
                return False
        def fileType(self):
            return 'Excel'

'''Office Finder
any MS office document'''
class OfcFinder(FileFinder):
        def matches(self, buffer):
            mag=magic.from_buffer(buffer)
            if re.search("Composite Document File", str(mag)):
                return True
            elif (re.search("PowerPoint", str(mag)) or
                re.search("Microsoft Word", str(mag)) or
                re.search("Microsoft WinWord", str(mag)) or
                re.search("Microsoft Excel", str(mag))):
                return True
            else:
                return False
        def fileType(self):
            return 'Office'
```

Each of these derived classes relies on the from_buffer method in the magic module. In most cases a call to magic.from_buffer is used to get the file magic string. This string is then searched for the desired contents using re.search. The regular expressions passed to re.search are literal strings. As a result, the re module is not strictly needed here (there are search functions built in to the string class). I opted to use re.search in order to introduce the re module that will be used more extensively later in this book. Several classes, such as ImageFinder, create lists of finder objects which are then iterated over in the matches method to search for multiple related file types.

The main function creates an OptionParser to easily parse command line options for the script. The "-s" or "--search" option allows the user to pass a comma separated list of file types for which to search. The "-c" or "--cluster" option permits the user to specify the cluster size in sectors. This can be used to speed up the search as only the first sector of each cluster will be checked (versus the default of checking every sector). The "-i" or "--image" flag is used to designate the filesystem image file. The offset to the start of the filesystem in sectors can be entered using the "-o" or "--offset" flag.

The split method in the string class is used to transform the comma separated list of file types to search for (option "-s") to a list of FileFinder objects. The existence of the filesystem image is checked with os.path.exists before the file is opened and scanned. The complete script follows.

```
#!/usr/bin/python2
'''Simple Python script to find
various types of files from an
image file.  Sectors are searched
directly and the offset and sector number
are returned.

As developed by Dr. Phil Polstra
for PentesterAcademy.com.'''

# import the file info library
# note this is Python 2.x only
# and that is why this script is
# in Python2
import magic
# process command line options
import optparse
# Regular Expressions
import re
# file existance
import os

'''Base class for file finder
merely defines some methods.'''
class FileFinder:
    def matches(self, buffer):
        return False
    def fileType(self):
        return 'Generic'
```

```python
'''JPEG Finder'''
class JpegFinder(FileFinder):
    def matches(self, buffer):
        mag=magic.from_buffer(buffer)
        if re.search("JPEG image", str(mag)):
            return True
        else:
            return False
    def fileType(self):
        return 'JPEG'

'''PNG Finder'''
class PngFinder(FileFinder):
    def matches(self, buffer):
        mag=magic.from_buffer(buffer)
        if re.search("PNG image", str(mag)):
            return True
        else:
            return False
    def fileType(self):
        return 'PNG'

'''GIF Finder'''
class GifFinder(FileFinder):
    def matches(self, buffer):
        mag=magic.from_buffer(buffer)
        if re.search("Gif image", str(mag)):
            return True
        else:
            return False
    def fileType(self):
        return 'GIF'

'''BMP Finder'''
class BmpFinder(FileFinder):
    def matches(self, buffer):
        mag=magic.from_buffer(buffer)
        if re.search("PC bitmap", str(mag)):
            return True
        else:
            return False
    def fileType(self):
        return 'Bitmap'
```

```python
'''Image Finder works will all image types'''
class ImageFinder(FileFinder):
    def __init__(self):
        self.finders=[]
        self.finders.append(JpegFinder())
        self.finders.append(PngFinder())
        self.finders.append(GifFinder())
        self.finders.append(BmpFinder())

    def matches(self, buffer):
        for finder in self.finders:
            if finder.matches(buffer):
                return True
        return False
    def fileType(self):
        return 'Image'

'''PDF Finder'''
class PdfFinder(FileFinder):
    def matches(self, buffer):
        mag=magic.from_buffer(buffer)
        if re.search("PDF document", str(mag)):
            return True
        else:
            return False
    def fileType(self):
        return 'PDF'

'''EXE Finder'''
class ExeFinder(FileFinder):
    def matches(self, buffer):
        mag=magic.from_buffer(buffer)
        if re.search("executable", str(mag)):
            return True
        else:
            return False
    def fileType(self):
        return 'Executable'

'''Zip Finder'''
class ZipFinder(FileFinder):
    def matches(self, buffer):
        mag=magic.from_buffer(buffer)
        if re.search("archive", str(mag)):
            return True
```

```python
            else:
                    return False
        def fileType(self):
            return 'Zip'

'''Powerpoint Finder'''
class PptFinder(FileFinder):
    def matches(self, buffer):
            mag=magic.from_buffer(buffer)
            if re.search("Composite Document File", str(mag)):
                    return True
            elif re.search("PowerPoint", str(mag)):
                return True
            else:
                    return False
        def fileType(self):
            return 'Powerpoint'

'''Word Finder'''
class DocFinder(FileFinder):
    def matches(self, buffer):
            mag=magic.from_buffer(buffer)
            if re.search("Composite Document File", str(mag)):
                    return True
            elif re.search("Microsoft Word", str(mag)):
                return True
            elif re.search("Microsoft WinWord", str(mag)):
                return True
            else:
                    return False
        def fileType(self):
            return 'Word'

'''Excel Finder'''
class XlsFinder(FileFinder):
    def matches(self, buffer):
            mag=magic.from_buffer(buffer)
            if re.search("Composite Document File", str(mag)):
                    return True
            elif re.search("Microsoft Excel", str(mag)):
                return True
            else:
                    return False
        def fileType(self):
            return 'Excel'
```

```
'''Office Finder
any MS office document'''
class OfcFinder(FileFinder):
    def matches(self, buffer):
        mag=magic.from_buffer(buffer)
        if re.search("Composite Document File", str(mag)):
            return True
        elif (re.search("PowerPoint", str(mag)) or
            re.search("Microsoft Word", str(mag)) or
            re.search("Microsoft WinWord", str(mag)) or
            re.search("Microsoft Excel", str(mag))):
            return True
        else:
            return False
    def fileType(self):
        return 'Office'


def main():
    # parse command line options
    parser=optparse.OptionParser(
    'usage %prog [-s searchList] [-c clusterSize] <-i imageFile>
        [-o offset]')
    parser.add_option('-s', '--search', dest='findList',
        help='comma separated list of things to search for')
    parser.add_option('-c', '--cluster', dest='clusterSize',
        help='sectors to search at a time')
    parser.add_option('-i', '--image', dest='imageFilename',
        help='image file (raw format) to search')
    parser.add_option('-o', '--offset', dest='offset',
        help='offset to start of filesystem in sectors')
    (options, args)=parser.parse_args()
    imageFilename=options.imageFilename
    if options.offset:
        offset=int(options.offset)
    else:
        offset=0
    if options.clusterSize:
        clusterSize=int(options.clusterSize)
    else:
        clusterSize=1
    # parse comma separated search list
    findList=options.findList.split(',')
    finders=[] # start with empty list
    for f in findList:
```

```python
            if f=='jpeg' or f=='jpg':
                finders.append(JpegFinder())
            elif f=='png':
                finders.append(PngFinder())
            elif f=='gif':
                finders.append(GifFinder())
            elif f=='bmp':
                finders.append(BmpFinder())
            elif f=='img' or f=='image':
                finders.append(ImageFinder())
            elif f=='pdf':
                finders.append(PdfFinder())
            elif f=='exe':
                finders.append(ExeFinder())
            elif f=='zip':
                finders.append(ZipFinder())
            elif f=='ppt' or f=='powerpoint':
                finders.append(PptFinder())
            elif f=='doc' or f=='word':
                finders.append(DocFinder())
            elif f=='xls' or f=='excel':
                finders.append(XlsFinder())
            elif f=='ofc' or f=='office':
                finders.append(OfcFinder())

    if not os.path.exists(imageFilename):
        print('Image file not found!')
        return(1)
    # now parse through the file
    pos=offset * 512
    with open(imageFilename, 'rb') as f:
        f.seek(pos)
        buffer=f.read(512*clusterSize)
        while len(buffer)>0:
            for finder in finders:
                if finder.matches(buffer):
                    print('Matching %s found at offset 0x%X, '+
                        'sector %d' % (finder.fileType(),pos, pos//512))
                    break
            pos+=512*clusterSize
            buffer=f.read(512*clusterSize)

if __name__=='__main__':
    main()
```

```
phil@i7laptop:~/book-windows/07-File Forensics$ ./find-files.py --help
Usage: usage find-files.py [-s searchList] [-c clusterSize] <-i imageFile> [-o offset]

Options:
  -h, --help            show this help message and exit
  -s FINDLIST, --search=FINDLIST
                        comma separated list of things to search for
  -c CLUSTERSIZE, --cluster=CLUSTERSIZE
                        sectors to search at a time
  -i IMAGEFILENAME, --image=IMAGEFILENAME
                        image file (raw format) to search
  -o OFFSET, --offset=OFFSET
                        offset to start of filesystem in sectors
phil@i7laptop:~/book-windows/07-File Forensics$
```

FIGURE 7.22.

Help screen for find-files.py script. This help screen was created by the optparse module.

One of the advantages of using a module like optparse to parse command line arguments is that it also automatically creates a help screen. This help screen is shown in Figure 7.22.

Partial results of running the find-files.py script to search for various image files are shown in Figure 7.23. Notice that the offset of 63 sectors to the start of the filesystem and cluster size of 8 sectors were both passed in via command line parameters in order to speed up the script. Partial results for a search of PDF and Microsoft Word files are shown in Figure 7.24.

Using Linux system tools to analyze an image

The script presented in the previous section is great for finding certain types of files. There are times, however, when you are more interested in finding certain words. When investigations concern possible illegal activities, a filesystem may be searched for keywords related to those activities.

Unless a filesystem is encrypted and/or most of its files are compressed, grep (GNU Regular Expression Parser) is one of the easiest ways to search it. The general syntax for this tool is `grep [options] <regular expression> [filename(s)]`. If no filename(s) is/are given then grep will search standard input. The command to search a filesystem image with grep and print out the offset of any matches is `grep --byte-offset --only-matching --text <regular expression> <filesystem image>`.

If you are familiar with regular expressions, feel free to skip over the rest of this section. A regular expression is a way of specifying a pattern. Regular expressions are so incredibly useful that they are found in many programming languages and tools. In many ways grep is the great

CHAPTER 7 File Forensics

```
phil@i7laptop:~/book-windows/07-File Forensics$ ./find-files.py -i /media/phil/TOSHIBA\ EXT/BU/image
s/filesigs.dd -o 63 -s img -c 8
Matching Image found at offset 0x8B6E00, sector 17847
Matching Image found at offset 0x8B7E00, sector 17855
Matching Image found at offset 0x8BBE00, sector 17887
Matching Image found at offset 0x8C3E00, sector 17951
Matching Image found at offset 0x8C7E00, sector 17983
Matching Image found at offset 0x78BFE00, sector 247295
Matching Image found at offset 0x8322E00, sector 268567
Matching Image found at offset 0x83F1E00, sector 270223
Matching Image found at offset 0x83F5E00, sector 270255
Matching Image found at offset 0x9A6BE00, sector 316255
Matching Image found at offset 0x9B6CE00, sector 318311
Matching Image found at offset 0x9E39E00, sector 324047
Matching Image found at offset 0xA4A6E00, sector 337207
Matching Image found at offset 0xAD4BE00, sector 354911
Matching Image found at offset 0xBB88E00, sector 384071
Matching Image found at offset 0xBBBFE00, sector 384511
Matching Image found at offset 0xBBC0E00, sector 384519
Matching Image found at offset 0xBBC1E00, sector 384527
Matching Image found at offset 0xBBC2E00, sector 384535
Matching Image found at offset 0xBD19E00, sector 387279
Matching Image found at offset 0xBD1DE00, sector 387311
Matching Image found at offset 0xBD20E00, sector 387335
Matching Image found at offset 0xBD23E00, sector 387359
Matching Image found at offset 0xBD37E00, sector 387519
Matching Image found at offset 0xBD43E00, sector 387615
```

FIGURE 7.23.

Partial results from using find-files.py to search for images in a filesystem image file.

```
phil@i7laptop:~/book-windows/07-File Forensics$ ./find-files.py -i /media/phil/T
s/filesigs.dd -o 63 -s pdf,doc -c 8
Matching Word found at offset 0xAB3E00, sector 21919
Matching Word found at offset 0x7E7BE00, sector 259039
Matching Word found at offset 0x9989E00, sector 314447
Matching Word found at offset 0xA2F4E00, sector 333735
Matching Word found at offset 0xA4ADE00, sector 337263
Matching Word found at offset 0xEC50E00, sector 483975
Matching Word found at offset 0xECBFE00, sector 484863
Matching Word found at offset 0xEDF7E00, sector 487359
Matching PDF found at offset 0xF36DE00, sector 498543
Matching PDF found at offset 0xF624E00, sector 504103
Matching Word found at offset 0x10892E00, sector 541847
Matching PDF found at offset 0x114C5E00, sector 566831
Matching Word found at offset 0x123DEE00, sector 597751
Matching Word found at offset 0x12869E00, sector 607055
Matching Word found at offset 0x12BB7E00, sector 613823
Matching Word found at offset 0x13187E00, sector 625727
Matching Word found at offset 0x1318CE00, sector 625767
Matching Word found at offset 0x1421CE00, sector 659687
Matching Word found at offset 0x20C69E00, sector 1073999
Matching Word found at offset 0x2BBF7E00, sector 1433535
Matching Word found at offset 0x2DD6EE00, sector 1502071
```

FIGURE 7.24.

Partial results from using find-files.py to search for PDF and Word documents.

Table 7.1. Regular expression items that match a single character.

Item	Meaning	Example
Any non-metacharacter	Literal character	B matches B
.	Anything but a newline	. matches anything but newline
[abc]	Matches anything inside []	[abc] matches a or b or c
[a-z]	Matches a range of characters	[a-z] matches any lowercase char
\	Escapes a metacharacter	\. matches a period

granddad of regular expression tools. It is primarily used for searching text files line by line, but as shown in the example in the previous paragraph it can be used on binary files as well.

Entire books have been written on regular expressions. There are also a plethora of online tools and references for those wishing to learn how to use regular expressions. I will give a very brief introduction to regular expressions here.

There are different components that make up a regular expression. These include things that match a single character, quantifiers, anchors, and miscellaneous items. Characters that have special meanings are known as metacharacters.

A few common items that match a single character are shown in Table 7.1. From the table we see that any non-metacharacter matches itself. If we do need to match a metacharacter, it can be escaped by preceding it with a \. For example, \. matches a period and \[matches an opening square bracket. The period is used to match any character except a newline (although this can often be changed to match everything using appropriate options). A list of characters any one of which will match can be enclosed in square brackets. For example, [0123456789] or [0-9] would match any single digit.

Quantifiers are used to match more than one character at a time. Quantifiers apply to the item that they follow. Notice that I said item. As we shall soon see, a quantifier can be applied to a single character, something that matches a single character, or a group. Some common quantifiers are shown in Table 7.2. The quantifiers in italics may not be available with all tools.

Combining items from Table 7.1 and Table 7.2 we can form a few simple regular expressions. These examples are shown in Table 7.3.

Anchors can be used to search for things at the beginning (^) or end ($) of a line. These are not often used in forensics as we normally do not care where on a line a match occurs. In fact, when dealing with binary files there are no lines.

The two most commonly used items in the miscellaneous category are grouping and alternation. By enclosing a regular expression in parentheses a quantifier can be applied to a group of items as opposed to a single character. Grouping has other purposes as well, but these are not commonly used in forensics. Separating two items by a vertical pipe (|) is known as alternation. The expression a|b will match either "a" or "b". With the addition of grouping and alternation to our toolbox we can create some more sophisticated regular expressions such as those shown in Table 7.4.

Table 7.2. Regular expression quantifiers.

Quantifier	Meaning
?	0 or 1
+	1 or more
*	0 or more
{n}	Exactly n
{n, m}	At least n, but no more than m
{n, }	At least n
{ , m}	No more than m

Table 7.3. A few simple regular expressions.

Regular Expression	Meaning
Dogs?	Dog or Dogs
[A-Z]+[a-z]*	Any capitalized word
[0-9]{3}\.[0-9]{3}\.[0-9]{4}	A US phone number in XXX.YYY.ZZZZ format
A*	Matches anything (zero or more A's)

Table 7.4. Regular expressions using grouping and/or alternation.

Regular Expression	Meaning
([0-9]{1,3}\.){3}[0-9]{1,3}	An IP address (will match other numbers too)
(Billy?)|(Willy?)|(William)	Bill, Billy, Will, Willy, or William
([0-9]{3}\.|\-){2}[0-9]{4}	US Phone XXX.YYY.ZZZZ or xxx-yyy-zzzz
(Kat)((hryn)|(hy)|(ie))?	Kat, Kathryn, Kathy, or Katie

Here are a couple of closing thoughts on regular expressions. Building regular expressions is an art. There are often multiple regular expressions which will give the same result. I recommend using the most straightforward regular expression that will work. This can help reduce the chance for errors. Always test a new regular expression on a test file to make sure it does what you think it should. If your regular expression seems right but is not working, try running egrep instead of grep. You may have accidentally used something the standard grep does not support, but egrep (extended grep) does. Partial results from applying the William regular expression to an image are shown in Figure 7.25.

File carving

File carving is the process of extracting files from a raw filesystem image. It relies on two items. The first is well known file signatures. As we discussed earlier in this chapter, most files start with a specific file signature. The second thing that file carving relies upon is the fact that the majority of files are contiguous.

There are a number of situations in which file carving really shines. Recently I was approached by a student that could not retrieve from her thumb drive any of the documents she needed to graduate. Upon examination, her drive had no recognizable filesystem whatsoever. Using file carving I was able to retrieve several thousand files from the drive. Locating files in unallocated space is another place that file carving is often useful.

```
phil@i7laptop:~/book-windows/07-File Forensics$ egrep --byte-offset --only-matching --text "(Billy?)
|(Willy?)|(William)" /media/phil/TOSHIBA\ EXT/BU/images/filesigs.dd
8599780:Will
8601882:Will
8601959:Will
10429668:Will
24736996:Will
30102023:Willy
30128135:William
127314578:Will
150545502:Will
150710733:Will
162787870:Will
164663808:Will
164663904:Will
164664012:Will
164664092:Will
164664192:Will
164664260:Will
165269236:Will
165269332:Will
165269440:Will
165269520:Will
165269620:Will
165269688:Will
165366576:Will
165366672:Will
```

FIGURE 7.25.

Partial results from running a regular expression search designed to locate variations on William against a filesystem image.

There are a number of general purpose file carvers. Scalpel is one of the most popular general carvers. This tool was written by Golden Richard and is based on another tool called Foremost. There are a number of specialized carvers for retrieving specific file types such as audio and video files. Some of these specialized carvers can extract corrupted and/or incomplete files.

Scalpel should be available in your Linux system repositories. If this is the case, installation is as simple as executing `sudo apt-get install scalpel`. The scalpel help screen can be displayed by running `scalpel -h`. Part of this help screen is shown in Figure 7.26. As can be seen in the figure, the general format is `scalpel [options] <image file> [image file...]`.

Scalpel supports a good number of options. The -b flag causes scalpel to carve a file even if the footer is not discovered within the maximum number of sectors. This option can be useful for retrieving partial files. Keep in mind that some file formats are unusable if the file is incomplete.

By default scalpel will looking for a configuration file in /etc/scalpel/scalpel.conf. This default location can be overridden with the -c option. This configuration file contains file signatures for files to be recovered, maximum file sizes, and other settings.

Normally the filesystem image file(s) is/are passed in on the command line. The -i option can be used to carve a list of filesystem images whose names are stored in a text file. This can be a useful option if you are attempting to recover files from multiple subjects simultaneously.

If you want to save any extracted files (which is what scalpel is all about) an output directory must be specified using the -o option. By default files are organized by type and placed in subdirectories. This behavior can be overridden using the -O option.

```
Scalpel version 1.60
Written by Golden G. Richard III, based on Foremost 0.69.
Carves files from a disk image based on file headers and footers.

Usage: scalpel [-b] [-c <config file>] [-d] [-h|V] [-i <file>]
               [-m blocksize] [-n] [-o <outputdir>] [-O num] [-q clustersize]
               [-r] [-s num] [-t <blockmap file>] [-u] [-v]
               <imgfile> [<imgfile>] ...

-b  Carve files even if defined footers aren't discovered within
    maximum carve size for file type [foremost 0.69 compat mode].
-c  Choose configuration file.
-d  Generate header/footer database; will bypass certain optimizations
    and discover all footers, so performance suffers.  Doesn't affect
    the set of files carved.  **EXPERIMENTAL**
-h  Print this help message and exit.
-i  Read names of disk images from specified file.
-m  Generate/update carve coverage blockmap file.  The first 32bit
    unsigned int in the file identifies the block size.  Thereafter
    each 32bit unsigned int entry in the blockmap file corresponds
    to one block in the image file.  Each entry counts how many
    carved files contain this block. Requires more memory and
    disk.  **EXPERIMENTAL**
-n  Don't add extensions to extracted files.
-o  Set output directory for carved files.
-O  Don't organize carved files by type. Default is to organize carved files
    into subdirectories.
```

FIGURE 7.26.

Part of the Scalpel help screen.

Analyzing filesystem image files

The -p option is used to preview what files will be carved. No files are actually carved when using this option. The audit log indicates what files would have been carved. This option can be useful for testing new file signatures.

A cluster size can be given using the -q option. When this is done only files that begin on cluster boundaries are carved. Care should be taken when using this option. This option should be used in conjunction with the -s option (not shown in Figure 7.26). The -s option requires a starting position in bytes (not sectors!) where the file carving should begin. The reason that it is important to use these together is that the reserved space before a filesystem may not be a multiple of the cluster size. We have seen this situation in some of the examples in this book including a filesystem with 63 reserved sectors and a cluster size of 16 sectors.

The scalpel.conf file is a typical Linux configuration file. It is a text file. A "#" begins a comment that continues to the end of the line. Many signatures for standard file types are included in the sample scalpel.conf file. Each of these is initially commented out.

The general format for a file signature in the scalpel.conf file is a single line consisting of file extension, case sensitivity (y or n), maximum size in bytes, header, and footer with each field separated by whitespace. As an example "gif y 5000000 GIF87a \x00\x3b" would match one of the two formats of GIF files. There are some additional flags that can be included in the file signatures. The sample scalpel.conf file is well documented and contains more information on how to correctly build a file signature. I recommend consulting Gary Kessler's website even when using signatures found in the example file in order to ensure you are using the most up-to-date information. Part of the scalpel.conf file used to extract some GIF files is shown in Figure 7.27.

```
#
#---------------------------------------------------------------
# GRAPHICS FILES
#---------------------------------------------------------------
#
#
# AOL ART files
#       art     y       150000     \x4a\x47\x04\x0e        \xcf\xc7\xcb
#       art     y       150000     \x4a\x47\x03\x0e        \xd0\xcb\x00\x00
#
# GIF and JPG files (very common)
        gif     y       5000000    \x47\x49\x46\x38\x37\x61    \x00\x3b
        gif     y       5000000    \x47\x49\x46\x38\x39\x61    \x00\x3b
#       jpg     y       200000000  \xff\xd8\xff\xe0\x00\x10    \xff\xd9
#
#
# PNG
#       png     y       20000000   \x50\x4e\x47?   \xff\xfc\xfd\xfe
#
#
# BMP     (used by MSWindows, use only if you have reason to think there are
#         BMP files worth digging for. This often kicks back a lot of false
#         positives
#
#       bmp     y       100000     BM??\x00\x00\x00
#
                                                            99,1         34%
```

FIGURE 7.27.

Part of the scalpel.conf file. Here the GIF lines have been uncommented in order to retrieve GIF files.

258 CHAPTER 7 File Forensics

```
phil@i7laptop:~$ scalpel -o scalpel-out /media/phil/TOSHIBA\ EXT/BU/images/filesigs.dd
Scalpel version 1.60
Written by Golden G. Richard III, based on Foremost 0.69.

Opening target "/media/phil/TOSHIBA EXT/BU/images/filesigs.dd"

Image file pass 1/2.
/media/phil/TOSHIBA EXT/BU/images/filesigs.dd: 100.0% |********************|   10.0 GB   00:00 ETA
Allocating work queues...
Work queues allocation complete. Building carve lists...
Carve lists built.  Workload:
gif with header "\x47\x49\x46\x38\x37\x61" and footer "\x00\x3b" --> 78 files
gif with header "\x47\x49\x46\x38\x39\x61" and footer "\x00\x3b" --> 1310 files
Carving files from image.
Image file pass 2/2.
/media/phil/TOSHIBA EXT/BU/images/filesigs.dd: 100.0% |********************|   10.0 GB   00:00 ETA
Processing of image file complete. Cleaning up...
Done.
Scalpel is done, files carved = 1388, elapsed = 133 seconds.
phil@i7laptop:~$ ls scalpel-out
audit.txt  gif-0-0  gif-1-0  gif-1-1
phil@i7laptop:~$
```

FIGURE 7.28.

Running scalpel against an image containing GIF files.

FIGURE 7.29.

Some GIF files extracted by scalpel. Not all of the files are valid GIF images.

Scalpel will make two passes through an image file. On the first pass it will locate potential files from their headers. On the second pass footers are used to attempt to find the end of the file. Running scalpel against an image containing GIF files is shown in Figure 7.28. It required just over two minutes to extract 1388 possible GIF files.

As seen in Figure 7.28, the GIF files have been extracted into three separate subdirectories. The easiest way to browse these extracted files is to use whatever file browser is included with your version of Linux. Some of the extracted files are shown in Figure 7.29. There are a few false positives such as 00000136.gif and 00000137.gif that were not actually GIF files. This is why the generic GIF icon is shown and an error message will be generated if the files are double clicked.

SUMMARY

In this chapter we have learned to extract information from a mounted subject filesystem or filesystem image. Many techniques were presented for extracting information without any low-level filesystem knowledge. Now that we have taken a break from examining filesystems at a low level, in the next chapter we will again dive deep into another filesystem, NTFS.

CHAPTER 8

NTFS Filesystems

INFORMATION IN THIS CHAPTER:

- NTFS basics
- NTFS Volume Boot Records
- Master File Table
- Files small and large
- Directories
- Deleted files
- Automation with Python
- Creating timelines

In this chapter we will discuss the NTFS filesystem. Despite the fact that it was introduced over two decades ago, this is the default filesystem in use on Windows systems today. In fact, modern versions of Windows cannot be installed on the older FAT filesystem.

NTFS BASICS

NTFS stands for Windows NT File System. It was introduced with Windows NT in 1993. It was not completely new, however. The original version of NTFS was an update and extension of the High Performance File System (HPFS) that Microsoft developed for OS/2 (an operating system written for IBM by Microsoft which IBM later took over when it became evident that Microsoft was more interested in pushing Windows than advancing OS/2).

On an NTFS filesystem files are a collection of attributes. Files and directories are stored in the Master File Table (MFT). As we will see, the MFT is a very central item for NTFS. The overall layout of an NTFS partition is shown in Figure 8.1.

Similar to a FAT partition, an NTFS begins with a Volume Boot Record (VBR). This VBR does have a different format as we will see later. Recall that FAT32 has a backup boot sector which is normally located in sector 6 of the multi-sector VBR. NTFS also has a backup boot record, but it is placed at the end of the partition. This location makes more sense as having a backup physically close to the primary increases the chance they are both unusable if the media becomes physically damaged.

Immediately after the VBR (which includes the boot code) we find an MFT mirror. The MFT is rather large and a complete backup would be impractical. Rather than mirror the entire MFT, only the first four entries are replicated in the MFT mirror. These four entries are needed to successfully read the NTFS filesystem. Because of its importance the MFT is placed in the middle of the partition. There is an algorithm used to calculate the MFT's initial size and

262 CHAPTER 8 NTFS Filesystems

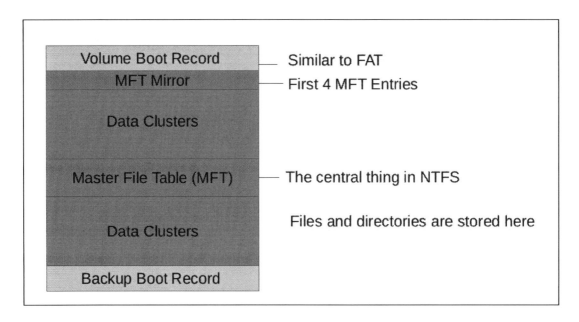

FIGURE 8.1.

Layout of an NTFS partition.

location. Space after the MFT, known as the MFT zone, is reserved for future expansion of the MFT in an attempt to avoid MFT fragmentation.

Just as with FAT, the VBR in NTFS allows the filesystem to tell the operating system about itself. It is most similar to the FAT32 VBR. This and other NTFS components will be described in more detail later in this chapter.

The MFT has entries for every file and directory on the partition. Each entry consists of a collection of attributes. In Linux everything is a file. In NTFS filesystems everything has an MFT entry. Speaking of Linux, an MFT entry is like an inode on an extended filesystem (it holds all the metadata), but with the addition of a filename.

The first several MFT entries have predefined uses. Microsoft refers to these as metadata files. The metadata files are summarized in Table 8.1.

The first entry is a self-reference to the MFT itself. This might seem pointless at first, but there are a couple reasons for this entry. First, if the MFT becomes fragmented, this entry is required to find the non-contiguous parts of the MFT. Second, if the start of the MFT is corrupted, this information must be read from the MFT mirror. The filename in this entry is $MFT.

The second entry is called $MFTMirr. This entry is a backup of the first four MFT entries. These contain the minimum information required to read an NTFS filesystem.

The third entry is named $LogFile. This entry contains journal records. NTFS is a journaling filesystem. What this means is that certain information is not written directly to disk. Rather, entries are made into a journal about what changes need to be made. Later the operating system performs the requested operations. This enhances performance by minimizing disk operations and read/write head movement. If the system were to go down before all operations are complete this is easily detected and repaired when the system comes back up. This is one

Table 8.1. NTFS Metadata files.

Entry	Filename	Description
0	$MFT	Self-reference for MFT
1	$MFTMirr	Backup of first 4 MFT entries
2	$LogFile	Journal records
3	$Volume	Volume info-label, identifier, version
4	$AttrDef	Attribute definitions
5	.	Root directory
6	$Bitmap	Allocation status of clusters
7	$Boot	Boot sector and boot code
8	$BadClus	Bad clusters in alternate data stream
9	$Secure	Security info and ACLs
10	$Upcase	Uppercase conversion table
11	$Extend	Optional extensions
16-23		Used if MFT is highly fragmented

reason why pulling the plug on a compromised system is often a better choice than it was in the past.

The fourth entry contains volume information. It has the name $Volume. Some of the things stored in this entry include the volume label, identifier, and version. This is the last entry in the MFT mirror as it is the last bit of information absolutely required to read an NTFS volume.

The fifth entry contains attribute definitions. It has the filename $AttrDef. The interesting thing about this metadata file is that it contains attribute definitions, but an understanding of some of the attribute definitions is required in order to read this entry. It seems like a chicken and egg situation (which came first?). I believe the intention is for this to allow new attributes to be added later. It does contain definitions for all attributes.

The sixth entry (entry 5) is the only metadata file that does not have a name that begins with $. This entry which is simply named "." (a period) houses the root directory. The way directories are stored is vastly different from the FAT filesystem. This will be discussed in detail later in this chapter.

The seventh entry contains the allocation status of clusters. It is named $Bitmap. The cluster chains are stored in MFT entries. This bitmap is rather simple. Each cluster on the volume has a bit in the bitmap that is either zero or one depending on whether it is unallocated or allocated, respectively.

The eighth entry points to the boot sector and boot code. This code is normally in cluster 1 (yes, NTFS does have a cluster 1). The metadata file is called $Boot.

The ninth entry is called $BadClus. It contains a list of bad clusters in something called an alternate data stream. This list operates much like $Bitmap except that a 1 in a cluster's bit indicates that it is bad. Because most modern media handle bad sectors at the hardware level, it is unusual to have any bad clusters in this list. Any bad clusters should be investigated as there is a good chance they were created in an attempt to hide data.

The tenth entry contains security information and Access Control Lists (ACL). It is called $Secure. This entry may not be populated in all versions of Windows.

The eleventh entry is called $Upcase. It is used to convert filenames to uppercase in order to perform comparisons. This table might seem silly at first. Given that filenames are stored in Unicode case conversions can be non-trivial for certain characters. Because this table is stored on each volume and not within Windows, someone could tamper with it. Such tampering might cause searches for some files to fail.

Optional extensions are stored in the twelfth entry named $Extend. There are a few blank entries (12 – 15). Entries 16 – 23 are reserved and only used if the MFT becomes highly fragmented. Regular files are stored in the MFT beginning with entry 24.

THE NTFS VOLUME BOOT RECORD

The Volume Boot Record (VBR) for an NTFS partition starts out similar to the FAT VBR, but it quickly diverges. The NTFS VBR does not have an extended BIOS parameter block. Rather, all of the parameters are considered primary (or essential). The NTFS VBR is summarized in Table 8.2.

The VBR begins with a jump instruction. This is a short jump (op code 0xEB), followed by an offset (should be 0x52) and then a no-operation (NOP) filler (0x90). After this comes the OEM name. Unlike FAT, the OEM name for NTFS volumes should be "NTFS". The version of Windows used to create an NTFS volume cannot be determined from the OEM name.

Starting at offset 11 (0x0B) we find the bytes per sector (should be 512 or 0x0200), sectors per cluster (most likely will be 0x08) and then reserved clusters. These values are in the same position as those in a FAT VBR. The next three bytes starting at offset 16 (0x10) must always be zero. If you consult the FAT VBR documentation, you will see that these bytes are used to store the number of copies of the FAT and number of root directory entries. If an NTFS VBR was misinterpreted as a FAT VBR, these numbers are nonsensical.

Bytes 19 and 20 (0x13 and 0x14) must be zero. These bytes are used in a FAT VBR to store the total sectors if the volume is under 32 MB (64k sectors). The media descriptor at offset 21 (0x15) will almost certainly be 0xF8 (hard disk). The number of sectors per FAT are stored in bytes 22 and 23 in the FAT VBR and must be zero for an NTFS VBR.

Beginning at offset 24 (0x18) we find sectors per track, number of heads, and number of hidden sectors (sectors before this partition). These are in the exact same locations as with the FAT VBR. The FAT VBR stores a 4-byte value for the total number of sectors for volumes over 32 MB at position 32 (0x20). For an NTFS VBR these bytes must be zeros. In other words, both fields for total sectors (both 2-byte and 4-byte) are zero if an NTFS VBR is mistakenly interpreted as a FAT VBR.

Table 8.2. The Volume Boot Record for an NTFS partition.

Offset	Length	Description (default)
0 (0x00)	3	Jump code (short jump, offset, NOP: 0xEB 0x52 0x90)
3 (0x03)	8	OEM name ("NTFS")
11 (0x0B)	2	Bytes per sector (512 = 0x0200)
13 (0x0D)	1	Sectors per cluster (0x08)
14 (0x0E)	7	Must be zeros to distinguish NTFS from FAT
21 (0x15)	1	Media descriptor (0xF8)
22 (0x16)	2	Must be zeros
24 (0x18)	2	Sectors per track
26 (0x1A)	2	Number of heads (probably 0xFF)
28 (0x1C)	4	Hidden sectors (sectors before the partition)
32 (0x20)	4	Must be zeros
36 (0x24)	4	Signature (0x80 0x00 0x80 0x00)
40 (0x28)	8	Total sectors in volume
48 (0x30)	8	Starting logical cluster number for MFT
56 (0x38)	8	Starting logical cluster number for MFT Mirror
64 (0x40)	4	Clusters per file record segment (see text for interpretation)
68 (0x44)	1	Clusters per index buffer (1)
69 (0x45)	3	Must be zeros
72 (0x48)	8	Volume serial number
80 (0x50)	4	Currently unused checksum value
84 (0x54)	427	Bootstrap code
511 (0x01FE)	2	Signature (0x55 0xAA)

The signature 0x80 0x00 0x80 0x00 at position 36 (0x24) indicates an NTFS volume. The total number of sectors follows the signature (position 40 or 0x28). This field is 8 bytes long which is enough to accommodate any media size. As we will later see, other factors effectively limit this field to 6 bytes.

CHAPTER 8 NTFS Filesystems

The logical cluster numbers for the start of the MFT and MFT mirror are stored in location 48 (0x30) and 56 (0x38), respectively. A logical cluster number (LCN) is measured from the start of a volume. In other words, it is just the sector number divided by the number of sectors per cluster. The starting cluster for the MFT varies, but is normally set so that the midpoint of the MFT and volume coincide. The standard place for the MFT mirror is cluster 2.

The entry at position 64 (0x40) houses the clusters per file record segment. If the number is between 0x00 and 0x7F, it represents the number of clusters. If, however, the value is between 0x80 and 0xFF, it represents 2 raised to the two's complement of the value. Recall that the two's complement is used to store negative integers. For example, the value 0xF6 has a two's complement of 0x0A and represents the value -10. A common value found in this field is 0xF6 which corresponds to 2 raised to the 10th power or 1024 clusters. This field is not important for forensics.

The first sector of the NTFS VBR ends with the clusters per index block (used to store directories, should be one), volume serial number, an unused checksum, bootstrap code, and the standard signature of 0x55 0xAA. As with FAT32, additional boot code is found in the second sector. A backup of the first VBR sector is stored in the last sector of the partition. An NTFS VBR opened in Active@ Disk Editor (ADE) is shown in Figure 8.2. Notice that ADE displays the information from both the primary and backup boot sector in the template view.

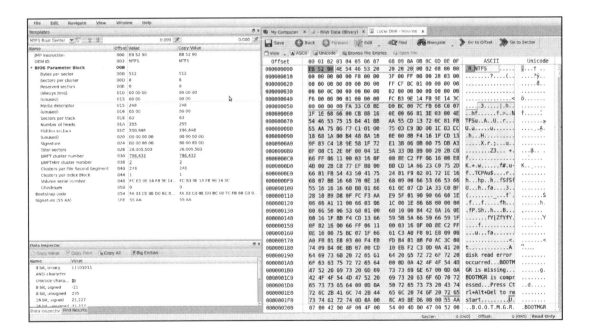

FIGURE 8.2.

Examining an NTFS boot sector in Active@ Disk Editor. Note that the backup boot sector information is also displayed in the template view.

THE MASTER FILE TABLE

The MFT is a key component of the NTFS filesystem. It is impossible to understand NTFS without a good understanding of how the MFT works. In this section we will dive down into the MFT in order to obtain the required enlightenment.

MFT basics

Every file or directory has at least one entry in the MFT. Every MFT entry has the same structure. It begins with a standard header which is followed by several attributes and ends with a standard terminator. Each attribute begins with a standard attribute header. After the attribute header the attribute data stream appears. The format for each type of attribute data stream is defined in the $AttrDef metadata file. These attributes may be resident (contained within the MFT entry) or non-resident (stored in data clusters).

The standard MFT entry is two sectors or 1024 bytes (1 KB) long. The standard cluster size is 8 sectors or 4096 bytes (4 KB) in size. This means that there are four MFT entries in a standard cluster. When an NTFS partition is first formatted, a largely empty MFT is created roughly in the middle of the partition.

The MFT record header is summarized in Table 8.3. This header is 56 (0x38) bytes long. It should be noted that extremely old versions of Windows used a slightly different header. This should not be an issue unless you plan on investigating Windows NT and Windows 2000 systems.

The MFT entry header begins with the signature "FILE" in ASCII. This is followed by an offset to the update sequence number (which should normally be 0x30). This leads to the question "What is an update sequence?" As an integrity check the last 2 bytes of each sector in an entry are replaced with an update sequence number (sometimes called a fix up code). The update sequence array contains the 2 bytes that should have been at the end of each sector. As MFT entries are two sectors long, the size of the update sequence and array should be three (one plus two). It is important to substitute the correct bytes from the update sequence array into the end of each sector when interpreting an MFT entry.

The log file sequence number is stored at offset 8. This is a reference number to entries in the filesystem log. This log is normally referred to as a journal. Recall that this is a place where transactions are stored while waiting to be committed to disk. Unless the filesystem was not closed cleanly, this value is uninteresting to forensic investigators.

The sequence number is stored in position 16 (0x10). This is just a use count for the entry. In other words, this is a counter that is incremented each time the entry is reused to store a different file or directory. The sequence number is used for integrity checking of MFT references as we shall soon see. The hard link count at offset 18 (0x12) corresponds to the number of names the file or directory has. As you may know, files in Windows can have both long and short filenames. The most common hard link count values are one and two.

The offset to the start of attributes is found at position 20 (0x14). This value should normally be 0x38. The flags field at offset 22 (0x16) is 16 bits wide. Only two bits are used, however. Bit 0 is an in-use flag and bit 1 is a directory flag. There are four possible values in this field: 0x00, 0x01, 0x02, and 0x03 for a deleted file, allocated file, deleted directory, and allocated directory, respectively.

Table 8.3. The MFT Record Header.

Offset	Size	Description (expected value)
0 (0x00)	4	"FILE" identifier
4 (0x04)	2	Offset to update sequence (0x30)
6 (0x06)	2	Size of update sequence array in words (0x03)
8 (0x08)	8	Log file sequence number or LSN
16 (0x10)	2	Sequence number
18 (0x12)	2	Hard link count
20 (0x14)	2	Offset to start of attributes (0x38)
22 (0x16)	2	Flags: Bit 0 = in use; Bit 1 = directory
24 (0x18)	4	MFT entry logical size
28 (0x1C)	4	MFT entry physical size (0x0400 or 1024)
32 (0x20)	8	Base file record (zero unless this is a continuation)
40 (0x28)	2	Next available attribute ID number
42 (0x2A)	2	Padding
44 (0x2C)	4	MFT record number
48 (0x30)	2	Update sequence number
50 (0x32)	2	Fix up codes for first sector of entry
52 (0x34)	2	Fix up codes for second sector of entry
54 (0x36)	2	Padding

The MFT logical record size is at position 24 (0x18). This is the portion of the entry that contains valid data. This is followed by the MFT physical record size, which should be 1024, at position 28 (0x1C). Windows does not clean up after itself if entries grow and shrink. As a result it is common to see data in the MFT entry slack space.

The base MFT entry number is stored as an 8-byte value at offset 32 (0x20). This is only used if a list of attributes for a file or directory has grown too large to be fully stored within a single MFT entry and must be continued in additional entries. An MFT reference consists of a 6-byte MFT entry number and a 2-byte sequence number. The sequence number is stored in the most significant 2 bytes.

The next available attribute ID is stored at position 40 (0x28). This number should not be interpreted to mean the number of attributes in an entry. The attribute ID seems to serve no useful purpose in the current version of NTFS.

The MFT entry number is located at offset 44 (0x2C). Unless the MFT is fragmented, this number should be the number of sectors from the start of the MFT divided by two. This is a 4-byte value. Note that the MFT reference allows for a 6-byte MFT entry number (the top 2 bytes are unused). A consequence of this is that the maximum number of files on an NTFS filesystem is 4,294,967,296. The update sequence number and array round out the MFT entry header. Two bytes of padding are added to make the header 56 (0x38) bytes long. As we will learn, many items in NTFS are aligned on 8 byte boundaries. The start of an MFT entry is shown in Figure 8.3.

A collection of attributes follows the header. The first attribute normally starts at offset 56 (0x38). Each attribute has a standard header. The first entry in this attribute header is the attribute type. Attributes are sorted by type, ascending. The value 0xFFFFFFFF is a terminator used to indicate the end of the list of attributes.

The attribute header is the same for all attributes. As a result, some fields that do not make sense for certain attributes must still be populated. Attributes may be resident or non-resident. The fields in the first 16 bytes of the header are common to all attributes regardless of residency. The remaining entries are different for resident and non-resident attributes. The first part of the attribute header is summarized in Table 8.4.

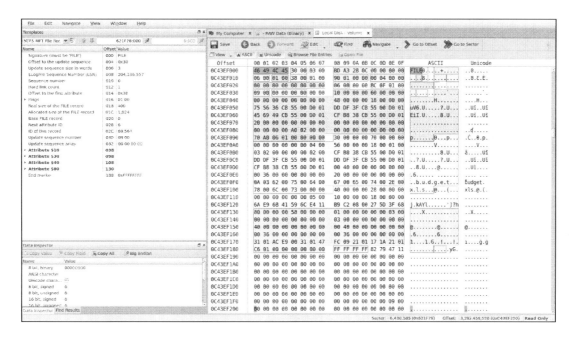

FIGURE 8.3.

Examining an MFT entry header in Active@ Disk Editor.

Table 8.4. The common fields at the start of an attribute header.

Offset	Length	Description
0 (0x00)	4	Attribute identifier code
4 (0x04)	4	Total length of the attribute including header (offset to next attribute)
8 (0x08)	1	Non-resident flag: 1 = non-resident, 0 = resident
9 (0x09)	1	Length of the attribute name (0 = not named)
10 (0x0A)	2	Offset to the attribute name (0 if not named)
12 (0x0C)	2	Flags (see text)
14 (0x0E)	2	Attribute ID

The total length of the attribute is normally padded as required in order to align the next attribute start on an 8-byte boundary. Most attributes are unnamed. We will discuss those that are later in this chapter. Only 3 of the available 16 bits in the flags field are used. These are bit 0 (0x0001), bit 14 (0x4000), and bit 15 (0x8000) which indicate an attribute is compressed, encrypted, and sparse, respectively. The attribute ID is a number used to identify the attribute. This field seems to serve no real purpose in the current version of NTFS.

It is common for many of the attributes to be resident. Some are required to be resident. The particulars of common attributes will be discussed later in this chapter. The remaining attribute header for resident attributes is summarized in Table 8.5.

Table 8.5. Attribute header fields specific to resident attributes.

Offset	Length	Description
16 (0x10)	4	Length of the attribute (without the header, data stream only)
20 (0x14)	2	Offset to start of attribute data stream (from start of header)
22 (0x16)	1	Indexed flag: 0x00 = no, 0x01 = yes
23 (0x17)	1	Padding to align on 8-byte boundary
24 (0x18)	Varies	Name of the attribute, if named (if unnamed, this field is skipped)

Table 8.6. Attribute header fields specific to non-resident attributes.

Offset	Length	Description
16 (0x10)	8	First Virtual Cluster Number (VCN)
24 (0x18)	8	Last VCN
32 (0x20)	2	Offset to data run(s)
34 (0x22)	2	Compression unit size: stored as 2 to power of this field
36 (0x24)	4	Padding
40 (0x28)	8	Physical size of attribute (should be a multiple of the cluster size)
48 (0x30)	8	Logical size of attribute
56 (0x38)	8	Initialized size of attribute data stream
64 (0x40)	Varies	Name of attribute, if named (not present for unnamed attributes)

The length of the attribute data stream is required because each entry is padded to have a size that is a multiple of 8 bytes. The offset to the start of this data stream is needed because the attribute can have a name and the length of that name varies. Indexed items are more easily searched. Generally speaking, only attributes likely to be searched, such as filenames, are indexed.

Some attributes are too large to store directly in the MFT. As we shall see, a file's contents (data) are just another attribute in NTFS. A structure known as a data run is used to list the clusters that contain attributes. Data runs will be discussed in detail later in this chapter. The remainder of the attribute header for non-resident attributes is summarized in Table 8.6.

A virtual cluster number is simply the cluster number within the set of clusters used to store the attribute. Numbering for virtual clusters begins at zero. The offset to the data run(s) is required because attributes may be named and the size of the name varies. The compression unit size is normally zero, meaning that the attributes are compressed by a factor of 2 to the 0 power which is 1, no compression. The physical size should be a multiple of the cluster size. Logical size is the actual size of the attribute (physical size minus total slack space). Examining attribute headers for both resident and non-resident attributes in ADE is shown in Figure 8.4.

272 CHAPTER 8 NTFS Filesystems

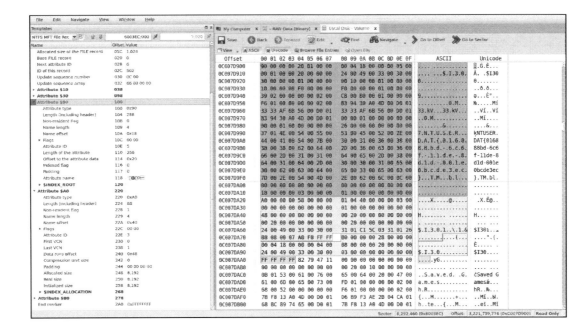

FIGURE 8.4.

Examining attribute headers with Active@ Disk Editor.

Attributes $10 and $30

Every file or directory stored on an NTFS filesystem must have an attribute with type code 0x10. This attribute is commonly known as $STANDARD_INFORMATION or $10. It must be resident. This attribute is used to store four timestamps and some other file attributes. Table 8.7 summarizes the fields in this attribute's data stream.

The four timestamps in this attribute store 100's of nanoseconds (0.0000001 second intervals) since January 1, 1601. Recall that FAT filesystem timestamps only have a resolution of two seconds. This is certainly quite the improvement, but still not as good as the 1 nanosecond accuracy found in the Linux extended filesystem. As we shall see later in this chapter, these timestamps are stored in multiple places. Discrepancies in these timestamps can be used to detect tampering.

NTFS offers additional file attributes not found in FAT. These are summarized in Table 8.8. Only four of these file attributes are found in FAT filesystems.

The read-only, hidden, system, and archive file attributes work the same as they do on a FAT filesystem. The new attributes will be discussed later in this chapter. Very few files have any of these new file attributes.

NTFS supports file versioning. If a file is versioned, the fields at offsets 36 (0x24) and 40 (0x28) are used to store version information. Use of the remaining fields varies depending on the version of Windows. Thankfully, these fields are rarely of interest to forensic examiners. Examining a $10 attribute in ADE is shown in Figure 8.5.

The Master File Table 273

Table 8.7. The $STANDARD_INFORMATION attribute data stream.

Offset	Length	Description
0 (0x00)	8	File creation timestamp
8 (0x08)	8	File modification timestamp
16 (0x10)	8	MFT record change timestamp
24 (0x18)	8	Last access timestamp
32 (0x20)	4	File attributes
36 (0x24)	4	Highest version number allowed (0 = versioning disabled)
40 (0x28)	4	Version number (0 = versioning disabled)
44 (0x2C)	4	Class ID
48 (0x30)	4	Owner ID
52 (0x34)	4	Security ID
56 (0x38)	8	Disk quota size
64 (0x40)	8	Update sequence number

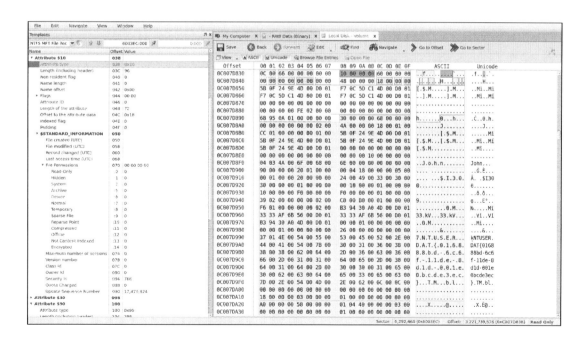

FIGURE 8.5.
Examining the $STANDARD_INFORMATION attribute in Active@ Disk Editor.

Table 8.8. File attributes stored in the $STANDARD_INFORMATION data stream.

Bit	Value	Description
0	0x0001	Read only
1	0x0002	Hidden
2	0x0004	System file
5	0x0020	Archive
6	0x0040	Device file
7	0x0080	Normal (standard) file
8	0x0100	Temporary file
9	0x0200	Sparse file
10	0x0400	Reparse point
11	0x0800	Compressed file
12	0x1000	Offline file
13	0x2000	Not content indexed
14	0x4000	Encrypted

Just as every file or directory must have a $STANDARD_INFORMATION attribute, it must have at least one $FILE_NAME attribute. The type code for this attribute is 0x30. As a result it is frequently referred to simply as $30. Files and directories can have more than one name. If a file has an 8.3 compliant name it may have a single filename. However, if this is not the case, a second short filename is required. Note that this is handled differently in NTFS than it is in FAT. On a FAT filesystem the second name is created in a directory. For NTFS all of the filenames are a part of the file itself.

Like the $10 attribute, the $30 attribute(s) must be resident. Unlike the $10 attribute, the $30 attribute(s) is (are) normally indexed. Both of these policies allow quick searches by filename. The $FILE_NAME ($30) attribute data stream is summarized in Table 8.9.

The MFT reference for the parent directory in the $30 attribute works the same as MFT references found elsewhere, such as the base MFT reference in the MFT entry header. The least significant 6 bytes house the MFT record number (only the lower 4 bytes are used), and the most significant 2 bytes hold the sequence number for that MFT entry. This serves as a double check in case the MFT record is changed and the changes are not pushed out to everything that references that entry.

The $30 attribute has the same four timestamps found in $10. These occur in the same order in both places. Later we will discuss the rules for which timestamps get updated in vari-

Table 8.9. The $FILE_NAME ($30) attribute data stream.

Offset	Length	Description
0 (0x00)	8	MFT reference (entry and sequence number) for parent directory
8 (0x08)	8	File creation timestamp
16 (0x10)	8	Modification timestamp
24 (0x18)	8	MFT record change timestamp
32 (0x20)	8	File access timestamp
40 (0x28)	8	Physical (allocated) file size
48 (0x30)	8	Logical (actual) file size
56 (0x38)	4	File attributes (see text for meanings)
60 (0x3C)	4	Extended file attributes (see text for meanings)
64 (0x40)	1	Length of the filename in characters
65 (0x41)	1	Filename namespace (see text)
66 (0x42)	Varies	Filename in Unicode

ous scenarios. We will also learn that there is yet another place that these redundant timestamps are stored.

The physical (allocated) and logical (actual) file sizes follow the timestamps. These sizes represent space used in clusters to store the file's data. Zeros are stored in these fields for directories and small files stored entirely in the MFT. The DOS file attributes are located at offset 56 (0x38) in the data stream. These values are summarized in Table 8.10. Note the similarity to the file attributes in $10.

The filename namespace is new. Four namespace types are defined. The Posix namespace has type 0x00. This namespace is used primarily for files that are internal to Windows. Posix is an old standard for writing Unix applications that work on various flavors of Unix. The POS stands for Portable Operating System and the "ix" suffix was added to make it sound Unix-related.

The Win32 namespace has type 0x01. This namespace is used for long filenames that are not DOS 8.3 compliant. Files and directories with this namespace in a $30 attribute should have another $30 attribute with a filename in the DOS 8.3 namespace (type 0x02). If a name is compatible with both of these namespaces the type 0x03 Win32/DOS namespace is used. Namespaces are summarized in Table 8.11.

A $FILE_NAME attribute for a directory is shown in Figure 8.6. Note that it has the directory attribute and its sizes are zero. The $FILE_NAME attribute for a typical file can be seen in Figure 8.7. Notice that the namespace is Win32/DOS (0x03).

Table 8.10. DOS file attributes stored in the $FILE_NAME ($30) attribute data stream.

Bit	Value	Description
0	0x0001	Read only
1	0x0002	Hidden
2	0x0004	System file
5	0x0020	Archive
6	0x0040	Device file
7	0x0080	Normal (standard) file
8	0x0100	Temporary file
9	0x0200	Sparse file
10	0x0400	Reparse point
11	0x0800	Compressed file
12	0x1000	Offline file
13	0x2000	Not content indexed
14	0x4000	Encrypted
28	0x10000000	Directory
29	0x20000000	Index View

Table 8.11. Filename namespace types.

Type code	Namespace
0x00	Posix
0x01	Win32
0x02	DOS 8.3 filenames
0x03	Win32/DOS

The Master File Table

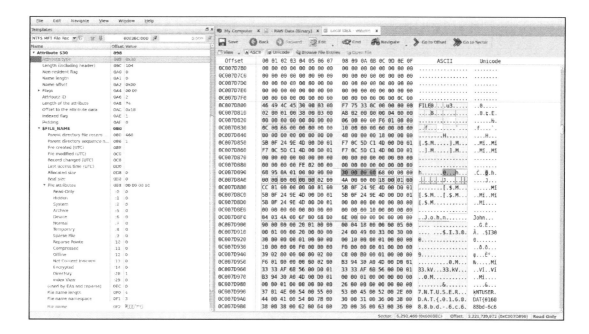

FIGURE 8.6.
Examining a $FILE_NAME attribute for a directory in Active@ Disk Editor.

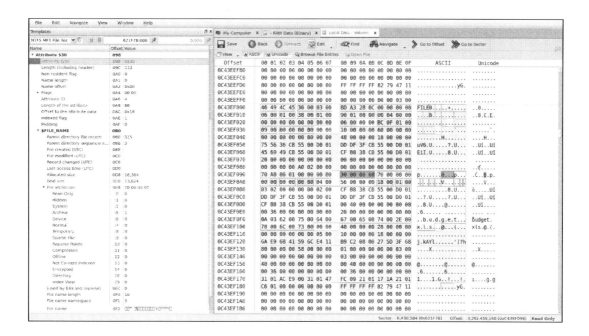

FIGURE 8.7.
Examining a $FILE_NAME attribute for a file in Active@ Disk Editor.

The data attribute

As previously mentioned, everything related to a file is stored in attributes in its MFT entry or entries. This includes the file contents (data). File contents are stored in the $DATA attribute which has the type code 0x80. The $DATA attribute is often referred to as $80. This attribute may be resident or non-resident.

FILES SMALL AND LARGE

Let us begin with the simplest case: a very small file. Every file must have a $STANDARD_INFORMATION ($10), at least one $FILE_NAME ($30), and at least one $DATA ($80) attribute. The file might have other attributes as well. There are 1024 bytes (2 sectors) in each MFT entry. Given the required items, there are typically 500-700 bytes that can be used to store file data. If the file is small enough, the $DATA attribute will be resident.

The performance implications of having files stored completely in the MFT are huge. Retrieving the file requires only one read operation. Contrast this with the FAT situation where even a small file requires reading a directory entry, reading in part of the first FAT, reading in part of the second FAT, and then reading in a single cluster that contains the file data. You will see many desktop.ini files on an NTFS filesystem used to store users' customized settings, etc. for certain directories. While the majority of Windows configuration information is stored in the registry, storing some of these items in small files represents a performance improvement. The $DATA attribute for one of these desktop.ini files is shown in Figure 8.8.

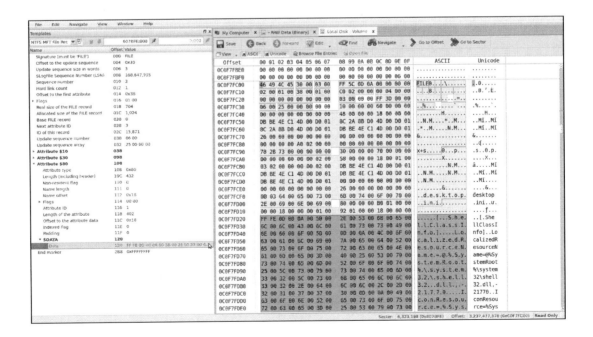

FIGURE 8.8.

Examining a small resident file in Active@ Disk Editor. Note that the data is 402 bytes long.

Once a file has become too large, the $DATA attribute becomes non-resident. All of the non-resident attributes use a series of data runs to describe the clusters they are stored in. A data run is comprised of three elements: a size byte, cluster count, and cluster offset. The size byte tells the size of the remaining two items. The high nybble (4 bits) indicates how many bytes are used to store the cluster offset and the low nybble specifies the size of the cluster count field in bytes. For example, the value 0x31 indicates that a 1 byte cluster count and 3 byte offset follow. A size byte value of 0x00 terminates a list of data runs.

The cluster count is stored as an unsigned integer. Data runs of up to 255 and 65,535 clusters can be stored in 1 and 2 byte cluster counts, respectively. It is somewhat rare to have cluster counts that are more than 2 bytes long as this represents more than 256 MB in contiguous clusters. Given that up to 64 GB in contiguous clusters can be represented by a data run with a 3 byte cluster count, you may never see a 4 byte cluster count.

The cluster offset is stored as a signed integer. This can make calculating the correct cluster number slightly tricky. The cluster offset in the first data run is simply the starting cluster. Every other data run requires adding the offset to the starting cluster of the previous data run. This is straightforward when all the offsets are positive. Where it gets difficult is when the offset is negative and the value is not one of the standard sizes (1, 2, 4, or 8 bytes).

Before discussing how to handle negative offsets, you need to know how to identify a negative signed integer. Negative integers are stored using two's complement format. There are a variety of ways of calculating two's complements, none of which are important for us. A negative number will always have the highest bit set. Said another way, the highest byte will be greater than or equal to 0x80. Remember that little endian format is used, so the last byte is the highest order one.

Data runs are best learned by walking through some examples. We will begin with a data run with only positive cluster offsets. As shown in Figure 8.9, the data runs for the file are 0x31 0x01 0xAC 0xE9 0x00, 0x31 0x01 0x47 0xFC 0x09, 0x21 0x01 0x17 0x1A, 0x21 0x01 0xC6 0x01, and 0x00.

The first data run is 0x31 x01 0xAC 0xE9 0x00. The 0x31 indicates 1 byte for the cluster count and 3 bytes for the offset. The cluster count is 0x01. The offset is 0x00E9AC (remember it is stored in little endian format). Notice how the highest byte of 0x00 is necessary to prevent this number from being negative. Converting 0xE9AC to decimal using the standard Linux calculator in programming mode as shown in Figure 8.10 yields 59,820 which agrees with Figure 8.9.

The second data run is 0x31 0x01 0x47 0xFC 0x09. This translates to a cluster count of 0x01 and cluster offset of 0x09FC47. Adding 0x09FC47 to 0xE9AC yields 0xAE5F3 or 714,227 which agrees with Figure 8.9.

The third data run is 0x21 0x01 0x17 0x1A. Translating this yields a cluster count of 0x01 and offset of 0x1A17. Adding 0x1A17 to 0xAE5F3 yields 0xB000A or 720,906. This agrees with Figure 8.9.

The final data run is 0x21 0x01 0xC6 0x01. This corresponds to a cluster count of 0x01 and offset of 0x01C6. Adding 0x01C6 to 0xB000A yields 0xB01D0 or 721,360. This is consistent with what ADE calculated as shown in Figure 8.9. The size byte of 0x00 terminates the data run.

Now that we have walked through a simple case we are ready to tackle a problem with negative cluster offsets. A file with negative cluster offsets is shown in Figure 8.11. Notice that the last two data runs have starting clusters that are lower than that of the previous data run.

280 CHAPTER 8 NTFS Filesystems

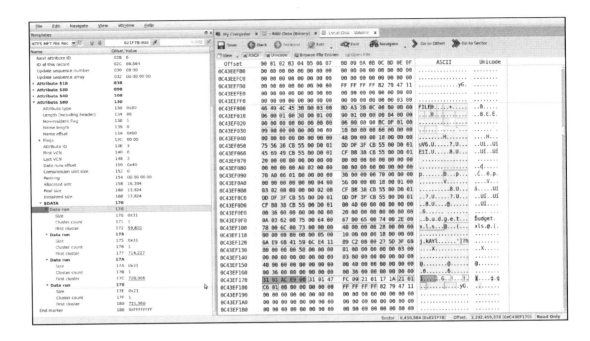

FIGURE 8.9.

A medium-sized file with only positive offsets in its data runs.

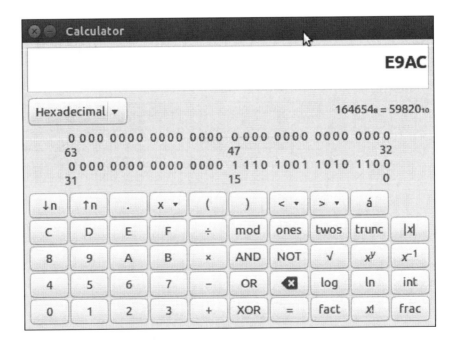

FIGURE 8.10.

Converting numbers to decimal using the Linux calculator. Notice how binary, octal, and decimal numbers are all displayed.

Files small and large 281

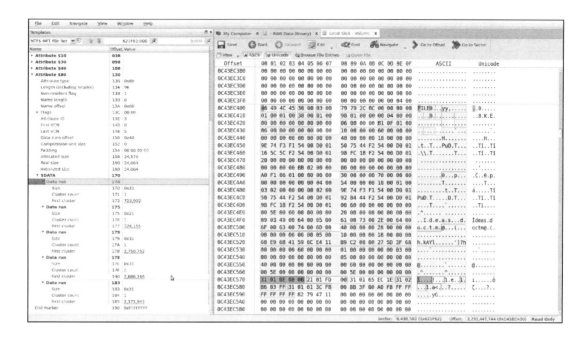

FIGURE 8.11.

Examining a medium-sized file with negative cluster offsets in Active@ Disk Editor.

The data runs for this file are 0x31 0x01 0xBE 0x0B 0x0B, 0x21 0x01 0xFD 0x00, 0x31 0x01 0x65 0xEC 0x1E, 0x31 0x02 0xB6 0x03 0xFF, 0x31 0x01 0x61 0x3C 0xFB, and the 0x00 terminator. The first data run translates to 1 cluster starting at 0x0B0BBE or 723,902. This agrees with Figure 8.11.

The second data run translates to 1 cluster at an offset of 0x00FD from 0x0B0BBE. The cluster is 0x0B0BBE + 0x00FD = 0xB0CBB or 724,155. The third data run translates to 1 cluster at an offset of 0x1EEC65 from 0xB0CBB. The cluster is 0xB0CBB + 0x1EEC65 = 0x29F920 or 2,750,752. Both of these are in agreement with Figure 8.11.

The fourth data run translates to 2 clusters at an offset of 0xFF03B6 from 0x29F920. The highest bit in the offset is set (highest byte >= 0x80) which indicates the offset is negative. In order to determine the appropriate offset we must calculate the two's complement of this value. The built-in Linux calculator stores numbers as 64-bit (8 byte) values when used in programming mode. In order to receive the correct answer the offset must be padded with leading bytes of 0xFF out to the full 8 bytes before calculating the two's complement. Our 3-byte offset requires 5 bytes of padding. We must calculate the two's complement of 0xFFFFFFFFFFFF03B6 as shown in Figure 8.12. The answer returned was 0xFC4A.

With the two's complement of the offset in hand the starting cluster is easily calculated as 0x29F920 − 0xFC4A = 0x28FCD6 or 2,686,166. This agrees with Figure 8.11. The easiest way to get this using the built-in calculator is via the "ans" memory. Memory locations, including "ans" (the previous answer to last calculation), are accessed using the button with the x and a downward pointing triangle on the first row. Typing the previous starting cluster (0x29F920) − ans, as shown in Figure 8.13, leads to the correct result.

282 CHAPTER 8 NTFS Filesystems

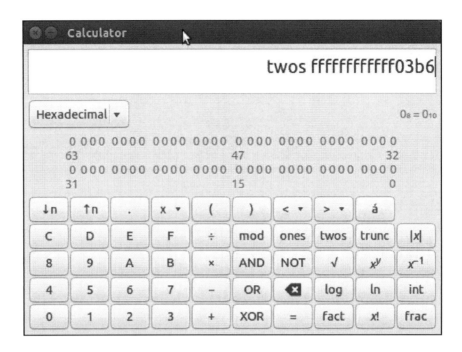

FIGURE 8.12.

Calculating the two's complement with the Linux calculator. In this case the offset of 0xFF03B6 is padded with 5 bytes of 0xFF.

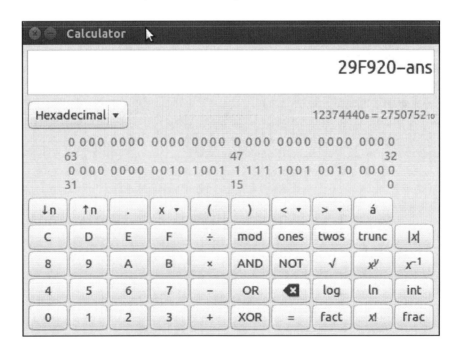

FIGURE 8.13.

Using the previously calculated two's complement stored in the calculator memory to calculate the starting cluster with the Linux calculator.

Files small and large

The last data run for this file is 0x31 0x01 0x61 0x3C 0xFB. This translates to one cluster at offset 0xFB3C61 from 0x28FCD6. This offset is once again negative. After padding the offset with leading bytes of 0xFF we must calculate the two's complement of 0xFFFFFFFFFFB3C61. The calculator returns 0x4C39F. The last cluster is then 0x28FCD6 − 0x4C39F = 0x243937 or 2,373,943 which agrees with Figure 8.11. Putting all of these together the file is stored in the following clusters: 723,902, 724,15, 2,750,752, 2,686,166, 2,686,167, and 2,373,943.

What happens when a file is large? One of the nice features of NTFS is that it allows large contiguous files to be accessed much quicker than on a FAT filesystem because it does not need to navigate the FAT to build a cluster chain. A 1 gigabyte page (swap) file is shown in Figure 8.14. The single data run for this file is 0x33 0x00 0x00 0x04 0x59 0xFA 0x1E. This translates to 0x040000 (262,144) clusters beginning at cluster 0x1EFA59 (2,030,169).

What happens when files are extremely large and fragmented? The list of data runs can become so large that a single MFT entry cannot house them all. Once multiple MFT entries are required, a new attribute, $ATTRIBUTE_LIST (type 0x20) must be added. This attribute list will have an entry for all attributes (including those stored in the first base MFT entry) with the exception of itself. Because attributes are sorted by type code, the $ATTRIBUTE_LIST ($20) entry should always be in the base entry. In theory it may be possible for the attribute list to grow too large to be stored in a single MFT entry, but I have never seen this actually happen. The $ATTRIBUTE_LIST data stream is summarized in Table 8.12.

The entries in each attribute list item are straightforward. The first field gives the type of attribute. The second is the record length which includes any padding and should be a multiple

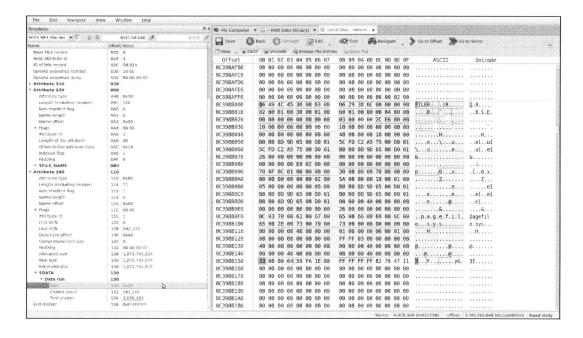

FIGURE 8.14.

A large contiguous file.

Table 8.12. The $ATTRIBUTE_LIST ($20) attribute data stream.

Offset	Length	Description
0 (0x00)	4	Attribute identifier
4 (0x04)	2	Record length (offset to next record)
6 (0x06)	1	Name length in characters
7 (0x07)	1	Offset to name
8 (0x08)	8	Starting Virtual Cluster Number (VCN)
16 (0x10)	8	MFT reference for record where attribute is stored
24 (0x18)	2	Attribute ID

of eight. Most attributes are unnamed and should have a name length of zero. Unlike some other items in the MFT, the name offset normally points just after the attribute ID even if there is no name. Because some attributes may only apply to certain clusters, a starting VCN is part of each attribute list entry. The MFT references work in the usual way with the lower 6 bytes (only 4 of which are used) giving the MFT entry number and the upper 2 bytes storing the sequence number.

Part of an MFT entry for a large (215 MB) fragmented file is shown in Figure 8.15. The $10 attribute is not shown in the figure. Notice that the base MFT entry contains $10, $20, and two $30 attributes. There are two additional MFT entries that both contain only a $80 attribute. The first $80 attribute (stored in MFT entry 21,913 with sequence number 9) covers VCN 0 – 11,583 and the second (stored in MFT entry 22,144 with sequence number 24) covers VCN 11,584 and higher. Part of the first secondary MFT entry is shown in Figure 8.16. Notice that this entry has only a $80 attribute (no $10, etc.).

DIRECTORIES

Having covered all of the possible file scenarios we now turn our attention to NTFS directories. In NTFS, directories are stored as an index of $FILE_NAME ($30) items. An index is used to store items in such a way that they are easily retrieved by a certain attribute, usually a name. NTFS directories are stored in a tree structure.

Tree structures are used in computer science in order to sort and quickly retrieve items. There are many different kinds of trees that are used depending on the situation. As we shall see, the trees used by NTFS are not particularly good in terms of retrieval speed, but this is balanced with the speed by which the tree may be altered. With few exceptions, most directories do not contain enough files to justify the processing time required to create and maintain a balanced tree. Most NTFS indexes are relatively flat (few levels and many nodes per level).

Directories 285

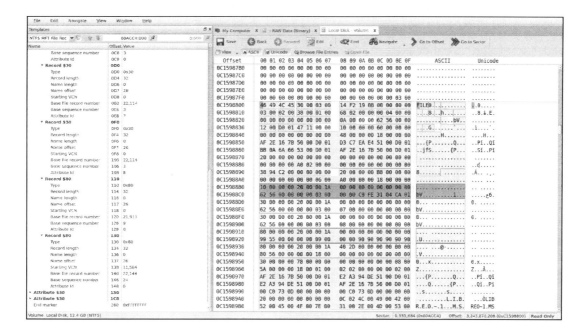

FIGURE 8.15.

Examining part of the MFT base entry for a large fragmented file in Active@ Disk Editor.

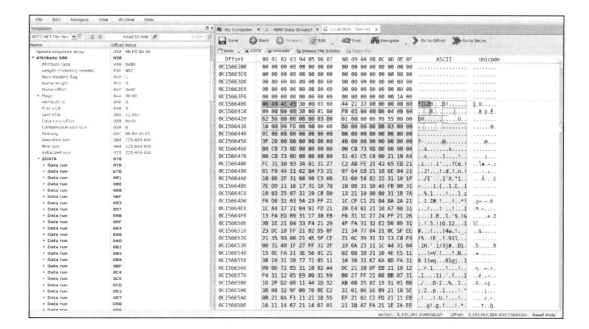

FIGURE 8.16.

Examining a part of a secondary (continued) MFT entry for a large fragmented file in Active@ Disk Editor. Note that the entry contains a single $80 attribute.

The $90 attribute

All trees must have a root or starting point for traversing the tree. For NTFS indexes this root is stored in a $INDEX_ROOT (type code 0x90) attribute commonly referred to as a $90 attribute. As it turns out, the $90 attribute stores more than just the index (tree) root. It also contains an index header and several index entries. This dual purpose attribute tends to be confusing to people first learning how NTFS works. Once the $90 attribute grows beyond a certain point the index entries are then stored in data clusters. Rest assured that we will walk through this slowly and show you what happens as a directory is first created and then starts to grow. The $90 attribute data stream layout is summarized in Table 8.13. Because indexes are used for other purposes (not just directories), the $90 attribute is named "$I30" in order for Windows to know this index houses a directory.

The index root entry is summarized in Table 8.14. This item begins with the type of attribute being indexed. In the case of directories, filenames which have a type of 0x30 are being indexed. The second field is a collation (sorting) rule. The most likely value to be found here is 0x01 which corresponds to a Unicode sort (essentially alphabetical). The buffer size will almost certainly be one standard 4096-byte cluster. The index root entry is used to describe the index overall.

An index header entry follows the index root entry in the $90 attribute data stream. The purpose of this header is to describe the index entries that follow. This 16-byte header is summarized in Table 8.15.

Table 8.13. $INDEX_ROOT ($90) data stream layout.

Index Root Entry (what is being indexed, collation rule, and index buffer size)
Index Header Entry (offset to first entry, logical/physical size of entries, resident or non-resident)
Index Entry
Index Entry
... (Additional Index Entries until the index becomes too large to be resident)

Table 8.14. The index root entry found in $INDEX_ROOT ($90) data stream.

Offset	Length	Description
0 (0x00)	4	Attribute type identifier (should be 0x30 for directories)
4 (0x04)	4	Collation rule (probably 0x01 for Unicode sort)
8 (0x08)	4	Buffer size (probably 0x1000 or 4096 bytes)
12 (0x0C)	4	Clusters per index buffer (probably 1)

Table 8.15. The index header entry found in the $INDEX_ROOT ($90) data stream.

Offset	Length	Description
0 (0x00)	4	Offset to first index entry
4 (0x04)	4	Logical size of index entries
8 (0x08)	4	Physical (allocated) size of index entries
12 (0x0C)	4	Non-resident flag (00 = resident; 01 = uses index buffers)

One or more index entries follow the index header. If the directory is empty, a single entry which is flagged as the last entry and points to MFT entry zero with sequence number zero will be present. Each entry is essentially a 16-byte preamble followed by a $FILE_NAME data stream. The index entry is summarized in Table 8.16.

An empty directory's $90 attribute is shown in Figure 8.17. Notice that it has the attribute name $I30, is indexing type 0x30 items, is using Unicode sort as a collation rule (rule 0x01), and uses one 4096-byte cluster per index buffer. From the header only 32 bytes are being used to store index entries (half of this in the 16-byte header), and the entries are resident. The single index entry points to the null MFT reference and is 16 (0x10) bytes long with the last entry flag (value 0x02) set. Note that ADE templates do not interpret these index entries, so this must be done manually. In case you are wondering, none of the expensive commercial tools in common use interpret these values either.

The $90 attribute for a directory containing only one item (a subdirectory) is shown in Figure 8.18. The cursor is at the start of the first index entry (offset 0x0C000E948). As can be seen in the Data Inspector window, this is for MFT entry 59 (0x3B) with sequence number 01. The length of the entry is 96 (0x60) bytes, and the $FILE_NAME data stream is 76 (0x4C) bytes long. The index entry is resident, and the MFT entry for the parent directory

Table 8.16. Format for index entries found in $INDEX_ROOT ($90) data stream.

Offset	Length	Description
0 (0x00)	8	MFT reference
8 (0x08)	2	Total length of this index entry
10 (0x0A)	2	Length of index entry data stream ($30 data stream)
12 (0x0C)	1	Index flags: Bit 0 = index buffers in use, Bit 1 = last entry
16 (0x10)	Varies	Index entry ($30) data stream if MFT reference not null
Last 8 bytes	8	Index buffer VCN if non-resident (index buffers in use)

288 CHAPTER 8 NTFS Filesystems

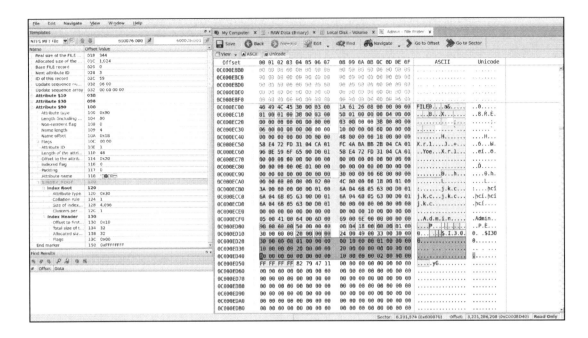

FIGURE 8.17.

The $INDEX_ROOT attribute for an empty directory.

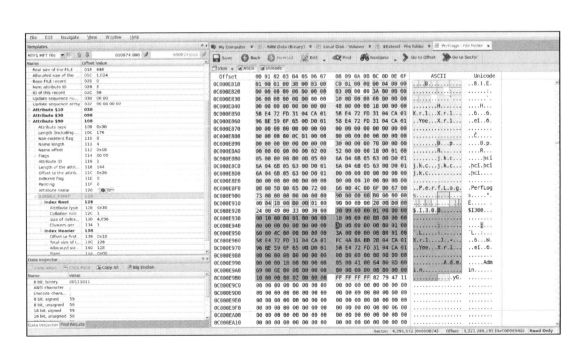

FIGURE 8.18.

The $INDEX_ROOT attribute for a directory containing one item.

is 58 (0x3A) with sequence number 01. The filename is Admin, and its attributes indicate it is a directory.

The second index entry begins at offset 0x0C000E9A8 (0x0C000E948 + 0x60). This entry points to the null MFT reference, has a length of 16 (0x10) bytes, and has the last entry flag set (value 0x02). The number of index entries that can be stored in the $90 attribute before things get pushed out to data clusters varies but is typically between two and five, depending on filename length and other items. Part of the $90 attribute for a directory with five items is shown in Figure 8.19. Note that the last item is again the null index entry (offset 0x0C0002F38).

The $A0 attribute and index buffers

What happens when a directory grows beyond what can be stored in the $INDEX_ROOT attribute? A new attribute $INDEX_ALLOCATION (type code 0xA0) is added. This new attribute is commonly called $A0. This attribute is used to describe index buffers. It is analogous to the $80 attribute for non-resident files in that it simply consists of a list of data runs for clusters containing index buffers. These buffers contain a header and then a list of index entries. As we will see, the $90 attribute does not go away and the entry or entries in $90 will point toward index buffers.

Like the $90 attribute, the new $A0 attribute is named "$I30". Another new attribute also named $I30 is added once index buffers become necessary. This new attribute is $BITMAP (type code 0xB0) and is commonly called $B0. We will discuss the $B0 attribute further in the

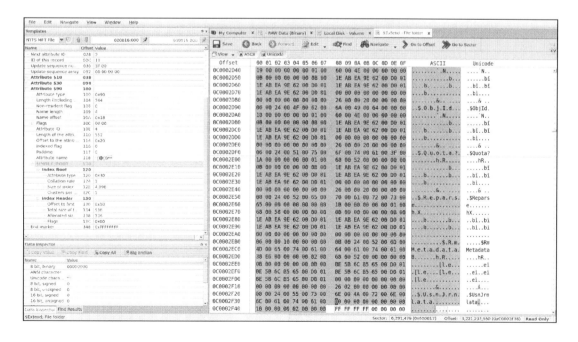

FIGURE 8.19.

Part of the $INDEX_ROOT attribute for a directory containing five items.

next section when we discuss large directories. The $A0 attribute for a directory using a single index buffer is shown in Figure 8.20. The single data run 0x11 0x01 0x2A indicates one cluster starting at cluster 42 (0x2A).

Each index buffer begins with a header. This header is normally 64 (0x40) bytes long including the padding to make entries start on an 8-byte boundary. This header is summarized in Table 8.17. Note that, as with with index entries in $90, none of the standard forensic tools (including the expensive commercial ones) interpret this header for you.

The string "INDX" at the start of an index buffer is used to verify that the cluster contains a valid set of index entries. Because the fields leading up to the update sequence array are all of a fixed size, the offset to the update sequence number should always be 40 (0x28). The update sequence here works the same as the one found in the MFT. Because the index buffer is 8 sectors long the size for the array should always be 9 (8 sectors + 1 update sequence number).

The log file sequence number is a reference to the filesystem journal. Virtual Cluster Numbers (VCN) are used to identify index buffers. The first index buffer has a VCN of zero. The offset to the start of index entries is relative to the position in which this offset is stored (0x18). The most likely value to be found here is 0x28 which indicates that entries begin at offset 0x40 (0x18 + 0x28).

When examining index buffers, be sure to check the logical size stored at offset 28 (0x1C). The value stored in this field plus 24 (0x18) indicates the start of the index buffer slack space. As items are added and removed from a directory the valid data in index buffer(s) will grow and shrink. When the logical size decreases, Windows does not zero out index buffer slack

Table 8.17. The index buffer header.

Offset	Length	Description
0 (0x00)	4	"INDX" in ASCII
4 (0x04)	2	Offset to update sequence number (probably 0x28 = 40)
6 (0x06)	2	Size of update sequence number & array in words (probably 9)
8 (0x08)	8	Log file sequence number
16 (0x10)	8	VCN of this index buffer
24 (0x18)	4	Offset to start of index entries from here (probably 0x28)
28 (0x1C)	4	Logical size of index entries (how much of buffer is used)
32 (0x20)	4	Physical size of index entries (4096 − 24 = 4072 or 0x0FE8)
36 (0x24)	4	Flags (00 = leaf buffer, 01 = buffer has children)
40 (0x28)	2	Update sequence number
42 (0x2A)	16	Update sequence array (8 values for the 8 sectors in buffer)

space. As a result, it is extremely common to see entries in the slack space that appear to be valid but are not.

The physical size should be 4096 minus 24 bytes for the header or 4072 (0x0FE8). The flags indicate if this buffer is a leaf in the tree (00) or a middle node that has children (01). The index buffer header ends with the update sequence number followed by the update sequence array and a few bytes of padding to ensure the index entries begin on an 8-byte boundary.

The index buffer header for the directory shown in Figure 8.20 is displayed in Figure 8.21. This was reached by clicking on the hyperlink in the $INDEX_ALLOCATION data run. The logical size of entries for this index buffer is 0x0CB0 or 3,248 bytes. This means that the slack space begins at offset 0x0CC8 (0x0CB0 + 0x18) into the cluster.

The index entries in the index buffer are very similar to those found in $INDEX_ROOT with two small differences. First, the flags field has a slightly different meaning. Here Bit 0 is used to indicate that subnodes exist (this is not a leaf node in the tree) and Bit 1 is used to indicate the final entry in a node as before. Second, if a subnode does exists, the VCN for the subnode index allocation is in the last 8 bytes of the entry. The index entry is summarized in Table 8.18.

The $INDEX_ROOT attribute for the directory shown in Figure 8.20 and Figure 8.21 appears in Figure 8.22. Notice the single index entry that begins at offset 0x0C000F1C0. Decoding this entry we see that it refers to the null MFT reference (entry zero with sequence number zero), is 0x18 (24) bytes long, has both the non-resident and last entry flags (value 0x03), and is pointing to the index buffer VCN zero.

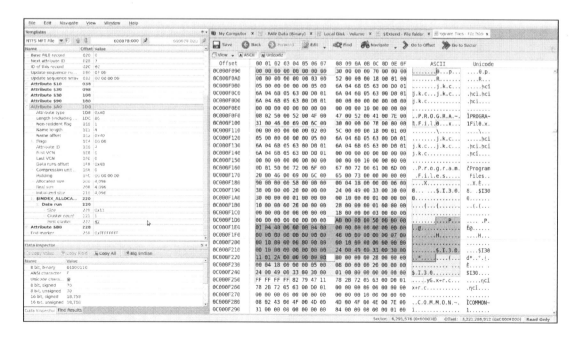

FIGURE 8.20.

The $INDEX_ALLOCATION ($A0) attribute for a directory stored in a single index buffer.

292 CHAPTER 8 NTFS Filesystems

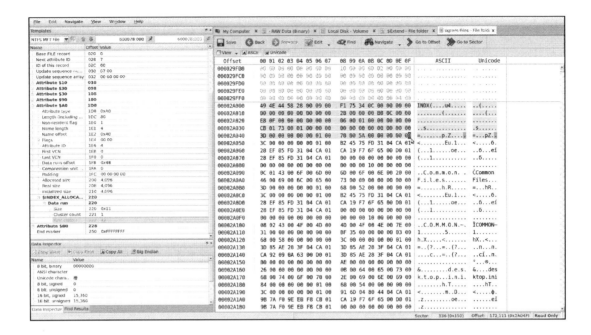

FIGURE 8.21.

Examining an index buffer header in Active@ Disk Editor.

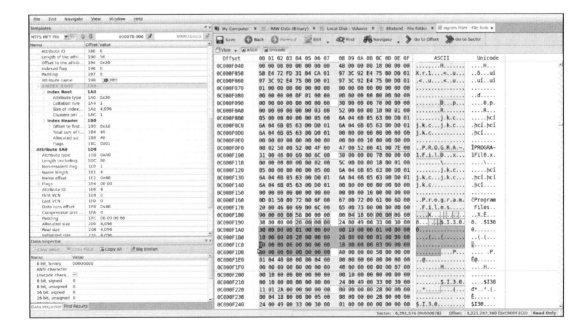

FIGURE 8.22.

$INDEX_ROOT attribute for a directory with an index buffer.

Table 8.18. Format for index entries contained in index buffers.

Offset	Length	Description
0 (0x00)	8	MFT reference
8 (0x08)	2	Total length of this index entry
10 (0x0A)	2	Length of index entry data stream ($30 data stream)
12 (0x0C)	1	Index flags: Bit 0 = has subnode, Bit 1 = last entry
16 (0x10)	Varies	$FILE_NAME data stream
Last 8 bytes	8	VCN of subnode index buffer (only present if subnode exits)

Once a directory has grown past the capacity of a single index buffer another will be added. It should be noted that even though index buffers are being used, there can still be index entries in the $INDEX_ROOT. A $90 attribute for a directory with two index buffers and a single resident entry in the $90 attribute (at offset 0x0C007D940) is shown in Figure 8.23.

Decoding the first index entry in Figure 8.23, we see it is for MFT entry 569 (0x0239) sequence number 2, it is 0xC8 bytes long (next entry begins at offset 0x0C007DA08), the

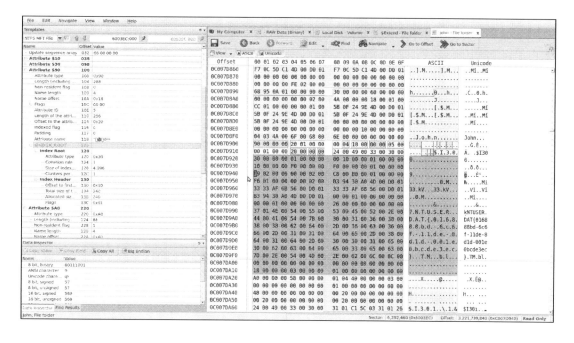

FIGURE 8.23.

The $INDEX_ROOT attribute for a directory with two index buffers.

294 CHAPTER 8 NTFS Filesystems

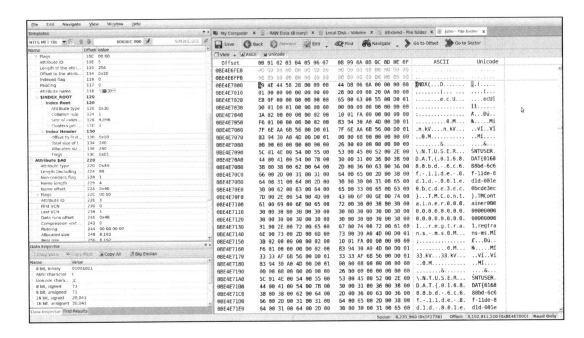

FIGURE 8.24.

The start of the second index buffer in a medium-sized directory.

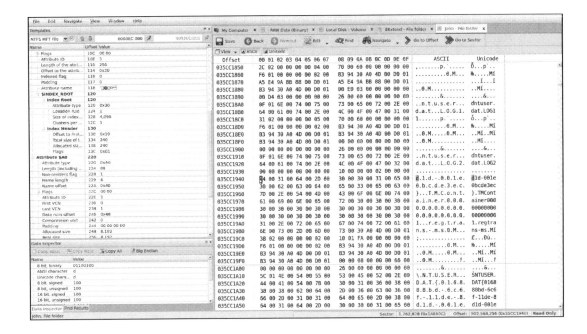

FIGURE 8.25.

The end of the first index buffer in a medium-sized directory.

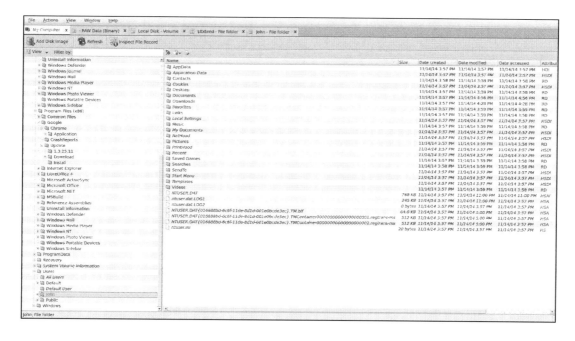

FIGURE 8.26.

A medium-sized directory. Figure 8.23, Figure 8.24, and Figure 8.25 all correspond to this directory.

$FILE_NAME data stream is 0xB0 bytes long, index buffers are in use, the parent directory is stored in MFT entry 502 (0x01F6) sequence number 2, the really long filename begins with "NTUSER.DAT" and has extension ".blf" (the update sequence array was used to get the correct value for the last character), and the index buffer VCN for the subnode is zero.

Decoding the second index entry in Figure 8.23, we see it is for the null MFT reference, is 0x18 bytes long, has both the uses index buffers and last entry flags set, and points to index buffer VCN 01. The beginning of the second index buffer is shown in Figure 8.24. Notice how the first entry in this index buffer looks like it might come right after the "NTUSER...blf" entry from Figure 8.23. This demonstrates the proper use of a tree. If a filename occurs before the entry, it should be in the left node (VCN 00) and if after the entry, it can be found in the right node (VCN 01). Examination of the end of the first index buffer reveals the entry right before that from $90 is stored. This is shown in Figure 8.25. The file is "ntuser.dat.LOG2", and the slack space begins at offset 0x035CC1940. The directory corresponding to Figure 8.23, Figure 8.24, and Figure 8.25 is shown in Figure 8.26.

Large directories

What happens when directories grow beyond the capacity of a pair of index buffers? Let us examine a larger directory to answer this question. The example we will use is the main \Windows directory from a Windows 7 subject. Part of this directory's MFT entry is shown in Figure 8.27. Note that four index buffers are required to store this directory.

296 CHAPTER 8 NTFS Filesystems

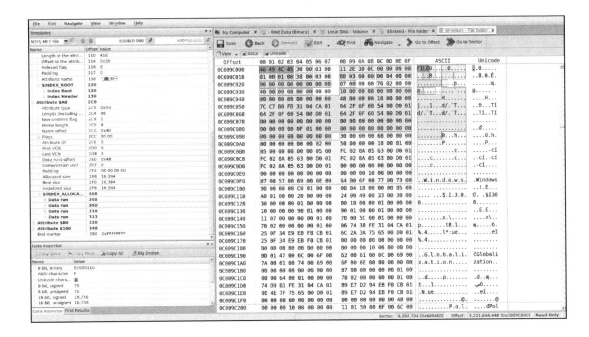

FIGURE 8.27.

Part of the MFT entry for the \Windows directory from a Windows 7 subject.

The $90 attribute for the directory in Figure 8.27 is shown in Figure 8.28. The index header begins at offset 0x0C009130 and has the flag that indicates index buffers are being used. The first index entry begins at offset 0x0C009C140. Decoding this entry yields the following information: it is for MFT entry 1,809 (0x0711) sequence number 1, is 0x78 bytes long, has a 0x5C byte $FILE_NAME data stream, has a subnode in index buffer VCN 00, is located in the directory stored in MFT entry 624 (0x0270) sequence number 1, and is a directory called "Globalization".

The second index entry begins at offset 0x0C009C1B8. Decoding this entry yields the following information: it is for MFT entry 2,183 (0x0887) with sequence number 1, is 0x80 bytes long with 0x64 of those bytes holding the $FILE_NAME data stream, has a subnode in index buffer VCN 01, is located in the directory stored in MFT entry 624 (0x0270) sequence number 1, and is named "PolicyDefinitions".

The third index entry begins at offset 0x0C009C238. Decoding this entry yields the following information: it is for MFT entry 15,964 (0x03E5C) sequence number 1, is 0x70 bytes long with 0x58 bytes holding the $FILE_NAME data stream, has a subnode in index buffer VCN 02, is located in the directory stored in MFT entry 624 (0x0270) sequence 1, and is named "Starter.xml". The final index entry which begins at offset 0x0C009C2A8 is for a null MFT reference with a subnode in index buffer VCN 03.

If we look at the filenames and subnodes for each entry, we discover that the names are "Globalization", "PolicyDefinitions", "Starter.xml", and nothing with subnodes stored in index buffer VCN 00, 01, 02, and 03, respectively. These filenames serve as dividing points which

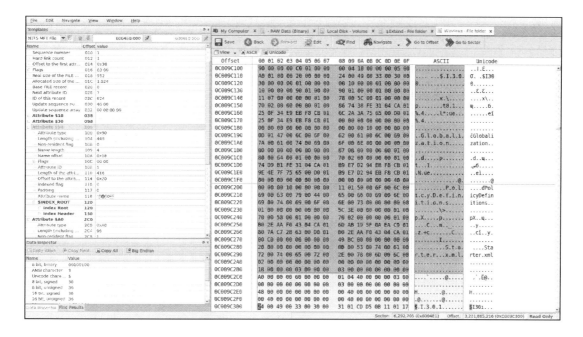

FIGURE 8.28.

The $INDEX_ROOT ($90) attribute for the \Windows directory from a Windows 7 subject.

allow you to know which index buffer to check for a particular entry. The location for any given entry based on the filename sort order are presented in Table 8.19.

The last entry in the first index buffer is for the file "fveupdate.exe" as shown in Figure 8.29. The first entry in the second index buffer is "GLOBAL~1" (the short filename entry for Globalization) as shown in Figure 8.30. The last entry in this index buffer is the "PLA" directory as shown in Figure 8.31. If we were to examine the last two index buffers, we would find that the first and last entries should come right before or after the values stored in the $90 attribute index entries.

Table 8.19. Location of entries from the directory in Figure 8.27 based on filename.

After	Before	Location
	Globalization	Index buffer in VCN 00
Globalization	PolicyDefinitions	Index buffer in VCN 01
PolicyDefinitions	Starter.xml	Index buffer in VCN 02
Starter.xml		Index buffer in VCN 03

298 CHAPTER 8 NTFS Filesystems

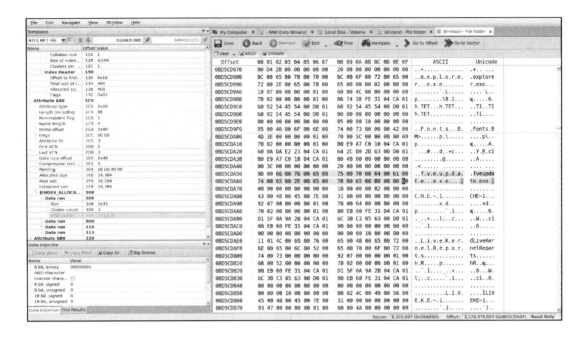

FIGURE 8.29.

The last entry in the first index buffer for the directory in Figure 8.27. The slack space begins at offset 0x0BD5CDA80.

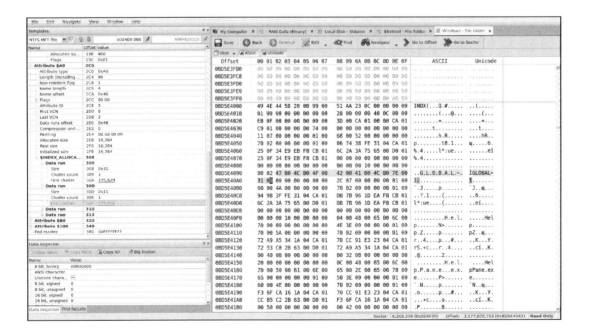

FIGURE 8.30.

The first entry in the second index buffer for the directory in Figure 8.27.

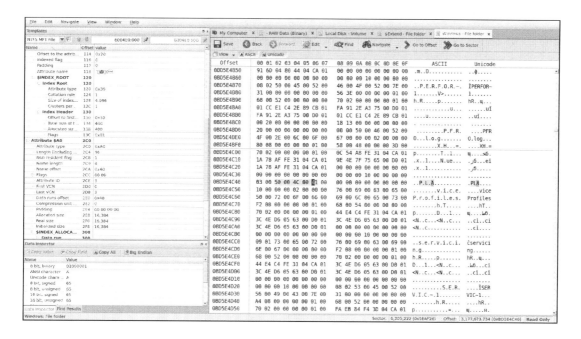

FIGURE 8.31.

The last entry in the second index buffer for the directory in Figure 8.27. The slack space begins at offset 0x0BD5E4C58.

In the \Windows directory example we saw that the entries were stored in a rather flat tree. Not counting the root node there are only two levels in this tree. The upper level is stored in the $90 attribute and the bottom level in the four index buffers.

The \Windows directory might be fairly large, but it is tiny compared to the \Windows\System32 directory. This directory for the same Windows 7 subject requires 160 index buffers. The first sector of the corresponding MFT entry can be seen in Figure 8.32. Note that in this case the single index entry points to a null MFT reference and has a subnode in index buffer VCN 112 (0x70).

You may be wondering why the subnode from the $90 attribute index entry does not point at VCN 000 or VCN 159. Part of the reason for this is the manner in which Windows allocates index buffers. Some of the index allocation data runs are shown in Figure 8.33. Notice how the data runs start to increase in size as a directory grows, doubling every few data runs until the final data run contains 32 clusters in this case. This allocation algorithm improves performance both by having clusters in the index near each other and by decreasing the chance that a directory will become so fragmented that it will require multiple MFT entries to store the $INDEX_ALLOCATION data runs.

You might be wondering how any unused clusters in these $INDEX_ALLOCATION data runs are handled. The answer lies in the $BITMAP ($B0) attribute. This bitmap (which is named $I30) is used in the same manner as the overall NTFS bitmap. A value of 1 in bit 0 indicates VCN 0 is in use, a value of 1 in bit 8 indicates that VCN 8 is in use, etc.

CHAPTER 8 NTFS Filesystems

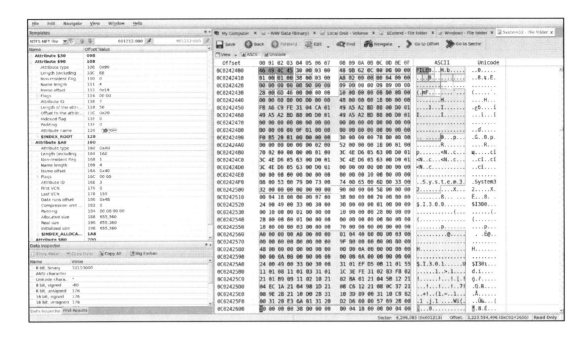

FIGURE 8.32.

The first sector for the MFT entry corresponding to the \Windows\System32 directory on a Windows 7 subject.

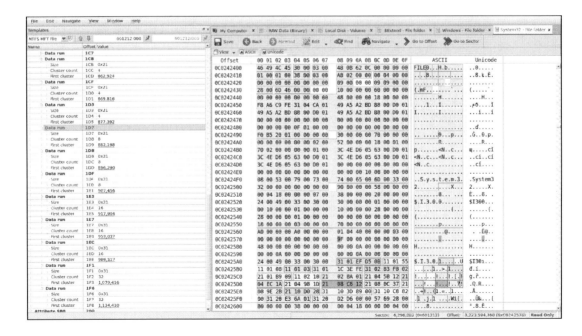

FIGURE 8.33.

Index allocation data runs of ever increasing size.

The $BITMAP attribute for the \Windows\System32 directory is shown in Figure 8.34. These bitmaps are always a multiple of 8 bytes long. All of the 128 bits in the first row in Figure 8.34 are set (all 16 bytes are 0xFF) indicating that the first 128 index buffers are in use. The value on the second line of 0x7FFF (0111 1111 1111 1111 in binary) indicates that the next 15 index buffers are also in use. In other words, of the 160 index buffers only 143 (128 + 15) are used. These index buffers are in VCN 000 through VCN 0142.

We now have a partial answer to our earlier question concerning why the $90 attribute index entry did not point to an index buffer in VCN 000 or VCN 159. VCN 159 is not in use. Why not VCN 000? For the answer we should examine VCN 112. The start of this index buffer is shown in Figure 8.35. From the flags at offset 0x107888024 we see that this index buffer has children (it is not a leaf node).

The index buffer shown in Figure 8.35 has a logical size of only 0x02E0 bytes. Decoding the first entry which begins at offset 0x107888040, we see that it has a subnode in VCN 006 and a filename of "CPFilters.dll". The second entry which begins at offset 0x1078880B8 also has a subnode (in VCN 037 (0x25)) and is for a directory named "en". The third entry which begins at offset 0x107888118 has a subnode in VCN 55 (0x37) and is for a file named "KBDINMAL.DLL". It seems rather clear that this index buffer is used to store the top level of the index tree.

If you were to examine all of the index buffers for the \Windows\System32 directory you would find that the index tree is only three to four levels deep. While this might sound pretty shallow for a directory containing several thousand files, it still represents a vast improvement over traversing this many FAT directory entries. Recall that FAT directory entries are unsorted and that many deleted entries might need to be read as well.

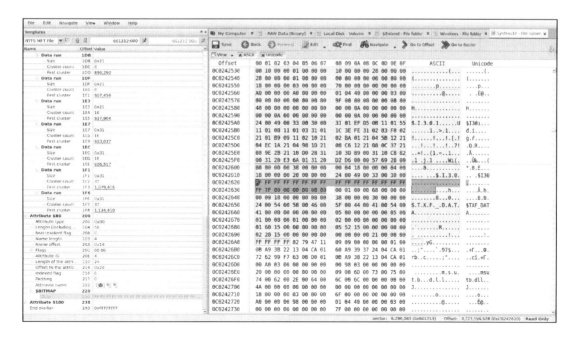

FIGURE 8.34.

The $BITMAP ($BO) for the \Windows\System32 directory for a Windows 7 subject.

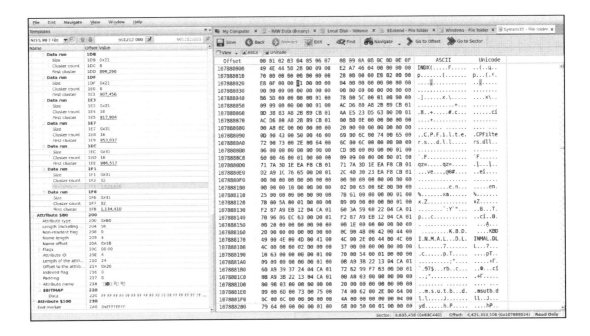

FIGURE 8.35.

The start of the index buffer in VCN 112 (0x70) for the \Windows\System32 directory from a Windows 7 subject.

Off-the-shelf tools for examining directories

As should be evident by now, NTFS directories are rather complicated, and interpreting all of the entries by hand is rather tedious. However, there are a few off-the-shelf packages that can help with this. The first tool I will present is FTK Imager from Access Data.

If you are trying to make disk images from Windows, FTK Imager is a popular tool. As we discussed previously in this book, there is no need for this tool if your forensic workstation runs Linux. It does have some nice features, though. One of the relevant features is the ability to extract the index buffers into an $I30 file. This tool was discussed in Chapter 3 where it was used to capture RAM. This tool easily runs on Linux with the WINE tool.

FTK Imager will create a pseudo file called $I30 in every directory that is stored in index buffers. To extract this file for processing simply right-click it and select export from the popup menu. Exporting the \Windows\System32 $I30 file is shown in Figure 8.36. It is important to realize that you are not getting the full directory in the $I30 file. Any index entries stored in the $90 attribute will be omitted.

William Ballenthin has created a Python script called INDXParse that will parse through the $I30 file and retrieve some of the information. This tool can get downloaded from github at https://github.com/williballenthin/INDXParse. This can be downloaded as a zip file or directly with git using the command `git clone https://github.com/williballenthin/INDXParse`.

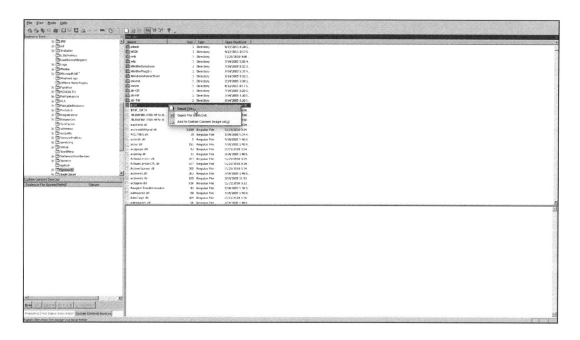

FIGURE 8.36.

Extracting a $I30 file with FTK Imager.

Unfortunately INDXParse only interprets and displays a portion of the information available in the $I30 file. This tool was developed with the intention of allowing an easy way to generate a body file for use in Autopsy and The Sleuth Kit. Only the information contained within a body file is reported. Body files are used in timeline generation. Later in this chapter we will learn a more powerful and general way to create timelines.

The help screen for INDXParse is shown in Figure 8.37. We see that it supports output in Comma Separated Value (CSV) and body file formats. It also has the ability to report on entries in index buffer slack space. Partial results from running this with the -c option against the \Windows\System32 $I30 file are shown in Figure 8.38. Notice that warnings are issued for the unused index buffers which are completely empty.

Normally the output from INDXParse would be redirected into a file which can then be opened in a spreadsheet program like LibreOffice Calc or imported into a database. The techniques for importing a CSV file and sorting spreadsheets by timestamps in LibreOffice Calc were discussed in Chapter 3. Part of the \Windows\System32 $I30 file that has been imported into a spreadsheet is shown in Figure 8.39. It is recommended that the timestamp fields are changed from the "Standard" type to an appropriate date type when importing into LibreOffice Calc for proper sorting.

We have come to the end of our discussion of NTFS directories. I believe this to be one of the hardest topics in all of Windows forensics. If you are not certain that you fully understand this topic I recommend you reread this section and walk through some examples yourself.

```
phil@i7laptop:~$ INDXParse.py --help
usage: INDXParse.py [-h] [-c | -b] [-d] [-v] [-t {dir,sdh,sii}] filename

Parse NTFS INDX files.

positional arguments:
  filename              Input INDX file path

optional arguments:
  -h, --help            show this help message and exit
  -c                    Output CSV
  -b                    Output Bodyfile
  -d                    Find entries in slack space
  -v                    Print debugging information
  -t {dir,sdh,sii}      Choose index type (dir, sdh, or sii)
phil@i7laptop:~$
```

FIGURE 8.37.

INDXParse help screen.

```
VBoxOGLpassthroughspu.dll,    98304,   98080, 2014-03-26 17:53:50,   2014-11-15 01:45:56.064453,2
014-11-15 01:45:56.064453,    2014-03-26 17:53:50
VBOXOG~1.DLL,    630784,  628512, 2014-03-26 17:53:50,   2014-11-15 01:45:55.611328,    2014-11-15 0
1:45:55.626953, 2014-03-26 17:53:50
VBOXOG~2.DLL,   1490944,         1489184,      2014-03-26 17:52:40,   2014-11-15 01:45:55.626953,2
014-11-15 01:45:55.658203,    2014-03-26 17:52:40
VBOXOG~3.DLL,    143360,  142624, 2014-03-26 17:53:50,   2014-11-15 01:45:55.658203,    2014-11-15 0
1:45:55.658203, 2014-03-26 17:53:50
VBOXOG~4.DLL,   1695744,         1693472,      2014-03-26 17:53:50,   2014-11-15 01:45:55.658203,2
014-11-15 01:45:55.705078,    2014-03-26 17:53:50
VBoxService.exe,          1744896,              1743648,       2014-03-26 17:53:50,   2014-11-15 01:45:55.
548828, 2014-11-15 01:45:55.595701,    2014-03-26 17:53:50
VBOXSE~1.EXE,   1744896,         1743648,      2014-03-26 17:53:50,   2014-11-15 01:45:55.548828,2
014-11-15 01:45:55.595701,    2014-03-26 17:53:50
VBoxTray.exe,    1507328,        1507104,      2014-03-26 17:53:52,   2014-11-15 01:45:55.486328,2
014-11-15 01:46:22.720701,    2014-03-26 17:53:52
vbscript.dll,    614400, 612864, 2010-11-21 03:24:00.883310,     2010-11-21 03:24:00.867710,      2014
-11-14 23:38:49.781248, 2010-11-21 03:24:00.867710
vds.exe,         536576, 533504, 2010-11-21 03:23:51.195694,     2010-11-21 03:23:51.195694,      2014
-11-14 23:38:49.906248, 2010-11-21 03:23:51.195694
vdsbas.dll,      192512, 190976, 2010-11-21 03:24:09.634926,     2010-11-21 03:24:09.619326,      2014
-11-14 23:38:49.921875, 2010-11-21 03:24:09.619326
vdsdyn.dll,      585728, 582656, 2009-07-14 01:41:56.136000,     2009-07-13 23:36:43.742266,      2014
-11-14 23:38:49.937500, 2009-07-13 23:36:43.742266
WARNING:INDXParse:Null block encountered at offset 585728.
WARNING:INDXParse:Null block encountered at offset 589824.
WARNING:INDXParse:Null block encountered at offset 593920.
```

FIGURE 8.38.

Partial results from running INDXParse against the \Windows\System32 $I30 file from a Windows 7 subject.

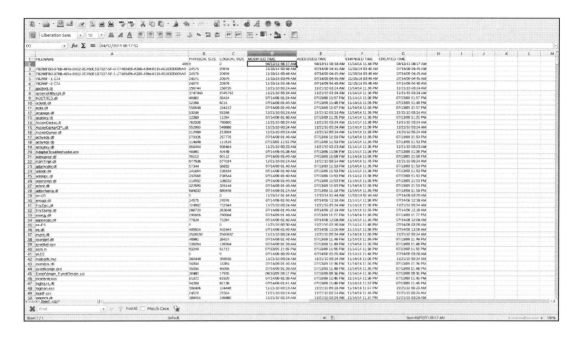

FIGURE 8.39.

Examining the CSV file generated by running INDXParse against the \Windows\System32 $I30 file from a Windows 7 subject.

DELETED FILES

Recovering deleted files is much simpler on NTFS filesystems than FAT filesystems. The biggest reason that this is so is the fact that the cluster chain stored in the the deleted file's $80 attribute is unchanged. There is no guessing required to rebuild the cluster chain. If the clusters have not been reallocated, the file should be recoverable, period.

Recall that when a file or directory is deleted from an NTFS filesystem the in-use flag in the MFT entry is unset and the appropriate bits in the filesystem $BITMAP are changed to indicate the clusters are available. The MFT entry flags are stored at offset 0x16 (22) in the MFT entry as shown in Figure 8.40. A deleted file should have the value of zero in this byte and a deleted directory results in this byte being equal to two.

Identifying potential deleted files is as simple as searching through the filesystem cluster by cluster checking for the "FILE" signature and the value 0x00 (0x02 for directories) at offset 0x16. The MFT entry number is also found in the MFT entry header at position 0x2C (44). This allows potential deleted entries to be identified even if the MFT is fragmented.

The header and $10 attribute must be at the beginning of an entry and are a fixed size. This allows a filename to be located in all but one case. The one exception is a file that has become fragmented to the point of requiring an $ATTRIBUTE_LIST ($20). Recall that attributes are sorted by type code. Other than this one edge case, a filename (which is not necessarily the only filename) should be found at offset 0xF0 (240) as seen in Figure 8.40.

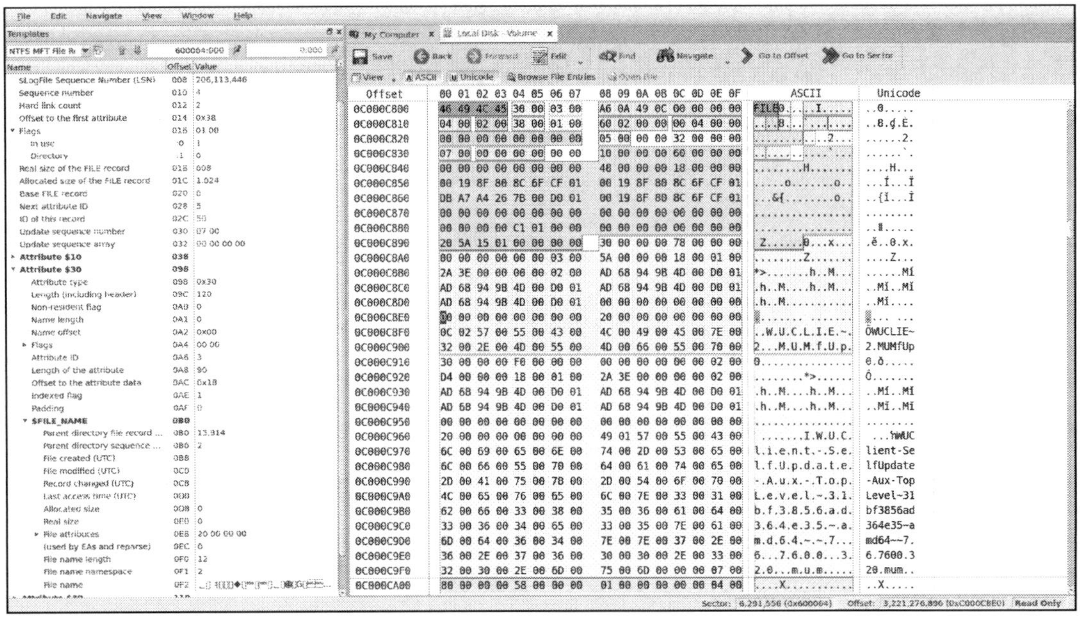

CHAPTER 8 NTFS Filesystems

FIGURE 8.40.

The first sector in an MFT entry for a file.

These facts can be combined to write a very simple script that locates potential deleted files and directories. Later we will discuss a better script that handles the edge case as well. The beauty of this little script is that only a few bytes must be interpreted. A full decoding of each MFT entry is not required. There may be a few false positives and the filenames for the edge case might be nonsensical, but the script is fast and the MFT entry number printed should be correct. The script follows.

```
#!/usr/bin/python2

"""
Simple script to parse a raw image
file or a file containining the MFT
and print out MFT entries that
might have deleted files in them.
by Dr. Phil Polstra (@ppolstra)
"""

import sys, os.path, struct

def getU32(data, offset=0):
    return struct.unpack('<L', data[offset:offset+4])[0]
```

```python
def getU16(data, offset=0):
  return struct.unpack('<H', data[offset:offset+2])[0]

def getU8(data, offset=0):
  return struct.unpack('B', data[offset:offset+1])[0]

def getU64(data, offset=0):
  return struct.unpack('<Q', data[offset:offset+8])[0]

def getU48(data, offset=0):
  return struct.unpack('<Q', data[offset:offset+6]+"\x00\x00")[0]

def usage():
  print("usage " + sys.argv[0] + "<image file> [offset in sectors]")
  exit(1)

def checkForDeleted(buff):
  if buff[0:4] == 'FILE':
    for i in range (0, 4):
      offset = i * 1024
      if buff[offset:offset+4] == 'FILE':
        # are the flags zero or two
        try:
          flags = getU16(buff, offset+22)
        except:
          pass
        if flags == 0 or flags == 2:
          mft = getU32(buff, offset+44)
          if mft != 0:
            # is it totally blank?
            if getU32(buff, offset+152) == 48:
              nameLen = getU8(buff, offset+240)
              if nameLen > 0:
                filename = buff[offset+242: offset+242 + nameLen * 2]
                if flags == 0:
                  print("Found potential deleted file %s at MFT %s" %
                        (filename, mft))
                else:
                  print("Found potential deleted directory %s at MFT %s" %
                    (filename, mft))

def main():
  if len(sys.argv) < 2:
    usage()
```

```
# read file
if not os.path.isfile(sys.argv[1]):
  print("File " + sys.argv[1] + " connot be openned for reading")
  exit(1)

if len(sys.argv) > 2:
  offset = int(sys.argv[2]) * 512 # offset was given
else:
  offset = 0
# read 512 byte chunks till MFT entry is found
# then read 4096 byte chunks = 4 MFT entries at a time
foundMFT = False
with open(str(sys.argv[1]), 'rb') as f:
  f.seek(offset)
  while not foundMFT:
    buff = str(f.read(512))
    if buff[0:4] == 'FILE':
      foundMFT = True
      break
    offset+=512
# now that we are properly aligned get a cluster at a time
# if searching through a raw image we may encounter MFT
# fragments before the start of the MFT
with open(str(sys.argv[1]), 'rb') as f:
  f.seek(offset)
  while buff:
    buff = str(f.read(4096))
    if buff[0:4] == 'FILE':
      checkForDeleted(buff)
    offset += 4096

if __name__ == '__main__':
  main()
```

The first thing to notice about this script is that it is a Python 2 script. This was done to simplify the handling of the Unicode filenames. Our old friend struct.unpack is used extensively to interpret fields in the MFT entry. The script imports sys, os.path, and struct for retrieving command line arguments, checking for the existence of the image file, and performing conversions, respectively.

The main part of the script is in the checkForDeleted function. This function expects a whole cluster (4 MFT entries). It will check for the "FILE" string in the header, check for a zero or two at offset 22 (MFT entry flags), check that the MFT entry number at offset 44 is not zero (which would indicate a yet to be used entry), verify that the value at offset 152 (0x98) is 48 (0x30) indicating that a filename entry can be found at offset 240, retrieve the file name length at offset 240, and if the length is non-zero, retrieve the filename string offset 242 and print a message.

```
Found potential deleted file AME542~1.MAN at MFT 70066
Found potential deleted file AM8AF5~1.MAN at MFT 70067
Found potential deleted file AM94B8~1.MAN at MFT 70068
Found potential deleted file AM347C~1.MAN at MFT 70069
Found potential deleted file AM4664~1.MAN at MFT 70070
Found potential deleted file AMA358~1.MAN at MFT 70071
Found potential deleted file AM9840~1.MAN at MFT 70072
Found potential deleted file AMCF32~1.MAN at MFT 70073
Found potential deleted file AMA4B5~1.MAN at MFT 70074
Found potential deleted file AM876F~1.MAN at MFT 70075
Found potential deleted file AM7EE0~1.MAN at MFT 70076
Found potential deleted file AM586A~1.MAN at MFT 70077
Found potential deleted file AM3BEB~1.MAN at MFT 70078
Found potential deleted file AM62A5~1.MAN at MFT 70079
Found potential deleted file AM7C1F~1.MAN at MFT 70080
Found potential deleted file AMA4B8~1.MAN at MFT 70081
Found potential deleted directory CBSHAN~1 at MFT 70082
Found potential deleted file PACKAG~1.CAT at MFT 70084
Found potential deleted file PACKAG~1.MUM at MFT 70085
Found potential deleted file PACKAG~2.CAT at MFT 70086
Found potential deleted file PACKAG~2.MUM at MFT 70087
Found potential deleted file PACKAG~3.CAT at MFT 70088
Found potential deleted file PACKAG~3.MUM at MFT 70089
Found potential deleted file PACKAG~4.CAT at MFT 70090
Found potential deleted file PACKAG~4.MUM at MFT 70091
Found potential deleted file PA6391~1.CAT at MFT 70092
Found potential deleted file PA329F~1.MUM at MFT 70093
```

FIGURE 8.41.

Partial output from running del-ntfs.py against a Windows 7 subject filesystem image.

The first part of the main method will read the filesystem one sector at a time until something that looks like an MFT (probably the MFT mirror unless the offset to the start of the MFT is passed) is found. This is done to make sure we are aligned on cluster boundaries as the script reads whole clusters at a time in order to enhance performance. Once things are aligned, a simple while loop is used to read the filesystem one cluster at a time. Because the entire filesystem is scanned, deleted files should be discovered even if the MFT is fragmented. Partial output from running this script against a Windows 7 subject is shown in Figure 8.41.

Recall that the MFT itself is stored in the $MFT metadata file. This MFT can be extracted using a tool such as FTK Imager. The simple script could then be run against the MFT file itself instead of the entire filesystem. This has two advantages. First, it should eliminate false positives from clusters that look like MFT entries but are not. Second, this will greatly speed up the scan by only looking through the pertinent clusters. Extracting the MFT is shown in Figure 8.42. Partial results of running the script against the MFT are displayed in Figure 8.43. The script execution time dropped from over a minute to under one second by operating on the MFT file directly.

PYTHON AND NTFS

You can do a lot of forensics by mounting a filesystem image on your Linux forensic workstation. You can also accomplish quite a bit with the tools described thus far in this book.

310 CHAPTER 8 NTFS Filesystems

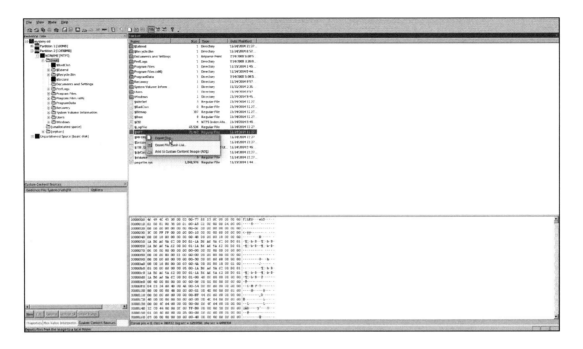

FIGURE 8.42.

Extracting the $MFT file with FTK Imager.

```
phil@i7laptop:~/book-windows/08-NTFS Filesystems$ ./del-ntfs.py /tmp/\$MFT
Found potential deleted file ETWRTE~3.ETL at MFT 45
Found potential deleted file ETWRTU~1.ETL at MFT 46
Found potential deleted file COMPON~3.REG at MFT 22361
Found potential deleted file COMPON~4.REG at MFT 22395
Found potential deleted file COOEF0~1.REG at MFT 22490
Found potential deleted file TMP000~1 at MFT 58855
Found potential deleted file 000000000000019C at MFT 69761
Found potential deleted file 000000000000019D at MFT 69762
Found potential deleted file 000000000000019E at MFT 69763
Found potential deleted file 00000000000001A0 at MFT 69765
Found potential deleted file IMPSER~1.LOC at MFT 69771
Found potential deleted file TMP509B.tmp at MFT 69863
Found potential deleted file TMP9CF9.tmp at MFT 69886
Found potential deleted file tmp.edb at MFT 69958
Found potential deleted file PADA67~1.CAT at MFT 69959
Found potential deleted file PA9E27~1.MUM at MFT 69960
Found potential deleted file AM7C1F~1.MAN at MFT 69961
Found potential deleted file AM8331~1.MAN at MFT 69962
Found potential deleted file PA43D0~1.MUM at MFT 69963
Found potential deleted file PA6D25~1.CAT at MFT 69964
Found potential deleted file AM62A5~1.MAN at MFT 69965
Found potential deleted file AM849D~1.MAN at MFT 69966
Found potential deleted file PA827B~1.CAT at MFT 69967
Found potential deleted file PA0EAA~1.MUM at MFT 69968
Found potential deleted file AM0A05~1.MAN at MFT 69970
Found potential deleted file PA329F~1.MUM at MFT 69971
```

FIGURE 8.43.

Partial results from running del-ntfs.py against the $MFT file. The script ran in under a second.

Any deep analysis of an NTFS filesystem can be sped up considerably using scripting. In this section we will develop a rich set of Python scripts for interpreting various NTFS components found in filesystem images. As we shall see, there are many practical uses for these scripts.

The VBR

As we did with FAT, we will begin by writing code to interpret the NTFS Volume Boot Record (VBR). The Vbr class in the following script is similar to the one we developed for FAT filesystems. I have chosen to implement this as a new class. I could have incorporated this in the existing Vbr class for FAT, but chose not to do so as the filesystem type should be known before any attempts are being made to interpret an image. The code for the new Vbr class follows.

```
#!/usr/bin/python3
'''
NTFS Volume Boot Record Parser
Created by Dr. Phil Polstra
for PentesterAcademy.com
'''

__all__=['Vbr']

import struct    # for interpreting the VBR
import optparse  # for command line options

class Vbr:
    def __init__(self, buffer):
        '''Create a Vbr object from a buffer that is at least
        512 bytes (1 sector) long.'''
        formatStr=('<3s' +  # jump instruction 0
            '8s' +          # OEM name (NTFS) 1
            'H' +           # bytes/sector (512) 2
            'B' +           # sectors/cluster (8) 3
            '7s' +          # padding (all zeroes) 4
            'B' +           # media descriptor (F8) 5
            'H' +           # should be 0 6
            'H' +           # sectors/track 7
            'H' +           # number of heads 8
            'L' +           # hidden sectors (before partition) 9
            'L' +           # padding 10
            'L' +           # signature (0x80 0x00 0x80 0x00) 11
            'Q' +           # total sectors 12
            'Q' +           # LCN for $MFT 13
            'Q' +           # LCN for $MFTMirr (2) 14
```

312 CHAPTER 8 NTFS Filesystems

```python
                 'L'    +    # clusters/file record segment 15
                 'B'    +    # clusters/index buffer (1) 16
                 '3s'   +    # padding 17
                 '8s'   +    # volume serial number 18
                 'L'    +    # checksum (unused) 19
                 '426s' +    # boot code 20
                 '2s'   )    # signature
        self._vbrTuple=struct.unpack(formatStr, buffer[:512])

    def jumpInstruction(self):
        return self._vbrTuple[0]

    def oemName(self):
        return self._vbrTuple[1]

    def bytesPerSector(self):
        return self._vbrTuple[2]

    def sectorsPerCluster(self):
        return self._vbrTuple[3]

    def bytesPerCluster(self):
        return self.bytesPerSector() * self.sectorsPerCluster()

    def clusterOffset(self, cluster=0):
        return (self.hiddenSectors() * self.bytesPerSector() +
            self.bytesPerCluster() * cluster )

    def mediaDescriptor(self):
        return self._vbrTuple[5]

    def isFloppy(self):
        return self._vbrTuple[5]==0xF0

    def isHardDisk(self):
        return self._vbrTuple[5]==0xF8

    def sectorsPerTrack(self):
        return self._vbrTuple[7]

    def heads(self):
        return self._vbrTuple[8]

    def hiddenSectors(self):
        return self._vbrTuple[9]
```

```python
    def totalSectors(self):
        return self._vbrTuple[12]

    def mftLcn(self):
        return self._vbrTuple[13]

    def mftMirrLcn(self):
        return self._vbrTuple[14]

    def clustersPerRecordSegment(self):
        return self._vbrTuple[15]

    def clustersPerIndexBuffer(self):
        return self._vbrTuple[16]

    def volumeSerialNumber(self):
        return self._vbrTuple[18]

    def checksum(self):
        return self._vbrTuple[19]

    def bootCode(self):
        return self._vbrTuple[20]

    def signature(self):
        return self._vbrTuple[21]

    def isSignatureValid(self):
        return self._vbrTuple[21]=='\x55\xaa'

    def getCluster(self, cluster, imageFilename):
        '''Opens an image file and retrieves data stored in
        a single cluster.'''
        with open(imageFilename, 'rb') as f:
            f.seek(self.clusterOffset(cluster))
            data=f.read(self.bytesPerCluster())
        return data

    def __str__(self):
        retStr=('OEM Name: ' + str(self.oemName()) +
            '\nBytes/sector: ' + str(self.bytesPerSector()) +
            '\nSectors/cluster: ' + str(self.sectorsPerCluster()) +
            '\nMedia descriptor: ' +
            str('%X' % self.mediaDescriptor()) +
            '\nSectors/track: ' + str(self.sectorsPerTrack()) +
```

```python
                    '\nHeads: ' + str(self.heads()) +
                    '\nHidden sectors: ' + str(self.hiddenSectors()) +
                    '\nTotal sectors: ' + str(self.totalSectors()) +
                    '\nMFT LCN: ' + str(self.mftLcn()) +
                    '\nMFT Mirror: ' + str(self.mftMirrLcn()) +
                    '\nClusters/Rec Seg: ' +
                    str(self.clustersPerRecordSegment()) +
                    '\nClusters/INDX: ' + str(self.clustersPerIndexBuffer()) +
                    '\nSerial Number: '+ str(self.volumeSerialNumber()) +
                    '\nChecksum: ' + str(self.checksum()) )
        return retStr

def main():
    parser=optparse.OptionParser()
    parser.add_option("-f", "--file", dest="filename",
                help="image filename")
    parser.add_option("-o", "--offset", dest='offset',
                help='offset in sectors to start of volume')

    (options, args)=parser.parse_args()
    filename=options.filename
    if options.offset:
        offset=512 * int(options.offset)
    else:
        offset=0

    with open(filename, 'rb') as f:
        f.seek(offset)
        buffer=f.read(512)

    vbr=Vbr(buffer)
    print(vbr)


if __name__=='__main__':
    main()
```

The script begins with the usual she-bang line, then it defines items to be exported with the __all__ list and imports the struct and optparse modules for interpreting binary values and parsing command line options, respectively. The Vbr constructor is very similar to that for the FAT VBR in that a format string is built and then struct.unpack is used to interpret the VBR and store the fields in a tuple. Note how a slice is used (buffer[:512]) to truncate the passed in buffer in case someone calls the constructor and supplies more than the first sector.

Several accessors are defined. A helper function called getCluster has been created.

```
phil@i7laptop:~/book-windows/08-NTFS Filesystems$ ./vbr-ntfs.py -f /media/phil/TOSHIBA\ EXT/BU/image
s/mystery.dd -o 206848
OEM Name: b'NTFS    '
Bytes/sector: 512
Sectors/cluster: 8
Media descriptor: F8
Sectors/track: 63
Heads: 255
Hidden sectors: 206848
Total sectors: 26005503
MFT LCN: 786432
MFT Mirror: 2
Clusters/Rec Seg: 246
Clusters/INDX: 1
Serial Number: b'\xfc\xb3\x9e\x14\xf8\x9e\x14<'
Checksum: 0
phil@i7laptop:~/book-windows/08-NTFS Filesystems$
```

FIGURE 8.44.

Results from running the VBR processing test script against an NTFS partition from a Windows 7 subject.

This method accepts a cluster number and an image filename and returns a cluster of data. It uses another helper method, clusterOffset, in order to calculate the position of a cluster in the filesystem image. The Vbr class also defines a __str__ method which is used to convert an object of this type to a string. This method is called (among other reasons) if the object is printed.

The main function uses the optparse module to define two command line parameters. The first parameter "-f" or "--file" is use to specify the filesystem image. The second optional parameter "-o" or "--offset" is used to specify the starting location of a filesystem in sectors. This option should be used whenever a full disk image is provided. The main method simply reads a VBR, creates a Vbr object, and then prints out the VBR information using print (which implicitly calls __str__). Results from running this script against the main partition (C: drive) of a Windows 7 subject are shown in Figure 8.44.

MFT headers

Recall that every MFT entry begins with a standard 54-byte header as described earlier in this chapter. A simple script containing an MFT header class and an example main method follows. No new techniques are used in this script. The main function builds on that of the previous section by adding an option to specify an MFT entry and printing out the header information. Running this script against the Windows 7 subject is shown in Figure 8.45. Note that the main

```
phil@i7laptop:~/book-windows/08-NTFS Filesystems$ ./mft1.py -f /media/phil/TOSHIBA\ EXT/BU/images/my
stery.dd -o 206848 -e 460
OEM Name: b'NTFS    '
Bytes/sector: 512
Sectors/cluster: 8
Media descriptor: F8
Sectors/track: 63
Heads: 255
Hidden sectors: 206848
Total sectors: 26005503
MFT LCN: 786432
MFT Mirror: 2
Clusters/Rec Seg: 246
Clusters/INDX: 1
Serial Number: b'\xfc\xb3\x9e\x14\xf8\x9e\x14<'
Checksum: 0
MFT entry: 460/1
        Size: 472/1024
        Base Record: 0/0
phil@i7laptop:~/book-windows/08-NTFS Filesystems$
```

FIGURE 8.45.

Testing the new MFT header interpretation code.

method will not work correctly with fragmented MFTs. We will see how to handle this situation in future scripts.

```
#!/usr/bin/python3
'''Set of classes to read and interpret
MFT entries.  Each MFT entry is created
by passing in a 1024 byte binary string.
Created by Dr. Phil Polstra
for PentesterAcademy.com'''

import struct    # for interpreting entries
import optparse # command line options
from vbr import Vbr

class MftHeader:
    def __init__(self, buffer):
        '''Expects a 1024-byte buffer
        containing a MFT record.'''
        formatStr=( '<4s' +     # FILE id 0
                    'H' +       # update seq offset (0x30) 1
                    'H' +       # size of update seq (3) 2
                    'Q' +       # log file seq number 3
```

```
                    'H'   +      # sequence number 4
                    'H'   +      # hard link count 5
                    'H'   +      # start of attributes 6
                    'H'   +      # flags b0=used b1=directory 7
                    'L'   +      # logical MFT record size 8
                    'L'   +      # physics MFT rec size (1024) 9
                    'Q'   +      # MFT base file reference 10
                    'H'   +      # next attribute ID 11
                    '2s'  +      # padding 12
                    'L'   +      # MFT Record number 13
                    '6s'  )      # update seq array 14
        self._headerTuple=struct.unpack(formatStr, buffer[:54])

def updateSequenceOffset(self):
    return self._headerTuple[1]

def updateSequenceSize(self):
    return self._headerTuple[2]

def updateSequenceArray(self):
    return self._headerTuple[14]

def logFileSequenceNumber(self):
    return self._headerTuple[3]

def sequenceNumber(self):
    return self._headerTuple[4]

def hardLinkCount(self):
    return self._headerTuple[5]

def attributeStart(self):
    return self._headerTuple[6]

def flags(self):
    return self._headerTuple[7]

def inUse(self):
    return (self._headerTuple[7] & 0x01) != 0

def isDirectory(self):
    return (self._headerTuple[7] & 0x02) != 0

def logicalRecordSize(self):
    return self._headerTuple[8]
```

CHAPTER 8 NTFS Filesystems

```python
        def physicalRecordSize(self):
            return self._headerTuple[9]

        def baseFileReference(self):
            return self._headerTuple[10]

        def baseFileMft(self):
            return self._headerTuple[10] & 0x0000FFFFFFFFFFFF

        def baseFileSequenceNumber(self):
            return self._headerTuple[10] >> 48

        def nextAttributeId(self):
            return self._headerTuple[11]

        def recordNumber(self):
            return self._headerTuple[13]

        def __str__(self):
            retStr=('MFT entry: ' + str(self.recordNumber()) +
                '/' + str(self.sequenceNumber()) +
                '\n\tSize: ' + str(self.logicalRecordSize()) +
                '/' + str(self.physicalRecordSize()) +
                '\n\tBase Record: ' + str(self.baseFileMft()) +
                '/' + str(self.baseFileSequenceNumber()) )
            return retStr

def main():
    parser=optparse.OptionParser()
    parser.add_option("-f", "--file", dest="filename",
                  help="image filename")
    parser.add_option("-o", "--offset", dest='offset',
                  help='offset in sectors to start of volume')

    parser.add_option("-e", "--entry", dest='entry',
                  help='MFT entry number')

    (options, args)=parser.parse_args()
    filename=options.filename
    if options.offset:
        offset=512 * int(options.offset)
    else:
        offset=0
    if options.entry:
        entry=int(options.entry)
```

```
        else:
                entry=0

        with open(filename, 'rb') as f:
                f.seek(offset)
                buffer=f.read(512)

        vbr=Vbr(buffer)
        print(vbr)

        # calculate the offset to the MFT entry
        mftOffset = (offset + # offset to start of partition
                     vbr.mftLcn() * # logical cluster number
                     vbr.bytesPerSector() * # sector size
                     vbr.sectorsPerCluster() + # sectors/cluster
                     1024 * entry ) #
        with open(filename, 'rb') as f:
                f.seek(mftOffset)
                buffer=f.read(1024)
        mftHeader=MftHeader(buffer)
        print(mftHeader)

if __name__=='__main__':
        main()
```

MFT attribute headers

Recall that every file attribute begins with a standard header. This header differs depending on whether the attribute is resident or non-resident. Non-resident attributes utilize data runs, so code for interpreting data runs is required in order to interpret the attribute header. We will use good object-oriented design and develop an Attribute base class that contains the code required to interpret the attribute header.

Because it makes sense to have all of the MFT processing code in one module, we will add to the script from the previous section. We start by creating a DataRun class. This class is little more than a wrapper around the built-in range class. It will be used to create a clusterList for non-resident attributes. The start of the new file follows.

```
#!/usr/bin/python3

'''Set of classes to read and interpret
MFT entries.  Each MFT entry is created
by passing in a 1024 byte binary string.
Created by Dr. Phil Polstra
for PentesterAcademy.com'''
```

```python
import struct      # for interpreting entries
import optparse    # command line options
import time        # time conversion functions
from vbr import Vbr

class MftHeader:
    def __init__(self, buffer):
        '''Expects a 1024-byte buffer
           containing a MFT record.'''
        formatStr=( '<4s' +     # FILE id 0
                    'H' +       # update seq offset (0x30) 1
                    'H' +       # size of update seq (3) 2
                    'Q' +       # log file seq number 3
                    'H' +       # sequence number 4
                    'H' +       # hard link count 5
                    'H' +       # start of attributes 6
                    'H' +       # flags b0=used b1=directory 7
                    'L' +       # logical MFT record size 8
                    'L' +       # physics MFT rec size (1024) 9
                    'Q' +       # MFT base file reference 10
                    'H' +       # next attribute ID 11
                    '2s' +      # padding 12
                    'L' +       # MFT Record number 13
                    '6s' )      # update seq array 14
        self._headerTuple=struct.unpack(formatStr, buffer[:54])

    def updateSequenceOffset(self):
        return self._headerTuple[1]

    def updateSequenceSize(self):
        return self._headerTuple[2]

    def updateSequenceArray(self):
        return self._headerTuple[14]

    def logFileSequenceNumber(self):
        return self._headerTuple[3]

    def sequenceNumber(self):
        return self._headerTuple[4]

    def hardLinkCount(self):
        return self._headerTuple[5]

    def attributeStart(self):
        return self._headerTuple[6]
```

```python
    def flags(self):
        return self._headerTuple[7]

    def inUse(self):
        return (self._headerTuple[7] & 0x01) != 0

    def isDirectory(self):
        return (self._headerTuple[7] & 0x02) != 0

    def logicalRecordSize(self):
        return self._headerTuple[8]

    def physicalRecordSize(self):
        return self._headerTuple[9]

    def baseFileReference(self):
        return self._headerTuple[10]

    def baseFileMft(self):
        return self._headerTuple[10] & 0x0000FFFFFFFFFFFF

    def baseFileSequenceNumber(self):
        return self._headerTuple[10] >> 48

    def nextAttributeId(self):
        return self._headerTuple[11]

    def recordNumber(self):
        return self._headerTuple[13]

    def __str__(self):
        retStr=('MFT entry: ' + str(self.recordNumber()) + '/' +
                    str(self.sequenceNumber()) +
                '\n\tSize: ' + str(self.logicalRecordSize()) + '/' +
                str(self.physicalRecordSize()) +
                '\n\tBase Record: ' + str(self.baseFileMft()) + '/' +
                str(self.baseFileSequenceNumber()) )
        return retStr

class DataRun:
    '''This class represents a single data run.
    it is little more than a wrapper around
    the range object.'''
    def __init__(self, start, count):
        self._range=range(start, count+1)
```

```python
def numberOfClusters(self):
    return len(self._range)

def startingCluster(self):
    return self._range[0]

def clusterList(self):
    retList=[]
    for i in self._range:
        retList.append(i)
    return retList
```

We then create a couple of helper functions that can interpret arbitrarily sized unsigned and signed integers. These are required because the size of cluster counts and offsets in data runs vary. The unsigned conversion is simple. The value is padded with an appropriate number of leading zero bytes in order to get an 8-byte unsigned integer which is converted to a Python value using struct.unpack. The signed conversion is slightly more complicated. The sign of the value must be determined, and if it is positive or negative, the value is padded to 8 bytes with leading bytes of 0x00 or 0xFF, respectively. The code for these methods follow.

```python
def bytesToUnsigned(buffer, bytes, pos=0):
    '''Take a slice of a binary string and
    converts it to an unsigned integer.'''
    paddedStr=buffer[pos:pos+bytes]
    for x in range(bytes, 8):
        paddedStr+='\x00'
    return struct.unpack('<Q', paddedStr)[0]

def bytesToSigned(buffer, bytes, pos=0):
    '''Take a slice of a binary string and
    converts it to a signed integer.'''
    paddedStr=buffer[pos:pos+bytes]
    # is it negative?
    if ord(buffer[pos+bytes-1]) >= 0x80:
        fillStr='\xff'
    else:
        fillStr='\x00'
    for x in range(bytes, 8):
        paddedStr+=fillStr
    return struct.unpack('<q', paddedStr)[0]
```

A third helper function, dataRuns, which accepts a buffer and optional offset is used to decode a set of data runs and return a list of DataRun objects. The function begins by creating an empty list and setting the startCluster (to be used in calculating cluster numbers from offsets) to zero. The data run(s) are read until the terminating 0x00 size byte or end of the buffer is encountered. The count size is obtained by performing a bitwise AND with the size byte and 0x0F in order to isolate the low nybble. An arithmetic shift right of 4 bits (equivalent to integer division by 2 to the 4th power) is used to isolate the offset size in the high nybble. The conversion helper functions are then used to create DataRun objects and add them to a list that is returned at the end of the function. The function follows.

```
def dataRuns(buffer, offset=0):
    '''This function will decode a binary stream of
    data runs and return a list of data run objects.'''
    pos=offset
    if pos >= len(buffer):
        return
    retList=[]
    startCluster=0
    # loop till size of next run is zero
    while buffer[pos]!='\x00' and pos < len(buffer):
        # get sizes for run
        countSize=ord(buffer[pos]) & 0x0F
        offsetSize=ord(buffer[pos]) >> 4
        pos+=1
        count=bytesToUnsigned(buffer[pos:pos+countSize], countSize)
        pos+=countSize
        startCluster+=bytesToSigned(buffer[pos:pos+offsetSize],
            offsetSize)
        pos+=offsetSize
        retlist.append(DataRun(startCluster, count))
    return retList
```

Armed with these helper functions we are now ready to create the Attribute class. This class is straightforward, and no new techniques are required to build it. The accessors for the Attribute class check whether the attribute is resident when returning certain residency dependent fields. If the item does not apply, the value of None is returned. Note that this is done implicitly as functions that do not explicitly return a value will evaluate to None. The complete script follows. Here we have added a single call to print the attribute header information for the first attribute which is probably $10. Running this new script is shown in Figure 8.46.

```
#!/usr/bin/python3

'''Set of classes to read and interpret
MFT entries.  Each MFT entry is created
by passing in a 1024 byte binary string.
Created by Dr. Phil Polstra
for PentesterAcademy.com'''

import struct      # for interpreting entries
```

324 CHAPTER 8 NTFS Filesystems

```python
import optparse  # command line options
import time      # time conversion functions
from vbr import Vbr

class MftHeader:
    def __init__(self, buffer):
        '''Expects a 1024-byte buffer
        containing a MFT record.'''
        formatStr=( '<4s' +      # FILE id 0
                    'H'  +       # update seq offset (0x30) 1
                    'H'  +       # size of update seq (3) 2
                    'Q'  +       # log file seq number 3
                    'H'  +       # sequence number 4
                    'H'  +       # hard link count 5
                    'H'  +       # start of attributes 6
                    'H'  +       # flags b0=used b1=directory 7
                    'L'  +       # logical MFT record size 8
                    'L'  +       # physics MFT rec size (1024) 9
                    'Q'  +       # MFT base file reference 10
                    'H'  +       # next attribute ID 11
                    '2s' +       # padding 12
                    'L'  +       # MFT Record number 13
                    '6s' )       # update seq array 14
        self._headerTuple=struct.unpack(formatStr, buffer[:54])

    def updateSequenceOffset(self):
        return self._headerTuple[1]

    def updateSequenceSize(self):
        return self._headerTuple[2]

    def updateSequenceArray(self):
        return self._headerTuple[14]

    def logFileSequenceNumber(self):
        return self._headerTuple[3]

    def sequenceNumber(self):
        return self._headerTuple[4]

    def hardLinkCount(self):
        return self._headerTuple[5]

    def attributeStart(self):
        return self._headerTuple[6]
```

```python
    def flags(self):
        return self._headerTuple[7]

    def inUse(self):
        return (self._headerTuple[7] & 0x01) != 0

    def isDirectory(self):
        return (self._headerTuple[7] & 0x02) != 0

    def logicalRecordSize(self):
        return self._headerTuple[8]

    def physicalRecordSize(self):
        return self._headerTuple[9]

    def baseFileReference(self):
        return self._headerTuple[10]

    def baseFileMft(self):
        return self._headerTuple[10] & 0x0000FFFFFFFFFFFF

    def baseFileSequenceNumber(self):
        return self._headerTuple[10] >> 48

    def nextAttributeId(self):
        return self._headerTuple[11]

    def recordNumber(self):
        return self._headerTuple[13]

    def __str__(self):
        retStr=('MFT entry: ' + str(self.recordNumber()) +
                '/' + str(self.sequenceNumber()) +
              '\n\tSize: ' + str(self.logicalRecordSize()) +
                '/' + str(self.physicalRecordSize()) +
              '\n\tBase Record: ' + str(self.baseFileMft()) +
                '/' + str(self.baseFileSequenceNumber()) )
        return retStr

class DataRun:
    '''This class represents a single data run.
    it is little more than a wrapper around
    the range object.'''
    def __init__(self, start, count):
        self._range=range(start, count+1)
```

```python
    def numberOfClusters(self):
        return len(self._range)

    def startingCluster(self):
        return self._range[0]

    def clusterList(self):
        retList=[]
        for i in self._range:
            retList.append(i)
        return retList

def bytesToUnsigned(buffer, bytes, pos=0):
    '''Take a slice of a binary string and
    converts it to an unsigned integer.'''
    paddedStr=buffer[pos:pos+bytes]
    for x in range(bytes, 8):
        paddedStr+='\x00'
    return struct.unpack('<Q', paddedStr)[0]

def bytesToSigned(buffer, bytes, pos=0):
    '''Take a slice of a binary string and
    converts it to a signed integer.'''
    paddedStr=buffer[pos:pos+bytes]
    # is it negative?
    if ord(buffer[pos+bytes-1]) >= 0x80:
        fillStr='\xff'
    else:
        fillStr='\x00'
    for x in range(bytes, 8):
        paddedStr+=fillStr
    return struct.unpack('<q', paddedStr)[0]

def dataRuns(buffer, offset=0):
    '''This function will decode a binary stream of
    data runs and return a list of data run objects.'''
    pos=offset
    if pos >= len(buffer):
        return
    retList=[]
    startCluster=0
    # loop till size of next run is zero
    while buffer[pos]!='\x00' and pos < len(buffer):
        # get sizes for run
        countSize=ord(buffer[pos]) & 0x0F
```

```
            offsetSize=ord(buffer[pos]) >> 4
            pos+=1
            count=bytesToUnsigned(buffer[pos:pos+countSize], countSize)
            pos+=countSize
            startCluster+=bytesToSigned(buffer[pos:pos+offsetSize], offsetSize)
            pos+=offsetSize
            retlist.append(DataRun(startCluster, count))
        return retList

class Attribute:
    def __init__(self, buffer, offset=0):
        '''Accept a buffer and optional offset to
        interpret an attribute header.  This is normally
        called when creating an attribute object, in
        which case the buffer is probably a 1K MFT entry.'''
        # header starts the same for resident/not
        formatStr=('<L' + # Attribute type 0
                    'L' + # total attribute length 1
                    'B' + # flag 00/01 resident/not 2
                    'B' + # name length 3
                    'H' + # offset to name 4
                    'H' + # flags 5
                    'H')  # attribute ID 6
        # if this is resident header continues
        if buffer[offset+8:offset+9]==b'\x00':
            formatStr+=('L' + # length of attribute 7
                        'H' + # offset to start of attribute 8
                        'B' + # indexed? 9
                        'B')  # padding 10
            self._headerTuple=struct.unpack(formatStr,
              buffer[offset:offset+24])
            if self.hasName():
                self._name=buffer[offset+
                  self.nameOffset(): offset+self.nameOffset() +
                  self.nameLength()*2]
            else:
                self._name=None
        else:
            # non-resident attribute
            formatStr+=('Q' +       # first VCN 7
                        'Q' +       # last VCN 8
                        'H' +       # offset to data runs 9
                        'H' +       # compression 2^x 10
                        '4s' +      # padding 11
                        'Q' + # physical size of attribute 12
```

```python
                            'Q' + # logical size of attribute 13
                            'Q')  # initialized size of stream 14
                self._headerTuple=struct.unpack(formatStr,
                    buffer[offset:offset+64])
                if self.hasName():
                    self._name=buffer[offset+
                        self.nameOffset():
                        offset+self.nameOffset() + self.nameLength()*2]
                else:
                    self._name=None
                self._dataRuns=dataRuns(buffer,
                    offset+self._headerTuple[9])

        def dataRuns(self):
            if not self.isResident():
                return self._dataRuns

        def clusterList(self):
            if not self.isResident():
                retList=[]
                for dr in self._dataRuns:
                    retList+=dr.clusterList()
                return retList

        def firstVcn(self):
            if not self.isResident():
                return self._headerTuple[7]

        def lastVcn(self):
            if not self.isResident():
                return self._headerTuple[8]

        def dataRunOffset(self):
            if not self.isResident():
                return self._headerTuple[9]

        def compression(self):
            if not self.isResident():
                return 2**self._headerTuple[10]

        def physicalSize(self):
            if not self.isResident():
                return self._headerTuple[12]

        def logicalSize(self):
            if not self.isResident():
                return self._headerTuple[13]
```

```python
    def initializedSize(self):
        if not self.isResident():
            return self._headerTuple[14]

    def attributeLength(self):
        if self.isResident():
            return self._headerTuple[7]

    def attributeOffset(self):
        if self.isResident():
            return self._headerTuple[8]

    def isIndexed(self):
        if self.isResident():
            return self._headerTuple[9]==0x01
        else:
            return False

    def attributeType(self):
        return self._headerTuple[0]

    def totalLength(self):
        return self._headerTuple[1]

    def isResident(self):
        return self._headerTuple[2]==0

    def nameLength(self):
        return self._headerTuple[3]

    def nameOffset(self):
        return self._headerTuple[4]

    def hasName(self):
        return self._headerTuple[3]!=0

    def name(self):
        self._name

    def flags(self):
        return self._headerTuple[5]

    def isCompressed(self):
        return (self._headerTuple[5] & 0x0001) != 0
```

```python
        def isEncrypted(self):
            return (self._headerTuple[5] & 0x4000) != 0

        def isSparse(self):
            return (self._headerTuple[5] & 0x8000) != 0

        def attributeId(self):
            return self._headerTuple[6]

        def __str__(self):
            retStr=('Attribute Type: ' + '%02X' % self.attributeType() +
                '\nAttribute Length: ' + '%04X' % self.totalLength() +
                '\nResident: ' + str(self.isResident()) +
                '\nName: ' + str(self.name()) +
                '\nAttribute ID: ' + str(self.attributeId()) )
            return retStr

def main():
    parser=optparse.OptionParser()
    parser.add_option("-f", "--file", dest="filename",
                  help="image filename")
    parser.add_option("-o", "--offset", dest='offset',
                  help='offset in sectors to start of volume')

    parser.add_option("-e", "--entry", dest='entry',
                  help='MFT entry number')

    (options, args)=parser.parse_args()
    filename=options.filename
    if options.offset:
        offset=512 * int(options.offset)
    else:
        offset=0
    if options.entry:
        entry=int(options.entry)
    else:
        entry=0

    with open(filename, 'rb') as f:
        f.seek(offset)
        buffer=f.read(512)

    vbr=Vbr(buffer)
    print(vbr)
```

```
        # calculate the offset to the MFT entry
        mftOffset = (offset + # offset to start of partition
                 vbr.mftLcn() * # logical cluster number
                 vbr.bytesPerSector() * # sector size
                 vbr.sectorsPerCluster() + # sectors/cluster
                 1024 * entry ) #
        with open(filename, 'rb') as f:
            f.seek(mftOffset)
            buffer=f.read(1024)
        mftHeader=MftHeader(buffer)
        print(mftHeader)
        stdInfo=Attribute(buffer, mftHeader.attributeStart())
        print(stdInfo)

if __name__=='__main__':
    main()
```

Standard information attribute

We will now create a StandardInfo class that inherits from Attribute to represent $STANDARD_INFORMATION ($10) attributes. Before we can process this attribute we need a way to convert the ridiculous Windows 64-bit timestamps (100's of nanoseconds since January 1, 1601) to something standard libraries can process. The easiest way to do this is to create a helper function, convertFileTime, that will convert this timestamp to seconds since January 1, 1970 (the Unix epoch). After a little reverse engineering and research of leap years and leap seconds, I have determined that there are 11,644,473,600 seconds between these two dates. This can easily be verified with Python using time.gmtime (which is also used in the convertFileTime helper function).

The StandardInfo class is straightforward with only one new technique employed. Because StandardInfo is derived from Attribute it must explicitly call the Attribute constructor from is constructor. The syntax for doing this is super(StandardInfo, self).__init__(buffer, offset). The super function is used to convert the StandardInfo reference self into an Attribute reference that points to the same object (self).

The main method is expanded to read in the first attribute under the assumption that it is a $STANDARD_INFORMATION attribute. The same assumptions concerning a non-fragmented MFT apply. The complete script follows. A test run of this script is shown in Figure 8.47.

```
#!/usr/bin/python3

'''Set of classes to read and interpret
MFT entries.  Each MFT entry is created
by passing in a 1024 byte binary string.
Created by Dr. Phil Polstra
for PentesterAcademy.com'''
```

```python
import struct      # for interpreting entries
import optparse    # command line options
import time        # time conversion functions
from vbr import Vbr

class MftHeader:
    def __init__(self, buffer):
        '''Expects a 1024-byte buffer
        containing a MFT record.'''
        formatStr=( '<4s' +     # FILE id 0
                    'H'   +     # update seq offset (0x30) 1
                    'H'   +     # size of update seq (3) 2
                    'Q'   +     # log file seq number 3
                    'H'   +     # sequence number 4
                    'H'   +     # hard link count 5
                    'H'   +     # start of attributes 6
                    'H'   +     # flags b0=used b1=directory 7
                    'L'   +     # logical MFT record size 8
                    'L'   +     # physics MFT rec size (1024) 9
                    'Q'   +     # MFT base file reference 10
                    'H'   +     # next attribute ID 11
                    '2s'  +     # padding 12
                    'L'   +     # MFT Record number 13
                    '6s' )      # update seq array 14
        self._headerTuple=struct.unpack(formatStr, buffer[:54])

    def updateSequenceOffset(self):
        return self._headerTuple[1]

    def updateSequenceSize(self):
        return self._headerTuple[2]

    def updateSequenceArray(self):
        return self._headerTuple[14]

    def logFileSequenceNumber(self):
        return self._headerTuple[3]

    def sequenceNumber(self):
        return self._headerTuple[4]

    def hardLinkCount(self):
        return self._headerTuple[5]
```

```python
    def attributeStart(self):
        return self._headerTuple[6]

    def flags(self):
        return self._headerTuple[7]

    def inUse(self):
        return (self._headerTuple[7] & 0x01) != 0

    def isDirectory(self):
        return (self._headerTuple[7] & 0x02) != 0

    def logicalRecordSize(self):
        return self._headerTuple[8]

    def physicalRecordSize(self):
        return self._headerTuple[9]

    def baseFileReference(self):
        return self._headerTuple[10]

    def baseFileMft(self):
        return self._headerTuple[10] & 0x0000FFFFFFFFFFFF

    def baseFileSequenceNumber(self):
        return self._headerTuple[10] >> 48

    def nextAttributeId(self):
        return self._headerTuple[11]

    def recordNumber(self):
        return self._headerTuple[13]

    def __str__(self):
        retStr=('MFT entry: ' + str(self.recordNumber()) +
            '/' + str(self.sequenceNumber()) +
            '\n\tSize: ' + str(self.logicalRecordSize()) +
            '/' + str(self.physicalRecordSize()) +
            '\n\tBase Record: ' + str(self.baseFileMft()) +
            '/' + str(self.baseFileSequenceNumber()) )
        return retStr

class DataRun:
    '''This class represents a single data run.
    it is little more than a wrapper around
```

```python
        the range object.'''
        def __init__(self, start, count):
            self._range=range(start, count+1)

        def numberOfClusters(self):
            return len(self._range)

        def startingCluster(self):
            return self._range[0]

        def clusterList(self):
            retList=[]
            for i in self._range:
                retList.append(i)
            return retList

def bytesToUnsigned(buffer, bytes, pos=0):
    '''Take a slice of a binary string and
    converts it to an unsigned integer.'''
    paddedStr=buffer[pos:pos+bytes]
    for x in range(bytes, 8):
        paddedStr+='\x00'
    return struct.unpack('Q', paddedStr)[0]

def bytesToSigned(buffer, bytes, pos=0):
    '''Take a slice of a binary string and
    converts it to a signed integer.'''
    paddedStr=buffer[pos:pos+bytes]
    # is it negative?
    if ord(buffer[pos+bytes-1]) >= 0x80:
        fillStr='\xff'
    else:
        fillStr='\x00'
    for x in range(bytes, 8):
        paddedStr+=fillStr
    return struct.unpack('q', paddedStr)[0]

def dataRuns(buffer, offset=0):
    '''This function will decode a binary stream of
    data runs and return a list of data run objects.'''
    pos=offset
    if pos >= len(buffer):
        return
    retList=[]
    startCluster=0
```

```python
        # loop till size of next run is zero
        while buffer[pos]!='\x00' and pos < len(buffer):
            # get sizes for run
            countSize=ord(buffer[pos]) & 0x0F
            offsetSize=ord(buffer[pos]) >> 4
            pos+=1
            count=bytesToUnsigned(buffer[pos:pos+countSize], countSize)
            pos+=countSize
            startCluster+=bytesToSigned(buffer[pos:pos+offsetSize],
                    offsetSize)
            pos+=offsetSize
            retlist.append(DataRun(startCluster, count))
        return retList

class Attribute:
    def __init__(self, buffer, offset=0):
        '''Accept a buffer and optional offset to
        interpret an attribute header.  This is normally
        called when creating an attribute object, in
        which case the buffer is probably a 1K MFT entry.'''
        # header starts the same for resident/not
        formatStr=('<L' + # Attribute type 0
                    'L' + # total attribute length 1
                    'B' + # flag 00/01 resident/not 2
                    'B' + # name length 3
                    'H' + # offset to name 4
                    'H' + # flags 5
                    'H')  # attribute ID 6
        # if this is resident header continues
        if buffer[offset+8:offset+9]==b'\x00':
            formatStr+=('L' + # length of attribute 7
                        'H' + # offset to start of attribute 8
                        'B' + # indexed? 9
                        'B')  # padding 10
            self._headerTuple=struct.unpack(formatStr,
                    buffer[offset:offset+24])
            if self.hasName():
                self._name=buffer[offset+self.nameOffset():
                    offset+self.nameOffset() + self.nameLength()*2]
            else:
                self._name=None
        else:
            # non-resident attribute
            formatStr+=('Q' +      # first VCN 7
                        'Q' +      # last VCN 8
```

```
                                    'H' +      # offset to data runs 9
                                    'H' + # compression 2^x 10
                                    '4s' +     # padding 11
                                    'Q' + # physical size of attribute 12
                                    'Q'   +    # logical size of attribute 13
                                    'Q') # initialized size of stream 14
                self._headerTuple=struct.unpack(formatStr,
                    buffer[offset:offset+64])
                if self.hasName():
                    self._name=buffer[offset+self.nameOffset():
                        offset+self.nameOffset() + self.nameLength()*2]
                else:
                    self._name=None
                self._dataRuns=dataRuns(buffer,
                    offset+self._headerTuple[9])

    def dataRuns(self):
        if not self.isResident():
            return self._dataRuns

    def clusterList(self):
        if not self.isResident():
            retList=[]
            for dr in self._dataRuns:
                retList+=dr.clusterList()
            return retList

    def firstVcn(self):
        if not self.isResident():
            return self._headerTuple[7]

    def lastVcn(self):
        if not self.isResident():
            return self._headerTuple[8]

    def dataRunOffset(self):
        if not self.isResident():
            return self._headerTuple[9]

    def compression(self):
        if not self.isResident():
            return 2**self._headerTuple[10]

    def physicalSize(self):
        if not self.isResident():
            return self._headerTuple[12]
```

```python
    def logicalSize(self):
        if not self.isResident():
            return self._headerTuple[13]

    def initializedSize(self):
        if not self.isResident():
            return self._headerTuple[14]

    def attributeLength(self):
        if self.isResident():
            return self._headerTuple[7]

    def attributeOffset(self):
        if self.isResident():
            return self._headerTuple[8]

    def isIndexed(self):
        if self.isResident():
            return self._headerTuple[9]==0x01
        else:
            return False

    def attributeType(self):
        return self._headerTuple[0]

    def totalLength(self):
        return self._headerTuple[1]

    def isResident(self):
        return self._headerTuple[2]==0

    def nameLength(self):
        return self._headerTuple[3]

    def nameOffset(self):
        return self._headerTuple[4]

    def hasName(self):
        return self._headerTuple[3]!=0

    def name(self):
        self._name

    def flags(self):
        return self._headerTuple[5]
```

```python
    def isCompressed(self):
        return (self._headerTuple[5] & 0x0001) != 0

    def isEncrypted(self):
        return (self._headerTuple[5] & 0x4000) != 0

    def isSparse(self):
        return (self._headerTuple[5] & 0x8000) != 0

    def attributeId(self):
        return self._headerTuple[6]

    def __str__(self):
        retStr=('Attribute Type: ' + '%02X' % self.attributeType() +
                '\nAttribute Length: ' + '%04X' % self.totalLength() +
                '\nResident: ' + str(self.isResident()) +
                '\nName: ' + str(self.name()) +
                '\nAttribute ID: ' + str(self.attributeId()) )
        return retStr

def convertFileTime(stupid):
    '''Converts idiotic Win32 filetimes to something reasonable.'''
    t = stupid * 100/ 1000000000
    t -= 11644473600 # seconds from 1/1/1601 to 1/1/1970
    if t > 0:
        return time.gmtime(t)
    else:
        return time.gmtime(0)

class StandardInfo(Attribute):
    '''This class is use to represent the $10 Standard Info
    attribute.  It is created from a buffer containing the
    MFT entry (1024 bytes) and an offset to the start of
    the attribute.'''
    def __init__(self, buffer, offset=0):
        super(StandardInfo, self).__init__(buffer, offset)
        # $10 is always resident so header is 24 bytes
        formatStr=('<Q' + # creation 0
                    'Q' + # modification 1
                    'Q' + # record change 2
                    'Q' + # access      3
                    'L' + # flags 4
                    'L' + # highest version 5
                    'L' + # version number 6
                    'L' + # class ID (XP) 7
```

```
                        'L' +       # owner ID (xp) 8
                        'L' +       # security ID (xp) 9
                        'Q' +       # quota disk size (xp) 10
                        'Q')        # update sequence (xp) 11
        self._10Tuple=struct.unpack(formatStr,
            buffer[offset+24:offset+24+72])

    def creationTime(self):
        return convertFileTime(self._10Tuple[0])

    def modificationTime(self):
        return convertFileTime(self._10Tuple[1])

    def recordChangeTime(self):
        return convertFileTime(self._10Tuple[2])

    def accessTime(self):
        return convertFileTime(self._10Tuple[3])

    def flags(self):
        '''Flags are
        0123456789ABCDE-bits
        RHS0DADSTSRCONE
        Oiy0iretmpeofon
         ds0rcvdpapmftc
          nt0thi  raplir'''
        return self._10Tuple[4]

    def isReadOnly(self):
        return (self.flags() & 0x01) !=0

    def isHidden(self):
        return (self.flags() & 0x02) !=0

    def isSystem(self):
        return (self.flags() & 0x04) !=0

    def isDirectory(self):
        return (self.flags() & 0x10) !=0

    def isArchive(self):
        return (self.flags() & 0x20) !=0

    def isStandardFile(self):
        return (self.flags() & 0x80) !=0
```

```python
    def isTemporaryFile(self):
        return (self.flags() & 0x100) !=0

    def isSparseFile(self):
        return (self.flags() & 0x200) !=0

    def isReparsePoint(self):
        return (self.flags() & 0x400) !=0

    def isCompressed(self):
        return (self.flags() & 0x800) !=0

    def isOffline(self):
        return (self.flags() & 0x1000) !=0

    def isNotIndexed(self):
        return (self.flags() & 0x2000) !=0

    def isEncrypted(self):
        return (self.flags() & 0x4000) !=0

    def highestVersion(self):
        return self._10Tuple[5]

    def versionNumber(self):
        return self._10Tuple[6]

    def hasVersioning(self):
        return self._10Tuple[5]!=0

    def classID(self):
        return self._10Tuple[7]

    def ownerID(self):
        return self._10Tuple[8]

    def securityID(self):
        return self._10Tuple[9]

    def quota(self):
        return self._10Tuple[10]

    def updatedSequenceNumber(self):
        return self._10Tuple[11]
```

```python
    def __str__(self):
        retStr=Attribute.__str__(self)
        retStr+=('\nCreated: ' +
            str(time.asctime(self.creationTime())) +
            '\nModified: '     +
            str(time.asctime(self.modificationTime())) +
            '\nRec Changed: ' +
            str(time.asctime(self.recordChangeTime())) +
            '\nAccessed: '    +
            str(time.asctime(self.accessTime())) +
            '\nFlags: ' + str('%04X' % self.flags()) +
            '\nHas Versioning: ' + str(self.hasVersioning()) )
        return retStr

def main():
    parser=optparse.OptionParser()
    parser.add_option("-f", "--file", dest="filename",
                  help="image filename")
    parser.add_option("-o", "--offset", dest='offset',
                  help='offset in sectors to start of volume')

    parser.add_option("-e", "--entry", dest='entry',
                  help='MFT entry number')

    (options, args)=parser.parse_args()
    filename=options.filename
    if options.offset:
        offset=512 * int(options.offset)
    else:
        offset=0
    if options.entry:
        entry=int(options.entry)
    else:
        entry=0

    with open(filename, 'rb') as f:
        f.seek(offset)
        buffer=f.read(512)

    vbr=Vbr(buffer)
    print(vbr)

    # calculate the offset to the MFT entry
    mftOffset = (offset + # offset to start of partition
            vbr.mftLcn() * # logical cluster number
```

```
                              vbr.bytesPerSector() * # sector size
                              vbr.sectorsPerCluster() + # sectors/cluster
                              1024 * entry ) #
        with open(filename, 'rb') as f:
            f.seek(mftOffset)
            buffer=f.read(1024)
        mftHeader=MftHeader(buffer)
        print(mftHeader)
        stdInfo=StandardInfo(buffer, mftHeader.attributeStart())
        print(stdInfo)
if __name__=='__main__':
    main()
```

Filename attribute

The development of the Filename class for handling $FILE_NAME ($30) attributes is straightforward. One new item is the use of str.decode to convert the filename to easily printable text using UTF-16 Unicode encoding in the __str__ method. The new class and updated main function follow. A test run of the new code is shown in Figure 8.48.

```
Sectors/cluster: 8
Media descriptor: F8
Sectors/track: 63
Heads: 255
Hidden sectors: 206848
Total sectors: 26005503
MFT LCN: 786432
MFT Mirror: 2
Clusters/Rec Seg: 246
Clusters/INDX: 1
Serial Number: b'\xfc\xb3\x9e\x14\xf8\x9e\x14<'
Checksum: 0
MFT entry: 460/1
        Size: 472/1024
        Base Record: 0/0
Attribute Type: 10
Attribute Length: 0060
Resident: True
Name: None
Attribute ID: 0
Created: Tue Jul 14 03:20:08 2009
Modified: Fri Nov 14 20:57:35 2014
Rec Changed: Fri Nov 14 20:57:35 2014
Accessed: Fri Nov 14 20:57:35 2014
Flags: 0001
Has Versioning: False
phil@i7laptop:~/book-windows/08-NTFS Filesystems$
```

FIGURE 8.47.

Testing the new StandardInfo class.

```
MFT entry: 460/1
        Size: 472/1024
        Base Record: 0/0
Attribute Type: 10
Attribute Length: 0060
Resident: True
Name: None
Attribute ID: 0
Created: Tue Jul 14 03:20:08 2009
Modified: Fri Nov 14 20:57:35 2014
Rec Changed: Fri Nov 14 20:57:35 2014
Accessed: Fri Nov 14 20:57:35 2014
Flags: 0001
Has Versioning: False
Attribute Type: 30
Attribute Length: 0068
Resident: True
Name: b'U\x00s\x00e\x00r\x00s\x00'
Attribute ID: 2
Filename: Users
Created: Fri Nov 14 23:30:48 2014
Modified: Fri Nov 14 23:30:48 2014
Rec Changed: Fri Nov 14 23:30:48 2014
Accessed: Fri Nov 14 23:30:48 2014
Flags: 10000000
Extended Flags: 0000
phil@i7laptop:~/book-windows/08-NTFS Filesystems$
```

FIGURE 8.48.

Testing the new Filename class.

```
class Filename(Attribute):
    '''This class is used to represent the $30 or Filename
    attribute.  It is created by passing in a MFT entry
    to the class.'''
    def __init__(self, buffer, offset=0):
        super(Filename, self).__init__(buffer, offset)
          # this attribute must be resident
        formatStr=('<L'    +    # MFT entry of parent 0
                   'H'     +    # MFT entry of parent upper 2 bytes 1
                   'H'     +    # Update sequence of parent 2
                   'Q'     +    # Created 3
                   'Q'     +    # Modified 4
                   'Q'     +    # record change 5
                   'Q'     +    # accessed 6
                   'Q'     +    # physical size 7
                   'Q'     +    # logical size 8
                   'L'     +    # flags 9
                   'L'     +    # extended flags 10
                   'B'     +    # filename length 11
                   'B')         # namespace 12
```

```python
        self._30Tuple=struct.unpack(formatStr, \
            buffer[offset+24:offset+24+66])
        self._name=buffer[offset+90:offset+90+self._30Tuple[11]*2]

    def parentMft(self):
        return self._30Tuple[0]

    def parentSequenceNumber(self):
        return self._30Tuple[2]

    def creationTime(self):
        return convertFileTime(self._30Tuple[3])

    def modificationTime(self):
        return convertFileTime(self._30Tuple[4])

    def recordChangeTime(self):
        return convertFileTime(self._30Tuple[5])

    def accessTime(self):
        return convertFileTime(self._30Tuple[6])

    def physicalSize(self):
        return self._30Tuple[7]

    def logicalSize(self):
        return self._30Tuple[8]

    def flags(self):
        return self._30Tuple[9]

    def isReadOnly(self):
        return (self.flags() & 0x01) !=0

    def isHidden(self):
        return (self.flags() & 0x02) !=0

    def isSystem(self):
        return (self.flags() & 0x04) !=0

    def isDirectory(self):
        return (self.flags() & 0x10000000) !=0

    def isIndexView(self):
        return (self.flags() & 0x20000000) !=0
```

```python
    def isArchive(self):
        return (self.flags() & 0x20) !=0
    
    def isStandardFile(self):
        return (self.flags() & 0x80) !=0
    
    def isTemporaryFile(self):
        return (self.flags() & 0x100) !=0
    
    def isSparseFile(self):
        return (self.flags() & 0x200) !=0
    
    def isReparsePoint(self):
        return (self.flags() & 0x400) !=0
    
    def isCompressed(self):
        return (self.flags() & 0x800) !=0
    
    def isOffline(self):
        return (self.flags() & 0x1000) !=0
    
    def isNotIndexed(self):
        return (self.flags() & 0x2000) !=0
    
    def isEncrypted(self):
        return (self.flags() & 0x4000) !=0
    
    def extendedFlags(self):
        return self._30Tuple[10]
    
    def nameLength(self):
        return self._30Tuple[11]
    
    def namespace(self):
        return self._30Tuple[12]
    
    def name(self):
        return self._name
    
    def __str__(self):
        retStr=Attribute.__str__(self)
        retStr+=('\nFilename: ' +    str(self.name().decode('utf-16')) +
                '\nCreated: ' +
                 str(time.asctime(self.creationTime())) +
                '\nModified: ' +
```

```python
                    str(time.asctime(self.modificationTime())) +
                    '\nRec Changed: ' +
                    str(time.asctime(self.recordChangeTime())) +
                    '\nAccessed: ' +
                    str(time.asctime(self.accessTime())) +
                    '\nFlags: ' + str('%04X' % self.flags()) +
                    '\nExtended Flags: ' +
                    str('%04X' % self.extendedFlags()) )
        return retStr


def main():
    parser=optparse.OptionParser()
    parser.add_option("-f", "--file", dest="filename",
                      help="image filename")
    parser.add_option("-o", "--offset", dest='offset',
                      help='offset in sectors to start of volume')

    parser.add_option("-e", "--entry", dest='entry',
                      help='MFT entry number')

    (options, args)=parser.parse_args()
    filename=options.filename
    if options.offset:
        offset=512 * int(options.offset)
    else:
        offset=0
    if options.entry:
        entry=int(options.entry)
    else:
        entry=0

    with open(filename, 'rb') as f:
        f.seek(offset)
        buffer=f.read(512)

    vbr=Vbr(buffer)
    print(vbr)

    # calculate the offset to the MFT entry
    mftOffset = (offset +   # offset to start of partition
                 vbr.mftLcn() *  # logical cluster number
                 vbr.bytesPerSector() *  # sector size
                 vbr.sectorsPerCluster() +  # sectors/cluster
                 1024 * entry )  #
```

```
        with open(filename, 'rb') as f:
            f.seek(mftOffset)
            buffer=f.read(1024)
        mftHeader=MftHeader(buffer)
        print(mftHeader)
        stdInfo=StandardInfo(buffer, mftHeader.attributeStart())
        print(stdInfo)
        filename=Filename(buffer, mftHeader.attributeStart() +
                        stdInfo.totalLength())
        print(filename)

if __name__=='__main__':
    main()
```

Data attribute

If a file is small, the $DATA attribute can be resident. Otherwise, it is stored in data clusters described by data runs. The functionality for handling data runs is already built into the Attribute class. I have added a _data element to the Data class that is only populated if the file is resident. This new (short) class follows.

```
class Data(Attribute):
    '''This class represents the data attribute.'''
    def __init__(self, buffer, offset=0):
        super(Data, self).__init__(buffer, offset)
        # is it resident
        if self.isResident():
            self._data=buffer[offset+self.attributeOffset():
             offset+self.attributeOffset()+self.attributeLength()]
        else:
            self._data=None

    def data(self):
        '''Return data if resident otherwise None'''
        return self._data

    def __str__(self):
        retStr=Attribute.__str__(self)
        if self.isResident():
            retStr+='\nData bytes: ' + str(len(self._data))
        else:
            retStr+='\nData runs: ' + str(len(self._dataRuns))
            retStr+='\nData clusters: ' + str(self.clusterList())
        return retStr
```

```
Rec Changed: Fri Nov 14 20:57:31 2014
Accessed: Fri Nov 14 20:57:31 2014
Flags: 0020
Extended Flags: 0000
Data run start/count: 37081/210
Attribute Type: 80
Attribute Length: 0048
Resident: False
Name: None
Attribute ID: 4
Data runs: 1
Data clusters: [37081, 37082, 37083, 37084, 37085, 37086, 37087, 37088, 37089, 37090, 37091, 37092,
37093, 37094, 37095, 37096, 37097, 37098, 37099, 37100, 37101, 37102, 37103, 37104, 37105, 37106, 37
107, 37108, 37109, 37110, 37111, 37112, 37113, 37114, 37115, 37116, 37117, 37118, 37119, 37120, 3712
1, 37122, 37123, 37124, 37125, 37126, 37127, 37128, 37129, 37130, 37131, 37132, 37133, 37134, 37135,
 37136, 37137, 37138, 37139, 37140, 37141, 37142, 37143, 37144, 37145, 37146, 37147, 37148, 37149, 3
7150, 37151, 37152, 37153, 37154, 37155, 37156, 37157, 37158, 37159, 37160, 37161, 37162, 37163, 371
64, 37165, 37166, 37167, 37168, 37169, 37170, 37171, 37172, 37173, 37174, 37175, 37176, 37177, 37178
, 37179, 37180, 37181, 37182, 37183, 37184, 37185, 37186, 37187, 37188, 37189, 37190, 37191, 37192,
37193, 37194, 37195, 37196, 37197, 37198, 37199, 37200, 37201, 37202, 37203, 37204, 37205, 37206, 37
207, 37208, 37209, 37210, 37211, 37212, 37213, 37214, 37215, 37216, 37217, 37218, 37219, 37220, 3722
1, 37222, 37223, 37224, 37225, 37226, 37227, 37228, 37229, 37230, 37231, 37232, 37233, 37234, 37235,
 37236, 37237, 37238, 37239, 37240, 37241, 37242, 37243, 37244, 37245, 37246, 37247, 37248, 37249, 3
7250, 37251, 37252, 37253, 37254, 37255, 37256, 37257, 37258, 37259, 37260, 37261, 37262, 37263, 372
64, 37265, 37266, 37267, 37268, 37269, 37270, 37271, 37272, 37273, 37274, 37275, 37276, 37277, 37278
, 37279, 37280, 37281, 37282, 37283, 37284, 37285, 37286, 37287, 37288, 37289, 37290]
phil@i7laptop:~/book-windows/08-NTFS Filesystems$
```

FIGURE 8.49.

Testing the new Data class.

Another helper function, getAttribute, has been added. This function accepts a buffer which contains an attribute (possibly the entire MFT entry) and an optional offset. It will first create a generic Attribute object in order to determine its type and then create and return the specific type of attribute object. This function and the updated main follow. Partial output from a test run of this script is shown in Figure 8.49.

```python
def getAttribute(buffer, offset=0):
    '''create a MFT attribute from
    a buffer and offset.  Will create
    a specific type if possible or
    a generic attribute if not.'''
    if buffer[offset:offset+4]==b'\xff\xff\xff\xff':
        return
    attr=Attribute(buffer, offset)
    if attr.attributeType() == 0x10:
        attr=StandardInfo(buffer, offset)
    elif attr.attributeType() == 0x30:
        attr=Filename(buffer, offset)
    elif attr.attributeType() == 0x80:
        attr=Data(buffer, offset)
    return attr
```

```
def main():
    parser=optparse.OptionParser()
    parser.add_option("-f", "--file", dest="filename",
                      help="image filename")
    parser.add_option("-o", "--offset", dest='offset',
                      help='offset in sectors to start of volume')

    parser.add_option("-e", "--entry", dest='entry',
                      help='MFT entry number')

    (options, args)=parser.parse_args()
    filename=options.filename
    if options.offset:
        offset=512 * int(options.offset)
    else:
        offset=0
    if options.entry:
        entry=int(options.entry)
    else:
        entry=0

    with open(filename, 'rb') as f:
        f.seek(offset)
        buffer=f.read(512)

    vbr=Vbr(buffer)
    print(vbr)

    # calculate the offset to the MFT entry
    mftOffset = (offset + # offset to start of partition
                 vbr.mftLcn() * # logical cluster number
                 vbr.bytesPerSector() * # sector size
                 vbr.sectorsPerCluster() + # sectors/cluster
                 1024 * entry ) #
    with open(filename, 'rb') as f:
        f.seek(mftOffset)
        buffer=f.read(1024)
    mftHeader=MftHeader(buffer)
    print(mftHeader)
    pos = mftHeader.attributeStart()
    while pos < mftHeader.logicalRecordSize():
        attr=getAttribute(buffer, pos)
        if not attr:
            break
```

```
            print(attr)
            pos+=attr.totalLength()

if __name__=='__main__':
    main()
```

Index root

We now turn our attention to directories. We begin with an IndexRoot class which represents an $INDEX_ROOT ($90) attribute. Before we can create this class, another class, IndexEntry, is required to represent the index entries possibly stored in this attribute. Recall that an index entry is essentially a 16-byte header followed by a standard $FILE_NAME data stream. If the entry has a subnode (as indicated by the index flags) the last 8 bytes contain the VCN for the subnode index buffer. The IndexEntry class follows.

```
class IndexEntry:
    '''Represents an index entry whether
    or not it is resident.'''
    def __init__(self, buffer, offset=0, resident=False):
        formatStr=('<Q'     +      # MFT ref 0
            'H'     +      # total record length 1
            'H'     +      # record length 2
            'B'     +      # index flag 3
            '3s'    +      # padding 4
            'L'     +      # MFT entry of parent 5
            'H'     +      # MFT entry of parent upper 2 bytes 6
            'H'     +      # Update sequence of parent 7
            'Q'     +      # Created 8
            'Q'     +      # Modified 9
            'Q'     +      # record change 10
            'Q'     +      # accessed 11
            'Q'     +      # physical size 12
            'Q'     +      # logical size 13
            'L'     +      # flags 14
            'L'     +      # extended flags 15
            'B'     +      # filename length 16
            'B')           # namespace 17
        self._entryTuple=struct.unpack(formatStr,
            buffer[offset:offset+82])
        self._name=buffer[offset+82:offset+82+self._entryTuple[16]*2]
        if not self.isResident():
            # vcn of subentries in last 8 bytes
            self._vcn=struct.unpack('<Q',
                buffer[offset+self._entryTuple[1]-
                    8:offset+self._entryTuple[1]])
```

```python
            else:
                self._vcn=None
    def __str__(self):
        retStr=('Index Entry:' +
            '\n\tMFT: ' + str(self.mft()) + '/' +
            str(self.sequenceNumber()) +
            '\n\tIs Resident: ' + str(self.isResident()) +
            '\n\tIs Last: ' + str(self.isLast()) +
            '\n\tParent MFT: ' + str(self.parentMft()) + '/' +
            str(self.parentSequenceNumber()) +
            '\n\tFilename: ' + str(self.name().decode('utf-16')) )
        return retStr

    def mft(self):
        return self._entryTuple[0] & 0xffffffffffff

    def sequenceNumber(self):
        return self._entryTuple[0] >> 48

    def totalLength(self):
        return self._entryTuple[1]

    def recordLength(self):
        return self._entryTuple[2]

    def indexFlags(self):
        return self._entryTuple[3]

    def isResident(self):
        return (self.indexFlags() & 0x01) == 0

    def isNonresident(self):
        return (self.indexFlags() & 0x01) != 0

    def isLast(self):
        return (self.indexFlags() & 0x02) != 0

    def parentMft(self):
        return self._entryTuple[5] + ((self._entryTuple[6] & 0xffff) <<32)

    def parentSequenceNumber(self):
        return self._entryTuple[7]

    def creationTime(self):
        return convertFileTime(self._entryTuple[8])
```

```python
        def modificationTime(self):
            return convertFileTime(self._entryTuple[9])

        def recordChangeTime(self):
            return convertFileTime(self._entryTuple[10])

        def accessTime(self):
            return convertFileTime(self._entryTuple[11])

        def physicalSize(self):
            return self._entryTuple[12]

        def logicalSize(self):
            return self._entryTuple[13]

        def flags(self):
            return self._entryTuple[14]

        def isReadOnly(self):
            return (self.flags() & 0x01) !=0

        def isHidden(self):
            return (self.flags() & 0x02) !=0

        def isSystem(self):
            return (self.flags() & 0x04) !=0

        def isDirectory(self):
            return (self.flags() & 0x10000000) !=0

        def isIndexView(self):
            return (self.flags() & 0x20000000) !=0

        def isArchive(self):
            return (self.flags() & 0x20) !=0

        def isStandardFile(self):
            return (self.flags() & 0x80) !=0

        def isTemporaryFile(self):
            return (self.flags() & 0x100) !=0

        def isSparseFile(self):
            return (self.flags() & 0x200) !=0
```

```
        def isReparsePoint(self):
            return (self.flags() & 0x400) !=0

        def isCompressed(self):
            return (self.flags() & 0x800) !=0

        def isOffline(self):
            return (self.flags() & 0x1000) !=0

        def isNotIndexed(self):
            return (self.flags() & 0x2000) !=0

        def isEncrypted(self):
            return (self.flags() & 0x4000) !=0

        def extendedFlags(self):
            return self._entryTuple[15]

        def nameLength(self):
            return self._entryTuple[16]

        def namespace(self):
            return self._entryTuple[17]

        def name(self):
            return self._name

        def childVcn(self):
            return self._vcn
```

With the IndexEntry class in hand, the IndexRoot class is easily written. This class follows, along with the updated getAttribute and main functions. A test run of this new class is shown in Figure 8.50.

```
class IndexRoot(Attribute):
    '''Index root $90 including any entries.'''
    def __init__(self, buffer, offset=0):
        super(IndexRoot, self).__init__(buffer, offset)
        formatStr=('<L'   +    # attribute type 0
                    'L'   +    # collation rule 1
                    'L'   +    # buffer size 2
                    'L'   +    # clusters/indx 3
                    'L'   +    # offset to 1st entry 4
                    'L'   +    # logical size 5
```

```
                              'L' +     # physical size  6
                              'L' )     # 00/01 resident/not  7
        self.__headerTuple=struct.unpack(formatStr, buffer[offset+
            self.attributeOffset():offset+self.attributeOffset()+32])
        pos=offset+self.attributeOffset()+16+self.__headerTuple[4]
        self.__indexEntries=[]
        # we only care about indexed filenames
        if self.__headerTuple[0] !=0x30:
            return
        while pos < offset+self.logicalIndexSize():
            entry=IndexEntry(buffer, pos)
            self.__indexEntries.append(entry)
            pos+=entry.totalLength()
            if entry.isLast():
                break

    def indexedAttributeType(self):
        return self.__headerTuple[0]

    def collationRule(self):
        return self.__headerTuple[1]

    def indexBufferSize(self):
        return self.__headerTuple[2]

    def clustersPerIndexBuffer(self):
        return self.__headerTuple[3]

    def offsetToFirstEntry(self):
        return self.__headerTuple[4]

    def logicalIndexSize(self):
        return self.__headerTuple[5]

    def physicalIndexSize(self):
        return self.__headerTuple[6]

    def isIndexResident(self):
        return self.__headerTuple[7]==0

    def isIndexNonresident(self):
        return self.__headerTuple[7]==1

    def indexEntries(self):
        return self.__indexEntries
```

```python
    def numberOfIndexEntries(self):
        return len(self._indexEntries)

    def __str__(self):
        retStr=Attribute.__str__(self)
        retStr+=('\nIndexed Type: ' +
          str('%0X' % self.indexedAttributeType())      +
              '\nIndex Entries: ' + str(self.numberOfIndexEntries()) )
        for i in range(self.numberOfIndexEntries()):
            retStr+= '\n' + self._indexEntries[i].__str__()
        return retStr
def getAttribute(buffer, offset=0):
    '''create a MFT attribute from
    a buffer and offset.  Will create
    a specific type if possible or
    a generic attribute if not.'''
    if buffer[offset:offset+4]==b'\xff\xff\xff\xff':
        return
    attr=Attribute(buffer, offset)
    if attr.attributeType() == 0x10:
        attr=StandardInfo(buffer, offset)
    elif attr.attributeType() == 0x30:
        attr=Filename(buffer, offset)
    elif attr.attributeType() == 0x80:
        attr=Data(buffer, offset)
    elif attr.attributeType() == 0x90:
        attr=IndexRoot(buffer, offset)
    return attr

def main():
    parser=optparse.OptionParser()
    parser.add_option("-f", "--file", dest="filename",
                    help="image filename")
    parser.add_option("-o", "--offset", dest='offset',
                    help='offset in sectors to start of volume')

    parser.add_option("-e", "--entry", dest='entry',
                    help='MFT entry number')

    (options, args)=parser.parse_args()
    filename=options.filename
    if options.offset:
        offset=512 * int(options.offset)
    else:
        offset=0
```

```
        if options.entry:
              entry=int(options.entry)
        else:
              entry=0

        with open(filename, 'rb') as f:
              f.seek(offset)
              buffer=f.read(512)

        vbr=Vbr(buffer)
        print(vbr)

        # calculate the offset to the MFT entry
        mftOffset = (offset +      # offset to start of partition
                    vbr.mftLcn() *  # logical cluster number
                    vbr.bytesPerSector() *  # sector size
                    vbr.sectorsPerCluster() +  # sectors/cluster
                    1024 * entry ) #
        with open(filename, 'rb') as f:
              f.seek(mftOffset)
              buffer=f.read(1024)
        mftHeader=MftHeader(buffer)
        print(mftHeader)
        pos = mftHeader.attributeStart()
        while pos < mftHeader.logicalRecordSize():
              attr=getAttribute(buffer, pos)
              if not attr:
                    break
              print(attr)
              pos+=attr.totalLength()

if __name__=='__main__':
     main()
```

Index allocations

The data stored in the MFT for an $INDEX_ALLOCATION ($A0) attribute is little more than a list of data runs. All of the real data is found in the index buffers. The IndexAllocation class used to represent a $INDEX_ALLOCATION attribute is created from the 1024-byte MFT entry. Depending on the operation it might be pointless to read, interpret, and store all the index entries (especially for large directories with thousands of entries).

Because the index entries from the index buffers are not stored in the MFT, a mechanism for obtaining this information is required. I have created a method in IndexAllocation called getEntries that accepts a buffer with the contents of a $I30 file. Recall that this file is essentially

```
Has Versioning: False
Attribute Type: 30
Attribute Length: 0070
Resident: True
Name: b'P\x00e\x00r\x00f\x00L\x00o\x00g\x00s\x00'
Attribute ID: 2
Filename: PerfLogs
Created: Fri Nov 14 23:30:48 2014
Modified: Fri Nov 14 23:30:48 2014
Rec Changed: Fri Nov 14 23:30:48 2014
Accessed: Fri Nov 14 23:30:48 2014
Flags: 10000000
Extended Flags: 0000
Attribute Type: 90
Attribute Length: 00B0
Resident: True
Name: None
Attribute ID: 1
Indexed Type: 30
Index Entries: 1
Index Entry:
        MFT: 59/1
        Is Resident: True
        Is Last: False
        Parent MFT: 58/1
        Filename: Admin
phil@i7laptop:~/book-windows/08-NTFS Filesystems$
```

FIGURE 8.50.

Testing the new IndexEntry and IndexRoot classes.

the concatenation of the index buffers. Such a file could be obtained with a tool such as FTK Imager or via some scripts appearing later in this chapter. The method hasEntries is used to determine if the index buffers have been loaded.

A class, IndexBuffer, has been created to represent each index buffer. It stores the header information and also a list of IndexEntry items. This class is used by the IndexAllocation getEntries method to create a master list of index entries that are stored in the IndexAllocation class. This list can be quite large and may not be in the proper sorted order. For our purposes this is not really a concern as the entries are likely to be resorted by one of the timestamps by our scripts or simply stored in a database. The new IndexBuffer and IndexAllocation classes, and updated versions of getAttribute and main follow. A test run of this new code is shown in Figure 8.51.

```
class IndexBuffer:
    '''This class is used to process a
    4096 byte index buffer.'''
    def __init__(self, buffer, offset=0):
        # process the header
        formatStr=('<4s' +      # INDX 0
                    'H' +       # offset to update seq 1
                    'H' +       # update seq size in words 2
                    'Q' +       # log file seq number 3
```

CHAPTER 8 NTFS Filesystems

```
                            'Q' +        # VCN 4
                            'L' +        # offset to entries 5
                            'L' +        # logical size 6
                            'L' +        # physical size 7
                            'L' +        # flags 00/01 leaf/parent 8
                            'H' +        # update seq 9
                            '8H' )       # update seq array 10
        self._headerTuple=struct.unpack(formatStr,
            buffer[offset:offset+58])
        # copy data to new buffer so we can apply fix up codes
        self._data=buffer[offset:]
        for i in range(0, self._headerTuple[2]-1):
            replaceIndex = offset + 512 * i + 510
            self._data = (self._data[0: replaceIndex] +
                        self._data[42+i*2:42+i*2+2] +
                        self._data[replaceIndex + 2: ])
        # now read the entries
        pos=offset+self._headerTuple[5]
        self._entries=[]
        while pos < offset + self._headerTuple[6]+24:
            entry=IndexEntry(data, pos)
            self._entries.append(entry)
            pos+=entry.totalLength()
            if entry.isLast():
                break

    def isValid(self):
        return self._headerTuple[0]=='INDX'

    def updateSequenceOffset(self):
        return self._headerTuple[1]

    def updateSequenceSize(self):
        return self._headerTuple[2]

    def logFileSequence(self):
        return self._headerTuple[3]

    def vcn(self):
        return self._headerTuple[4]

    def offsetToEntries(self):
        return self._headerTuple[5]

    def logicalSize(self):
        return self._headerTuple[6]
```

```python
    def physicalSize(self):
        return self._headerTuple[7]

    def flags(self):
        return self._headerTuple[8]

    def isLeaf(self):
        return (self.flags() & 0x01) == 0

    def hasChildren(self):
        return (self.flags() & 0x01) == 1

    def entries(self):
        return self._entries

class IndexAllocation(Attribute):
    '''This class represents the $A0 attribute.
    This attribute is really just a list of
    data runs.'''
    def __init__(self, buffer, offset=0):
        super(IndexAllocation, self).__init__(buffer, offset)
        self._entries=None

    def __str__(self):
        retStr=Attribute.__str__(self)
        retStr+='\nIndex Buffer Data runs: ' + str(len(self._dataRuns))
        retStr+='\nNumber of Index Buffers: ' +
            str(self.numberOfIndexBuffers())
        retStr+='\nIndex Buffer Clusters: ' + str(self.clusterList())
        return retStr

    def numberOfIndexBuffers(self):
        return self.lastVcn()+1

    def getEntries(self, i30buffer):
        '''Returns the entire list of index entries
        stored in this $A0 attribute.
        Warning: This list can be quite large!
        Entries are returned in the order in
        which they are stored in index buffers which
        may not be the correct order per the collation
        rule.'''
        self._entries=[]
        for i in range(self.numberOfIndexBuffers()):
            indexBuffer=IndexBuffer(i30buffer, i*4096)
            self._entries+=indexBuffer.entries()
```

```python
    def hasEntries(self):
        '''Have the entries been retrieved?'''
        return self._entries!=None

    def numberOfEntries(self):
        if self.hasEntries():
            return len(self._entries)
        else:
            return 0

    def entries(self):
        return self._entries

    def entry(self, index):
        if self._entries:
            return self._entries[index]

def getAttribute(buffer, offset=0):
    '''create a MFT attribute from
    a buffer and offset.  Will create
    a specific type if possible or
    a generic attribute if not.'''
    if buffer[offset:offset+4]==b'\xff\xff\xff\xff':
        return
    attr=Attribute(buffer, offset)
    if attr.attributeType() == 0x10:
        attr=StandardInfo(buffer, offset)
    elif attr.attributeType() == 0x30:
        attr=Filename(buffer, offset)
    elif attr.attributeType() == 0x80:
        attr=Data(buffer, offset)
    elif attr.attributeType() == 0x90:
        attr=IndexRoot(buffer, offset)
    elif attr.attributeType() == 0xA0:
        attr=IndexAllocation(buffer, offset)
    return attr

def main():
    parser=optparse.OptionParser()
    parser.add_option("-f", "--file", dest="filename",
                      help="image filename")
    parser.add_option("-o", "--offset", dest='offset',
                      help='offset in sectors to start of volume')
    parser.add_option("-e", "--entry", dest='entry',
                      help='MFT entry number')
```

```
            (options, args)=parser.parse_args()
            filename=options.filename
            if options.offset:
                    offset=512 * int(options.offset)
            else:
                    offset=0
            if options.entry:
                    entry=int(options.entry)
            else:
                    entry=0

            with open(filename, 'rb') as f:
                    f.seek(offset)
                    buffer=f.read(512)

            vbr=Vbr(buffer)
            print(vbr)

            # calculate the offset to the MFT entry
            mftOffset = (offset + # offset to start of partition
                        vbr.mftLcn() * # logical cluster number
                        vbr.bytesPerSector() * # sector size
                        vbr.sectorsPerCluster() + # sectors/cluster
                        1024 * entry ) #
            with open(filename, 'rb') as f:
                    f.seek(mftOffset)
                    buffer=f.read(1024)
            mftHeader=MftHeader(buffer)
            print(mftHeader)
            pos = mftHeader.attributeStart()
            while pos < mftHeader.logicalRecordSize():
                    attr=getAttribute(buffer, pos)
                    if not attr:
                            break
                    print(attr)
                    pos+=attr.totalLength()

if __name__=='__main__':
    main()
```

Bitmap attributes

Bitmaps are used to keep track of allocations in NTFS. The filesystem has a $BITMAP metadata file that keeps track of which clusters on an NTFS filesystem are allocated. Recall that as directories grow, Windows will allocate index buffers in chunks of ever increasing size. A

```
Modified: Fri Nov 14 23:30:48 2014
Rec Changed: Fri Nov 14 23:30:48 2014
Accessed: Fri Nov 14 23:30:48 2014
Flags: 10000000
Extended Flags: 0000
Attribute Type: 90
Attribute Length: 0058
Resident: True
Name: None
Attribute ID: 5
Indexed Type: 30
Index Entries: 0
Data run start/count: 214136/1
Attribute Type: A0
Attribute Length: 0050
Resident: False
Name: None
Attribute ID: 3
Index Buffer Data runs: 1
Number of Index Buffers: 1
Index Buffer Clusters: [214136]
Attribute Type: B0
Attribute Length: 0028
Resident: True
Name: None
Attribute ID: 4
phil@i7laptop:~/book-windows/08-NTFS Filesystems$
```

FIGURE 8.51.

Partial output from a test run of the new IndexBuffer and IndexAllocation code.

$BITMAP ($B0) attribute named $I30 is used in this case to keep track of which index buffers are actually in use.

As mentioned earlier in this chapter, the bitmap itself will be a multiple of 8 bytes long. As a result, there are often leftover bits in the bitmap (more bits in the bitmap than index buffers). The simple Bitmap class presented here only works for resident $BITMAP attributes.

There are two reasons I did not write this class to handle non-resident bitmaps. First, that data is not available when the Bitmap object is created (stored outside of the MFT entry). Second, I have never observed a $I30 bitmap that grew so large it became non-resident. The new Bitmap class and updated getAttribute and main follow. A test run of this new code is shown in Figure 8.52.

```
class Bitmap(Attribute):
    '''This class is used to decode a $Bitmap ($B0) attribute.
    This attribute is normally used to keep track of index
    buffer allocation.'''
    def __init__(self, buffer, offset):
        super(Bitmap, self).__init__(buffer, offset)
        self._bitmap=buffer[offset+self.attributeOffset():
            offset+self.attributeOffset()+self.attributeLength()]

    def inUse(self, cluster):
        if cluster > len(self._bitmap) * 8:
```

```python
                return False
            byteNumber = cluster // 8
            bitNumber = cluster % 8
            bitmapByte = self._bitmap[byteNumber]
            return (bitmapByte & 2**bitNumber) != 0

    def clustersInMap(self):
        return 8 * len(self._bitmap)

    def clustersInUse(self):
        inuse=0
        for i in range(self.clustersInMap()):
            if self.inUse(i):
                inuse+=1
        return inuse

    def __str__(self):
        retStr=Attribute.__str__(self)
        retStr+='\nClusters in use/bitmap: ' + \
          str(self.clustersInUse()) + \
          '/' + str(self.clustersInMap())
        return retStr

def getAttribute(buffer, offset=0):
    '''create a MFT attribute from
    a buffer and offset.  Will create
    a specific type if possible or
    a generic attribute if not.'''
    if buffer[offset:offset+4]==b'\xff\xff\xff\xff':
        return
    attr=Attribute(buffer, offset)
    if attr.attributeType() == 0x10:
        attr=StandardInfo(buffer, offset)
    elif attr.attributeType() == 0x30:
        attr=Filename(buffer, offset)
    elif attr.attributeType() == 0x80:
        attr=Data(buffer, offset)
    elif attr.attributeType() == 0x90:
        attr=IndexRoot(buffer, offset)
    elif attr.attributeType() == 0xA0:
        attr=IndexAllocation(buffer, offset)
    return attr

def main():
    parser=optparse.OptionParser()
```

CHAPTER 8 NTFS Filesystems

```python
    parser.add_option("-f", "--file", dest="filename",
                     help="image filename")
    parser.add_option("-o", "--offset", dest='offset',
                     help='offset in sectors to start of volume')

    parser.add_option("-e", "--entry", dest='entry',
                     help='MFT entry number')

    (options, args)=parser.parse_args()
    filename=options.filename
    if options.offset:
        offset=512 * int(options.offset)
    else:
        offset=0
    if options.entry:
        entry=int(options.entry)
    else:
        entry=0

    with open(filename, 'rb') as f:
        f.seek(offset)
        buffer=f.read(512)

    vbr=Vbr(buffer)
    print(vbr)

    # calculate the offset to the MFT entry
    mftOffset = (offset + # offset to start of partition
            vbr.mftLcn() * # logical cluster number
            vbr.bytesPerSector() * # sector size
            vbr.sectorsPerCluster() + # sectors/cluster
            1024 * entry ) #
    with open(filename, 'rb') as f:
        f.seek(mftOffset)
        buffer=f.read(1024)
    mftHeader=MftHeader(buffer)
    print(mftHeader)
    pos = mftHeader.attributeStart()
    while pos < mftHeader.logicalRecordSize():
        attr=getAttribute(buffer, pos)
        if not attr:
            break
        print(attr)
        pos+=attr.totalLength()

if __name__=='__main__':
    main()
```

```
Number of Index Buffers: 160
Index Buffer Clusters: [775663, 775748, 775756, 775759, 660587, 855278, 855279, 857767, 857783, 8577
84, 858225, 858226, 862924, 862925, 862926, 862927, 869816, 869817, 869818, 869819, 877392, 877393,
877394, 877395, 882198, 882199, 882200, 882201, 882202, 882203, 882204, 882205, 896290, 896291, 8962
92, 896293, 896294, 896295, 896296, 896297, 907456, 907457, 907458, 907459, 907460, 907461, 907462,
907463, 917904, 917905, 917906, 917907, 917908, 917909, 917910, 917911, 917912, 917913, 917914, 9179
15, 917916, 917917, 917918, 917919, 953037, 953038, 953039, 953040, 953041, 953042, 953043, 953044,
953045, 953046, 953047, 953048, 953049, 953050, 953051, 953052, 986517, 986518, 986519, 986520, 9865
21, 986522, 986523, 986524, 986525, 986526, 986527, 986528, 986529, 986530, 986531, 986532, 1079416,
 1079417, 1079418, 1079419, 1079420, 1079421, 1079422, 1079423, 1079424, 1079425, 1079426, 1079427,
1079428, 1079429, 1079430, 1079431, 1079432, 1079433, 1079434, 1079435, 1079436, 1079437, 1079438, 1
079439, 1079440, 1079441, 1079442, 1079443, 1079444, 1079445, 1079446, 1079447, 1134410, 1134411, 11
34412, 1134413, 1134414, 1134415, 1134416, 1134417, 1134418, 1134419, 1134420, 1134421, 1134422, 113
4423, 1134424, 1134425, 1134426, 1134427, 1134428, 1134429, 1134430, 1134431, 1134432, 1134433, 1134
434, 1134435, 1134436, 1134437, 1134438, 1134439, 1134440, 1134441]
Attribute Type: B0
Attribute Length: 0038
Resident: True
Name: None
Attribute ID: 4
Clusters in use/bitmap: 143/192
Attribute Type: 100
Attribute Length: 0068
Resident: True
Name: None
Attribute ID: 8
phil@i7laptop:~/book-windows/08-NTFS Filesystems$
```

FIGURE 8.52.

Partial output from a test run of the new Bitmap class. This was run against a \Windows\System32 directory. Note that only 143 of the 160 index buffers are in use.

Attribute lists

So far we have developed code to handle nearly every scenario. However, we have not covered the case of the large fragmented file with an $ATTRIBUTE_LIST ($20) attribute. The attribute list contains 26-byte entries for each attribute associated with the file. The AttributeItem class is used to represent these entries. The AttributeList class contains information found in the standard attribute header and a list of AttributeItem objects.

The code for the new classes and updated getAttribute and main follow. A test run against a large fragmented file is shown in Figure 8.53. Notice that there are two additional MFT entries and each contains a single $DATA ($80) attribute.

```python
class AttributeItem:
    '''An item in an attribute list.'''
    def __init__(self, buffer, offset=0):
        formatStr=('<L'   +     # Attribute ID   0
                   'H'    +     # record length  1
                   'B'    +     # name length    2
                   'B'    +     # offset to name 3
                   'Q'    +     # VCN            4
                   'Q'    +     # MFT reference  5
                   'H'    )     # attribute ID   6
```

```python
            self._itemTuple=struct.unpack(formatStr,
                buffer[offset:offset+26])
            if self._itemTuple[2] > 0:
                self._name=(buffer[offset+self._itemTuple[3]:
                    offset+self._itemTuple[3]+2*self._itemTuple[2]])
            else:
                self._name=None
        def name(self):
            return self._name

        def hasName(self):
            return self._itemTuple[2] > 0

        def vcn(self):
            return self._itemTuple[4]

        def recordLength(self):
            return self._itemTuple[1]

        def attributeType(self):
            return self._itemTuple[0]

        def mft(self):
            return self._itemTuple[5] & 0xffffffffffff

        def attributeId(self):
            return self._itemTuple[6]

        def updateSequence(self):
            return self._itemTuple[5] >> 48

        def __str__(self):
            retStr=('AttributeList type: ' + str('%0X' %
                self.attributeType()) +
                    '\nStored in MFT: ' + str(self.mft()) + '/' +
                    str(self.updateSequence()) +
                    '\nName: ' + str(self.name()) )
            return retStr

class AttributeList(Attribute):
    '''Attribute list created from MFT entry
    1024 byte data stream.'''
    def __init__(self, buffer, offset=0):
        super(AttributeList, self).__init__(buffer, offset)
        # standard header is 24 bytes (must be resident)
        pos=offset+24
        self._list=[]
```

```python
            while pos < offset + self.totalLength():
                item=AttributeItem(buffer, pos)
                pos+=item.recordLength()
                self._list.append(item)

    def length(self):
        return len(self._list)

    def list(self):
        return self._list

    def __str__(self):
        retStr=Attribute.__str__(self)
        retStr+='\nAttribute List:'
        for i in range(self.length()):
            retStr+='\n\t'+str(self._list[i].__str__())
        return retStr

def getAttribute(buffer, offset=0):
    '''create a MFT attribute from
    a buffer and offset. Will create
    a specific type if possible or
    a generic attribute if not.'''
    if buffer[offset:offset+4]==b'\xff\xff\xff\xff':
        return
    attr=Attribute(buffer, offset)
    if attr.attributeType() == 0x10:
        attr=StandardInfo(buffer, offset)
    elif attr.attributeType() == 0x20:
        attr=AttributeList(buffer, offset)
    elif attr.attributeType() == 0x30:
        attr=Filename(buffer, offset)
    elif attr.attributeType() == 0x80:
        attr=Data(buffer, offset)
    elif attr.attributeType() == 0x90:
        attr=IndexRoot(buffer, offset)
    elif attr.attributeType() == 0xA0:
        attr=IndexAllocation(buffer, offset)
    elif attr.attributeType() == 0xB0:
        attr=Bitmap(buffer, offset)
    return attr

def main():
    parser=optparse.OptionParser()
    parser.add_option("-f", "--file", dest="filename",
                      help="image filename")
```

```python
        parser.add_option("-o", "--offset", dest='offset',
                    help='offset in sectors to start of volume')
        parser.add_option("-e", "--entry", dest='entry',
                    help='MFT entry number')
        (options, args)=parser.parse_args()
        filename=options.filename
        if options.offset:
            offset=512 * int(options.offset)
        else:
            offset=0
        if options.entry:
            entry=int(options.entry)
        else:
            entry=0

        with open(filename, 'rb') as f:
            f.seek(offset)
            buffer=f.read(512)

        vbr=Vbr(buffer)
        print(vbr)

        # calculate the offset to the MFT entry
        mftOffset = (offset +  # offset to start of partition
                    vbr.mftLcn() *  # logical cluster number
                    vbr.bytesPerSector() *  # sector size
                    vbr.sectorsPerCluster() +  # sectors/cluster
                    1024 * entry ) #
        with open(filename, 'rb') as f:
            f.seek(mftOffset)
            buffer=f.read(1024)
        mftHeader=MftHeader(buffer)
        print(mftHeader)
        pos = mftHeader.attributeStart()
        while pos < mftHeader.logicalRecordSize():
            attr=getAttribute(buffer, pos)
            if not attr:
                break
            print(attr)
            pos+=attr.totalLength()

if __name__=='__main__':
    main()
```

```
Rec Changed: Fri Nov 14 21:38:59 2014
Accessed: Fri Nov 14 21:18:05 2014
Flags: 0020
Has Versioning: False
Attribute Type: 20
Attribute Length: 00B8
Resident: True
Name: None
Attribute ID: 6
Attribute List:
        AttributeList type: 10
Stored in MFT: 22114/3
Name: None
        AttributeList type: 30
Stored in MFT: 22114/3
Name: None
        AttributeList type: 30
Stored in MFT: 22114/3
Name: None
        AttributeList type: 80
Stored in MFT: 21913/9
Name: None
        AttributeList type: 80
Stored in MFT: 22144/24
Name: None
Attribute Type: 30
Attribute Length: 0078
```

FIGURE 8.53.

Partial results from a test run of the new AttributeItem and AttributeList classes against a large fragmented file.

We have developed classes to handle all of the important attributes in the MFT. Now all that remains is to clean up this code and package it for easy importing into other scripts. To facilitate this we add an __all__ list containing the classes and functions to be exported and add a new class, MftEntry, to represent a 1024-byte MFT entry. The MftEntry class will apply the fixup codes from the update sequence array automatically to facilitate creating objects that represent attributes. The complete MFT module follows.

```
#!/usr/bin/python3

'''Set of classes to read and interpret
MFT entries.  Each MFT entry is created
by passing in a 1024 byte binary string.
Created by Dr. Phil Polstra
for PentesterAcademy.com'''

__all__=['MftHeader', 'DataRun', 'dataRuns', 'Attribute',
'StandardInfo', 'AttributeItem', 'AttributeList', 'Filename',
'Data', 'IndexRoot', 'IndexEntry', 'IndexAllocation', 'Bitmap',
'IndexBuffer', 'getAttribute', 'MftEntry']
```

CHAPTER 8 NTFS Filesystems

```python
import struct    # for interpreting entries
import optparse  # command line options
import time      # time conversion functions
from vbr import Vbr

class MftHeader:
    def __init__(self, buffer):
        '''Expects a 1024-byte buffer
        containing a MFT record.'''
        if buffer[0:4]==b'FILE':
            self._isValid=True
            formatStr=( '<4s' +      # FILE id 0
                        'H'  +       # update seq offset (0x30) 1
                        'H'  +       # size of update seq (3) 2
                        'Q'  +       # log file seq number 3
                        'H'  +       # sequence number 4
                        'H'  +       # hard link count 5
                        'H'  +       # start of attributes 6
                        'H'  +       # flags b0=used b1=directory 7
                        'L'  +       # logical MFT record size 8
                        'L'  +       # physics MFT rec size (1024) 9
                        'Q'  +       # MFT base file reference 10
                        'H'  +       # next attribute ID 11
                        '2s' +       # padding 12
                        'L'  +       # MFT Record number 13
                        '6s' )       # update seq array 14
            self._headerTuple=struct.unpack(formatStr, buffer[:54])
        else:
            self._isValid=False

    def isValid(self):
        return self._isValid

    def updateSequenceOffset(self):
        return self._headerTuple[1]

    def updateSequenceSize(self):
        return self._headerTuple[2]

    def updateSequenceArray(self):
        return self._headerTuple[14]

    def logFileSequenceNumber(self):
        return self._headerTuple[3]
```

```python
    def sequenceNumber(self):
        return self._headerTuple[4]

    def hardLinkCount(self):
        return self._headerTuple[5]

    def attributeStart(self):
        return self._headerTuple[6]

    def flags(self):
        return self._headerTuple[7]

    def inUse(self):
        return (self._headerTuple[7] & 0x01) != 0

    def isDirectory(self):
        return (self._headerTuple[7] & 0x02) != 0

    def logicalRecordSize(self):
        return self._headerTuple[8]

    def physicalRecordSize(self):
        return self._headerTuple[9]

    def baseFileReference(self):
        return self._headerTuple[10]

    def baseFileMft(self):
        return self._headerTuple[10] & 0x0000FFFFFFFFFFFF

    def baseFileSequenceNumber(self):
        return self._headerTuple[10] >> 48

    def nextAttributeId(self):
        return self._headerTuple[11]

    def recordNumber(self):
        return self._headerTuple[13]

    def __str__(self):
        retStr=('MFT entry: ' + str(self.recordNumber()) +
                '/' + str(self.sequenceNumber()) +
                '\n\tSize: ' + str(self.logicalRecordSize()) +
                '/' + str(self.physicalRecordSize()) +
                '\n\tBase Record: ' + str(self.baseFileMft()) +
                '/' + str(self.baseFileSequenceNumber()) )
        return retStr
```

```python
class DataRun:
    '''This class represents a single data run.
    it is little more than a wrapper around
    the range object.'''
    def __init__(self, start, count):
        self._start=start
        self._count=count

    def numberOfClusters(self):
        return self._count

    def startingCluster(self):
        return self._start

    def clusterList(self):
        retList=[]
        for i in range(self._start, self._start+self._count):
            retList.append(i)
        return retList

    def __str__(self):
        return ('Data run start/count: ' +
                    str(self.startingCluster()) +
                    '/' + str(self.numberOfClusters()) )

def bytesToUnsigned(buff, sz, pos=0):
    '''Take a slice of a binary string and
    converts it to an unsigned integer.'''
    paddedStr=buff[pos:pos+sz]
    for x in range(sz, 8):
        paddedStr+=b'\x00'
    return struct.unpack('<Q', paddedStr)[0]

def bytesToSigned(buff, sz, pos=0):
    '''Take a slice of a binary string and
    converts it to a signed integer.'''
    paddedStr=buff[pos:pos+sz]
    # is it negative?
    if ord(buff[pos+sz-1:pos+sz]) >= 0x80:
        fillStr=b'\xff'
    else:
        fillStr=b'\x00'
    for x in range(sz, 8):
        paddedStr+=fillStr
    return struct.unpack('<q', paddedStr)[0]
```

Python and NTFS

```python
def dataRuns(buff, offset=0):
    '''This function will decode a binary stream of
    data runs and return a list of data run objects.'''
    pos=offset
    if pos >= len(buff):
        return
    retList=[]
    startCluster=0
    # loop till size of next run is zero
    while buff[pos]!=b'\x00' and pos < len(buff):
        # get sizes for run
        size=ord(buff[pos:pos+1])
        if size==0:
            break
        countSize=size & 0x0F
        offsetSize=size >> 4
        pos+=1
        count=bytesToUnsigned(buff, countSize, pos)
        pos+=countSize
        startCluster+=bytesToSigned(buff, offsetSize, pos)
        pos+=offsetSize
        retList.append(DataRun(startCluster, count))
    return retList

class Attribute:
    def __init__(self, buffer, offset=0):
        '''Accept a buffer and optional offset to
        interpret an attribute header.  This is normally
        called when creating an attribute object, in
        which case the buffer is probably a 1K MFT entry.'''
        # header starts the same for resident/not
        formatStr=('<L' + # Attribute type 0
                    'L' + # total attribute length 1
                    'B' + # flag 00/01 resident/not 2
                    'B' + # name length 3
                    'H' + # offset to name 4
                    'H' + # flags 5
                    'H')  # attribute ID 6
        # if this is resident header continues
        if buffer[offset+8:offset+9]==b'\x00':
            formatStr+=('L' +       # length of attribute 7
                        'H' + # offset to start of attribute 8
                        'B' + # indexed? 9
                        'B')  # padding 10
            self.__headerTuple=struct.unpack(formatStr,
                buffer[offset:offset+24])
```

```python
                    if self.hasName():
                        self.__name=buffer[offset+self.nameOffset():
                            offset+self.nameOffset() + self.nameLength()*2]
                    else:
                        self.__name=None
            else:
                # non-resident attribute
                formatStr+=('Q'    +      # first VCN 7
                            'Q'    +      # last VCN 8
                            'H'    +      # offset to data runs 9
                            'H'    + # compression 2^x 10
                            '4s'   +      # padding 11
                            'Q'    + # physical size of attribute 12
                            'Q'    +      # logical size of attribute 13
                            'Q')   # initialized size of stream 14
                self.__headerTuple=struct.unpack(formatStr,
                        buffer[offset:offset+64])
                if self.hasName():
                    self.__name=buffer[offset+self.nameOffset():
                        offset+self.nameOffset() + self.nameLength()*2]
                else:
                    self.__name=None
                self._dataRuns=dataRuns(buffer,
                        offset+self.__headerTuple[9])

    def dataRuns(self):
        if not self.isResident():
            return self._dataRuns

    def clusterList(self):
        if not self.isResident():
            retList=[]
            for dr in self._dataRuns:
                retList+=(dr.clusterList())
            return retList


    def firstVcn(self):
        if not self.isResident():
            return self.__headerTuple[7]

    def lastVcn(self):
        if not self.isResident():
            return self.__headerTuple[8]
```

```
def dataRunOffset(self):
    if not self.isResident():
        return self.__headerTuple[9]

def compression(self):
    if not self.isResident():
        return 2**self.__headerTuple[10]

def physicalSize(self):
    if not self.isResident():
        return self.__headerTuple[12]

def logicalSize(self):
    if not self.isResident():
        return self.__headerTuple[13]

def initializedSize(self):
    if not self.isResident():
        return self.__headerTuple[14]

def attributeLength(self):
    if self.isResident():
        return self.__headerTuple[7]

def attributeOffset(self):
    if self.isResident():
        return self.__headerTuple[8]

def isIndexed(self):
    if self.isResident():
        return self.__headerTuple[9]==0x01
    else:
        return False

def attributeType(self):
    return self.__headerTuple[0]

def totalLength(self):
    return self.__headerTuple[1]

def isResident(self):
    return self.__headerTuple[2]==0

def nameLength(self):
    return self.__headerTuple[3]
```

```python
        def nameOffset(self):
            return self.__headerTuple[4]

        def hasName(self):
            return self.__headerTuple[3]!=0

        def name(self):
            self.__name

        def flags(self):
            return self.__headerTuple[5]

        def isCompressed(self):
            return (self.__headerTuple[5] & 0x0001) != 0

        def isEncrypted(self):
            return (self.__headerTuple[5] & 0x4000) != 0

        def isSparse(self):
            return (self.__headerTuple[5] & 0x8000) != 0

        def attributeId(self):
            return self.__headerTuple[6]

        def __str__(self):
            retStr=('Attribute Type: ' + '%02X' % self.attributeType() +
                    '\nAttribute Length: ' + '%04X' % self.totalLength() +
                    '\nResident: ' + str(self.isResident()) +
                    '\nName: ' + str(self.name()) +
                    '\nAttribute ID: ' + str(self.attributeId()) )
            return retStr

    def convertFileTime(stupid):
        '''Converts idiotic Win32 filetimes to something reasonable.'''
        t = stupid * 100/ 1000000000
        t -= 11644473600
        if t > 0:
            return time.gmtime(t)
        else:
            return time.gmtime(0)

    class StandardInfo(Attribute):
        '''This class is use to represent the $10 Standard Info
        attribute.  It is created from a buffer containing the
        MFT entry (1024 bytes) and an offset to the start of
```

```python
        the attribute.'''
    def __init__(self, buffer, offset=0):
        super(StandardInfo, self).__init__(buffer, offset)
        # $10 is always resident so header is 24 bytes
        formatStr=('<Q' + # creation     0
                   'Q' + # modification  1
                   'Q' + # record change 2
                   'Q' + # access        3
                   'L' + # flags         4
                   'L' + # highest version 5
                   'L' + # version number 6
                   'L' + # class ID (XP)  7
                   'L' + # owner ID (xp)  8
                   'L' + # security ID (xp) 9
                   'Q' + # quota disk size (xp) 10
                   'Q')  # update sequence (xp) 11
        self._10Tuple=struct.unpack(formatStr,
              buffer[offset+24:offset+24+72])

    def creationTime(self):
        return convertFileTime(self._10Tuple[0])

    def modificationTime(self):
        return convertFileTime(self._10Tuple[1])

    def recordChangeTime(self):
        return convertFileTime(self._10Tuple[2])

    def accessTime(self):
        return convertFileTime(self._10Tuple[3])

    def flags(self):
        '''Flags are
        0123456789ABCDE-bits
        RHS0DADSTSRCONE
        Oiy0iretmpeofon
         ds0rcvdpapmftc
         nt0thi  raplir'''
        return self._10Tuple[4]

    def isReadOnly(self):
        return (self.flags() & 0x01) !=0

    def isHidden(self):
        return (self.flags() & 0x02) !=0
```

```python
def isSystem(self):
    return (self.flags() & 0x04) !=0

def isDirectory(self):
    return (self.flags() & 0x10) !=0

def isArchive(self):
    return (self.flags() & 0x20) !=0

def isStandardFile(self):
    return (self.flags() & 0x80) !=0

def isTemporaryFile(self):
    return (self.flags() & 0x100) !=0

def isSparseFile(self):
    return (self.flags() & 0x200) !=0

def isReparsePoint(self):
    return (self.flags() & 0x400) !=0

def isCompressed(self):
    return (self.flags() & 0x800) !=0

def isOffline(self):
    return (self.flags() & 0x1000) !=0

def isNotIndexed(self):
    return (self.flags() & 0x2000) !=0

def isEncrypted(self):
    return (self.flags() & 0x4000) !=0

def highestVersion(self):
    return self._10Tuple[5]

def versionNumber(self):
    return self._10Tuple[6]

def hasVersioning(self):
    return self._10Tuple[5]!=0

def classID(self):
    return self._10Tuple[7]
```

```python
    def ownerID(self):
        return self._10Tuple[8]

    def securityID(self):
        return self._10Tuple[9]

    def quota(self):
        return self._10Tuple[10]

    def updatedSequenceNumber(self):
        return self._10Tuple[11]

    def __str__(self):
        retStr=Attribute.__str__(self)
        retStr+=('\nCreated: ' +
            str(time.asctime(self.creationTime())) +
            '\nModified: '     +
            str(time.asctime(self.modificationTime())) +
            '\nRec Changed: ' +
            str(time.asctime(self.recordChangeTime())) +
            '\nAccessed: '    +
            str(time.asctime(self.accessTime())) +
            '\nFlags: ' + str('%04X' % self.flags()) +
            '\nHas Versioning: ' + str(self.hasVersioning()) )
        return retStr

class AttributeItem:
    '''An item in an attribute list.'''
    def __init__(self, buffer, offset=0):
        formatStr=('<L' +      # Attribute ID 0
                   'H' +       # record length 1
                   'B' +       # name length    2
                   'B' +       # offset to name 3
                   'Q' +       # VCN 4
                   'Q' +       # MFT reference 5
                   'H' )       # attribute ID 6
        self._itemTuple=struct.unpack(formatStr,
            buffer[offset:offset+26])

        if self._itemTuple[2] > 0:
            self._name=buffer[offset+self._itemTuple[3]:
                offset+self._itemTuple[3]+2*self._itemTuple[2]]
        else:
            self._name=None
```

```python
        def name(self):
            return self._name

        def hasName(self):
            return self._itemTuple[2] > 0

        def vcn(self):
            return self._itemTuple[4]

        def recordLength(self):
            return self._itemTuple[1]

        def attributeType(self):
            return self._itemTuple[0]

        def mft(self):
            return self._itemTuple[5] & 0xffffffffffff

        def attributeId(self):
            return self._itemTuple[6]

        def updateSequence(self):
            return self._itemTuple[5] >> 48

        def __str__(self):
            retStr=('AttributeList type: ' + str('%0X' %
                self.attributeType()) +
                '\nStored in MFT: ' + str(self.mft()) + '/' +
                str(self.updateSequence()) +
                '\nName: ' + str(self.name()) )
            return retStr

class AttributeList(Attribute):
    '''Attribute list created from MFT entry
    1024 byte data stream.'''
    def __init__(self, buffer, offset=0):
        super(AttributeList, self).__init__(buffer, offset)
        self._list=[]
        if not self.isResident():
            return # we don't support non-resident attribute lists
        # standard header is 24 bytes (if resident)
        # non-resident attribute lists are not supported
        pos=offset+24
        while pos < offset + self.totalLength():
            item=AttributeItem(buffer, pos)
            pos+=item.recordLength()
            self._list.append(item)
```

```python
    def length(self):
        return len(self._list)

    def list(self):
        return self._list

    def __str__(self):
        retStr=Attribute.__str__(self)
        if not self.isResident():
            retStr+='\n****Non-resident Attribute lists not
                supported****'
            return retStr
        retStr+='\nAttribute List:'
        for i in range(self.length()):
            retStr+='\n\t'+str(self._list[i].__str__())
        return retStr

class Filename(Attribute):
    '''This class is used to represent the $30 or Filename
    attribute.  It is created by passing in a MFT entry
    to the class.'''
    def __init__(self, buffer, offset=0):
      super(Filename, self).__init__(buffer, offset)
          # this attribute must be resident
      formatStr=('<L'    +     # MFT entry of parent 0
                 'H'     +     # MFT entry of parent upper 2 bytes 1
                 'H'     +     # Update sequence of parent 2
                 'Q'     +     # Created 3
                 'Q'     +     # Modified 4
                 'Q'     +     # record change 5
                 'Q'     +     # accessed 6
                 'Q'     +     # physical size 7
                 'Q'     +     # logical size 8
                 'L'     +     # flags 9
                 'L'     +     # extended flags 10
                 'B'     +     # filename length 11
                 'B')          # namespace 12
      self._30Tuple=struct.unpack(formatStr, buffer[offset+24:offset+24+66])
      self._name=buffer[offset+90:offset+90+self._30Tuple[11]*2]

    def parentMft(self):
      return self._30Tuple[0]

    def parentSequenceNumber(self):
        return self._30Tuple[2]
```

```python
def creationTime(self):
    return convertFileTime(self._30Tuple[3])

def modificationTime(self):
    return convertFileTime(self._30Tuple[4])

def recordChangeTime(self):
    return convertFileTime(self._30Tuple[5])

def accessTime(self):
    return convertFileTime(self._30Tuple[6])

def physicalSize(self):
    return self._30Tuple[7]

def logicalSize(self):
    return self._30Tuple[8]

def flags(self):
    return self._30Tuple[9]

def isReadOnly(self):
    return (self.flags() & 0x01) !=0

def isHidden(self):
    return (self.flags() & 0x02) !=0

def isSystem(self):
    return (self.flags() & 0x04) !=0

def isDirectory(self):
    return (self.flags() & 0x10000000) !=0

def isIndexView(self):
    return (self.flags() & 0x20000000) !=0

def isArchive(self):
    return (self.flags() & 0x20) !=0

def isStandardFile(self):
    return (self.flags() & 0x80) !=0

def isTemporaryFile(self):
    return (self.flags() & 0x100) !=0
```

```python
    def isSparseFile(self):
        return (self.flags() & 0x200) !=0

    def isReparsePoint(self):
        return (self.flags() & 0x400) !=0

    def isCompressed(self):
        return (self.flags() & 0x800) !=0

    def isOffline(self):
        return (self.flags() & 0x1000) !=0

    def isNotIndexed(self):
        return (self.flags() & 0x2000) !=0

    def isEncrypted(self):
        return (self.flags() & 0x4000) !=0

    def extendedFlags(self):
        return self._30Tuple[10]

    def nameLength(self):
        return self._30Tuple[11]

    def namespace(self):
        return self._30Tuple[12]

    def name(self):
        return self._name

    def filename(self):
      return self._name.decode('utf-16', errors='ignore')

    def __str__(self):
        retStr=Attribute.__str__(self)
        retStr+=('\nFilename: ' +
           str(self.name().decode('utf-16', errors='ignore')) +
               '\nCreated: ' + str(time.asctime(self.creationTime())) +
               '\nModified: ' +
               str(time.asctime(self.modificationTime())) +
               '\nRec Changed: '   +
               str(time.asctime(self.recordChangeTime())) +
               '\nAccessed: ' + str(time.asctime(self.accessTime())) +
               '\nFlags: ' + str('%04X' % self.flags()) +
               '\nExtended Flags: ' + str('%04X' %
               self.extendedFlags()) )
        return retStr
```

```python
class Data(Attribute):
    '''This class represents the data attribute.'''
    def __init__(self, buffer, offset=0):
        super(Data, self).__init__(buffer, offset)
        # is it resident
        if self.isResident():
            self._data=buffer[offset+self.attributeOffset():
                offset+self.attributeOffset()+self.attributeLength()]
        else:
            self._data=None

    def data(self):
        '''Return data if resident otherwise None'''
        return self._data

    def __str__(self):
        retStr=Attribute.__str__(self)
        if self.isResident():
            retStr+='\nData bytes: ' + str(len(self._data))
        else:
            retStr+='\nData runs: ' + str(len(self._dataRuns))
            retStr+='\nData clusters: ' + str(self.clusterList())
        return retStr

class IndexEntry:
    '''Represents an index entry whether
    or not it is resident.'''
    def __init__(self, buffer, offset=0, resident=False):
        if struct.unpack('<Q', buffer[offset:offset+8])[0] ==0:
            # we are all done here
            formatStr=('<Q'  +      # MFT ref 0
                       'H'   +      # total record length 1
                       'H'   +      # record length 2
                       'B'   +      # index flag 3
                       '3s'  )      # padding 4
            self._entryTuple=(struct.unpack(formatStr,
                    buffer[offset:offset+16]) +
                    (0,0,0,0,0,0,0,0,0,0,0,0,0,0) )
            self._name=b''
            self._vcn=None
        else:
            formatStr=('<Q'  +      # MFT ref 0
                       'H'   +      # total record length 1
                       'H'   +      # record length 2
                       'B'   +      # index flag 3
```

```
                              '3s'   +      # padding 4
                              'L'    +      # MFT entry of parent 5
                              'H'    +      # MFT entry of parent upper
                                                2 bytes 6
                              'H'    +      # Update sequence of parent 7
                              'Q'    +      # Created 8
                              'Q'    +      # Modified 9
                              'Q'    +      # record change 10
                              'Q'    +      # accessed 11
                              'Q'    +      # physical size 12
                              'Q'    +      # logical size 13
                              'L'    +      # flags 14
                              'L'    +      # extended flags 15
                              'B'    +      # filename length 16
                              'B')          # namespace 17
            self._entryTuple=struct.unpack(formatStr,
                buffer[offset:offset+82])
            self._name=buffer[offset+82:offset+82+
                self._entryTuple[16]*2]
            if not self.isResident():
                # vcn of subentries in last 8 bytes
                self._vcn=struct.unpack('<Q',
                    buffer[offset+self._entryTuple[1]-
                    8:offset+self._entryTuple[1]])
            else:
                self._vcn=None

    def __str__(self):
        retStr=('Index Entry:' +
            '\n\tMFT: ' + str(self.mft()) + '/' +
            str(self.sequenceNumber()) +
            '\n\tIs Resident: ' + str(self.isResident()) +
            '\n\tIs Last: ' + str(self.isLast()) +
            '\n\tParent MFT: ' + str(self.parentMft()) +
            '/' + str(self.parentSequenceNumber()) +
            '\n\tFilename: ' +
            str(self.name().decode('utf-16', errors='ignore')) )
        return retStr

    def mft(self):
        return self._entryTuple[0] & 0xffffffffffff

    def sequenceNumber(self):
        return self._entryTuple[0] >> 48
```

```python
    def totalLength(self):
        return self._entryTuple[1]

    def recordLength(self):
        return self._entryTuple[2]

    def isEmpty(self):
        return self.recordLength()==0

    def indexFlags(self):
        return self._entryTuple[3]

    def isResident(self):
        return (self.indexFlags() & 0x01) == 0

    def isNonresident(self):
        return (self.indexFlags() & 0x01) != 0

    def isLast(self):
        return (self.indexFlags() & 0x02) != 0

    def parentMft(self):
        return self._entryTuple[5] + ((self._entryTuple[6] &
            0xffff) <<32)

    def parentSequenceNumber(self):
        return self._entryTuple[7]

    def creationTime(self):
        return convertFileTime(self._entryTuple[8])

    def modificationTime(self):
        return convertFileTime(self._entryTuple[9])

    def recordChangeTime(self):
        return convertFileTime(self._entryTuple[10])

    def accessTime(self):
        return convertFileTime(self._entryTuple[11])

    def physicalSize(self):
        return self._entryTuple[12]

    def logicalSize(self):
        return self._entryTuple[13]
```

```python
    def flags(self):
        return self._entryTuple[14]

    def isReadOnly(self):
        return (self.flags() & 0x01) !=0

    def isHidden(self):
        return (self.flags() & 0x02) !=0

    def isSystem(self):
        return (self.flags() & 0x04) !=0

    def isDirectory(self):
        return (self.flags() & 0x10000000) !=0

    def isIndexView(self):
        return (self.flags() & 0x20000000) !=0

    def isArchive(self):
        return (self.flags() & 0x20) !=0

    def isStandardFile(self):
        return (self.flags() & 0x80) !=0

    def isTemporaryFile(self):
        return (self.flags() & 0x100) !=0

    def isSparseFile(self):
        return (self.flags() & 0x200) !=0

    def isReparsePoint(self):
        return (self.flags() & 0x400) !=0

    def isCompressed(self):
        return (self.flags() & 0x800) !=0

    def isOffline(self):
        return (self.flags() & 0x1000) !=0

    def isNotIndexed(self):
        return (self.flags() & 0x2000) !=0

    def isEncrypted(self):
        return (self.flags() & 0x4000) !=0
```

```python
    def extendedFlags(self):
        return self._entryTuple[15]

    def nameLength(self):
        return self._entryTuple[16]

    def namespace(self):
        return self._entryTuple[17]

    def name(self):
        return self._name

    def filename(self):
        return self._name.decode('utf-16', errors='ignore')

    def childVcn(self):
        return self._vcn

class IndexRoot(Attribute):
    '''Index root $90 including any entries.'''
    def __init__(self, buffer, offset=0):
        super(IndexRoot, self).__init__(buffer, offset)
        formatStr=('<L' +       # attribute type 0
                   'L' +        # collation rule 1
                   'L' +        # buffer size 2
                   'L' +        # clusters/indx 3
                   'L' +        # offset to 1st entry 4
                   'L' +        # logical size 5
                   'L' +        # physical size 6
                   'L' )        # 00/01 resident/not 7
        self.__headerTuple=struct.unpack(formatStr,
            buffer[offset+self.attributeOffset():
            offset+self.attributeOffset()+32])
        pos=offset+self.attributeOffset()+16+self.__headerTuple[4]
        self._indexEntries=[]
        # we only care about indexed filenames
        if self.__headerTuple[0] !=0x30:
            return
        while pos < offset+self.logicalIndexSize():
            entry=IndexEntry(buffer, pos, True)
            self._indexEntries.append(entry)
            pos+=entry.totalLength()
            if entry.isLast():
                break
```

```python
    def indexedAttributeType(self):
        return self.__headerTuple[0]

    def collationRule(self):
        return self.__headerTuple[1]

    def indexBufferSize(self):
        return self.__headerTuple[2]

    def clustersPerIndexBuffer(self):
        return self.__headerTuple[3]

    def offsetToFirstEntry(self):
        return self.__headerTuple[4]

    def logicalIndexSize(self):
        return self.__headerTuple[5]

    def physicalIndexSize(self):
        return self.__headerTuple[6]

    def isIndexResident(self):
        return self.__headerTuple[7]==0

    def isIndexNonresident(self):
        return self.__headerTuple[7]==1

    def indexEntries(self):
        return self._indexEntries

    def numberOfIndexEntries(self):
        return len(self._indexEntries)

    def __str__(self):
        retStr=Attribute.__str__(self)
        retStr+=('\nIndexed Type: ' + str('%0X' %
            self.indexedAttributeType())  +
            '\nIndex Entries: ' +
            str(self.numberOfIndexEntries()) )
        for i in range(self.numberOfIndexEntries()):
            retStr+= '\n' + self._indexEntries[i].__str__()
        return retStr
```

```python
class IndexBuffer:
    '''This class is used to process a
    4096 byte index buffer.'''
    def __init__(self, buffer, offset=0):
        # process the header
        formatStr=('<4s'   +     # INDX 0
                   'H'     +     # offset to update seq 1
                   'H'     +     # update seq size in words 2
                   'Q'     +     # log file seq number 3
                   'Q'     +     # VCN 4
                   'L'     +     # offset to entries 5
                   'L'     +     # logical size 6
                   'L'     +     # physical size 7
                   'L'     +     # flags 00/01 leaf/parent 8
                   'H'     +     # update seq 9
                   '8H'    )     # update seq array 10
        self._headerTuple=struct.unpack(formatStr,
            buffer[offset:offset+58])
        if not self.isValid():
            self._entries=[]
            return

        # copy data to new buffer so we can apply fix up codes
        self._data=buffer[offset:offset+4096]
        for i in range(0, self._headerTuple[2]-1):
           replaceIndex = offset + 512 * i + 510
           upSeqPos=self._headerTuple[1]+2
           self._data = (self._data[0: replaceIndex] +
                   self._data[upSeqPos+i*2:upSeqPos+i*2+2] +
                   self._data[replaceIndex + 2: ])
        # now read the entries
        pos=self._headerTuple[5] + 24
        self._entries=[]
        while pos < self._headerTuple[6] + 24:
            entry=IndexEntry(self._data, pos)
            if entry.recordLength()==0:
                break
            self._entries.append(entry)
            pos+=entry.totalLength()
            if entry.isLast():
                break

    def isValid(self):
        return self._headerTuple[0]==b'INDX'
```

```python
    def updateSequenceOffset(self):
        return self._headerTuple[1]

    def updateSequenceSize(self):
        return self._headerTuple[2]

    def logFileSequence(self):
        return self._headerTuple[3]

    def vcn(self):
        return self._headerTuple[4]

    def offsetToEntries(self):
        return self._headerTuple[5]

    def logicalSize(self):
        return self._headerTuple[6]

    def physicalSize(self):
        return self._headerTuple[7]

    def flags(self):
        return self._headerTuple[8]

    def isLeaf(self):
        return (self.flags() & 0x01) == 0

    def hasChildren(self):
        return (self.flags() & 0x01) == 1

    def entries(self):
        return self._entries

class IndexAllocation(Attribute):
    '''This class represents the $A0 attribute.
    This attribute is really just a list of
    data runs.'''
    def __init__(self, buffer, offset=0):
        super(IndexAllocation, self).__init__(buffer, offset)
        self._entries=None

    def __str__(self):
        retStr=Attribute.__str__(self)
        retStr+='\nIndex Buffer Data runs: ' + str(len(self._dataRuns))
        retStr+='\nNumber of Index Buffers: ' + \
            str(self.numberOfIndexBuffers())
```

```python
                    retStr+='\nIndex Buffer Clusters: ' + str(self.clusterList())
                    return retStr

            def numberOfIndexBuffers(self):
                return self.lastVcn()+1

            def getEntries(self, i30buffer):
                '''Returns the entire list of index entries
                stored in this $A0 attribute.
                Warning: This list can be quite large!
                Entries are returned in the order in
                which they are stored in index buffers which
                may not be the correct order per the collation
                rule.'''
                self._entries=[]
                for i in range(self.numberOfIndexBuffers()):
                    indexBuffer=IndexBuffer(i30buffer, i*4096)
                    self._entries+=indexBuffer.entries()

            def hasEntries(self):
                '''Have the entries been retrieved?'''
                return self._entries!=None

            def numberOfEntries(self):
                if self.hasEntries():
                    return len(self._entries)
                else:
                    return 0

            def entries(self):
                return self._entries

            def entry(self, index):
                if self._entries:
                    return self._entries[index]

    class Bitmap(Attribute):
        '''This class is used to decode a $Bitmap ($B0) attribute.
        This attribute is normally used to keep track of index
        buffer allocation.'''
        def __init__(self, buffer, offset):
            super(Bitmap, self).__init__(buffer, offset)
            if self.isResident():
                self._bitmap=buffer[offset+self.attributeOffset():
                    offset+self.attributeOffset()+self.attributeLength()]
```

```python
    def inUse(self, cluster):
        if not self.isResident():
            return False
        if cluster > len(self._bitmap) * 8:
            return False
        byteNumber = cluster // 8
        bitNumber = cluster % 8
        bitmapByte = self._bitmap[byteNumber]
        return (bitmapByte & 2**bitNumber) != 0

    def clustersInMap(self):
        if not self.isResident():
            return 0
        return 8 * len(self._bitmap)

    def clustersInUse(self):
        inuse=0
        for i in range(self.clustersInMap()):
            if self.inUse(i):
                inuse+=1
        return inuse

    def __str__(self):
        retStr=Attribute.__str__(self)
        retStr+='\nClusters in use/bitmap: ' +
            str(self.clustersInUse()) + '/' +
            str(self.clustersInMap())
        return retStr

def getAttribute(buffer, offset=0):
    '''create a MFT attribute from
    a buffer and offset.  Will create
    a specific type if possible or
    a generic attribute if not.'''
    if buffer[offset:offset+4]==b'\xff\xff\xff\xff':
        return
    attr=Attribute(buffer, offset)
    if attr.attributeType() == 0x10:
        attr=StandardInfo(buffer, offset)
    elif attr.attributeType() == 0x20:
        attr=AttributeList(buffer, offset)
    elif attr.attributeType() == 0x30:
        attr=Filename(buffer, offset)
    elif attr.attributeType() == 0x80:
        attr=Data(buffer, offset)
```

```python
        elif attr.attributeType() == 0x90:
            attr=IndexRoot(buffer, offset)
        elif attr.attributeType() == 0xA0:
            attr=IndexAllocation(buffer, offset)
        elif attr.attributeType() == 0xB0:
            attr=Bitmap(buffer, offset)
    return attr

class MftEntry:
    '''This class represents an MFT entry.
    It is normally created by passing in
    a 1024 byte buffer with the data stream.'''
    def __init__(self, buffer, offset=0):
        self._mftHeader=MftHeader(buffer)
        pos = self._mftHeader.attributeStart()
        self._attrList=[]
        if self._mftHeader.isValid():
            # apply the fixup at the end of sectors
            data=buffer[offset:offset+1024]
            for i in range(self._mftHeader.updateSequenceSize()-1):
                data=(data[:512*i+510] +
                    buffer[offset+
                    self._mftHeader.updateSequenceOffset()+2*i+2:
                    offset+
                    self._mftHeader.updateSequenceOffset()+2*i+4] +
                    data[512*i+512:])
            # get attributes
            while pos < self._mftHeader.logicalRecordSize():
                attr=getAttribute(data, pos)
                if not attr:
                    break
                self._attrList.append(attr)
                pos+=attr.totalLength()

    def numberOfAttributes(self):
        return len(self._attrList)

    def attributes(self):
        return self._attrList

    def attribute(self, number):
        return self._attrList[number]

    def attributesOfType(self, attrType):
        retList=[]
```

```python
        for attr in self._attrList:
            if attr.attributeType()==attrType:
                retList.append(attr)
        return retList

    def __str__(self):
        retStr=self._mftHeader.__str__()
        for attr in self._attrList:
            retStr+=attr.__str__()
        return retStr

    def updateSequenceOffset(self):
        return self._mftHeader.updateSequenceOffset()

    def updateSequenceSize(self):
        return self._mftHeader.updateSequenceSize()

    def updateSequenceArray(self):
        return self._mftHeader.updateSequenceArray()

    def logFileSequenceNumber(self):
        return self._mftHeader.logFileSequenceNumber()

    def sequenceNumber(self):
        return self._mftHeader.sequenceNumber()

    def hardLinkCount(self):
        return self._mftHeader.hardLinkCount

    def attributeStart(self):
        return self._mftHeader.attributeStart()

    def flags(self):
        return self._mftHeader.flags()

    def inUse(self):
        return self._mftHeader.inUse()

    def isDirectory(self):
        return self._mftHeader.isDirectory()

    def logicalRecordSize(self):
        return self._mftHeader.logicalRecordSize()

    def physicalRecordSize(self):
        return self._mftHeader.physicalRecordSize()
```

```python
    def baseFileReference(self):
        return self._mftHeader.baseFileReference()

    def baseFileMft(self):
        return self._mftHeader.baseFileMft()

    def baseFileSequenceNumber(self):
        return self._mftHeader.baseFileSequenceNumber()

    def nextAttributeId(self):
        return self._mftHeader.nextAttributeId()

    def recordNumber(self):
        return self._mftHeader.recordNumber()


def main():
    parser=optparse.OptionParser()
    parser.add_option("-f", "--file", dest="filename",
                      help="image filename")
    parser.add_option("-o", "--offset", dest='offset',
                      help='offset in sectors to start of volume')

    parser.add_option("-e", "--entry", dest='entry',
                      help='MFT entry number')

    (options, args)=parser.parse_args()
    filename=options.filename
    if options.offset:
        offset=512 * int(options.offset)
    else:
        offset=0
    if options.entry:
        entry=int(options.entry)
    else:
        entry=0

    with open(filename, 'rb') as f:
        f.seek(offset)
        buffer=f.read(512)

    vbr=Vbr(buffer)
    print(vbr)
```

```
      # calculate the offset to the MFT entry
      mftOffset = (offset +  # offset to start of partition
              vbr.mftLcn() * # logical cluster number
              vbr.bytesPerSector() * # sector size
              vbr.sectorsPerCluster() + # sectors/cluster
              1024 * entry ) #
      with open(filename, `rb') as f:
          f.seek(mftOffset)
          buffer=f.read(1024)
      mftEntry=MftEntry(buffer)
      print(mftEntry)

if __name__=='__main__':
    main()
```

Extracting files and directories

Active@ Disk Editor is a nice free tool for working with filesystem images. The biggest limitation this tool has is that it will not permit files to be extracted. While it is certainly true that FTK Imager could be used for this purpose or the image could be mounted, having a Python script to extract files and directory $I30 files would be very convenient.

The script presented in this section can be used to extract files by MFT entry number from an image. This script has a few nice features. First, it will extract a file regardless of whether or not the file is deleted. If the filesystem image is mounted on your Linux forensic workstation, deleted files are not visible and hence cannot be extracted. Second, when extracting $I30 files for directories, the user can exclude or include the unused index buffers. Third, the script will handle fragmented MFTs. It will check for a fragmented MFT when performing the extract by verifying that the MFT entry number is correct. If the MFT is fragmented, this script can be used to extract the MFT and then pass that into the script when extracting other files. Because the MFT is stored in entry zero, it is guaranteed not to be in the fragmented portion of the MFT (if it is fragmented at all). Fourth, it is much faster to use scripting to extract a bunch of files than to navigate a graphical application such as FTK Imager. Fifth, any alternate data streams are automatically retrieved by this script. Alternate data streams are named $DATA attributes that are often abused by attackers and others trying to hide data. These will be covered more thoroughly in future chapters. Sixth, $I30 files are named "index-<directory name>" instead of having every file with the same name.

You might be concerned that a script that does all of these things must be extremely long. In actuality, the script is only 205 lines long and that is including the comments and whitespace. The complete script follows.

```
#!/usr/bin/python3
'''Simple script to extract a file or
directory using its MFT entry number.
Create by Dr. Phil Polstra (@ppolstra)
for PentesterAcademy.com.'''
```

CHAPTER 8 NTFS Filesystems

```python
from mft import *
import optparse
from vbr import Vbr

def mftOffset(entry, vbr):
   '''Given a Vbr object and MFT entry number
   this function will return the correct offset
   into a filesystem image assuming the MFT is
   NOT FRAGMENTED.'''
   return (vbr.mftLcn() *  # logical cluster number
   vbr.bytesPerSector() *  # sector size
   vbr.sectorsPerCluster() +  # sectors/cluster
   1024 * entry )  # MFT entry is 1k long

def main():
   parser=optparse.OptionParser()
   parser.add_option("-f", "--file", dest="filename",
            help="image filename")
   parser.add_option("-o", "--offset", dest='offset',
            help='offset in sectors to start of volume')
   parser.add_option("-e", "--entry", dest='entry',
            help='MFT entry number')
   parser.add_option('-d', '--directory', dest='directory',
            help='output directory')
   parser.add_option('-m', '--mft', dest='mftFile',
            help='MFT file')
   parser.add_option('-s', '--slack', dest='indxSlack', action='store_true',
            help='Included INDX buffer slack')

   (options, args)=parser.parse_args()
   filename=options.filename
   if options.offset:
      offset=512 * int(options.offset)
   else:
      offset=0
   if options.entry:
      entry=int(options.entry)
   else:
      entry=0

   if options.directory:
      outDir=options.directory
      if outDir[len(outDir)-1]!='/':
         outDir+='/'
   else:
      outDir='./'
```

```python
    with open(filename, 'rb') as f:
        f.seek(offset)
        buffer=f.read(512)

vbr=Vbr(buffer)

# calculate the offset to the MFT entry
mOffset = (offset + # offset to start of partition
           mftOffset(entry, vbr))

# did they supply a MFT files?
# only needed if MFT is fragmented
if options.mftFile:
    with open(options.mftFile, 'rb') as f:
        f.seek(entry * 1024)
        buffer=f.read(1024)
else:
    with open(filename, 'rb') as f:
        f.seek(mOffset)
        buffer=f.read(1024)

mftEntry=MftEntry(buffer)
# check for fragmented MFT
if mftEntry.recordNumber()!=entry:
    print('Fragmented MFT detected...Exiting')
    return -1

# get the filename attribute(s)
filenames=mftEntry.attributesOfType(0x30)
if len(filenames)==0:
    return

# if there is more than one filename get longest
if len(filenames) > 0:
    fnLength=0
    for fnEntry in filenames:
        if fnEntry.nameLength() > fnLength:
            fname=fnEntry.filename()
            fnLength=fnEntry.nameLength()
# take care of special cases
if fname[0]=='.':
    fname='root'
elif fname[0]=='$':
    fname='dollar'+fname[1:]
# file or directory?
```

```python
          if filenames[0].isDirectory():
             # get the $I30 file
             indexAllocs=mftEntry.attributesOfType(0xa0)
             if len(indexAllocs) > 0:
                # we don't handle the case of A0 in Attribute list
                # I have never seen this happen
                clusterList=[]
                for indexAlloc in indexAllocs:
                   clusterList+=indexAlloc.clusterList()
             bitmaps=mftEntry.attributesOfType(0xb0)
             if len(bitmaps)==1:
                print('Creating INDX file index-'+str(fname))
                with open(outDir+'index-'+str(fname), 'wb') as outFile:
                   for i in range(len(clusterList)):
                      if options.indxSlack or bitmaps[0].inUse(i):
                         outFile.write(vbr.getCluster(clusterList[i], filename))
          else:
             # get the file data
             # check for attribute list case
             attributeLists=mftEntry.attributesOfType(0x20)
             if len(attributeLists) > 0:
                # get the MFT entries that contain $80 attributes
                firstVcn=-1
                mftList=[]
                for attributeList in attributeLists:
                   recordList=attributeList.list()
                   for record in recordList:
                      if record.attributeType()==0x80:
                         if record.vcn()>firstVcn:
                            mftList.append(record.mft())
                            firstVcn=record.vcn()
                         else:
                            mftList.insert(0, record.mft())
                dataAttributes=[]
                for mftNo in mftList:
                   # get the MFT
                   # calculate the offset to the MFT entry
                   eOffset = (offset + # offset to start of partition
                         mftOffset(mftNo, vbr))

                   if options.mftFile:
                      with open(options.mftFile, 'rb') as f:
                         f.seek(mftNo * 1024)
                         buffer2=f.read(1024)
```

```python
        else:
            with open(filename, 'rb') as f:
                f.seek(eOffset)
                buffer2=f.read(1024)
        tEntry=MftEntry(buffer2)
        # check for fragmented MFT
        if tEntry.recordNumber()!=mftNo:
            print('Fragmented MFT detected...exiting')
            return -1
        dataAttributes+=tEntry.attributesOfType(0x80)
else:
    # get the cluster list or inline data
    dataAttributes=mftEntry.attributesOfType(0x80)
clusterList=[]
adsClusterList=[]
adsName=None
adsData=None
data=None
lastVcn=-1
adsLastVcn=-1

for dataAttr in dataAttributes:
    if dataAttr.hasName():
        # we have an alternate data stream
        adsName=dataAttr.name()
        if dataAttr.data():
            adsData=dataAttr.data()
        else:
            if dataAttr.firstVcn() > adsLastVcn:
                adsClusterList+=(dataAttr.clusterList())
                adsLastVcn=dataAttr.lastVcn()
            else:
                adsClusterList=dataAttr.clusterList()+adsClusterList
    else:
        # normal data stream
        if dataAttr.data():
            data=dataAttr.data()
        else:
            if dataAttr.firstVcn() > lastVcn:
                clusterList+=(dataAttr.clusterList())
                lastVcn=dataAttr.lastVcn()
            else:
                clusterList=dataAttr.clusterList()+clusterList
```

```
            # now write to the file(s)
            print("Extracting file "+str(fname))
            with open(outDir+str(fname), 'wb') as outFile:
               if data:
                  outFile.write(data)
               else:
                  for cluster in clusterList:
                     outFile.write(vbr.getCluster(cluster, filename))
            if adsName:
              print("Extracting alternate data stream", adsName, "for file", fname)
              with open(outDir+str(fname)+'-ads-'+adsName, 'wb') as outFile:
                 if adsData:
                    outFile.write(adsData)
                 else:
                    for cluster in adsClusterList:
                       outFile.write(vbr.getCluster(cluster, filename))

if __name__=='__main__':
   main()
```

The script begins by importing the modules created earlier and optparse (for processing command line arguments). The main method first creates an option parser and adds six options. The first three, "--file", "--offset", and "--entry", have been used in previous scripts. The new "--directory" option is used to specify an output directory for extracted files. The "--mft" option allows an MFT file to be passed in to speed things up and/or handle fragmented MFTs. The "--slack" option allows any empty index buffers to be included in the $I30 file. This option exists because many tools such as INDXParse will fail if these empty index buffers are omitted.

The VBR is read from the image. Using information from the VBR the offset to the MFT entry is calculated and the MFT entry is retrieved from the filesystem image or MFT file if one was supplied. The MFT entry number is verified in either case and the script will exit if it does not check out.

Filenames are retrieved from the MFT entry. If there are no filenames, this is not a valid base MFT entry and the script exits. We loop through the filenames and keep only the longest one. If the filename is "." (indicating the root directory) we change the filename to "root". If the name begins with "$" we change that to "dollar" to avoid complications with filenames beginning with a character used to reference environment variables in Linux.

Next we determine if the entry points to a file or directory. If it is a directory, the index buffer clusters numbers are retrieved and stored in a list. Then the $BITMAP ($B0) attribute is retrieved. A for loop is used to retrieve each index buffer and write it to the output file if the index buffer is marked as in-use in the $BITMAP or the "--slack" option was specified.

If the entry points to a file, we first check for the edge case of the large fragmented file which will have an attribute list. The attribute list is used to retrieve all of the MFT entries which house $DATA attributes. These MFT entries are then iterated in order to build a list

```
phil@i7laptop:~/book-windows/08-NTFS Filesystems$ ./extract.py -f /media/phil/TOSHIBA\ EXT/BU/images
/mystery.dd -o 206848 -e 2313 -d /tmp -s
Creating INDX file index-System32
phil@i7laptop:~/book-windows/08-NTFS Filesystems$ ls -l /tmp/index-System32
-rw-rw-r-- 1 phil phil 655360 Jun 15 15:18 /tmp/index-System32
phil@i7laptop:~/book-windows/08-NTFS Filesystems$ ./extract.py -f /media/phil/TOSHIBA\ EXT/BU/images
/mystery.dd -o 206848 -e 22114 -d /tmp
Extracting file LibreOffice_4.3.4_Win_x86.msi
phil@i7laptop:~/book-windows/08-NTFS Filesystems$ ls -l /tmp/LibreOffice_4.3.4_Win_x86.msi
-rw-rw-r-- 1 phil phil 225689600 Jun 15 15:19 /tmp/LibreOffice_4.3.4_Win_x86.msi
phil@i7laptop:~/book-windows/08-NTFS Filesystems$ ./extract.py -f /media/phil/TOSHIBA\ EXT/BU/images
/mystery.dd -o 206848 -e 0 -d /tmp
Extracting file dollarMFT
phil@i7laptop:~/book-windows/08-NTFS Filesystems$ ./extract.py -f /media/phil/TOSHIBA\ EXT/BU/images
/mystery.dd -o 206848 -e 22000 -m /tmp/dollarMFT -d /tmp
Extracting file 8EA86C033C277996C7EE317E0F0E3B25_FA28DE7789074807CA48B6AD8BDB213C
phil@i7laptop:~/book-windows/08-NTFS Filesystems$ ls -l /tmp/8EA86C033C277996C7EE317E0F0E3B25_FA28DE
7789074807CA48B6AD8BDB213C
-rw-rw-r-- 1 phil phil 4096 Jun 15 15:21 /tmp/8EA86C033C277996C7EE317E0F0E3B25_FA28DE7789074807CA48B
6AD8BDB213C
phil@i7laptop:~/book-windows/08-NTFS Filesystems$ ./extract.py -f /media/phil/TOSHIBA\ EXT/BU/images
/mystery.dd -o 206848 -e 460 -m /tmp/dollarMFT -d /tmp
Creating INDX file index-Users
phil@i7laptop:~/book-windows/08-NTFS Filesystems$ ls -l /tmp/index-Users
-rw-rw-r-- 1 phil phil 4096 Jun 15 15:22 /tmp/index-Users
phil@i7laptop:~/book-windows/08-NTFS Filesystems$
```

FIGURE 8.54.

Some example uses of the extract.py script.

of $DATA attributes. For the normal case the list of $DATA attributes will contain the single $DATA attribute from the only MFT entry.

We loop over the $DATA attribute list in order to build a cluster list. We also build an alternate data stream cluster list if a named $DATA attribute exists. I should point out that I have not handled the edge case of a file that has more than one alternate data stream. Once the cluster list is complete, it is used to create the extracted file. If an alternate data stream was found, a second file is created. Several examples of using this new script (including extracting and using the MFT) are shown in Figure 8.54.

The script presented in this section offers a glimpse into what is possible with a suite of NTFS Python classes in hand. This script could be easily expanded to analyze extracted files to determine the file type, etc. Our codebase could be used to search a filesystem for deleted files and directories and automatically extract them. A similar script that finds and extracts files with alternate data streams could be written. The possibilities are endless. In the next section we will leverage our work in order to create timelines.

TIMELINES

Building a proper timeline can help you understand what happened on the subject system. Earlier in this book we discussed how to build a miniature timeline. In this section we will show you how to extract all of the timestamps from a filesystem and use them to maximum advantage.

Extracting information from an image

The script presented in this section will extract Modified, Accessed, Record changed, and Created (MARC) timestamps. The script requires an MFT file and will optionally accept a filesystem image and offset to the start of a partition. All timestamps from the $STANDARD_INFORMATION and $FILE_NAME attributes are retrieved from the MFT and printed in Comma Separated Value (CSV) format. If a filesystem image is passed to the script, the MARC timestamps from all index buffers are also retrieved. In order to avoid collisions with dates, times, and filenames a semicolon (rather than a comma) is used as a separator. The script follows.

```
#!/usr/bin/python3
'''Simple script to extract timeline info.
This script will extract just infomation
found in MFT or also include index buffers
if an image file is given.
Create by Dr. Phil Polstra (@ppolstra)
for PentesterAcademy.com.'''

from mft import *
import optparse
from vbr import Vbr
import time

def printHeader():
    '''Prints the header listing columns.'''
    print('Source;AccessDate;AccessTime;ModifyDate;ModifyTime;'
        'CreateDate;CreateTime;RecordChangeDate;RecordChangeTime;'
        'MftEntry;UpdateSequence;'
        'Attributes;FileSize;AllocatedSize;Filename')

def printLine(source, accessTs, modifyTs, createTs, recordChangeTs,
            mftNo, updateSeq,
            attributes, fileSize=0, allocatedSize=0,
filename='<unknown>'):
    '''This function creates the CSV line.'''
    print(source,              # where is this from
        time.strftime('%Y-%m-%d', accessTs),
        time.strftime('%H:%M:%S', accessTs),
        time.strftime('%Y-%m-%d', modifyTs),
        time.strftime('%H:%M:%S', modifyTs),
        time.strftime('%Y-%m-%d', createTs),
        time.strftime('%H:%M:%S', createTs),
        time.strftime('%Y-%m-%d', recordChangeTs),
        time.strftime('%H:%M:%S', recordChangeTs),
        mftNo, updateSeq,
```

```python
            attributes, fileSize, allocatedSize, '"'+str(filename)+'"',
            sep=';')

def main():
    parser=optparse.OptionParser()
    parser.add_option("-f", "--file", dest="filename",
            help="image filename")
    parser.add_option("-o", "--offset", dest='offset',
            help='offset in sectors to start of volume')
    parser.add_option('-m', '--mft', dest='mftFile',
            help='MFT file')

    (options, args)=parser.parse_args()
    filename=options.filename
    if options.offset:
        offset=512 * int(options.offset)
    else:
        offset=0
    # if we have an image file grab VBR
    if options.filename:
        with open(options.filename, 'rb') as f:
            f.seek(offset)
            buffer=f.read(512)

        vbr=Vbr(buffer)

    # MFT file is a required option
    if not options.mftFile:
        print('Sorry, this script requires an MFT file')
        return -1

    # now open the MFT file and get all the info for each entry
    with open(options.mftFile, 'rb') as mftF:
        buffer=mftF.read(1024)
        printHeader()
        while buffer:
            mftEntry=MftEntry(buffer)
            # do filenames first
            fnames = mftEntry.attributesOfType(0x30)
            if len(fnames)>0:
                for fnameAttr in fnames:
                    printLine('F', fnameAttr.accessTime(),
                        fnameAttr.modificationTime(),
                        fnameAttr.creationTime(),
                        fnameAttr.recordChangeTime(),
```

```
                        mftEntry.recordNumber(), mftEntry.sequenceNumber(),
                        fnameAttr.flags(),
                        fnameAttr.logicalSize(),
                        fnameAttr.physicalSize(),
                        fnameAttr.filename())
                # now get the standard info
                # this is done second so we can get size and filename
                for stdInfo in mftEntry.attributesOfType(0x10):
                    printLine('S', stdInfo.accessTime(),
                        stdInfo.modificationTime(),
                        stdInfo.creationTime(),
                        stdInfo.recordChangeTime(),
                        mftEntry.recordNumber(), mftEntry.sequenceNumber(),
                        stdInfo.flags(),
                        fnameAttr.logicalSize(),
                        fnameAttr.physicalSize(),
                        fnameAttr.filename())
                # now get the index buffers, but only if you gave
                # me an image file
                if options.filename and mftEntry.isDirectory():
                    indexAllocs=mftEntry.attributesOfType(0xA0)
                    for indexAlloc in indexAllocs:
                        # we don't handle the case of A0 in Attribute list
                        # I have never seen this happen
                        clusterList=[]
                        clusterList+=indexAlloc.clusterList()
                        # build $I30 file in memory
                        indxBuffer=b''
                        for clusterNo in clusterList:
                            indxBuffer+=vbr.getCluster(clusterNo, filename)
                        indexAlloc.getEntries(indxBuffer)
                        for i in range(indexAlloc.numberOfEntries()):
                            indexEntry=indexAlloc.entry(i)
                            printLine('I', indexEntry.accessTime(),
                                indexEntry.modificationTime(),
                                indexEntry.creationTime(),
                                indexEntry.recordChangeTime(),
                               indexEntry.mft(), indexEntry.sequenceNumber(),
                                indexEntry.flags(),
                                indexEntry.logicalSize(),
                                indexEntry.physicalSize(),
                                indexEntry.filename())
            buffer=mftF.read(1024)

if __name__=='__main__':
    main()
```

The script begins with the usual she-bang line followed by a few imports. Two helper functions are defined. The printHeader function prints a header at the start of the output in order to identify all of the fields and make it easier to import this data into a spreadsheet or database. The other helper function, printLine, is used to print out each line of data. It uses the "sep" option for print to change the default separator from a space to a semicolon. In order to make report generation easier the timestamps are broken out into separate date and time fields. The filenames are surrounded by double quotes in order to avoid trouble with filenames containing spaces or characters with special meanings in Linux.

The main function is straightforward. It begins by setting up an option parser to handle the command line parameters. If a filesystem image was given, the VBR is retrieved (in order to grab index buffers later). We then walk through the MFT and extract $FILE_NAME timestamps and then $STANDARD_INFORMATION timestamps. If a filesystem image was given and an MFT entry points to a directory, the appropriate index buffers are retrieved and all of the timestamps from the index entries are extracted as well. Note that any index entries in the $INDEX_ROOT are not extracted by this script, but that could easily be added if desired. The first lines of output from this script run against a Windows 7 subject are shown in Figure 8.55. It took less than 45 seconds to run this script against a 20 GB filesystem image.

```
phil@i7laptop:~/book-windows/08-NTFS Filesystems$
phil@i7laptop:~/book-windows/08-NTFS Filesystems$ ./get-macs.py -f /media/phil/TOSHIBA\ EXT/BU/image
s/mystery.dd -o 206848 -m /tmp/dollarMFT |more
Source;AccessDate;AccessTime;ModifyDate;ModifyTime;CreateDate;CreateTime;RecordChangeDate;RecordChan
geTime;MftEntry;UpdateSequence;Attributes;FileSize;AllocatedSize;Filename
F;2014-11-14;23:27:49;2014-11-14;23:27:49;2014-11-14;23:27:49;2014-11-14;23:27:49;0;1;6;16384;16384;
"$MFT"
S;2014-11-14;23:27:49;2014-11-14;23:27:49;2014-11-14;23:27:49;2014-11-14;23:27:49;0;1;6;16384;16384;
"$MFT"
F;2014-11-14;23:27:49;2014-11-14;23:27:49;2014-11-14;23:27:49;2014-11-14;23:27:49;1;1;6;4096;4096;"$
MFTMirr"
S;2014-11-14;23:27:49;2014-11-14;23:27:49;2014-11-14;23:27:49;2014-11-14;23:27:49;1;1;6;4096;4096;"$
MFTMirr"
F;2014-11-14;23:27:49;2014-11-14;23:27:49;2014-11-14;23:27:49;2014-11-14;23:27:49;2;2;6;67108864;671
08864;"$LogFile"
S;2014-11-14;23:27:49;2014-11-14;23:27:49;2014-11-14;23:27:49;2014-11-14;23:27:49;2;2;6;67108864;671
08864;"$LogFile"
F;2014-11-14;23:27:49;2014-11-14;23:27:49;2014-11-14;23:27:49;2014-11-14;23:27:49;3;3;6;0;0;"$Volume
"
S;2014-11-14;23:27:49;2014-11-14;23:27:49;2014-11-14;23:27:49;2014-11-14;23:27:49;3;3;6;0;0;"$Volume
"
F;2014-11-14;23:27:49;2014-11-14;23:27:49;2014-11-14;23:27:49;2014-11-14;23:27:49;4;4;6;36000;36864;
"$AttrDef"
S;2014-11-14;23:27:49;2014-11-14;23:27:49;2014-11-14;23:27:49;2014-11-14;23:27:49;4;4;6;36000;36864;
"$AttrDef"
F;2014-11-14;23:27:49;2014-11-14;23:27:49;2014-11-14;23:27:49;2014-11-14;23:27:49;5;5;268435462;0;0;
"."
```

FIGURE 8.55.

The start of output from the get-macs.py script.

Importing into a spreadsheet

Importing the timestamp information into a spreadsheet is fairly simple. Run the script from the previous section and redirect the output to a file by appending >myfile.csv to the end of the command line. Open the file in LibreOffice Calc and ensure that the semicolon box is checked in the "Separator options" as shown in Figure 8.56. Be sure to set the format for the date fields correctly as shown in Figure 8.57.

Sorting spreadsheets was discussed earlier in this book. The spreadsheet in Figure 8.56 con-

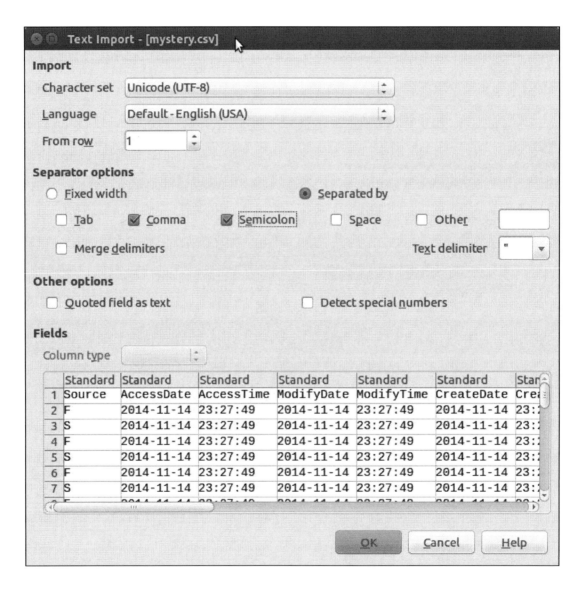

FIGURE 8.56.

Importing a timeline CSV file into LibreOffice Calc.

tains 300,000 rows. Depending on your installed memory it can take some time (possibly hours) to sort such a large file. Recall that the procedure is to select the relevant rows and then chose Sort from the Data menu. You should be greeted with a dialog like the one in Figure 8.58. If columns are listed by letter, be sure to check "Range contains column labels" on the options tab.

Sorting a large spreadsheet can bring a computer to its knees. An alternative would be to sort the CSV file on the command line before importing. The sort utility can be used for this purpose. A better alternative is to import the information into a proper database for maximum performance and flexibility.

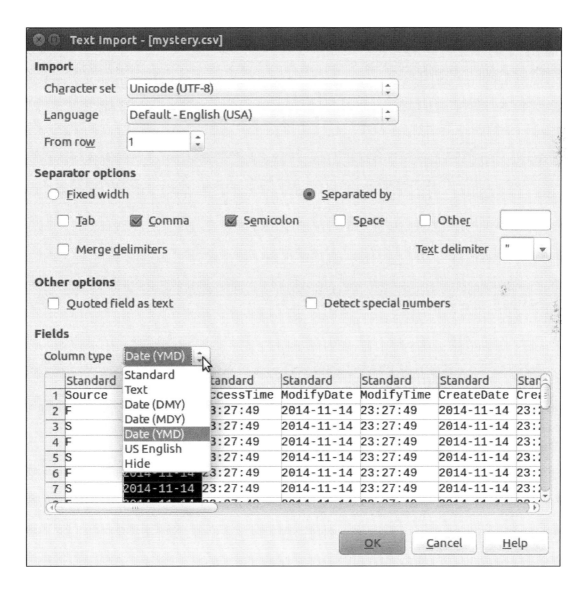

FIGURE 8.57.

Setting the field format for dates.

CHAPTER 8 NTFS Filesystems

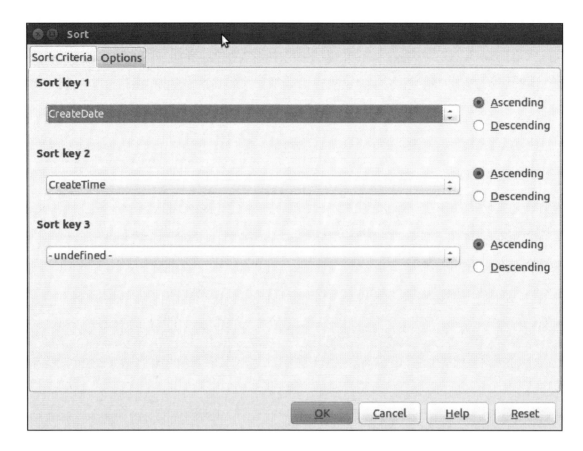

FIGURE 8.58.

Sorting timestamps by creation date and time.

Importing into a database

The timestamp information in a CSV file is easily imported into a database. There are several choices for a database management system on Linux. MySQL is one of the top choices. If it is not already installed, running `sudo apt-get install mysql-server` should remedy the situation for any Debian or Ubuntu based Linux distributions.

Once the MySQL program is installed, a database needs to be created. The mysqladmin tool is used to create a database. The syntax for creating a database is `mysqladmin -u <username> -p create <databases name>`. The -u option allows you to specify a user and the -p causes it to ask for a password (there are other methods of authentication possible, but this is the easiest and set up by default). There are other ways of creating databases, but this is one of the simplest. I like to create a new database for each case to keep things simple.

A database with no tables is not very useful. To create some tables first log into the MySQL client using `mysql -u <username> -p`. You must connect to a database by typing `connect <database name>` in the client. Creating a database and connecting to it from

```
phil@i7laptop:~$ mysqladmin -u root -p create winfor-book
Enter password:
phil@i7laptop:~$ mysql -u root -p
Enter password:
Welcome to the MySQL monitor.  Commands end with ; or \g.
Your MySQL connection id is 38
Server version: 5.5.49-0ubuntu0.14.04.1 (Ubuntu)

Copyright (c) 2000, 2016, Oracle and/or its affiliates. All rights reserved.

Oracle is a registered trademark of Oracle Corporation and/or its
affiliates. Other names may be trademarks of their respective
owners.

Type 'help;' or '\h' for help. Type '\c' to clear the current input statement.

mysql> connect winfor-book
Connection id:    39
Current database: winfor-book

mysql>
```

FIGURE 8.59.

Creating and connecting to a MySQL database.

the MySQL client is shown in Figure 8.59. The following SQL command will create a table called files that stores all the pertinent metadata.

```
create table files (
       Source char(1) not null,
       AccessDate date not null,
       AccessTime time not null,
       ModifyDate date not null,
       ModifyTime time not null,
       CreateDate date not null,
       CreateTime time not null,
       RecordModDate date not null,
       RecordModTime time not null,
       MftEntry bigint not null,
       SequenceNumber smallint not null,
       Permissions int not null,
       FileSize bigint not null,
       AllocatedSize bigint not null,
       Filename varchar(256) not null,
       recno bigint not null auto_increment,
       primary key(recno)
);
```

This command can be typed into the MySQL client, copied and pasted from a file, or run directly in MySQL. If you are not familiar with MySQL, it is a relational database. These types of databases have been around for decades. Complete coverage of MySQL is well out of scope for this book on forensics. As you will see, when you initially start the MySQL client, help is available by typing "help" into the tool.

Like many other databases, MySQL uses semicolons to terminate commands. The syntax for the create table command used here is `create table <tablename> (<field 1> <type> [not null] [options], <field 2> <type> [not null] [options], ... <field n> <type> [not null] [options], [primary key(<field>)] );`. MySQL supports several data types including fixed and variable length strings, dates, times, integers of various sizes, and floating point numbers.

Relational databases have the concept of a field being null. In this context null means that something does not exist. It is different from being blank. By declaring a field to be "not null", records (also called rows) cannot be inserted into a database table if the field is omitted. A primary key is used to uniquely identify a record in a table. The recno field is used as the primary key in this table. The line `recno bigint not null auto_increment` declares recno to be the largest size integer possible and every time a new record is inserted in this table MySQL will increment an internal counter and insert its current value into recno automatically. Creating this table is shown in Figure 8.60.

Tables can be listed in the MySQL client by typing `show tables;`. Table details are displayed using `desc <tablename>;`. Data can be loaded using normal SQL statements such as INSERT. In our case we want to use a MySQL command that will accept a CSV file in

```
mysql> create table files (
    -> Source char(1) not null,
    -> AccessDate date not null,
    -> AccessTime time not null,
    -> ModifyDate date not null,
    -> ModifyTime time not null,
    -> CreateDate date not null,
    -> CreateTime time not null,
    -> RecordModDate date not null,
    -> RecordModTime time not null,
    -> MftEntry bigint not null,
    -> SequenceNumber smallint not null,
    -> Permissions int not null,
    -> FileSize bigint not null,
    -> AllocatedSize bigint not null,
    -> Filename varchar(256) not null,
    -> recno bigint not null auto_increment,
    -> primary key(recno)
    -> );
Query OK, 0 rows affected (0.10 sec)

mysql>
```

FIGURE 8.60.

Creating a table in MySQL to store file metadata.

order to load the file metadata we retrieved from the filesystem image. The required command follows.

```
load data infile '/tmp/case-mystery.csv' into table files
fields terminated by ';'
enclosed by '"'
lines terminated by '\n'
ignore 1 rows
(Source, @AccessDate, AccessTime, @ModifyDate, ModifyTime, @CreateDate,
CreateTime, @RecordModDate, RecordModTime, MftEntry,
SequenceNumber, Permissions, FileSize, AllocatedSize, Filename)
set AccessDate=str_to_date(@AccessDate, "%Y-%m-%d"),
ModifyDate=str_to_date(@ModifyDate, "%Y-%m-%d"),
CreateDate=str_to_date(@CreateDate, "%Y-%m-%d"),
RecordModDate=str_to_date(@RecordModDate, "%Y-%m-%d");
```

Let us walk through this command. The first line says we would like to load data in a file stored in /tmp into the files table. There is a reason that /tmp is used for the load. Only files from approved directories can be loaded into MySQL. This is done to prevent certain attacks when MySQL is used with a webserver. The /tmp directory is on the approved list by default and it is easier to use it than to reconfigure MySQL to accept files from another location. In addition to location, the files should be owned by the mysql user. The file ownership is easily changed by running `sudo chown mysql <filename>` at the command line.

The second line says that fields are separated by semicolons and the next says that string may be enclosed in double quotes. The following two lines say that each line (which contains one record) is terminated by a newline and the first row should be ignored because it contains a header.

If all of the fields were simple strings and numbers this SQL command would be very simple. Unfortunately, the date fields make things more complicated. Because dates can be in several different formats the str_to_date function is used to convert a string containing a date in a certain format to a MySQL date object. The items beginning with "@" create a user variable from the input. For example, @AccessDate causes the second field in the input line to be assigned to @AccessDate. Later the line `set AccessDate=str_to_date(@AccessDate, "%Y-%m-%d")` uses this @AccessDate variable as an input to str_to_date in order to insert the correct value into the AccessDate field (column). The loading process is shown in Figure 8.61. Notice that it took only 11 seconds to load 299,904 rows.

With all of the file metadata now in the database all kinds of queries can be performed. The date sort that brought LibreOffice Calc to its knees can be done in MySQL. The SQL command is simply `select * from files order by AccessDate desc, AccessTime desc;`. The output from this command should be stored in a file (possibly a CSV file for import into Calc?). If you run this command in the MySQL client, it may appear to take a long time. In actuality the query runs quickly (under a second), but displaying the results to the screen can be slow. We will discuss ways of printing proper timelines in the next section.

```
mysql> load data infile '/tmp/case-mystery.csv' into table files
    -> fields terminated by ';'
    -> enclosed by '"'
    -> lines terminated by '\n'
    -> ignore 1 rows
    -> (Source, @AccessDate, AccessTime, @ModifyDate, ModifyTime, @CreateDate,
    -> CreateTime, @RecordModDate, RecordModTime, MftEntry,
    -> SequenceNumber, Permissions, FileSize, AllocatedSize, Filename)
    -> set AccessDate=str_to_date(@AccessDate, "%Y-%m-%d"),
    -> ModifyDate=str_to_date(@ModifyDate, "%Y-%m-%d"),
    -> CreateDate=str_to_date(@CreateDate, "%Y-%m-%d"),
    -> RecordModDate=str_to_date(@RecordModDate, "%Y-%m-%d");
Query OK, 299904 rows affected, 1 warning (11.12 sec)
Records: 299904  Deleted: 0  Skipped: 0  Warnings: 1

mysql>
```

FIGURE 8.61.

Loading file metadata into MySQL.

Printing timelines

To create a proper timeline with operations listed in chronological order (not separated by operation) we need a new table in the database. This table will store an operation code, source, date, time, and a reference to a record in the files table (the appropriate recno as this is the primary key for the files table). This new table, timeline, is a cross reference table. These types of tables do not normally have primary keys. The command to create this table follows.

```
create table timeline (
Operation char(1),
Source char(1),
Date date not null,
Time time not null,
Recno bigint not null
);
```

Information is inserted into the new table by performing a set of queries and using the results for the insert operation. This is not as difficult as it sounds. Figure 8.62 shows this table being created and populated. Notice that this entire process took about 17 seconds. The required queries follow.

```
insert into timeline (Operation, Source, Date, Time, recno)
select "A", Source, AccessDate, AccessTime, recno from files;
```

```
insert into timeline (Operation, Source, Date, Time, recno)
select "M", Source, ModifyDate, ModifyTime, recno from files;
insert into timeline (Operation, Source, Date, Time, recno)
select "C", Source, CreateDate, CreateTime, recno from files;
insert into timeline (Operation, Source, Date, Time, recno)
select "R", Source, RecordModDate, RecordModTime, recno from files;
```

Creating a timeline report using this new table requires a SQL query. To display the operation, source, date, time, and filename, the syntax for the query is as follows: `select operation, timeline.source, timeline.date, timeline.time, filename from files, timeline where timeline.date >= str_to_date('<start date>', '%Y-%m-%d') and timeline.date < str_to_date('<end date>', '%Y-%m-%d') and files.recno = timeline.recno order by timeline.date desc, timeline.time desc;`. For example, the query to obtain a full timeline for November 14, 2014, is as follows: `select operation, timeline.source, timeline.date, timeline.time, filename from files, timeline where timeline.date >= str_to_date('2014-11-14', '%Y-%m-%d') and timeline.date < str_to_date('2014-11-15', '%Y-%m-%d') and files.recno = timeline.recno order by timeline.date desc, timeline.time desc;`. This query retrieved 726,008 rows in under two seconds.

The SQL query in the previous paragraph selects information from multiple tables (files and timeline). Because of this, columns that are common to both tables must be prefixed with

```
mysql> create table timeline (
    -> Operation char(1),
    -> Source char(1),
    -> Date date not null,
    -> Time time not null,
    -> Recno bigint not null
    -> );
Query OK, 0 rows affected (0.11 sec)

mysql> insert into timeline (Operation, Source, Date, Time, recno)
    -> select "A", Source, AccessDate, AccessTime, recno from files;
Query OK, 299904 rows affected (3.89 sec)
Records: 299904  Duplicates: 0  Warnings: 0

mysql> insert into timeline (Operation, Source, Date, Time, recno)
    -> select "M", Source, ModifyDate, ModifyTime, recno from files;
Query OK, 299904 rows affected (5.09 sec)
Records: 299904  Duplicates: 0  Warnings: 0

mysql> insert into timeline (Operation, Source, Date, Time, recno)
    -> select "C", Source, CreateDate, CreateTime, recno from files;
Query OK, 299904 rows affected (4.28 sec)
Records: 299904  Duplicates: 0  Warnings: 0

mysql> insert into timeline (Operation, Source, Date, Time, recno)
    -> select "R", Source, RecordModDate, RecordModTime, recno from files;
Query OK, 299904 rows affected (4.26 sec)
```

FIGURE 8.62.

Creating and populating the timeline table.

"<tablename>." to avoid any ambiguity. One of the where clauses must join (link) the two tables together. This is the purpose of the files.recno = timeline.recno clause.

It is quite likely that you will want to run a query like the one in the preceding paragraph many times. A simple shell script can make this a lot less tedious. The shell script that follows will accept a database name, starting date, and optional ending date and print out the relevant timeline records.

```bash
#!/bin/bash
#
# print-timeline.sh
#
# Simple script to print a timeline
#
# Created by Dr. Phil Polstra (@ppolstra)
# for PentesterAcademy.com

usage () {
        echo "usage: $0 <database> <starting date> [ending date]"
        echo "Simple script to get timeline from the database"
        exit 1
}

if [ $# -lt 2 ] ; then
      usage
fi

# no end date given
if [ $# -lt 3 ] ; then
      cat << EOF | mysql $1 -u root -p
      select Operation, timeline.source, timeline.date, timeline.time,
      filename, mftEntry, sequenceNumber, filesize, allocatedSize
      from files, timeline
      where timeline.date >= str_to_date("$2", "%Y-%m-%d") and
      files.recno = timeline.recno
      order by timeline.date desc, timeline.time desc;
EOF
else
      cat << EOF | mysql $1 -u root -p
      select Operation, timeline.source, timeline.date, timeline.time,
      filename, mftEntry, sequenceNumber, filesize, allocatedSize
      from files, timeline
      where timeline.date >= str_to_date("$2", "%Y-%m-%d") and
      timeline.date < str_to_date("$3", "%Y-%m-%d") and
      files.recno = timeline.recno
      order by timeline.date desc, timeline.time desc;
EOF
fi
```

Timelines   417

The script begins with the standard she-bang line. A usage function is defined. If the number of command line arguments ($#) is less than two, the usage function is called and the script exits. The script branches based on whether or not an end date was specified. This script could have been shorter and more elegant, but I chose simplicity instead.

The lines `cat << EOF | mysql $1 -u root -p` might require a little explanation if you are unfamiliar with shell scripting. The construct `cat << <marker>` is used to send a multi-line string to standard out. This string terminates when the marker occurs on a line by itself. The marker "EOF" is traditionally used, but any string will work. In this script what happens is that the SQL query is sent to standard out. Because this is piped to MySQL, the query is run and the results sent to standard out. The passed in database, start date, and end date are substituted for $1, $2, and $3, respectively.

The output from this script can be captured to a file which is then opened in LibreOffice Calc or some other tool. The default out format from MySQL is tab delimited. Be sure to check the Tab box under "Separator options" when importing this file into Calc. A query for a one month period returning 758,752 records ran in only 6.2 seconds. This is less time than what Calc required to just open the file. The advantages of using a real database should be pretty obvious. This spreadsheet is over twice the size of the previous one that LibreOffice Calc could not sort in an hour and it was generated already sorted in seconds. The sorted spreadsheet is shown in Figure 8.63.

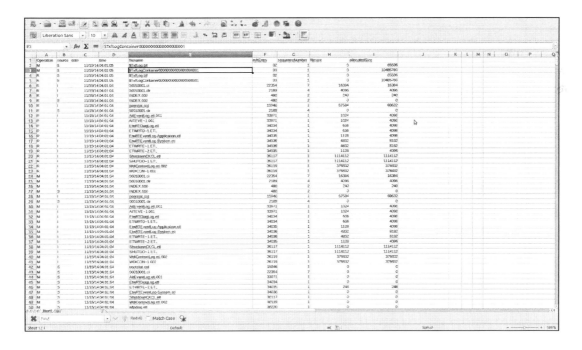

FIGURE 8.63.

Opening a large sorted set of timeline records in LibreOffice Calc.

Understanding timestamps

NTFS timestamp rules are often confusing to new forensic investigators. This is not surprising given that Microsoft has changed the timestamp rules in the past and probably will do so again in the future. Be warned that the rules presented in this section may change in the future. Microsoft has some knowledge base articles that outline these rules, including what happens if files move between NTFS and FAT filesystems.

We will examine what happens to $FILE_NAME and $STANDARD_INFORMATION timestamps when performing common file operations. We will begin with a file copy operation. The timestamp changes for this situation are summarized in Table 8.20. As can be seen from the table, only the modification time in $STANDARD_INFORMATION is unchanged.

What happens when a file is accessed? This scenario is summarized in Table 8.21. In this case nothing is changed, except for the $STANDARD_INFORMATION access time and then only if running a pre-Vista version of Windows. For newer versions of Windows the only changes are in the index entries.

What does it mean to modify a file? From Windows' perspective this means that the data in a file was written to disk. If you write the same contents to disk (perhaps because you have a dumb editor that will re-save the file even when it is unchanged) this still counts as a modification. Timestamp changes for file modifications are summarized in Table 8.22. Note that only the $STANDARD_INFORMATION modification timestamp is changed.

Table 8.20. Timestamp changes when copying a file.

	$STANDARD_INFOFORMATION	$FILE_NAME
Modification	No change	Changed
Access	Changed	Changed
Creation	Changed	Changed
Record Change	Changed	Changed

Table 8.21. Timestamp changes when accessing a file.

	$STANDARD_INFORMATION	$FILE_NAME
Modification	No change	No change
Access	Changed if pre-Vista	No change
Creation	No change	No change
Record Change	No change	No change

What happens when a file is deleted? None of the timestamps in the MFT are changed. As a consequence, when deleted files are recovered, they retain all of the original metadata. This scenario is summarize in Table 8.23.

As shown in Table 8.24. When a file is renamed only the record change time in $STANDARD_INFORMATION is updated. This might seem a bit bizarre, but the $FILE_NAME attributes do not reflect any changes when the filename is changed.

What happens when a file is moved? The answer depends on whether the file was moved to a different location on the same volume or a totally different volume. Timestamp updates for a

Table 8.22. Timestamp changes when modifying a file.

	$STANDARD_INFORMATION	$FILE_NAME
Modification	Changed	No change
Access	No change	No change
Creation	No change	No change
Record Change	No change	No change

Table 8.23. Timestamp changes when deleting a file.

	$STANDARD_INFORMATION	$FILE_NAME
Modification	No change	No change
Access	No change	No change
Creation	No change	No change
Record Change	No change	No change

Table 8.24. Timestamp changes when renaming a file.

	$STANDARD_INFORMATION	$FILE_NAME
Modification	No change	No change
Access	No change	No change
Creation	No change	No change
Record Change	Changed	No change

Table 8.25. Timestamp changes when moving a file within a volume.

	$STANDARD_INFORMATION	$FILE_NAME
Modification	No change	Changed to $SI time
Access	No change	No change
Creation	No change	No change
Record Change	Changed	Changed to $SI time

Table 8.26. Timestamp changes when moving a file to another volume.

	$STANDARD_INFORMATION	$FILE_NAME
Modification	No change	Changed
Access	Changed	Changed
Creation	No change	Changed
Record Change	Changed	Changed

file moved within a volume are summarized in Table 8.25. The new timestamps in the $FILE_NAME attribute are changed to match the $STANDARD_INFORMATION timestamps from before the move.

When a file is moved to a new volume, the rules are very different. This scenario is summarized in Table 8.26. Note that only the modification and creation times in $STANDARD_INFORMATION remain unchanged.

Because the timestamp rules are a bit complicated and have been known to change over time, examining timestamp information might uncover meddling from attackers. When looking at timelines such as those generated from the script in the previous section, an understanding of these rules will help an investigator separate the normal from the abnormal.

Printing timelines on a file-by-file basis

Sometimes it is more convenient to examine an individual file's timeline than to look at file operations on a system-wide chronological timeline. This can help you examine key system files. It is also easier to see altered timestamps when examining all timestamps for a file. The script presented in this section allows timeline records to be extracted for a single MFT entry or the entire volume. The script follows.

```bash
#!/bin/bash
#
# print-timeline.sh
#
# Simple script to print a timeline on a
# file-by-file basis.
#
# Created by Dr. Phil Polstra (@ppolstra)
# for PentesterAcademy.com

usage () {
      echo "usage: $0 <database> [mft record ID]"
      echo "Simple script to get timeline from the database"
      echo "on a file-by-file basis."
      exit 1
}

if [ $# -lt 1 ] ; then
      usage
fi

# no MFT record given
if [ $# -lt 2 ] ; then
      cat << EOF | mysql $1 -u root -p
      select Operation, timeline.source, timeline.date, timeline.time,
      filename, mftEntry, sequenceNumber, filesize, allocatedSize
      from files, timeline
      where files.recno = timeline.recno
      order by mftEntry, timeline.date, timeline.time;
EOF
else
      cat << EOF | mysql $1 -u root -p
      select Operation, timeline.source, timeline.date, timeline.time,
      filename, mftEntry, sequenceNumber, filesize, allocatedSize
      from files, timeline
      where files.recno = timeline.recno and
      files.mftEntry = $2
      order by mftEntry, timeline.date, timeline.time;
EOF
fi
```

This script is very similar to our other timeline script presented earlier. The only real difference is the SQL query. This query returns more fields, but the primary difference lies in the order by clause. Whereas the previous script ordered results by date and time, the new script orders them first by MFT entry, then date and time. An example of running this script for the \Windows\System32 directory only is shown in Figure 8.64.

```
phil@i7laptop:~/book-windows/08-NTFS Filesystems$ ./print-file-timeline.sh winfor-book 2313
Enter password:
Operation    source  date        time      filename    mftEntry    sequenceNumber    filesize    allocatedSize
C            I       2009-07-14  03:20:10  System32    2313        1                 0           0
C            S       2009-07-14  03:20:10  System32    2313        1                 0           0
R            F       2014-11-14  23:30:49  System32    2313        1                 0           0
C            F       2014-11-14  23:30:49  System32    2313        1                 0           0
M            F       2014-11-14  23:30:49  System32    2313        1                 0           0
A            F       2014-11-14  23:30:49  System32    2313        1                 0           0
R            I       2014-11-15  04:00:49  System32    2313        1                 0           0
R            S       2014-11-15  04:00:49  System32    2313        1                 0           0
M            I       2014-11-15  04:00:49  System32    2313        1                 0           0
M            S       2014-11-15  04:00:49  System32    2313        1                 0           0
A            I       2014-11-15  04:00:49  System32    2313        1                 0           0
A            S       2014-11-15  04:00:49  System32    2313        1                 0           0
phil@i7laptop:~/book-windows/08-NTFS Filesystems$
```

FIGURE 8.64.

All available timestamps for the \Windows\System32 directory on a Windows 7 subject.

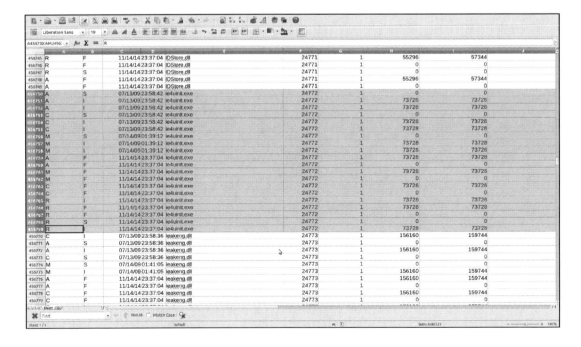

FIGURE 8.65.

All available timestamps for the \Windows\System32 directory on a Windows 7 subject.

Partial results from running the script against the entire filesystem image are shown in Figure 8.65. When examining all files or individual files, you are looking for inconsistencies. Note how only three different timestamps appear in all of the highlighted entries in the figure. This is generally what you should expect to see. If you see more than three different timestamps for one file some further investigation might be warranted.

SUMMARY

In this chapter we have learned to extract information from an NTFS filesystem. We also learned a bit more Python along the way and leveraged this to interpret NTFS filesystem structures, extract files, and create timelines. In the next chapter we will investigate something unique to Windows, the registry.

CHAPTER 9

The Windows Registry

INFORMATION IN THIS CHAPTER:

- Registry basics
- The system hive
- The software hive
- The SAM hive
- The user hive
- Registry viewing tools
- Information extraction with RegRipper

REGISTRY BASICS

Prior to Windows NT (the first real operating system version of Windows) configuration information for Windows and Windows applications could be found in .ini (pronounced eye-in-eye or inny) files. These text files were scattered all about the filesystem. Some were stored in the same location as the application, some in Windows directories, and some in seemingly random places. In order to improve the situation, Microsoft introduced the registry with the release of Windows NT in 1993.

What is the registry? It is a tree structure that houses nearly all configuration for Windows and applications. As we saw in the last chapter, some .ini files still remain. The registry uses a tree structure. This fact combined with centralizing the information in a few files (not lots of files scattered everywhere) leads to improved performance.

The registry editor, regedit, that ships with every version of Windows since Windows NT makes the registry appear to be a single large file. Regedit running on Windows 7 is shown in Figure 9.1. In fact, the registry is stored in at least five files that are called hive files. Most of these hives are stored in \Windows\System32\Config. Each user also has a user hive that is stored in their user directory. For Windows versions XP up to, but not including, Vista, this is the "\Documents and Settings\<username>" folder. For Windows Vista and newer systems it is \Users\<username>.

As can be seen in Figure 9.1, the registry is organized into several main branches: HKEY_CLASSES_ROOT, HKEY_CURRENT_USER, HKEY_LOCAL_MACHINE, HKEY_USERS, AND HKEY_CURRENT_CONFIG. Based on this, one might incorrectly assume that these branches correspond to the five hive files referenced earlier. In reality, all but the user hives are subbranches of HKEY_LOCAL_MACHINE.

The HKEY_CLASSES_ROOT branch is used to house information such as what programs can handle certain file types. HKEY_CURRENT_USER contains user specific settings for the currently logged in user. This branch is really just a symbolic link to the appropriate branch

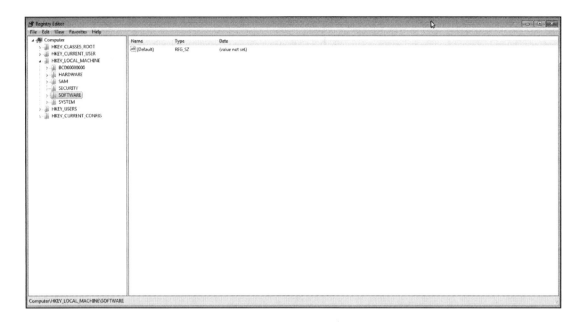

FIGURE 9.1.

Running regedit on a Windows 7 system.

under HKEY_USERS. Similarly, HKEY_CURRENT_CONFIG and HKEY_CLASSES_ROOT link to subbranches located under HKEY_LOCAL_MACHINE.

Because nearly everything is stored under HKEY_LOCAL_MACHINE, it is often abbreviated as HKLM. Four of the HKLM subbranches come directly from hive files. These are stored in files in \Windows\System32\Config named SAM, SECURITY, SOFTWARE, and SYSTEM. Some additional hives have been added in recent versions of Windows, but these four have been there since the beginning. Files with the same name but extensions such as .LOG, .LOG1, .LOG2, etc. may exist in this same directory. These log files store recent changes to the corresponding hive with .LOG being the most recent, then .LOG1, and so on.

Unlike the other hives, the user hive files have an extension. They are named NTUSER.DAT. These files also have log files stored in ntuser.dat.log1, ntuser.dat.log2, etc.

What is stored in each of these hives? The SAM hive is used to store login information. This includes user accounts (complete with password hashes) and groups. This hive is not normally viewable in tools such as regedit on a running system. Attackers will try to get this hive and then crack all of the user passwords offline. Surprisingly, the SECURITY hive contains no valuable security information and is also uninteresting to forensic investigators.

The SOFTWARE hive contains mappings of programs to file types. This part of the hive is typically uninteresting to forensic investigators. Installed programs have their configuration stored in this hive. This includes Windows and many of its components.

The SYSTEM hive contains system-wide configuration information and also information

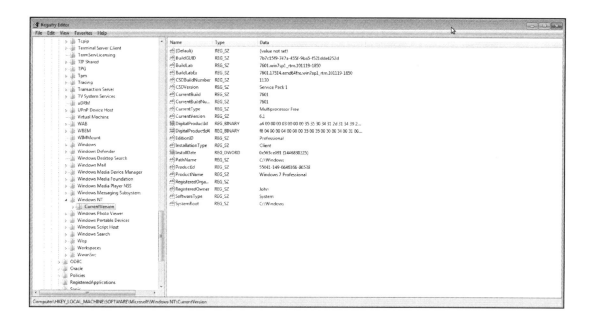

FIGURE 9.2.

Examining a registry node that contains multiple values.

that pertains to the system as a whole (such as the computer name). The user hive has System and Software branches that are used to store a user's overrides to items from SYSTEM and SOFTWARE. In a sense there is a hierarchy of hives with SYSTEM at the top, then SOFTWARE, and finally the user hives.

The original version of the registry allowed nodes to be created which could contain a single unnamed value. This was quickly changed to allow each node in the tree to have multiple named values. As seen in Figure 9.2, even when values are added to a node (sometimes called a key) a value named "(Default)" may also be present. There are a number of data types that may be stored in the registry. Some of the more common ones are summarized in Table 9.1.

The registry is a treasure trove of data for the forensic examiner. Because it stores so much data, many people do not realize the extent to which their actions can be tracked solely with examination of the registry. For example, the registry keeps track of every USB device ever connected (including thumb drives). As another example, uninstalling many applications does not remove all of the registry keys created during installation. We will examine several tools for extracting information from the registry in the remainder of this chapter.

EXTRACTING HIVE FILES

The easiest way to examine the registry is to first extract the hive files from a filesystem image. If you prefer a graphical tool for this purpose, FTK Imager is a good choice. As has been men-

Table 9.1. Common registry data types.

Data type	Description
REG_BINARY	Binary data that is not interpreted by Windows
REG_SZ	Null-terminated string (default type)
REG_EXPAND_SZ	Like REG_SZ, but environment variables are expanded when read
REG_DWORD	32-bit number in little endian format
REG_LINK	Unicode symbolic link
REG_QWORD	64-bit number in little endian format
REG_MULTI_SZ	Array of null-terminated strings (two nulls terminate the array)
REG_NONE	No defined type

tioned previously, this tool easily runs on Linux using the WINE (Wine Is Not an Emulator) tool that translates Win32 API calls to native Linux system calls. To run FTK Imager simply change to the directory where you have extracted it and type `wine ./FTK\ Imager.exe`.

Once the subject filesystem image has been loaded (using "Add evidence item") browse to the \Windows\System32\Config directory and select the SAM, SOFTWARE, and SYSTEM hives (Control-click for multiple selection). Right-click and select "Export Files" from the popup menu as shown in Figure 9.3. Do not forget to grab any user hives (NTUSER.DAT) from the user directories in \Users or "\Documents and Settings".

If you prefer to stay away from Windows applications, this extraction is easily done with the extract.py script presented in the previous chapter. This script requires the MFT entry number for each file to be extracted. This is easily found in Active@ Disk Editor (ADE). The Python modules from the previous chapter could also be used to obtain the MFT entry numbers for a fully scripted solution. Alternatively the filesystem image could be mounted and the hives copied or accessed directly.

EXAMINING THE REGISTRY

On a running Windows system most of the registry (everything but the SAM hive) can be viewed with regedit, assuming you have the proper permissions. When working with a filesystem image or hive files, different tools are required. These tools fall into two basic categories: offline registry viewers and analyzers.

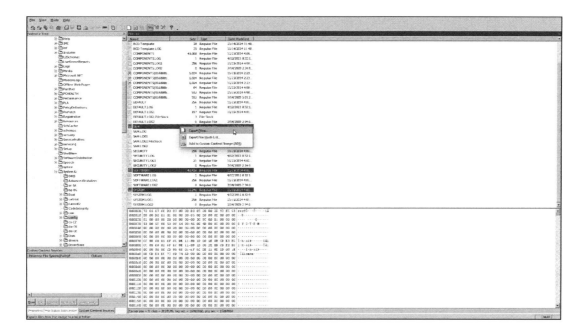

FIGURE 9.3.

Extracting some of the hive files from \Windows\System32\Config with FTK Imager.

Registry viewing tools

There are a number of tools available to view an offline registry. One of my personal favorites is the Forenic Registry Editor (FREd). FREd is an open source tool that is available for Linux and Windows. It is probably in your Linux system repositories. Installation on a Debian or Ubuntu based Linux is as simple as running `sudo apt-get install fred`.

While FREd might be available in standard repositories, the same is not usually true for the default reports provided. These can be downloaded as Debian packages from https://www.pinguin.lu/pkgserver and then installed by running `sudo dpkg -i <package file name>`. Alternatively, the appropriate software repository can be added using instructions on the same page.

Once FREd is running, a hive can be loaded by selecting "Open hive" from the File menu. As shown in Figure 9.4, FREd looks similar to regedit in that it has a tree view and key value view. To this basic functionality it adds a hex viewer and standard reports. These will be discussed in more detail shortly.

Access Data (makers of FTK Imager) offers a complete line of forensic tools. One of the tools in their suite is a registry viewer. This product can be downloaded from http://accessdata.com. If you do not have a security key (USB dongle) for their suite of products, this tool will be run in demo mode. In case you were to somehow miss this fact, two popups will be displayed to tell you this is only a demo. This tool is shown in Figure 9.5. As can be seen in the figure, this tool has a nice key properties pane that is displayed for a limited number of registry keys. This same information is displayed using reports in FREd.

430 CHAPTER 9 The Windows Registry

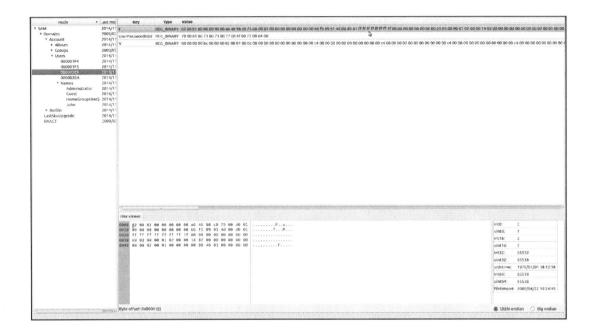

FIGURE 9.4.
The Forensic Registry Editor (FREd).

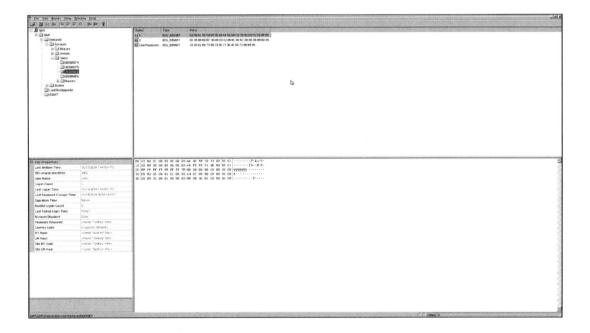

FIGURE 9.5.
The Access Data Registry Viewer tool.

The SAM hive

As previously mentioned, the SAM hive houses user account information. A user's account data can be found under SAM/SAM/Domains/Account/Users/<user ID> where <user ID> is the user number as a 32-bit hexadecimal number with leading zeros as required. Just as with Linux, the first regular user is normally assigned user ID 1001 (0x03E9). The user used to install Windows will have account information stored in SAM/SAM/Domains/Account/Users/000003E9 as shown in Figure 9.6.

As seen in Figure 9.6, user information is stored in three binary values: F, V, and UserPasswordHint. The password hint is simply the hint as a Unicode string. Decoding the F and V values is best left to automated tools. The user name to ID mapping is done by storing the user ID value in the default key in SAM/SAM/Domains/Account/Users/Names/<user name> as shown in Figure 9.7.

To easily get all of the pertinent information from the SAM hive, select "Generate report" from the Reports menu in FREd. If you do not see any reports listed, you likely forgot to download and install the reports as described earlier in this section. You should be greeted by a screen like the one shown in Figure 9.8.

A SAM report in FREd is shown in Figure 9.9. Looking at the John account we see that he has user ID 1001 (0x03E9), he last logged in 2014/11/15, he last changed his password on 2014/11/14, he has no failed logins, his account does not expire, he is not required to enter a password to log in, he has logged in twice, and his password hint is "password". Running this report is considerably easier than interpreting the F and V entries manually.

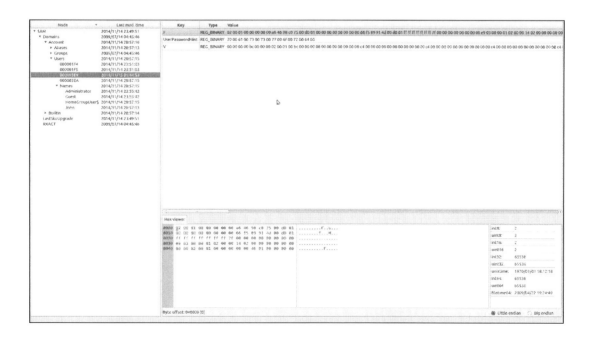

FIGURE 9.6.

Examining user account information in FREd.

CHAPTER 9 The Windows Registry

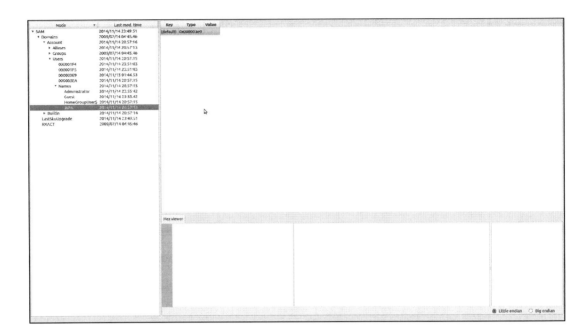

FIGURE 9.7.

Mapping user names to user IDs.

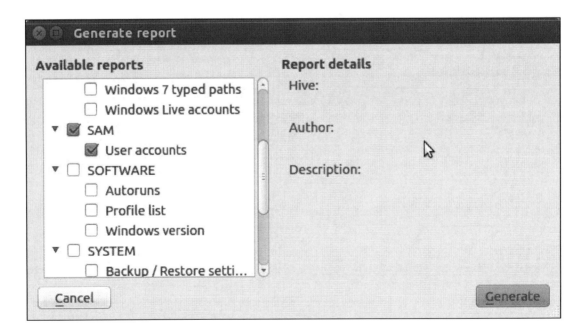

FIGURE 9.8.

Generating a report in FREd.

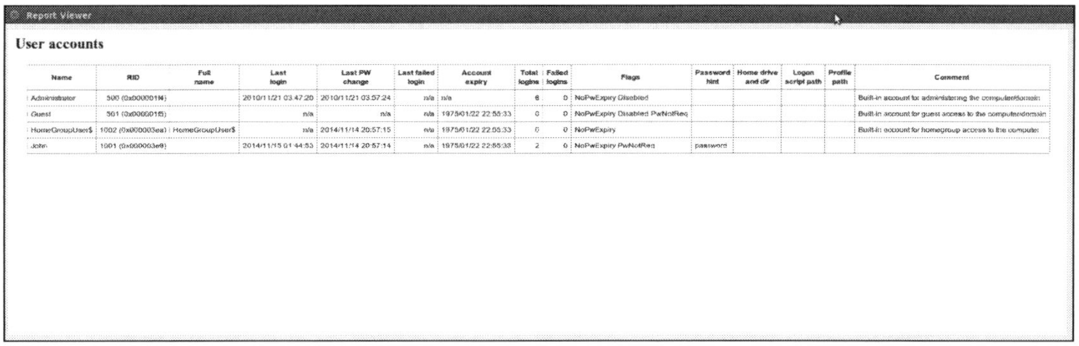

FIGURE 9.9.

The FREd SAM User accounts report.

The System hive

The system hive is at the top level of the registry hive hierarchy. What I mean by this is that it contains system-wide configuration information, whereas the software hive contains settings on a per software package basis and the user hives contain personal overrides and individual user activity information. Before we get started I should point out that many things have been pushed down to lower levels in the hierarchy with successive Windows releases. In other words, things that used to be system-wide settings have drifted toward being configurable by the individual users.

The top level of the system hive is shown in Figure 9.10. The first two branches are ControlSet001 and ControlSet002. ControlSet001 is the default configuration that is normally used. When the system is running, this SYSTEM/ControlSet001 branch is linked to HKEY_CURRENT_CONFIG. The remaining branches are used to store system-wide settings. Nearly everything that is interesting to the forensic examiner is found in the ControlSet001 branch of this hive.

The two subbranches under SYSTEM/ControlSet001 that contain the most interesting information for forensic examiners are Control and Enum. The Enum branch contains information on various types of devices that have been attached to a system. A somewhat expanded view of this branch is shown in Figure 9.11. The majority of relevant information is found in the Control branch.

As shown in Figure 9.12, the computer name can be found in SYSTEM/ControlSet001/Control/ComputerName/ComputerName/ComputerName. This repetition of names is common in the registry. For older versions of Windows this information might be found in SYSTEM/ControlSet001/Control/ComputerName/ActiveComputerName/ComputerName.

The last shutdown time can be found in SYSTEM/ControlSet001/Control/Windows/ShutdownTime as seen in Figure 9.13. This is a 64-bit timestamp just like the one used in NTFS. FREd will interpret these timestamps. The system in the figure was last shutdown on 2014/11/15 at 04:01:02 UTC.

Timezone information can be found in SYSTEM/ControlSet001/Control/TimeZoneInformation as seen in Figure 9.14. Windows stores the timezone name, daylight savings time

CHAPTER 9 The Windows Registry

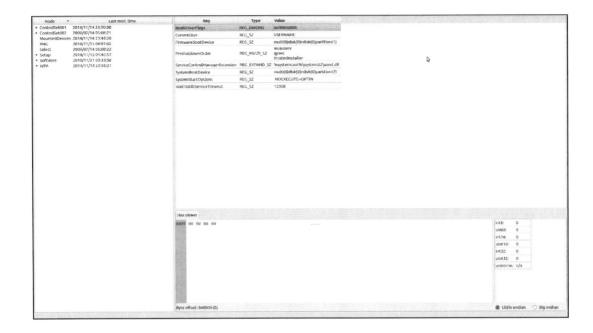

FIGURE 9.10.

The top level of the System hive as seen in FREd.

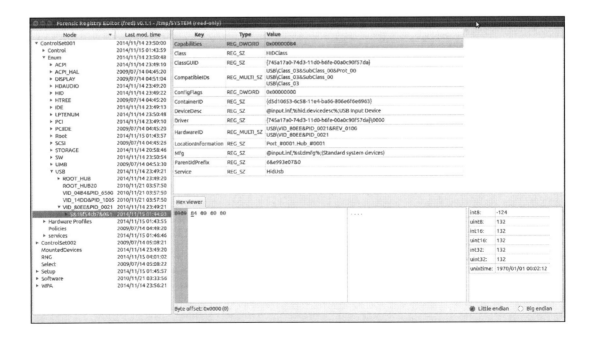

FIGURE 9.11.

The partially expanded SYSTEM/ControlSet001/Enum branch.

Examining the registry

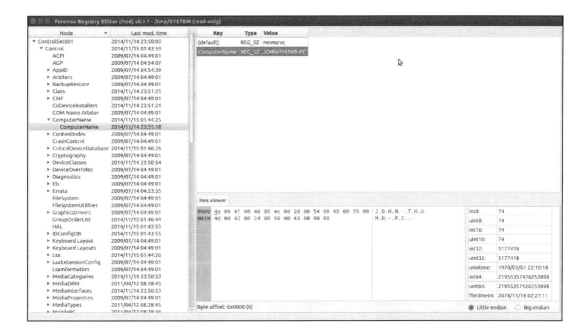

FIGURE 9.12.
Retrieving the computer name from the registry.

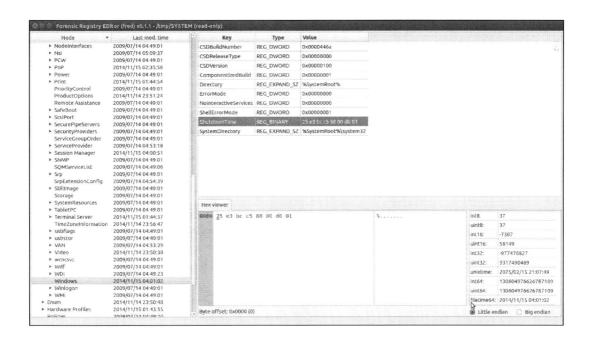

FIGURE 9.13.
Retrieving the last shutdown time from the registry.

436 CHAPTER 9 The Windows Registry

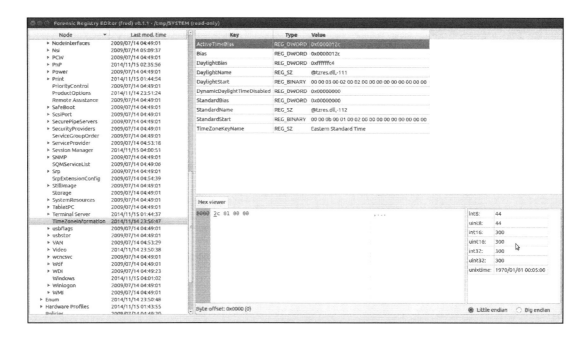

FIGURE 9.14.

Retrieving timezone information from the registry.

information, and offset from UTC in minutes in various keys in this node. The subject system in the figure is using Eastern Standard Time which is offset 300 minutes (5 hours) from UTC. It is important to know the timezone when interpreting timestamps because the UTC time in the timestamps is normally derived from the system clock which is usually set to local time. If the timezone is set incorrectly, these timestamps will be skewed.

Various networking information is available under SYSTEM/ControlSet001/Services/Tcpip. Drilling down a little further in this branch to Parameters/Interfaces/{GUID}, where GUID is the globally unique identifier for a network interface, will provide detailed information on installed network cards, including last assigned addresses and gateways. Examining this information is shown in Figure 9.15.

Information on any folders or printers being shared via Windows file sharing can be found under SYSTEM/ControlSet001/Services/LanmanServer. The Parameters branch contains configuration information. A list of shares can be found in the Shares branch. A share of the C:\Users directory under the name Users is shown in Figure 9.16.

Recall that the FAT filesystem did not store file and directory access times, only dates. With the introduction of NTFS this was changed and the access timestamps are stored with the same resolution as the rest (100s of nanoseconds). Because this resulted in poor performance, access timestamp updating for directories that are listed (either via the file explorer or command prompt) can be disabled by creating the key SYSTEM/ControlSet001/Control/FileSystem/NtfsDisableLastAccessUpdate and setting its value to 1. This is the default and recommended setting for recent versions of Windows. It is important to know if access timestamp

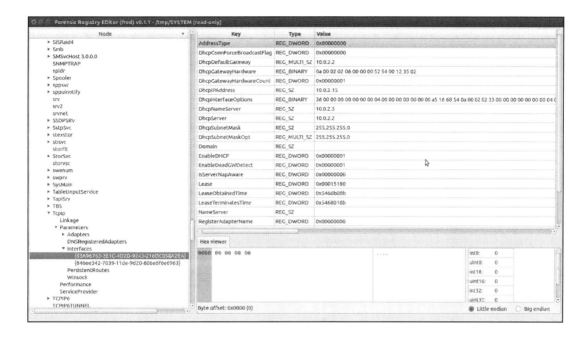

FIGURE 9.15.

Examining network card information in the system hive.

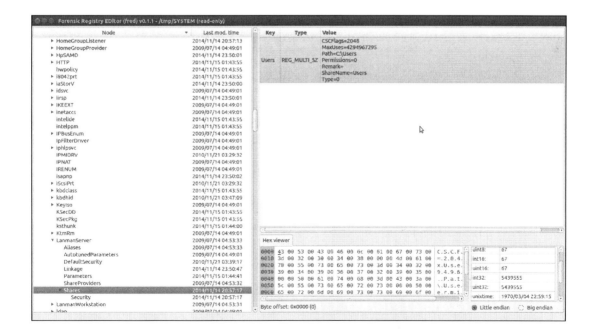

FIGURE 9.16.

Retrieving folder and printer network shares from the system hive.

438 CHAPTER 9 The Windows Registry

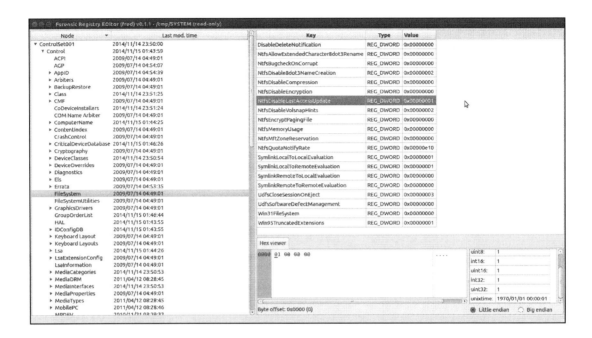

FIGURE 9.17.

Determining if directory access timestamp updating has been disabled.

updating has been disabled when examining timelines. Examining this key for a Windows 7 subject is shown in Figure 9.17. Note that this system has the default setting (access timestamps are not updated).

Information on devices that have been connected to a system can be found under SYSTEM/ControlSet001/Enum. Some of the more interesting subbranches are HID, STORAGE, USB, and USBSTOR which are used to store information on USB Human Interface Devices (keyboards, mice, etc.), various types of media, all USB devices, and USB mass storage devices (thumb drives, backup drives, etc.), respectively. If you suspect data

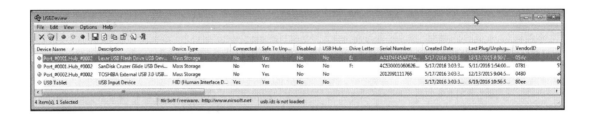

FIGURE 9.18.

USBDeview from NirSoft.

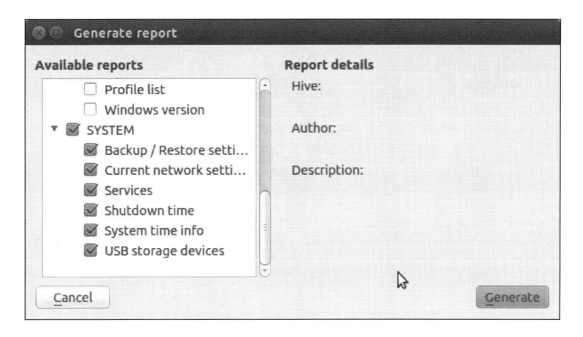

FIGURE 9.19.

Built-in system hive reports in FREd.

has been exfiltrated from a network, the information in USBSTOR will tell you what make, model, and serial number USB mass storage devices have been connected. The last connection time and user who connected the device are also stored here. NirSoft makes a nice tool called USBDeview that will display USB device information from a live system or a system hive file. USBDeview is available from http://www.nirsoft.net/utils/usb_devices_view.html. This tool is shown in Figure 9.18.

FREd provides several system hive reports as shown in Figure 9.19. These reports can provide all of the information from this section in a nice format that is easily imported to your case documentation. If you are feeling adventurous, you can create your own reports.

The Software hive

Because Windows itself is a piece of software, the software hive file contains a lot of pertinent information for forensic investigators. Recall that generally speaking information is stored under an <organization>/<product> branch. For backward compatibility much of the Windows information is stored under SOFTWARE/Microsoft/Windows NT. Items added in newer versions of Windows may be found under SOFTWARE/Microsoft/Windows.

Earlier in this book we saw how to determine the approximate version of Windows based on the directory structure of the C: drive. Much more precise information can be found under SOFTWARE/Microsoft/Windows NT/CurrentVersion. Viewing this information in FREd is shown in Figure 9.20.

440 CHAPTER 9 The Windows Registry

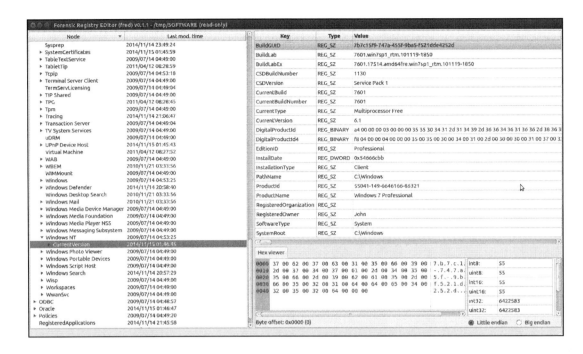

FIGURE 9.20.

Examining Windows version information in the software hive.

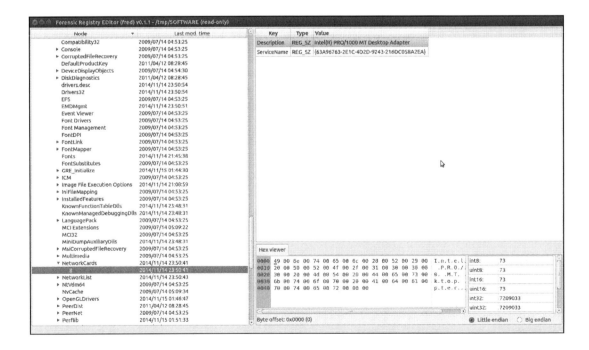

FIGURE 9.21.

Examining network card information in the software hive.

Examining the registry

As we shall see, there is a wealth of information stored under SOFTWARE/Microsoft/Windows NT/CurrentVersion. Information on network cards can be found under SOFTWARE/Microsoft/Windows NT/CurrentVersion/NetworkCards/<number> as shown in Figure 9.21. Microsoft released a Big Brother application called "Windows Genuine Advantage". Their claim was this was done for the users' advantage. In reality this software existed to detect versions of Windows running on well-known product keys. If installed, this software stores the MAC (hardware) address in a value under SOFTWARE/Microsoft/Windows Genuine Advantage. If a system has wireless network cards, information concerning previously connected networks can be found under SOFTWARE/Microsoft/WZCSVC/Parameters/Interfaces/{GUID} where GUID is the globally unique identifier assigned to a wireless interface.

Microsoft added a registry key that could be used to override the recycle bin's normal behavior and just delete files stored there. In pre-Vista versions of Windows creating a NukeOnDelete key in SOFTWARE/Microsoft/Windows/CurrentVersion/Explorer/BitBucket and setting its value to 1 will override the normal behavior. This override was moved to the user hives for later versions of Windows. This key for a Windows XP system is shown in Figure 9.22.

FREd provides several software hive reports as shown in Figure 9.23. The results of running these reports on a Windows 7 subject are shown in Figure 9.24. Note the detailed Windows version information given. This information can be helpful if a breach is suspected as it allows you to research known vulnerabilities in various versions of Windows.

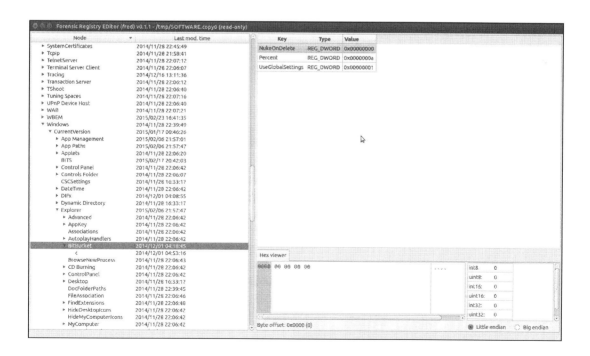

FIGURE 9.22.

Examining the NukeOnDelete key for a Windows XP subject.

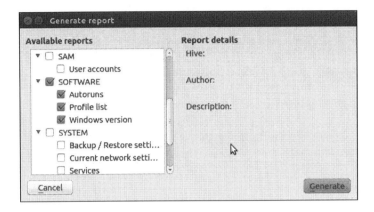

FIGURE 9.23.

FREd software hive reports.

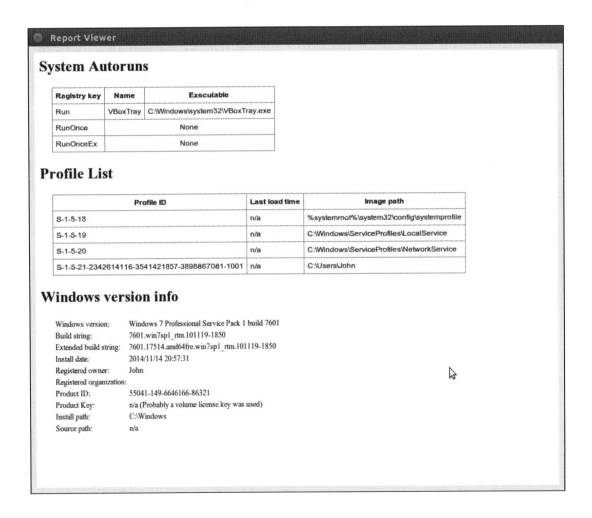

FIGURE 9.24.

FREd software hive reports results for a Windows 7 subject.

The User hive

When it comes to tracking user behavior there is no better place to look for evidence than the user hives (stored in NTUSER.DAT files). As was previously mentioned, Microsoft added a key that can cause files to be deleted instead of stored in the recycle bin. In pre-Vista versions of Windows this key was stored in the software hive. In newer versions of Windows it has moved down to the user hive(s) and can also be configured on a volume-by-volume basis. Creating the key NTUSER/Software/Microsoft/Windows/CurrentVersion/Explorer/BitBucket/Volume/{volume GUID}/NukeOnDelete where "volume GUID" is the globally unique identifier assigned to a volume and setting its value to 1 will override the default recycle bin behavior for a particular volume. This key is shown in Figure 9.25.

Windows stores some user activity information concerning what a user has run under NTUSER/Software/Microsoft/Windows/CurrentVersion/Explorer/UserAssist/{GUID}/Count. In a perfect example of security through obscurity, Microsoft encodes (not encrypts!) this information with a ROT13 cipher. The ROT13 cipher simply shifts each character 13 places in alphabetical order. An "A" becomes "N", "B" becomes "O", etc. Several registry tools can decipher this information. Some of these values are shown in Figure 9.26. Note that ".rkr" decodes to ".exe".

Information concerning recently used documents is stored under NTUSER/Software/Microsoft/Windows/CurrentVersion/Explorer/RecentDocs. Here you will find a list of values

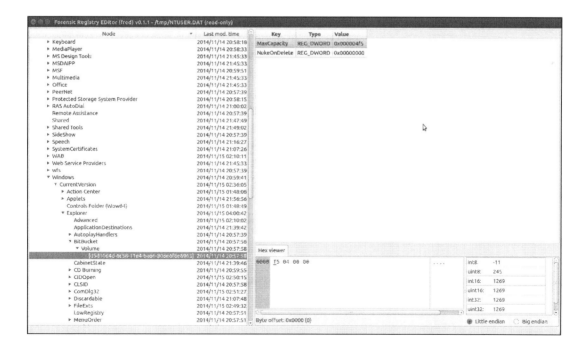

FIGURE 9.25.

Examining the NukeOnDelete key for a Windows 7 subject.

444 CHAPTER 9 The Windows Registry

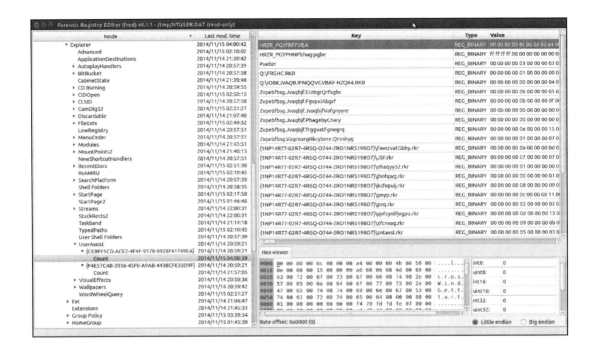

FIGUE 9.26.

Examining the UserAssist information in FREd. Note that the values have been ROT13 encoded.

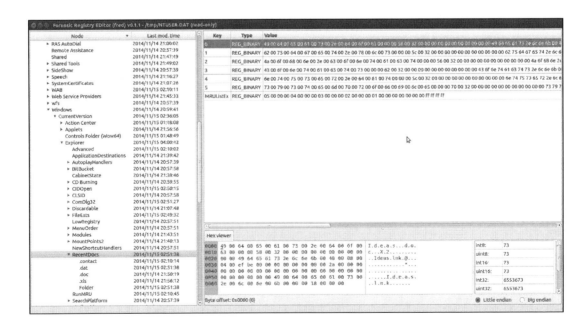

FIGURE 9.27.

Examining most recently used documents in a user hive.

that have numbers as names and also an MRUListEx value. The MRUListEx value stores the actual order in which documents were used with the most recent listed first. For the hive shown in Figure 9.27 the MRUListEx indicates that documents 5, 4, 3, 2, 1, and 0 were recently accessed with 5 being the most recent and 0 the least. The top level RecentDocs branch stores information on all documents. Subkeys under RecentDocs show the same information, but for specific file types.

In a similar manner to how recent document information is stored, most recently run (by selecting Run from start menu or using Window-R hotkey) programs are stored under NTUSER/Software/Microsoft/Windows/CurrentVersion/Explorer/RunMRU. Unlike RecentDocs which uses numbers for documents, RunMRU uses letters for recently run programs. There are no subkeys of RunMRU. The RunMRU values for a Windows 7 system are shown in Figure 9.28.

As shown in Figure 9.29, there are a number of FREd reports for the user hives. The results from three of these reports are shown in Figure 9.30. If there is more than one user on the system, each user hive should be examined.

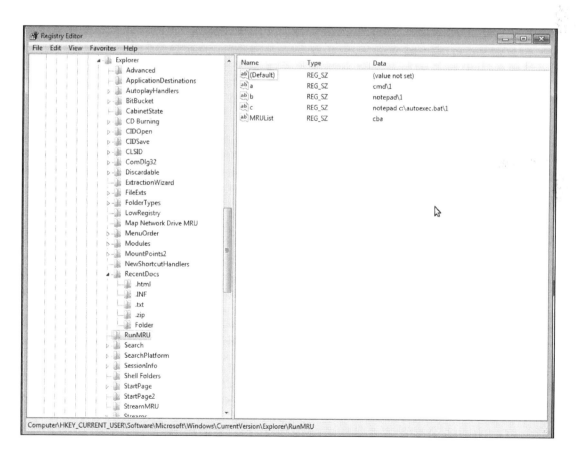

FIGURE 9.28.

Examining recently run programs.

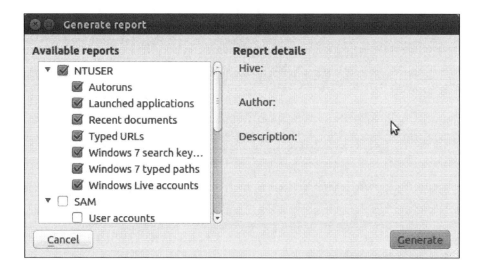

FIGURE 9.29.

User hive reports provided by FREd.

USING REGRIPPER

Harlan Carvey, a noted Windows forensics expert, has created a tool called RegRipper for examining registry hives. This tool was written in Perl. The Perl (Practical Extraction and Report Language) programming language was created by Larry Wall in 1987, four years before the first version of Python. While Python has replaced Perl as the preferred language for many information security professionals, Perl is still widely used by many system administrators and programmers. Like Python, Perl is likely pre-installed on most Linux systems. Perl is known for its ability to easily search and manipulate text and files. Prior to the introduction of PHP (which is based on Perl) Perl was widely used to create interactive websites via the Common Gateway Interface (CGI).

The RegRipper tool is likely in your standard Linux system repositories. Installing it on Debian or Ubuntu based systems is as easy as running `sudo apt-get install regripper`. Alternatively, it may be downloaded from github by running `git clone https://github.com/keydet89/RegRipper2.8`. RegRipper includes both a graphical tool and a command line tool. The graphical tool is started by running `regripper`. This is shown in Figure 9.31. The rip.pl script can be used on the command line or within scripts. The rip.pl help screen is shown in Figure 9.32.

As can be seen from Figure 9.31, RegRipper is very easy to use. Simply select a hive file, name the output report text file, select the appropriate profile for your hive, and click "Rip it". If you prefer the command line version, then run `rip.pl -r <hive file> -f <profile>`. RegRipper uses a plugin architecture. Plugins are written in Perl. A profile is nothing more than a text file that lists all of the plugins that pertain to a particular hive. RegRipper plugins for each hive will be discussed in greater detail in following sections of this chapter.

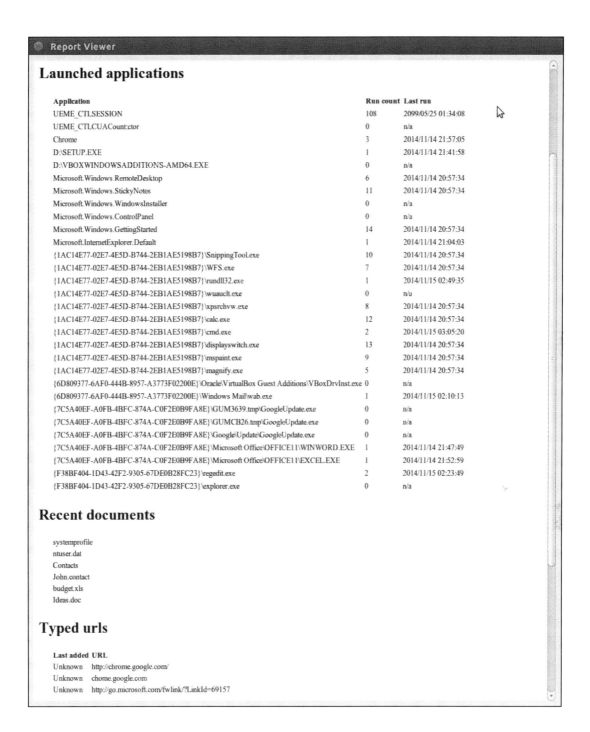

FIGURE 9.30.

Partial results from running FREd user hive reports.

448 CHAPTER 9 The Windows Registry

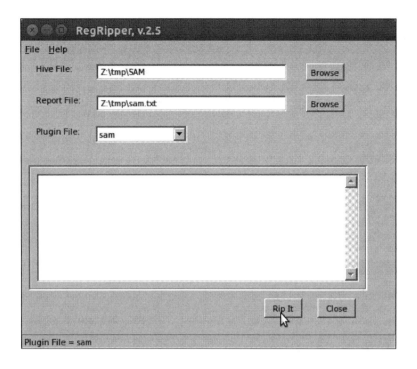

FIGURE 9.31.

The graphical version of RegRipper.

```
phil@i7laptop:~/RegRipper2.8$ ./rip.pl -h
Rip v.2.8_20130801 - CLI RegRipper tool
Rip [-r Reg hive file] [-f plugin file] [-p plugin module] [-l] [-h]
Parse Windows Registry files, using either a single module, or a plugins file.

  -r Reg hive file...Registry hive file to parse
  -g ................Guess the hive file (experimental)
  -f [profile].......use the plugin file (default: plugins\plugins)
  -p plugin module...use only this module
  -l ................list all plugins
  -c ................Output list in CSV format (use with -l)
  -s system name.....Server name (TLN support)
  -u username........User name (TLN support)
  -h.................Help (print this information)

Ex: C:\>rip -r c:\case\system -f system
    C:\>rip -r c:\case\ntuser.dat -p userassist
    C:\>rip -l -c

All output goes to STDOUT; use redirection (ie, > or >>) to output to a file.

copyright 2013 Quantum Analytics Research, LLC
phil@i7laptop:~/RegRipper2.8$
```

FIGURE 9.32.

Help screen for the command line version of RegRipper.

SAM hive

There is only a single module in the SAM RegRipper profile. It will parse the SAM and print out details on each user. These details include user name, user ID, full name, account type, account flags, and dates for account creation, last login, password reset, and login failure. Partial results from running this module against a Windows 7 SAM hive are shown in Figure 9.33.

System hive

Over 300 plugins are provided in the current version of RegRipper. Sometimes it might seem as though there are too many plugins to fully understand the purpose of all of them. You can get a list of available plugins in CSV format by `running rip.pl -l -c >plugins.csv`. This list is easily viewed in LibreOffice Calc (or your favorite spreadsheet program). Using techniques described earlier, this spreadsheet may be sorted by hive. There are over sixty plugins that may be used on the system hive.

I recommend running all of the plugins in the standard RegRipper profiles. It never hurts to have extra data. Which data is most pertinent will vary depending on the nature of your investigation. Some of the top plugins that are relevant to most investigations are listed in Table 9.2.

Many of the system hive plugins not listed in Table 9.2 are used to detect malware infections. If you are investigating a system as a part of an incident response, I would check these plugins carefully. In many ways these plugins are like a diagnostic blood test. Rather than look for the malware directly, the plugins look for byproducts of various bits of malware in the registry.

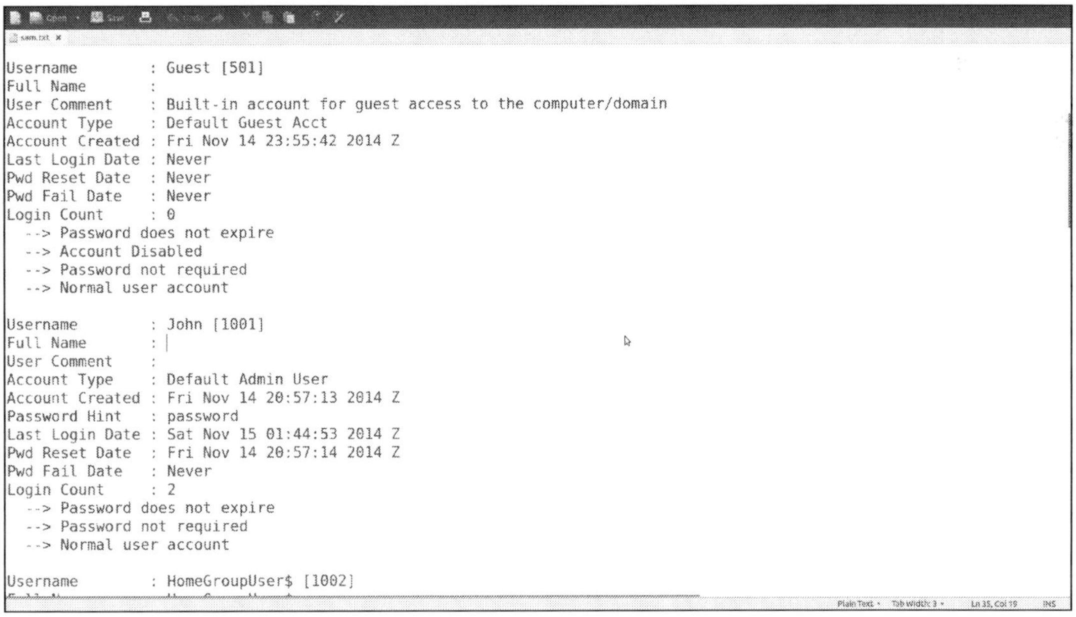
```
Username        : Guest [501]
Full Name       :
User Comment    : Built-in account for guest access to the computer/domain
Account Type    : Default Guest Acct
Account Created : Fri Nov 14 23:55:42 2014 Z
Last Login Date : Never
Pwd Reset Date  : Never
Pwd Fail Date   : Never
Login Count     : 0
  --> Password does not expire
  --> Account Disabled
  --> Password not required
  --> Normal user account

Username        : John [1001]
Full Name       :
User Comment    :
Account Type    : Default Admin User
Account Created : Fri Nov 14 20:57:13 2014 Z
Password Hint   : password
Last Login Date : Sat Nov 15 01:44:53 2014 Z
Pwd Reset Date  : Fri Nov 14 20:57:14 2014 Z
Pwd Fail Date   : Never
Login Count     : 2
  --> Password does not expire
  --> Password not required
  --> Normal user account

Username        : HomeGroupUser$ [1002]
```

FIGURE 9.33.

Partial results from running the RegRipper SAM parse module against a Windows 7 subject.

Table 9.2. System hive plugins pertinent to most investigations.

Plugin	Description
Compname	Retrieves both the computer name and TCP/IP computer name
Disablelastaccess	Checks the NtfsDisableLastAccessUpdate flag (directory timestamps)
fw_config	Firewall information such as if enabled and if notifications are disabled
Hibernate	Is hibernation supported – if so, hibernation file used in RAM analysis
Mountdev	Retrieves information on mounted filesystems
Network	Retrieves network GUIDs
Nic, nic2	Retrieves network card info such as DHCP, last address, etc.
Nolmhash	Checks for disabling of LanManager password hashes (default=disabled)
Pagefile	Get location of pagefile and whether it is cleared on shutdown
Prefetch	Get info on level of prefetching (more about this in a later chapter)
Rdpport	Is remote desktop enabled - if so, what is the port (default=3389)
Routes	Are there any persistent routes (normally there should not be any)
Services	Get info on services (should be checked for additions/deletions)
Shares	Get network shares
Shutdown	Get time of last shutdown (reboot after compromise?)
Time	Get timezone name and offsets from UTC
Usbdevices	Parses USB device information (was USB device used in an attack?)
Usbstor	Get info on previously connected USB drives (data exfiltration?)

Software hive

There are over eighty plugins available for the software hive. Many of these are uninteresting unless you are investigating a suspected breach. The plugins that are more likely to be relevant in all investigations are summarized in Table 9.3. As with all hives, I recommend running the plugins from the RegRipper profile even though much of the data will not be relevant.

User hive

There are over 140 RegRipper plugins for the user hives. As with the other hives, many of these are mostly relevant when a breach is suspected. The user hive plugins pertinent to most investigations are summarized in Table 9.4.

In these RegRipper sections we have touched on some of the most useful RegRipper plugins. Many of these relate to the registry discussion from earlier in this chapter. The utility of some of these plugins will become clearer in future chapters when we examine Windows artifacts and suspected malware. I would strongly encourage you to walk through the RegRipper reports from all of the hives on both a pre-Vista and newer Windows subject in order to become familiar with this extremely useful tool.

Table 9.3. Software hive plugins pertinent to most investigations.

Plugin	Description
Banner	Is there a login banner (perhaps one that should be there?)
Bitbucket	Check for NukeOnDelete flag (pre-Vista only)
Defbrowser	Get default browser (if IE could have been source of compromise)
Installer	What was installed via the standard MS installer program
Networkcards	Get information on network cards
soft_run	Get autostart items from software hive
startmenuinternetapps	Get installed Internet apps (good when looking at browser history, etc.)
Uac	Is User Account Control enabled requiring password for admin tasks?
winnt_cv	What is the exact version of Windows running on this system

Table 9.4. User hive plugins pertinent to most investigations.

Plugin	Description
bitbucker_user	Get user recycle bin settings
Ccleaner	Is the popular ccleaner tool installed (might clear some cache files if run)
Environment	Get user environment variables such as temporary file directories
ie_settings	What are the Internet Explorer settings (helpful for examining history)
Officedocs	Get recent MS Office documents
Printers	What printers does the user use (including printing to file)
Privoxy	Is Privoxy, the privacy-oriented proxy, installed?
Proxysettings	Get proxy settings
Putty	Is this popular SSH client installed?
Recentdocs	Get recent documents overall and broken down by type
Runmru	Get programs recently run by run on start button or Window-R hotkey
Ssh_host_keys	Get SSH authentication keys for this user
startmenuinternetapps_cu	This user's Internet apps and default browser
Typedurls	Get recently visited webpages
Userassist	Get most recently run programs from the UserAssist key
vista_bitbucket	Get the user's NukeOnDelete setting (Vista and later)

SUMMARY

In this chapter we learned about the data treasure trove known as the Windows registry. Tools and procedures for extracting the registry hive files were presented. The overall registry structure and most pertinent registry keys were discussed at length. With this knowledge in hand, we showed you how to easily extract information using RegRipper. In the next chapter we will learn about Windows artifacts (interesting files on the filesystem).

CHAPTER 10

Windows Artifacts

INFORMATION IN THIS CHAPTER:

- Recycle bin
- Event logs
- Prefetch files
- User directories
- Miscellaneous artifacts
- Web browser history

THE RECYCLE BIN

When users "delete" files in Windows, they are normally stored in the recycle bin; that is, unless the NukeOnDelete registry key was created and set to 1 as discussed in the previous chapter. The recycle bin is housed in a hidden directory. The name of this directory varies depending on the version of Windows. Old versions of Windows such as Windows 95/98 use C:\Recycler as the recycle bin. Windows XP uses C:\Recycled. Vista and newer versions of Windows use C:\$Recycle.Bin.

The way deleted files are stored in the recycle bin is different for pre-Vista and Vista or newer versions of Windows. In the older versions of Windows deleted files are named DX###.ext where X is the drive letter from which the file was deleted, ### is an ordinal number, and ext is the original file extension. For example, a file named Dc2.pptx was deleted from the C: drive and is a new format PowerPoint file (at least that is what the extension indicates). Because the file extension is retained, deleted files are easily opened if the filesystem image is mounted on your Linux forensic workstation.

In addition to any deleted files there will normally be a desktop.ini configuration file and an INFO2 file in the recycle bin directory. The purpose of the INFO2 file is to tell you what the files used to be called and what directory they came from. An example \Recycled folder from a Windows XP subject is shown in Figure 10.1. From the figure we can see that an OpenOffice (or LibreOffice) presentation and PowerPoint presentation were both deleted from the C: drive and stored in the recycle bin.

In order to determine the original filename and location for the two deleted files from Figure 10.1 we must look inside the INFO2 file. The start of the corresponding INFO2 file is shown in Figure 10.2. The first 16 (0x10) bytes of this file are a header. The first four bytes will be 0x05 0x00 0x00 0x00 or 0x04 0x00 0x00 0x00 depending on the version of Windows in use. The 2-byte unsigned integer at offset 12 (0x0C) holds the record size. The most common record size is 800 (0x0320) bytes.

The first entry begins on the second line at offset 16 (0x10). The fully qualified pathname

456 CHAPTER 10 Windows Artifacts

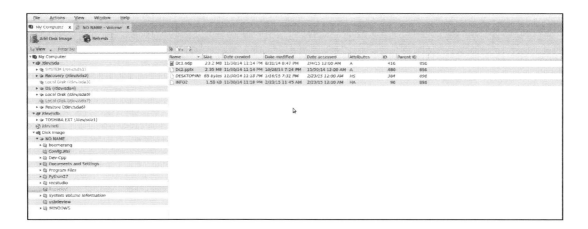

FIGURE 10.1.

The recycle bin folder for a Windows XP subject.

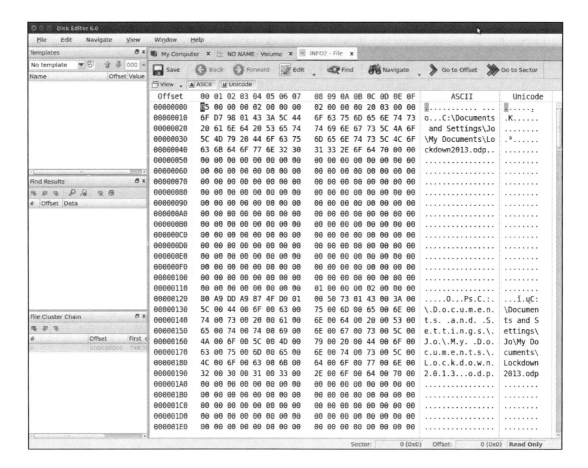

FIGURE 10.2.

The INFO2 file from the recycle bin in Figure 10.1.

in ASCII begins 4 bytes into each record (offset 20 or 0x14 for the first record). From the figure we can see that the file Dc1.odp used to be Lockdown2013.odp that was stored in the Jo user's "My Documents" directory.

The ordinal number (record number) is stored as a 4-byte unsigned integer 264 (0x108) bytes into the record (offset 0x118 for first record). From Figure 10.2 the number for the first file is 1. The next four bytes hold the drive designator (also as a 4-byte unsigned integer) where 0x00 = A:, 0x01=B:, 0x02=C:, 0x03=D, etc.

A 64-bit file timestamp (100s of nanoseconds since January 1, 1601) is found at offset 272 (0x0110) of each record. This is followed by a 4-byte physical size in bytes (which should be a multiple of the cluster size) at offset 280 (0x0118). The deleted Lockdown2013.odp file has a physical size of 0x01735000 or 24,334,336 bytes. The filename in Unicode is found at offset 284 (0x011C). For filenames in English the ASCII and Unicode names will normally agree.

The second deleted file is shown in Figure 10.3. We see that the file used to be stored in the Jo user's "My Documents" folder as ciso.pptx. Looking at offset 0x0438 we see this is file number 2 deleted from C:. It has a physical size (offset 0x448) of 2,461,696 (0x00259000) bytes.

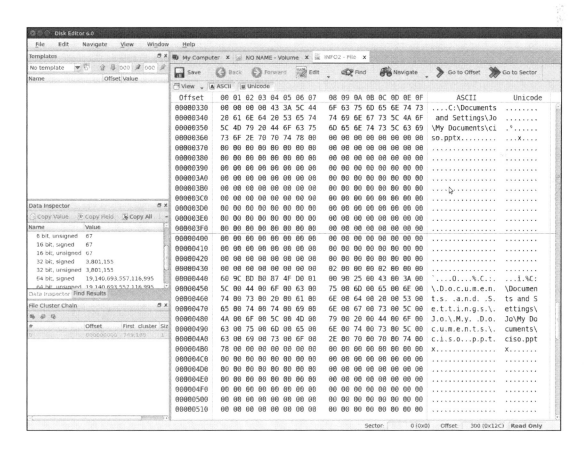

FIGURE 10.3.

The second deleted file record in INFO2 from the recycle bin in Figure 10.1.

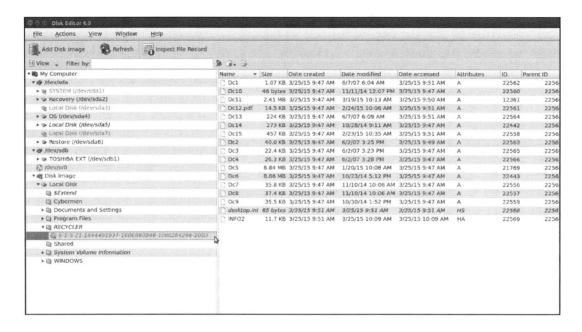

FIGURE 10.4.

A subfolder in the recycle bin housing the deleted files for the user with ID 1003.

You might wonder if there is any benefit to interpreting the INFO2 file. Given that the deleted files may be opened directly this is certainly a fair question. Whether or not knowing the original filename is useful depends on the type of investigation. In most cases having the original pathname will tell you the owner of the deleted file.

Depending on the exact version of Windows being run the recycle bin folder may contain subfolders named as users' GUIDs. Such a recycle bin is shown in Figure 10.4. From the GUID folder name, these files belong to the user with ID 1003. Notice that all but one of the deleted files have also had their extensions removed in an attempt to hide data.

As was previously mentioned, deleted files are stored in the recycle bin using a different system for later versions of Windows beginning with Vista. As with older versions of Windows, there may be subdirectories in the $Recycle.Bin folder for each user of the system. The recycle bin folder for the user with ID 1001 on a Windows 7 subject is shown in Figure 10.5.

Note that there is no INFO2 file in Figure 10.5. Under the new recycle bin system deleted files are named $Rxxxxxx.ext where xxxxxx is six random characters and ext is the original file extension. As with the DX####.ext files in the old recycle bin, these files are easily opened directly if the filesystem image has been mounted.

The INFO2 file has been replaced by a 544 byte file named $Ixxxxxx.ext where xxxxxx and ext match that of the corresponding $Rxxxxxx.ext file. In a sense each file gets its own INFO2 file. The start of the $IAP6NZA.xls file from Figure 10.5 is shown in Figure 10.6.

The $Ixxxxxx.ext files begin with an 8-byte header of 0x01 0x00 0x00 0x00 0x00 0x00 0x00 0x00. This is followed by the original file size as an 8-byte unsigned integer at offset 8 (0x08). The file size in the figure is 0x3600 or 13,824 bytes. The time the file was deleted is

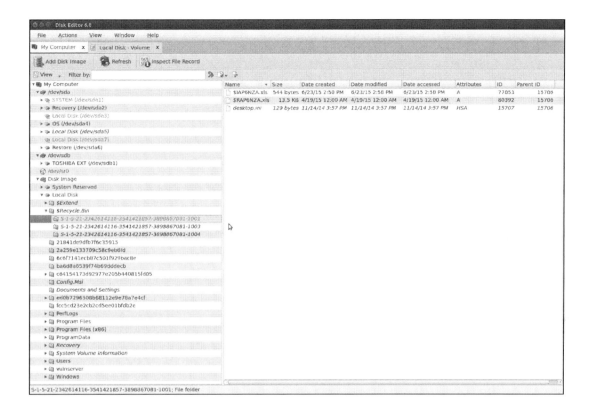

FIGURE 10.5.

The recycle bin for the user with ID 1001 on a Windows 7 subject.

stored as a 64-bit timestamp at offset 16 (0x10). The remainder of the $Ixxxxxx.ext file contains the filename in Unicode. Unlike the INFO2 files the filename is not also stored in ASCII. NTFS filenames may be up to 255 characters long without the path. There are only 265 characters of storage available in this file. As a result, there is always a chance that the pathname will be truncated.

EVENT LOGS

Windows stores event logs in a set of compressed XML files in the \Windows\System32\Winevt\Logs directory on systems running Vista and later Windows versions. These event log files have evtx extensions. Unlike the XML based Microsoft Office documents, these files are compressed in blocks, not as a whole. The reason for this is that items are constantly added to the logs and performance would be extremely poor if the entire log file had to be re-compressed with each new entry. Several event log files from a Windows 7 subject are shown in FTK Imager in Figure 10.7. These files must be exported or the filesystem image must be mounted in order to use the event log analysis tools discussed in this section.

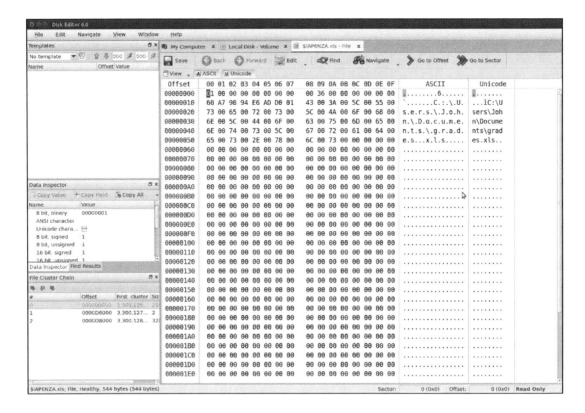

FIGURE 10.6.

The start of a $Ixxxxxx.ext file from a Windows 7 recycle bin.

One of the best tools for interpreting the XML based event log files is python-evtx by William Ballenthin. If the name sounds familiar it could be because he is also the author of INDX-Parse. According to Ballenthin this tool is based on a Perl module by Andreas Schuster. The main project page for python-evtx is located at http://www.williballenthin.com/evtx. This will point you to the github page at https://github.com/williballenthin/python-evtx. To install python-evtx download it with `git clone https://github.com/williballenthin/python-evt`, change to the directory with `cd python-evtx`, and then install the tool with `sudo python setup.py install`.

The python-evtx module comes with a few sample scripts in a scripts subdirectory. One of these scripts, evtxdump.py, can be used to dump the contents of an event log in the native XML format. In other words, it will read an evtx file and uncompress it. The syntax for calling this script is `evtxdump.py <evtx file>`.

The evtxdump.py script accepts only a single evtx file (wildcards are not supported). This limitation is easily overcome by wrapping a call to this script in a bash for loop. The one-liner bash script that will process all evtx files and extract XML files is `IFS=$(echo -en "\n\b"); for i in $(ls .evtx); do <path-to-python-evtx>/scripts/evtxdump.py "$i" 1>"$(basename $i .evtx).xml" 2>"$(basename

Event logs

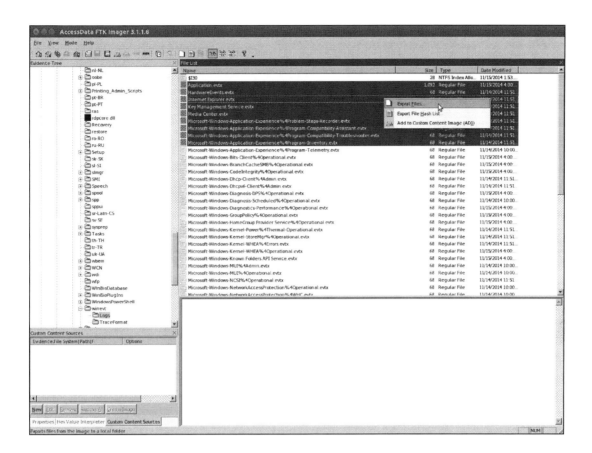

FIGURE 10.7.

Exporting Windows event log files in FTK Imager.

$i .evtx).log" ; done. This one-liner would be much simpler if Windows did not tend to throw spaces and other troublesome characters into filenames.

The elements in this one-liner have been used in previous scripts in this book. One small difference is the use of basename (basename <file> <known extension>) where a known file extension is stripped from the filename. This alternate form is used to generate output filenames. All of the quotes around filenames are to prevent problems with spaces in the names. Here is the one-liner from the previous paragraph broken up into multiple lines with comments.

```
IFS=$(echo -en "\n\b"); # reset filename separator to not include space
for i in $( ls .evtx ); # list all evtx files set value to $i for the loop
do # begin the for loop
  <path-to-python-evtx>/scripts/evtxdump.py "$i" \#dump current evtx file
  1>"$(basename $i .evtx).xml" \ # redirect stdout to XML file
  2>"$(basename $i .evtx).log" ; # redirect any errors to log file
done # end the for loop
```

462 CHAPTER 10 Windows Artifacts

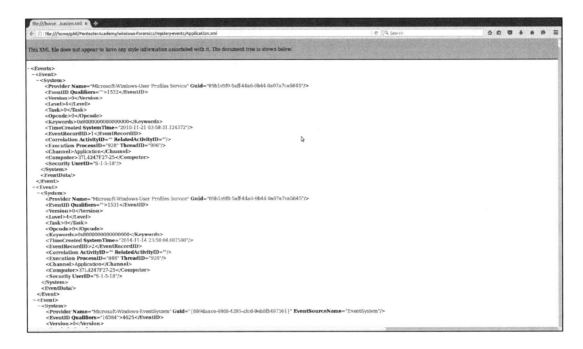

FIGURE 10.8.

Viewing an XML file with the Firefox browser.

You have extracted all of the XML files. Now what? There are a few options for viewing these files. One option is to use a web browser. An XML file being viewed in Firefox is shown in Figure 10.8. While initially it may not appear advantageous to view XML files in a browser, they all support expanding and collapsing the various levels in the XML document which can be useful. Files can also be viewed in any text editor. Some text editors will smartly interpret the XML, but most will just treat it as normal text.

Because the XML files are simple text files, they are easily searched using tools like GREP (GNU Regular Expression Parser). This has the advantage of being very simple. The downside is that it is not easy to search for values in specific event elements. One of the most powerful tools for parsing XML files is the Python Beautiful Soup module. This module is easily installed with `sudo easy_install beautifulsoup4`. Coverage of this tool is well outside the scope of this book. You can find out more at https://www.crummy.com/software/BeautifulSoup/bs4/doc/.

Pre-Vista versions of Windows use a binary format for event log files. These logs on old systems are stored in files with evt extensions in the \Windows\System32\Config directory (the same place registry hives can be found). A directory containing event logs for a Windows XP subject is shown in Figure 10.9.

As can be seen in Figure 10.10, the evt files store event information strings in Unicode. There are a number of options for interpreting these evt files. One simple option is to use an event viewer from a Windows XP system to open the file by either running this program in a virtual machine or using WINE. A tool such as GREP could be used to search through the

Event logs

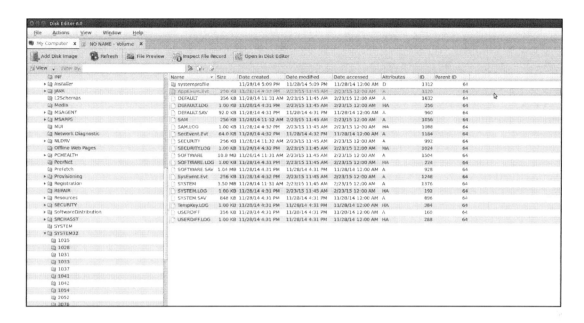

FIGURE 10.9.
Windows XP event log files.

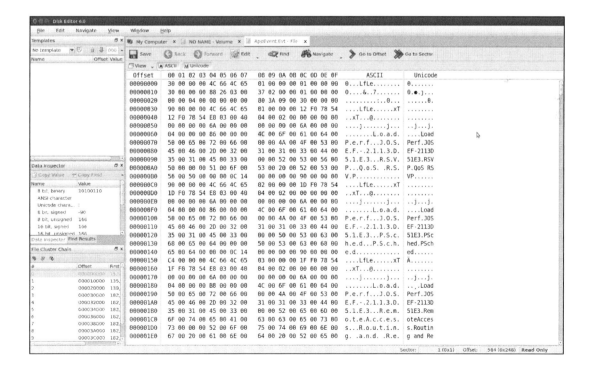

FIGURE 10.10.
Part of a Windows XP event log file.

```
phil@i7laptop:~/readevt$ sudo mkdir /etc/perl/File
phil@i7laptop:~/readevt$ sudo cp ReadEvt.pm /etc/perl/File/.
phil@i7laptop:~/readevt$ perl lsevt3.pl ~/PentesterAcademy/windows-forensics/win
xp-events/AppEvent.Evt |more
Record Number : 1
Source         : LoadPerf
Computer Name  : STARFLEET1
Event ID       : 1000
Event Type     : EVENTLOG_INFORMATION_TYPE
Time Generated : Wed Apr 29 17:44:28 2015
Time Written   : Wed Apr 29 17:44:28 2015
Message Str    : RSVP
Message Data   : 0c 14 00 00

Record Number : 2
Source         : LoadPerf
Computer Name  : STARFLEET1
Event ID       : 1000
Event Type     : EVENTLOG_INFORMATION_TYPE
Time Generated : Wed Apr 29 17:44:28 2015
Time Written   : Wed Apr 29 17:44:28 2015
Message Str    : PSched
Message Data   : 0c 14 00 00
```

FIGURE 10.11.

Installing and using the File::ReadEvt Perl module.

evt binary files for certain keywords. There is a set of scripts in GrokEVT that can be used to parse evt files and also correlate them with information from the registry. GrokEVT is rather complicated to set up and use. More information on GrokEVT can be found at http://projects.sentinelchicken.org/grokevt/.

Harlan Carvey, author of RegRipper, has written a Perl module for parsing evt files called File::ReadEVT. This module is availabe for download from http://www.cpan.org/modules/by-authors/id/H/HC/HCARVEY/File-ReadEvt-0.1a.zip. To install this module first unzip this module and change to the directory where you extracted the files. Create a directory for the required module to live with `sudo mkdir /etc/perl/File`, then copy the module to this directory with `sudo cp ReadEvt.pm /etc/perl/File/`.. The included lsevt3.pl file can then be used to list entries in an evt file with `perl lsevt3.pl <evt file>`. These steps are shown in Figure 10.11.

PREFETCH FILES

Prefetch files were introduced in Windows XP in order to speed up the loading of common applications and Windows components. Prefetch files have pf extensions and reside in the \Windows\prefetch directory. A prefetch file contains a list of other files that must be loaded (fetched) in order to run an executable. This includes DLL files among other things. Recall from the previous chapter that there is a registry setting that determines if prefetch files are created for boot processes, applications, or both.

You may be wondering what use prefetch files could be for a forensic examiner. There are a couple of scenarios where these can be helpful. If a user has installed and then removed an application, any prefetch files created will remain. This can be used to disprove the person that claims he or she never installed an application. The access timestamp on a prefetch file can be used to show the most recent time an application was executed.

Another use of prefetch files requires actually interpreting the file. If a program has been trojaned, it may access additional files (mostly DLLs) when compared to the original version. By having a list of files that are touched, the alteration of the executable might be detected. Windows might also create a prefetch file for malware. Knowing what files and libraries a program uses can help a person understand what it does and, more importantly, whether or not it is malicious.

There are a few prefetch file parsing tools available. Red Wolf Computer Forensics has developed a free (but not open source) prefetch parser that may be downloaded from their website at http://redwolfcomputerforensics.com. After you have downloaded and unzipped the appropriate file from the website, you will notice that it contains a few executables and a Perl script. For simplicity you may wish to run one of the executables using WINE. The Perl script depends on several Perl modules that are not installed on your system by default. The graphical tool shown in Figure 10.12 was started using `wine prefetch_parser_gui.exe`.

As can be seen in Figure 10.12, using the Prefetch Parser is straightforward. Supply a case number which is used to create a database file, point it toward the directory where the prefetch files are located (this could be the \Windows\prefetch directory if you mounted the filesystem image), tell it where to output the reports, tell it whether you are running pre-Vista Windows or not, select your desired output format from HTML, CSV, TAB, or XML, and click "Parse Prefetch Files".

When the HTML format is selected, a set of HTML files will be generated, including an index.html file. An example index.html file is shown in Figure 10.13. From this screen we can see the program executable, number of times it has run, and last execution time. Partial results from clicking on the Google Chrome prefetch file link are shown in Figure 10.14.

USER DIRECTORIES

Each user has an AppData subdirectory in his or her user's folder (C:\Users\<username>) for Vista and later versions of Windows. As seen in Figure 10.15, there are three subdirectories in AppData: Local, LocalLow, and Roaming. The Local directory is used for things that would not make sense to follow you around as you move from machine to machine on a network, such as application caches. The Roaming directory is used for things that should follow you from one machine to the next, such as program settings and recently used documents. The LocalLow directory is used for certain data that would be stored in Local, but the data is being isolated from other user data in Local for security reasons.

Software developers may create directories in AppData\Local to store any data that they

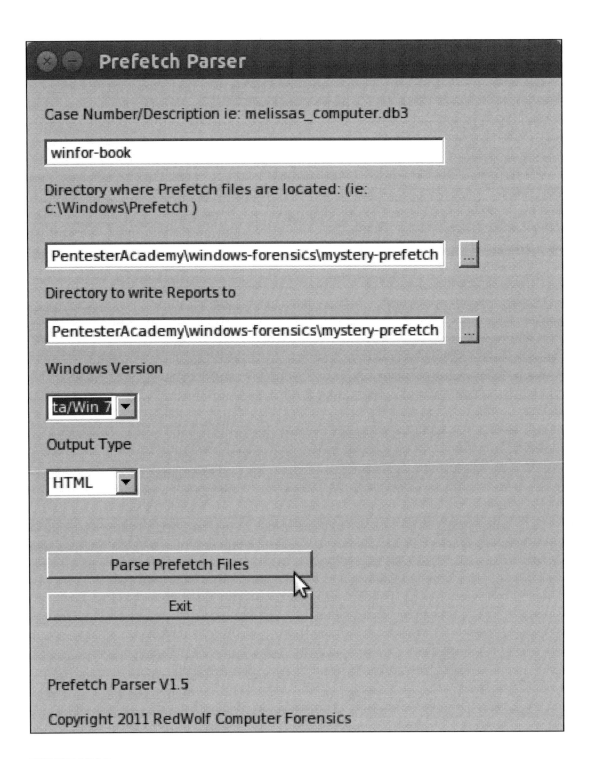

FIGURE 10.12.

Running the Red Wolf Prefetch Parser.

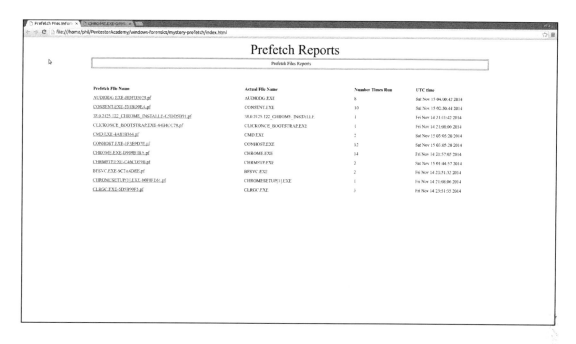

FIGURE 10.13.

The index.html file output by Prefetch Parser.

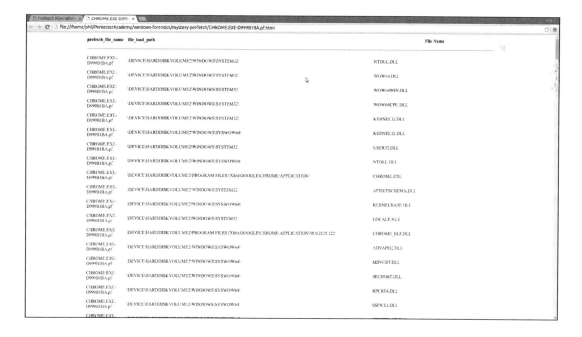

FIGURE 10.14.

Part of the report for the Google Chrome prefetch file.

468 CHAPTER 10 Windows Artifacts

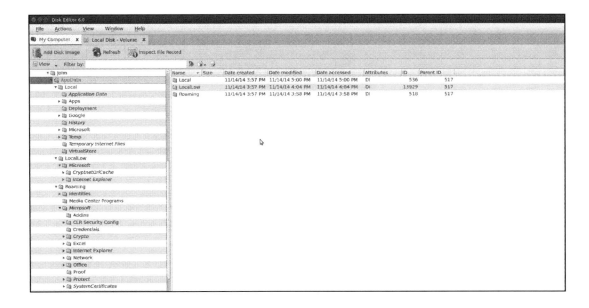

FIGURE 10.15.

The three subdirectories under a user's AppData folder.

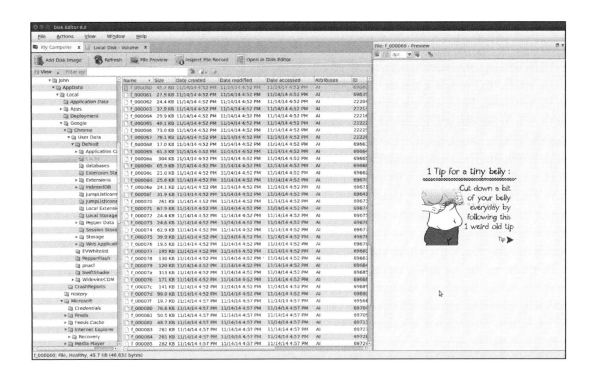

FIGURE 10.16.

Viewing Google Chrome cache files in Active@ Disk Editor.

wish to be a part of a user's local profile. The preferred procedure is to create a directory with the organization's name and product subdirectories underneath. For example, Google Chrome files are stored under AppData\Local\Google\Chrome. Cached files for this browser are stored in AppData\Local\Google\Chrome\User Data\Default\Cache. A tool such as Active@ Disk Editor (ADE), Autopsy, or FTK Imager can be used to view these cached files. A preview of a graphic file in this directory is shown in Figure 10.16. Note that you could also mount the filesystem image on your Linux forensic workstation and view the files that way.

Each user has a temporary directory under AppData\Local\Temp. Because this directory is virtually guaranteed to be writable, many applications store temporary files here. Few of those applications delete these files. This directory is much like /tmp on Linux/Unix systems with one important difference. The /tmp directories are normally cleared each time a system restarts, but the AppData\Local\Temp directories are not. An AppData\Local\Temp directory is shown in Figure 10.17. Note that several applications have created logs in this directory and some have also created directories.

Webmail seems to be the new norm for most users. Having said that, if a user is running Microsoft Outlook, any e-mail messages saved for offline viewing might be found in .ost files inside the AppData\Local\Microsoft\Outlook directory. A free tool for viewing these .ost files can be found at http://freeviewer.org/ost.

If a user runs Internet Explorer, cached files may be present in "AppData\Local\

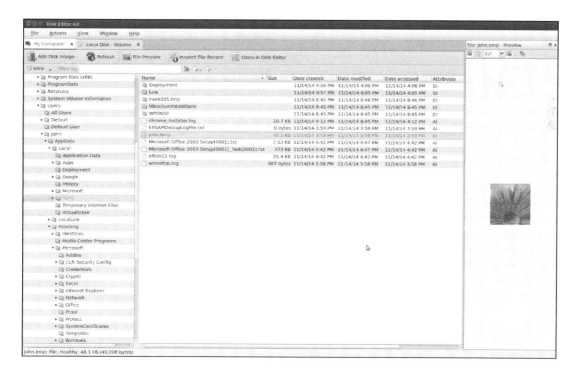

FIGURE 10.17.

A user's AppData\Local\Temp directory.

470 CHAPTER 10 Windows Artifacts

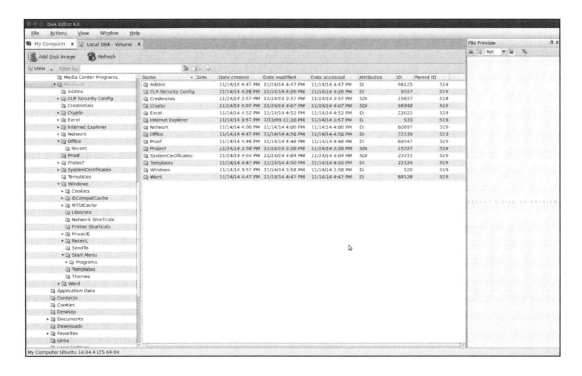

FIGURE 10.18.

The AppData\Roaming\Microsoft directory.

Microsoft\Windows\Temporary Internet Files". Browsing history is stored in AppData\Local\Microsoft\Windows\History. Tools for interpreting these files will be discussed later in this chapter.

Applications can create directories under AppData\Roaming. As with AppData\Local, the preferred procedure is to create a folder for the organization and subfolders for products. Not surprisingly, there are a number of directories under AppData\Roaming\Microsoft. The AppData\Roaming\Microsoft directory is shown in Figure 10.18. Note that the tree view on the left has been partially expanded.

As we learned in the last chapter, recently opened documents are recorded in the registry. On newer versions of Windows (Vista and later) this is also recorded via link (.lnk) files stored in AppData\Roaming\Microsoft\Windows\Recent. This directory is shown in Figure 10.19. The files to which the links point are easily divined by opening the link files in ADE and browsing through the text inside the files.

If the user has created any network or printer shortcuts they will be stored in "AppData\Roaming\Microsoft\Windows\Network Shortcuts" or "AppData\Roaming\Microsoft\Windows\Printer Shortcuts", respectively. Any Internet Explorer cookies can be found in AppData\Roaming\Microsoft\Windows\Cookies. If the user employs Macromedia Flash Player to play Flash animations, Flash cookies may be found in "AppData\Roaming\Macromedia\Flash Player\#SharedObjects\<random value>\". Flash cookies can be a good thing to check as most users do not know to clear them.

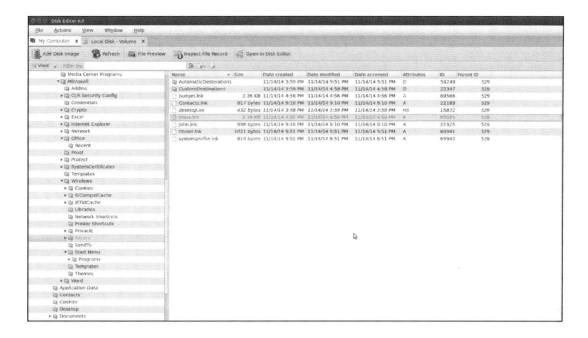

FIGURE 10.19.

Recently opened files stored as links in AppData\Roaming\Microsoft\Windows\Recent.

Just as recently opened documents are tracked system-wide, Microsoft Office will keep a record of recent Office documents. This information is stored in link files under AppData\Roaming\Microsoft\Office\Recent. This directory is shown in Figure 10.20.

MISCELLANEOUS ARTIFACTS

When documents are printed, they are not immediately sent to the printer. Rather, they are sent to a print spool until the printer is ready to print them. There are a couple of reasons that this is done. Relative to other peripherals, printers are very slow. As anyone who has ever cleared a paper jam can attest, there is also a greater chance that something will go wrong. Occasionally print jobs get stuck in the spool. The most likely reason for this to happen is that nobody replenished the paper in the printer. It is always worth checking for documents caught in the spool. These documents can be found in \Windows\System32\spool\PRINTERS.

There may be some useful log files in the \Windows\debug directory. One of these is the network setup log which gives useful information on network settings and installed network cards (much of this is also found in the registry). If the Microsoft Malicious Software Removal Tool (MRT) has been installed, its log file will also be in this directory. The MRT file contains a lot of useful system information.

Information on installed devices can be found in \Windows\inf\setupapi.dev.log. This can be useful when investigating USB devices (including USB mass storage devices) that have been attached to the system. Part of this log file is shown in Figure 10.21.

472 CHAPTER 10 Windows Artifacts

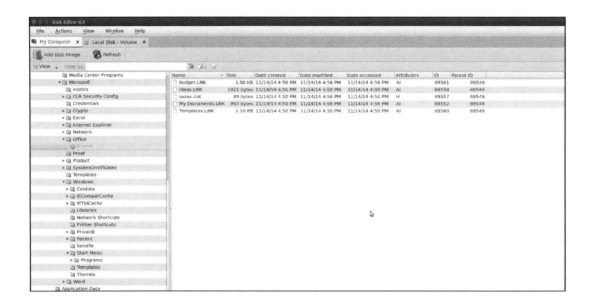

FIGURE 10.20.

Recently used Microsoft Office documents stored in link files inside the AppData\Roaming\Microsoft\Office\Recent directory.

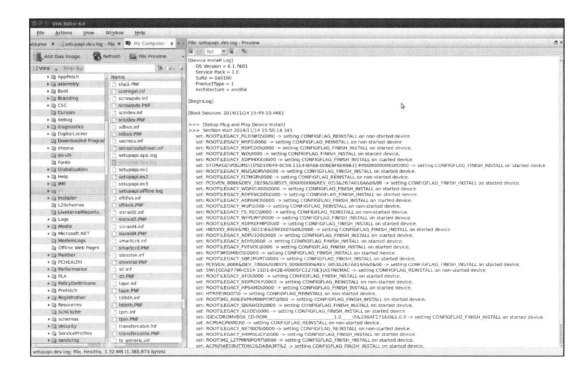

FIGURE 10.21.

Part of the setupapi.dev.log file.

There are a few other miscellaneous interesting places to look on the filesystem. Adrian Crenshaw (aka IronGeek) has a nice list of Windows artifacts at http://www.irongeek.com/i.php?page=security/windows-forensics-registry-and-file-system-spots. If you do visit this page, be sure to check out Adrian's archive of conference videos (many of which he personally recorded).

WEB BROWSER HISTORY

Earlier in this chapter we mentioned where some of the web browser cache and history files can be found. Because there are several browsers available and they all store information in different formats, it would be convenient to have a single tool that processes files for the most popular browsers. One such tool is Browser History View by Nirsoft. This tool can be downloaded from https://nirsoft.net/utils/browsing_history_view.html.

The Browser History View (BHV) is a Windows executable. It is easily run with WINE on your Linux forensic workstation by changing to the directory where you uncompressed the zip file and executing `wine ./BrowsingHistoryView.exe &`. BHV has several modes of operation. One of my favorites allows you to point the tool at the \Users directory, and it will retrieve web history for all users. The easiest way to use this mode is to mount your filesystem image with the mount-image.py script presented earlier in this book. The command is `sudo mount-image.py <filesystem image>`. The initial BHV screen (called Advanced Options) is shown in Figure 10.22.

As can be seen in Figure 10.22, BHV supports nine of the most popular browsers. History may be filtered by time, a list of keywords to include, and a list of keywords or URLs to exclude. I see no reason not to retrieve all available information as this tool is quite fast. Some results from this tool run against a Windows 7 subject with three users are shown in Figure 10.23. Here the results have been sorted by user.

From the results in Figure 10.23, it would appear that Sue likes to visit pinterest.com. It would also appear that Johnny, Jr. is interested in Jessica Alba. Any URL in the list can be visited by selecting an item and pressing F6 or right-clicking an item and selecting "Open URL in web browser" from the popup menu. BHV can be used to create HTML reports and individual items may be saved in text, CSV, XML, or HTML format. BHV is a very useful free tool.

Many of the large tools, such as Autopsy, process web history from a few of the top browsers. As discussed earlier in this book, Autopsy can take considerable time to load a typical filesystem image. For this and other reasons a standalone tool like BHV is often preferred.

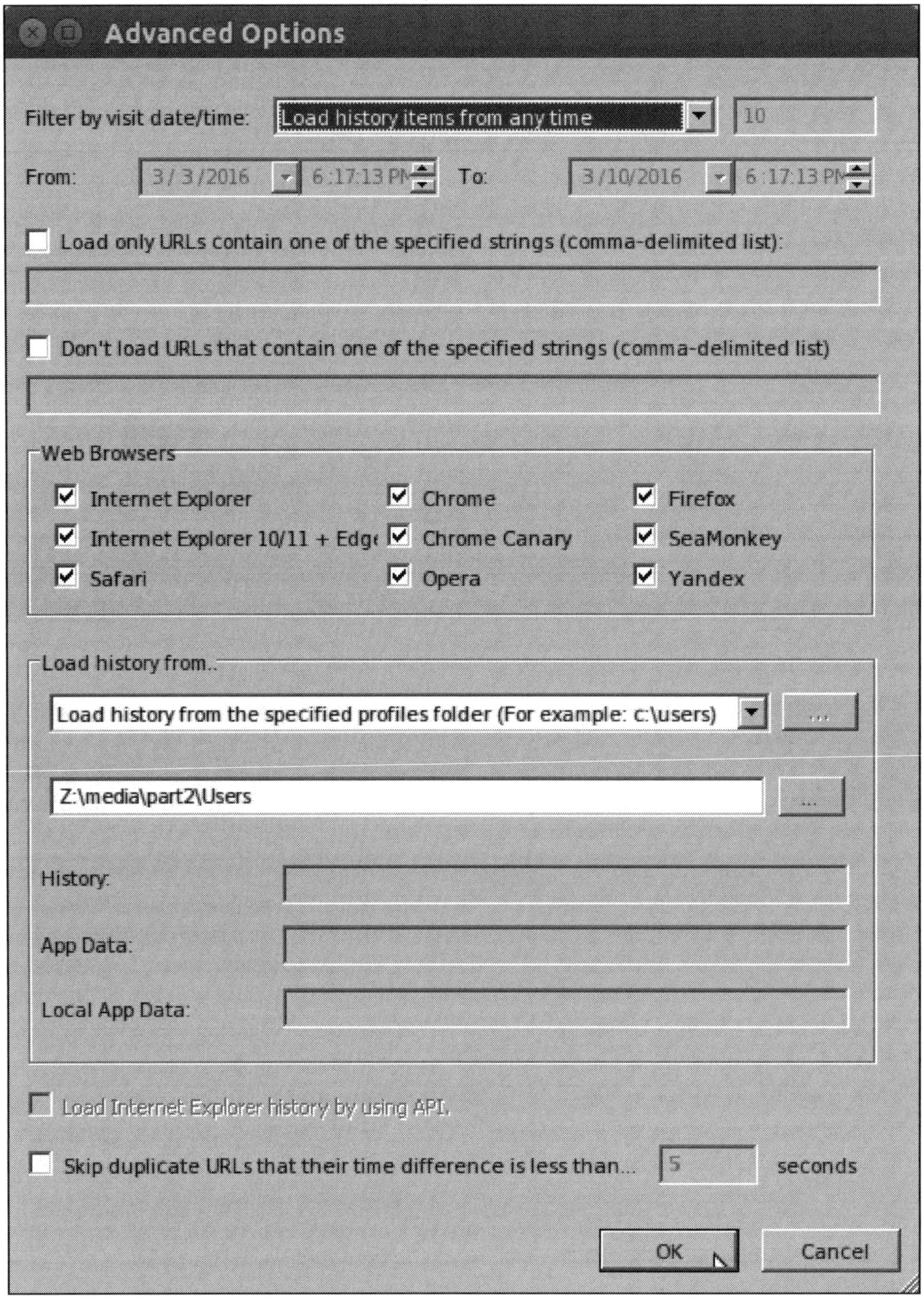

FIGURE 10.22.

The initial Browser History Viewer screen.

FIGURE 10.23.

Browser history sorted by user.

SUMMARY

In this chapter we have examined various interesting items that can be found in files on a Windows system. Several useful tools were presented to that aim. In the next chapter we will show you how to learn a lot about a system solely based on a memory image.

CHAPTER 11

Memory Forensics

INFORMATION IN THIS CHAPTER:

- Introducing Volatility
- Volatility basics
- Processes
- Finding malware
- Volatility commands

INTRODUCING VOLATILITY

Interest in memory forensics has increased dramatically in the last several years. This is due in large part to the release of the Volatility framework. Volatility is a collection of Python scripts used to analyze memory images. I do not say this to trivialize Volatility. After all, Metasploit is similarly a collection of Ruby scripts.

If you go to enough conferences, you will likely hear someone say that evidence from memory (and hence Volatility) cannot be used in court. I have never seen anyone produce a law, regulation, or rule to back up this statement, however. As with any new tool, an attorney certainly might attempt to challenge findings from Volatility. Fortunately, this is likely a non-issue as anything found in Volatility will most certainly point you to evidence on a filesystem that can be used in court (because as an industry we have been doing dead analysis for decades). I have yet to find an incident where evidence existed solely in memory.

Volatility can be downloaded from http://volatilityfoundation.org. I recommend you download the latest version of Volatility directly from this site. Volatility may be downloaded as a standalone executable for Windows, OS X, or Linux. You can download the Python scripts directly either as a zip file on the website or from the github repository using `git clone https://github.com/volatilityfoundation/volatility`. If you downloaded the source code version of Volatility, be sure to install it by changing to the appropriate directory and running `sudo python setup.py install`.

If you want to better understand how Volatility works, I recommend downloading the source code version. This will allow you to walk through the various Python scripts. In this book we will focus on using Volatility. If you want to learn more about how it works and understand memory models at a deeper level, you might consider picking up a copy of *The Art of Memory Forensics* by members of the Volatility team.

```
phil@i7laptop:~/PentesterAcademy/windows-forensics$ vol.py -f pawin7subject.img --profile=Win7SP1x64
 pslist|more
Volatility Foundation Volatility Framework 2.5
Offset(V)          Name                    PID   PPID   Thds    Hnds   Sess  Wow64 Start
                   Exit
------------------ ----------------------- ----- ------ ------  ------ ----- ----- ----------------
----------------   ------------------------
0xfffffa80018ad040 System                    4      0     80     656   ------    0 2015-12-10 15:10
:51 UTC+0000
0xfffffa800213e8d0 smss.exe                248      4      2      29   ------    0 2015-12-10 15:10
:51 UTC+0000
0xfffffa8002e11b30 csrss.exe               320    312      9     448       0     0 2015-12-10 15:11
:02 UTC+0000
0xfffffa80018be060 csrss.exe               368    360      7     209       1     0 2015-12-10 15:11
:03 UTC+0000
0xfffffa8002e26b30 wininit.exe             376    312      3      77       0     0 2015-12-10 15:11
:03 UTC+0000
0xfffffa8002e2f920 winlogon.exe            404    360      3     110       1     0 2015-12-10 15:11
:03 UTC+0000
0xfffffa8002ec3b30 services.exe            464    376      5     185       0     0 2015-12-10 15:11
:07 UTC+0000
0xfffffa8002ed5b30 lsass.exe               472    376      7     695       0     0 2015-12-10 15:11
:08 UTC+0000
0xfffffa8002ed99d0 lsm.exe                 480    376     10     141       0     0 2015-12-10 15:11
:08 UTC+0000
0xfffffa8002f3f340 svchost.exe             576    464      9     349       0     0 2015-12-10 15:11
:18 UTC+0000
```

FIGURE 11.1.

Listing processes from a memory image in Volatility.

VOLATILITY BASICS

If you have installed Volatility from source code, it can be run by typing `vol.py` in a shell. If you opted for the standalone executable, you must either place the executables in one of the directories in your $PATH environment variable or fully specify the pathname each time you run it. The executables are named `volatility_2.5_linux_x64` and `volatiliy_2.5_linux_x86` for 64 and 32 bit executables, respectively, assuming you are running Volatility 2.5 (the most recent as of this writing).

Running Volatility without any command line options will generate an error. Most Volatility commands require a memory image file (-f option), profile (--profile option), and a command (plugin). Readers of *Linux Forensics* will recall that working with a Linux image required building a profile thanks to the large number of Linux versions available. Life is simpler when dealing with Windows images as all of the supported profiles are already built in. These profiles are required to account for subtle differences in how things are handled in the operating system kernel from one version (including patch level) to the next. Partial results from running `vol.py -f pawin7subject.img --profile=Win7SP1x64 pslist` in order to list processes for a Windows 7 subject are shown in Figure 11.1.

Part of the Volatility help screen (obtained with vol.py -h) is shown in Figure 11.2. A few of the options on this screen are commonly used. The --info option will print a list of supported plugins and profiles. The -f (or --filename) option is required by nearly every command, as is the --profile option. Another popular option not shown in the figure is --output which is used to select an output format. The list of supported output formats is plugin specific.

Because nearly every Volatility command requires an image file and profile, it can become quite tedious to type in these values over and over. Volatility does support setting these values in environment variables. There are some who would advocate for this method. Personally, I prefer to use aliases in Linux as this is a generally useful thing and very easy to set up. As an added bonus, aliases can be made for examining multiple images simultaneously.

Setting up an alias is as easy as typing `alias <name>='<command to alias>'`. For example, to create an alias named vpaw (Volatility Pentester Academy Windows subject) that runs Volatility with the correct profile and image file I might use `alias vpaw='vol.py --profile=Win7SP1x64 -f ~/PentesterAcademy/windows-forensics/pawin7 subject-memory.img'`.

There are a number of files that are loaded each time you log in to a Linux machine and/or start a new shell. Two of these files are .profile and .bashrc, both of which are located in a user's home directory (i.e. /home/phil). In Linux, files that start with a period are hidden by default but can be viewed using the -a option to the ls command (similar to dir in Windows). Adding this alias near the end of the ~/.bashrc file (~/ is a shortcut that resolves to the current user's home directory) is shown in Figure 11.3. It should be noted that the standard .bashrc file will load any aliases stored in ~/.bash_aliases if the file exists, so this same line could have been added to that file. If you want this to take effect without starting a new shell, you must source the file by typing `. ~/.bashrc`.

```
Usage: Volatility - A memory forensics analysis platform.

Options:
  -h, --help            list all available options and their default values.
                        Default values may be set in the configuration file
                        (/etc/volatilityrc)
  --conf-file=/home/phil/.volatilityrc
                        User based configuration file
  -d, --debug           Debug volatility
  --plugins=PLUGINS     Additional plugin directories to use (colon separated)
  --info                Print information about all registered objects
  --cache-directory=/home/phil/.cache/volatility
                        Directory where cache files are stored
  --cache               Use caching
  --tz=TZ               Sets the (Olson) timezone for displaying timestamps
                        using pytz (if installed) or tzset
  -f FILENAME, --filename=FILENAME
                        Filename to use when opening an image
  --profile=WinXPSP2x86
                        Name of the profile to load (use --info to see a list
                        of supported profiles)
  -l LOCATION, --location=LOCATION
                        A URN location from which to load an address space
  -w, --write           Enable write support
  --dtb=DTB             DTB Address
  --shift=SHIFT         Mac KASLR shift address
--More--
```

FIGURE 11.2.

Part of the Volatility help screen.

```
    . ~/.bash_aliases
fi

# enable programmable completion features (you don't need to enable
# this, if it's already enabled in /etc/bash.bashrc and /etc/profile
# sources /etc/bash.bashrc).
if ! shopt -oq posix; then
  if [ -f /usr/share/bash-completion/bash_completion ]; then
    . /usr/share/bash-completion/bash_completion
  elif [ -f /etc/bash_completion ]; then
    . /etc/bash_completion
  fi
fi

alias upd='sudo apt-get update && sudo apt-get -y upgrade'
alias vpa='vol.py --profile=LinuxUbuntu-14_04-3_16_0-30x64 -f ~/PentesterAcademy/linux-forensics/cas
es/2015-3-9/ram.lime'
alias vpas2='vol.py --profile=LinuxUbuntu-14_04-3_16_0-30x64 -f /home/phil/cases/pas2/ram.lime'
alias vpaw='vol.py --profile=Win7SP1x64 -f ~/PentesterAcademy/windows-forensics/pawin7subject-memory
.img'

PERL_MB_OPT="--install_base \"/home/phil/perl5\""; export PERL_MB_OPT;
PERL_MM_OPT="INSTALL_BASE=/home/phil/perl5"; export PERL_MM_OPT;
export PATH=/home/phil/jdk1.8.0_66/bin:/home/phil/jdk1.8.0_66/jre/bin:$PATH;

export PATH="$PATH:$HOME/.rvm/bin" # Add RVM to PATH for scripting
                                                                    107,1         Bot
```

FIGURE 11.3.

Adding an alias near the end of ~/.bashrc to more easily run Volatility with a specific image and profile.

EXAMINING PROCESSES

Process lists

A good starting point when working with Volatility is to examine process information. A list of processes can be obtained from the pslist plugin. This is one of the most basic plugins that will look in the same memory locations as the tasklist utility. In other words, if an attacker has tried to cover his or her tracks, you may not be able to tell that from running this command alone. Partial results from running this command on a Windows 7 subject are shown in Figure 11.4. The execution time for this command against a 2GB memory image was 13.5 seconds.

There are a couple things to note about the output in Figure 11.4. First of all, you would normally want to capture all of this output to a file using > `<filename>` or |tee `<filename>` (in order to send results to the screen and a file). Second, most plugins will output a memory offset. Some of the lower level commands might require this offset as an input. Third, every process has an ID number (PID) and also knows the ID number of the process that launched it (PPID for parent PID). Fourth, each process may have multiple threads of execution (Thds) and will surely have multiple handles (Hnds). A handle is essentially a pointer that is used to refer to objects across processes.

The pslist plugin provides a flat view. In order to better understand what process started

```
phil@i7laptop:~/PentesterAcademy/windows-forensics$ vpaw pslist|more
Volatility Foundation Volatility Framework 2.5
Offset(V)          Name                    PID   PPID   Thds    Hnds   Sess  Wow64 Start
                   Exit
---------------------------------------------------------------------------------------
0xfffffa80018ad040 System                    4      0     80     662   ------     0 2015-12-10 15:10
:51 UTC+0000
0xfffffa800213e8d0 smss.exe                248      4      2      29   ------     0 2015-12-10 15:10
:51 UTC+0000
0xfffffa8002e11b30 csrss.exe               320    312      9     476        0     0 2015-12-10 15:11
:02 UTC+0000
0xfffffa80018be060 csrss.exe               368    360      9     285        1     0 2015-12-10 15:11
:03 UTC+0000
0xfffffa8002e26b30 wininit.exe             376    312      3      77        0     0 2015-12-10 15:11
:03 UTC+0000
0xfffffa8002e2f920 winlogon.exe            404    360      3     110        1     0 2015-12-10 15:11
:03 UTC+0000
0xfffffa8002ec3b30 services.exe            464    376      8     191        0     0 2015-12-10 15:11
:07 UTC+0000
0xfffffa8002ed5b30 lsass.exe               472    376      7     695        0     0 2015-12-10 15:11
:08 UTC+0000
0xfffffa8002ed99d0 lsm.exe                 480    376     10     141        0     0 2015-12-10 15:11
:08 UTC+0000
0xfffffa8002f3f340 svchost.exe             576    464      9     349        0     0 2015-12-10 15:11
:18 UTC+0000
0xfffffa8002e12060 VBoxService.ex          636    464     11     116        0     0 2015-12-10 15:11
```

FIGURE 11.4.

Partial results from running the pslist plugin against a Windows 7 subject.

other processes, the pstree plugin can be used. This will list processes as before, but children are listed under their parent and the name is preceded by a period for each level down in the tree. Partial output from this command is shown in Figure 11.5. This plugin required 2.6 seconds when run against a 2GB image.

The pslist plugin just searches through the usual list of processes that are stored in a linked list. A linked list is a way of storing items in which every item has a link to the next item (and sometimes the previous item). The psscan plugin, on the other hand, searches through memory for the same process information. Because of this, psscan might uncover hidden processes related to malware or some kind of attack. Partial output from this plugin is shown in Figure 11.6. This plugin required 4.4 seconds when run against a 2GB image.

The psscan plugin is able to output DOT files. A DOT file is used to describe a graph (directed tree structure). The command to run psscan and create a DOT file using our alias is `vpaw psscan --output=dot --output-file=psscan.dot`. The output file can be viewed with an appropriate viewer such as dotty. Part of the psscan.dot file being viewed in dotty is shown in Figure 11.7.

Volatility supplies a number of cross-referencing plugins. The purpose of these plugins is to detect inconsistencies when attackers or malware attempt to hide their presence. The cross-referencing command for processes is psxview. Partial output from running this command is shown in Figure 11.8. This plugin required 22.2 seconds to run against a 2GB image.

You might be wondering what you are looking for in the psxview results. Inconsistency is what you seek. A process that was detected by psscan, but not pslist, is worth investigating. Be

CHAPTER 11 Memory Forensics

```
phil@i7laptop:~/PentesterAcademy/windows-forensics$ time vpaw pstree
Volatility Foundation Volatility Framework 2.5
Name                                          Pid    PPid   Thds   Hnds  Time
------------------------------------------    ----   ----   ----   ----  ----
0xfffffa8002e11b30:csrss.exe                   320    312     9     476  2015-12-10 15:11:02 UTC+0000
0xfffffa8002e26b30:wininit.exe                 376    312     3      77  2015-12-10 15:11:03 UTC+0000
. 0xfffffa8002ec3b30:services.exe              464    376     8     191  2015-12-10 15:11:07 UTC+0000
.. 0xfffffa8002f6e390:svchost.exe              848    464    31     965  2015-12-10 15:11:26 UTC+0000
.. 0xfffffa8002f3f340:svchost.exe              576    464     9     349  2015-12-10 15:11:18 UTC+0000
.. 0xfffffa800357b740:svchost.exe             2156    464     9     360  2015-12-10 15:12:21 UTC+0000
.. 0xfffffa8003151b30:svchost.exe             1164    464    19     294  2015-12-10 15:11:38 UTC+0000
.. 0xfffffa80030aeb30:svchost.exe              532    464    16     472  2015-12-10 15:11:32 UTC+0000
.. 0xfffffa800366d060:svchost.exe             2968    464    12     318  2015-12-10 15:13:50 UTC+0000
.. 0xfffffa8003499b30:SearchIndexer.          1828    464    13     606  2015-12-10 15:12:17 UTC+0000
.. 0xfffffa8034ec9e0:wmpnetwk.exe             1328    464    13     442  2015-12-10 15:12:18 UTC+0000
.. 0xfffffa8002f0c060:svchost.exe              824    464    26     550  2015-12-10 15:11:26 UTC+0000
... 0xfffffa80033aeb30:dwm.exe                1940    824     3      69  2015-12-10 15:12:08 UTC+0000
.. 0xfffffa8001b04b30:WUDFHost.exe             160    824     8     197  2015-12-10 15:16:05 UTC+0000
.. 0xfffffa8002f44350:svchost.exe              700    464     6     244  2015-12-10 15:11:21 UTC+0000
.. 0xfffffa800337e9d0:taskhost.exe            1872    464     7     184  2015-12-10 15:12:08 UTC+0000
.. 0xfffffa8002e12060:VBoxService.ex           636    464    11     116  2015-12-10 15:11:19 UTC+0000
.. 0xfffffa800312c060:spoolsv.exe             1132    464    13     282  2015-12-10 15:11:36 UTC+0000
.. 0xfffffa8003068700:svchost.exe             1012    464    16     451  2015-12-10 15:11:30 UTC+0000
.. 0xfffffa8002f11060:svchost.exe              788    464    21     562  2015-12-10 15:11:24 UTC+0000
.. 0xfffffa80031bbb30:svchost.exe             1276    464    24     317  2015-12-10 15:11:40 UTC+0000
. 0xfffffa8002ed5b30:lsass.exe                 472    376     7     695  2015-12-10 15:11:08 UTC+0000
. 0xfffffa8002ed99d0:lsm.exe                   480    376    10     141  2015-12-10 15:11:08 UTC+0000
0xfffffa80018ad040:System                        4      0    80     662  2015-12-10 15:10:51 UTC+0000
. 0xfffffa800213e8d0:smss.exe                  248      4     2      29  2015-12-10 15:10:51 UTC+0000
0xfffffa800339e2e0:explorer.exe               1964   1932    21     830  2015-12-10 15:12:09 UTC+0000
. 0xfffffa80033738e0:VBoxTray.exe             1368   1964    13     171  2015-12-10 15:12:13 UTC+0000
. 0xfffffa8001d80060:cmd.exe                   284   1964     1      20  2015-12-11 16:21:38 UTC+0000
.. 0xfffffa8001c67b30:bc.exe                  3316    284     1      18  2015-12-11 16:22:30 UTC+0000
... 0xfffffa8001cd5060:bc.exe                 3700   3316     3     124  2015-12-11 16:22:31 UTC+0000
.... 0xfffffa80036a6060:cmd.exe               3676   3700     1      35  2015-12-11 16:22:31 UTC+0000
0xfffffa80018be060:csrss.exe                   368    360     9     285  2015-12-10 15:11:03 UTC+0000
```

FIGURE 11.5.

Partial output from the pstree plugin.

```
phil@i7laptop:~/PentesterAcademy/windows-forensics$ time vpaw psscan |tee psscan.txt
Volatility Foundation Volatility Framework 2.5
Offset(P)           Name              PID    PPID  PDB                Time created
Time exited
------------------  ----------------  -----  ----  -----------------  ---------------------------
0x0000000010e0f0f0  chrome.exe        3448   2412  0x000000006ca4a000 2015-12-11 16:13:14 UTC+0000
2015-12-11 16:21:05 UTC+0000
0x000000005d9d4740                       0      0 0xfffffa80040221a0

0x000000007dab40f0  chrome.exe        4016   2412  0x00000000007e0000 2015-12-11 16:04:31 UTC+0000
2015-12-11 16:21:05 UTC+0000
0x000000007dd4de20  chrome.exe        2952   2412  0x000000006e69c000 2015-12-11 16:02:46 UTC+0000
2015-12-11 16:03:06 UTC+0000
0x000000007dfd2b30  chrome.exe        3428   2412  0x000000006d702000 2015-12-11 16:03:05 UTC+0000
2015-12-11 16:03:24 UTC+0000
0x000000007e06f620  svchost.exe       2968    464  0x000000000897d000 2015-12-10 15:13:50 UTC+0000

0x000000007e0a8620  cmd.exe           3676   3700  0x00000000323a6000 2015-12-11 16:22:31 UTC+0000

0x000000007e29c0f0  SearchIndexer.    1828    464  0x000000000fcbd000 2015-12-10 15:12:17 UTC+0000

0x000000007e2eefa0  wmpnetwk.exe      1328    464  0x000000000e942000 2015-12-10 15:12:18 UTC+0000

0x000000007e37dd00  svchost.exe       2156    464  0x000000000d849000 2015-12-10 15:12:21 UTC+0000

0x000000007e575ea0  VBoxTray.exe      1368   1964  0x0000000012602000 2015-12-10 15:12:13 UTC+0000
```

FIGURE 11.6.

Partial output from the psscan plugin.

Examining processes 483

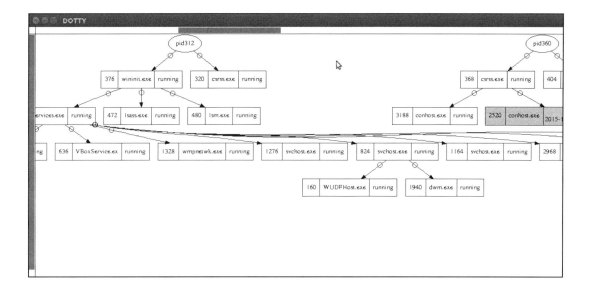

FIGURE 11.7.

Using dotty to examine psscan results in graph format.

```
phil@i7laptop:~/PentesterAcademy/windows-forensics$ time vpaw psxview |tee psxview.txt
Volatility Foundation Volatility Framework 2.5
Offset(P)          Name              PID  pslist psscan thrdproc pspcid csrss session deskthrd
ExitTime
------------------ ----------------- ---- ------ ------ -------- ------ ----- ------- --------
--------
0x000000007e941900 svchost.exe        576 True   True   True     True   True  True    True
0x000000007e37dd00 svchost.exe       2156 True   True   True     True   True  True    False
0x000000007e8290f0 wininit.exe        376 True   True   True     True   True  True    True
0x000000007fa6a0f0 bc.exe            3316 True   True   True     True   True  True    False
0x000000007e5a08a0 explorer.exe      1964 True   True   True     True   True  True    True
0x000000007fa6e620 conhost.exe       3188 True   True   True     True   True  True    True
0x000000007e8dbf90 lsm.exe            480 True   True   True     True   True  True    False
0x000000007e06f620 svchost.exe       2968 True   True   True     True   True  True    False
0x000000007e90e620 svchost.exe        824 True   True   True     True   True  True    True
0x000000007e7540f0 svchost.exe       1164 True   True   True     True   True  True    True
0x000000007e814620 VBoxService.ex     636 True   True   True     True   True  True    True
0x000000007e5b10f0 dwm.exe           1940 True   True   True     True   True  True    True
0x000000007e6b10f0 svchost.exe        532 True   True   True     True   True  True    True
0x000000007fad7620 bc.exe            3700 True   True   True     True   True  True    True
0x000000007e575ea0 VBoxTray.exe      1368 True   True   True     True   True  True    True
0x000000007e66acc0 svchost.exe       1012 True   True   True     True   True  True    True
0x000000007e72e620 spoolsv.exe       1132 True   True   True     True   True  True    True
0x000000007e8d80f0 lsass.exe          472 True   True   True     True   True  True    False
0x000000007e2eefa0 wmpnetwk.exe      1328 True   True   True     True   True  True    True
0x000000007e970950 svchost.exe        848 True   True   True     True   True  True    True
0x000000007e29c0f0 SearchIndexer.    1828 True   True   True     True   True  True    True
```

FIGURE 11.8.

Partial output from running the psxview plugin.

aware that some legitimate processes might be hidden in the normal process list. Just because something looks inconsistent does not mean it is malware. By the same token, some malware and attackers do a poor job of hiding themselves and their processes might not be flagged by this tool.

Drilling down into a single process

The process listing plugins discussed in the previous section might identify processes that warrant further investigation. The getsids plugin can be used to retrieve security identifiers (SIDs) for a particular process. This information can be used to identify processes that belong to specific users. If a process has had its privileges escalated inappropriately by an attacker or malware, it will show up in the results from getsids. Partial results from running getsids against a couple processes on a Windows 7 system are shown in Figure 11.9. You can specify a process for getsids using the -p option.

The top of Figure 11.9 shows SIDs for a Chrome process. Notice the the first SID listed is for the John user. This indicates that John is running this process. The same is also true for the command prompt shown in the bottom portion of the figure.

The privs plugin is used to list any privileges that have been granted to a process. This information can be used to identify processes that have been trojaned and/or malware. For example, a word processor or web browser should not have administrative privileges such as the ability to add machines to the domain or increase user disk quotas. Because privileges

```
phil@i7laptop:~/PentesterAcademy/windows-forensics$ vpaw getsids -p 2412
Volatility Foundation Volatility Framework 2.5
chrome.exe (2412): S-1-5-21-3073187811-2502202371-618229334-1001 (John)
chrome.exe (2412): S-1-5-21-3073187811-2502202371-618229334-513 (Domain Users)
chrome.exe (2412): S-1-1-0 (Everyone)
chrome.exe (2412): S-1-5-21-3073187811-2502202371-618229334-1000
chrome.exe (2412): S-1-5-32-544 (Administrators)
chrome.exe (2412): S-1-5-32-545 (Users)
chrome.exe (2412): S-1-5-4 (Interactive)
chrome.exe (2412): S-1-2-1 (Console Logon (Users who are logged onto the physical console))
chrome.exe (2412): S-1-5-11 (Authenticated Users)
chrome.exe (2412): S-1-5-15 (This Organization)
chrome.exe (2412): S-1-5-5-0-122847 (Logon Session)
chrome.exe (2412): S-1-2-0 (Local (Users with the ability to log in locally))
chrome.exe (2412): S-1-5-64-10 (NTLM Authentication)
chrome.exe (2412): S-1-16-8192 (Medium Mandatory Level)
phil@i7laptop:~/PentesterAcademy/windows-forensics$ vpaw getsids -p 284
Volatility Foundation Volatility Framework 2.5
cmd.exe (284): S-1-5-21-3073187811-2502202371-618229334-1001 (John)
cmd.exe (284): S-1-5-21-3073187811-2502202371-618229334-513 (Domain Users)
cmd.exe (284): S-1-1-0 (Everyone)
cmd.exe (284): S-1-5-21-3073187811-2502202371-618229334-1000
cmd.exe (284): S-1-5-32-544 (Administrators)
cmd.exe (284): S-1-5-32-545 (Users)
cmd.exe (284): S-1-5-4 (Interactive)
cmd.exe (284): S-1-2-1 (Console Logon (Users who are logged onto the physical console))
cmd.exe (284): S-1-5-11 (Authenticated Users)
```

FIGURE 11.9.

Using getsids to determine process owners and/or privileges.

can be inherited from a parent process, the --silent option can be useful as it will only show the privileges explicitly enabled by a process. Partial output from running privs against the Chrome process from Figure 11.9 is shown in Figure 11.10. Rerunning this plugin with the --silent option produced no output which indicates that no privileges were explicitly enabled by the process.

As mentioned previously, handles are used in Windows to refer to system objects. There are many types of system objects. Forensic investigators might be particularly interested in key, directory, file, and process handles which refer to registry keys, directories, files, and managed processes, respectively. The handles plugin will list handles used by a process. Running this plugin against our Chrome process produced no results. The same cannot be said when running this plugin against a command prompt process. Partial results from this plugin are shown in Figure 11.11.

Due to the vastness of the registry some malware will attempt to hide information inside registry keys. The handles plugin allows those keys to be identified. A tool such as FREd can then be used to examine the appropriate parts of the registry. Volatility does have the ability to access the in-memory registry image, but navigating this registry image with Volatility is much more tedious than using full-feature registry viewers to examine hive files. The file and directory handles can alert you to things a process is touching that it should not.

Many programs support command line arguments. For example, to run notepad and directly open a file one would type `notepad <filename>`. By retrieving the command line from such a notepad process we can determine what file was being edited. Some poorly written

```
phil@i7laptop:~/PentesterAcademy/windows-forensics$ vpaw privs -p 2412
Volatility Foundation Volatility Framework 2.5
Pid      Process            Value Privilege                      Attributes              Descr
iption
-------- ------------------ ----- ------------------------------ ----------------------- -----
------
    2412 chrome.exe             2 SeCreateTokenPrivilege                                 Creat
e a token object
    2412 chrome.exe             3 SeAssignPrimaryTokenPrivilege                          Repla
ce a process-level token
    2412 chrome.exe             4 SeLockMemoryPrivilege                                  Lock
pages in memory
    2412 chrome.exe             5 SeIncreaseQuotaPrivilege                               Incre
ase quotas
    2412 chrome.exe             6 SeMachineAccountPrivilege                              Add w
orkstations to the domain
    2412 chrome.exe             7 SeTcbPrivilege                                         Act a
s part of the operating system
    2412 chrome.exe             8 SeSecurityPrivilege                                    Manag
e auditing and security log
    2412 chrome.exe             9 SeTakeOwnershipPrivilege                               Take
ownership of files/objects
    2412 chrome.exe            10 SeLoadDriverPrivilege                                  Load
and unload device drivers
    2412 chrome.exe            11 SeSystemProfilePrivilege                               Profi
le system performance
    2412 chrome.exe            12 SeSystemtimePrivilege                                  Chang
```

FIGURE 11.10.

Partial output from running the privs plugin on a Chrome process.

```
phil@i7laptop:~/PentesterAcademy/windows-forensics$ vpaw handles -p 284
Volatility Foundation Volatility Framework 2.5
Offset(V)           Pid     Handle              Access  Type            Details
------------------  ------  ------------------  ------  --------------  -------
0xffff8a00cf07060   284     0x4                 0x9     Key             MACHINE\SOFTWARE\MI
CROSOFT\WINDOWS NT\CURRENTVERSION\IMAGE FILE EXECUTION OPTIONS
0xffff8a000b4e520   284     0x8                 0x3     Directory       KnownDlls
0xfffffa80031c4290  284     0xc                 0x100020 File           \Device\Mup\;E:\vbo
xsrv\shared\aesshell
0xfffffa8003578ae0  284     0x10                0x1f0003 Event
0xffff8a001d569b0   284     0x14                0x20019 Key             MACHINE\SYSTEM\CONT
ROLSET001\CONTROL\NLS\SORTING\VERSIONS
0xfffffa80039449d0  284     0x18                0x1f0001 ALPC Port
0xfffffa8003a1bbb0  284     0x1c                0x1f0001 ALPC Port
0xffff8a0128017c0   284     0x20                0x1     Key             MACHINE\SYSTEM\CONT
ROLSET001\CONTROL\SESSION MANAGER
0xfffffa8001c43430  284     0x24                0x804   EtwRegistration
0xfffffa8004051bc0  284     0x28                0x21f0003 Event
0xfffffa8002e41940  284     0x2c                0xf037f WindowStation   WinSta0
0xfffffa8002e7bd30  284     0x30                0xf01ff Desktop         Default
0xfffffa8002e41940  284     0x34                0xf037f WindowStation   WinSta0
0xffff8a00b234f10   284     0x38                0x20019 Key             MACHINE
0xfffffa8001d30060  284     0x3c                0x1fffff Thread         TID 3784 PID 284
0xffff8a00857b550   284     0x40                0xf003f Key             USER\S-1-5-21-30731
87811-2502202371-618229334-1001
0xffff8a00933e5c0   284     0x44                0x20019 Key             MACHINE\SYSTEM\CONT
ROLSET001\CONTROL\NLS\LOCALE
```

FIGURE 11.11.

Partial results from running the handles plugin against a command prompt.

programs will accept usernames and passwords as command line arguments. The Volatility cmdline plugin allows the command line used to launch a process to be retrieved. Running this plugin for a couple of processes named bc.exe is shown in Figure 11.12. Note the comma-separated list of process IDs in the -p option.

The results shown in Figure 11.12 are suspicious. It appears that this program is being passed a remote IP address and port number. On Linux and Unix systems, bc is the basic calculator program. Some research into this process is justified, especially given that it may be performing some network communications (which is not something it sounds like a calculator would be doing).

The dlllist plugin can be used to list any executables and DLLs used by a process. Running this plugin against the Chrome process leads to an error because the Program Execution Block (PEB) cannot be read for the process. This error is fairly common and does not necessarily mean that a process is malicious. The most common reason for this error is that some of the process memory is currently paged out (stored in the page file).

Running this module against one of the bc.exe processes is shown in Figure 11.13. Note that Volatility recommends running the ldrmodules plugin as this process uses WoW64 (Windows on Windows 64-bit). WoW64 is used to run 32-bit applications on 64-bit versions of Windows. The results from running the recommended ldrmodules plugin against the bc.exe are shown in Figure 11.14.

A few of the DLLs in Figure 11.14 look a bit suspicious. In particular, sechost.dll, rpcrt4.dll, nsi.dll, and cyrptbase.dll make it look like this program is performing some sort of encrypted

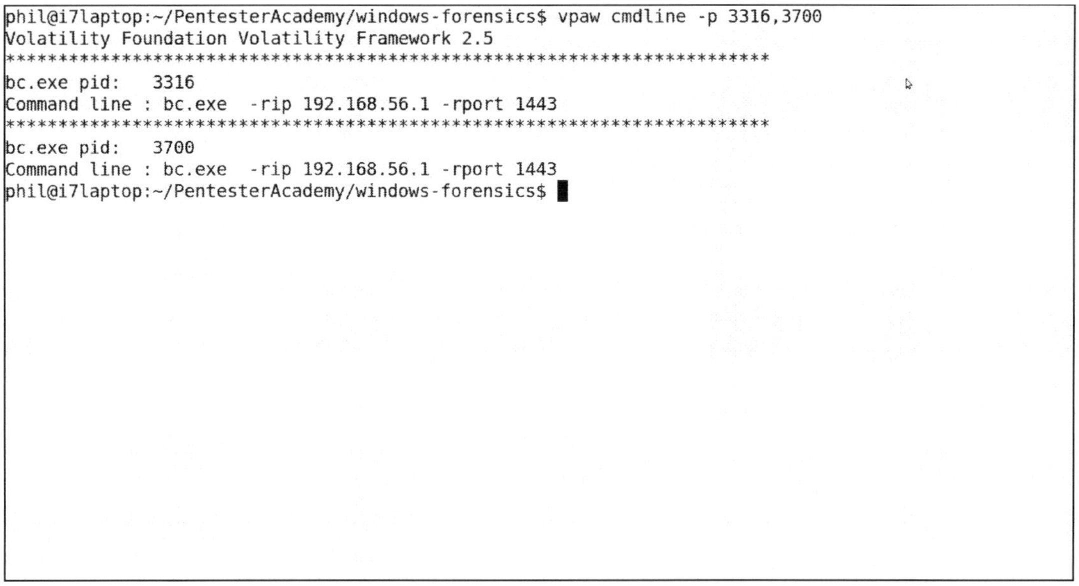

```
phil@i7laptop:~/PentesterAcademy/windows-forensics$ vpaw cmdline -p 3316,3700
Volatility Foundation Volatility Framework 2.5
************************************************************************
bc.exe pid:    3316
Command line : bc.exe  -rip 192.168.56.1 -rport 1443
************************************************************************
bc.exe pid:    3700
Command line : bc.exe  -rip 192.168.56.1 -rport 1443
phil@i7laptop:~/PentesterAcademy/windows-forensics$
```

FIGURE 11.12.

Running the Volatility cmdline plugin on two suspicious processes.

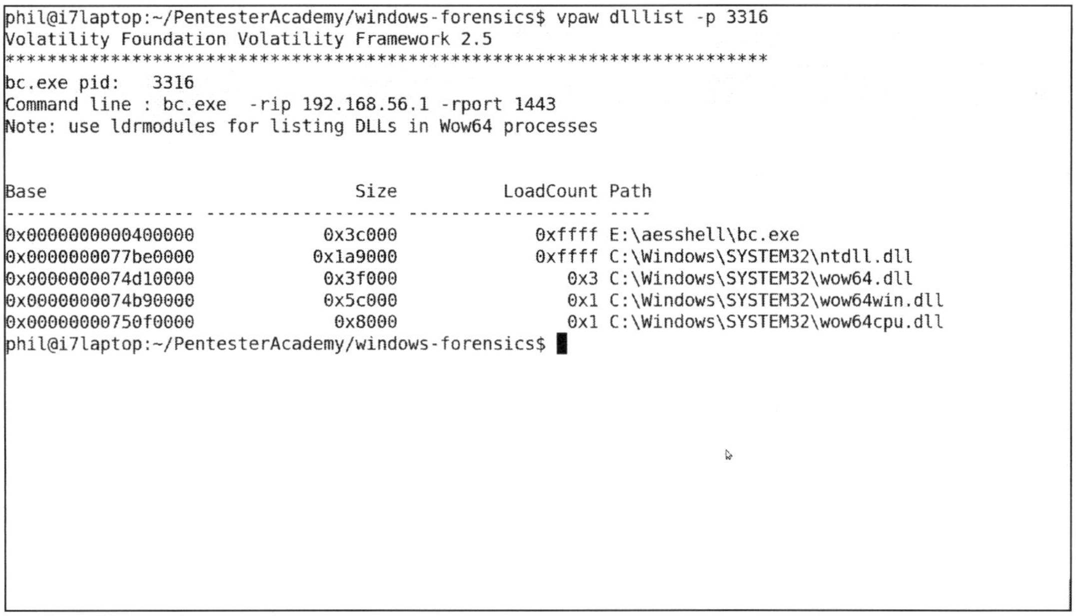

```
phil@i7laptop:~/PentesterAcademy/windows-forensics$ vpaw dlllist -p 3316
Volatility Foundation Volatility Framework 2.5
************************************************************************
bc.exe pid:    3316
Command line : bc.exe  -rip 192.168.56.1 -rport 1443
Note: use ldrmodules for listing DLLs in Wow64 processes

Base                Size             LoadCount Path
------------------  ---------------  --------- ----
0x0000000000400000  0x3c000             0xffff E:\aesshell\bc.exe
0x0000000077be0000  0x1a9000            0xffff C:\Windows\SYSTEM32\ntdll.dll
0x0000000074d10000  0x3f000                0x3 C:\Windows\SYSTEM32\wow64.dll
0x0000000074b90000  0x5c000                0x1 C:\Windows\SYSTEM32\wow64win.dll
0x00000000750f0000  0x8000                 0x1 C:\Windows\SYSTEM32\wow64cpu.dll
phil@i7laptop:~/PentesterAcademy/windows-forensics$
```

FIGURE 11.13.

Running the dlllist plugin against a bc.exe process running on Windows 7. Note that Volatility suggests running the ldrmodule to list DLLs in a WoW64 process.

488 CHAPTER 11 Memory Forensics

```
phil@i7laptop:~/PentesterAcademy/windows-forensics$ vpaw ldrmodules -p 3316
Volatility Foundation Volatility Framework 2.5
Pid        Process              Base                InLoad InInit InMem MappedPath
--------   ------------------   ------------------  ------ ------ ----- ----------
    3316   bc.exe               0x0000000075ee0000  False  False  False \Windows\SysWOW64\KernelBase.dll
    3316   bc.exe               0x0000000000400000  True   False  True  \;E:\vboxsrv\shared\aesshell\bc.exe
    3316   bc.exe               0x0000000075f30000  False  False  False \Windows\SysWOW64\rpcrt4.dll
    3316   bc.exe               0x0000000074b40000  False  False  False \Windows\SysWOW64\apphelp.dll
    3316   bc.exe               0x0000000076020000  False  False  False \Windows\SysWOW64\sechost.dll
    3316   bc.exe               0x0000000075a70000  False  False  False \Windows\SysWOW64\ws2_32.dll
    3316   bc.exe               0x0000000074b90000  True   True   True  \Windows\System32\wow64win.dll
    3316   bc.exe               0x0000000075c70000  False  False  False \Windows\SysWOW64\msvcrt.dll
    3316   bc.exe               0x00000000762b0000  False  False  False \Windows\SysWOW64\kernel32.dll
    3316   bc.exe               0x0000000077dc0000  False  False  False \Windows\SysWOW64\ntdll.dll
    3316   bc.exe               0x0000000077be0000  True   True   True  \Windows\System32\ntdll.dll
    3316   bc.exe               0x00000000750f0000  True   True   True  \Windows\System32\wow64cpu.dll
    3316   bc.exe               0x0000000077490000  False  False  False \Windows\SysWOW64\nsi.dll
    3316   bc.exe               0x0000000075920000  False  False  False \Windows\SysWOW64\sspicli.dll
    3316   bc.exe               0x0000000075910000  False  False  False \Windows\SysWOW64\cryptbase.dll
    3316   bc.exe               0x0000000074d10000  True   True   True  \Windows\System32\wow64.dll
phil@i7laptop:~/PentesterAcademy/windows-forensics$
```

FIGURE 11.14.

Running the ldrmodules plugin against a bc.exe process running on Windows 7.

network communication. When combined with the command line information found previously, this program is suspicious enough to justify further investigation.

A process' memory space can be dumped to disk using the memdump plugin. This can be useful when investigating a suspicious process in order to determine what it does. When dumping a process with memdump the --dump-dir option must be used to specify an output directory. Files are saved as <process ID>.dmp. A utility such as strings and/or grep can be used to extract text from the dump file in order to divine its function. If you are not familiar with strings, it is a simple program that will walk through a file and print out anything that looks like it might be text. The syntax for this tool is just `strings <filename>`.

The memmap plugin will display resident memory pages. This plugin will also map virtual and physical addresses. Partial results from running this plugin against a bc.exe process are shown in Figure 11.15. Notice that all of the pages in the figure are 4096 (0x1000) bytes in size.

The dump file obtained using the memdump plugin is good for searching. It is not as useful for examining the actual program code. A process' executable may be dumped using the procdump plugin. The --dump-dir option must be used with this plugin. Files are saved as executable.<process ID>.exe. The start of the bc.exe executable is shown in Figure 11.16.

You may be wondering why anyone would need to use procdump when the executable can be read from the filesystem image directly. As we will see in the next chapter, some malware authors will use various techniques in order to obfuscate their code. Having the code as it appears in memory can be helpful in such situations. Even some legitimate executables will do things that make reading the code directly from the executable file challenging.

```
phil@i7laptop:~/PentesterAcademy/windows-forensics$ vpaw memmap -p 3316|more
Volatility Foundation Volatility Framework 2.5
bc.exe pid:   3316
Virtual               Physical              Size          DumpFileOffset
------------------    ------------------    ----------    ------------------
0x0000000000010000    0x000000005d171000    0x1000        0x0
0x0000000000020000    0x000000002eef5000    0x1000        0x1000
0x0000000000021000    0x00000000023f7000    0x1000        0x2000
0x000000000002f000    0x000000002ff76000    0x1000        0x3000
0x0000000000040000    0x000000002a22b000    0x1000        0x4000
0x000000000008d000    0x0000000057252000    0x1000        0x5000
0x000000000008e000    0x000000006cbc9000    0x1000        0x6000
0x000000000008f000    0x000000006fdbd000    0x1000        0x7000
0x0000000000183000    0x000000002d5d8000    0x1000        0x8000
0x0000000000184000    0x000000002aed7000    0x1000        0x9000
0x0000000000185000    0x000000009bd6000     0x1000        0xa000
0x0000000000186000    0x00000000389d5000    0x1000        0xb000
0x0000000000187000    0x0000000078bd4000    0x1000        0xc000
0x0000000000188000    0x000000002e853000    0x1000        0xd000
0x0000000000189000    0x0000000052fd2000    0x1000        0xe000
0x000000000018a000    0x000000003f9d1000    0x1000        0xf000
0x000000000018b000    0x000000006f9ce000    0x1000        0x10000
0x000000000018c000    0x00000000288cd000    0x1000        0x11000
0x000000000018d000    0x0000000037e4c000    0x1000        0x12000
0x000000000018e000    0x000000007416d000    0x1000        0x13000
0x000000000018f000    0x000000005dfde000    0x1000        0x14000
0x0000000000190000    0x000000005c3bf000    0x1000        0x15000
```

FIGURE 11.15.

Running the memmap plugin against a bc.exe process running on Windows 7.

```
00000000  4D 5A 90 00  03 00 00 00  04 00 00 00  FF FF 00 00  B8 00 00 00   MZ..............
00000014  00 00 00 00  40 00 00 00  00 00 00 00  00 00 00 00  00 00 00 00   ....@...........
00000028  00 00 00 00  00 00 00 00  00 00 00 00  00 00 00 00  00 00 00 00   ................
0000003C  D8 00 00 00  0E 1F BA 0E  00 B4 09 CD  21 B8 01 4C  CD 21 54 68   ............!..L.!Th
00000050  69 73 20 70  72 6F 67 72  61 6D 20 63  61 6E 6E 6F  74 20 62 65   is program cannot be
00000064  20 72 75 6E  20 69 6E 20  44 4F 53 20  6D 6F 64 65  2E 0D 0D 0A    run in DOS mode....
00000078  24 00 00 00  00 00 00 00  13 C4 5C C3  57 A5 32 90  57 A5 32 90   $.........\.W.2.W.2.
0000008C  57 A5 32 90  5E DD B6 90  7A A5 32 90  5E DD A7 90  49 A5 32 90   W.2.^...z.2.^...I.2.
000000A0  5E DD A1 90  52 A5 32 90  57 A5 33 90  2D A5 32 90  5E DD B1 90   ^...R.2.W.3.-.2.^...
000000B4  ED A5 32 90  5E DD A6 90  56 A5 32 90  5E DD A3 90  56 A5 32 90   ..2.^...V.2.^...V.2.
000000C8  52 69 63 68  57 A5 32 90  00 00 00 00  00 00 00 00  50 45 00 00   RichW.2.........PE..
000000DC  4C 01 04 00  2E 2C 4E 51  00 00 00 00  00 00 00 00  E0 00 03 01   L....,NQ............
000000F0  0B 01 09 00  00 9C 01 00  00 F6 01 00  00 00 00 00  F7 B2 00 00   ....................
00000104  00 10 00 00  00 B0 01 00  00 00 40 00  00 10 00 00  00 02 00 00   ..........@.........
00000118  05 00 00 00  00 00 00 00  05 00 00 00  00 00 00 00  00 C0 03 00   ....................
0000012C  00 04 00 00  00 00 00 00  03 00 00 80  00 00 10 00  00 10 00 00   ....................
00000140  00 00 10 00  00 10 00 00  00 00 00 00  10 00 00 00  00 00 00 00   ....................
00000154  00 00 00 00  14 08 02 00  3C 00 00 00  00 D0 02 00  38 EA 00 00   ........<.......8...
00000168  00 00 00 00  00 00 00 00  00 00 00 00  00 00 00 00  00 00 00 00   ....................
0000017C  00 00 00 00  00 00 00 00  00 00 00 00  00 00 00 00  00 00 00 00   ....................
00000190  00 00 00 00  00 00 00 00  00 00 00 00  00 00 00 00  E0 00 02 00   ....................
000001A4  40 00 00 00  00 00 00 00  00 00 00 00  00 B0 01 00  A8 01 00 00   @...................
000001B8  00 00 00 00  00 00 00 00  00 00 00 00  00 00 00 00  00 00 00 00   ....................
000001CC  00 00 00 00  2E 74 65 78  74 00 00 00  B6 9A 01 00  00 10 00 00   .....text...........
000001E0  00 9C 01 00  00 04 00 00  00 00 00 00  00 00 00 00  00 00 00 00   ....................
000001F4  20 00 00 60  2E 72 64 61  74 61 00 00  A4 61 00 00  00 B0 01 00   ...`.rdata...a......
--- executable.3316.exe       --0x0/0x30600-------------------------------
```

FIGURE 11.16.

The start of an executable extracted from memory with the procdump plugin.

FINDING MALWARE

Volatility provides several plugins that will attempt to locate malware somewhat automatically. The first such plugin we will discuss is apihooks. API hooking is something that malware might do in order to avoid detection. In most cases administrative privileges are required to create an API hook. There are a number of different types of API hooks. Regardless of the exact method employed, an API hook redirects a call to a legitimate function (usually a system function which requires an API call) to point at a malicious substitute.

Generally speaking the Volatility plugins for detecting malware take a while to run. The apihooks plugin is no exception. Running this plugin against a 2GB memory image required approximately 13 minutes. This plugin does seem to suffer from a large number of false positives. To be fair, it is not always possible to distinguish between a legitimate function that immediately branches and one that has been hooked. Partial results from running this plugin against a Windows 7 subject are shown in Figure 11.17.

If you suspect a system breach, you might wonder about the audit policies in place. As we have seen earlier in this book, this information can be obtained from the registry. It can also be retrieved using the Volatility auditpol plugin. Partial results from running this against a Windows 7 subject are shown in Figure 11.18.

Windows applications can ask to be notified of certain events. One method of implementing this notification is to register a call back function. A call back function is something that is executed whenever a certain type of event occurs. There are a large number of events for which

```
************************************************************************
Hook mode: Usermode
Hook type: Import Address Table (IAT)
Process: 576 (svchost.exe)
Victim module: umpo.dll (0x7fefce20000 - 0x7fefce4c000)
Function: advapi32.dll!PerfDeleteInstance
Hook address: 0x7fefd0b1ed4
Hooking module: pcwum.DLL

Disassembly(0):
0xfd0b1ed4 48               DEC EAX
0xfd0b1ed5 895c2408         MOV [ESP+0x8], EBX
0xfd0b1ed9 57               PUSH EDI
0xfd0b1eda 48               DEC EAX
0xfd0b1edb 83ec30           SUB ESP, 0x30
0xfd0b1ede 48               DEC EAX
0xfd0b1edf 8bfa             MOV EDI, EDX
0xfd0b1ee1 48               DEC EAX
0xfd0b1ee2 8bd9             MOV EBX, ECX
0xfd0b1ee4 e8dffbffff       CALL 0xfd0b1ac8
0xfd0b1ee9 33d2             XOR EDX, EDX
0xfd0b1eeb 48               DEC EAX

************************************************************************
Hook mode: Usermode
Hook type: Import Address Table (IAT)
"apihooks.txt" 1258L, 44390C                            1,1        Top
```

FIGURE 11.17.

Partial results from running the apihooks plugin against a Windows 7 subject.

an application can request to be notified. One event that is often checked by malware is system shutdown. This is one reason why pulling the plug on a subject system can sometimes (but not always) be a better idea than performing a normal shutdown. Partial results from running the Volatility callbacks plugin are shown in Figure 11.19.

Some malware might try to infect a system by installing new device drivers. Alternatively, existing device drives could be replaced. The device tree can be retrieved using the Volatility devicetree plugin. Partial results from running this plugin against a Windows 7 system are shown in Figure 11.20.

If you are suspicious of a device driver the driverirp plugin may provide helpful information. This plugin will list driver Input/Output Request Packet (IRP) addresses. Altering the driver IRP addresses is another form of hooking. Any addresses that do not point to system binaries should be investigated. Partial output from this plugin is shown in Figure 11.21.

Applications can hook various events and cause code to be executed when the event occurs. Volatility provides an eventhooks plugin for detecting these event hooks. Results from running this plugin against a Windows 7 subject are shown in Figure 11.22. Note that one process (1964) has hooked the menu start events. Two processes (1368 and 1964) have hooked the desktop switch event. Some investigation reveals that these processes are explorer (1964) and the Virtual Box Tray (1368). These hooks appear legitimate for these two applications.

Windows allows applications to create timers. Once the specified time has elapsed, an application is notified either via a message or a call to a callback function. Timers can be used to avoid while loops that spend most of their time sleeping. The gditimers plugin can be used to

```
phil@i7laptop:~/PentesterAcademy/windows-forensics$ vpaw auditpol
Volatility Foundation Volatility Framework 2.5
System Events:
        Security State Change: S
        Security System Extention: Not Logged
        System Integrity: S/F
        IPSec Driver: Not Logged
        Other System Events: S/F
Logon/Logoff Events:
        Logon: S
        Logoff: S
        Account Lockout: S
        IPSec Main Mode: Not Logged
        Special Logon: S
        IPSec Quick Mode: Not Logged
        IPSec Extended Mode: Not Logged
        Other Logon Events: Not Logged
        Network Policy Server: S/F
Object Access Events:
        File System: Not Logged
        Registry: Not Logged
        Kernel Object: Not Logged
        SAM: Not Logged
        Other Object Events: Not Logged
        Certification Services: Not Logged
        Application Generated: Not Logged
        Handle Manipulation: Not Logged
```

FIGURE 11.18.

Partial results from running the Volatility auditpol plugin.

```
phil@i7laptop:~/PentesterAcademy/windows-forensics$ vpaw callbacks |tee callbacks.txt
Volatility Foundation Volatility Framework 2.5
Type                                  Callback           Module           Details
------------------------------------- ------------------ ---------------- ----------
EventCategoryTargetDeviceChange       0xfffff88001925850 volsnap.sys      volsnap
GenericKernelCallback                 0xfffff8800263bd2c peauth.sys       -
EventCategoryDeviceInterfaceChange    0xfffff96000190bd0 win32k.sys       Win32k
EventCategoryTargetDeviceChange       0xfffff96000191304 win32k.sys       Win32k
EventCategoryDeviceInterfaceChange    0xfffff96000190bd0 win32k.sys       Win32k
EventCategoryDeviceInterfaceChange    0xfffff96000190bd0 win32k.sys       Win32k
EventCategoryDeviceInterfaceChange    0xfffff96000190a88 win32k.sys       Win32k
EventCategoryTargetDeviceChange       0xfffff96000191304 win32k.sys       Win32k
EventCategoryTargetDeviceChange       0xfffff96000190870 win32k.sys       Win32k
EventCategoryTargetDeviceChange       0xfffff96000191304 win32k.sys       Win32k
EventCategoryTargetDeviceChange       0xfffff96000191304 win32k.sys       Win32k
EventCategoryTargetDeviceChange       0xfffff96000191304 win32k.sys       Win32k
GenericKernelCallback                 0xfffff960001a7860 win32k.sys       -
EventCategoryHardwareProfileChange    0xfffff880035770e8 i8042prt.sys     i8042prt
EventCategoryTargetDeviceChange       0xfffff800027fc180 ntoskrnl.exe     mouclass
EventCategoryDeviceInterfaceChange    0xfffff88001949370 volsnap.sys      volsnap
EventCategoryTargetDeviceChange       0xfffff88001925850 volsnap.sys      volsnap
EventCategoryHardwareProfileChange    0xfffff88001401138 VIDEOPRT.SYS     VBoxVideo
EventCategoryHardwareProfileChange    0xfffff88003427890 HDAudBus.sys     HDAudBus
EventCategoryDeviceInterfaceChange    0xfffff880035f68a4 CompositeBus.sys CompositeBus
EventCategoryTargetDeviceChange       0xfffff88000ce5914 mountmgr.sys     mountmgr
EventCategoryDeviceInterfaceChange    0xfffff880035f68a4 CompositeBus.sys CompositeBus
IoRegisterFsRegistrationChange        0xfffff880010f17f0 fltmgr.sys       -
```

FIGURE 11.19.

Partial output from running the Volatility callbacks plugin against a Windows 7 system.

```
phil@i7laptop:~/PentesterAcademy/windows-forensics$ vpaw devicetree
Volatility Foundation Volatility Framework 2.5
DRV 0x7e38e900 \Driver\PROCEXP152
---| DEV 0xfffffa8001992a40 PROCEXP152 UNKNOWN
DRV 0x7e40c7c0 \FileSystem\srvnet
---| DEV 0xfffffa800320b2e0 SrvNet FILE_DEVICE_NETWORK_FILE_SYSTEM
---| DEV 0xfffffa800320b790 SrvAdmin FILE_DEVICE_UNKNOWN
DRV 0x7e428970 \Driver\secdrv
---| DEV 0xfffffa8003101060 Secdrv UNKNOWN
---| DEV 0xfffffa8003228750 AscKmd UNKNOWN
DRV 0x7e43c370 \Driver\tcpipreg
DRV 0x7e45d400 \FileSystem\srv2
---| DEV 0xfffffa80031d8260 Srv2 FILE_DEVICE_NETWORK_FILE_SYSTEM
DRV 0x7e473060 \FileSystem\srv
---| DEV 0xfffffa8003272560 LanmanServer FILE_DEVICE_NETWORK
DRV 0x7e553a80 \Driver\AsyncMac
---| DEV 0xfffffa800367b050 NDMP13 FILE_DEVICE_PHYSICAL_NETCARD
---| DEV 0xfffffa8001992cb0 ASYNCMAC FILE_DEVICE_NETWORK
DRV 0x7e553e70 \Driver\USBSTOR
---| DEV 0xfffffa8001a91b60 00000053 FILE_DEVICE_DISK
------| ATT 0xfffffa8001ae8060 DR1 - \Driver\Disk FILE_DEVICE_DISK
---------| ATT 0xfffffa8001acb040 - \Driver\partmgr FILE_DEVICE_DISK
---| DEV 0xfffffa8001ae5850 00000052 FILE_DEVICE_BUS_EXTENDER
DRV 0x7e69a2e0 \Driver\rspndr
---| DEV 0xfffffa800308ce40 rspndr FILE_DEVICE_NETWORK
DRV 0x7e69b060 \Driver\lltdio
---| DEV 0xfffffa800309bc80 lltdio FILE_DEVICE_NETWORK
```

FIGURE 11.20.

Partial results from running devicetree against a Windows 7 subject.

```
phil@i7laptop:~/PentesterAcademy/windows-forensics$ vpaw driverirp |more
Volatility Foundation Volatility Framework 2.5
----------------------------------------------------
DriverName: PROCEXP152
DriverStart: 0xfffff88002a31000
DriverSize: 0xc000
DriverStartIo: 0x0
  0 IRP_MJ_CREATE                      0xfffff88002a33000 PROCEXP152.SYS
  1 IRP_MJ_CREATE_NAMED_PIPE           0xfffff800026ce1d4 ntoskrnl.exe
  2 IRP_MJ_CLOSE                       0xfffff88002a33000 PROCEXP152.SYS
  3 IRP_MJ_READ                        0xfffff800026ce1d4 ntoskrnl.exe
  4 IRP_MJ_WRITE                       0xfffff800026ce1d4 ntoskrnl.exe
  5 IRP_MJ_QUERY_INFORMATION           0xfffff800026ce1d4 ntoskrnl.exe
  6 IRP_MJ_SET_INFORMATION             0xfffff800026ce1d4 ntoskrnl.exe
  7 IRP_MJ_QUERY_EA                    0xfffff800026ce1d4 ntoskrnl.exe
  8 IRP_MJ_SET_EA                      0xfffff800026ce1d4 ntoskrnl.exe
  9 IRP_MJ_FLUSH_BUFFERS               0xfffff800026ce1d4 ntoskrnl.exe
 10 IRP_MJ_QUERY_VOLUME_INFORMATION    0xfffff800026ce1d4 ntoskrnl.exe
 11 IRP_MJ_SET_VOLUME_INFORMATION      0xfffff800026ce1d4 ntoskrnl.exe
 12 IRP_MJ_DIRECTORY_CONTROL           0xfffff800026ce1d4 ntoskrnl.exe
 13 IRP_MJ_FILE_SYSTEM_CONTROL         0xfffff800026ce1d4 ntoskrnl.exe
 14 IRP_MJ_DEVICE_CONTROL              0xfffff88002a33000 PROCEXP152.SYS
 15 IRP_MJ_INTERNAL_DEVICE_CONTROL     0xfffff800026ce1d4 ntoskrnl.exe
 16 IRP_MJ_SHUTDOWN                    0xfffff800026ce1d4 ntoskrnl.exe
 17 IRP_MJ_LOCK_CONTROL                0xfffff800026ce1d4 ntoskrnl.exe
 18 IRP_MJ_CLEANUP                     0xfffff800026ce1d4 ntoskrnl.exe
 19 IRP_MJ_CREATE_MAILSLOT             0xfffff800026ce1d4 ntoskrnl.exe
```

FIGURE 11.21.

Partial output from the driverirp Volatility plugin.

```
phil@i7laptop:~/PentesterAcademy/windows-forensics$ vpaw eventhooks
Volatility Foundation Volatility Framework 2.5
Handle: 0x20071, Object: 0xfffff900c1acab60, Session: 1
Type: TYPE_WINEVENTHOOK, Flags: 0, Thread: 1304, Process: 1964
eventMin: 0x4 EVENT_SYSTEM_MENUSTART
eventMax: 0x7 EVENT_SYSTEM_MENUPOPUPEND
Flags: , offPfn: 0xffc18248, idProcess: 0, idThread: 0
ihmod: -1

Handle: 0x300ed, Object: 0xfffff900c1b61a70, Session: 1
Type: TYPE_WINEVENTHOOK, Flags: 0, Thread: 1376, Process: 1368
eventMin: 0x20 EVENT_SYSTEM_DESKTOPSWITCH
eventMax: 0x20 EVENT_SYSTEM_DESKTOPSWITCH
Flags: , offPfn: 0x7fef93c1090, idProcess: 0, idThread: 0
ihmod: -1

Handle: 0x10119, Object: 0xfffff900c1aa5550, Session: 1
Type: TYPE_WINEVENTHOOK, Flags: 0, Thread: 1800, Process: 1964
eventMin: 0x20 EVENT_SYSTEM_DESKTOPSWITCH
eventMax: 0x20 EVENT_SYSTEM_DESKTOPSWITCH
Flags: , offPfn: 0x7fefaf52fd4, idProcess: 0, idThread: 0
ihmod: -1

phil@i7laptop:~/PentesterAcademy/windows-forensics$
```

FIGURE 11.22.

Results from running the eventhooks plugin against a Windows 7 subject.

494 CHAPTER 11 Memory Forensics

```
phil@i7laptop:~/PentesterAcademy/windows-forensics$ vpaw gditimers
Volatility Foundation Volatility Framework 2.5
 Sess            Handle Object             Thread  Process                    nID Rate(m
s)   Countdown(ms) Func
-----  --------------- ------------------  ------  -------------------------  ------- ------
----  --------------- ------------------
    0           0x10083 0xffff900c00e08e0     440  csrss.exe:320             0x7ffe       3
5000           35000 0xffff96000102be4
    0           0x10092 0xffff900c1abd430    2216  wmpnetwk.exe:1328          0x0        30
0000            5640 0x000007fefdf0b5f4
    0           0x1009e 0xffff900c1abb360    2216  wmpnetwk.exe:1328         0x7ffd
2000            2000 0x000007fef3eb6380
    0           0x100df 0xffff900c01a8360    2452  svchost.exe:848            0x0        30
0000          229640 0x000007fefdf0b5f4
    1           0x20043 0xffff900c0134410     436  csrss.exe:368             0x7ffe
1000             546 0xffff960001a5cb4
    1           0xc0069 0xffff900c1ba4730    1304  explorer.exe:1964         0x7ff4       6
0000           50171 0x0000000000000000
    1           0x3006f 0xffff900c1aaa110    1304  explorer.exe:1964          0x15       60
0000          589671 0x0000000000000000
    1           0x9008d 0xffff900c00d5200    1376  VBoxTray.exe:1368          0x0         1
0000            5046 0x0000000000000000
    1           0x1008f 0xffff900c1aa3ed0     436  csrss.exe:368             0x7ffc       3
5000           35000 0xffff96000102be4
    1           0x10093 0xffff900c1aa3d80     436  csrss.exe:368             0x7ffb
   32              32 0xffff96000155718
    1           0x200b5 0xffff900c1f677e0    1304  explorer.exe:1964          0xa        30
```

FIGURE 11.23.

Partial output from the gditimers Volatility plugin.

find applications that have registered timers. One piece of information provided by this plugin is the address of the function called when the timer expires. That code at this address can be examined if it is thought to be malicious. Partial results from running this plugin are shown in Figure 11.23.

There is a somewhat generic malware finder in Volatility called malfind. This plugin relies primarily on memory page permissions. Memory pages have permissions similar to files such as read, write, and execute. A well-constructed program will ensure that no writable and executable pages exist. Partial results from running malfind against a Windows 7 subject are shown in Figure 11.24.

MORE VOLATILITY COMMANDS

There are a good number of Volatility commands that we have yet to cover. The plugins covered in previous sections were ones that might apply to most investigations. In this section we will cover some of the Volatility commands that may be helpful for certain types of investigations and a complete waste of time in others. Because there is not a clear way to organize these miscellaneous plugins, they will be covered in alphabetical order with the exception of related plugins that will be discussed together.

The first miscellaneous plugin we will cover is clipboard. This plugin will retrieve anything stored in the Windows clipboard. Running this command is shown in Figure 11.25. The only real information displayed here is the text "ntuser.dat".

```
phil@i7laptop:~/PentesterAcademy/windows-forensics$ vpaw malfind
Volatility Foundation Volatility Framework 2.5
Process: svchost.exe Pid: 788 Address: 0x1410000
Vad Tag: VadS Protection: PAGE_EXECUTE_READWRITE
Flags: CommitCharge: 16, MemCommit: 1, PrivateMemory: 1, Protection: 6

0x01410000  41 ba 80 00 00 00 48 b8 38 a1 0d fe fe 07 00 00   A.....H.8.......
0x01410010  48 ff 20 90 41 ba 81 00 00 00 48 b8 38 a1 0d fe   H...A.....H.8...
0x01410020  fe 07 00 00 48 ff 20 90 41 ba 82 00 00 00 48 b8   ....H...A.....H.
0x01410030  38 a1 0d fe fe 07 00 00 48 ff 20 90 41 ba 83 00   8.......H...A...

0x01410000 41                 INC ECX
0x01410001 ba80000000         MOV EDX, 0x80
0x01410006 48                 DEC EAX
0x01410007 b838a10dfe         MOV EAX, 0xfe0da138
0x0141000c fe07               INC BYTE [EDI]
0x0141000e 0000               ADD [EAX], AL
0x01410010 48                 DEC EAX
0x01410011 ff20               JMP DWORD [EAX]
0x01410013 90                 NOP
0x01410014 41                 INC ECX
0x01410015 ba81000000         MOV EDX, 0x81
0x0141001a 48                 DEC EAX
0x0141001b b838a10dfe         MOV EAX, 0xfe0da138
0x01410020 fe07               INC BYTE [EDI]
0x01410022 0000               ADD [EAX], AL
0x01410024 48                 DEC EAX
```

FIGURE 11.24.

Partial results from malfind.

```
phil@i7laptop:~/PentesterAcademy/windows-forensics$ vpaw clipboard
Volatility Foundation Volatility Framework 2.5
Session    WindowStation  Format                    Handle  Object              Data
---------- -------------- ------------------------- ------- ------------------- --------
         1 WinSta0        CF_UNICODETEXT           0x710287 0xffffff900c1aa9440 ntuser.dat

         1 WinSta0        CF_TEXT                     0x10 ------------------

         1 WinSta0        0x240265L            0x200000000000 ------------------

         1 WinSta0        CF_TEXT                      0x1 ------------------

         1 -------------- ------------------       0x240265 0xffffff900c1aef750

phil@i7laptop:~/PentesterAcademy/windows-forensics$
```

FIGURE 11.25.

Running the clipboard plugin.

496 CHAPTER 11 Memory Forensics

```
phil@i7laptop:~/PentesterAcademy/windows-forensics$ vpaw cmdscan
Volatility Foundation Volatility Framework 2.5
**************************************************
CommandProcess: conhost.exe Pid: 3188
CommandHistory: 0x7ee90 Application: cmd.exe Flags: Allocated, Reset
CommandCount: 5 LastAdded: 4 LastDisplayed: 4
FirstCommand: 0 CommandCountMax: 50
ProcessHandle: 0x60
Cmd #0 @ 0x7e1c0: e:
Cmd #1 @ 0x5d380: cd aesshell
Cmd #2 @ 0x7e000: dir
Cmd #3 @ 0x83230: bc.exe -rip 192.168.56.1.1 -rport 1443
Cmd #4 @ 0x7f170: bc.exe -rip 192.168.56.1 -rport 1443
Cmd #15 @ 0x40158:
Cmd #16 @ 0x7e000: dir
**************************************************
CommandProcess: conhost.exe Pid: 3188
CommandHistory: 0x7f1e0 Application: bc.exe Flags: Allocated
CommandCount: 0 LastAdded: -1 LastDisplayed: -1
FirstCommand: 0 CommandCountMax: 50
ProcessHandle: 0x58
**************************************************
CommandProcess: conhost.exe Pid: 3188
CommandHistory: 0x7f490 Application: bc.exe Flags: Allocated
CommandCount: 0 LastAdded: -1 LastDisplayed: -1
FirstCommand: 0 CommandCountMax: 50
ProcessHandle: 0xd4
```

FIGURE 11.26.

Partial results from the cmdscan plugin.

The cmdscan plugin can be used to retrieve command line history. This can be helpful if you are attempting to trace a user's activities. Partial results from this plugin are shown in Figure 11.26. Starting the suspicious bc.exe processes is shown in the figure.

More extensive command history can be obtained using the consoles plugin. In some cases it will provide a rather complete history of commands entered and responses. Partial results from running this command are shown in Figure 11.27. The figure shows several commands the John user ran at a command prompt complete with responses.

Some malware may manipulate desktops. In Windows a desktop is essentially a container for applications. If programs are launched in another desktop, they may not be easily visible to a logged-in user. Some ransomware operates by restricting access to a user's desktop. The deskscan plugin will retrieve information on various desktops present on a system. Partial results from running this plugin are shown in Figure 11.28.

While you will most likely have the registry hives from a filesystem image, Volatility does provide a plugin for dumping the registry hives from memory called dumpregistry. This plugin requires the --dump-dir option. Another occasionally useful plugin is editbox. It will report any text in edit boxes or other text controls currently displayed on the screen. If you are examining an older (pre-Vista) Windows subject, the evtlogs plugin can be used to retrieve the resident portion of these old format log files.

When a breach or malware infection is suspected, having a list of open files can be helpful. The Volatility filescan plugin can be used to find and list open files. Partial output from running this plugin against a Windows 7 system is shown in Figure 11.29.

```
CommandHistory: 0x7ee90 Application: cmd.exe Flags: Allocated, Reset
CommandCount: 5 LastAdded: 4 LastDisplayed: 4
FirstCommand: 0 CommandCountMax: 50
ProcessHandle: 0x60
Cmd #0 at 0x7e1c0: e:
Cmd #1 at 0x5d380: cd aesshell
Cmd #2 at 0x7e000: dir
Cmd #3 at 0x83230: bc.exe -rip 192.168.56.1.1 -rport 1443
Cmd #4 at 0x7f170: bc.exe -rip 192.168.56.1 -rport 1443
----
Screen 0x61cf0 X:80 Y:300
Dump:
Microsoft Windows [Version 6.1.7601]
Copyright (c) 2009 Microsoft Corporation.  All rights reserved.

C:\Users\John>e:

E:\>cd aesshell

E:\aesshell>dir
 Volume in drive E is VBOX_shared
 Volume Serial Number is 0000-0805

 Directory of E:\aesshell

06/25/2015  02:10 AM                551 bc.spec
06/25/2015  02:10 AM            569,680 MSVCP90.dll
```

FIGURE 11.27.

Partial results from the consoles plugin.

```
phil@i7laptop:~/PentesterAcademy/windows-forensics$ vpaw deskscan
Volatility Foundation Volatility Framework 2.5
******************************************************
Desktop: 0x7e2b95c0, Name: mswindowstation\mssrestricteddesk, Next: 0x0
SessionId: 0, DesktopInfo: 0xfffff900c1ec0a70, fsHooks: 0
spwnd: 0xfffff900c1ec0b90, Windows: 18
Heap: 0xfffff900c1ec0000, Size: 0xc0000, Base: 0xfffff900c1ec0000, Limit: 0xfffff900c1f80000
******************************************************
Desktop: 0x7e87bd30, Name: WinSta0\Default, Next: 0xfffffa8002e41bf0
SessionId: 1, DesktopInfo: 0xfffff900c0600a70, fsHooks: 0
spwnd: 0xfffff900c0600b90, Windows: 156
Heap: 0xfffff900c0600000, Size: 0x1400000, Base: 0xfffff900c0600000, Limit: 0xfffff900c1a00000
 3788 (taskhost.exe 1872 parent 464)
 2860 (cmd.exe 3676 parent 3700)
 3696 (bc.exe 3700 parent 3316)
 3784 (cmd.exe 284 parent 1964)
 3816 (conhost.exe 3188 parent 368)
 3224 (conhost.exe 3188 parent 368)
 444 (csrss.exe 368 parent 360)
 436 (csrss.exe 368 parent 360)
 884 (explorer.exe 1964 parent 1932)
 2000 (explorer.exe 1964 parent 1932)
 332 (explorer.exe 1964 parent 1932)
 1144 (explorer.exe 1964 parent 1932)
 1188 (explorer.exe 1964 parent 1932)
 1800 (explorer.exe 1964 parent 1932)
 1492 (explorer.exe 1964 parent 1932)
```

FIGURE 11.28.

Partial results from running the deskscan plugin.

```
phil@i7laptop:~/PentesterAcademy/windows-forensics$ vpaw filescan
Volatility Foundation Volatility Framework 2.5
Offset(P)           #Ptr   #Hnd Access Name
------------------  -----  ---- ------ ----
0x0000000000660d10  16     0    -W-rw- \Device\HarddiskVolume2\Users\John\AppData\Local\Temp\scoped
_dir_2412_30080\CRX_INSTALL\_locales\ca\messages.json
0x0000000000c26070  2      0    -W-rw- \Device\HarddiskVolume2\Users\John\AppData\Local\Temp\scoped
_dir_2412_14862\CRX_INSTALL\_locales\vi\messages.json
0x0000000000c261a0  16     0    R--r-d \Device\HarddiskVolume2\Users\John\AppData\Local\Temp\ad_dri
ver.sys
0x0000000000c26820  2      0    -W-rw- \Device\HarddiskVolume2\Users\John\AppData\Local\Temp\scoped
_dir_2412_14862\CRX_INSTALL\_locales\zh_CN\messages.json
0x0000000000fd5980  2      0    -W-rw- \Device\HarddiskVolume2\Users\John\AppData\Local\Temp\scoped
_dir_2412_23805\CRX_INSTALL\_locales\uk\messages.json
0x00000000014e7580  16     0    R--r-d \Device\HarddiskVolume2\Windows\System32\en-US\SoundRecorder
.exe.mui
0x00000000014e7760  2      0    -W-rw- \Device\HarddiskVolume2\Users\John\AppData\Local\Temp\scoped
_dir_2412_13836\CRX_INSTALL\_locales\bg\messages.json
0x00000000014e7a20  16     0    R--r-d \Device\HarddiskVolume2\Windows\System32\en-US\PerfCenterCPL
.dll.mui
0x0000000005984280  2      0    -W-rw- \Device\HarddiskVolume2\Users\John\AppData\Local\Temp\scoped
_dir_2412_13836\CRX_INSTALL\_locales\sk\messages.json
0x0000000005984c60  2      0    -W-rw- \Device\HarddiskVolume2\Users\John\AppData\Local\Temp\scoped
_dir_2412_13836\CRX_INSTALL\_locales\ru\messages.json
0x0000000005bd83d0  2      0    -W-rw- \Device\HarddiskVolume2\Users\John\AppData\Local\Temp\scoped
_dir_2412_23805\CRX_INSTALL\_locales\vi\messages.json
0x0000000005bd8f20  2      0    -W-rw- \Device\HarddiskVolume2\Users\John\AppData\Local\Temp\scoped
```

FIGURE 11.29.

Partial output from the filescan plugin.

Users can create objects on Windows systems. When they do, handles are needed in order to reference them. The Volatility gahti plugin can be used to retrieve information on the types of user objects present in each session. There are at least twenty types of user objects with later versions of Windows having a few new object types. The userhandles plugin can be used to display information on the objects themselves (not just the type of objects present). Information from both of these plugins can be useful when studying malware. Partial output from the userhandles plugin is shown in Figure 11.30. Note that objects are presented one session at a time.

The Volatility getservicesids plugin can be used to retrieve Security IDs (SIDs) for services on a Windows system. This plugin is useful for checking if a service is owned by someone it should not be (such as an interactive user). Partial results from running this plugin are shown in Figure 11.31. It took approximately 2.5 minutes to run this plugin against a 2GB image.

User hashes are a common target for attackers wishing to crack passwords offline. As we discussed in a previous chapter, these hashes are in the SAM hive. There are a number of tools for extracting these hashes from the hive file. Volatility provides the hashdump plugin to retrieve this information from memory. The results from running this plugin are shown in Figure 11.32. Notice how many of the hashes are the same. This is because Windows stupidly does not salt the password hashes. This and the way passwords are hashed in chunks makes Windows passwords extremely easy to crack.

If a system is using hibernation, the hibernation information can be listed using the hibinfo plugin (recall that RegRipper also provides this information). Hives can be listed with the hivelist plugin. The hivedump plugin allows hives to be dumped to disk. These plugins are unneeded if you have a filesystem image.

```
phil@i7laptop:~/PentesterAcademy/windows-forensics$ vpaw userhandles|more
Volatility Foundation Volatility Framework 2.5
******************************************************
SharedInfo: 0xfffff9600031e520, SessionId: 0 Shared delta: 0
aheList: 0xfffff900c0400000, Table size: 0x2000, Entry size: 0x18

Object(V)             Handle  bType           Flags   Thread  Process
---------             ------  -----           -----   ------  -------
0xfffff900c05824b0    0x10001 TYPE_MONITOR    0       ------- -
0xfffff900c01a9970    0x10002 TYPE_WINDOW     64      448     320
0xfffff900c00bf5a0    0x10003 TYPE_CURSOR     0       ------- 320
0xfffff900c05b0b90    0x10004 TYPE_WINDOW     0       448     320
0xfffff900c00deb90    0x10005 TYPE_CURSOR     0       ------- 320
0xfffff900c05b0e60    0x10006 TYPE_WINDOW     0       448     320
0xfffff900c00dea60    0x10007 TYPE_CURSOR     0       ------- 320
0xfffff900c05b1070    0x10008 TYPE_WINDOW     0       448     320
0xfffff900c00dfb90    0x10009 TYPE_CURSOR     0       ------- 320
0xfffff900c05e0b90    0x1000a TYPE_WINDOW     0       448     320
0xfffff900c00dfa60    0x1000b TYPE_CURSOR     0       ------- 320
0xfffff900c05e0d90    0x1000c TYPE_WINDOW     0       448     320
0xfffff900c00e04f0    0x1000d TYPE_CURSOR     0       ------- 320
0xfffff900c05e0fa0    0x1000e TYPE_WINDOW     0       448     320
0xfffff900c00e03c0    0x1000f TYPE_CURSOR     0       ------- 320
0xfffff900c0600b90    0x10010 TYPE_WINDOW     0       448     320
0xfffff900c00e1b90    0x10011 TYPE_CURSOR     0       ------- 320
0xfffff900c0600d90    0x10012 TYPE_WINDOW     0       448     320
0xfffff900c00e1710    0x10013 TYPE_CURSOR     0       ------- 320
```

FIGURE 11.30.

Partial output from the userhandles plugin.

```
servicesids = {
    'S-1-5-80-4151353957-356578678-4163131872-800126167-2037860865': '.NET CLR Networking 4.0.0.0',
    'S-1-5-80-1135273183-3738781202-689480478-891280274-255333391': '.NET Memory Cache 4.0',
    'S-1-5-80-712059680-203367400-2977813368-4125985704-79366942': 'ASP.NET',
    'S-1-5-80-2913627202-1669313743-594640567-3758707557-1808359087': 'ASP.NET_4.0.30319',
    'S-1-5-80-2132180438-3108490898-1075229718-3888178202-2916226535': 'aspnet_state',
    'S-1-5-80-2676549577-1911656217-2625096541-4178041876-1366760775': 'AudioSrv',
    'S-1-5-80-957945053-4060038483-2323299089-2025834768-4289255912': 'b57nd60a',
    'S-1-5-80-289285388-4137671665-1240080895-2344186716-3552465961': 'clr_optimization_v2.0.50727_6
4',
    'S-1-5-80-2611951811-1959136347-1062071333-3982815153-2811717512': 'clr_optimization_v4.0.30319_
32',
    'S-1-5-80-2839768381-3691089589-2614646340-3191585287-3380622033': 'clr_optimization_v4.0.30319_
64',
    'S-1-5-80-2597136289-665204401-1725106016-1253143166-1853691573': 'dmvsc',
    'S-1-5-80-1628851891-332911214-942992855-2381080451-357317118': 'gupdate',
    'S-1-5-80-1391398224-2746689181-3888380295-1755171859-6364376': 'gupdatem',
    'S-1-5-80-1708301557-710215499-1045718168-382692165-3542596111': 'HdAudAddService',
    'S-1-5-80-2876499719-392125430-158013367-819050375-2387260967': 'ksthunk',
    'S-1-5-80-61387632-1770052757-913906803-2764154990-1232092381': 'MSDTC Bridge 4.0.0.0',
    'S-1-5-80-89244771-1762554971-1007993102-348796144-2203111529': 'NetMsmqActivator',
    'S-1-5-80-2943419899-937267781-4189664001-1229628381-3982115073': 'NetPipeActivator',
    'S-1-5-80-3579033775-2824656752-1522793541-1960352512-462907086': 'NetTcpActivator',
    'S-1-5-80-1598306103-1873062032-3786967184-80952375-3176933300': 'npf',
    'S-1-5-80-3596911058-2952229928-1888671852-1743692427-614402820': 'PerfHost',
    'S-1-5-80-217413056-3833387362-178569430-1954288181-1272411947': 'SMSvcHost 4.0.0.0',
    'S-1-5-80-3182985763-1431228038-2757062859-428472846-3914011746': 'stisvc',
```

FIGURE 11.31.

Partial output from the getservicesids plugin.

```
phil@i7laptop:~/PentesterAcademy/windows-forensics$ vpaw hashdump
Volatility Foundation Volatility Framework 2.5
Administrator:500:aad3b435b51404eeaad3b435b51404ee:31d6cfe0d16ae931b73c59d7e0c089c0:::
Guest:501:aad3b435b51404eeaad3b435b51404ee:31d6cfe0d16ae931b73c59d7e0c089c0:::
John:1001:aad3b435b51404eeaad3b435b51404ee:ca7e37203ec3131dda33b440cbb6ef35:::
HomeGroupUser$:1002:aad3b435b51404eeaad3b435b51404ee:93cbb18886589ad8e06b4d7741d7e385:::
phil@i7laptop:~/PentesterAcademy/windows-forensics$
```

FIGURE 11.32.

Output from the hashdump plugin.

Internet Explorer history can be retrieved from memory with the iehistory plugin. Of course if you already have a filesystem image, there are a number of tools that will provide this same information (and likely for multiple browsers). Partial output from running this plugin is shown in Figure 11.33.

Networking information for Vista and later versions of Windows can be obtained with the netscan plugin. This information can be compared with information collected during a live response. Partial results from this plugin are shown in Figure 11.34. The sockets and sockscan plugins provide similar information for pre-Vista versions of Windows.

The last shutdown time (before shutting down the system after getting the memory image) can be obtained from the shutdown plugin. This information is retrieved from the registry. One use of this information would be to determine if some malware or an attack forced a system restart.

Service information can be obtained using the svcscan plugin. This plugin will retrieve how a service is started (system start, on demand, etc.) and its current state. Partial output from this command is shown in Figure 11.35.

The Volatility timeliner plugin can be used to generate a timeline for objects currently in memory. The information presented includes when something was started, process ID, and end time, if applicable. Partial output from this command is shown in Figure 11.36.

If you believe a user might be utilizing the TrueCrypt disk encryption software, the truecryptsummary plugin can be used to retrieve more information. If TrueCrypt is not found, this plugin returns nothing. If, on the other hand, TrueCrypt is in use, the truecryptmaster

```
phil@i7laptop:~/PentesterAcademy/windows-forensics$ vpaw iehistory |more
Volatility Foundation Volatility Framework 2.5
****************************************************
Process: 1964 explorer.exe
Cache type "URL " at 0x44d5000
Record length: 0x100
Location: :2015121120151212: John@http://www.msn.com/?ocid=iehp
Last modified: 2015-12-11 11:00:23 UTC+0000
Last accessed: 2015-12-11 16:00:23 UTC+0000
File Offset: 0x100, Data Offset: 0x0, Data Length: 0x0
****************************************************
Process: 1964 explorer.exe
Cache type "URL " at 0x44d5100
Record length: 0x100
Location: :2015121120151212: John@:Host: www.msn.com
Last modified: 2015-12-11 11:00:23 UTC+0000
Last accessed: 2015-12-11 16:00:23 UTC+0000
File Offset: 0x100, Data Offset: 0x0, Data Length: 0x0
****************************************************
Process: 1964 explorer.exe
Cache type "URL " at 0x44d5200
Record length: 0x100
Location: :2015121120151212: John@https://www.google.com/chrome
Last modified: 2015-12-11 11:00:49 UTC+0000
Last accessed: 2015-12-11 16:00:49 UTC+0000
File Offset: 0x100, Data Offset: 0x0, Data Length: 0x0
****************************************************
```

FIGURE 11.33.

Partial output from the iehistory plugin.

```
phil@i7laptop:~/PentesterAcademy/windows-forensics$ vpaw netscan
Volatility Foundation Volatility Framework 2.5
Offset(P)         Proto    Local Address           Foreign Address         State       Pid
     Owner                 Created
0x660990          TCPv4    -:49540                 204.186.48.39:443       CLOSED      241
2    chrome.exe
0x37bad630        TCPv4    -:49507                 -:443                   CLOSED      241
2    chrome.exe
0x385be010        TCPv4    -:49506                 -:443                   CLOSED      241
2    chrome.exe
0x5ecb79d0        TCPv4    -:49513                 -:443                   CLOSED      241
2    chrome.exe
0x62d6b7f0        TCPv4    -:49560                 204.186.48.39:443       CLOSED      241
2    chrome.exe
0x7d9d2a90        TCPv4    -:49503                 -:443                   CLOSED      241
2    chrome.exe
0x7da196a0        UDPv6    fe80::340b:9e62:23d3:d5b8:546    *:*                        788
     svchost.exe           2015-12-11 16:20:23 UTC+0000
0x7da7a830        UDPv4    0.0.0.0:5355            *:*                                 532
     svchost.exe           2015-12-11 16:31:48 UTC+0000
0x7da7a830        UDPv6    :::5355                 *:*                                 532
     svchost.exe           2015-12-11 16:31:48 UTC+0000
0x7dc33530        UDPv4    0.0.0.0:0               *:*                                 636
     VBoxService.ex        2015-12-11 16:32:20 UTC+0000
0x7de3b310        UDPv4    0.0.0.0:0               *:*                                 636
     VBoxService.ex        2015-12-11 16:32:15 UTC+0000
0x7dea3ce0        UDPv4    0.0.0.0:5355            *:*                                 532
```

FIGURE 11.34.

Partial output from the netscan plugin.

```
phil@i7laptop:~/PentesterAcademy/windows-forensics$ vpaw svcscan |more
Volatility Foundation Volatility Framework 2.5
Offset: 0xcbdc50
Order: 393
Start: SERVICE_DEMAND_START
Process ID: -
Service Name: WwanSvc
Display Name: WWAN AutoConfig
Service Type: SERVICE_WIN32_SHARE_PROCESS
Service State: SERVICE_STOPPED
Binary Path: -

Offset: 0xcbdb60
Order: 392
Start: SERVICE_AUTO_START
Process ID: 824
Service Name: wudfsvc
Display Name: Windows Driver Foundation - User-mode Driver Framework
Service Type: SERVICE_WIN32_SHARE_PROCESS
Service State: SERVICE_RUNNING
Binary Path: C:\Windows\System32\svchost.exe -k LocalSystemNetworkRestricted

Offset: 0xcbda70
Order: 391
Start: SERVICE_DEMAND_START
Process ID: -
Service Name: WUDFRd
```

FIGURE 11.35.

Partial output from the svcscan plugin.

```
phil@i7laptop:~/PentesterAcademy/windows-forensics$ vpaw timeliner|more
Volatility Foundation Volatility Framework 2.5
2015-12-11 16:32:22 UTC+0000|[LIVE RESPONSE]| (System time)|
2015-12-11 11:00:23 UTC+0000|[IEHISTORY]| explorer.exe->:2015121120151212: John@http://www.msn.com/?
ocid=iehp| PID: 1964/Cache type "URL " at 0x44d5000 End: 2015-12-11 16:00:23 UTC+0000
2015-12-11 11:00:23 UTC+0000|[IEHISTORY]| explorer.exe->:2015121120151212: John@:Host: www.msn.com|
PID: 1964/Cache type "URL " at 0x44d5100 End: 2015-12-11 16:00:23 UTC+0000
2015-12-11 11:00:49 UTC+0000|[IEHISTORY]| explorer.exe->:2015121120151212: John@https://www.google.c
om/chrome| PID: 1964/Cache type "URL " at 0x44d5200 End: 2015-12-11 16:00:49 UTC+0000
2015-12-11 11:00:49 UTC+0000|[IEHISTORY]| explorer.exe->:2015121120151212: John@:Host: www.google.co
m| PID: 1964/Cache type "URL " at 0x44d5300 End: 2015-12-11 16:00:49 UTC+0000
2015-12-11 11:01:02 UTC+0000|[IEHISTORY]| explorer.exe->:2015121120151212: John@https://www.google.c
om/chrome/browser/desktop/index.html| PID: 1964/Cache type "URL " at 0x44d5400 End: 2015-12-11 16:01
:02 UTC+0000
2015-12-11 11:01:17 UTC+0000|[IEHISTORY]| explorer.exe->:2015121120151212: John@https://www.google.c
om/chrome/browser/thankyou.html?platform=win&clickonceinstalled=1&installdataindex=defaultbrowser| P
ID: 1964/Cache type "URL " at 0x44d5500 End: 2015-12-11 16:01:17 UTC+0000
2015-12-11 11:05:11 UTC+0000|[IEHISTORY]| explorer.exe->:2015121120151212: John@file:///C:/Users/Joh
n/Downloads/Imager_Lite_3.1.1.zip| PID: 1964/Cache type "URL " at 0x44d5600 End: 2015-12-11 16:05:11
 UTC+0000
2015-12-11 11:05:11 UTC+0000|[IEHISTORY]| explorer.exe->:2015121120151212: John@:Host: Computer| PID
: 1964/Cache type "URL " at 0x44d5700 End: 2015-12-11 16:05:11 UTC+0000
2013-10-19 01:08:06 UTC+0000|[IEHISTORY]| explorer.exe->http://www.bing.com/favicon.ico| PID: 1964/C
ache type "URL " at 0x4fc6000 End: 2015-11-09 03:07:23 UTC+0000
2013-10-19 01:08:06 UTC+0000|[IEHISTORY]| explorer.exe->https://ieonline.microsoft.com/favicon.ico|
PID: 1964/Cache type "URL " at 0x4fc6100 End: 2015-11-09 03:07:30 UTC+0000
2009-07-15 17:44:20 UTC+0000|[IEHISTORY]| explorer.exe->http://download.microsoft.com/download/7/A/B
```

FIGURE 11.36.

Partial output from the timeliner plugin.

and truecryptpassphrase plugins can be used to retrieve master keys and passphrases, respectively.

The User Assist information can be retrieved with the userassist plugin. Recall that this is information on recently run programs and commands which is stored in a user's registry hive. This is the ROT13 encoded information discussed in a previous chapter. This information is more easily obtained with RegRipper if the hive files are available.

Information on currently open windows can be obtained with the windows plugin. This can be useful when some malware infection is suspected. Malware can do work in hidden windows (either not visible or underneath other windows). It is also possible to overlay legitimate windows with bogus ones that might capture user input (among other things). The wintree plugin shows parent/child relationships for currently displayed windows. While the wintree information is not nearly as verbose as that of windows, it is more easily used to identify windows hiding underneath other windows.

The final Volatility plugin we will discuss is yarascan. YARA is a very popular tool among malware researchers. YARA is a pattern matching tool that has its own simple syntax. Patterns are organized into rules where each rule specifies a set of conditions that will cause a file (or object) to match the rule. More information on YARA can be found at http://virustotal.github.io/yara/.

The yarascan plugin allows YARA rules to be specified directly in text or supplied in a file. The -Y or --yara-rules option is used to enter YARA rules directly. When supplying a file full of YARA rules, the -y or --yara-file option is used. However the rules are provided, the scan can be applied to a single process (-p or --pid option), set of processes matching a regular expression pattern (-n or --name option), kernel modules only (-K or --kernel option), or everything (-A or --all option).

SUMMARY

We have not covered every available Volatility plugin in this chapter. Rather, we have attempted to cover the most frequently used plugins in some detail and introduced some others that may prove useful in certain types of investigations. The focus of this chapter has been on integrating Volatility into the overall investigation process. More detailed information on specific plugins is easily found on the Internet. Many of the Volatility plugins discussed in this chapter are useful for identifying potentially malicious programs. In the next chapter we will see how to safely investigate suspicious files further.

CHAPTER

Malware

12

INFORMATION IN THIS CHAPTER:

* Checking databases
* First steps in examining an unknown file
* Program packers
* Setting up a sandbox
* 32-bit executables
* 64-bit executables

IS IT IN A DATABASE?

After analyzing filesystem images and possibly memory images, you might end up with a list of suspicious files. In this chapter we will discuss some next steps for investigating these suspicious binaries. It should be said at the start that this chapter is not an attempt to teach you how to reverse engineer Windows applications in just a few short pages. Rather, this chapter is about some simple things that can be done to determine if something is malicious. If you are interested in delving into the world of reverse engineering, the 32-bit and 64-bit Assembly courses from PentesterAcademy.com are a good starting point. I have also authored a video course entitled "Reverse Engineering and Exploit Development" (O'Reilly, 2015) that serves as a nice introduction to reverse engineering on Linux, Windows, OS X, and Android.

One of the first things that you can do with a suspicious file is calculate a hash value for it. This hash value can then be used to see if the file has an entry in any standard databases. While it is no longer considered strong enough for use in cryptography, the MD5 (Message Digest version 5) hash is still widely used in file reference databases. Some databases also support SHA (Secure Hash Algorithm) or SHA256 (SHA with 256-bit values).

To examine suspicious files they should first be extracted using one of the scripts presented earlier in this book or a tool such as FTK Imager. If you have a memory image, it can be helpful to also extract the in-memory executable as well. Hashes should be calculated on the executable stored on disk (not the in-memory version). Calculating an MD5 checksum is as simple as running `md5sum <filename(s)>`. Calculating a few hashes is shown in Figure 12.1. To calculate other hashes use sha1sum, sha224sum, sha256sum, sha384sum, or sha512sum for SHA, SHA224, SHA256, SHA384, or SHA512, respectively.

One of the most complete databases of known files is maintained by the National Institute of Standards and Technology (NIST). This database is known as the National Software Reference Library (NSRL) project. This project is housed at http://www.nsrl.nist.gov. The NSRL database is available in several formats. One format is a DVD image that is updated four times a year. A number of commercial tools will use the NSRL databases from such a DVD image directly.

```
phil@i7laptop:~/PentesterAcademy/windows-forensics/suspect-exes$ md5sum *
966fe904599b9a0f80ea498851180829  chrome.exe
e83d2495d5867e224fbf42ef40d8856c  DVDMaker.exe
4c38bafadebf64402a9743247f5b105d  notepad.exe
phil@i7laptop:~/PentesterAcademy/windows-forensics/suspect-exes$ sha1sum *
89ecea555b949082d9f6839a883868bfed79301f  chrome.exe
fec908e0e7bc469875ab8f68d936225c635a6ac2  DVDMaker.exe
95f77e0524931a0176967d98a349ab173b483c99  notepad.exe
phil@i7laptop:~/PentesterAcademy/windows-forensics/suspect-exes$ sha256sum *
a95a67df82fd40a0173c08919e7ab4b3cc207c8b8e07d850cc9c8ad0a44bf0cb  chrome.exe
2c806d9b932f24c4bc84e86ced7962a75c0161ff732f77eb1827a3a14976b2c1  DVDMaker.exe
a70e59518a532947878fadbd76a44cedba9f1bd05a0672c6bd8dbb5e7bbccea6  notepad.exe
phil@i7laptop:~/PentesterAcademy/windows-forensics/suspect-exes$ sha512sum *
df877cf4658455df6ac68d4c522fc66dbc477420c69c543349b15df1135f0d6d5d5ad249ea9848642074363b4d93cd369418
5f090723f494ced87f61722f4ddc  chrome.exe
e22f36cb40fff2672e9e49aa991656a0cc1188c7ba2583efae2d238a4e864bd5f8bdc532a5c35285ca2b4b105097454eb06d
5860c41e618c44bab6e300408b8d  DVDMaker.exe
bc8d404e91cc370df033e77a669ed40d4b1c1e35e8f775ef9e2f0cf6cbf34216ee323f5546b2ae358ea93fed4fc6c5b3a60f
043e4b55baa0a88cfad216ff0262  notepad.exe
phil@i7laptop:~/PentesterAcademy/windows-forensics/suspect-exes$
```

FIGURE 12.1.

Calculating hash values for suspicious files.

There is a project called NSRLquery that allows a user to download an nsrllookup client which can be used to query machines running a nsrlsvr for NSRL information. More details on this project can be found at the NSRL website. An online NSRL search hosted by hashsets.com is also available. Using the online lookup to search for the notepad.exe MD5 hash is shown in Figure 12.2.

Some of the results from the query in Figure 12.2 are shown in Figure 12.3. Note that more than one match was returned by the search engine despite the fact that a single MD5 was supplied for the search. The results supplied by hashsets.com can be sorted by file size or other columns. This might make it easier to match a file to the correct result from the set returned.

FIRST STEPS WHEN EXAMINING AN UNKNOWN FILE

If there was no entry in the NSRL or similar database, it is time to start looking inside the suspicious file. The first thing you can do is use the strings utility on the file. The strings tool will scan through a file and print anything that looks like it might be a string to standard out. The syntax for running strings is `strings [options] [file(s)]`. The help screen for strings is shown in Figure 12.4.

When you use the strings utility on an executable, it is likely that many of the items displayed first will not look much like strings. This is due to the fact that the source code (in machine code) appears at the beginning of the file and some of the operation codes could be

First steps when examining an unknown file 507

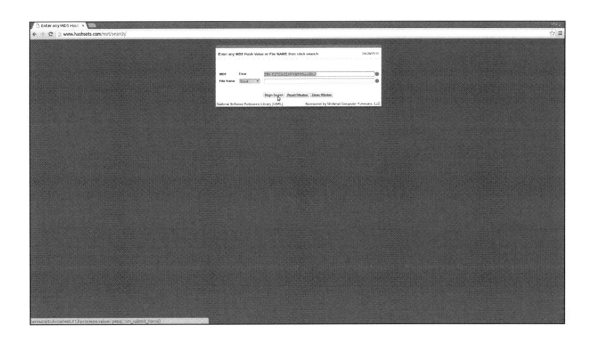

FIGURE 12.2.
Searching the NSRL database for a single MD5 value.

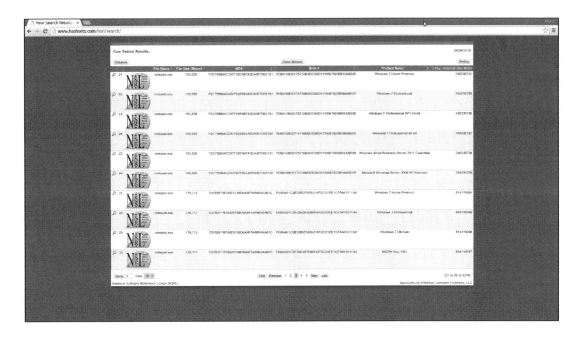

FIGURE 12.3.
Results from the search in Figure 12.2.

```
phil@i7laptop:~/PentesterAcademy/windows-forensics/suspect-exes$ strings --help
Usage: strings [option(s)] [file(s)]
 Display printable strings in [file(s)] (stdin by default)
 The options are:
  -a - --all                Scan the entire file, not just the data section [default]
  -d --data                 Only scan the data sections in the file
  -f --print-file-name      Print the name of the file before each string
  -n --bytes=[number]       Locate & print any NUL-terminated sequence of at
  -<number>                   least [number] characters (default 4).
  -t --radix={o,d,x}        Print the location of the string in base 8, 10 or 16
  -o                        An alias for --radix=o
  -T --target=<BFDNAME>     Specify the binary file format
  -e --encoding={s,S,b,l,B,L} Select character size and endianness:
                            s = 7-bit, S = 8-bit, {b,l} = 16-bit, {B,L} = 32-bit
  @<file>                   Read options from <file>
  -h --help                 Display this information
  -v -V --version           Print the program's version number
strings: supported targets: elf64-x86-64 elf32-i386 elf32-x86-64 a.out-i386-linux pei-i386 pei-x86-6
4 elf64-l1om elf64-k1om elf64-little elf64-big elf32-little elf32-big pe-x86-64 pe-i386 plugin srec
symbolsrec verilog tekhex binary ihex
Report bugs to <http://www.sourceware.org/bugzilla/>
phil@i7laptop:~/PentesterAcademy/windows-forensics/suspect-exes$
```

FIGURE 12.4.

The strings help screen.

interpreted as text. The exceptions to this are strings that begin with a period or at sign, such as .text @.data, @.reloc, etc. These items indicate the start of sections in the executable file. The first part of the output from running strings on notepad.exe is shown in Figure 12.5.

Scanning further into the strings results should reveal a list of imported DLLs and functions. This information can be used to get a better idea about what sort of operations are being performed by the program. Some of these values for the notepad.exe file are shown in Figure 12.6.

The remaining results from strings should be walked through and checked for any keywords or phrases that might give some clue as to the program's function. GREP can be used to make this process quicker, provided you know what you are seeking. For example, `strings <file> | grep -i pass` could be used to search for a value that might be associated with a password.

The unknown binary could be examined in a hex editor as shown in Figure 12.7. The executable should begin with 0x4D 0x5A ("MZ"). There will likely be a message such as the one at offset 0x4E stating that the program cannot be run in DOS mode. There should be a few more entries followed by ".text" which indicates the start of the text section.

Examining an executable in a hex editor is not the best way to go for a number of reasons. First, the data is not organized according to standard executable file sections (sometimes called segments). Second, the machine code is not presented in Assembly (disassembled) which makes it nearly impossible to follow the code. Third, there can be large gaps full of empty space in the file, especially if it is an in-memory executable image.

```
!This program cannot be run in DOS mode.
\zRich
.text
`.rdata
@.data
.pdata
@.rsrc
@.reloc
d$0L
L$@E3
|$HP
H WATAUH
\$@H
l$HH
t$PH
 A]A\_
L$ SUVWH
(_^][
L$@D
UVWATAUAVAWH
@A_A^A]A\_^]
L$4L
D$0H
|$0+
UVWATAUAVAWH
A_A^A]A\_^]
"notepad.txt" 1748L, 13298C                                          1,1          Top
```

FIGURE 12.5.

The first part of output from running strings on notepad.exe. The highlighted lines are for file section headers.

```
notepad.pdb
VERSION.dll
ntdll.dll
OLEAUT32.dll
COMCTL32.dll
SHLWAPI.dll
ole32.dll
WINSPOOL.DRV
SHELL32.dll
COMDLG32.dll
msvcrt.dll
USER32.dll
GDI32.dll
KERNEL32.DLL
ADVAPI32.dll
RegSetValueExW
RegQueryValueExW
RegCreateKeyW
RegCloseKey
RegOpenKeyExW
IsTextUnicode
CloseServiceHandle
OpenSCManagerW
OpenServiceW
QueryServiceConfigW
GetLocalTime
                                                                    633,1         35%
```

FIGURE 12.6.

DLLs and functions imported by notepad.exe in the strings results.

```
00000000  4D 5A 90 00  03 00 00 00  04 00 00 00  FF FF 00 00  B8 00 00 00  MZ..............
00000014  00 00 00 00  40 00 00 00  00 00 00 00  00 00 00 00  00 00 00 00  ....@...........
00000028  00 00 00 00  00 00 00 00  00 00 00 00  00 00 00 00  00 00 00 00  ................
0000003C  E8 00 00 00  0E 1F BA 0E  00 B4 09 CD  21 B8 01 4C  CD 21 54 68  ............!..L.!Th
00000050  69 73 20 70  72 6F 67 72  61 6D 20 63  61 6E 6E 6F  74 20 62 65  is program cannot be
00000064  20 72 75 6E  20 69 6E 20  44 4F 53 20  6D 6F 64 65  2E 0D 0D 0A   run in DOS mode....
00000078  24 00 00 00  00 00 00 00  83 C2 32 29  C7 A3 5C 7A  C7 A3 5C 7A  $.........2)..\z..\z
0000008C  C7 A3 5C 7A  CE DB D8 7A  C6 A3 5C 7A  CE DB C9 7A  C5 A3 5C 7A  ..\z...z..\z...z..\z
000000A0  CE DB CF 7A  DA A3 5C 7A  C7 A3 5D 7A  33 A3 5C 7A  CE DB DF 7A  ...z..\z..]z3.\z...z
000000B4  D3 A3 5C 7A  CE DB D5 7A  CC A3 5C 7A  CE DB C8 7A  C6 A3 5C 7A  ..\z...z..\z...z..\z
000000C8  CE DB CD 7A  C6 A3 5C 7A  52 69 63 68  C7 A3 5C 7A  00 00 00 00  ...z..\zRich..\z....
000000DC  00 00 00 00  00 00 00 00  00 00 00 00  50 45 00 00  64 86 06 00  ............PE..d...
000000F0  B3 C9 5B 4A  00 00 00 00  00 00 00 00  F0 00 22 00  0B 02 09 00  ..[J.........."....
00000104  00 A8 00 00  00 58 02 00  00 00 00 00  70 35 00 00  00 10 00 00  .....X......p5......
00000118  00 00 00 00  01 00 00 00  00 10 00 00  00 02 00 00  06 00 01 00  ................
0000012C  06 00 01 00  06 00 01 00  00 00 00 00  00 50 03 00  00 10 00 00  .............P......
00000140  00 00 00 00  02 00 40 81  00 00 08 00  00 00 00 00  00 10 01 00  ......@.........
00000154  00 00 00 00  00 00 10 00  00 00 00 00  00 10 00 00  00 00 00 00  ................
00000168  00 00 00 00  10 00 00 00  00 00 00 00  00 00 00 00  F8 CF 00 00  ................
0000017C  2C 01 00 00  00 40 01 00  60 F1 01 00  00 30 01 00  B4 06 00 00  ,....@..`....0......
00000190  00 00 00 00  00 00 00 00  00 00 00 00  00 00 00 00  00 00 00 00  ................
000001A4  00 00 00 00  00 00 00 00  00 00 00 00  00 00 00 00  00 00 00 00  ................
000001B8  00 00 00 00  00 00 00 00  00 00 00 00  00 00 00 00  00 00 00 00  ................
000001CC  00 00 00 00  00 00 00 00  00 00 00 00  00 00 00 00  00 00 00 00  ................
000001E0  00 00 00 00  00 00 00 00  00 00 00 00  00 00 00 00  2E 74 65 78  .............tex
000001F4  74 00 00 00  70 A7 00 00  00 10 00 00  00 A8 00 00  00 06 00 00  t...p...........
--- notepad.exe       --0x0/0x2F400-----------------------------------------
```

FIGURE 12.7.

The start of an executable in hexedit.

There are a number of tools available that can interpret Portable Executable (PE) files. One such program is PEBrowse by SmidgeonSoft. This program is available as both a 32-bit and 64-bit Windows executable from http://smidgeonsoft.prohosting.com/pebrowse-pro-file-viewer.thml. Both versions will interpret 32 and 64 bit executables.

After downloading the PEBrowse zip file, unzip the archive. The program must be installed by changing to the appropriate directory and running `wine pebinstp.exe`. You will be presented with a dialog box asking if you agree to the license. Once you complete the installation of PEBrowse it will be located in your .wine folder in your home directory. Recall that files and directories beginning with a period are hidden in Linux. The .wine folder is used to storeWindows programs that have been installed using WINE. The PEBrowse program is most likely found in "~/.wine/drive_c/Program Files (x86)/SmidgeonSoft/PEBrowse-Pro/PEBrowsePro.exe" (recall that ~/ indicates a user's home directory). If you intend to run this program often, you might want to create a symbolic link to it using `ln -s <source> <destination>` or create a link on your desktop by right-clicking on the PEBrowsePro.exe file and selecting "Make Link" and then dropping the link file onto your desktop. Creating a link is shown in Figure 12.8.

The initial PEBrowse screen is shown in Figure 12.9. From this screen a file can be loaded using the Control-O shortcut or by selecting Open from the File menu. The file loading screen is shown in Figure 12.10. It is normal to get a message after loading a file stating that the file contains no debugging information.

The notepad.exe file loaded into PEBrowse is shown in Figure 12.11. From the tree view

First steps when examining an unknown file 511

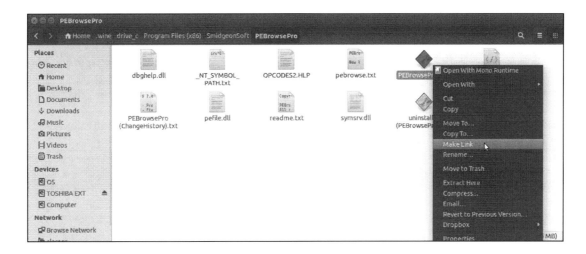

FIGURE 12.8.

Creating a link. Once the link is created it may be dropped on the desktop for easy launching.

on the left we can see this is a 64-bit executable as it has an "Optional Header64" branch on the tree. The first part of this tree that should be examined is the Imports branch. Earlier we saw how strings could be used to determine what DLLs and functions were being imported. PEBrowse allows us to get the same information in a much more convenient format.

FIGURE 12.9.

PEBrowse initial screen.

512 CHAPTER 12 Malware

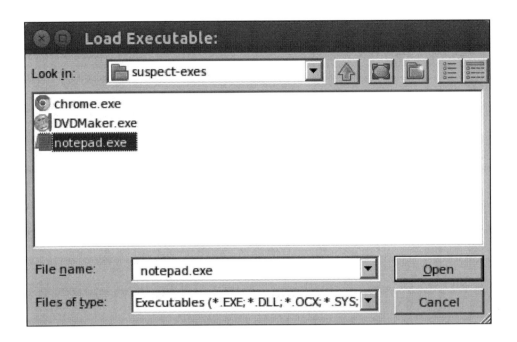

FIGURE 12.10.
PEBrowse Load File dialog box.

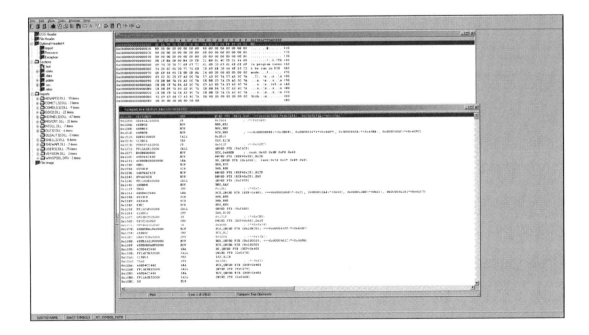

FIGURE 12.11.
The notepad.exe file loaded into PEBrowse.

The program source code is normally located in the .text section. Part of the disassembled program from .text is shown in Figure 12.11. The program is displayed in 64-bit Assembly. While this section might look intimidating to those who do not know Assembly, knowledge of Assembly is rarely required in order to make the determination as to whether or not something is malicious. Rather, the imported DLLs and functions are the keys to understanding what a program does.

The .rdata and .data sections shown in Figure 12.11 are used to store data (program variables). The difference between the two is that .rdata is used to store constants and .data is used for variables. It is not unusual to find things such as hardcoded passwords in .rdata and/or .text (the program code itself). Tools like PEBrowse allow you to see these values in context which can make things easier than it is with strings alone.

PACKERS

A packer is a program used to compress executables into an executable program that will uncompress and launch the original program. Packing a program can create a smaller executable. If the media used to store a program has slow read speeds, a packer can decrease loading time. Less information must be read from disk, but the tradeoff is increased memory and computation requirements at application launch.

Packers have legitimate uses. They are also used by malware authors in an attempt to obfuscate their code. Before a packed program can be examined, it must be unpacked. If a memory image was collected, Volatility can be used to capture an in-memory version of a program. Another option is to determine the packer used and unpack the binary.

While there are a number of packers available, the most popular by far is called UPX (Ultimate Packer for eXecutables). UPX offers good performance and supports Windows, Linux, DOS, OS X, and several other types of executables. The main webpage for this open source tool is http://upx.sourceforge.net. UPX can be installed on Debian and Ubuntu based systems with `sudo apt-get install upx-ucl`.

How do you know if a program has been packed? There are a couple telltale signs. First, the program will import very few functions. The ones imported will likely be for loading libraries and other things the packer requires. Second, the sections will have nonstandard names and there will likely be no .text section. Figure 12.12 shows how a packed version of notepad.exe appears in PEBrowse. The notepad.exe file was packed using the command `upx notepad.exe`. The file size decreased from 193,536 to 153,600 bytes.

It is extremely obvious that the file in Figure 12.12 is packed. The section names UPX0 and UPX1 indicate that the UPX packer is in use. As can be seen in the tree view in the left of the figure, only 17 functions are imported. The functions imported from kernel32.dll are used for starting processes, loading libraries, and allocating memory.

Once the packer has been identified, it can be used to unpack the file. In the rare case that something other than UPX was used, a little Internet research will likely lead to the proper program to unpack a file. For files packed by UPX the command to unpack them is `upx -d <filename>`. The unpacked notepad.exe is shown in Figure 12.13. Notice that all of the standard sections such as .text have returned and over 100 functions are now imported.

514 CHAPTER 12 Malware

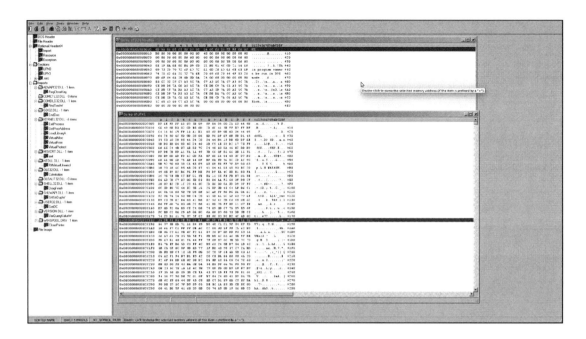

FIGURE 12.12.
Examining a packed file in PEBrowse.

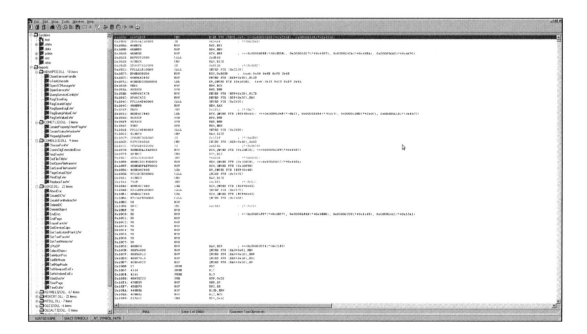

FIGURE 12.13.
Examining a packed binary after it has been unpacked.

SETTING UP A SANDBOX

If after looking at the file in PEBrowse you are still unsure of the file's maliciousness, you might want to set up a sandbox in order to somewhat safely perform some dynamic analysis. You need to proceed with caution when running suspected malware. If not done properly, there is a chance you might infect your forensic workstation and/or other systems connected to your network!

One of the safest ways to run suspected malware is to set up Windows on a machine that is not connected to any network. This can be a good use for old hardware. While this is the safest way to go, it is not the most convenient. Such a system must be reinitialized each time it is used. Because it is disconnected, there is no easy way to move files to/from the system other than via a USB drive. One advantage of this method is that some sophisticated malware will refuse to run in a virtual environment as a deterrent to reverse engineering.

Creating a sandbox virtual machine is much more convenient than setting up a physical machine. Personally, I recommend using VirtualBox from Oracle. VirtualBox is free and widely used which makes life easier if you should run into any problems. I recommend setting up a Windows XP system for 32-bit executables and a Windows 7 system for 64-bit executables. Newer versions of Windows could be used if desired, but Windows 7 should be acceptable in nearly every case.

Creating a new machine in VirtualBox is straightforward. From the main screen click on the New button and you will be greeted by a dialog box like the one shown in Figure 12.14.

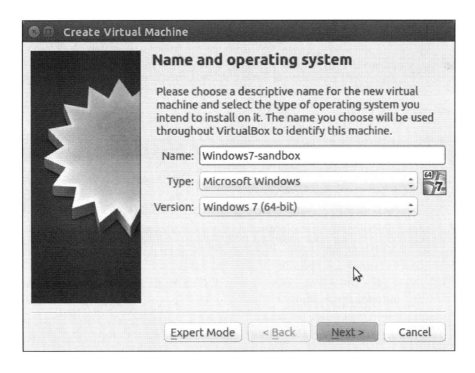

FIGURE 12.14.

Creating a new virtual machine in VirtualBox step 1.

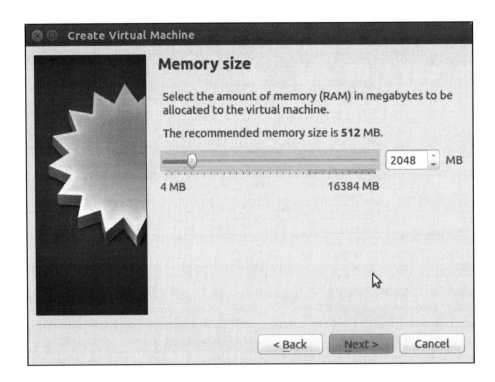

FIGURE 12.15.

Specifying RAM for a virtual machine in VirtualBox.

After clicking Next from the dialog in Figure 12.14, you will be prompted to enter the amount of memory the virtual machine should have in a dialog box like that shown in Figure 12.15. There is no need to give the virtual machine a large amount of RAM as only one application will be run at a time (possibly inside a debugger).

Once the memory has been specified, a hard disk image must be created. A dialog like the one in Figure 12.16 will be displayed. After clicking Create you will be prompted for a format by a Dialog like the one shown in Figure 12.17.

As seen in Figure 12.18, after clicking Next in the dialog shown in Figure 12.17, you will be asked if the virtual hard disk should be dynamically allocated or fixed size. I recommend the default of dynamically allocated for the sandbox. The fixed size option is good when creating images which you intend to use for practicing forensics (because the dynamically allocated drives lead to complications such as fragmented MFTs).

The final virtual hard disk creation dialog is shown in Figure 12.19. On this screen you must select a file name for the virtual disk and also its size. The defaults should be fine for the sandbox.

After clicking Create in the dialog shown in Figure 12.19, the new virtual machine will have been created. By default there will be one enabled network adapter that is attached to a NAT (Network Address Translation) network. The NAT network is essentially a pipe straight out to the Internet (it does not connect to your LAN). You will want to leave this as is while

Setting up a sandbox 517

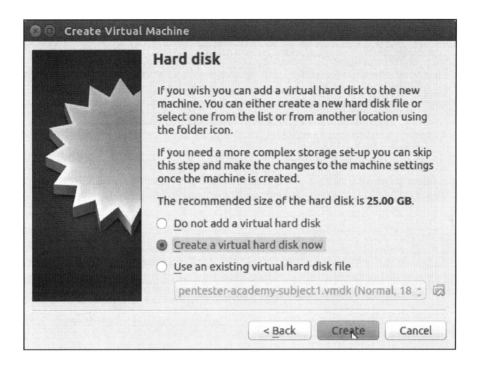

FIGURE 12.16.
The first virtual hard drive creation dialog in VirtualBox.

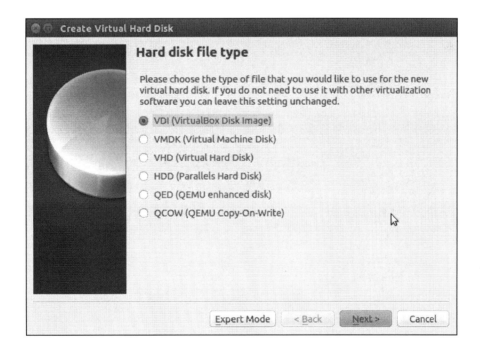

FIGURE 12.17.
Specifying a virtual hard drive format in VirtualBox.

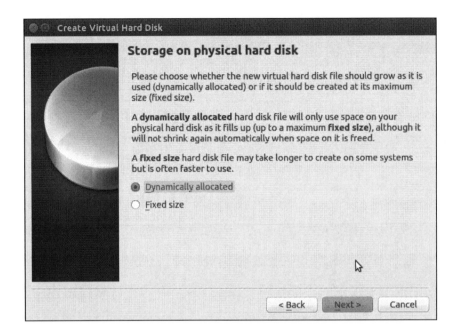

FIGURE 12.18.

Picking between dynamically allocated and fixed size virtual hard disks in VirtualBox.

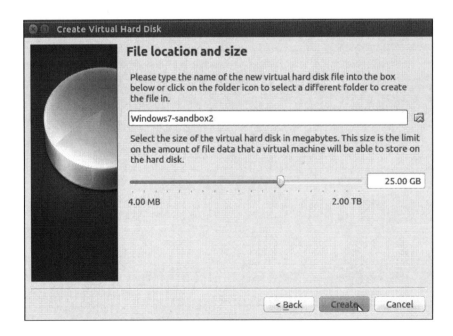

FIGURE 12.19.

Specifying the filename and size for a virtual hard disk in VirtualBox.

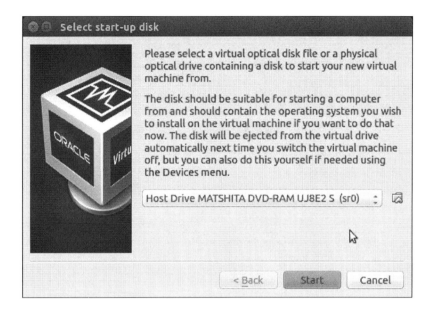

FIGURE 12.20.

The first run dialog box for VirtualBox which prompts for a start-up disk.

installing Windows, but it must be changed before running any suspicious programs in your sandbox.

When running your new virtual machine for the first time you will be prompted for start-up media by a dialog box like the one shown in Figure 12.20. Either an ISO (image) file or a physical DVD can be used to install Windows into the new virtual machine. Once Start is pressed in this dialog the normal Windows setup procedure will commence.

Once Windows has been installed in the new virtual machine, the network settings must be changed. There are two options. The safest option is to disable the network adapter completely. There are a couple of downsides to this method. First, some malware will not run properly if there is no network connectivity. Second, any executables must be manually moved to the virtual machine via a USB drive. To use this option simply uncheck the "Enable Network Adapter" box in the Network Settings dialog shown in Figure 12.21.

The slightly more dangerous, but much more convenient, option is to connect the network adapter to a host-only network. A host-only network is connected to the host machine and any virtual machines, but nothing else (unless you foolishly set up the host to route this traffic off this network). There are a few advantages to this method. First, it is much easier to copy files between the host and virtual machine. Second, malware is more likely to run properly. Third, any malware network traffic is easily sniffed and displayed using WireShark or a similar program.

The correct settings for a network adapter connected to a host-only network are shown in Figure 12.21. If this is the first virtual machine to be connected to a host-only network, one must first be created. To create a host-only network select Preferences from the File menu, then click on Network in the list on the left, click on the "Host-only Networks" tab, and press the "+" button on the right. The Network Preferences dialog is shown in Figure 12.22.

CHAPTER 12 Malware

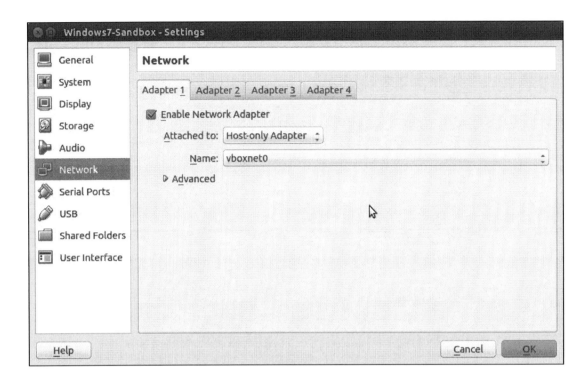

FIGURE 12.21.
The Network Settings dialog from VirtualBox.

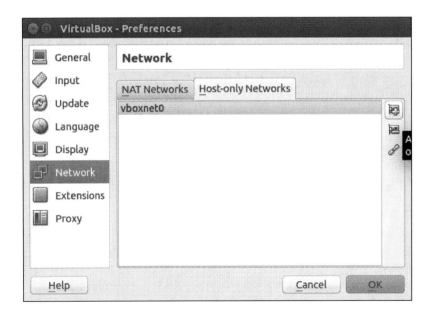

FIGURE 12.22.
Creating a host-only network in VirtualBox.

EXAMINING EXECUTABLES

Any in-depth examination of executables will require a debugger. Most debuggers are geared toward debugging programs you have written. As a result, they are most effective when a debug build has been created and the source code (in C, C++, or whatever language was used) is available. There are a few debuggers created specifically for reverse engineering.

32-bit executables

IDA Pro is one of the most popular debuggers for professional reverse engineers. It supports a number of different platforms. Unfortunately for the casual reverse engineer, licensing for IDA Pro starts at over US$1000. You read that correctly, I said licensing, not purchasing. A free version of IDA Pro is available that is over 18 versions behind the commercial version, cannot be used commercially, can only be used with 32-bit Windows executables, is only available as a Windows program (licensed versions are available on multiple platforms), and comes with no technical support. This free version can be downloaded from https://www.hex-rays.com/products/ida/support/download_freeware.shtml.

The freeware version of IDA can be downloaded onto the Linux forensic workstation and then transferred to the virtual machine via a host-only network or USB drive. As an alternative a NAT network interface can be temporarily enabled in the virtual machine and then disabled before running any suspicious programs. The IDA freeware program with the 32-bit chrome.exe file loaded is shown in Figure 12.23.

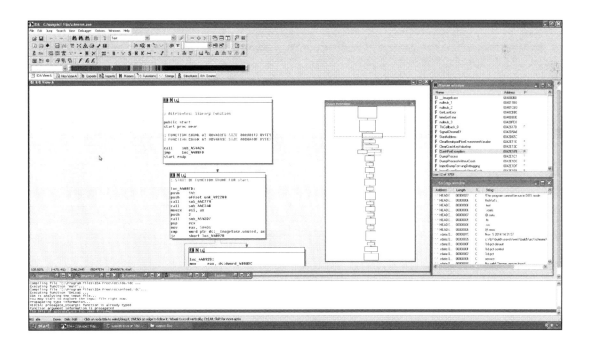

FIGURE 12.23.

Examining a 32-bit executable in the freeware version of IDA.

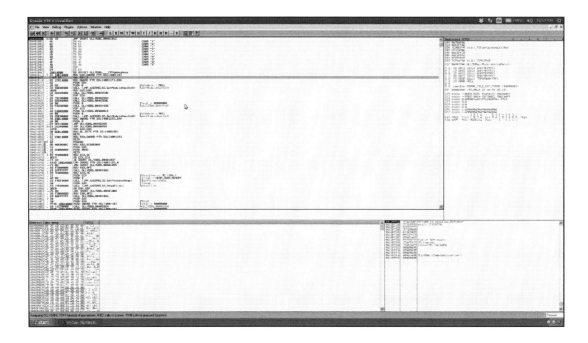

FIGURE 12.24.

Examining OllyDbg inside of OllyDbg.

If you prefer an open source debugger for 32-bit executables Olly Debugger (OllyDbg) is a popular choice. OllyDbg can be downloaded from http://ollydbg.de. Many third party plugins are available for OllyDbg thanks to its open architecture. OllyDbg examining itself is shown in Figure 12.24.

Knowing Assembly certainly helps when examining programs in IDA. Regardless of whether or not you know Assembly, the primary thing IDA provides over other debuggers is the IDA View-A window. This will provide a flow chart view of the program showing what is called and under what conditions. The IDA View-A windows for chrome.exe is shown in Figure 12.25.

Clicking on the Functions tab in IDA will display the functions window as shown in Figure 12.26. Unless the program was built with debugging information (unlikely) the function names will primarily be sub_<address>. The length of each function is given. This length can be used to easily determine what functions have significant functionality and which ones merely call another function (likely an API function).

Clicking on the Exports and Imports tabs in IDA will display exported and imported functions, respectively. This is the same information that was available with PEBrowse. Because the imports are sorted by address, they are listed in roughly the same order that they are called. One advantage of the imports list in IDA over PEBrowse is that any imported function can be double-clicked which will bring you to the place in the code (in IDA View-A) where the function is imported. The results of double-clicking the RegOpenKeyExW import are shown in Figure 12.27. Notice how IDA provides some comments for a few functions

Examining executables 523

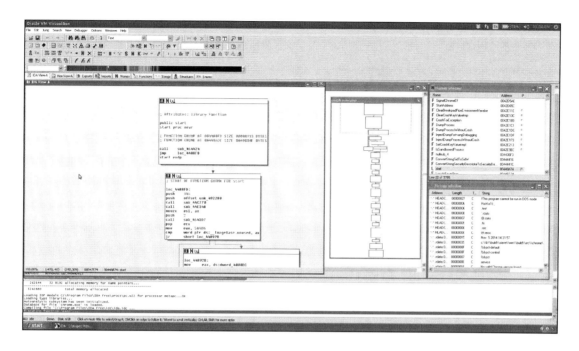

FIGURE 12.25.
The IDA View-A window for chrome.exe.

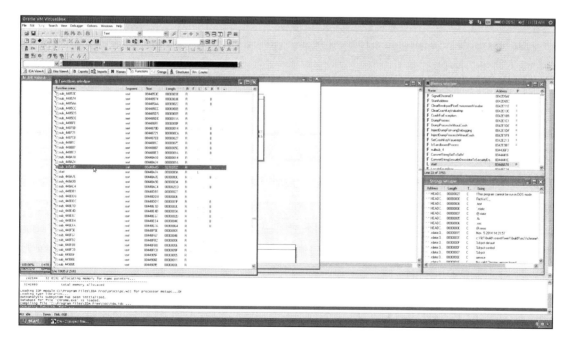

FIGURE 12.26.
The functions window in IDA.

FIGURE 12.27.

Results from double-clicking an import in IDA.

that describe what they do. Also note that function parameters have descriptive names. If you are still uncertain about a particular API call, you can find documentation for most of them on the Internet.

If after examining a program in IDA you are still uncertain as to whether or not it is malicious, it may be time to attempt to run the program. If the program requires networking to work, you might consider enabling a host-only network and then sniffing any traffic coming out of the virtual machine with WireShark or something similar. If the program was started with command line parameters (as determined with the Volatility cmdlines plugin), those command line parameters can be entered into IDA by selecting "Process options" from the Debugger menu and entering any parameters in the displayed dialog box. Alternatively a process can be launched on the command line and then IDA can be attached to this running process by selecting "Attach to process" from the Debugger menu. At a minimum you should have some C programming experience if you are attempting to run any programs in the debugger. IDA has all of the usual debugger features that one would expect if he or she has ever used a debugger before.

64-bit executables

What if you have a 64-bit executable and lack the funds to license IDA Pro? There are a number of free 64-bit Windows debuggers available. One option is PEBrowseDbg64 Interactive by SmidgeonSoft. These are the same people who produce PEBrowse described earlier in this

Examining executables 525

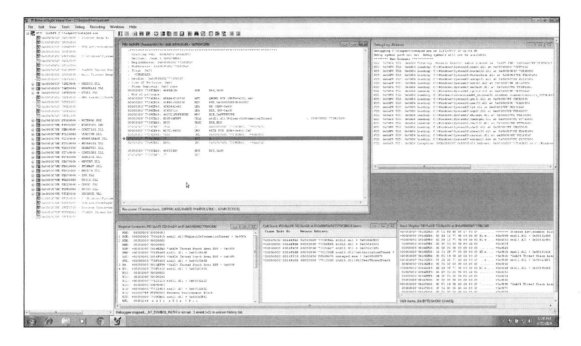

FIGURE 12.28.

Examining notepad.exe in PEBrowseDbg64.

chapter. This can be downloaded from http://smidgeonsoft.prohosting.com/pebrowse-pro-interactive-debugger.html. PEBrowseDbg64 is shown in Figure 12.28 with notepad.exe loaded. Note that this debugger requires .NET to be installed. When you attempt to launch it the first time, you will likely be greeted with a dialog asking you to download the appropriate .NET libraries. For this reason you might want to have networking enabled the first time you run this application.

If you prefer an open source debugger, x64dbg is an option. This debugger is available from http://x64dbg.com. When you click on the download link, you will be redirected to sourceforge.net. For reasons unknown, x64dbg is distributed as a 7zip archive. Windows does not natively know how to process these archives, so another program such as WinZip must be downloaded. The x64dbg debugger is shown in Figure 12.29 with notepad.exe loaded.

As debuggers go, x64dbg is fairly typical. There are four main windows that are displayed: code (in Assembly unless you have a debug build), CPU registers, memory, and the stack. The code, registers, memory, and stack windows are shown in the upper left, upper right, lower left, and lower right of Figure 12.29, respectively.

Regardless of which of these debuggers you choose you will not get the advanced analysis that IDA provides in the IDA View-A window. Practically speaking, this means that you will need a better understanding of C programming. At least a basic understanding of 64-bit Assembly is also required in order to get much out of these 64-bit debuggers.

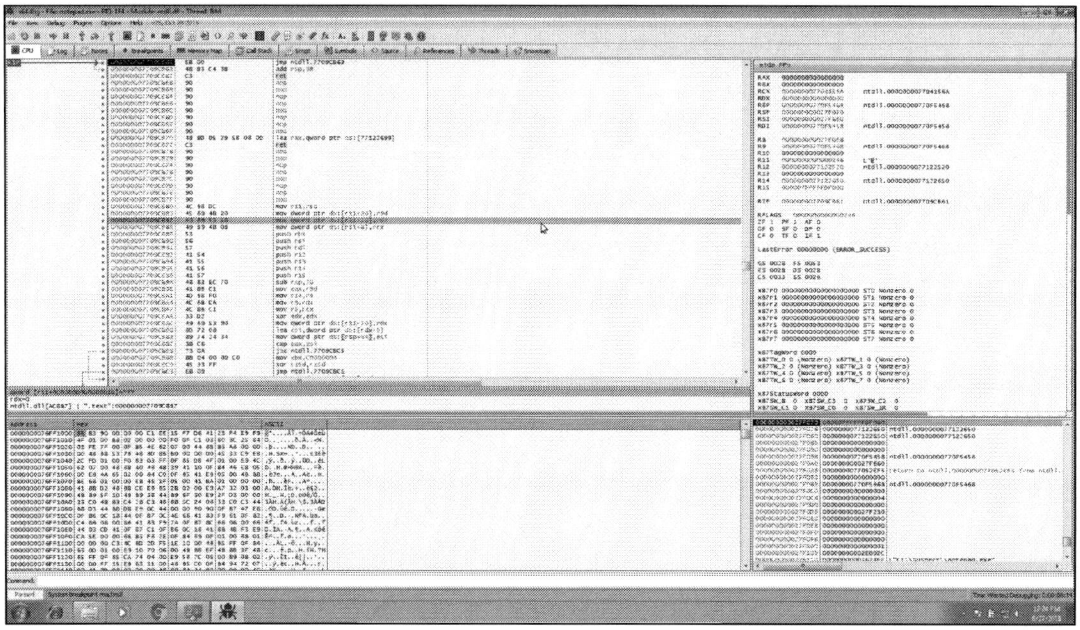

FIGURE 12.29.

Examining notepad.exe in x64dbg.

SUMMARY

In this chapter we learned some simple ways to examine suspicious programs. Much of what was discussed required only limited knowledge of the inner workings of Windows programs. In the next chapter we will look at what is required to finish an investigation and move on to the next one.

CHAPTER 13

The Road Ahead

INFORMATION IN THIS CHAPTER:

- Finishing an investigation
- Preparing for the next investigation

FINISHING THE INVESTIGATION

After all of the fun work of figuring out what happened and how is complete, the investigation is not quite over. An investigation is not truly finished until the necessary reports have been written. Reporting is often one of the least favorite tasks for forensic investigators. If you have been diligently taking notes in your bound notebook with numbered pages, this process should be a little less painful.

I would create the same type of report when performing a forensic investigation or penetration test. The report should consist of three parts: an executive summary, the main report body, and appendices. If you are not a native speaker of the language in which the report is to be written or do not feel confident in your writing abilities, it may be in your best interest to have someone look over the report before sending it to the client. Even a few minor grammatical errors can make you appear unprofessional.

The executive summary is meant for high level managers (CEO, etc.). These people do not have time to read the full report and may also lack low-level technical knowledge. The executive summary should ideally be less than a page. It should include a high-level description of what happened on the system(s) of interest. Major findings should be listed. An example of a major finding would be that a thumb drive belonging to John Smith was used to exfiltrate data from the organization. The executive summary should not include low-level details such as how this exfiltration was discovered using RegRipper on the system registry hive, etc. The executive summary should be easily transformed into an Impress or PowerPoint presentation that you might give to the client when delivering your report.

The main body of the report should be systematic. In other words, it should have some sense of organization. The exact form of organization will vary depending on the type of investigation. A system breach or malware infection might be organized chronologically. An investigation into corporate espionage or illegal activity could be organized based on significance of findings.

All of the findings should be presented here, not just the major ones. To the maximum extent possible the report should be free of technical jargon. If jargon is required, all terms should be clearly defined. If the nature of the investigation requires more than just a few jargon terms, consider creating a glossary.

Resist the urge to dump the raw output from various tools into the main body of a report. You are not adding value unless you are interpreting the output from tools used and presenting their findings in non-technical terms. Shorter is better when it comes to the main body of the report.

> ## LOOK AT MY REPORT
>
> ### Bigger is not always better
> Recently, while having lunch at a conference, I heard a somewhat new forensic investigator bragging to his friends about an investigation his company had recently performed. Apparently, as the new guy on the team, he was responsible for writing the report for this investigation. He was extremely proud of the 250+ page report that he was generating. From his description, not only was this report extremely long, but it was bogged down with technical details.
>
> The reality is that nobody is interested in reading such a report. Delivering a report that cannot be read and understood by the technical people working for your client is going to decrease, not improve, the client's impression of you and your organization. Show the client what you really know and impress them with your ability to describe things in a way they can understand.

All of the gory details should be contained in appendices. The main body of your report should refer to information in the appendices in order to guide the more technical members of your client's organization without bogging down the less technical people in the details. Any output from tools and scripts can be pasted into an appendix. If you created any custom scripts for this investigation, these should appear in the appendices. If any standard procedures were customized or new procedures were developed, they should be thoroughly documented in the appendices.

With the written report (possibly with an accompanying presentation) complete, you are now ready to archive the case. I recommend burning a CD or DVD containing the report, presentation (if any), any custom scripts, digital copies of any notes (possibly scans from your bound notebook), and anything else you feel might be relevant. You might wonder why I suggest burning this information to disk versus storing it on a hard drive with any system images collected. There are a few reasons for this recommendation. A CD or DVD has a shelf life of many years. The hard drive containing any images collected is best left alone to the maximum extent possible. Also, if your investigation results in some sort of court case, you do not want all of your notes and final report included in evidence for the opposing side to see. It is much cleaner to separate your notes and findings from images that may become evidence.

Once everything is complete you should package your backup drive(s) with images, CD or DVD, and any hard copies (including your bound notebook) together. A large zip lock bag works well for this purpose. This package should be stored in a secure and climate controlled location.

PREPARING FOR THE NEXT INVESTIGATION

Now that the investigation is over you might be wondering what you can do to prepare yourself for the next investigation. The best thing you can do whenever there is some down time is to educate yourself. There are so many specializations in forensics and taking a class or reading a book is always a fun way to become better at specific areas of forensics.

Another thing that you might attempt to improve your forensic skills is looking at test images and forensic challenges that are available on the Internet. A good list of images and challenges can be found at http://forensicfocus.com/images-and-challenges. This page links to many other pages, such as the Computer Forensic Reference Data Sets (CFReDS) from NIST. The CFReDS site is nice because it contains images for various types of cases (system breach, malware infection, etc.). A link to some of Brian Carrier's tool testing images (http://dftt.sourceforge.net) is also present on the forensicfocus.com page. These images are good for testing technical knowledge of NTFS and FAT filesystems. There are links to network captures for those wishing to learn more about network forensics and even links to images from real cases (such as the Enron case).

Several challenges are also listed at forensicfocus.com. The nice thing about challenges is that once they are over some of the winning submissions are normally posted. Do not be shy about trying your hand at some of these challenges. You probably will not win the first few you try, but you will likely learn a lot. You may even discover a passion for a certain area of forensics.

If you are looking for some online training, PentesterAcademy.com is certainly a great place to start. Most of the courses at PentesterAcademy are just as applicable to forensics as they are to penetration testing. There are also a growing number of courses specifically on forensics (almost forty hours worth at the time of this writing). These courses include Windows Forensics, Linux Forensics, and USB Forensics.

Finally, do not do forensics in isolation. Find some good forensic conferences to attend. Many information security conferences feature forensic talks and challenges. Do some research and find local forensics groups in your area. If you do not live in a large city, search for virtual conferences and webinars where you can learn more about forensics and network with other interested people.

SUMMARY

We have reached the end of our journey into Windows forensics. It is my sincere wish that this book will spark your interest in the exciting world of forensic science. I hope that you have enjoyed reading this book and following along with the forensic exercises as much as I have enjoyed writing it. So long, until next time.